THE ARDEN SHAKESPEARE

THIRD SERIES

General Editors: Richard Proudfoot, Ann Thompson,
David Scott Kastan and H.R. Woudhuysen

HAMLET

REVISED EDITION

THE ARDEN SHAKESPEARE

* Second series

HAMLET

Edited by
ANN THOMPSON AND
NEIL TAYLOR

Bloomsbury Arden Shakespeare
An imprint of Bloomsbury Publishing PLC

B L O O M S B U R Y

LONDON · OXFORD · NEW YORK · NEW DELHI · SYDNEY

Bloomsbury Arden Shakespeare

An imprint of Bloomsbury Publishing Plc

50 Bedford Square	1385 Broadway
London	New York
WC1B 3DP	NY 10018
UK	USA

www.bloomsbury.com

Bloomsbury is a registered trade mark of Bloomsbury Publishing Plc

This edition of HAMLET, edited by Ann Thompson and Neil Taylor, 2006
Revised Edition published 2016 by the Arden Shakespeare

Editorial matter © 2006, 2016 Ann Thompson and Neil Taylor

The general editors of the Arden Shakespeare have been
W. J. Craig and R. H. Case (first series 1899–1944)
Una Ellis-Fermor, Harold F. Brooks, Harold Jenkins and
Brian Morris (second series 1946–82)

Present general editors (third series)
Richard Proudfoot, Ann Thompson, David Scott Kastan and H. R. Woudhuysen

British Library Cataloguing-in-Publication Data
A catalogue record for this book is available from the British Library.

ISBN:	HB:	978-1-4725-1839-2
	PB:	978-1-4725-1838-5
	ePDF:	978-1-4742-7389-3
	ePub:	978-1-4742-7388-6

Library of Congress Cataloging-in-Publication Data
A catalog record for this book is available from the Library of Congress.

Typeset by RefineCatch Limited, Bungay, Suffolk
Printed and bound in India

The Editors

Ann Thompson is Emeritus Professor of English Language and Literature at King's College London. She has edited *The Taming of the Shrew* and *Cymbeline*, and her other publications include *Shakespeare's Chaucer, Shakespeare, Meaning and Metaphor* (with John O. Thompson) and *Women Reading Shakespeare, 1600–1900* (with Sasha Roberts). She has also published widely on editing Shakespeare, feminist criticism of Shakespeare and Shakespeare's language. She is one of the General Editors of the Arden Shakespeare Third Series.

Neil Taylor is Emeritus Professor of English Literature at the University of Roehampton. He has edited *Henry IV, Part 2, Henry VI, Part 3* and (with Bryan Loughrey) *Thomas Middleton: Five Plays*. He has also published widely on Shakespeare, Shakespeare on film and television, and other aspects of Renaissance and modern drama.

For John, Sarah and Dixie

CONTENTS

Contents

LIST OF
ILLUSTRATIONS

xi

GENERAL EDITORS' PREFACE

The earliest volume in the first Arden series, Edward Dowden's *Hamlet*, was published in 1899. Since then the Arden Shakespeare has been widely acknowledged as the pre-eminent Shakespeare edition, valued by scholars, students, actors and 'the great variety of readers' alike for its clearly presented and reliable texts, its full annotation and its richly informative introductions.

In the third Arden series we seek to maintain these well-established qualities and general characteristics, preserving our predecessors' commitment to presenting the play as it has been shaped in history. Each volume necessarily has its own particular emphasis which reflects the unique possibilities and problems posed by the work in question, and the series as a whole seeks to maintain the highest standards of scholarship, combined with attractive and accessible presentation.

Newly edited from the original documents, texts are presented in fully modernized form, with a textual apparatus that records all substantial divergences from those early printings. The notes and introductions focus on the conditions and possibilities of meaning that editors, critics and performers (on stage and screen) have discovered in the play. While building upon the rich history of scholarly activity that has long shaped our understanding of Shakespeare's works, this third series of the Arden Shakespeare is enlivened by a new generation's encounter with Shakespeare.

THE TEXT

On each page of the play itself, readers will find a passage of text supported by commentary and textual notes. Act and scene divisions (seldom present in the early editions and often the product of eighteenth-century or later scholarship) have been retained for ease of reference, but have been given less prominence than in previous series. Editorial indications of location of the action have been removed to the textual notes or commentary.

In the text itself, elided forms in the early texts are spelt out in full in verse lines wherever they indicate a usual late twentieth-century pronunciation that requires no special indication and wherever they occur in prose (except where they indicate non-standard pronunciation). In verse speeches, marks of elision are retained where they are necessary guides to the scansion and pronunciation of the line. Final -ed in past tense and participial forms of verbs is always printed as -ed, without accent, never as -'d, but wherever the required pronunciation diverges from modern usage a note in the commentary draws attention to the fact. Where the final -ed should be given syllabic value contrary to modern usage, e.g.

> Doth Silvia know that I am banished?
>
> > (*TGV* 3.1.214)

the note will take the form

> 214 **banished** banishèd

Conventional lineation of divided verse lines shared by two or more speakers has been reconsidered and sometimes rearranged. Except for the familiar *Exit* and *Exeunt*, Latin forms in stage directions and speech prefixes have been translated into English and the original Latin forms recorded in the textual notes.

COMMENTARY AND TEXTUAL NOTES

Notes in the commentary, for which a major source will be the *Oxford English Dictionary*, offer glossarial and other explication of verbal difficulties; they may also include discussion of points of interpretation and, in relevant cases, substantial extracts from Shakespeare's source material. Editors will not usually offer glossarial notes for words adequately defined in the latest edition of *The Concise Oxford Dictionary* or *Merriam-Webster's Collegiate Dictionary*, but in cases of doubt they will include notes. Attention, however, will be drawn to places where more than one likely interpretation can be proposed and to significant verbal and syntactic complexity. Notes preceded by * discuss editorial emendations or variant readings.

Headnotes to acts or scenes discuss, where appropriate, questions of scene location, the play's treatment of source materials, and major difficulties of staging. The list of roles (so headed to emphasize the play's status as a text for performance) is also considered in the commentary notes. These may include comment on plausible patterns of casting with the resources of an Elizabethan or Jacobean acting company and also on any variation in the description of roles in their speech prefixes in the early editions.

The textual notes are designed to let readers know when the edited text diverges from the early edition(s) or manuscript sources on which it is based. Wherever this happens the note will record the rejected reading of the early edition(s) or manuscript, in original spelling, and the source of the reading adopted in this edition. Other forms from the early edition(s) or manuscript recorded in these notes will include some spellings of particular interest or significance and original forms of translated stage directions. Where two or more early editions are involved, for instance with *Othello*, the notes also record all important differences between them. The textual notes take a form that has been in use since the nineteenth century. This comprises, first: line reference, reading adopted in the text and closing square bracket; then: abbreviated reference, in italic, to the earliest edition to adopt the accepted reading, italic semicolon and noteworthy alternative reading(s), each with abbreviated italic reference to its source.

Conventions used in these textual notes include the following. The solidus / is used, in notes quoting verse or discussing verse lining, to indicate line endings. Distinctive spellings of the base text follow the square bracket without indication of source and are enclosed in italic brackets. Names enclosed in italic brackets indicate originators of conjectural emendations when these did not originate in an edition of the text, or when the named edition records a conjecture not accepted into its text. Stage directions (SDs) are referred to by the number of the line within or immediately after which they are placed. Line numbers with a decimal point relate to centred entry SDs not falling within a verse line and to SDs more than one line long, with the number after the point indicating the line within the SD: e.g. 78.4 refers to the fourth line of the SD following line 78. Lines of SDs at the start of a scene are numbered 0.1, 0.2, etc. Where only a line number precedes a square bracket, e.g. 128], the note relates to the whole line; where SD is added to the number, it relates to the whole of a SD within or immediately following the line. Speech prefixes (SPs) follow similar conventions, 203 SP] referring to the speaker's name for line 203. Where a SP reference takes the form, e.g. 38+ SP, it relates to all subsequent speeches assigned to that speaker in the scene in question.

Where, as with *King Henry V*, one of the early editions is a so-called 'bad quarto' (that is, a text either heavily adapted, or reconstructed from memory, or both), the divergences from the present edition are too great to be recorded in full in the notes. In these cases, with the exception of *Hamlet*, which prints an edited text of the Quarto of 1603, the editions will include a reduced photographic facsimile of the 'bad quarto' in an appendix.

INTRODUCTION

Both the introduction and the commentary are designed to present the plays as texts for performance, and make appropriate reference to stage, film and television versions, as well as introducing the reader to the range of critical approaches to the plays. They discuss the history of the reception of the texts within the theatre and scholarship and beyond, investigating the interdependency of the literary text and the surrounding 'cultural text' both at the time of the original production of Shakespeare's works and during their long and rich afterlife.

PREFACE

We are very privileged to be able to take our place in the long line of those who have been involved in the transmission of the texts of *Hamlet* for over 400 years. Our debts to our predecessors are apparent on every page, and it has given us great pleasure to enter into a kind of dialogue (a virtual one, in most cases) with so many people who have been this way before. Our immediate predecessor in the Arden Shakespeare series, Harold Jenkins, did his job so well that we felt there was no need to do it again in the same way – one of the many reasons why we are offering a totally different approach to the play. Other editors of the 1980s, notably Philip Edwards and George Hibbard, have been important influences, as have the editorial team (Stanley Wells, Gary Taylor, John Jowett and William Montgomery) that produced the Oxford *Complete Works* and its *Textual Companion*. We have been working on our edition at the same time as the Variorum team (Hardin Aasand, Nick Clary, Bernice Kliman and Eric Rasmussen) and have enjoyed many conversations with them as our work progressed; Bernice's 'Enfolded *Hamlet*', generously given away with the *Shakespeare Newsletter* in 1996, has been an excellent quick-reference tool. Outside the Anglo-American tradition of editing, fully annotated editions of *Hamlet* have recently appeared in Germany (edited by Holger M. Klein), Italy (*Il primo Amleto* and *Amleto*, edited by Alessandro Serpieri) and Spain (*A Synoptic 'Hamlet'*, edited by Jesús Tronch-Pérez), and we have valued these perspectives.

We owe an enormous debt to our colleagues on the Arden team, especially to Richard Proudfoot and David Scott Kastan, first for sanctioning this three-text edition from the start (despite some understandable misgivings), and then for helping us through every stage. They have read and reread with unfailing patience and have been overwhelmingly generous in making constructive suggestions and saving us from egregious errors. We must mention support from the publishers during changing and challenging times, especially Jane Armstrong and Talia Rodgers at Routledge, in the early days of the project; Jessica Hodge, first at Thomas Nelson and then at Thomson Learning, who guided it through the next stage; and finally Margaret Bartley at Thomson Learning, who saw it through to completion. We would also like to thank Fiona Freel, Giulia Vincenzi and Philippa Gallagher at Thomson Learning. We were intimidated to learn that our copy-editor, Linden Stafford, was also the copy-editor for Harold Jenkins's edition of *Hamlet* in the second series of the Arden Shakespeare in 1982, but we have been hugely impressed with her positive attitude to our own enterprise and with her detailed and careful work; she certainly deserves a PhD in Shakespeare studies in general and Arden house style in particular. Our professional proofreader, Annette Clifford-Vaughan, was also most helpful, especially in suggesting numerous minor changes to commentary notes to get the page layout right.

We have benefited from informal consultations with fellow Arden editors at regular meetings in London and Stratford-upon-Avon and at the conferences of the Shakespeare Association of America. Many friends and colleagues have invited us to give papers on our work as it has progressed, and we have learnt a lot from the feedback on these occasions. Students taking Ann's course on '*Hamlet* and its afterlife' in the 'Shakespeare Studies: Text and Playhouse' MA programme (jointly taught by King's College London and Shakespeare's Globe theatre) have been a valued source of input and encouragement. It could be invidious to name individuals, but Peter Donaldson, Akiko Kusunoki, Gordon McMullan, Reiko Oya, Peter Reynolds and Ron Rosenbaum deserve special mention for specific contributions.

We began this project when we were both working at Roehampton Institute (now Roehampton University), and we are grateful for support from colleagues, especially Bryan Loughrey, and for institutional support, including sabbatical leave. Roehampton also employed Sasha Roberts as a research assistant, and her hard work and enthusiasm were particularly valued in the first years of the project. Since 1999 Ann has received institutional support from King's College London. The Arts and Humanities Research Board (now Council), the British Academy and the Leverhulme Trust have all provided financial support, as have the Folger Shakespeare Library and the Huntington Library, in terms of residential fellowships. Librarians have been very helpful, especially Georgianna Ziegler at the Folger, who alerted us to their wide range of illustrative materials.

We have been able to benefit from a great deal of recent research on Elizabethan theatres and acting companies, and from the experience of seeing several of Shakespeare's plays (including *Hamlet*) performed at the reconstructed Globe theatre in London. New reference works have greatly facilitated our editorial labours: we might instance Alan C. Dessen and Leslie Thomson's *A Dictionary of Stage Directions in English Drama 1580–1642*, Naseeb Shaheen's *Biblical References in Shakespeare's Plays*, and B.J. Sokol and Mary Sokol's *Shakespeare's Legal Language: A Dictionary*. And at last two works on Shakespeare's language have replaced E.A. Abbott's venerable *A Shakespeare Grammar* of 1869, namely Norman F. Blake's *A Grammar of Shakespeare's Language* and Jonathan Hope's *Shakespeare's Grammar*. These have played their part in our work, along with extensive documentation and discussion of UK and overseas performance and criticism. Just as our edition goes to press, we are grateful to Tony Howard for letting us read the typescript of his book on *Women as Hamlet*.

And finally there are the people to whom we are dedicating this edition, who have lived with it patiently for far too long and who will share our profound relief at seeing it in print.

A NOTE ON THE TEXT

This volume contains an edited and annotated text of the 1604–5 (Second Quarto) printed version of *Hamlet*, with passages that are found only in the 1623 text (the First Folio) printed as Appendix 1. It is a fully self-contained, free-standing edition which includes in its Introduction and appendices all the supporting materials that a reader would expect to find in an Arden edition. Uniquely, however, we are also offering readers a second volume, *Hamlet: The Texts of 1603 and 1623*, which contains edited and annotated texts of the other two early versions. This second volume is an entirely optional supplement: the present volume does not depend upon it in any way, and we imagine the majority of readers will be content with just one *Hamlet*. We explain in our Introduction and Appendix 2 our rationale for offering all three texts in this way, and the headnotes to each scene in the commentary contain brief summaries of the principal differences in the handling of the material in the three texts.

Quotations from the three texts, as well as act, scene and line numbers, are taken from these two volumes unless otherwise stated. Of course we hope that some readers will want to study all three texts, since we feel that making them all available in the Arden format is our main justification for adding to the long list of existing editions of *Hamlet*.

Ann Thompson and Neil Taylor
London

INTRODUCTION

THE CHALLENGES OF *HAMLET*

Lastly, let me entreat, and beseech, and adjure, and implore you not to write an essay on Hamlet. In the catalogue of a library which is very dear to me, there are about four hundred titles of separate editions, essays, commentaries, lectures, and criticisms of this sole tragedy, and I know that this is only the vanguard of the coming years. To modify the words, on another subject, of my ever dear and revered Master, the late Professor Child, I am convinced that were I told that my closest friend was lying at the point of death, and that his life could be saved by permitting him to divulge his theory of Hamlet, I would instantly say, 'Let him die! Let him die! Let him die!'

Thus spoke Horace Howard Furness, one of our many distinguished predecessors as an editor of *Hamlet*, when he addressed the Phi Beta Kappa society at Harvard University almost one hundred years ago in 1908 (Gibson, 220).[1] He was certainly right about the 'four hundred titles' being 'only the vanguard' of the army of publications which was to march through the twentieth century: by the 1990s the average number of publications *every year* on *Hamlet*, as recorded in the *Shakespeare Quarterly Annual Bibliography*, was running at well over 400, an exponential advance comparable to that in 4.4 of the play (in the Second Quarto text only), where Hamlet's

---

1 Furness edited the massive two-volume Variorum *Hamlet* published in 1877. The library he mentions is presumably the one he helped to create at the University of Philadelphia, and Professor Child is Francis James Child (1825–96), philologist and collector of English and Scottish ballads and songs, who had taught Furness at Harvard from 1857 to 1858, and with whom he maintained contact: see Gibson, 25, 100.

1

estimate of the Norwegian forces moves from 2,000 to 20,000 men in thirty-five lines. We must therefore begin by acknowledging the extraordinary size of 'the *Hamlet* phenomenon' and the challenge it represents to everyone who confronts it.

The challenge of acting Hamlet

The sheer depth and breadth of tradition weigh heavily on those who tackle *Hamlet*, whether as actor, director, editor or critic. Actors are haunted by their predecessors as well as by their contemporary rivals. Simon Russell Beale's success in the role at the National Theatre, London, in 2000 and on international tour 2000–1, was ascribed by Dennis Quilley (who played Polonius and the Gravedigger) in part to the fact that 'he's said, Let's forget Gielgud and Olivier and John Neville, and just see what the character means' (quoted in Croall, 33); but in a joint *New York Times* interview (8 April 2001) with Adrian Lester, who played Hamlet for Peter Brook at the Bouffes du Nord, Paris, and on tour in New York and London, also in 2000–1, Beale reflected on the difficulty of 'wiping the slate clean':

> There has never been a time when there aren't 800 Hamlets . . . You are aware consciously that there is a history about it. You see this list of Hamlets and you think, 'Oh, my God, no. And there's Adrian opening in five minutes. There's Olivier. There's Gielgud . . . But there's an extraordinary shutoff point when the rehearsal room door closes. Gielgud died the morning we started rehearsals for our *Hamlet*, and you thought, 'This is really weird.' But you have to – as Adrian says – start from scratch.

Gielgud himself made a similar point when asked if he had modelled his performance on any of his predecessors:

> No, I didn't. I thought I had. I thought I would copy all the actors I'd ever seen, in turn, and by then I'd

seen about a dozen or fifteen Hamlets [including H.B. Irving (Sir Henry's son), Ernest Milton, Henry Baynton, Arthur Phillips, Colin Keith-Johnston and John Barrymore]. Of course, [the elder, Sir Henry] Irving was my god, although I'd never seen him . . . I didn't try to copy, I only took note of all the things he'd done and looked at the pictures of him and so on. But when it came to the [London Old] Vic, the play moved so fast and there was so much of it that I suddenly felt, 'Well, I've just got to be myself', and I really played it absolutely straight as far as I could.

(quoted in Burton, 140)

Previous generations were equally affected: a cartoon from 1804 (see Fig. 1) shows John Philip Kemble (who performed the role from 1783 to 1817) with William Betty on his back, illustrating the sensational competition between the adult performer (Kemble was forty-seven in 1804) and the child actor who astonished London by undertaking the role at the age of thirteen and becoming known as 'the infant Roscius' (see 2.2.327 and n.). Kemble is exclaiming (in a parody of Ophelia's lines at 3.1.159–60), 'Alas! is it come to this / Ah! woe is me / Seeing what I have seen / Seeing what I see!! Oh Roscious –'. There were well-known rivalries between contemporaries like William Charles Macready (who performed the role from 1823 to 1851) and Edwin Forrest (1829–72), and John Gielgud (1930–44) and Laurence Olivier (1937–48) (on the former, see Phelps, 20–21, and Hapgood, 75; on the latter, see Maher, 26, and Olivier, 50).

One of the most famous American Hamlets, Edwin Booth (who performed the role from 1853 to 1891), was apparently haunted by the ghost of his father, Junius Brutus Booth, who had himself played Hamlet from 1829 to 1849: a cartoon of 1875 shows the 'Spirit of the Elder B——h' appearing to 'B——h the Younger' (see Fig. 2). Edwin claimed to have heard his father's voice speaking through the Ghost, and he

1 Cartoon of John Philip Kemble with William Betty on his back, dated 30 November 1804; see p. 3

2 Cartoon of the spirit of Junius Brutus Booth appearing to Edwin Booth, from *New York Times Dramatic News* (October 1875). In the caption the Spirit of the Elder Booth is saying, 'I am thy father's Ghost', and Booth the Younger replies, 'I'll call THEE Hamlet, Father' (see 1.5.9 and 1.4.44–5)

used a miniature of his father in the closet scene. Junius Brutus had died before Edwin's first Hamlet and he saw the performance as a 'sacred pledge'; his biographer records that the role became 'almost an autopsychography' for him (see Shattuck, 3–6).[1] Daniel Day Lewis withdrew from the part in mid-run in 1989 after he allegedly began seeing *his* father (the recently deceased poet Cecil Day-Lewis) on stage at the National Theatre in London (see Davison). The Ghost is indeed often played by an actor who has himself played Hamlet in the past: Gielgud as director used his own voice for the Ghost when he directed Richard Burton in 1964 (the Ghost did not actually appear in this production), and Paul Scofield played the Ghost to Mel Gibson's Hamlet in Franco Zeffirelli's 1990 film.

In the past, actors of Hamlet were very much aware of a heritage of 'points', that is details of stage business which had been introduced by their predecessors and had become in effect canonized as part of the acting tradition. They had to make conscious decisions whether, for example, to crawl menacingly across the stage during the acting of *The Murder of Gonzago* in 3.2 (as Edmund Kean had first done in 1814), and whether to overturn a chair on the appearance of the Ghost in 3.4 (as David Garrick had first done in 1742); reviewers would be equally aware of such 'points' and would regularly comment on how they were handled (see more examples at pp. 97–111). This was in part a consequence of what seems to us the extraordinary longevity of particular performances: Thomas Betterton played Hamlet from 1661 until 1709 (when he was seventy-four), Garrick from 1742 to 1776, John Philip Kemble from 1783 to 1817, Edmund Kean from 1814 to 1832 and William Charles Macready from 1823 to 1851. Thus a performance could be polished and embellished over a period of twenty, thirty or

---

1   It was Edwin's elder brother, John Wilkes Booth, who assassinated Abraham Lincoln on 26 April 1865, an event that caused Edwin to retire from the stage for nine months; he returned, triumphantly, in the role of Hamlet.

more years, with audiences returning again and again expecting minor modifications but no radical changes. Even in the first half of the twentieth century, John Gielgud performed the part occasionally from 1929 to 1945. This simply does not happen in the modern theatre. An individual actor may get the chance to play Hamlet in more than one run (for example, Mark Rylance at Stratford in 1988 and at the London Globe in 2000), but the surrounding production will be completely different and audiences will expect the individual performance to be tailored accordingly. Actors are concerned, if anything, to avoid the 'points' associated with previous Hamlets, though they may unconsciously reinvent them, as when Michael Pennington (212) describes Stephen Dillane in 1994 'copying' a piece of business from a Russian Hamlet in 1839. Film confers a different kind of longevity on a performance, though it is notable in this context that Laurence Olivier's Richard III has proved to be a more dominant (and in some ways inhibiting) influence than his Hamlet.

From the late nineteenth century onwards, the director began to succeed the actor-manager and to occupy a dominant role in the theatre. In the 1950s Eric Bentley imagined a world in which even the author, let alone the actor, was eclipsed by the director: 'To speak of Shakespeare's *Hamlet* will soon be as unusual and eccentric as to speak of Schikaneder's *Magic Flute*. The playwright is just a librettist; the composer's name is Reinhardt, Meyerhold, Piscator, Baty, Logan, or Kazan' (Bentley, 112). The name of William Shakespeare has hardly become as obscure as that of Emanuel Schikaneder, but in some cases the director does indeed triumph over the performer, especially in the continental European theatre and for those working within it, from Edward Gordon Craig's Moscow *Hamlet* in 1911 to Peter Brook's Paris *Hamlet* in 2000. This also applies to films, unless the actor is very well known: we usually speak of the 1964 Russian film as Grigori Kozintsev's *Hamlet* rather than as Innokenty Smoktunovsky's *Hamlet*, but we might speak of the 1990 film either as Franco Zeffirelli's *Hamlet* or as Mel Gibson's *Hamlet*. Hamlet's own presentation of *The Murder of Gonzago*, given a new title, *The Mousetrap*, and altered by the insertion of 'a speech of some dozen or sixteen lines', prefigures the power of the director to reinterpret and reinvent the play, and 'directors' theatre' has its own history of the anxiety of influence and the pressure to be original (see Wilcock for an extended study of this). In addition to many 'straight' productions of *Hamlet* powered by a strong directorial vision, the twentieth century saw a number of versions of the play presented through a directorial collage or kaleidoscope, including those by Charles Marowitz (*Hamlet Collage*, 1965), Heiner Müller (*Hamletmachine*, 1979), Peter Brook (*Qui est là?*, 1995), Robert Lepage (*Elsinore*, 1995) and Robert Wilson (*Hamlet: A Monologue*, 1995). All these are 'variations' of the play, rearranged for the directors' purposes far more radically than Hamlet proposes to rewrite *The Murder of Gonzago*, but still trading on the cultural capital of 'Shakespeare' and 'Hamlet' and indeed depending on the audience's familiarity with the original. (For more on 'directors' theatre', see pp. 111–17.)

The challenge of editing Hamlet

Of the earliest printed texts of *Hamlet*, three stand out as being significant for the modern editor – those known as the First Quarto or Q1 (1603), the Second Quarto or Q2 (1604–5) and the First Folio or F (1623). Q1 is the shortest of these texts, the only one of the three that could plausibly have been acted in its entirety, but quite different from the others in much of its dialogue and even in the names of some of its characters ('Ofelia' and 'Leartes' have a father called 'Corambis'). Q2 is almost twice the length of Q1 and lacks some famous passages of F's dialogue (including Hamlet's observation that 'Denmark's a prison' at 2.2.242). F is a little shorter than Q2 and lacks some substantial passages of Q2's dialogue (including the whole of Hamlet's soliloquy 'How all occasions do inform against me' at 4.4.31).

While modern actors consciously aim to reject the burden of tradition and 'just see what the character means', 'start from scratch' or 'be themselves', editors do not have this option. We are well aware that we stand (if at all) on the shoulders of giants, or, in Stanley Wells's more modest metaphor, that we constitute merely 'one thin layer in the coral reef of editorial effort' (Wells, *Re-Editing*, 3). On the one hand we must indeed 'start from scratch', having an obligation to edit our text(s) as if no one had ever done it before, but on the other hand, if we emend a word, add a stage direction or even make a significant alteration to a piece of punctuation, we must check to see if any of our predecessors made the same change and be scrupulous about acknowledging that precedent. At times we may envy the very earliest editors their freedom to intervene in the interests of clarification, as with Pope's 1723 emendation of F's 'like most' to 'most like' at 2.2.347 (Folio text only; see Appendix 1), Theobald's 1733 emendation of Q2's 'And Anchors' to 'An anchor's' at 3.2.213 (Q2 text only) or Hanmer's 1744 emendation of F's 'fond' to 'fanned' at 5.2.155 (Folio text only; see Appendix 1): most of these readings now seem obvious and have been accepted by the vast majority of editors. At other times we may deplore the influence of early editions, as with the imposition of an act break in the middle of the closet scene (at 3.4/4.1), first found in the Quarto of 1676 (Q6) and adopted by almost all subsequent editors, despite their inability to justify it (see Appendix 4). The nature of our work involves a laborious reinvention of the wheel and an extreme nervousness about claiming anything at all as original to this edition.

Nevertheless, we would not have undertaken a task on this scale if we had not felt we had something genuinely new and indeed 'original' to offer. When we started, we were aware of the three fine editions of the play that had appeared in the 1980s: Harold Jenkins's for the Arden Shakespeare in 1982, Philip Edwards's for the New Cambridge Shakespeare in 1985 and G.R. Hibbard's for the Oxford Shakespeare in 1987. We were also aware of the massive and radical work of the Oxford team (Stanley Wells, Gary Taylor, John Jowett and William Montgomery) on the *Complete Works* (modern spelling and original spelling versions, 1986) and the *Textual Companion* (1987). Those volumes famously included two texts of *King Lear*, the 1608 Quarto version as well as the 1623 Folio version, and the editors argued, building on the work of scholars such as Steven Urkowitz, Gary Taylor and Michael Warren, that the latter represented an authorial revision of the former. The 'two texts of *King Lear*' became further 'canonized' in the *Norton Shakespeare*, edited by Stephen Greenblatt, Walter Cohen, Jean E. Howard and Katherine Eisaman Maus (1997).

The Oxford team took a similar line on the relationship between the 1604–5 Quarto and the 1623 Folio texts of *Hamlet* (as did both Edwards and Hibbard in the single-play volumes), namely that the latter is a revision of the former, but they printed only one version. Stanley Wells and Gary Taylor later recorded their regret at this decision:

> It now seems obvious that we should have included two versions of *Hamlet*, as we did of *King Lear*, a Folio-based version and one based on Q2 [but] . . . It was not yet at all clear that the rewriting of *Hamlet* was as important for anyone's interpretation of the play as the rewriting of *Lear* . . . [and] *Hamlet* was one of the last plays we edited; we were tired.
>
> (Wells & Taylor, 16–17)

They conceded that the solution they had adopted of printing the Q2–only lines as 'additional passages' was 'hopelessly confusing' and that only a 'determined scholar' with access to the expensive *Textual Companion* would be in a position to reconstruct the Q2 text they had chosen not to print (Wells & Taylor, 16–17). They expressed a hope that their publishers would subsequently make a parallel-text *Hamlet* available but this has not happened. Our decision to print not two but all three of the early texts of *Hamlet* can be seen on one level as making up for this deficit.

This edition is in two volumes, which print Q2 in the first and Q1 and F in the second. Ideally, we would have printed the three texts either in one volume (printing them in the order in which they were originally published – Q1, Q2, F) or in three, but a variety of practical considerations has led us to settle for a two-volume format. Given that decision, it became necessary to decide on the distribution of the texts between the two volumes. As Q2 is the longest text, it makes sense to put it on its own, since that allows the two volumes to be not too dissimilar in size. Although we have edited, modernized and annotated the texts in such a way that a reader can choose to read each version separately, we are aware nevertheless that not all readers will wish to do this, and we have therefore chosen to provide the F-only lines as 'additional passages' within the Q2 volume. This decision certainly does not arise out of any conviction that Q2 is the one authoritative text, or that if F has any authority it is limited to only those 'additional passages', or that Q1 is a mere curiosity. On the contrary, we believe that each of the three texts has sufficient merit to be read and studied on its own. We fervently hope that readers will study both volumes, experience the imaginative power of all three texts, and explore and weigh the scholarly debates surrounding their origins.

Yet, however much we are committed to the project of producing a multiple-text edition, we have to concede that the Arden Shakespeare is associated with single-text, eclectic editions. We have not produced an eclectic edition, but we feel we must at least provide our readers with the material to read a *Hamlet* within that tradition. And we also have to concede that, if one were forced to choose just one of the three early texts of *Hamlet* as, on the balance of the evidence, the most likely to have authority, it would have to be Q2. This is because (a) the evidence is strong, and there is general agreement among scholars, that Q2 derives from an authorial manuscript; (b) few scholars in the last hundred years have ever claimed that Q1 is based on an authorial manuscript, no one has ever claimed that it is the most authoritative of the three texts, and Q2 was printed during Shakespeare's lifetime not long after the play was first staged and apparently as a deliberate attempt on the part of Shakespeare's company, and presumably with his consent, to correct and displace Q1; and (c) forceful and, for many, persuasive as the arguments are that F derives from an authorial revision of the play, or a more 'theatrical' text than Q2, there is less than general agreement on either of these points, and, were it to be there, agreement on either point would not necessarily be a reason for attributing more authority to F than to Q2.

Hence we have provided in this volume a self-contained 'Arden *Hamlet*' with all the usual apparatus, including full information about the other text traditionally regarded as 'good' (F) in Appendices 1 and 2 as well as in the textual notes and commentary. But we have also provided modernized and annotated texts of both F and Q1 in a second volume, entitled *Hamlet: The Texts of 1603 and 1623* (abbreviated henceforth as Ard Q1/F, and to which quotations from these texts refer unless otherwise stated). We are assuming that those who consult this second volume will have the first volume to hand (but not vice versa), so, while the commentary on Q1 is quite extensive, that on F concentrates exclusively on its differences from Q2 (and what previous editors have made of them) and does not repeat glossarial and interpretative notes where F is substantially identical to Q2. (For more extensive discussion of the texts and composition of *Hamlet*, see pp. 76–96 and Appendix 2.)

The choice of text (or in our case the refusal to choose) is perhaps the most fundamental decision an editor has to make, but it is by no means the only one. Arden editions have always been valued for their wealth of annotation and commentary, and, while we were facing a formidably thorough model in Jenkins's Arden edition, it was published as long ago as 1982, and the Cambridge and Oxford single-play editions had followed soon afterwards. It was apparent that by the time our work appeared there would be some serious updating to be done: there would be twenty or twenty-five years' worth of productions, adaptations, scholarship and criticism to be assimilated and incorporated. Readerships change all the time, and perhaps the UK undergraduate readership has altered most of all in the last twenty years, during which period an elite higher education system where around 10 per cent of school-leavers went to university has developed into a 'mass' system where nearly 50 per cent participate. Pedagogical methods have changed, both at school and at university, so student readers require different kinds of annotation. There is much more emphasis on the plays in performance in modern editions of Shakespeare: editors now engage with issues of staging not just in a 'stage history' section of an introduction but throughout their commentaries. We are also aware of an international readership who will rightly expect *Hamlet* to be treated as an international phenomenon, not as a play exclusively 'owned' by the Anglo-American tradition.

The challenge to the greatness of Hamlet: Hamlet *versus* Lear

Despite what seems to us the formidable status of 'the *Hamlet* phenomenon', we should acknowledge that during the last decade of the twentieth century the status and pre-eminence of *Hamlet* was challenged by R.A. Foakes, who claimed that in about 1960 *King Lear* had replaced *Hamlet* as 'the best, the greatest, or the chief masterpiece of Shakespeare' (Foakes, *Hamlet*, 1), citing numerous critics who take this relative judgement for granted. This late twentieth-century primacy of *King Lear* rested in part on its belated emergence as a stageable text after a long period during which it was regarded as 'Shakespeare's greatest work . . . but not the best of his plays', as A.C. Bradley put it in his influential *Shakespearean Tragedy*

(202), and in part, as Foakes demonstrates, on a shift in interpretation away from readings which had seen it as a kind of redemptive parable in which Lear 'loses the world but gains his soul' and towards those which saw it as a bleak vision of suffering and despair.

This shift may well have been related to the global context of the Cold War when the ever-present threat of nuclear destruction made 'the promised end' envisaged by Kent (*Lear* 5.3.261) seem imminent. Tracing the traditional interpretations of *Hamlet* and *Lear*, and in particular their perceived relevance to political issues, Foakes draws a contrast between them:

> Although Hamlet was, as a character, abstracted from the play and privatized as a representative of everyman by Romantic and later critics, he also became in the nineteenth century an important symbolic political figure, usually typifying the liberal intellectual paralysed in will and incapable of action. By contrast, *King Lear* was depoliticized . . . and until the 1950s the play was, in the main, seen as a tragedy of personal relations between father and daughter, or as a grand metaphysical play about Lear's pilgrimage to discover his soul. All this changed after 1960, since when *King Lear* has come to seem richly significant in political terms, in a world in which old men have held on to and abused power, often in corrupt and arbitrary ways; in the same period *Hamlet* has lost much of its political relevance, as liberal intellectuals have steadily been marginalized in Britain and in the United States.
>
> (*Hamlet*, 6)

He concludes that 'for the immediate future, *King Lear* will continue to be regarded as the central achievement of Shakespeare, if only because it speaks more largely than the other tragedies to the anxieties of the modern world' (224). Foakes repeated these claims when he edited *King Lear* in

1997, but in the same year E.A.J. Honigmann edited *Othello* and argued that *his* play really deserved to be acknowledged as 'the greatest tragedy' (Honigmann, Ard[3] *Oth*, 1 and 102–11). One does often become partisan on behalf of the play one is editing (though there are exceptions to this, as when a woman edits *The Taming of the Shrew*), but this is not just an academic game: as editors of this text (or, rather, these texts) of *Hamlet*, we feel we must engage with the formidable status of the play and the historical and cultural contexts which have generated and continue to generate that status.

Clearly, from the publication statistics mentioned on p. 1, *Hamlet* continues to attract attention both inside and outside the scholarly community: those 400-plus publications per year are categorized in the *Shakespeare Quarterly Annual Bibliography* for 2001 under the headings 'Bibliographies and Checklists', 'Editions and Texts', 'Translations and Adaptations', 'Sources and Influences', 'Textual and Bibliographical Studies', 'Criticism', 'Pedagogy', 'Other', 'Actors, Acting, Directing', 'Film, Cinema, Radio, Television', 'Music', 'Readings, Audio Recordings', 'Stage and Theater History', 'Stage Productions' and 'Theatrical Techniques'. The average number of publications relating to *King Lear* is under 200 and that play has never had the high level of recognition enjoyed by *Hamlet*: it seems unlikely that the average person in London, New York, Moscow or Delhi could quote or identify any lines from *Lear*, while 'To be or not to be' must be the most frequently quoted (and parodied) speech in western and indeed global cultural tradition. Partly because of its supposed unstageability, *Lear* lacks the visual icons generated by *Hamlet*: its most frequently illustrated moments – the opening scene with Lear dividing up a map of his kingdom, and the final scene with Lear's entry carrying his dead daughter Cordelia – would probably not instantly signify '*Lear*' to most people in the same way that the man with the skull, the ghost on the battlements or the woman dead in the water signify '*Hamlet*'. For actors, of course, the title role of Hamlet remains one in which a young (or younger middle-aged) actor can make his (or indeed her) mark as a potential 'star' early on, while the title role of *King Lear* is an older man's part, the confirmation or culmination of an already successful career. It is even arguable that the political topicality of *King Lear* is already dated, relating as it did to a particular period of history and the dominance of elderly politicians such as Leonid Brezhnev and Ronald Reagan; certainly, as we shall see, *Hamlet* was perceived as being more topical than ever during the final years and collapse of the Soviet Union.

Indeed, there is not much evidence of *Hamlet* being in decline outside the Anglo-American tradition. Books on 'foreign' Shakespeare have proliferated in recent years: a brief list would have to include *Shakespeare on the German Stage*, volume 1, *1586–1914*, by Simon Williams (1990), and volume 2, *The Twentieth Century*, by Wilhelm Hortmann (1998); *Foreign Shakespeare: Contemporary Performance* by Dennis Kennedy (1993); *Shakespeare in the New Europe*, edited by Michael Hattaway, Boika Sokolova and Derek Roper (1994); *Hamlet and Japan*, edited by Yoshiko Ueno (1995); *Shakespeare and South Africa* by David Johnson (1996); *Shakespeare in China* by Xiao Yang Zhang (1996); *Shakespeare and Hungary* edited by Holger Klein and Peter Davidhazi (1996); *Post-Colonial Shakespeares*, edited by Ania Loomba and Martin Orkin (1998); *Shakespeare and the Japanese Stage*, edited by Takashi Sasayama, J.R. Mulryne and Margaret Shewring (1999); *Shakespeare and Eastern Europe* by Zdeněk Stříbrný (2000); *Performing Shakespeare in Japan*, edited by Minami Ryuta, Ian Carruthers and John Gillies (2001); *Painting Shakespeare Red: An East-European Appropriation* by Alexander Shurbanov and Boika Sokolova (2001); and *Shakespeare and Scandinavia* by Gunnar Sorelius (2002). Relevant studies have also appeared in collections such as *Shakespeare and National Culture*, edited by John J. Joughin (1997), and *Shakespeare and Appropriation*, edited by Christy Desmet and Robert Sawyer (1999). Most of these books attest to the traditional and virtually worldwide dominance of *Hamlet*; as indeed does the evidence from the international film industries: *Hamlet* has been knowledgeably described as 'the world's most filmed story after Cinderella', generating over fifty versions and, in that respect, in a completely different league from any other play.[1] The demise of *Hamlet* may have been exaggerated, but what, in fact, does this play mean to modern audiences and readers?

HAMLET IN OUR TIME

At one time, this must obviously have been an interesting play written by a promising Elizabethan playwright. However, equally obviously, that is no longer the case. Over the years, *Hamlet* has taken on a huge and complex symbolizing function and, as a part of the institution called 'English literature', it has become far more than a mere play by a mere playwright.

(Hawkes, *Meaning*, 4)

Most Americans know by heart a few tags from Shakespeare's plays even if they have not read them. A man on the street interviewed by Al Pacino for his documentary *Looking for Richard* [1996], or a Congressman in Washington, D.C. providing sound bites for the six o'clock news, can quote or parody the same rusty speech from *Hamlet* ('B2 or not B2').

(Taylor, 'Bard', 202)

What does *Hamlet* mean today? How can one get beyond its sheer iconic status and unpack that 'huge and complex

---

1   This claim is made by Luke McKernan and Olwen Terris, authors of *Walking Shadows: Shakespeare in the National Film and Television Archive* (1994), in their unpublished programme note to the June 1994 season at the National Film Theatre in London, which featured twelve *Hamlet* films.

symbolizing function' to discover why this apparently primitive drama, with its reliance on ghosts and the revenge ethic, nevertheless maintains its power in the twenty-first century? The question is of course impossible to answer in the space of this Introduction: we can only give some pointers towards current debates and hope that readers will also find suggestions in the remainder of the Introduction and in the commentary as to how modern performers and critics are interpreting the play, questioning or reaffirming old readings and finding new ones.

The soliloquies and the modernity of Hamlet

As Gary Taylor implies, and despite his overall argument that Shakespeare's reputation peaked during the Victorian period and is now in decline, *Hamlet* remains famous for its soliloquies, so let us begin with that 'same rusty speech', 'To be or not to be'. If one wants to argue that the First Quarto of *Hamlet* is in any sense a 'memorial reconstruction' of a 'better' text, it seems now incredible that the actor or reporter failed to remember this particular line, which appears in Q1 as 'To be, or not to be – ay, there's the point' (7.115 in our text). Moreover, the entire speech appears in a different place in Q1, during the equivalent of 2.2, much earlier than in the other texts (see pp. 76–96 and Appendix 2), and several modern stagings of Q2/F *Hamlet* have adopted the Q1 placing as being, for their purposes, more logical than the Q2/F placing in 3.1.[1] While Hamlet's soliloquies

---

1 British examples in the second half of the twentieth century include Michael Benthall directing John Neville at London's Old Vic in 1957; Tony Richardson directing Nicol Williamson at London's Roundhouse in 1969; Ron Daniels directing Mark Rylance at the Royal Shakespeare Theatre, Stratford-upon-Avon, in 1989; and Matthew Warchus directing Alex Jennings at the Royal Shakespeare Theatre, Stratford-upon-Avon, in 1997. Further examples at the beginning of the twenty-first century include Trevor Nunn directing Ben Whishaw at the London Old Vic and Michael Boyd directing Toby Stephens at the Royal Shakespeare Theatre, Stratford-upon-Avon, both in 2004. Franco Zeffirelli's 1990 film version, starring Mel Gibson, also adopted the Q1 placing.

are among the best-known and indeed best-loved features of the play, they seem, on the basis of the three earliest texts, to be movable or even detachable: there is no sign in Q1 or F of Hamlet's last soliloquy, delivered after his encounter with the Norwegian Captain at 4.4.31–65 in Q2, and in one modern production this speech was not only cut but replaced by 'To be or not to be' on the grounds that this much later moment is Hamlet's nadir.[1]

'To be or not to be' has of course taken on a life of its own, featuring in endless burlesques, parodies, cartoons and advertisements from the early seventeenth century to the present day. An unusual example of the speech being quoted out of context but quite seriously is when the character played by Robert Lepage in Denys Arcand's 1989 film *Jesus of Montreal* insists on including a version of 'Hamlet's soliloquy' as his condition for taking part in an updated version of a mystery play. The lines from 'to die: to sleep' up to 'fly to others that we know not of' (3.1.63–81) – spoken, of course, in French – make perfect sense as delivered by one of the disciples after the crucifixion and before the resurrection of Jesus.[2] Actors and directors put a great deal of work into the delivery of the soliloquies,[3] and audiences and reviewers repay these efforts by focusing much of their attention on these very famous speeches. Editors and critics build entire theories of the play and its hero on what he says in these monologues. The significance of the last soliloquy, for example, has ironically been highlighted by recent editors who think Shakespeare decided to omit it:

1 See Lavender, 233, discussing Peter Brook's 2000 production with Adrian Lester at the Bouffes du Nord, Paris.
2 Within the film, Lepage's character remarks that he will never be cast as Hamlet, but a fascination with *Hamlet* pervades Lepage's own work as a director and performer in theatre and film up to and including his 1995 multimedia show *Elsinore*, in which he played all the characters.
3 See, for example, the accounts in Shattuck, Gilder, Berkoff, Pennington, Maher and Holmes.

Philip Edwards (who prints it in square brackets) argues that 'it is not one of the great soliloquies' and that it is 'insufficient and inappropriate for Act 4 of *Hamlet*' (Cam², 17), while G.R. Hibbard (who consigns it to an appendix) writes that the lines 'do nothing to advance the action, nor do they reveal anything new about Hamlet and his state of mind' (Oxf¹, 362).

These comments prompt one to ask what exactly is 'great' about 'the great soliloquies' and what is their function in the play. Certainly, it has been widely assumed that they tell us something about Hamlet's state of mind and that in doing so they render him a modern hero.

> Since the end of the nineteenth century, *Hamlet* has been hailed as Shakespeare's most modern play, as the play that itself breaks out of the medieval and into the modern. Hamlet's consciousness, it is said, as dramatized primarily through his soliloquies, is what makes it so precocious.
>
> (de Grazia, 'Soliloquies', 80–1)

As de Grazia herself is aware, this simplistic division between the medieval and the modern has been challenged, not least by medievalists, who argue that the kind of interiority or subjectivity identified by scholars working on the Renaissance as modern can be found much earlier, in the poetry of William Langland and Geoffrey Chaucer, for example (see Aers). And the whole debate has been problematized by recent modes of criticism which associate the process of 'self-fashioning' and the exploration of the essentialist self with a particular historical moment, usually related to the concept of 'bourgeois individualism', which, it is claimed, did not exist before 1660 (see Lee). In a later contribution to the debate, de Grazia ('Time') sees Hamlet's interiority as an early nineteenth-century invention and argues for a rejection of the 'presentist' approach to the play. Nevertheless, it is difficult to deny that one of the things about Hamlet that has always fascinated actors, audiences and readers has been precisely the scope the play gives us to speculate about what he means when he says he has 'that within which passes show' (1.2.85).

But is it accurate to conclude that the soliloquies 'dramatize Hamlet's consciousness'? They surely fulfil a number of different functions, ranging from exposition of the plot to meditation on commonplace topics, and they are often less 'personal' than the soliloquies of, say, Richard III, Iago in *Othello* or Edmund in *King Lear*. The first one (1.2.129–59) is introduced with the stage direction '*Exeunt all but Hamlet*' in both Q1 and Q2 and the equivalent '*Exeunt. Manet Hamlet*' in F, while the third (2.2.484–540) begins 'Now I am alone.' But some of them are not even 'soliloquies' at all: Ophelia is on stage throughout 'To be or not to be' (3.1.55–87), and the audience knows that the King and Polonius are overhearing the speech; in some productions Hamlet addresses it specifically to Ophelia and in some he shows he is aware of the spies. Again in 4.4 Hamlet asks his companions to 'Go a little before' (30), and Q2 has no exit direction for them before his long speech; since they have been instructed to 'Follow him at foot' (4.3.51), it seems more likely that they go upstage rather than just walk off. So the mental picture we all seem to have of *Hamlet*, which is Hamlet alone on stage, is actually realized rather less often than one might think, though some theatrical conventions of act and scene division have tended to emphasize it (see Appendix 4). Curiously, there is an analogy here with one of the most common among illustrations of *Hamlet* (including paintings and photographs of actual performances), which consists of Hamlet alone contemplating a skull that he is holding in his hand: he is not in fact alone at all at this moment in 5.1, but in conversation with the Gravedigger and Horatio. Hamlet-as-icon, however, has to be alone, which is perhaps one reason why many illustrations (and cartoons) show him delivering 'To be or not to be' while holding a skull, conflating two very different moments in the play (see Figs 3 and 4).

3 Cartoon by Phil May of Hamlet with a skull, 1894

In any case, when Hamlet is alone, is he simply thinking aloud or is he rather talking to the audience? Centuries of performance in theatres equipped with proscenium arches and footlights separating the audience from the stage have

4 Cartoon by Patrick Blower of Tony Blair, UK Prime Minister, as Hamlet with a sheep's skull during the 2001 general election campaign when there was speculation that the epidemic of foot and mouth disease would cause a postponement of the poll (taken from the London *Evening Standard*, 16 March 2001)

encouraged the 'thinking aloud' approach and the cinema's convention of the 'voiceover' has enhanced it (notably, for example, in Laurence Olivier's 1948 film, where the camera seems to go inside the actor's head), but from the later twentieth century onwards, performances 'in the round', in smaller studio spaces and in reconstructions of Elizabethan theatres have allowed Hamlets to choose to direct the speeches outwards instead of inwards. Even in conventional theatres, the expectations of actors and audiences have changed: the recording of Richard Burton's performance (directed by John Gielgud and filmed in the Lunt-Fontanne Theatre in New York in 1964) shows him delivering the soliloquies in an internalized way, making no direct contact with the audience (who feel they can applaud after each speech without breaking the illusion). But in the proscenium–arch Royal Shakespeare Theatre in Stratford-upon-Avon in the following year David Warner, in Peter Hall's production, electrified audiences by addressing them directly. Though some reviewers put this down to an instinctual young actor's ignorance of the proper conventions, most commented on the power of this approach as well as its relative novelty. Clearly it could also be dangerous: one night, when Warner asked 'Am I a coward?' (2.2.506), someone shouted, 'Yes!' – which he remembered as one of the most exhilarating moments in his career (see Maher, 41, 51–3). That particular soliloquy, as Emrys Jones points out (*Scenic*, 104–5), has much in common with Richard III's 'Was ever woman in this humour wooed?' (1.2.232–68), in which the character shares with the audience his amazement at what we have just witnessed.

Other soliloquies are more reflective in tone, but the reflections are not always intimate or personal. Hamlet tends to ask 'what is this quintessence of dust?' (2.2.274) rather than 'What am I?', and it has been possible for scholars and critics to disagree totally over whether his most famous speech does or does not tell us of his own suicidal tendencies. The rediscovery of Q1 in 1823 contributed significantly to this debate, since 'To be or not to be' in that text follows a mere five lines after the King's 'See where he comes, poring upon a book' (7.110) (equivalent to 'But look where sadly the poor wretch comes reading' (2.2.165) in Q2, where 'To be or not to be' follows some 430 lines later), allowing those who do not want Hamlet to be suicidal to argue that he is simply meditating on what he has read. Whatever one's view of this (and it should be noted that Hamlet's discussion of 'self-slaughter' at 1.2.129–34 is not prompted by any book), it is surely clear that, even if he begins from his own situation, he moves on to more general speculations about the human condition – a tendency featured again in the maligned 'How all occasions do inform against me' (4.4.31–65), where again Hamlet asks 'What is a man?' (32). Indeed, one of the problems with this particular soliloquy might be that its more personal reflections are downright inaccurate: how can Hamlet claim he has 'strength and means / To do't [kill the King]' (44–5) when he is being escorted out of the country?

Hamlet has the largest part in the play, indeed in the entire Shakespearean canon, but the sheer number of words he utters, in conversation as well as in monologue, does not automatically give us access to 'that within'. The soliloquies give us a sense of his intelligence and his frustration (qualities with which we can easily identify), and dramaturgically they serve the usual end of allowing the character with superior awareness to set up situations of dramatic irony by his confidences in the audience. But centuries of debate demonstrate that in many ways Hamlet remains an opaque character, much in need of Horatio's posthumous interpretation; in the lighter tradition of *Hamlet* offshoots, Horatio's failure to complete and publish his exhaustive *Life and Letters of Hamlet the Dane* becomes something of a standing joke (see, for example, pp. 134–5).

Another problematic legacy of the formidable '*Hamlet* tradition' is the sheer (over-)familiarity of the play's language: it can seem a mere tissue of quotations, causing actors difficulty in making the lines sound fresh. We have lost the rhetorical training of Shakespeare's time and the technical vocabulary of linguistic effects which went with it: we are often impatient with studies of style, rhetoric and metre, preferring to move straight to 'the meaning of the play', that is, to larger patterns relating to themes, characters, historical and religious contexts. Editors are privileged to be able to engage with a text at the level of word-by-word detail, and actors, given enough rehearsal time, are obliged to undertake similar inquiries, but the general tendency of modern criticism has been to overlook verbal intricacy in favour of the larger picture. A scattering of late twentieth-century exceptions to this would include Patricia

Parker's *Literary Fat Ladies* and her essay on '*Othello* and *Hamlet*' ('Dilation'), George T. Wright's 'Hendiadys and *Hamlet*' and Ann Thompson and John O. Thompson's chapter on *Hamlet* in *Shakespeare, Meaning and Metaphor*; all of these explore new versions of traditional 'close reading' approaches, not just to the soliloquies but to the language of the play more generally.

Hamlet *and Freud*

> Though conclusive evidence is hard to come by, it is difficult to read Shakespeare without feeling that he was almost certainly familiar with the writings of Hegel, Marx, Nietzsche, Freud, Wittgenstein and Derrida.
>
> (Eagleton, ix–x)

Is this because in so many ways Shakespeare got in first, anticipating many of the major concerns of later writers, or is it because they were themselves overwhelmingly influenced by him? *Hamlet* has certainly featured in some of the key texts in modern philosophy and psychoanalysis. Marx developed a revolutionary theory of history in the *Eighteenth Brumaire* (1852) through a subversive reading of the Ghost of Hamlet's father (see Stallybrass, 'Mole'). Freud famously first sketched his theory of the Oedipus complex (later developed in *The Interpretation of Dreams*, 1900) in a letter to Wilhelm Fliess in October 1897 in which he argued that, in *Hamlet*, Shakespeare's 'unconscious understood the unconscious of his hero' in this way (see Garber, 124–71). More than any other of Shakespeare's plays, *Hamlet* has attracted psychoanalytic critics, and Hamlet and Ophelia have become respectively the iconic representatives of male and female instability.

In his identification of the 'Ophelia complex', Gaston Bachelard discussed the symbolic connections between women, water and death, seeing drowning as an appropriate merging into the female element for women, who are always associated with liquids: blood, milk, tears and amniotic fluid. Visual images of Ophelia either about to drown or drowning became increasingly popular in the nineteenth century (see Figs 5 and 6, and 4.7.164–81n.). Moreover, as Elaine Showalter has demonstrated, the particular circumstances of Ophelia's madness have made her 'a potent and obsessive figure in our cultural mythology' (78): she represents a powerful archetype in which female insanity and female sexuality are inextricably intertwined. Men may go mad for a number of reasons, including mental and spiritual stress, but women's madness is relentlessly associated with their bodies and their erotic desires. Melancholy was a fashionable disease among young men in London in the late sixteenth century, but it was associated with intellectual and imaginative genius in them, whereas 'women's melancholy was seen instead as biological and emotional in its origins' (Showalter, 81; see also Schiesari). The very word 'hysteria' implies a female physiological condition, originating as it does from the Greek *hystera* meaning womb. King Lear, fighting off his own impending madness, equates '*Hysterica passio*' with the medical condition involving feelings of suffocation and giddiness known to Elizabethans as 'the mother'. Stagings of Ophelia's mad scene (4.5) have always been influenced by prevailing stereotypes of female insanity, from sentimental wistfulness in the eighteenth century to full-blown schizophrenia in the twentieth.

To risk a very crude generalization, the Anglo-American *Hamlet* has often been read through Freud as primarily a domestic drama, with some productions to this day omitting Fortinbras and most of the play's politics (this happened, for example, when John Caird directed Simon Russell Beale at the National Theatre in London in 2000), while in other parts of the world, notably in eastern and east-central Europe during the dominance of the Soviet Union and the Cold War, *Hamlet* has been primarily a political play enacting the possibility of dissent from various forms of totalitarianism (see pp. 117–22;

5 1794 etching by Francesco Bartolezzi from a painting by Henry Tresham of an upright pre-Millais Ophelia 'clambering' to hang her garlands; see 4.7.164–81 and n.

6 Jean Simmons as a post-Millais Ophelia in a photograph taken on set
during the making of Laurence Olivier's 1948 film

Stříbrný; Shurbanov & Sokolova). There is, of course, an irony
here: would-be subversives in countries of the former Soviet
Union have re-read *Hamlet* in order to rebel against the very
regimes set up in the name of revolutionary Marxism: the 'old
mole' quality of the play can undermine Stalinism as well as
capitalism.

Psychoanalytic readings have been particularly influential in
the United Kingdom and North America, as we shall illustrate
from three representative examples. Janet Adelman's 1992
book, *Suffocating Mothers*, takes the same starting-point as
John Caird's production by explicitly eliminating the play's
politics. She sees the *Henry IV* plays and *Julius Caesar*
as 'oedipal dramas from which the chief object of contention
[i.e. the mother] has been removed', so that the father–son
relationship can be explored in an uncomplicated way, and she

29

continues: 'Before *Hamlet*, this relationship tends to be enacted in the political rather than the domestic sphere' (Adelman, 11). Her powerful reading of *Hamlet* makes it exclusively a family drama. It foregrounds the return of the mother and the subsequent release of infantile fantasies and desires involving maternal malevolence and the submerged anxiety of the male regarding subjection to the female. *Hamlet* also becomes the watershed between the mother-free romantic comedies and the later tragedies, mainly by admitting the difficult and, for Shakespeare, inevitably tragic presence of a fully imagined female sexuality. This is not to say that Gertrude herself is a completely realized character for Adelman; she sees her as 'less powerful as an independent character than as the site for fantasies larger than she is' (30) – fantasies concerning the need for masculine identity to free itself from the contaminated maternal body. And it is those fantasies which set the scene for all the plays that follow: after *Hamlet*'s failure to bring back from the dead the good father who can stabilize female sexuality, the other tragedies 're-enact paternal absence' (35) as the heroes struggle to define themselves in relation to women: 'for the emergence of the annihilating mother in *Hamlet* will call forth a series of strategies for confining or converting her power' (36).

Jacqueline Rose puts politics back into *Hamlet* by tracing how influential male readers of the play, Ernest Jones as well as T.S. Eliot, have echoed Hamlet's misogyny and blamed Gertrude for what they saw as the aesthetic and moral failings of the play overall. Picking up on Eliot's analogy for Hamlet as 'the Mona Lisa of literature', she argues that in his reading

the question of the woman and the question of meaning go together. The problem with *Hamlet* is not just that the emotion it triggers is unreasonable and cannot be contained by the woman who is its cause, but that this excess of affect produces a problem of interpretation: how to read, or control by reading, a play whose

inscrutability (like that of the *Mona Lisa*) has baffled
– and seduced – so many critics.

(Rose, 97–8)

Femininity itself becomes the problem within the play, and
within attempts to interpret it, but paradoxically femininity is
also seen as the source of creativity and the very principle
of the aesthetic process in other psychoanalytic readings in
which the process shifts from character to author: Shakespeare,
unlike his hero, can be claimed to have effected a productive
reconciliation with the feminine in his own nature.

For Marjorie Garber, our third example of the psychoanalytic
approach, the play is more complicated: in her 1987 book,
Shakespeare's Ghost Writers: Literature as Uncanny Causality,
she writes, 'In *Hamlet* . . . Shakespeare instates the uncanny as
sharply as he does the Oedipus complex' (Garber, 127). Freud's
sense of the uncanny depends on the revival of repressed
infantile or primitive beliefs and the compulsion to repeat:
'What, indeed, is revenge but the dramatization and acculturation
of the repetition compulsion?' (129). The father–son relationship
is still central, but the Ghost becomes at least as important as
the Queen. Freud insisted (*Interpretation of Dreams* (1900);
cited in Garber, 165) that *Hamlet* was written immediately after
the death of Shakespeare's own father in 1601 and not long
after the death of his son Hamnet/Hamlet (in 1596), so was
affected by his personal sense of bereavement (see, however,
our discussion of dating on pp. 45–60) and his personal interest
in a character obliged to transform his mourning into revenge.
Garber draws on Jacques Lacan as well as on Freud, especially
on his 1959 essay 'Desire and the interpretation of desire in
Hamlet'. In this reading, the Ghost, as a marker of absence and
a reminder of loss, becomes 'the missing signifier, the veiled
phallus' (Garber, 130; see also Fink).

But, if the Ghost is absence, invoking him and addressing
him produces an effect of unbearable, petrifying presence:
Garber draws parallels with the Father-Commendatore visiting

statue in Mozart's *Don Giovanni*, but it is Hamlet who is turned into stone. And, in a dizzying final twist, Garber allegorizes not only *Hamlet* but 'Shakespeare' itself, the canon (' "Remember me!" The canon has been fixed against self-slaughter': Garber, 176), as working through the same dynamic as the transference relationship in psychoanalytic practice. 'The transferational relationship Freud describes as existing between the analyst and the patient is . . . precisely the kind of relation that exists between "Shakespeare" and western culture . . . "Shakespeare" is the love object of literary studies . . . The Ghost is Shakespeare' (xiv, 176).

Reading against the Hamlet *tradition*

In an essay on *Hamlet* published in 2002, Richard Levin claimed 'a certain uniqueness in the current critical scene' in that 'I think [the play] presents Hamlet as an individual with a personality and I admire him' (Levin, 215). A few years earlier, Harold Bloom had taken a similar, self-consciously old-fashioned stance when he announced that 'After Jesus, Hamlet is the most cited figure in Western consciousness' and that 'Perhaps indeed it is Falstaff and Hamlet, rather than Shakespeare, who are mortal gods' (Bloom, xix, 4). Both critics can be seen to represent a kind of backlash against contemporary modes of criticism that have, for them, turned away from traditional readings of the play and, in the process, lost touch with the general reader, and indeed the general audience. Their response is to reinstate the importance of Hamlet himself as a character with whom audiences and readers can sympathize and identify. But what is the 'traditional' reading of *Hamlet* and how has it been challenged?

The history of what Levin (215) calls 'the megagigantic body of commentary on *Hamlet*' is a subject of study in itself which has produced a number of helpful surveys and anthologies, from Paul S. Conklin's *History of 'Hamlet' Criticism 1601– 1821* in 1947 to David Farley-Hills's ongoing four-volume

Critical Responses to 'Hamlet' 1600–1900, which commenced publication in 1995 (see also Weitz and Gottschalk). New volumes of essays appear all the time, and it is perhaps not surprising that many modern readings of *Hamlet* are as much concerned with interpreting the play 'against' or in opposition to what are taken to be traditional readings of it as they are with producing distinctive new readings. This is quite challenging because, especially when compared with the critical reception of *King Lear*, the critical reception of *Hamlet* was generally positive before the appearance of some of the Freudian and Marxist readings in which Hamlet as a character became more or less 'sick', either through a fixation on his mother or through an intellectual inability to take political action. There have been a few anti-*Hamlet* voices, but by and large Anglo-American and other cultures have taken a favourable view of the play and its hero. So has recent criticism been merely perverse in choosing to read *Hamlet* differently?

A characteristic approach among critics reading 'against' the older tradition is to find in the play itself contradictions and equivocations that challenge simple readings. Terence Hawkes, for example, in his 1986 chapter significantly entitled 'Telmah', sets out to 'read *Hamlet* backwards' (96) and to 'undermine our inherited notion of *Hamlet* as a structure that runs a satisfactorily linear course' (94) by drawing out 'countervailing patterns' such as an 'avuncular chord' (99) which operates against the paternal focus. He maintains that the vitality of *Hamlet* 'resides precisely in its plurality: in the fact that it contradicts itself and strenuously resists our attempts to resolve, to domesticate that contradiction' (117), so that simply to offer an 'alternative' reading would be inappropriate. But he in effect offers a very anti-Hamlet interpretation in which the usurping King is 'no simple villain, but a complex, compelling figure' (100) and he ends by suggesting that when Fortinbras gives orders for the conduct of 'his passage' (5.2.382) he has perhaps stopped talking about Hamlet and is referring to the King. A similar desire to 'unread' the play, to unsettle its meanings, can be found in Catherine Belsey's chapter 'Sibling rivalry, *Hamlet* and the first murder', which sees the play as a kind of Dance of Death, but one where we have to relinquish the desire for closure and allow the text to 'retain its mystery, its a-thetic knowlege, its triumphant undecidability – and its corresponding power to seduce' (Belsey, 172).

During the 1980s, when Hawkes's contribution appeared, editors and textual critics were making valiant efforts to unsettle *Hamlet* in a different way by displacing the standard conflated text, but some of them also indicated an increasing unease with the play's hero and his achievements. Philip Edwards, in the masterly introductory essay to his New Cambridge edition (1985), is eloquent on his struggle to distance himself from a sentimental, idealized view of Hamlet, especially as the play approaches its climax: 'It is hard to know what right Hamlet has to say ["I loved Ophelia"] when we think of how we have seen him treat her . . . For those of us who to any extent "believe in" Hamlet, Shakespeare makes things difficult in this scene [5.1]' (56). Examining Hamlet's demand for assurance from Horatio at [5.2.62–6[1]] he observes: 'It is difficult to see how we can take this speech except as the conclusion of a long and deep perplexity' (58). He adds, 'It is hard for us in the twentieth century to sympathise with Hamlet and his mission' (60), and he summarizes some of the ways in which the concerns of the play seem alien to a modern audience or reader:

> Hearing voices from a higher world belongs mainly in the realm of abnormal psychology. Revenge may be common but is hardly supportable. The idea of purifying violence belongs to terrorist groups. Gertrude's sexual behaviour and remarriage do not seem out of the ordinary.
>
> (Cam^2, 60)

1   Edwards prints the slightly longer version of this speech found in F: see Appendix 1.

In the next section of this Introduction we shall look at some of the attempts by modern critics to explore *Hamlet* through locating its belief systems and politics in a specifically Elizabethan context. But Edwards's Hamlet seems not only outdated but a failure who hardly deserves the 'flights of angels' that Horatio wishes would sing him to his rest:

> There is no doubt of the extent of Hamlet's failure. In trying to restore 'the beauteous majesty of Denmark' he has brought the country into an even worse state, in the hands of a foreigner. He is responsible, directly or indirectly, for the deaths of Polonius, Ophelia, Rosencrantz and Guildenstern. With more justification, he has killed Laertes and Claudius. But if his uncle is dead, so is his mother.
>
> (58)

Unsurprisingly, feminist critics have expressed difficulties with the play, deploring both the stereotypes of women depicted in it and the readiness of earlier critics to accept Hamlet's view of the Queen and Ophelia without questioning whether the overall view taken by the play (or its author) might be different. Marilyn French revived the definition 'problem play' (first applied to *Hamlet* by F.S. Boas in a chapter in *Shakspere and his Predecessors* in 1896 and previously revived by E.M.W. Tillyard when he included *Hamlet* in his 1950 book, *Shakespeare's Problem Plays*) in her 1982 study, *Shakespeare's Division of Experience*. When Carolyn Heilbrun reprinted her essay on 'Hamlet's mother' in 1990, she noted that when she had first published it in 1957 she had been 'a feminist waiting for a cause to join'. Subsequent studies have attempted to reclaim the play's women: Ellen J. O'Brien, in 'Revision by excision: rewriting Gertrude', demonstrates how the Queen's role was severely and consistently cut onstage from 1755 to 1900 (and frequently after that) so as to eliminate any possibility of the character being affected by the closet scene, while renewed interest in Q1 has also fuelled more sympathetic readings of the Queen (see Kehler and Shand).

All Shakespeare's plays mean different things at different times and in different places. Some of them have had their meanings changed quite radically by historical events: it is difficult, for example, for post-Holocaust and post-feminist generations to approach *The Merchant of Venice* and *The Taming of the Shrew* as straightforward comedies. *King Lear* took on new meanings during the Cold War, *The Tempest* comes to reflect the concerns of postcolonial societies and *Othello* is seen in the context of modern racism. Yet one of the most influential modes of recent criticism, New Historicism, has been largely concerned with putting the plays back into the context of their own time. In the next section we shall attempt to explore what this means for *Hamlet* and indeed whether we can be confident of when exactly that time was.

HAMLET IN SHAKESPEARE'S TIME

When he was working on *Hamlet*, towards the end of the sixteenth century and at the very beginning of the seventeenth, Shakespeare was in his mid-thirties. His previous experience of writing tragedy consisted of *Titus Andronicus* (1592), *Romeo and Juliet* (1595) and, very probably, *Julius Caesar* (1599, but see pp. 45–60).[1] All three of these generic predecessors had contained revenge as a motivation for the narrative, as had many of the English history plays he had produced during the 1590s. From the mid-1590s Shakespeare had enjoyed an unusual degree of stability in his career as a sharer in the Chamberlain's Men, acting as well as writing for the company. During the decade before *Hamlet*, he seems to have alternated

---

1 Dates are taken from 'The canon and chronology of Shakespeare's plays', in *TxC*, 69–144.

between writing histories and comedies, the former culminating in *Henry V* and the latter in *As You Like It* (both around 1599).

Hamlet *at the turn of the century*

Shakespeare's only son Hamnet or Hamlet died in August 1596, and his father John was to die in September 1601. It is difficult to dismiss the relevance of these experiences to the writing of *Hamlet*, a play which begins with the death of a father and ends with the death of a son, both called Hamlet, though it is equally difficult to define the precise nature of that relevance with any confidence. Shakespeare scholars, perhaps nervous of overtly biographical readings, have regularly referred to Shakespeare's son as Hamnet rather than Hamlet, pointing out that he and his twin sister Judith were named after Shakespeare's Stratford friends, Hamnet and Judith Sadler, but, as Park Honan notes, 'Hamnet' 'was interchangeable with "Hamlet" – in Shakespeare's will in a legal hand his friend would appear as "Hamlet Sadler" – and among abundant local variants of the same name were (for example) Amblet, Hamolet and even Hamletti' (Honan (90).[1] Shakespeare's father arguably appears twice in the graveyard scene. The Gravedigger's somewhat gratuitous reference to Adam as a 'gentleman' on the grounds that he was 'the first that ever bore arms' (5.1.32–3) reminds us that John Shakespeare had tried unsuccessfully several times to acquire a coat of arms and that his son apparently assisted him in his successful attempt in October 1596, ironically just two months after the death of his own son, who would have inherited this status (see Honan, 21, 38, 228–9). Slender's flattery of Shallow as one who 'writes himself *Armigero*' (i.e. claims the right to bear arms) in *The Merry Wives of Windsor* (1.1.8) is another

---

1   See also Greenblatt, 'Hamnet' and *Will*, for further speculations on this possible link.

turn-of-the-century reference to these events. Later in the graveyard scene, in response to Hamlet's question, 'How long will a man lie i'th' earth ere he rot?', the Gravedigger assures him that 'a tanner will last you nine year' (5.1.154–8): we may remember that John Shakespeare was a glover, sometimes described as a whittawer (that is, a specialist in the preparation of soft, white leather), whose trade involved tanning the skins of goats, deer and other animals before turning them into gloves. He was apparently illiterate and when he drew his mark on documents he regularly identified himself as a glover by using either a pair of glover's compasses or a glover's stitching clamp (Honan, 8). It is tempting to follow the suggestion of Robert N. Watson that 'Hamlet's guilt-ridden compulsion to help his tormented father may draw on Shakespeare's own guilt towards his recently deceased and reputedly Catholic father' (Watson, 75), but, as we shall demonstrate below, the play cannot definitely be dated after September 1601. It seems, however, that John Shakespeare had been in poor health for some years before his death, so the play may anticipate rather than reflect that event.

On the national scale, the long reign of Elizabeth was drawing towards its end and there was much anxiety and unease about the future. In the brief discussion of *Hamlet* in the 'Epilogue' to her recent history of the Tudor dynasty, Susan Brigden writes: 'Shakespeare's art is transcendent, Prince Hamlet's questions are for all time, but the play originated in a particular time and place, and its themes were quintessentially those of the Renaissance and Reformation' (Brigden, 364). For her, the lament of Shakespeare's hero that 'the time is out of joint' was topical in 1600. Hamlet embodies lingering doubts about the 'lost world' of traditional Catholicism; he lives in a court poisoned by corruption at the centre; he agonizes over the discrepancy between the 'new worlds' opening up to the human mind and spirit and the inadequacy of individuals to live up to their potential.

Certainly, *Hamlet* has been read as a *fin de siècle* text in a number of ways. A new kind of 'historicist' reading has in fact provided a way of addressing the 'problem' earlier critics had with what they perceived as an excess of sexuality in *Hamlet*. T.S. Eliot famously typified this approach in his statement in 1919 that 'Hamlet is up against the difficulty that his disgust is occasioned by his mother, but his mother is not an adequate equivalent for it; his disgust envelops and exceeds her'; hence the play lacks an 'objective correlative' – an appropriate matching of emotion to object (Eliot, 145). Recent interpretations have, in effect, accounted for the apparently excessive focus on Gertrude by identifying her with Elizabeth I and reading the play as a kind of meditation on the ageing and passing of the Virgin Queen.

Such readings have much in common with the influential interpretation of *A Midsummer Night's Dream* by Louis Adrian Montrose, whose essay, '"Shaping fantasies": figurations of gender and power in Elizabethan culture', discusses that play in relation to the cult of Elizabeth with particular attention to the ageing body of the Virgin Queen. The notion of political power being inherent in the body of a woman (particularly an ageing woman) is seen as troubling to male subjects, just like the representation of Hamlet's mother as 'Th'imperial jointress to this warlike state' (1.2.9). The extent to which the present King's marriage to the Queen has consolidated or even ensured his 'election' is not made clear in the play, but Leonard Tennenhouse reads *The Murder of Gonzago* as an effort to 'represent the queen's body as an illegitimate source of political authority':

> Hamlet's attempt at staging a play is very much an attempt on the playwright's part to imagine a situation in which political power was not associated with a female and the aristocratic female was not iconically bonded to the land.
>
> (Tennenhouse, 91)

He argues that it is important for Hamlet to distinguish two separate acts of treason, the seizing of the Queen's body and the seizing of political power, since it is only by separating them and by subordinating the former that the threat to the state can be diminished:

> Hamlet's obsession with the misuse of the queen's sexuality, more than his uncle's possession of the state, transforms the threat of dismemberment into pollution. We might say that, in redefining the nature of the threat against the body politic, Hamlet attempts to stage a Jacobean tragedy.
>
> (96)

In this reading, Hamlet himself seems to become a New Historicist critic who is more comfortable with representations of absolutist male power than with the idea of a powerful woman.

Hamlet has also been seen as a 'succession' play which reflects anxieties about female intervention in patrilinear culture and represents the exhaustion of the old dynasty. Stuart M. Kurland is confident that, 'Unlike some modern readers, Shakespeare's audience would have been unlikely to see in Hamlet's story merely a private tragedy or in Fortinbras' succession to the Danish throne a welcome and unproblematic restoration of order', but would have read the play as looking forward with some trepidation to the not yet certain accession of James I (Kurland, 291). Bruce Thomas Boehrer's more ambitious reading sees *Hamlet* as a play that 'reconstructs history so as to relieve English cultural myth of the twin burdens of Elizabeth's sex and her barrenness' (Boehrer, 64). Working through the complicated set of parallels whereby Gertrude's incestuous remarriage both recalls and refigures Henry VIII's remarriage to Elizabeth's mother, Anne Boleyn, he argues that the play's misogyny works to reassure its contemporary audience:

In facing and surviving the death of its royal house, *Hamlet* enacts the promised end of Tudor imperial culture: an end feared and contemplated by English monarchs and subjects at least since Henry VIII divorced Catherine of Aragon, and an end that was by 1599 almost inevitable. In affirming an order beyond this chaos, the play may at last manage through wishful thinking to free itself from female influence.

(Boehrer, 77; see also McCabe,
162–71, and Rosenblatt)

If this reading was available for Elizabethan audiences, it was curiously neglected in the Restoration when, as we have seen, Fortinbras (and any idea of the survival of the royal house associated with him) was summarily cut. It might be as reasonable to argue that *Hamlet* projects the possibility that the son of a foreign monarch formerly seen as an enemy (Mary, Queen of Scots) could be acceptable as a king. Steven Mullaney, another critic who finds the centrality of Gertrude in the play problematic, explains it in more forthright terms as a kind of misogyny that anticipated the mourning for the queen: 'The final progress of Elizabeth – the cultural processing of her age, in both senses of that term – was completed long after her funeral procession took place but begun some years before it, when her aging body first announced the proximity of her last days' (Mullaney, 142). But would Elizabethan audiences really have seen the ageing body of their Virgin Queen in Shakespeare's Gertrude, played by a boy actor and, at least according to Hamlet, sexually active to an alarming degree? While these readings have their interest, one would not want to reduce *Hamlet* to a play about the forthcoming demise of Elizabeth, any more than one would want to reduce it to a play about the deaths of John and Hamlet Shakespeare.

More limited claims for the topicality of *Hamlet* are made by Karin S. Coddon and Patricia Parker. Coddon's essay, '"Such strange desyns": madness, subjectivity and treason in *Hamlet* and Elizabethan culture', relates *Hamlet* to the decline and fall of Elizabeth's former favourite Robert Devereux, Earl of Essex, who was finally executed in February 1601, though his star had been declining since 1597 and he had notably lost the Queen's favour over his disastrous military expedition to Ireland. (The premature and perhaps unwise celebration of this expedition in the Chorus to Act 5 of *Henry V* is a very rare example of an unquestionable reference by Shakespeare to a current event.) She explores the question of Essex's melancholy or madness, seen at the time as a product of thwarted ambition that became displaced into treason. Hamlet after all complains, 'I lack advancement' (3.2.331), a remark which is closely followed by the King's pious justification for dispatching him to England on the grounds that in Denmark he is a threat to the security of the state (3.3.1–26). Without wanting to make an exact equation between the fictional Hamlet and the historical Essex, Coddon sees the representation of madness in the play as relating to the 'faltering of ideological prescriptions to define, order, and constrain subjectivity' (Coddon, 61) and she argues for madness as 'an instrument of social and political disorder' (62).

Parker's essay, '*Othello* and *Hamlet*: dilation, spying, and the "secret places" of woman', has a different sense of the topical relevance of the play. Beginning with Hamlet's obsession with the 'secret places' of women – not only his interest in Gertrude's sexuality but his lewd references to Ophelia's 'lap' in the dialogue before the dumb-show in 3.2 – she moves into a reading which brings out the play's representation of a Court full of spies and informers. The King employs Rosencrantz and Guildenstern to spy on Hamlet, to 'pluck out the heart of [his] mystery' (3.2.357–8), Polonius sends Reynaldo to spy on Laertes in Paris (2.1), and there are many instances of secrets being hidden or revealed. Parker sees *Hamlet* as being written at a 'crucial historical juncture' (Parker, 31) when a state secret service was being developed:

> This sense of both the holding and the withholding of secrets in *Hamlet* . . . [evokes] the emergent world of statecraft contemporary with the play, one that historians describe as increasingly involving the mediation of agents, go-betweens, and representatives across bureaucratic as well as geographic distances, along with the corresponding multiplication of informers and spies.
>
> (Parker, 134–5)

For Robert N. Watson (74–102), Michael Neill (216–61) and Stephen Greenblatt (*Purgatory*), the topical issues are to do with death, religion, and the shift from a culture in which the living could do something for the dead (specifically, they could shorten their time in purgatory by prayers and other actions) to one in which nothing could be done – or in which revenge becomes a problematic substitute. Watson specifically sees revenge tragedy as 'a displacement of prayers for the dead forbidden by the Reformation' (75), while Neill argues that *Hamlet* is written 'against' the popular genre, acknowledging that nothing can be done for the dead, though revenge can be a form of memory. Greenblatt's exploration of 'the poetics of Purgatory' and the intense power of the Ghost in *Hamlet* notes the paradox that 'a young man from Wittenberg, with a distinctly Protestant temperament, is haunted by a distinctly Catholic ghost' (Greenblatt, *Purgatory*, 240). Hamlet seems to accept the Ghost's claim to come from purgatory, although the whole conception of purgatory along with the practices that had developed around it had been explicitly denied and rejected by the Church of England in 1563 (235). Perhaps, he suggests, the play represents

> a fifty-year effect, a time in the wake of the great, charismatic ideological struggle in which the revolutionary generation that made the decisive break with the past is all dying out and the survivors hear

only hypocrisy in the sermons and look back with
longing at the world they have lost.

(248)

Or perhaps 'the Protestant playwright was haunted by the spirit
of his Catholic father pleading for suffrages to relieve his soul
from the pains of Purgatory' (249). But again we run into the
problem of the precise date of the play: Greenblatt would prefer
not to credit anyone other than Shakespeare with 'the single
most important alteration to the old story', the introduction of
the Ghost (205), but his desire to make the direct link with the
death of John Shakespeare requires him, reluctantly, to accept
that it was the anonymous author of the *Ur-Hamlet* (or 'pre-
Hamlet') who made this change. While no one doubts that
Shakespeare's *Hamlet* is a late Elizabethan play, it has proved
difficult to pin it down more precisely.

The challenge of dating Hamlet

Can we establish a precise date? Our predecessor, Harold
Jenkins, wrote in the Introduction to his 1982 Arden Shakespeare
edition that 'A conflict of evidence has made its precise
date, like most other things about *Hamlet*, a problem' (1). But
what do we mean by the 'precise date' of a Shakespeare play?
Some later Arden editors (Lois Potter in the 1997 edition of
The Two Noble Kinsmen, for example, or Edward Burns in the
2000 edition of *Henry VI, Part 1*) prioritize the date of the
first performance, whereas Ernst Honigmann, in his influential
essay on 'The date of *Hamlet*', set out to determine 'when
it was written' ('Date', 24). Jenkins was rightly concerned
with when *Hamlet* was 'written and produced' (1), but this
immediately suggests the possibility of two dates.

In fact, there must be at least three separate significant dates
for any Shakespeare play: those of the completion of the
manuscript, the first performance and the first printing. In the
case of this edition of *Hamlet*, however, we are not dealing with

one printed text but three. Neither are we necessarily dealing with one first performance: the performance history of Q1 is surely different from that of Q2, and F may be different again. And behind the printed text there may be more than one 'completed' manuscript. Furthermore, it is generally held that there was an earlier *Hamlet* play, the so-called *Ur-Hamlet*, either by Shakespeare or by someone else, with its own necessarily different set of dates, and this hypothetical lost play continues to complicate the issue of the date of Shakespeare's play and indeed the issue of its sources. We shall try to indicate in this section why scholars can continue to disagree about the dating evidence and its interpretation.

Was there an earlier Hamlet *play?*

Edmund Malone was the first to suggest that there was a *Hamlet* on the stage in 1589 when, in his Preface to Robert Greene's *Menaphon*, Thomas Nashe referred to 'whole Hamlets, I should say handfuls, of tragical speeches' (Nashe, 3.315). In 1594 Philip Henslowe recorded a performance of a play called *Hamlet* at Newington Butts; two years later Thomas Lodge's reference to a 'ghost which cried so miserably at the Theatre, like an oyster-wife, *Hamlet*, revenge' (*Wit's Misery*, 1596) inevitably suggests a play performed by the Lord Chamberlain's Men (Shakespeare's company), since they acted at The Theatre playhouse in Shoreditch until late 1596. A slightly later phrase in Nashe's Preface has long persuaded some scholars that this *Hamlet* play was by Thomas Kyd – he describes how Seneca's followers on 'our stage . . . imitate the kid in Aesop' – and Emma Smith ('Ghost writing') has reviewed the enormous lengths to which scholars have gone in order to reconstruct Kyd's lost *Hamlet* and its supposed relationship to Shakespeare's *Hamlet*. Attempts have nevertheless been made, repeatedly,[1]

---

1 See, for example, Lewis, 64–76; Gray, 'Reconstruction'; Parrott–Craig, 7–15; Bowers, *Tragedy*, 89–93; Whitaker, 329–46; Bullough, 7.45, 49, 51.

and they continue: G. Blakemore Evans ('An echo of the *Ur-Hamlet*?') has recently written about *Moderatus* (1595), a little-known chivalric romance by Robert Parry, which contains an incident in which a sealed letter is opened, read and then resealed with a signet ring. Evans points out that in all the proposed sources or analogues for the main Hamlet story – Saxo, Belleforest and *The Hystorie of Hamblet* – the King's letter to the King of England, which contains instructions that Amleth/Hamblet be killed, is cut in runic letters on a board, and Amleth has to scrape it clean, reinscribe it and sign it with the forged signature of Fengon. Since Shakespeare is unlikely to have been influenced by Parry, Evans speculates that Parry, who had visited London several times before 1595, may have been recalling the *Ur-Hamlet*.

On 24 June 1626 a company of English players performed a *Tragoedia von Hamlet einen Printzen in Dennemarck* in Dresden. This may well be the German drama, *Der bestrafte Brudermord oder: Prinz Hamlet aus Dännemark*, which was first published in Berlin in 1781 (from a manuscript dated 27 October 1710 but subsequently lost[1]). *Fratricide Punished*, as English scholars call it, is a much compressed version of Shakespeare's plot, done in prose, lacking almost all the soliloquies, Ophelia's songs and the graveyard scene, but with some added scenes, including a Senecan prologue, some added characters and some added farcical business. Scholars cannot agree whether the play derives from Q1 (parallels include the fact that its Polonius equivalent is called Corambus, and the nunnery scene precedes the entry of the players), from Q2 (with which it shares many features not present in Q1) or from the *Ur-Hamlet*. The last of these possibilities was dismissed by Jenkins and Hibbard, but was entertained by most of the nineteenth-century scholars who discussed *Der bestrafte*

---

1   It was published in the journal *Olla Potrida*, ed. H.A.O. Reichard (Berlin, 1781), pt 2, 18–68.

Brudermord,[1] and hence provides the opportunity for further speculation about the nature of the lost play.

There is general agreement that, stylistically, the texts of *Hamlet* printed in 1604–5 and 1623 'cannot belong to the years before 1590' (*TxC*, 138), but nevertheless it is not logically impossible that the play referred to by Nashe was an earlier version by Shakespeare and not by Kyd. Nor is it logically impossible that the play referred to by Lodge was an earlier version by Shakespeare. All three of the later texts involve a Ghost who commands his son to revenge his 'foul and most unnatural murder', though the two words 'Hamlet' and 'revenge' are not actually contiguous in any of them. Q1's version of the relevant dialogue reads:

> *Ghost* Hamlet, if euer thou didst thy deere father loue.
> *Ham.* O God.
> *Ghost* Reuenge his foule, and most vnnaturall murder:
> (5.17–20)

Q2's Ghost does not actually address Hamlet by name at this point:

> *Ghost.* . . . List, list, o list:
>   If thou did'st euer thy deare father loue.
> *Ham.* O God.
> *Ghost.* Reuenge his foule, and most vnnaturall murther.
> (1.5.22–5)

F's version reads:

> *Gho.* . . . list *Hamlet*, oh list,
>   If thou didst euer thy deare Father loue.
> *Ham.* Oh Heauen!
> *Gho.* Reuenge his foule and most vnnaturall Murther.
> (1.5.22–5)

---

1 Furness (2.116–20) traced the theory back to Bernhardy, to Cohn, and to Cam.

Nevertheless, a version of a play of *Hamlet* by Shakespeare containing the words 'Hamlet, revenge' might conceivably date back to at least 1589, though the play as we know it in the three surviving texts must have been written, or rewritten, a decade later.

Are there any early references to Shakespeare's play?

Early references, unfortunately, are no more decisive, and one of them consists of the significant absence of a reference: Honigmann ('Date') felt it was 'fairly safe' to assume that *Hamlet* could not have been written earlier than the autumn of 1598 when Francis Meres composed a list of Shakespeare's plays (*Palladis Tamia: Wits Treasury*; see Chambers, *Shakespeare*, 2.193–4) and made no mention of it. Almost all scholars agree, but an accidental omission by Meres, although unlikely, is not inconceivable: he was not to know how important his list would be for future scholars.

A reference by Gabriel Harvey is also problematic. At some point after buying a copy of Thomas Speght's 1598 edition of Chaucer's *Works*, Harvey made some annotations, among which is a note that 'The younger sort takes much delight in Shakespeares Venus, & Adonis: but his Lucrece, & his tragedie of Hamlet, prince of Denmarke, haue it in them, to please the wiser sort' (BL Add. MS 42518, fol. 394^v). But when did he make this note and which version of the play does he mean? Dating Harvey's marginalia is a confusing exercise. One of his annotations implies a very early date: he lists some 'florishing metricians' including not only Shakespeare but Spenser, who died on 16 January 1599, and Thomas Watson, who died in 1592. Since Harvey must have bought the book in 1598 or later, either he did not know Watson was dead or his use of 'florishing' did not imply 'living'. The note refers to literary works which 'the Earle of Essex commendes' but, since Essex died on 25 February 1601, it must have been written earlier. However, it also refers to

'Owens new Epigrams' and since these were not published until 1607 we seem to re-enter the world of the impossible.

Scholars twist and turn as they try to reconcile the seeming contradictions and impossibilities in Harvey.[1] They point out, for example, that elsewhere he uses 'flourishing' as a technical term descriptive of a writer's style: if so, neither Watson nor Spenser need have been living when Harvey wrote his note. They reckon that Harvey might have seen John Owen's epigrams in manuscript: if so, the note could have been written years before 1607. They also puzzle over the form in which Harvey came across the play. Honigmann rejects the idea that Harvey could be referring to the *Ur-Hamlet* because he cannot imagine 'the wiser sort' enjoying it, but, since the play is lost, such speculations are dubious. Jenkins uses the same argument to dismiss the idea that it was a performance from which 'the abridged and garbled Q1' might have derived (Ard[2], 6); Edwards concludes sensibly that Harvey 'is really of little use in trying to date *Hamlet*' (Cam[2], 5) and moves on to other material.

We should be on safer ground with the Stationers' Register. On 26 July 1602, James Roberts registered 'A booke called the Revenge of Hamlett Prince Denmarke as yt was latelie Acted by the Lord Chamberleyne his servantes' (Arber, 3.212). Almost every scholar assumes this is a reference to Shakespeare's play, and the reference to the Chamberlain's Men certainly supports the assumption, although the author is not mentioned and this is not precisely the play's title as it appears in any printed version. Roberts did go on to print the Second Quarto in 1604–5 (of the seven extant copies, three are dated 1604, the rest 1605), but not the First Quarto in 1603. As we shall see

---

1   Virginia F. Stern points out (127–8) that in his marginalia in another book (Guicciardini's *Detti et fatti* (Venice, 1571), sig. K2[r], acquired in the 1580s) Harvey mentions 'The Tragedie of Hamlet'; she argues that the reference to Owen postdates the rest of the relevant notes on fol. 422[v] in the Chaucer volume and concludes that the reference to *Hamlet* was written in June 1599.

(pp. 56–8 and 77), the title-page of the First Quarto makes its own rather puzzling claim about the play's early performances.

Finally, Andrew Gurr has added a further clue that points to 1600. This is the poem *Daiphantus* to which its author, 'An. Sc.' (perhaps Antony Scoloker), attached an epistle in which he noted that the poem 'this last year might have been burned'. Gurr recognizes that *Daiphantus* was published in 1604 (and it has long been noted that the poem itself contains references to 'mad Hamlet'), but he thinks the epistle was written earlier and refers to the burning of books resulting from the so-called 'Bishops' ban' of 1 June 1599. The implication is that the epistle was written in 1600, and, since the author expresses in it the hope that his poem might 'please all, like Prince Hamlet', Gurr concludes that *Hamlet* had only recently appeared (Gurr, 'Auto da fe', 15). Duncan-Jones incidentally supports the truth of Scoloker's claim (which implies that it was not only 'the wiser sort' who enjoyed the play) by noting 'the high incidence of boys given the name "Hamlet" in the first decade of the seventeenth century' (Duncan-Jones, 180). None of this is implausible, but again the hypotheses are unproven.

Can we date Hamlet *in relation to other contemporary plays?*

Many scholars believe that the allusions to Julius Caesar in *Hamlet* are references to Shakespeare's own play of that name. Jenkins, for example, hears an echo of *Julius Caesar* at 1.1.112–19, and reads 3.2.99–100 as a joke about *Julius Caesar* 'as performed by Shakespeare's company' (Ard², 1). Since the play that Thomas Platter saw at the Globe on 21 September 1599 was probably Shakespeare's *Julius Caesar* (though, as David Daniell points out (15–16), not necessarily its first performance),[1] he concludes that *Hamlet* cannot be earlier than that date. Others

---

1 Shapiro ('Biography') has suggested it might have been ten days earlier because Platter was using the old calendar; see also Shapiro, *1599*.

have noted that Plutarch's Caesar is killed in the Senate House, Shakespeare's is killed in the Capitol, and Polonius refers to the Capitol, so they claim Shakespeare must be referring back to his own dramatization (though, as we point out at 3.2.100n., he could have picked up this error from Chaucer's 'Monk's Tale' at any time). Honigmann finds support for this in the assumption that 'the two actors who played the original Hamlet and Polonius – almost certainly Burbage and Heminges – must have taken Brutus and Caesar in *Julius Caesar*, if we can trust modern casting methods and the researches of present-day scholars into "Shakespeare's personnel"' ('Date', 29). He also finds support in the 'coincidence' that Q1's title-page claims that *Hamlet* was played 'in the two Vniuersities of Cambridge and Oxford' and Polonius is given the 'completely gratuitous anecdote about playing "i'the university"' (29). Hibbard argues that the longer reference to the death of Caesar at 1.1.112–19 was 'intended to serve as an advertisement for *Julius Caesar*' and was therefore cut in F because that play was no longer being performed (Oxf[1], 355).

But, while there is a close relationship between *Hamlet* and *Julius Caesar* (Hamlet mentions 'Imperious Caesar' yet again at 5.1.202), it is not absolutely necessary to assume that references in the one play are 'echoes' of the other. Nor do we have to assume that a reference to a play about the death of Julius Caesar has to be read as a joke about a play by Shakespeare, a performance by the Lord Chamberlain's Men or, indeed, any event in real life at all. In its context (in all three texts), Hamlet's joke is primarily a pun on 'Brutus/brute' and 'Capitol/capital' and it does not depend on a topical allusion of any kind. There are similar problems with using as dating evidence a line in the 'bad quarto' of *The Merry Wives of Windsor* (registered 18 January 1602), 'What is the reason that you use me thus?' (1188). Jenkins assumes the line was 'lifted' from *Hamlet*, 5.1.278 (Ard[2], 1), but it could be the other way round, or Shakespeare might have used the line twice, or someone transcribing either play might have inadvertently recalled the other.

Can we date *Hamlet* with reference to plays by other people? There are many structural and verbal parallels between *Hamlet* and John Marston's *Antonio's Revenge*, which was entered in the Stationers' Register on 24 October 1601. These parallels may well be 'too strong to be merely coincidental', as G.K. Hunter wrote (Marston, *Revenge* (1965), xviii), but scholars have failed to agree on the relationship between the two plays. Some have thought that Shakespeare was following Marston; others, including Jenkins, that Marston was following Shakespeare; yet others, including Hunter, attribute the similarities to a common source: the *Ur-Hamlet*. In two recent studies, Charles Cathcart argues that echoes of *Hamlet* are present in Marston's earlier Antonio play, *Antonio and Mellida*, which he dates 1599/1600, and in the collaborative play *Lust's Dominion*, which he argues was written about the same time (Cathcart, '*Hamlet*' and '*Dominion*'), but MacDonald P. Jackson and Michael Neill had again invoked the *Ur-Hamlet* as an explanation of the *Antonio and Mellida* parallels (Marston, *Plays*, 4). W. Reavley Gair agrees about the influence of the lost *Hamlet* play but argues that Shakespeare and Marston were working at the same time and in direct competition with each other (Marston, *Revenge* (1978), 12–14), while Katherine Duncan-Jones replaces 'competition' with 'friendly emulation' or 'collusion', citing evidence of close links between the two playwrights and examples of their shared vocabulary (Duncan-Jones, 144–9). Regrettably, it has to be concluded that, as with *Julius Caesar* and *Merry Wives*, parallels with *Antonio's Revenge* cannot be conclusive in trying to date *Hamlet*.

Can we date *Hamlet* through the internal reference to the so-called 'war of the theatres'? Jenkins argued that 'a striking topical allusion would seem to place *Hamlet* firmly in 1601' (Ard[2], 1). This is the 'eyrie of children' who are 'now the fashion' and 'berattle the common stages' (2.2.336–60 in F; see

2.2.299n. in the Q2 commentary and Appendix 1). These, says Jenkins, are the boy actors, known as the Children of the Chapel, established from Michaelmas 1600 at the Blackfriars and acting, among other plays, Ben Jonson's *Cynthia's Revels* (before the end of 1600) and *Poetaster* (in 1601, possibly spring), both of which snipe at the plays in the public playhouses. Part of the 'throwing about of brains' (2.2.356–7 in F) and 'much to-do on both sides' (2.2.350–1 in F) was the retaliation of the public playwrights in Dekker's *Satiromastix* (entered in the Stationers' Register on 11 November 1601). The allusion to the boy actors is in F, and is represented in Q1, but absent from Q2. Jenkins followed Dover Wilson in regarding it as a 1601 topical addition to the original manuscript, cut for the printing of Q2 in 1604–5 but resurfacing in 1623 in F. He argued that 'the account of the theatre quarrel in *Hamlet* must date about or soon after the middle of 1601' (Ard², 2), and he thought that 'the late innovation' (2.2.296 in Q2, 2.2.331 in F) meant 'the recent insurrection' and referred to Essex's rebellion of 8 February 1601 (3). James P. Bednarz suggests a reason for the 1604–5 'cut', namely that by 1604 the Children of the Chapel had become the Children of Her Majesty's Chapel under the patronage of Queen Anne, so that this might be another 'diplomatic' cut, like that of the lines about Denmark being a prison at 2.2.237–67 in F (Bednarz, 248). Honigmann, citing Q1's use of the word 'novelty' (7.271) as support for a more modern use of 'innovation', took 'the late innovation' to be an allusion to the renewal of acting by the boys in 1600, which led in turn to the 'inhibition' of 22 June 1600 when the Privy Council stepped in to restrict the number of playhouses and their performances.

Another possible topical allusion in this F-only passage is in Rosencrantz's response to Hamlet's question about the child actors' success, 'Do the boys carry it away?', 'Ay, that they do, my lord – Hercules and his load too' (2.2.358–60 in F). It has been argued that the sign of the new Globe theatre showed

Hercules carrying the world on his shoulders (see Knutson, 82–3; and Dutton), so this would be a reference, probably an ironic one, to the triumph of the children over the adult actors. An added piquancy for the original audience would be that this concession of defeat was delivered to Richard Burbage (see List of Roles, 1n.), who was in effect the landlord of the boys' company at the Blackfriars. If we accept this as a reference to the sign of the Globe, we should note that Q2, like F, begins the whole passage with some lines of banter about Fortune that arguably allude to the sign of the Fortune theatre (see 2.2.224n.).[1]

Hamlet's first performances

It seems that the first performance of *Hamlet* of which we have a specific record took place, bizarrely, on board a ship anchored off the coast of Africa in 1607. The evidence is supplied by Thomas Rundall, editor of the 1849 Hakluyt Society publication *Narratives of Voyages towards the North-West 1496–1631*; he included parts of the journal of Captain William Keeling, who was in command of three ships sponsored by the East India Company which set out for the East Indies in March 1607 but got separated almost at once. One ship, the *Consent*, proceeded towards Bantam and the Moluccas, but the other two, the *Red Dragon* (captained by Keeling) and the *Hector* (captained by William Hawkins), were beset by storms and anchored off what is now Sierra Leone for six weeks. Keeling's journal refers to performances of two plays:

1   Jenkins (2) persuasively dismissed as false, unlikely or unprovable two further arguments in relation to the 'war of the theatres' – that Dekker's *Satiromastix* contains in the two pictures of Horace (5.2.251–64) an imitation of the two pictures Hamlet shows his mother (3.4.51), and that the phrase 'the Humorous Man' (2.2.288) is an allusion to the production of Jonson's *Everyman Out of His Humour* in 1599.

1607 September 5th
I sent the interpreter according to his desier abord the
Hector whear he brooke fast and after came abord me
wher we gave the tragedie of Hamlett.

September 30
Captain Hawkins dined with me wher my companions
acted Kinge Richard the Second.

September 31
I invited Captain Hawkins to a ffishe dinner and had
Hamlet acted abord me w[hi]ch I p[er]mit to keepe my
people from idleness and unlawful games or sleepe.

These entries were not printed by Samuel Purchas, Keeling's
first editor, in 1625, and an accusation of forgery was made by
Sidney Lee, who, in his *Life of Shakespeare* (1898), listed the
entries as fabrications by John Payne Collier and others. This
accusation was repeated by Sydney Race in a letter to *Notes
and Queries* in 1950 in which he asserted that the relevant
pages were now missing from the journal and claimed that 'a
crew of rude sailors' could not possibly have memorized 'two
of Shakespeare's most difficult plays' (Race, 345–6). William
Foster of the East India Office, however, had defended Rundall
in 1900, pointing out that not just a few pages but the whole
journal was now missing and that this was not surprising given
the general state of the archive. He argued that a captain at
sea would be more likely to write the impossible date of '31
September' than an ingenious forger, and he put forward
evidence of another play performed on an East India Company
ship (Foster, 'Forged'). Foster was (happily, as the editor
noted) still alive to respond to Race in 1950, when he made the
further points that there had been no public access to the East
India House records and that Collier made no reference to
these entries later. He assumed, moreover, that what the sailors
performed were 'their own rough versions of the *stories* of

Hamlet and *Richard II*' (Foster, 'Replies', 415). On the question of the 'impossible date', we would add that Henslowe's diary contains two entries for 31 September 1601 which have not been challenged as forgeries (see Henslowe, 182).

Ania Loomba provides a fascinating account of the whole controversy in her essay, 'Shakespearian transformations' (Loomba, 111–14), but her interest is not so much in the authenticity of the entries as in what the terms of the debate tell us about attitudes to Shakespeare's status in relation to class, race and national culture. She points out, however, that the most recent editors of Keeling accept the entries as authentic (see Stachan & Penrose), and it seems unlikely that they would be taken in by a nineteenth-century forgery. Park Honan (286) refers to the account and Charles R. Forker, editor of the 2002 Arden *King Richard II*, mentions it briefly as a record of an early 'amateur performance' of his play (122). Of course we cannot know what sort of text of *Hamlet* was used (both Q1 and Q2 were in print), but we need not resort to the condescension of Race and Foster, who perhaps underestimate the capacities of ordinary people at a time when there was much more incentive for everyone to have a well-trained memory. In the most recent discussion of this tantalizing journal, Gary Taylor ('Red Dragon') supports its authenticity by arguing that there is other evidence that English seamen voyaging to Africa took books with them, and that it would not be surprising if they put on plays, not only for their own recreation, but as a natural way of entertaining visitors from other cultures.

It is generally assumed, of course, that *Hamlet* had been acted in London before the two performances on the *Red Dragon*. The title-page of Q1 claims to present the play 'As it hath beene diuerse times acted by his Highnesse seruants in the Cittie of London: as also in the two Vniuersities of Cambridge and Oxford, and elsewhere', and (as mentioned above) the Stationers' Register refers to a *Hamlet* play as being 'latelie Acted by the Lord Chamberlayne his servantes'. Unfortunately, no one has been able to corroborate these statements by producing hard evidence of any particular performance in London, Cambridge or Oxford. Alan H. Nelson notes numerous attempts by the university authorities to ban professional performances in Cambridge from 1568, with companies being turned away in the 1590s and again in 1605–6. He concludes: 'though the lord chamberlain's players came to Cambridge at least once, in 1594–5, perhaps with Shakespeare among them, suggestions that Shakespeare's company succeeded in playing, and even presented *Hamlet* at Cambridge on this or another occasion, may be viewed with some scepticism' (*REED: Cambridge*, 2.725; see also his Appendix 10, 2.984–5). He assumes that the title-page claim is fraudulent, a false claim by the publisher trying to sell his book.

It seems, however, despite the lack of hard evidence, that Richard Burbage originated the role of Hamlet for the Chamberlain's Men at the Globe: an anonymous 'Funerall Ellegye on ye Death of the famous Actor Richard Burbedg' (1619) lists 'Young Hamlet' as one of his parts and notes, 'Oft have I seen him, leap into the Grave', which is usually taken to be a reference to his performance in the graveyard scene, though Q1 is the only text to contain a specific stage direction to this effect (see 5.1.247 SDn.). Another argument from original casting relates to the conspicuous absence of a part for a clown in *Hamlet*: Hamlet includes the clown in his enumeration of the stock dramatic characters when he is told that the players are about to arrive (this is in F and Q1 but not in Q2: see 2.2.288–9n. and Appendix 1), and he advises the other players not to allow the clown to extemporize when he gives them some instructions before *The Murder of Gonzago* in 3.2, but no clown appears among the players, and 'the King's jester', Yorick, has been dead for 'three and twenty years' (5.1.163–4; but 'this dozen year' in Q1, 16.86). It has been argued that this deficit was literally true of Shakespeare's company at the time he wrote *Hamlet*: the Chamberlain's Men had recently lost the popular comedian Will Kempe and had yet to acquire Robert Armin (see Gurr, *Playgoing*, 151–2; Wiles, 57–60; Barrie; and Thompson, 'Jest'). It is true that the Gravedigger and his companion in 5.1 (Scene 16 in Q1) are designated 'clowns' in the stage directions in all three texts, but this is a generic term meaning 'rustic' or 'lower class' as well as 'comedian', and the one-scene-only role of the Gravedigger would hardly satisfy Kempe (who had played Falstaff) or Armin (who was about to play Touchstone; but see List of Roles, 20n.).

In the end, the best evidence that *Hamlet* was not only performed but acclaimed soon after 1600 comes from the proliferation of allusions to it in other plays of the period. Interestingly, these are as often as not facetious or satirical. Thomas Dekker and Thomas Middleton's play *The Honest Whore* (Part 1, 1604) develops Hamlet's scene with the skull in knowing and parodic mode (4.1), and Middleton returned to this in the opening scene of *The Revenger's Tragedy* (1606), by which time the skull could daringly be represented as that of 'Gloriana'. In *Eastward Ho*, a comedy written by George Chapman, John Marston and Ben Jonson and first performed in 1605, the authors introduce a footman called Hamlet entirely, it would seem, so that someone can say to him '''Sfoot, Hamlet, are you mad?' (3.1.7). The Queen's description of the death of Ophelia is parodied in the description by Slitgut (4.1.66–75), a butcher's apprentice, of the plight of a usurer's wife, who eventually survives a shipwreck in the Thames which befalls her when she is running away with her lover, Sir Petronel Flash, who is in turn running away from his wife, who is called Gertrude. Several other allusions in this play indicate that *Hamlet* was not only well known by 1605 but already available as a text inviting less than serious treatment.[1] Parodic references are also found in Beaumont and Fletcher's *The Woman Hater*

---

1   See Van Fossen, 14; Horwich; and Farley-Hills, 'Crux'. See also commentary notes on 1.2.67, 179–80; 2.2.315; 4.5.44, 71, 182–91; 4.7.173–4.

(1606; see also 1.5.6–7n.) and their *The Scornful Lady* (1613; see also 3.1.60n.). This apparent lack of respect was troublesome for Brinsley Nicholson, one of the editors of the *Shakespere-Allusion Book*, who commented on an apparently irreverent reference to *Hamlet* in 1604: 'This and similar quotations show the fame and reputation of Shakespere [*sic*], being popularly known lines quoted or imitated for the purpose of causing a good-humoured laugh at their misappropriation' (Ingleby, 1.129).

When another editor introduced an allusion with the words 'This is plainly a sneer at *Hamlet*', Alexander Dyce felt obliged to add a footnote, 'Nonsense, more compliment than sneer' (Dyce, 1.200). More serious references and imitations also occur, notably in the influence of the representation of Ophelia's madness on that of Cornelia in 5.4 of John Webster's *The White Devil* (1609–12), and the Jailer's Daughter in scenes in *The Two Noble Kinsmen* (1613–14) attributed to John Fletcher (especially 4.1 and 4.3).

After all this, we have to admit that we are no nearer than previous scholars to establishing a 'precise date'. Both Honigmann and Jenkins argued that *Hamlet* was written at some point before the death of Essex on 28 February 1601 but after both *Julius Caesar* and *Antonio's Revenge*. Honigmann preferred a date 'either late in 1599 or early in 1600' ('Date', 24). Jenkins's position is more complex but easier to understand; he came up with two dates. Because he too believed that *Julius Caesar* came first and that Harvey was writing before Essex's death, he concluded that '*Hamlet* reached the stage in or shortly before 1600' (Ard², 6). But the addition to the text of reference to the boy actors meant that 'as it has come down to us it belongs to 1601' (13). Edwards and Hibbard both took a similar line; Edwards is less convinced by the Marston parallels and Hibbard does not mention them, but both are confident about the relationship to *Julius Caesar*, and both thought the boy actors were an afterthought added around 1601.

Yet there is surely little real substance to the arguments about *Antonio's Revenge*; they have a troubling tendency to work in both directions. The arguments about *Julius Caesar* are less evenhanded: no one, so far as we know, has found echoes of *Hamlet* in that play or argued that it is later, but the argument that *Hamlet* alludes to *Julius Caesar*, while attractive, remains unproven. Once this is conceded, and once it is further conceded that we are not looking for just one 'precise date' but a process of production which involves drafts of manuscripts, performances in different venues, and the publication of a number of different texts, then it becomes possible to admit that a version of *Hamlet* by Shakespeare may date back to 1589, or even earlier, and that the most reliable subsequent dates are those on the title-pages of the early editions, followed by the dates of plays and other surviving texts which can plausibly be seen as conscious allusions to *Hamlet*.

To summarize, the firmest external evidence is the Stationers' Register date of 26 July 1602 and the 1603 on Q1's title-page, which together make either 1602 or 1603 the *terminus ad quem* for a Shakespearean *Hamlet* of some kind. The best internal evidence may well be the reference to 'the late innovation': of course, it would only date one passage but, according to whether one is the more persuaded by Jenkins or by Honigmann, it would take the *terminus ad quem* back to either the spring of 1601 or some time in 1600.

THE STORY OF *HAMLET*

Murder most foul

Where did the story of *Hamlet* come from? What were Shakespeare's sources? The concept of the 'source' presupposes a model of a writer at work – reading books or seeing plays or listening to anecdotes or witnessing events – and 'using' this material as his own, either consciously or unconsciously. It offends against the idea of the artist as originator, creator, genius. Consider Hamlet's remark that he has heard 'That guilty creatures sitting at a play / Have by the very cunning of the scene / Been struck so to the soul that presently / They have proclaimed their malefactions' (2.2.524–7). The anonymous play, *A Warning for Fair Women*, was performed by Shakespeare's company in 1599, and includes a reference to the story of a Norfolk woman

> that had made away her husband,
> And sitting to behold a tragedy
> At Linne a towne in Norffolke,
> Acted by Players traveling that way,
> Wherein a woman that had murthered hers
> Was ever haunted with her husbands ghost:
>
> She was so mooved with the sight thereof,
> As she cryed out, the Play was made by her,
> And openly confesst her husbands murder.[1]

According to Jenkins (482), the story was well known (see also Proudfoot, 'Conscience'), but Geoffrey Bullough (7.38) believed *A Warning* itself 'was probably Shakespeare's source'. Such an assertion assumes that there must be a source, and that it is unlikely that Shakespeare could have thought of such an idea for himself.

But it also raises the issue of what significance can be attributed to the identification of a source. Source-hunting may tell us something biographical about the writer (how he spent his time, how his mind worked), but can it also tell us something about the nature and, possibly, the meaning of his work? If the study of sources sharpens our sense of what the work is and, by comparing and contrasting the finished product with the source, what is distinctive about it, it can be a useful exercise. Even

---

1   *A Warning for Fair Women: A Critical Edition*, ed. Charles Dale Cannon (The Hague and Paris, 1975), lines 2037–48.

where there is no agreement as to whether a body of material is a source or about the extent to which it has influenced the creation of *Hamlet*, there may still be illumination of *Hamlet* through the study of analogues (or even dissimilar material).

Source-hunters have proved to be ambitious and ingenious in their attempts to explain the origins of the multiple ingredients making up *Hamlet* – picking over not only the world's literature, but also any non-literary documentation of actual people and events from history (including Shakespeare's personal history) and, where they find any substantial similarity, calling it a matter of 'source' rather than 'coincidence'. Bullough was keen to consider the possibility that the title of the play in 3.2 – *The Murder of Gonzago* – came into Shakespeare's imagination because he knew something about the historical Francesco Maria I della Rovere, Duke of Urbino. The duke, who died in October 1538, was reputedly murdered by having poison poured in his ears at the instigation of a kinsman of the duchess, one Luigi Gonzago. Luigi may have suggested 'Lucianus', Gonzago has become the victim rather than the murderer, Leonora has become 'Baptista' (the name of an earlier Duchess of Urbino, Battista Sforza), the murderer is the nephew, and, despite Hamlet's assertion that 'Gonzago is the duke's name' (3.2.232–3), the duke and duchess are a king and queen. Having found in the Duke of Urbino a possible source for elements in the play-within-the-play, Bullough (7.33) went on to conjecture that the same duke prompted Shakespeare's description of the Ghost, arguing that old Hamlet's physical appearance was influenced by an engraving of Titian's portrait of the same Francesco Maria, which is in the Uffizi Gallery in Florence – a bearded figure in complete steel with hand on truncheon and a helmet behind him with beaver up.[1] As for the nature of old

---

1   Bullough reproduces the engraving (as plate 1, opposite 7.31), taking it from Paolo Giovio's *Elogia Virorum Bellica Virtute Illustrium* (Basle, 1575), a work that came out in a number of editions.

Hamlet's death, Eden and Opland have argued that the idea of pouring poison in the ear could have come from knowledge of an essay published in Venice in 1564 by the anatomist Eustachio, which establishes the internal connection between the ear and the throat. However, Shakespeare could more easily have been affected by Marlowe's *Edward II* (1592; 5.4.34–5), which refers to a Neapolitan method of dispatching one's sleeping enemies by blowing a little powder in their ears.

7 Drawing (*c.* 1755–60) by Francis Hayman of Barry Spranger as Hamlet in 3.4 with the Ghost appearing in armour (see 3.4.99.ln.)

Of course, Hamlet himself encourages source-hunting when he provides a kind of commentary note on *The Murder of Gonzago*: 'the story', he proclaims to the audience, 'is extant and written in very choice Italian' (3.2.255–6). If he is right, then we would have a literary source. As yet, no scholar has managed to track that Italian story down. As represented by the players, both in the dumb-show and in the dialogue version, it is a story about murder and remarriage, but not one about revenge. *Hamlet* has famously been associated with one of the most basic stories about murder and revenge, that identified by Freud as the Oedipus complex: 'How if', mused Freud's follower Ernest Jones, 'Hamlet had in years gone by, as a child, bitterly resented having had to share his mother's affection even with his own father, had regarded him as a rival, and had secretly wished him out of the way so that he might enjoy undisputed and undisturbed the monopoly of that affection?' (Ernest Jones, 51). When Hamlet's father died, he could not but feel guilty that his wish had been granted, so his grieving was contaminated by guilt and a manufactured idolization of the missing parent. Thus the story of Oedipus, who discovered that his mother had committed incest and who avenged his father's death by killing his father's murderer, could have been a source for *Hamlet*, either because Shakespeare knew of the Greek myth or because he was compelled by his unconscious to write about the psychic material to which Freud later applied the epithet 'Oedipal'.

If we are looking for parallels at the level of the main narrative and structure of the play, there are plenty of stories about sons who avenge the deaths of their fathers. They include the Persian legend of Kei Chosra, as well as the northern legends of King Horn, Bevis of Hampton, and Havelok the Dane. And ancient Greece provides the stories of Orestes. Louise Schleiner posits 'the possible mediated influence of Aeschylus' *Oresteia* and Euripides' *Orestes* on *Hamlet*, probably through . . . Latin translations and through a pair of

[lost] English plays of 1599 entitled *Agamemnon* and *Orestes' Furies*' (Schleiner, 29–30). Despite modern interest in a Freudian reading of the story, she argues that 'Shakespeare's Hamlet is much more a version – even a purposive revision – of Orestes than of Oedipus. Hamlet is at no risk of marrying or having sex with his mother. He is at considerable risk of killing her' (37). She sees in Horatio a version of Pylades, and in Laertes, when he catches the dead Ophelia in his arms (and in Hamlet, particularly in Q1 where he leaps into Ofelia's grave to join Leartes; see 5.1.247 SD), she sees a version of the graveyard scene in *Orestes*, where Orestes embraces his sister in the belief that they face death. Schleiner argues that, even if Shakespeare did not read these tragedies in Greek or in Latin translations, Latinist adapters such as Ben Jonson (whose library contained Latin translations), Chapman or Marston (or even Dekker) could easily have told him about them.

An antic disposition

In addition to stories about sons as avengers, there were also old stories about clever avenging sons who pretended to be stupid in order to outwit their enemies. Shakespeare knew at least one – the story of Lucius Junius Brutus, supposed founder of the Roman republic in 509 BC, who avenged the deaths of his father and brother, outwitting their murderer Tarquin the Proud by pretending to be an imbecile (hence 'Brutus', which means 'stupid'). Shakespeare could have read about Brutus, either in Livy's *History of Rome*, book 1, chapter 56 (possibly in a translation such as Philemon Holland's *Roman History*, which was published in 1600), or in Ovid's *Fasti*, where Brutus is described as *stulti sapiens imitator*, 'wise though pretending to be fool' (2.717). Shakespeare explicitly refers to Brutus' mask of stupidity in two of his works before or around *Hamlet* – the 1594 poem of *The Rape of Lucrece* (at 1813) and the 1599 play, *Henry V* (at 2.4.37–8). *Julius Caesar* also contains two references to this Brutus (1.2.157 and 2.1.53–4), though not specifically to his pretence.

But there is also an old Nordic story of a clever son whose name Amlodi or Amleth (Amblett, Hamblet or Hamlet in other treatments) also means 'stupid'. It was written down in Latin about AD 1200 by Saxo Grammaticus, as part of a collection of tales which were printed in Paris in 1514 as *Danorum Regum heroumque Historiae*. Shakespeare may possibly have read it in volume 5 of François de Belleforest's popular collection of *Histoires tragiques*, first published in French in 1570 (after all, both Q1 and Q2 describe Shakespeare's play as a 'Tragical History').

In Saxo's version, Rorik, King of Denmark, appoints two brothers, Horwendil and Fengo, joint governors of Jutland. When Horwendil kills the King of Norway in single combat, he marries Rorik's daughter Gerutha, and she gives birth to Amleth. But Fengo murders his brother and marries Gerutha himself. Amleth pretends to be mad, talks nonsense and wears rags, but some courtiers are suspicious and try to trap him into confessing he is planning revenge, first with a young woman and then by planting a spy in his mother's chamber. Amleth is warned of the first trap, and he himself identifies the spy, kills him and feeds him to the pigs. Fengo becomes suspicious, dare not offend Rorik or Gerutha, so sends Amleth to England with two retainers, who carry a letter to the King of England commanding him to execute Amleth. Amleth changes the letter so that it orders the death of the retainers instead – while also requiring Amleth's marriage to the Princess of England. Back in Denmark, back in his rags again, and finding himself at his own funeral, Amleth pretends to prick his finger on his sword; the courtiers render it harmless by riveting it into its scabbard. He then gets them drunk and sets fire to the banqueting hall, swaps his sword for Fengo's and kills Fengo with it. Amleth is proclaimed king.

Thus there is a villain who kills his brother, the king. He thereby inherits the throne and marries his sister-in-law, the

8 Hamlet (Innokenty Smoktunovsky) and Laertes (C. Olesenko) over the body of Ophelia (Anastasiya Vertinskaya) in the film directed by Grigori Kozintsev (1964)

queen. There is a hero, the late king's clever son (an inveterate punster and riddler), who protects himself from his uncle and provides a cover for his revenge by pretending to be an idiot. The villain suspects the hero is not stupid and tests him. He first tempts him to seduce an attractive young woman; but the hero makes it seem that he has resisted the temptation. The villain tests him a second time, by planting a spy in the queen's bedroom to overhear her talking to her son; but the spy is discovered by the hero, and killed. He then tests the hero a third time, by sending him to a foreign country with two escorts, who carry instructions to the foreign king to have him killed; but the hero outwits them and arranges for them to be killed instead. Finally, the hero arrives home during a funeral, kills the villain after an exchange of swords, and becomes king. All these plot elements are to be found in Shakespeare's versions of the Amleth legend.

While Saxo lacks a Laertes or a sister who goes mad and kills herself, an Osric or any gravediggers or players (or, indeed, a play), he provides equivalents of all Shakespeare's other major characters – old Hamlet and young Hamlet, old Fortinbras and young Fortinbras, the King and Queen, Polonius, Horatio, Ophelia, Rosencrantz and Guildenstern, and the King of England. Belleforest adds to Saxo the idea that Amleth is melancholic. He also suggests that, before killing his brother, Fengon (as he calls the villain) had seduced his brother's wife, and speculates as to whether or not she knew of or even encouraged the murder. In this treatment, as in Shakespeare's Q1 version, the queen conspires with the hero to keep his secret, encouraging him to take vengeance and become king. Belleforest is embarrassed by the primitive barbarity of the story and is interested in trying to give it a Christian reading: while private revenge is wrong, Amleth was nevertheless an agent of God's justice.

It seems unlikely that Shakespeare knew Saxo at first hand, but it is worth noting that while the ending of Saxo's story of

Amleth involves more adventures following his successful revenge, and while his Amleth marries twice, first the Princess of England and then the Queen of Scotland, there are features of these stages of the story which 'fit' with features of Shakespeare's treatment. Amleth displays more of his cunning and intelligence, and he is also shown to be concerned, as Hamlet is, with the retelling of his own story – a concern which leads him to have his adventures engraved on his shield. Herminthrud, the Scottish queen, whom he is sent to woo on behalf of the King of England, always has her suitors murdered, but, because she can 'read' Amleth's exploits in his shield, she decides not to kill him but to marry him instead – and *then* she kills him! Saxo comments:

> All vows of women become void with changes of fortune, are dissolved by the shifting of time, and disappear with the play of fate, for their faith stands on slippery feet. Though they are quick to promise you something, they are slow to keep it. Slaves of pleasure, they leap headfirst and gaping in their continual longing for something new, and forget the old.
>
> (Hansen, 117)

If anything, Belleforest's treatment increases the intensity of misogyny in Saxo.

Shakespeare may have known Belleforest's treatment, but, in a number of respects, his play differs from the legend he takes over. For example, in Belleforest it is no secret that Fengon has murdered Amleth's father. In Shakespeare, however, no one knows – unless Gertrude does, and there is no sound reason to believe she does – so Hamlet has to be told, and Shakespeare introduces a ghost to do the telling (this could possibly have been suggested to him by a couple of references in Belleforest to the king's '*ombre*'). Because the crime is public knowledge, Amleth needs the disguise of idiocy lest his uncle suspect he is up to something, but in Shakespeare the king has no reason to believe that Hamlet knows anything, so his antic disposition is unnecessary, except in so far as it reveals something about Hamlet's inner state of mind. In Belleforest, again, Amleth realizes that he is being tempted into seducing the girl. In Shakespeare it is unclear whether or not Hamlet knows that Ophelia is being used to make him reveal his secrets. On the other hand, sometimes the differences between the Nordic legend and Shakespeare are not as great as they appear. Shakespeare may be thought to have rejected that part of the story where, having killed the spy in his mother's bedchamber, Amleth cuts him up and feeds him to the pigs. But Hamlet displays no more respect for Polonius' corpse when he announces he will 'lug the guts' next door (3.4.210) and then jokes that the King's councillor has become a diet for worms and the smell of his decomposing body will soon give away where Hamlet has hidden it.

In Saxo and Belleforest, the villain has organized a funeral for Amleth (believing he will have been killed in England) but the body proves not to be dead at all. In Shakespeare it is a real ceremony with a real corpse, Ophelia. Yet, in Shakespeare's treatment, Laertes does protest that there is something less than genuine about the funeral, because the priest is unhappy about staging a ceremony for a supposed suicide. Secondly, there is an ironical sense in which the funeral in Shakespeare *is* the hero's funeral. It certainly seals Hamlet's death warrant, because he declares his presence and thereby reinforces the letter (4.7.43–6) in which he has informed his uncle that he has in effect outwitted him and survived the plot to have him killed by the King of England. Furthermore, in Q1 at least, Hamlet leaps into the grave as if he were claiming it for himself. Amleth carefully plans his revenge and achieves it by deliberately burning down the villain's hall while his retainers are inebriated in the funeral celebrations. Hamlet, on the other hand, has no straightforward revenge strategy, and the deaths of the King, Gertrude, and Laertes come about almost by accident. But at an earlier stage he has an elaborate stratagem, which involves a kind of equivalent to Amleth's firing of the hall: in order to catch not the life but the conscience of the King, Hamlet stages a play in the King's hall, and the outcome is that the King is 'frighted with false fire' (3.2.257 in F; 9.174 in Q1; not in Q2, but see 3.2.258–9n.).

Despite its popularity (it had been reissued seven times by 1601), Belleforest's Amleth story did not appear in English until 1608, by which time Shakespeare's play was already written, performed and published. He may have read Belleforest in French, but in any case, if Saxo/Belleforest is taken to be his major source, Shakespeare updates the story to a Christian Renaissance Court, emphasizes the generational gap between the parents and children by populating the Court with a large number of students (Hamlet, Horatio, Rosencrantz, Guildenstern and Laertes, and possibly Marcellus and Barnardo), and settles for a tragic ending.

Wherever *Hamlet*'s plot departs from Belleforest, some scholars have wondered whether the idea for that plot element was prompted, not by Shakespeare's imagination, but by the hypothetical *Ur-Hamlet*, which we have discussed earlier (pp. 45–8). There is no ghost in Belleforest, but, as we have seen, Thomas Lodge referred to one in 1596, and since he can hardly be referring to any of the known Shakespearean treatments, the inference may be that this is a reference to the *Ur-Hamlet*, and Shakespeare took it over. At the same time, Thomas Kyd's play *The Spanish Tragedy* (*c.* 1589) has many plot similarities to *Hamlet* which are not to be found in Belleforest, and these include a ghost. But they also include a play-within-a-play, a faithful friend called Horatio, a brother who kills his sister's lover, and a female suicide.[1] Perhaps

---

1 It is quite possible that Shakespeare knew, or knew of, a woman called 'Hamlett' – Katherine Hamlett – who drowned in the river Avon in Stratford in December 1579 when Shakespeare was fourteen, and that this event may have influenced his shaping of Ophelia's death (see Duncan-Jones, 152–3).

Shakespeare's play draws on Kyd's play, but perhaps both plays draw on the *Ur-Hamlet*. As we have also seen, the plot of John Marston's play *Antonio's Revenge* has many similarities to that of *Hamlet*, but scholars have been unable to agree which play is the earlier and therefore which may have borrowed from the other, or whether both borrowed from the *Ur-Hamlet*.

'Sentences', speeches and thoughts

Source material is not restricted to narrative. Robert S. Miola reminds us in *Shakespeare and Classical Tragedy* that Thomas Nashe encouraged a consideration of the *Ur-Hamlet*'s debt to Roman tragedy: 'English *Seneca* ... will affoord you whole *Hamlets*.' But Nashe's mind was on the play's 'sentences' and 'tragicall speeches' rather than its action. Miola argues that 'Seneca's real presence in *Hamlet* appears in transformed conventions – such as the Ghost – rather than in specifically imitated passages' (Miola, *Tragedy*, 36), for 'Seneca shapes *Hamlet*'s infrastructure, its internal logic and design, rather than its surface' (33). When Hamlet talks of Hercules and Pyrrhus he is probably drawing on *Hercules Furens* and *Troades*, but Hamlet 'continually rejects the Senecan models he seeks to embrace' (48). Similarly, the play as opposed to its hero directly challenges the dramatic models it evokes and imitates, and its author, while he 'recalls Seneca's depiction of extreme passion, his operatic, superbly playable rhetoric, his penchant for meditation, his concern with the supernatural', nevertheless 'struggles to transform the monomaniacal revenger of Senecan drama into a tragic hero who can develop in the course of the action and move pity as well as terror' (33).

The opening of the play, with its night-watchmen on the battlements, and a consciousness of something rotten in the state, has parallels with the opening of Aeschylus' *Agamemenon*, but then, as Cherrell Guilfoyle has pointed out, it also has parallels with the Shepherds' Play in the medieval Coventry mystery cycle, with its shepherds watching, its references to

Christmas and its consciousness of something otherworldly in the bitterly cold air (Guilfoyle, 25–6). Polonius claims that the players do both tragedy and comedy – 'Seneca cannot be too heavy nor Plautus too light' (2.2.336–7). When Hamlet looks back on his Senecan play of *The Murder of Gonzago*, with its *Agamemnon*-like plot and its Latinate villain Lucianus, and describes it as a 'comedy' (3.2.285), he is being characteristically mischievous and ironic. But Miola argues in *Shakespeare's Reading* that a major influence on Shakespeare's drama as a whole, and not just his comedies, was the great exponent of Roman comedy, Plautus. The *Menaechmi* is a well-established source for plays such as *The Comedy of Errors* and *Twelfth Night*, but

> Shakespeare works a final variation on Plautus's *Menaechmi* in *Hamlet*. Like Plautus's Traveller, Hamlet feigns madness ... Like Menaechmus or Antipholus, Hamlet wanders through a strange yet familiar world. He meets friends, family, and lovers but all are not who they claim to be ... Hamlet suffers a tragic version of errors-play *aporia*, a deep confusion about himself and the world. The play raises to a higher level Plautine questions about identity and the nature of illusion and the self in the world.
>
> (Miola, *Reading*, 80–1)

At a verbal level, it certainly looks as if the speech which Hamlet asks the Player to recite in 2.2 was influenced by a play by Christopher Marlowe and, possibly, Thomas Nashe, *The Tragedy of Dido Queen of Carthage* (written around 1585, published 1594), in which Pyrrhus, with 'harness dropping blood, . . . whiskt his sword about, / And with the wind thereof the King fell down' (2.1.253–4).[1] In a series of articles published

---

1 For further possible influence of *Dido*, see commentary notes on 1.1.62; 2.2.384, 392, 395, 411, 417, 436; 3.4.56

in the early 1980s, J.J.M. Tobin argued persuasively that *Hamlet*'s language displays a widespread influence of Nashe's work.[1] This time, it was primarily the pamphlets *Pierce Penniless his Supplication to the Devil* (1592), *Strange News* (1592), *Christ's Tears over Jerusalem* (1593), *The Terrors of the Night* (1594), *Have with you to Saffron-Walden* (1596) and *Lenten Stuff* (1599), but Tobin also found verbal traces of Nashe's play *Summer's Last Will and Testament* (1592, published 1600), and Gabriel Harvey's pamphlets *A New Letter of Notable Contents* (1593) and *Pierce's Supererogation or a New Praise of the Old Ass* (1593). Descriptions of the Danish court and Danish drinking, for example, are to be found in *Pierce Penniless*, which talks of 'the heavy-headed gluttonous house-dove' (1.210) and 'this surly swinish generation' (1.180), while *Christ's Tears* includes not just 'spleanative' (13), 'playstring' (149), 'nunnery' (meaning brothel) (152) and 'an inch thick' (180), but, in one passage (148–150), 'justice', 'corrupted', 'buyes', 'give evidence' (all of which, in Q2, occur in 3.3.57–64) and 'salary' (which, in F, is at 3.3.79).

As well as narrative and verbal sources, some scholars have been interested in the origins of Shakespeare's conceptual thinking. Starting with Edward Capell in 1780, a large number of scholars have argued that Shakespeare knew, and was influenced by, Michel Eyquem de Montaigne (1533–92), whose *Essays* were published between 1580 and 1588. If Shakespeare did not read them in French, Sir William Cornwallis referred to having read an English version in 1600, and this could have been by John Florio, whose translation was not published until 1603 but which had been under way since 1598. In his essay on 'Self-consciousness in Montaigne and Shakespeare', R. Ellrodt argues that *Hamlet* displays close parallels to the thought and/or phrasing of passages in Montaigne at 3.1.59–62 and 82–7, 4.3.19–24, 4.4.39–42, and 5.2.10–11 and 200–1, while three

---

1   See Tobin, 'Nashe', *'Teares'*, *'Lenten'*, *'Salary'*, 'Elements' and 'Harvey'.

consecutive essays in the second book of essays ('We taste nothing purely', 'Against idlenesse, or doing nothing' and 'Of bad meanes employed to a good end') not only offer close parallels but may have influenced the characterization of both Hamlet and Fortinbras. Ronald Knowles, pondering the larger question of '*Hamlet* and counter-humanism', wonders if the arguments Shakespeare gives Hamlet at 2.2.269–74 about man's dignity and misery ('What piece of work is a man . . . the paragon of animals. And yet to me what is this quintessence of dust?', etc.) derive ultimately not from Montaigne's extended essay, 'Apology of Raymond Sebond', but from Pierre Boaistuau's 'Bref discours de l'excellence et dignité de l'homme' (1558) and 'Le Théâtre du monde, où il est fait un ample discours des misères humaines' (1561), the latter having been translated into English in about 1566 and again in 1574 by John Alday (Knowles, 1049, 1052–3). But, above all, Ellrodt is struck by the closeness of Montaigne's discussion to Shakespeare's representation of 'modes of self-awareness'. He finds a very modern 'simultaneous awareness of experience and the experiencing self' in the patterns of Hamlet's mental life and in Montaigne's statements such as 'we are double in ourselves, which is the cause that what we believe, we believe it not', his descriptions of his 'irresolute imaginations, and sometimes contrary' and his frustrated wish to be able to 'resolve my selfe'.[1]

So *Hamlet* again seems 'modern', as we discussed earlier (pp. 18–21), even though it draws on archaic Nordic myths and has analogues in Greek and Latin drama. Wherever the story came from, Shakespeare was responsible for turning it into one of the most powerful and influential tragedies in the English language and, as we shall see in the sections on '*Hamlet* on stage and screen' and 'Novel Hamlets', making it available for seemingly endless retelling and rewriting by others.

1   Michel de Montaigne, *The Essayes*, trans. John Florio, Everyman's Library, 3 vols (1910), bk 2, ch. 16, 342; bk 3, ch. 2, 23.

THE COMPOSITION OF *HAMLET*

The quartos and the Folio

The quartos

There being no extant authorial manuscript of Shakespeare's *Hamlet* (or, indeed, of any other of his plays), our knowledge of the composition of his version of the story is restricted to the inferences we can draw from the early printed texts of the play and contemporary references to them. The earliest of these, as we have seen, is an entry in the Stationers' Register on 26 July 1602 made by James Roberts, a London printer. The entry describes 'A booke called the Revenge of Hamlett Prince Denmarke' as having been 'latelie Acted' by the Lord Chamberlain's Men,[1] the acting company to which Shakespeare belonged as actor, shareholder and resident dramatist.

The next year, Nicholas Ling and John Trundle published a play by William Shakespeare entitled *The Tragicall Historie of Hamlet Prince of Denmarke*. According to its title-page, the play had been performed a number of times by 'his Highnesse seruants' (Fig. 9). Soon after the accession of James I, Shakespeare's company acquired royal patronage and a new title, becoming 'The King's Men' on 19 May 1603, so this text must have been published after that date. It is in quarto format (the size of a modern paperback) and is thus known as the First Quarto of *Hamlet*.

Q1's printer was not James Roberts but Valentine Simmes. In 1604, however, Ling employed Roberts to print a somewhat different play with the same title, *The Tragicall Historie of*

---

1 By a royal charter of 1557, the Stationers' Company had acquired the monopoly of all printing in England outside the university presses of Oxford and Cambridge. On 23 June 1586, the Star Chamber decreed that all books had to be licensed for printing by the Archbishop of Canterbury or the Bishop of London (or, after 1588, by their deputies). A printer or publisher who secured a licence to print and entered his copy in the Stationers' Register thereby gained copyright.

THE
Tragicall Hiſtorie of
HAMLET
Prince of Denmarke

By William Shake-ſpeare.

As it hath beene diuerſe times acted by his Highneſſe ſer-
uants in the Cittie of London : as alſo in the two V-
niuerſities of Cambridge and Oxford, and elſe-where

At London printed for N.L. and Iohn Trundell.
1603.

9 Title-page of the First Quarto

Hamlet, Prince of Denmarke, and again attributed to William Shakespeare. This publication is the Second Quarto (Fig. 10). Some copies were dated 1604, others 1605, but the two dates do not indicate separate editions: printers made corrections as they worked and did not discard uncorrected

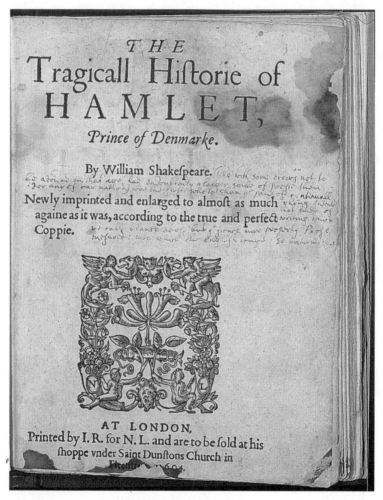

10 Title-page of the Second Quarto

pages, so individual copies of a book can include different readings; the date is just one of a number of variants in the case of Q2.

The only features that these three *Hamlet*s have in common are the name and designation of the chief character, and the fact that they are plays. But each is connected with one of the other two, whether through its printer, its publisher, its author or its acting company. The textual history of *Hamlet* is full of questions and largely empty of clear answers. Is 'The Revenge of Hamlett Prince Denmarke' in the Stationers' Register for 1602 the same play as *The Tragicall Historie of Hamlet Prince of Denmarke* that Simmes printed for Ling in 1603? Or is it, rather, *The Tragicall Historie of Hamlet, Prince of Denmarke*, which Roberts printed for Ling in 1604? If the latter, why did Roberts wait two years before printing it? Was Simmes violating Roberts's right to the play by printing a play with the same title in 1603, and was the wish to drive Q1 off the bookstalls the motivation behind Roberts's decision to print Q2 in 1604? This would seem to make sense, except that Roberts printed Q2 for Ling, and it was Ling who had published Q1 – so Ling would seem to have been in competition with himself.

Whatever reason Ling had to publish two very different plays by the same author and with the same name within a year of each other, he certainly seems to have ended up with the rights to *Hamlet*, since we know he transferred them in 1607 to another publisher, John Smethwick. Smethwick proceeded to reprint Q2 as the Third Quarto in 1611, the Fourth in about 1621 and the Fifth in 1637. Q3, Q4 and Q5 each contain some very minor alterations to the text. Further reprints of 1676, 1683, 1695 and 1703, known as 'Players' Quartos', were not only adapted to suit Restoration tastes, but include sections marked to record the cuts made by the Duke's Company as it acted the play at its Dorset Gardens and Drury Lane theatres.

The First Folio

Soon after the appearance of the Fourth Quarto, another Shakespearean *Hamlet* was published, under the title *The Tragedie of Hamlet, Prince of Denmarke*. It formed part of a 'folio' (i.e. large format) volume of thirty-six plays attributed to Shakespeare and printed in 1623 in the shop of William Jaggard and his son Isaac (Fig. 11). Reprints of this so-called 'First Folio' appeared in 1632 (F2), 1664 (F3) and 1685 (F4), each making editorial changes to its predecessor. The First Folio's full title is *Mr William Shakespeares Comedies, Histories, & Tragedies. Published according to the True Originall Copies*; but, for the purposes of this Introduction, except where a distinction needs to be made between F1 and any of these reprints, we shall refer to it simply as 'F'.

F's colophon lists four stationers as its publishers, Jaggard senior being one and Smethwick another. A list of twenty-six 'Principall Actors' in the plays includes the two editors of the volume, John Heminges and Henry Condell, as well as Shakespeare himself. *Hamlet* appears among the Tragedies, immediately succeeding *Macbeth* and immediately preceding *King Lear*. Its text is different again from the text found in either Q1 or Q2. For a start, at 27,602 words of dialogue, F's *Hamlet* is 73 per cent longer than Q1's 15,983, but 4 per cent shorter than Q2's 28,628.[1] Further, 1,914 words of F's dialogue (i.e. 7 per cent) are not to be found in Q2, while 2,887 words of Q2's dialogue (10 per cent) are not to be found in F. How is one to explain these differences? And how is an editor to choose which *Hamlet* to print?

---

1 Fleay (135–6 and 259) calculated that *Hamlet* has 3,924 lines, Chambers (*Shakespeare*, 2.398–405) reckoned 3,929, and Hart ('Number') came up with 3,762. Each took an eclectic edition as the source of the data (Fleay and Chambers used Globe; Hart used Cam). Lukas Erne drew on Hart (*Homilies*, 148, and 'Number') and concluded that Q2 has 3,668 lines and F has 3,537 (Erne, 141). But the length of a line of prose is not a constant, either within a publication or between publications. The more meaningful comparison is between numbers of words in the three texts.

11 Title-page of the First Folio

The relationship of Q2 to Q1

When one examines the texts of the two earliest quartos, most of Q1's plot is to be found in Q2, as are most of its characters and the rough gist of a great deal of its dialogue. Indeed, some stretches of dialogue are virtually identical. Nevertheless, most of the language and versification is markedly different, and Q2 is 79 per cent longer than Q1. This has given rise to many theories, including the following:

1   That Q1 is either Shakespeare's adaptation of a play by another playwright (Thomas Kyd, perhaps) or Shakespeare's first draft of an original play which he went on to expand and rewrite almost in its entirety.
2   That Q1 is not the work of Shakespeare but a poor reconstruction of a stage production of his *Hamlet*, sold to Simmes and/or Ling as a way of cashing in on its commercial success (either a 'bootleg' version made by someone in the audience, or else a memorial reconstruction made by one or more members of Shakespeare's company).

Both theories of Q1 require a theory of Q2. Traditionally it has been accorded a superior status to that of Q1. Those who regard Q1 as a first draft have always tended to see Q2 as based on a thorough revision and expansion of, and improvement on, that draft. However, the majority of twentieth-century scholars have argued that, despite its being printed after Q1, Q2 records a text which pre-dates the text of Q1. Either way, Q2's status has been high because it gives every impression of being based, at very few removes, on a manuscript in Shakespeare's own hand – what scholars term the author's 'foul papers'.[1]

But there are alternative interpretations to those that have won the most favour in the last hundred years. Q1's title-page describes the state of its text as being 'As it hath beene diuerse

---

1   The term 'foul papers' is first found in use by the King's Men in 1625, and refers to an author's uncorrected play manuscript, from which an acting company would have prepared a fair copy.

times acted'. Q2's title-page makes no mention of performance, preferring to describe its text as being 'Newly imprinted and enlarged to almost as much againe as it was, according to the true and perfect Coppie.' Presumably, Ling is comparing Q2 to Q1 when he talks of the text being enlarged, and he may well be claiming that Q2 has more authority than Q1 when he describes it as being true and perfect (implying that Q1's text was less true and less perfect). But, alternatively, he could be describing a difference not in the quality but in the origins of the two texts – explaining to his prospective readers that Q1 is based on the play as it has been acted, i.e. a version designed specifically for the stage, whereas Q2 is based on a different kind of manuscript and one which is designed for a quite different purpose. Writing in 1992, Giorgio Melchiori expressed his belief that 'behind Q2 there is a play for the closet, not for the stage' (Melchiori, 200).

The relationship of F to Q2

F lacks about 230 of Q2's lines, while Q2 lacks about 70 of F's lines. In his 1982 Arden edition, Harold Jenkins categorized three further main kinds of difference: (1) F has fuller and more systematic stage directions, (2) F has variants in the dialogue; and (3) there are many 'little scraps of dialogue incorporated in F for which Q2 gives no warrant' (Ard[2], 62). Much of the difference between the two texts he attributed to the influence on F of performance, or preparation for performance, in the theatre. He summarized it by saying that F differs from Q2 through 'theatrical modifications both deliberate and accidental, through literary sophistication and modernization, and through the inevitable corruptions incident to the processes of transcription and printing' (64).

But Jenkins nevertheless sees a direct relationship between F and Q2, believing that F is based partly on an annotated copy of Q2. His evidence takes the form of 'numerous little correspondences' scattered throughout the text (Ard[2], 65) –

common errors, unusual spellings, inessential commas, the adoption of a colon, wrong pointing, the abbreviation of stage directions, and small anomalous details already taken over from Q1. But, in Jenkins's opinion, the annotated Q2 was collated with and emended against a manuscript which, particularly in the second half of the play, seems to have been 'a theatrical abridgement' (56). At the same time, F is based partly on a transcript of a fair copy of Shakespeare's foul papers. This means that, for Jenkins, while Q2 normally has the greater authority because it derives directly from Shakespeare's foul papers, F sometimes has the greater authority because it derives ultimately from foul papers, and 'differs from Q2 partly by preserving what Q2 omits or misrenders' (64).

Gary Taylor, along with almost all other scholars, shares Jenkins's belief that the manuscript authority for Q2 was Shakespeare's foul papers, that F derives to a significant extent from another (manuscript) source, and that this source derives ultimately from foul papers. Bearing in mind that Ling and Smethwick between them provide continuity of ownership of Q1, Q2, Q3, Q4 and F, Taylor is prepared to entertain the possibility that, just as the printers of Q2 consulted Q1, any of Q2–4 editions could have been consulted by the printers of F to clarify substantive readings (*TxC*, 396–7). But this in no way dilutes his opinion that 'the manuscript authority for F was a late and apparently literary scribal transcript' (399). He rejects as expressions of 'personal distaste' the view of Jenkins and others, such as John Dover Wilson, that the manuscript behind F is a debasement of the text, deriving from a promptbook which incorporated, for example, 'actors' interpolations' and a prompter's faulty memory (400–1). F's repeated agreement with Q1 against Q2 in matters of verbal and theatrical substance indicates that they both derive from a theatrical manuscript that pre-dates the printing of Q2 in 1604 but post-dates the foul papers behind Q2. That manuscript could well have been the promptbook (which would normally be an annotated fair copy of foul papers), but Taylor cannot see why Shakespeare himself could not have had a hand in the preparation of that theatrical manuscript (after all, Shakespeare was the company's resident dramatist and, as one of the company's 'Principall Actors', perfectly capable of making the odd 'actor's interpolations' himself).[1] In agreement with Philip Edwards (Cam[2], 8–32), Taylor argues that 'a coherent literary strategy unites some of the Folio's cuts to some of the Folio's additions' (*TxC*, 400), that Shakespeare was responsible for at least some of the additions and almost all of the cuts, and that Q2 and F are slightly different works of art. Taylor goes further, however, in arguing that it is 'intrinsically probable that Shakespeare was responsible for much of the verbal variation between Q2 and F, ... that Shakespeare prepared a fair copy of the foul papers, that in making that fair copy he revised the text in a number of ways, and that F derives, at one or possibly more removes, from that fair copy' (401). Hence, the Oxford Shakespeare *Complete Works* adopts F as its copy-text.

So Jenkins and Taylor agree that Q2 is authoritative, since it derives more directly than any other extant printed text from Shakespeare's foul papers. But they represent alternative theories of F, one regarding it as a debasement of the authorial text which lies behind Q2, the other regarding it as deriving from a second, later authorial text.

Authoritative or not, both Q2 and F present a common problem – they are the two longest texts in the canon. Jenkins acknowledged the problem when he wrote that even the shorter 'contains more than can be supposed to have been regularly

1   R.A. Foakes has written that 'for a long time textual critics were seduced by the mirage of a single text that would be closest to the lost original of the author, and so supposed that printers' errors or playhouse interpolations and cuts could alone account for the differences between the variant texts of plays like *Hamlet* and *King Lear*, not merely corruptions, substitutions, misreadings and the like, but also substantive changes that are neatly dovetailed into the verse pattern, as well as what look like major authorial cuts or additions' (Foakes, *Hamlet*, 115–16).

played at the Globe' (Ard², 56). Lukas Erne has explored this idea, arguing that both Q2 and F are 'too long to have been performed – or to have been intended to be performed – in their entirety' (Erne, 172). In his opinion, the text recorded in Q2 was written in the knowledge that it needed abridgement and adaptation for the stage, while the shorter F is still probably only 'a preliminary abridgement rather than an acting text' (219, 183). Therefore, the Oxford Shakespeare *Complete Works*, far from recovering 'Shakespeare's plays as they were acted in London playhouses' (Oxf, xxxix), actually recovers 'conflations of theatrical scripts and reading texts' (Erne, 26). Both Q2 and F function according to a 'literary' logic, and 'correspond to what an emergent dramatic author wrote for readers in an attempt to raise the literary respectability of playtexts' (Erne, 220). Hence the references on their title-pages to 'the true original copy'.

What, then, of Q1?

When first discovered in 1823, and for most of the nineteenth century, Q1 was thought to be Shakespeare's first draft. But for most of the twentieth century that idea was dismissed (although it was re-explored towards the end of the century by, among others, Steven Urkowitz[1]). What replaced the 'first draft' theory was Q1's categorization as one of the 'bad quartos' – a term invented by A.W. Pollard to describe shorter, earlier, markedly different, and, in the opinion of most readers, artistically inferior versions of some of Shakespeare's plays which were subsequently reprinted in quarto format.[2] This theory explained a 'bad quarto' as being an unauthorized reconstruction of a 'good' text sold to the printing-house by disaffected actors or

---

1   See Urkowitz, 'Old mole', 'Good news' and 'Basics'; also Bains, 'Corrupt', and Sams, 'Taboo'. Irace, *Reforming* (95–114), argues against this position.

2   The phrase was coined by Pollard in 1909 in order to identify the 'stolne, and surreptitious copies' referred to by Heminges and Condell in the Preface to the First Folio of 1623.

commercial rivals of Shakespeare's company. W.W. Greg developed an influential theory of 'memorial reconstruction' to explain the mechanics of reconstruction (Greg, *Merry Wives*, Introduction).[1] Its implications are positive as well as negative: Q1 tells us nothing reliable about Shakespeare's contribution to the text, but it may tell us something about theatre history – namely how the play may have been acted.

Scholars have developed Greg's theory by debating the provenance of the performance behind Q1. It could be a (more or less problematic) record of a production mounted, either by the Lord Chamberlain's/King's Men[2] or by a rival company, and either touring in the provinces[3] or, as Lukas Erne has argued, performing in London (Erne, 94). But a further development has been to question the belief that Shakespeare had no hand in Q1. Giorgio Melchiori wondered whether, behind a 'very seriously debased' Q1, there might lie 'an authorially revised version for the public stage' (Melchiori, 208), and Erne has gone on to argue that Shakespeare wrote a *Hamlet* to be read (Q2) and a subsequent partial abridgement for theatrical performance (F), and then, working with his fellow actors, completed a theatrical abridgement which appeared on the London stage and which was then memorially reconstructed as Q1.[4]

Unlike Q2, and even F, and whatever its inadequacies, Q1 is at least of a performable length. It also makes theatrical good sense in respect of its cuts, as productions we have seen have demonstrated. In a detailed examination of its abridgement and reshaping, Erne includes consideration of the unique scene 14, which has often been taken to be invented to cover for a lapse in memory, but which he argues is more likely to be 'a conscious

1 The theory is attacked in Urkowitz, 'Good news', 193–205.
2 Dessen, 'Options'.
3 See Greg, *First Folio*, 300; Irace, 20.
4 Peter Blayney has argued that actors made copies of plays for their friends, writing down what they remembered having been spoken onstage. 'The quality of such texts would vary greatly (both from each other and from scene to scene within a single text)' (Blayney, 393–4).

reworking designed to shorten and speed up the action of the play in preparation for the stage' (Erne, 237).[1]

Editorial practice

The options open to editors of a Shakespeare play include producing

1   a photographic, or diplomatic, facsimile of a particular copy of a particular printed book, e.g. the British Library copy of Q2 *Hamlet*;
2   an old-spelling, or modernized, edition of such a copy of *Hamlet*;
3   an old-spelling, or modernized, edition of an 'ideal' (i.e. with its obvious errors corrected or any inconsistencies between particular copies ironed out) printed edition of a text, e.g. the text of *Hamlet* represented by Q2;
4   an old-spelling, or modernized, edition of the reconstructed text of a lost manuscript assumed to lie behind a printed edition, e.g. the text of *Hamlet* contained in Shakespeare's foul papers from which Q2 probably derives;

1   'Among the deliberate cuts in Q1 *Hamlet* reflecting stage abridgement are the first twenty-six lines of the King's opening speech of the second scene [1.2.1–26], all but the first lines of the Pyrrhus speech [2.2.406–12], Hamlet's "mirror up to nature" speech [3.2.16–28] and all but the first two and the last four lines of the Player King's long speech [3.2.182–205]' (Erne, 225). Q2's first six scenes all have a direct equivalent in Q1, but from 2.2 onwards Q1 deletes and restructures the action. In Q2/F, 2.2 (including plans for eavesdropping and the play) is on one day, 3.1 (including eavesdropping, 'To be' and the nunnery scene), 3.2, 3.3 and 3.4 (including the play) the next day. In Q1, Corambis' eavesdropping plan is followed immediately by 'To be' and the nunnery dialogue, the fishmonger episode, Hamlet's meeting with Rossencraft and Gilderstone, the entry of the players, the plans for a play and then the play – all in one day. Where in Q2/F both Corambis' and Hamlet's plans are for the next day and the two actions interfere with each other (i.e. a typical multiple action), Q1's action is quicker, simpler, more logical, more direct. Similarly, in the subsequent scenes, the Q2/F treatment involves an intricate series of events which have to be narrated because they occur offstage and which 'considerably slow down the pace of the action'. 'This fact seems to have been taken into account when the play was prepared for the stage' (Erne, 237): procrastination and delay may be part of the literary *Hamlet*, but not necessarily part of the theatrical *Hamlet*.

5 an old-spelling, or modernized, edition of a play (e.g. Shakespeare's *Hamlet*).

In the case of options 1–2, editors are attempting to record and make readable certain features of a particular material object produced by a number of contributors (including, in the case of a copy of Q2, probably Shakespeare, members of the Lord Chamberlain's Men, and compositors and others in Roberts's printing-house). In the case of options 2–5, there is always the possibility that editors will feel obliged occasionally to 'correct' the text, in which case they necessarily posit a more correct text which they either ascribe to the author or else acknowledge to be their own. In the case of options 3–4, the editors treat the early printed text or texts as clues in an attempt to recover something lost or never achieved – either a particular lost manuscript or an ideal text which, if it existed, would record the author's or printer's preferred intended version of the play at a particular moment of his life or, more likely, the editors' preferred version of the play which they claim either best represents the author's preferred intended version[1] or at least represents the play as a recognizable cultural phenomenon.

---

1 Most (but not all) editors claim to have an interest in their author's intentions, even if they recognize the impossibility of ever knowing those intentions and even if they also recognize that intentions may change over months or even days, let alone a lifetime. Proper names present a particularly interesting problem. Because Elizabethan spelling was fluid, editors feel free to 'modernize' (correct) the spelling in the quartos and the Folio. But how is one to spell Rosencrantz or Guildenstern, where the spelling varies, not only from text to text, but even within texts? These are not real people; they are the products of Shakespeare's imagination. In the absence of a manuscript, how could we ever know his intentions over such names? A persuasive theory about the authority of the quarto or Folio texts might shed light on how Shakespeare actually spelt these names in a particular manuscript, but, since Shakespeare seemed capable of spelling his own name differently on different occasions, how reliable a guide would such evidence be? What do publishers' editors do with authors who can't spell? Presumably they correct their errors. Mervyn Peake seems to have spelt the name of one his characters in the *Gormenghast* trilogy 'Fuschia' (at least he does so in one of his illustrations), but the 1968 Penguin edition of *Titus Groan* spells it 'Fuchsia' (as the flower is spelt). Who is correct?

In this edition of Shakespeare's *Hamlet*, we print three separate, edited, modernized texts, one based on Q1, one on Q2 and one on F. In other words, we are aiming at a modernized option 5, but attempting to achieve it by producing three of option 3. This is unprecedented, not just in the history of the Arden Shakespeare but, as far as we know, in the whole history of the play. Of course, we are not the first editors to print these *Hamlet*s: there have been many photographic or diplomatic facsimiles published either as separate entities or, in the case of F, as part of editions of the First Folio. Frequently, such facsimiles have been of particular copies (e.g. the two quartos produced by W.W. Greg in 1940 and 1951[1]), but sometimes they have been conflations of particular pages from different copies (e.g. Charlton Hinman's 1968 edition of the First Folio, and Graham Holderness and Bryan Loughrey's 1992 edition of Q1[2]). Paul Bertram and Bernice Kliman's 1991 diplomatic old-spelling *Three-Text 'Hamlet'* attempts to bring together Q1, Q2 and F in one volume but lacks any extended emendation, notes or commentary.[3] It prints the corrected readings wherever there is a variant, and then records the uncorrected reading. This means that it is edited, to a limited degree. It also means that it is a diplomatic edition of each text, rather than of any particular copy of that text. But the text is an ideal version of the printed text, rather than of any text lying behind the printed text.

---

1 *Hamlet: the Quarto of 1604–5: Shakespeare Quarto Facsimiles no. 4* (Oxford, 1940) is a facsimile of the Gorhambury copy in the Bodleian Library, Oxford, with the '1604' title-page from the Elizabethan Club, Yale copy. *Hamlet: the Quarto of 1603: Shakespeare Quarto Facsimiles no. 7* (Oxford, n.d. [1951]) is a facsimile of the British Library copy with the title-page from the Huntington Library, California. They were both reprinted with a 'Note to second impression' by Charlton Hinman (Oxford, 1964).

2 This edited diplomatic facsimile of the British Library copy of Q1 includes the title-page from the Huntington copy (Holderness & Loughrey, 32).

3 The *Three-Text 'Hamlet'* has been reissued in a second edition, revised and expanded, with an introduction by Eric Rasmussen (2003).

Kathleen O. Irace produced an edited, modernized text of Q1 in 1998. John Dover Wilson produced an old-spelling edition of Q2 in 1930, the so-called Cranach *Hamlet*, and Thomas Marc Parrott and Hardin Craig produced a Q2-based edition in 1938.[1] In 1986, Stanley Wells and Gary Taylor, the general editors of the Oxford Shakespeare *Complete Works*, explained that their text of *Hamlet* was 'based on the Folio' but 'passages present in the 1604 quarto but absent from the Folio are printed as Additional Passages because we believe that, however fine they may be in themselves, Shakespeare decided that the play as a whole would be better without them' (Oxf, 653). G.R. Hibbard produced a separate, edited, modernized text of F in 1987 (Oxf[1]), and followed the same procedure. Even so, both F-based editions printed a partly conflated text, drawing in material from Q2 and even Q1. The complexity of Wells and Taylor's approach is highlighted in their 1986 *Original-Spelling Edition* of the *Complete Works*. Introducing their *Hamlet* text, they repeat their earlier statement: 'our text is based on the Folio' (Oxf OS, 735), but a few lines later appear to contradict themselves by adding, 'Our edition is based upon the 1604 Quarto (printed from Shakespeare's foul papers), with additions and alterations from the Folio (printed from a scribal transcript)' (735). Their text is based on F in so far as it usually adopts F's substantive differences from Q2 and rejects Q2's substantive differences from F, but, as they explain, 'We follow the edition which we believe to be closest to Shakespeare's manuscript in spelling, punctuation, capitalization, and italicization' (*TxC*, 135)[2] – and that is usually Q2.

---

1   Parrott and Craig argued that, because all modern texts are a conflation of Q2 and F, 'they give us something that Shakespeare never wrote', whereas their edition provided 'the *Hamlet* that Shakespeare wrote' (Parrott–Craig, v). This is a misrepresentation of the principles underlying a conflated edition such as Jenkins's Ard[2] (see Appendix 2), which attempts to use conflation to get closer to 'the *Hamlet* that Shakespeare wrote' than the text supplied by either Q2 or F.

2   Greetham (333) attributes this principle of divided authority in copy-text – 'one text for accidentals and possibly several others for imported substantives' – to the 'Greg–Bowers school', i.e. the theoretical work of W.W. Greg and Fredson Bowers.

So, for as long as Wells and Taylor's substantive F text is the same as the substantive Q2 text, they choose to retain Q2's accidentals rather than F's – despite the fact that the substantive text *as a whole* is the one to be found in F and not in Q2. And words drawn exclusively from Q2 naturally appear in Q2's spelling. But how is an editor to spell text from other sources? Wells and Taylor's solutions are to use F's spelling when the chosen words are *only* present in F, Q1's spelling when the text is Q1's (e.g. the stage direction at Q1 11.57, '*Enter Ghost in his night gowne*'), and 'heritage' spelling when the text is the editor's own invention (e.g. in such stage directions as at 1.1.0, when Barnardo and Francisco enter '*at seuerall doores*', and at 1.38.1, when the Ghost enters '*in compleat Armor, holding a tronchion, with his beauer vp*'). There is, therefore, a sense in which almost all the text we end up reading is neither Q2 nor F, but F dressed in Q2's clothing.

In 2002 Jesús Tronch-Pérez produced *A Synoptic 'Hamlet'*, offering the reader 'a simultaneous and synthetic view of two of the originary texts from which the *Hamlet* of today is known' by printing both 'significant variants', one in superscript and the other in subscript, whenever the texts of Q2 and F diverge (Tronch-Pérez, 17). The result is a modernized edition of both Q2 and F, edited along the most conservative principles, i.e. emending variants only when they 'make no sense' (17).

Why a three-text edition?

Each of Q1, Q2 and F is a version of *Hamlet* which appeared either in, or soon after, Shakespeare's lifetime. Each includes a printed claim to be by him. Each has a case to be considered as 'authentic'. But almost all editors of a Shakespeare play are commissioned by publishers, or else driven by their own ambition, to establish a final, definitive text, choosing between alternative readings when they exist, or correcting perceived errors on the part of the author or those scribes, book-keepers, printers or proofreaders who have come between him and the editors' copy-text. At the same time, almost all editors seek to justify what they print by claiming that it represents either a lost text (a manuscript in Shakespeare's handwriting or an early performance of his play) or an ideal text (Shakespeare's intended definitive text or what he would or should have written if he hadn't gone wrong).[1] The former may be worth pursuing, but only if there is good reason for believing that the texts from which the editor is working do indeed derive from a single lost original. Pursuit of the ideal text is more problematic: while correcting obvious mistakes is regarded by most editors as part of the job, any further acts of 'correction' could well be regarded as either presumptuous or futile (see Thompson & Taylor, 'Text').

For as long as editors are seeking to establish a single text of *Hamlet*, they are driven to regard each of the three early texts, Q1, Q2 and F, as imperfect to some degree and, with extremely few exceptions, have produced a fourth, improved, eclectic text. Almost all such editors have conflated at least two existing texts, usually Q2 and F. As Barbara Mowat has pointed out, the history of the conflated *Hamlet* goes back to 1709, when Nicholas Rowe conflated the quarto of 1676 and the Folio of 1685: subsequent editors have displayed 'a seeming inability to be content with an F or a Q text alone' (Mowat, 118). Naturally, one motive for conflation is the wish to publish as much *Hamlet* as possible: in 1992 Mowat herself combined forces with Paul Werstine to produce the New Folger edition, and, in their words, it 'resembles most other modern editions in offering its readers a text of the Second Quarto combined with as much of the First Folio as it has been possible to include' (Folg[2], xlix). But the term 'conflation' can also be used to mean any individual act of emendation in which the editor who is faced with an

---

1   Holderness and Loughrey are the exceptions. See Appendix 2 for a discussion of the implications of their position.

unsatisfactory reading in the copy-text turns automatically to the other text as a possible source for a better reading. Harold Jenkins in his Q2-based edition of 1982 (Ard[2]) used both kinds of conflation, printing numerous emendations from F and incorporating in his text all the F-only passages. Gary Taylor and G.R. Hibbard in their F-based editions of 1986 (Oxf) and 1987 (Oxf[1]) used Q2 as their first source of emendation but nevertheless excluded the Q2-only passages and printed them as supplementary information after the 'full' text (Oxf, 775–7; Oxf[1], 335–69).

In this multiple edition of *Hamlet* we have eschewed both forms of conflation on principle, preferring to treat each text as an independent entity. This is not because we believe that they were, in fact, entirely independent, but because none of the evidence of possible dependence is sufficiently overwhelming or widespread to oblige us to make any particular act of conflation as a result. And these three texts are remarkably distinct entities. Anyone reading Q1, in its original printed form, in a facsimile or in a modern edition, is immediately struck by how different it is from Q2 or F. But anyone reading the original printed texts of Q2 and F should consider how very different they are from each other. Q2 contains 3,902 separate printed lines of text. A comparison of these lines (including any speech prefixes) with their counterparts in F reveals that only 220 are identical in every respect (including accidentals and decisions to italicize). This means that Q2 differs from F in 94 per cent of its printed lines of text, and even if one restricts the comparison to substantives the figure only comes down to 36 per cent. In addition, one still needs to bear in mind that there are about 70 lines in F for which there are no counterparts in Q2, and about 230 lines in Q2 with no counterparts in F.

If by '*Hamlet*' we mean a public representation of a 'Hamlet' narrative – that is, a story involving a character called Hamlet who has some continuity of identity with the Amlodi figure of Nordic myth – then these three texts are just three 'expressions' of *Hamlet* out of the infinite number of *Hamlet*s which have or could have come into existence. They are, to narrow the field, three representations of Shakespeare's *Hamlet*, and each representation takes the form of a scholarly edition. But the concepts embodied in the phrases 'Shakespeare's *Hamlet*' and 'scholarly edition' need careful handling, by us and by our readers. Our text (i.e. our multiple edition) is based on printed texts published between 1603 and 1623. We are not assuming that William Shakespeare was necessarily the sole author of every word in those early seventeenth-century texts, nor that we know the degree to which any of them represent the author's or authors' intentions, nor how it was that they came to be in print. We do know, however, that they have a claim to be regarded as separate plays as well as separate versions of the same play. Our approach to editing them ultimately lacks intellectual purity, since 'the dream of the original text'[1] inevitably informs every editor's mind and, therefore, practice. But we nevertheless offer three *Hamlet*s rather than one.

In a discussion of Kenneth Branagh's 1996 film of *Hamlet*, Peter Holland points out that 'The note in the screenplay [Branagh, 175] about "the choice of text" indicates that the screenplay is based on F1: "Nothing," we are told, "has been cut from the text, and some passages absent from it . . . have been supplied from the Second Quarto"' (Holland, 288). But Holland observes that 'more of Shakespeare is not, in this case, necessarily better' (288). By way of illustration he explores one brief snatch of dialogue from Act 5, comparing its effect in Q2, in F and in a conflation of the two.

> In Q2, after Hamlet has murdered Polonius, Gertrude enters with Claudius who is accompanied by Rosencrantz and Guildenstern; Gertrude asks the others

---

1 The phrase is employed by W.B. Worthen (83), who compares the textual critic's 'dream' with the attempt to reconstruct Shakespeare's Globe in London.

to leave so that she can tell Claudius what has happened in private: 'Bestow this place on us a little while' [4.1.4]. In the Folio text, Rosencrantz and Guildenstern do not appear and Gertrude's line is also, logically, cut. It makes them appear much less like Claudius's toadying acolytes, less willing accomplices than further victims of the King's plotting. The payoff is later: when Hamlet describes how he sent them to their deaths, Horatio comments in both Q2 and F, 'So Guildenstern and Rosencrantz go to't' [5.2.56], but it is only in F that Hamlet offers the vicious pun in response: 'Why, man, they did make love to this employment' [57], picking up on 'go to't' as a phrase for sexual activity. The text in which Hamlet criticizes his erstwhile schoolfellows for enjoying the sexiness of conspiracy is the text in which we do not see them doing that. The conflated text goes nearer to justifying Hamlet's callousness than either Q2 or F taken separately permits.

(Holland, 289)

As we have seen, Stanley Wells and Gary Taylor decided to print two texts of *King Lear* in the Oxford Shakespeare *Complete Works*. Stephen Greenblatt, the general editor of the 1997 Norton Shakespeare, which took over the Oxford texts, nevertheless decided not only to print the two texts of *King Lear* but to add a third, 'a conflated version . . . so that readers can encounter the tragedy in the form that it assumed in most editions from the eighteenth century until very recently' (Norton, 2315). Mercifully, you may feel, the general editors of the Arden Shakespeare have decided not to break all records by including a conflated text of *Hamlet* and making this the first four-text edition.[1]

---

1 Teena Rochfort Smith had begun a *Four-Text Hamlet in Parallel Columns* in 1883, but it was not completed. It was a diplomatic facsimile of Q1, Q2 and F, accompanied by an old-spelling conflated text based closely on Q2 with occasional emendation from F; see Thompson, 'Teena'.

HAMLET ON STAGE AND SCREEN

Hamlet and his points

Those who have seen other Hamlets are aghast.
Mr. Irving is missing his points, he is neglecting his
opportunities. Betterton's face turned as white as his
neck-cloth, when he saw the Ghost. Garrick thrilled the
house when he followed the spirit . . . But Mr. Irving's
intention is not to make points.

(Scott, 62)

Clement Scott is describing Sir Henry Irving's performance as
Hamlet in November 1874 (Scott, 62; quoted in Wells,
Anthology, 107) and invoking his two great predecessors from
the seventeenth and eighteenth centuries, Thomas Betterton
and David Garrick. Scott also discusses Irving's costume and
appearance: 'How is he dressed, and how does he look? No
imitation of the portrait of Sir Thomas Lawrence, no funereal
velvet, no elaborate trappings, no Order of the Danish elephant,
no flaxen wig after the model of M. Fechter, (Scott, 61; in
Wells, *Anthology*, 106). Here he adds into the equation two
more recent actors, John Philip Kemble (painted by Lawrence
in 1801; see Fig. 12) and Charles Albert Fechter, whose first
London appearance as Hamlet in 1861 introduced a naturalism
which coloured all subsequent portrayals of the character.

What Scott's essay reveals is, first, the importance of a
perceived stage tradition in the performance history of *Hamlet*;
second, the importance of Hamlet himself in that tradition;
and, third, the part in that tradition played by 'points', i.e.
trademark pieces of stage 'business' invented by an actor
and then, frequently, taken up and repeated by subsequent
actors (see pp. 6–7). Irving, Scott says, is deliberately breaking
with tradition, by dressing differently and by abandoning
established points. It is worth noting the introduction into
the discussion of Fechter, a Frenchman. The tradition is
conceived of as primarily, if not exclusively, an English

12 John Philip Kemble as Hamlet; portrait by Sir Thomas Lawrence (1801)

tradition: even when the Frenchman intrudes, it is in English and on the English stage.

An assumed English tradition conventionally dominates the history of the play in performance until the end of the nineteenth century. This assumption is accurate in so far as, for a long time, most professional performances were London-based. After 1660, the licence to perform Shakespeare was restricted to just two acting companies, each with its own theatre in London, and it was only in the nineteenth century that this arrangement really began to break down. But the conventional picture of a tradition is restrictive. There were theatres and actors elsewhere in the world, and actors toured. By the beginning of the twentieth century, the reading and, to a lesser extent, the performance of Shakespeare had become a global phenomenon.

The first absolutely definite record of an individual performance of Shakespeare's *Hamlet* in London was not until 1619, when it was done at Court, probably with Joseph Taylor playing the prince. But the entry of 26 July 1602 in the Stationers' Register states that it had been 'lately Acted', and the title-page of the 1603 Quarto claims that *The Tragicall Historie of Hamlet Prince of Denmarke* had been performed 'diuerse times . . . in the Cittie of London'. As we have seen, there is some uncertainty about which *Hamlet* is meant by some of the earliest references, but by the time it was done at Hampton Court in 1637 the play as we know it today had appeared in at least eight printed editions (those of 1603, 1604, 1611, 1619, *c.* 1621, 1623, 1632 and 1637), and this suggests a popularity that must surely have been largely generated by performance rather than print.

Indeed, there is evidence that the play was being seen outside London, and even outside the British Isles themselves in the very earliest years of the century. The First Quarto of 1603 refers to performances of the play in the universities of Cambridge and Oxford (although we don't know whether these performances actually took place, or, if they did, whether they were by professionals or by amateurs), and within four years it had taken on a life of its own, quite definitely independent of Shakespeare's acting company when, as we have seen, it was acted by William Keeling's crew off the coast of Africa on 5 September 1607 and on 31 March 1608. As we have also seen, there is evidence that English actors were touring a *Hamlet* in Germany in 1626, and possibly earlier.

Richard Burbage, the leading actor in Shakespeare's company, had 'young Hamlett' in his repertoire, and, at least according to Nicholas Rowe, Shakespeare himself played the ghost of Hamlet's father. But Shakespeare died in 1616, Burbage died in 1619 and Joseph Taylor joined the King's Men two months after Burbage's death. By this time, then, direct continuity with the 'original' conception of the play had already been significantly weakened or broken. Continuity was further demolished by the closing of the theatres in 1642, although while they were closed one of the 'pieces of plays' performed by itinerant actors was 'The Grave Makers', i.e. the opening of Act 5. When they reopened at the succession of Charles II, the rights to perform *Hamlet* passed from the King's Men to the Duke's Company, the latter run by Sir William Davenant. Davenant has been credited with coaching his Hamlet (Betterton) and his Ophelia (Betterton's wife) from his memories of performances by Taylor and the boys of the King's Men in the period before the theatres were closed, but in performance Davenant's *Hamlet* was already a distinct entity, in many respects unlike the play recorded in the quartos of 1604 onwards. As recorded in the so-called 'Players' Quarto' of 1676, Davenant had not only 'refined' the language but, 'This play being too long to be conveniently Acted', he had cut Voltemand, Cornelius and Reynaldo, Polonius' advice to Laertes, most of Laertes' advice to Ophelia, all of Hamlet's advice to the players, and Fortinbras's first appearance; while, of the famous longer speeches, only 'To be or not to be' survives in its entirety. The play as performed reduced the text to approximately 2,800 lines (i.e. about 25 per cent of Q2 was cut), and, as Lukas Erne has pointed out, this may reflect the shape and dimensions of the play as performed in Shakespeare's day too.[1]

Betterton played Hamlet from 1661 to 1709, by which time he was seventy-four: Colley Cibber recorded for posterity a description of the scene in which he first meets the Ghost. In contrast with those actors who get the house thundering with applause, by 'straining vociferation requisite to express rage and fury', Betterton ensured that the passion in Hamlet's beautiful speech never rose beyond 'an almost breathless astonishment, or an impatience, limited by filial reverence'; he first 'opened with a pause of mute amazement, then rising slowly to a solemn, trembling voice, he made the Ghost equally terrible to the spectator as to himself' (Lowe, 100–2; quoted in Wells, *Anthology*, 18). Clearly, the art of acting on the Restoration stage involved the generation of arresting and memorable moments of sensation. The German scientist Georg Lichtenberg described David Garrick in the same scene in 1774–5:

> Garrick turns sharply and at the same moment staggers back two or three paces with his knees giving way under him; his hat falls to the ground and both his arms, especially the left, are stretched out nearly to their full length, with the hands as high as his head, the right arm more bent and the hand lower, and the fingers apart; his mouth is open: thus he stands rooted to the spot, with legs apart, but no loss of dignity, supported by his friends.
>
> (Mare & Quarrell, 9; quoted in Wells, *Anthology*, 24)

---

1   Erne, 169. Erne notes that the 'Players' Quartos' of 1676, 1683, 1695 and 1703 offer the play in two forms, 'the original authorial and the then current theatrical text', and goes on to argue that 'the original authorial' (i.e. Q2) version was a 'literary' text, far too long to be performed but intended for publication, and therefore to be read rather than acted.

Lichtenberg also noted the fame already attached to 'To be or not to be': 'a large part of the audience not only knows it by heart as well as they do the Lord's Prayer, but listens to it, so to speak, as if it were a Lord's Prayer' (Mare & Quarrell, 15; in Wells, *Anthology*, 26). Another of Garrick's 'points' was to knock over Gertrude's chair on the appearance of the Ghost in the closet scene, a piece of business explicitly rejected by Charlotte Cushman (one of a long tradition of female Hamlets) in 1851: as she wrote in her promptbook (now at the Folger Shakespeare Library), 'I don't like the kicking of the chair, nor the Queen's sprawling on the ground.'[1]

From 1742 to 1776 Garrick was an active, energetic Hamlet, but interest was beginning to shift from the external action of the play as a whole to the inner life of the central protagonist. Though focused on revenge and in control throughout (his madness was entirely an act and he ended his life by running on Laertes' sword), Garrick's Hamlet was characterized primarily by grief for his father, and it was this emotional state that determined everything in his behaviour. Similarly, John Philip Kemble, whose Hamlet dominated the stage between 1783 and 1817, attempted to build a coherent characterization upon a single unifying idea, Hamlet's melancholy and noble suffering, which made him grave and pensive. It was a reflection of the Romantic emphasis on feeling, but also a precursor of the modern desire to find a unifying concept to explain a play.[2]

In 1661 *Hamlet* was the first Shakespeare play to be presented with perspective scenery. Starting with Kemble, the introduction into the theatre of specially painted (as opposed to stock)

1 The chair had become a bed as early as 1714, judging by the redrawing of the frontispiece for Rowe's second edition (see Rosenberg, 645–6).

2 Kemble's grandfather, John Ward, led a company performing *Hamlet* among other plays on a regular touring circuit of the West Midlands and the Welsh borders from 1744 to 1766: see Thompson, 'Ward'. His sister, Sarah Siddons, was an early female Hamlet, performing the role in Birmingham, Bristol, Liverpool and Manchester in the 1780s and reviving it in Dublin in 1802 (see Howard).

scenery provided a credibly 'real' environment, which supported the growing interest in the definition of characters who were individuals rather than types. As the nineteenth century developed, Hamlet became increasingly characterized as an extreme case of the individual. Edmund Kean (1787–1833) was an early manifestation of this process, and the kind of selfhood he projected was 'fragmented, uneven, divided . . . in keeping with Romantic sensibility' (Dawson, 46). Kemble's niece, Fanny, paid tribute to Kean's ability to deliver moments of 'overpowering passion' and looks and gestures of 'thrilling, piercing meaning' (Kemble, 430; quoted in Dawson, 45). William Hazlitt provides evidence of the epiphanic eloquence of one of Kean's famous 'points'. After the 'vehemence' of his attacks on Ophelia in the nunnery scene, Kean stopped at the edge of the stage, turned and walked back 'from a pang of parting tenderness to press his lips on Ophelia's hand. It had an electrical effect on the house. It was the finest commentary that was ever made on Shakespeare. It explained the character at once.'[1] But part of what it explained for Hazlitt was the fact that Hamlet is not consistent, that Kemble's approach was inadequate to Hamlet's ultimately incoherent nature.

Herbert Beerbohm-Tree was still kissing Ophelia's hand in this manner in 1892, but perhaps the most influential of Kean's 'points' was his famous crawl (see Fig. 13). In 1814 the *London Herald* deplored the fact that, in the play scene, Kean 'forgot that inalienable delicacy, which should eternally characterize a gentleman in his deportment before the ladies, that he not only exposed his *derrière* to his mistress, but positively crawled upon his belly towards the King like a wounded snake in a meadow, rather than a Prince' (quoted in Mills, 83), but it was still being done in France in 1886 by Jean Mounet Sully, in a German film in 1920 directed by Svend Gade and Heinz Schall and starring the Danish actress Asta Nielsen (see Fig. 14), and

---

1 William Hazlitt, *Morning Chronicle*, 14 March 1814.

13 Painting by Daniel Maclise (1842) of the Court watching *The Murder of Gonzago* (3.2), showing William Macready about to perform Edmund Kean's 'crawl'

14 Still from *Hamlet: the Drama of Vengeance* directed by Svend Gade and
   Heinz Schall (Germany, 1920), showing Asta Nielsen about to begin her
   'crawl'

by Laurence Olivier in his 1948 film (though he crawled into
the slightly later closet scene instead).

After Kean, Hamlets became increasingly sensitive,
oppressed, paralysed by consciousness. Typical of the kind was
Edwin Booth, the great American actor, who played Hamlet
first in San Francisco in 1853 at the age of twenty, took it to
Australia, played it for 100 nights in New York during 1864–5,
and played it when he retired from the stage in 1891. Booth
emphasized Hamlet's reflective intellectuality and spirituality:
he felt that Goethe got the play right when he described it as a
representation of 'the effects of a great action laid upon a soul
unfit for the performance of it'; and he wrote to the critic
William Winter on 10 February 1882 that 'I have always
endeavoured to make prominent the femininity of Hamlet's

character' (Watermeier, 203; quoted in Mills, 132). Charles Clarke, who made a detailed 60,000-word summary of Booth's interpretation based on nine separate performances in 1870, described his Hamlet as a man horrified by his success in killing Claudius – his 'consciousness was outraged. His will was appalled' (quoted in Hapgood, 34).

Clarke's is one of those voices that have the power to revive the experience of an audience from the past. When Booth delivers the 'To be or not to be' soliloquy, he is, significantly, seated, immobilized and silenced by his troubled thoughts:

> He comes down to the left hand and drops into a chair. Every moment is replete with thoughtfulness and mental absorption, and his face is almost condensed, so powerful seems the working of his mind. He looks over the side of the chair at his audience with one hand held up to his temple and two or three dark locks of hair falling over it. But although his eyes are resting directly on one he does not see a single external thing. He does not speak for ten or fifteen seconds – not with his tongue; but his eyes proclaim the thought almost as well as the voice could. I forget all about the man then; for the time I see right through his flesh and overlook his *mind*.[1]

In the same way, Henry Irving (1838–1905) was praised for unveiling the workings of Hamlet's mind. Whatever his technical eccentricities – E.R. Russell notes that he moved on the stage like 'a fretful man trying to get very quickly over a ploughed field' (Russell, 4) – those who saw his first performance in the role in 1874 claimed that 'We see Hamlet think.'[2] But Irving was more emotional than Booth, and, above all, more

---

1 Mills's transcript of Charles Clarke's manuscript in the Folger Shakespeare Library, Washington, DC (Mills, 140).
2 *Era*, 3 November 1874.

HAMLET (*To Mr. Irving*): "Nor do not saw the air too much with your hand thus; but use all gently; for in the very torrent, tempest, and (as I may say,) whirlwind of your passion, you must acquire and beget a temperance, that may give it smoothness."

15 Undated cartoon of Hamlet giving Henry Irving advice on acting, taken from an extra-illustrated copy of William Winter, *Henry Irving* (1885), opposite p. 94; see 3.2.4–8

natural. Too natural for some, who complained that his 'moody Dane, as enacted at the Lyceum, irresistibly reminds us of the effeminate loungers whom we are prone to encounter in the drawing rooms of London.'[1] But Irving's Hamlet was more

1 *Sporting Times*, 7 November 1874.

than moody: his sanity was at stake, and his inner torment derived largely from the intensity and ambivalence of his feelings towards those to whom he was closest. He devised business to encapsulate this complex psychological state. As he sprawled watching in total absorption the representation of his mother's treachery in *The Murder of Gonzago* (see Fig. 16), he gnawed away at Ophelia's peacock-feathered fan until he demolished it; then, with the play abandoned, hurled away the remains of the fan, shrieked and leapt into the King's empty chair.

> There was no crawling forward on the floor to watch the King during the play, as so many actors have done; and none of Ophelia's peacock fan for Hamlet to tap his breast with and fling into the air, as Irving used to do ... there is very little concern about external tradition.[1]

This is Stark Young reviewing the American actor, John Barrymore (1882–1942), playing Hamlet in New York, and continuing the practice of comparing and contrasting each new Hamlet with his predecessors – in this case, Kean and Irving. *Hamlet* had been introduced into France in 1745, Russia in 1748, Germany in 1776,[2] Sweden in 1787, Czechoslovakia in 1791, Poland in 1798, South Africa in 1799, Japan in 1903 and China in 1916, but you would not know it from Young's review. The tradition is conceived of as English, or possibly Anglo-American. Even as recently as 1985, John A. Mills ignored almost everything outside Britain and the United States when he published *Hamlet on Stage: The Great Tradition*.

John Gielgud (1904–2000) was an example of someone embroiled in, and always conscious of, a tradition. He starred in six different productions of *Hamlet* between 1930 and 1945,

---

1 Stark Young, *The New Republic*, 20 November 1922.
2 *Der bestrafte Brudermord*, of course, had been performed in Germany in *c.* 1710.

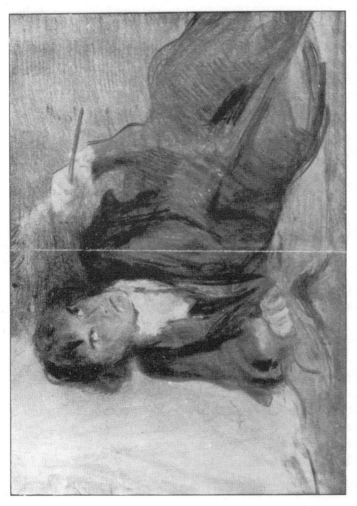

16 Illustration 'from the painting by F[rancis] W[ilford] Lawson' of Henry Irving speaking Lucianus' line at 3.2.247, taken from an extra-illustrated copy of the Variorum *Hamlet* (1877), vol. 1, opposite p. 336; see 3.2.248–53n.

and directed the play too, most famously in New York in 1964 with Richard Burton in the title role. His grandmother was Kate Terry, Fechter's Ophelia in 1864; his aunt was Ellen Terry, Irving's Ophelia in 1878; and his cousin was Edward Gordon Craig (Ellen Terry's son), the co-director with Konstantin Stanislavsky and designer of a hugely influential production in 1912 at the Moscow Art Theatre. In 1937, with good reason, Gielgud published an essay entitled 'The Hamlet tradition'.[1]

But the notion of 'tradition' is perhaps restrictive, because it assumes a hegemonic line of influence. Before 1900, our knowledge of the performances of *Hamlet* derives from written descriptions or drawings, paintings and prints made by people who were members of an audience or participants in a production. Since 1900, when Sarah Bernhardt was filmed in a scene from the play, visual and sound recordings have between them created a rich performance archive (as we have said, there are at least fifty films) which explodes both the idea that Hamlet is the possession of an English-speaking culture and the idea that one could trace a linear history of performance. Extracts from Gielgud's stage performances were captured for posterity on audiotape, and he made radio broadcasts, some of which were recorded, and commercial recordings of key speeches. His 1964 production with Burton was filmed and Gielgud himself appeared in two films, Humphrey Jennings's *A Diary for Timothy* (made in 1946 and including an extract from his stage performance) and Kenneth Branagh's 1996 production (in which he played 'Priam'). We can now hear or see historic Hamlets, not only from Britain and North America (Beerbohm-Tree, Frank Benson, Ernest Milton, Johnston Forbes-Robertson, John Barrymore, Maurice Evans, Laurence Olivier, Michael Redgrave, David Warner, Nicol Williamson, Peter O'Toole, Ian McKellen, Albert Finney, Ben Kingsley, Derek Jacobi, Jonathan

---

1   John Gielgud, 'The Hamlet tradition: notes on costume, scenery and stage business', in Gilder, 109–71.

Pryce, Michael Pennington, Mark Rylance, Daniel Day Lewis, Kevin Kline, Mel Gibson, Ethan Hawke and Simon Russell Beale, and many others) but from at least sixteen other countries, including France (Sarah Bernhardt, Jean Mounet Sully), Denmark (Asta Nielsen), Germany (Alexander Moissi), Italy (Ruggero Ruggeri) and Russia (Innokenti Smoktunovsky). Influence is no longer exclusively dependent upon an actor or director witnessing a live stage performance in the flesh.

Enter the director

The discovery in 1881 of the de Witt drawing of the Swan theatre prompted William Poel to argue for a bare Elizabethan acting space which could accommodate continuous, uninterrupted, ensemble playing. This was a reaction against the cumbersome, historically accurate, pictorial scenery of the Victorian stage, usually designed to concentrate attention on the star actor. Barrymore may have been a star, but his director, Arthur Hopkins, commissioned a simple, multi-purpose set intended to speed the action and, through its design, communicate an idea, an interpretation of the play. In January 1925 he brought the production to London's Haymarket Theatre, but at the Kingsway Theatre, a little later in the year, Barry Jackson and H.K. Ayliff sensationally demolished another tradition by updating the play and dressing Hamlet in plus-fours (see Fig. 17). Within a few months there were two more modern-dress *Hamlet*s, one in Prague, directed by Karel Hilar, the other in Berlin, directed by Leopold Jessner.

The modern-dress experiments of the 1920s, combined with the staging ideas of Poel and Gordon Craig, liberated design and opened up the play to new acting styles and new meanings. Subsequent directors have felt free to set the play in any period (Michael Benthall's 1948 Stratford-upon-Avon production was Victorian) or no period at all (Hans Gratzer in Vienna in 1979), and project their vision directly into the audience's mind by

17 The graveyard scene (5.1) from the first modern-dress *Hamlet*, directed by Barry Jackson and H.K. Ayliff, with Colin Keith-Johnston as Hamlet, at the Kingsway theatre, London, in 1925

means of an image on the retina (Otomar Krejča's 1977 production in Düsseldorf was dominated by a huge mirror, Jürgen Flimm's in Hamburg in 1986 by a huge wall, John Caird's at London's National Theatre in 2000 by a huge cross).

Jackson and Ayliff's *Hamlet* also reoriented readings of the play. 'The difference in the main is not to Hamlet himself . . . but in the others, who surprise one by suddenly leaping to life . . . *Hamlet* in all its parts is a great deal better play than any company of actors have ever dared to think it before.'[1] Colin Keith-Johnston's Hamlet was young, modern, casual and matter-of-fact; he smoked, he was confrontational, morose, even violent. But, while his was the main part, no longer was everything viewed from his perspective, and subsequent productions have chosen to allow other characters to be individuals with their own developing, tragic lives. When Patrick Stewart played the King in Rodney Bennett's BBC television production of 1980 he, 'rather than Hamlet, commanded the most respect . . . He loved Gertrude deeply and genuinely, had killed for her and wrestled with the guilt of having done so; at the same time, he was the King, and charged with the responsibility of his role. All this he took seriously and handled with dexterity and dispatch. If he was forced into hypocrisy, it seemed to go against the grain.'[2]

The major change which came about in the twentieth century – and which was itself probably accelerated by the development of the cinema – was the emergence of the director, who became as important as, or even more important than, the actor. Irving, while ensuring that his productions were star vehicles for himself, had made sure he controlled and perfected every element in his productions – the scenery, the lighting, the appearance and movements of his actors. As Dawson explains, 'he went back to the early texts, thought through the various

1 Hubert Griffith, *Observer*, 25 August 1925; quoted in Wells, *Anthology*, 205.
2 Anthony B. Dawson, *Watching Shakespeare: A Playgoers' Guide* (1988), 160.

possible readings, and made his many changes, cuts, and restorations on the basis of a full consideration of character and meaning' (59). Like Irving before them, some of the great English Hamlets since 1900 – Gielgud, Olivier, Branagh and Mark Rylance – have also combined the roles of actor and manager or director. Perhaps for this reason, their Hamlets have tended to be sympathetic, even heroic, figures. Rylance in the London Globe production of 2000 'extravagantly over-acted his madness with a wild frivolity, his laughter constantly bordering on hysterical despair, until in the nunnery scene he began to feel that he was no longer pretending' (Dobson, '2000', 262), but he ensured, by 'working' the groundlings, that his audience 'sided' with him throughout. Gielgud was always prepared to show Hamlet's cruelty when wounded, but he was a lonely and frustrated victim of circumstance, angry with himself as much as with others, and he grew in moral stature as the play progressed.

Yet many, and arguably most, of the key figures in the history of *Hamlet* in performance since 1900 have not been those of actors or actor-directors, but those of 'pure' directors – directors as *auteurs*. Poel, Gordon Craig and Stanislavsky, Jackson and Ayliff, Jessner, Guthrie, Grigori Kozintsev, Peter Hall, Yuri Lyubimov, Daniel Mesguich, Buzz Goodbody, Heiner Müller, Richard Eyre, Peter Brook, Franco Zeffirelli, Yukio Ninagawa and Michael Almereyda have each opened up new possibilities for the play's afterlife. Outside Britain and North America, the necessity of translation has brought with it less reverence for the verbal text, less inhibition in making new meanings and, indeed, new texts.

Michael Dobson wrote that John Caird's 2000 production at London's National Theatre, with Simon Russell Beale as Hamlet, 'was director's Shakespeare to the core: meticulously choreographed; expensively lit; ... equipped with an impressive, reverberating sound system and sumptuous incidental music; glossily designed; and informed by a single, powerful vision' (Dobson, '2000', 259). To suit his metaphysical vision, Caird cut Fortinbras, whom he found a boring distraction (Croall, 14, 15). Almost all directors cut the text, but beyond that most would hesitate to add to it. Jonathan Miller may have been prepared to defy conventional readings, with Anton Lesser playing Hamlet in 1982 as a distinctly unheroic, 'unattractive character, a tiresome, clever, destructive boy' (Miller, 111), but he was unprepared to alter a word of dialogue to make his readings easier to deliver. A very few directors have attempted to stage what actors call 'the entirety', that is, an eclectic incorporation of all the substantive action and dialogue of the Second Quarto and the First Folio texts: Frank Benson tried it at Stratford in 1899, Peter Hall at the Old Vic in 1975, and Kenneth Branagh in his 1996 film. Ben Greet staged the Second Quarto at the Old Vic in 1916, and at least twenty-five directors have staged the First Quarto – most famously William Poel at St George's Hall in 1881, and most recently Andrew Borba in Los Angeles in 2003.[1]

Of course, 'the text', as this edition attempts to demonstrate, is not a stable, unified, universally identified entity. Most directors have started with a printed text (probably ignorant of its relationship to the earliest printed versions) and then modified it. Davenant, and the actors and actor-managers who succeeded him, were all prepared to cut or change the text, informed either by the practical necessity to keep it short enough for audiences to bear with or else by a notion of propriety and decorum (cleansing it of obscenity, improving on Shakespeare's versification or plotting, ennobling the hero or communicating a moral message). The modern director has been happy to do all of these things, but has tended to concentrate on the last in the list. Caird was doing nothing new when he removed Fortinbras: Robert Wilks cut him as far back as 1732, he remained cut until Johnston Forbes-Robertson reinstated

1   See Ard Q1/F for more detail on the stage history of Q1.

him at the Lyceum in 1897, and he has often gone missing since, as in Michael Almereyda's 2000 film. In Germany, especially since the Second World War, directors have felt far less bound by the text and far more adventurous about its capacity to catalyse other texts. Peter Zadek, according to Ron Engle, 'perhaps best represents the German directorial vision that has aroused both praise and condemnation for its license with the text and interpretation' (Engle, 94). Zadek produced the play twice, at Bochum in 1977 and at Hamburg and the Edinburgh Festival in 1999. His postmodern alienation techniques deliberately created an incongruity between actors and their characters, but such alienation was not necessarily at the expense of emotional response. In 1999, for example, his Hamlet was played by the fifty-year-old Angela Winckler; her conception of the revenger was of an abused, damaged child in shock, reduced to a puppet. Horatio, who sat beside her as she died, held her head up as if he were her parent – or, perhaps, her ventriloquist. It was bizarre, but it was also involving, and moving.

It has been the complexity of Hamlet's psyche that has dominated most productions in the Anglo-American tradition, and this has probably been fuelled by the influence of the actor-manager, whose ego has been nourished by the size of the role and its variety and richness (the range of emotion, the wit, the soliloquies, and so on). For his only stage performance of the role, at London's Old Vic in 1937, Olivier was directed by Tyrone Guthrie, whose Freudian interpretation of the prince made him into a forceful, highly active man rendered passive because of the Oedipal conflicts forced on him by his mother. When Olivier went on to direct a film version in 1948, he deployed the same reading, commenting later that the story was seen through Hamlet's eyes, 'and when he's not present, through his imagination' (Olivier, 197). Since Olivier cast himself as Hamlet, that imagination may have elided with the director's: in an essay on 'Olivier, Hamlet and Freud' Peter S.

Donaldson found evidence in the film of the acting out of trauma in Olivier's early childhood (Donaldson, 31–67). However, Olivier further concentrated the audience's attention on himself by supplying the voice of the Ghost, by including a swashbuckling leap from a balcony in the final scene, and by ending the film once Hamlet had died. This somewhat narcissistic approach was continued in 1996 when Kenneth Branagh directed himself in a film version that was widely interpreted as an attempt to match, or cap, Olivier's.

Carol Rutter has protested at the diminution of Ophelia under the male gaze of Olivier and Branagh's films.[1] The stage versions by Jonathan Miller in 1982 and Ingmar Bergman in 1987 both tried to correct what they regarded as the traditional patronizing prettification of Ophelia's suffering by presenting her insanity as embarrassingly ugly and painful; but such an approach can objectify and demean Ophelia as much as it does her male abusers within the play. In 2003 another approach was demonstrated by the Grand Théâtre de Genève when presenting Ambroise Thomas's 1868 opera, *Hamlet*, in London. This piece is famous for a fourth act devoted almost entirely to Ophélie's madness and featuring her most beautiful death aria. As Natalie Dessay sang 'Ah, cruel! Je t'aime!' it gradually became apparent from the blood trickling down her dress that she was self-harming, slowly cutting into her breasts.

Hamlet *and politics*

Thomas's opera ends with Hamlet alive and ruling Denmark. The very act of translation has allowed many 'foreign' Hamlets to break free from the mesmeric intricacy of Shakespeare's language, modify his plot and allow neglected or new elements of *Hamlet* to emerge. One element is the political narrative and its implications for political action. In 1844 Ferdinand Freiligrath used the play as a stick with which to beat his native

1   See Rutter, 27–56; also Aebischer, 64–101, on '*Hamlet*'s unruly corpses'.

land for its cowardice ('Germany is Hamlet'), but by this time Shakespeare was already becoming appropriated as a German author and *Hamlet* went on to be used for a variety of political purposes. Jessner's updating of 1926 made Hamlet a political rebel and the production an all-out attack on Kaiser Wilhelm II: it was later cited by the Nazis as being an offence against the playwright, who seemed, at least to Werner Deubel, to belong more to Germany than to England (Deubel, 5; cited in London, 240). The play enjoyed ninety-four legal productions under the Third Reich, including 130 performances of a Berlin production starring Gustaf Gründgens in 1936 that led Goebbels to write in his diary, 'What a genius Shakespeare is!' (London, 243–5).

The First Folio's phrase about Denmark being a prison has always resonated with those living under oppressive regimes. Michael Chekhov's 1924–5 *Hamlet* at the Moscow Art Theatre was branded as decadent and reactionary by official communist critics, who also spread rumours that Stalin hated the character of the hero; the play was banned in Russia, but Boris Pasternak in his 1930s translation managed to turn it into a tragedy of duty and self-denial whose hero is 'a judge of his own time and servant of the future' (see Stříbrný, 79, 83, 99). Grigori Kozintsev staged Pasternak's translation immediately after Stalin's death in 1953, and his later film version (1964) presented Hamlet as an intellectual dissident in a totalitarian state – a reading that became standard throughout the countries of the Soviet Union. The otherwise bare set for Yuri Lyubimov's 1971–80 production at Moscow's Taganka Theatre featured a huge woollen curtain which moved mysteriously around the stage, suggesting a hostile force at work, but also a prison wall – with ears (see Fig. 18). Vladimir Vysotsky, a well-known ballad singer, a dissident and an alcoholic, played the prince, and the politics of resistance seemed to be exemplified in his starting the play by reading Boris Pasternak's poem 'Hamlet' from the epilogue to his banned novel *Doctor Zhivago* (see Stříbrný, 119–20).

18 Hamlet watches the King attempting to pray (3.3) from behind the huge
curtain in the version of Yuri Lyubimov's *Hamlet* staged at the Haymarket
theatre, Leicester, in 1989, with Daniel Webb as Hamlet, Andrew Jarvis
as the King

The contrasts between 'western' (Anglo-American) readings and 'eastern' (Soviet Communist) readings were perhaps particularly stark in Germany, where the divided country supported two Shakespeare societies and two Shakespeare journals throughout the Cold War period. In the east, it was necessary to present Hamlet as 'a truly utopian prefiguration of the socialist-humanist conscience' or even as 'a pioneering champion of socialist society', though this simplistic appropriation of Renaissance texts became increasingly challenged during the 'thaw' in the 1960s (see Weimann, 'Divided', and Pfister). A similar trajectory can be traced in Bulgaria, where

> The received picture of the Prince as an effete melancholy intellectual was ... castigated as a bourgeois fabrication. In fact, this young man, it was insisted, had a considerable willpower and energy as well as firm convictions for which he continued to fight to the bitter end.
>
> (Shurbanov & Sokolova, 180)

Heavily politicized versions of *Hamlet* became almost an index of the internal politics of various eastern European countries; Shurbanov and Sokolova suggest that the production staged by Vili Tsankov in Varna in 1956 'foreshadowed, and maybe even encouraged, the specifically national line of dissent, that of dogged non-cooperation rather than militant opposition' (185), whereas by 1982 Nedyalko Yordanov's production in Burgas was received as 'an oblique, yet quite transparent verdict on a dictatorial regime whose very nature would logically lead to a catastrophe' (197). The overtly oppositional production by Roman Zawistowski in Krakow in 1956 was 'full of pain and hatred against Stalinist oppression and surveillance' (Stříbrný, 100).

Meanwhile, in East Germany, Heiner Müller's play, *Hamletmachine*, written in 1977 and first performed in Paris two years later, consisted of two monologues, one by Hamlet and one by Ophelia, each exploring the plight of the intellectual under communism: Hamlet was impotent, but Ophelia was a terrorist chanting 'Long live hate and contempt.' In a more recent version, Sulayman Al-Bassam's *The Al-Hamlet Summit*, first performed in English at the Edinburgh Festival in 2002 and revived in Arabic at the Riverside Studios in London in 2004, the play is used 'to probe into the troubled heart of the modern day Middle East' (programme note), and Ophelia becomes a suicide bomber.

Attempts to politicize the play in Britain have been more muted and more spasmodic. But in the 1960s Peter Hall's Royal Shakespeare Company aspired to engage with political issues: the programme note for his 1965 production explained that his *Hamlet* was 'about the disillusionment which produces an apathy of the will so deep that commitment to politics, to religion or to life is impossible'. Elsinore was an efficient but oppressive court, Denmark was both a prison and itself imprisoned in a state of Cold War with Norway, 24-year-old David Warner's Hamlet was an unheroic student, trapped and helpless, and Glenda Jackson's Ophelia committed suicide in a futile act of rebellion. Ten years later, Buzz Goodbody's RSC studio production revisited the prison image: the whole auditorium was a playing space, the audience became participants rather than spectators, and, at the end, Hamlet's command that the door be locked (5.2.296) was followed by the theatre doors being slammed shut.

In 1980 Richard Eyre directed Jonathan Pryce at the Royal Court, London, in a production that tried to incorporate the psychological, the political and the metaphysical. William Dudley's claustrophobic set was full of doors behind which stood armed guards: 'the assertion of power linked to a control of information' (Dawson, 160). Pryce's Hamlet was possessed, as if by the devil; he retched up the Ghost's lines as if from the depths of his stomach; and when he died he gave a sudden epileptic shudder as if experiencing the relief of exorcism.

Pryce's performance was so extreme in its instability, such a physical and emotional *tour de force*, such a sensation in the old manner of a Garrick, a Kean or an Irving, that some spectators felt that the performer ended up taking precedence over the character.

Something similar happened with Eyre's subsequent dealings with the play. Following his success at the Royal Court, Eyre was due to direct it in Bucharest, but his plans changed and the job went to the Romanian director Alexandru Tocilescu. Eyre went to see it in 1985:

> As the regime tightened its grip and the corrosive effect of tyranny leaked into every area of public and private life, the theatre gathered more and more power as the sole public medium of expression where thoughts could be spoken . . . The code was one that could be read by an audience but not challenged by the censors . . . Hamlet was seen unambiguously as a man fighting against Claudius/Ceauçescu, and if he vacillated, accused himself of cowardice, cursed himself for his inaction, it only reflected the audience's awareness of their own frailty. They sat enraptured in an unheated theatre for several hours on uncomfortable seats or crouched on the edge of the stage, swathed in scarves and overcoats. Line after line was greeted with the applause of recognition; this was their story.

When the Romanian revolution came in 1989, the actor playing Hamlet, Ion Caramitru, led the storming of the television station, from which he could broadcast the words 'We're free, we've won' – and then, unlike Fortinbras, 'Don't shoot . . .' (Eyre, 160; see also Stříbrný, 134). Inevitably, perhaps, the post-communist *Hamlet* has become more inward-looking and domestic rather than political: Stříbrný notes that, unlike his highly political productions of 1960 and 1981, Andrzej Wajda's 1989 Krakow production, starring a female Hamlet, Teresa

Budzisz-Krzyzanowska, 'concentrated on personal, psychological probing, leaving larger social issues mostly aside' (137; see also Walaszek).

In the last fifty years, the play's iconic status has led to countless attempts to adapt, rethink, debunk and vandalize it. Jack J. Jorgens's seminal *Shakespeare on Film* established a distinction between the 'theatrical' and the 'filmic' (Jorgens, 7–35), and most film *Hamlet*s are something of both: Olivier's, for example, is theatrical in its origins and in its permanent expressionist set, but filmic in the mobility of the camera and the use of deep focus, voiceover and mood music. More recent *Hamlet*s have been increasingly conceived as exercises in screen conventions and values. In 1962, the hero of Claude Chabrol's film *Ophelia* was seduced by Olivier's film into believing that his uncle was a murderer. In 2000, Ethan Hawke in Michael Almereyda's film carried a Fisher Price PixelVision camera, his soliloquies were video diaries, and he debated whether to be or not to be in the 'Action Films' section of his local Blockbuster video store; Elsinore had become the New York offices of the Denmark Corporation, leading Deborah Cartmell to discuss the film in terms of urban 'teenpic', a modern city comedy ('*Hamlet* 2000: Michael Almereyda's City Comedy'). In 1996, Zeffirelli conceived of Mel Gibson's Hamlet as if he were a television cop or the hero of a western, reduced the text by two-thirds, shuffled the remaining speeches into a different sequence, and prompted some critics to recall Q1 (see Campbell; Howlett; and Hodgdon).

Returning to the theatre, Charles Marowitz's *Hamlet Collage* (1965), *The Marowitz Hamlet* (1972) and *Ham-omlet* (1972) had already disassembled the play, while Peter Brook's *Qui est là?* (1996) presented fragments modified by voices of past directors. In his 1990 production Heiner Müller added in his own *Hamletmachine* to create a monster performance lasting seven and a half hours, but Tom Stoppard has managed to boil the play down to fifteen minutes and then to ninety seconds.

Attempts to refocus on characters other than Hamlet have included plays such as Stoppard's *Rosencrantz and Guildenstern Are Dead* (1967), Jeff Wanshel's *Ophelia* (1992) and Howard Barker's *Gertrude the Cry* (2002). In 1986 Kevin Carr looked to audiences to prompt a *Hamlet Improvised*. Film spin-offs include Akira Kurosawa's *The Bad Sleep Well* (1960), Kenneth Branagh's comedy about an amateur production, *In the Bleak Midwinter* (1995), and Luca Damiano's exercise in porn, *Hamlet: For the Love of Ophelia Parts 1 and 2* (1996). There have been ballets choreographed by Kim Brandstrup (1993), Veronica Paeper (1994) and Peter Schaufuss (1996), and in 2001 Eleanor Lloyd directed *Hamlet the Musical* at the ADC Theatre in Cambridge. The play has been performed by five actors (*Carnal, Bloody and Unnatural Acts*, directed by Julie-Ann Robinson, 1989), four actors (in Maison Bertaux, a Soho cakeshop, 1993), three actors (*Haprdans* by Ivan Vyskočil, 1986), two actors (*Hamlet in the Mirror* by Manuel Dionis-Bayer, 1998) and one actor (Arthur Smith in Edinburgh, Robert Wilson in Houston, Texas, and Robert Lepage in Montreal, all in 1995).

Under the influence of Derridean and Lacanian post-structuralist theory, the French director Daniel Mesguich's production of *Le Hamlet de Shakespeare* in 1977 in Grenoble featured two Hamlets, two Ophelias and two texts – Shakespeare's written text and a second text, a kind of commentary of material from other authors 'made up of all the alluvial deposits which have accumulated and continue to accumulate around the first text'.[1] In a second production in 1986 in Paris, the curtain went up to reveal . . . a second curtain, and there were even more Hamlets. Mesguich's recognition that 'A text is by definition open and plural' led him to acknowledge that ultimately the director has no control over it:

---

1   Quoted in Guy Dumur, 'Les Classiques dans tous leurs états', *Nouvel Observateur*, 22 August 1977, 61; cited in Carlson, 231.

'during rehearsal I explain a good deal. I speak knowing that between saying and doing there is a gulf. That gulf is the actor's freedom.'[1]

NOVEL HAMLETS

Hamlet meets Fielding, Goethe, Dickens and others

Characters in novels, just like people in real life, are wont to experience close encounters with *Hamlet*. Sometimes they go to the theatre and watch the play; sometimes they get involved in a production of it; sometimes they read it, discuss it or otherwise allude to it. Novelists, for their part, rewrite the story and adapt it for their own times and purposes; they write sequels and prequels; encouraged perhaps by Hamlet's speech at the beginning of 3.2, they treat it as a mirror to reflect every conceivable aspect of 'the very age and body of the time'. Often they give us, explicitly or implicitly, original and searching interpretations of the play. As usual, we cannot claim to give a comprehensive survey, but in this section we shall look at what seem to us some representative examples of the enormous impact of *Hamlet* on prose fiction.[2]

The most memorable theatre visit probably occurs in Henry Fielding's *Tom Jones* (1749, book 16, chapter 5), when Tom goes to see *Hamlet* with Mr Partridge, who is set up as the naïve playgoer who scorns the skill required for the naturalistic acting of the hero: 'Why I could act as well as he myself. I am sure if I had seen a Ghost, I should have looked in the very same Manner, and done just as he did.' Partridge prefers the more artificial style of the man playing the King who 'speaks all his words distinctly, half as loud again as the other. Anybody may see he is an actor.' The assumption that Fielding is describing an actual performance by David Garrick is supported by

1   Daniel Mesguich, 'Hamlet c'est moi', *20 Ans* (December 1986).
2   We are indebted in this section to previous studies by Scofield and Welsh.

Hapgood and Dawson, both of whom quote the fictional Partridge when discussing one of the most famous features of Garrick's performance, his dramatic 'start' at his first encounter with the Ghost: 'if that little man there upon the stage is not frightened, I never saw any man frightened in my life' (Hapgood, 15; Dawson, 38).

A century later, Charles Dickens in *Great Expectations* (1861) sends Pip to the theatre with his friend Herbert Pocket to see a ludicrous performance by the visiting actor 'Waldengarver', in fact the over-ambitious Wopsle (book 2, chapter 31). Dickens takes the occasion to satirize how nineteenth-century Hamlets were careful to maintain their sartorial dignity despite Ophelia's graphic description of the hero's disarray (2.1.74–81): Wopsle appeared 'with his stocking disordered (its disorder expressed, according to usage, by one very neat fold in the top, which I suppose to be always got up with a flat-iron)'. Again an allusion to a real-life performance has been detected, this time to that of the French actor Charles Albert Fechter, whose first performance opened in London (to generally favourable reviews) in March 1861, a fortnight before the relevant episode of the novel appeared in Dickens's weekly *All the Year Round* (see Welsh, 107).

As for novels in which the characters get involved in productions of *Hamlet*, the most famous example must be Johann Wolfgang von Goethe's *Wilhelm Meister's Apprenticeship*, which was written over a long period from 1776 to 1796 and whose first draft was called *Wilhelm Meister's Theatrical Calling*. After his father dies, the hero joins an acting company on condition that they produce the play with himself in the title role. Somewhat improbably, no one is cast to play the Ghost, but a letter informs Wilhelm that an actor will appear on the night, and this duly happens, the mystery figure having a voice which reminds him of that of his own father (Goethe, book 5, 11.195) A more recent example of a novel that revolves around a staging of *Hamlet* would be Alan Isler's *The Prince of West End Avenue*

(1994), in which the play is put on by a group of elderly Jewish people, residents of a retirement home on the Upper West Side of Manhattan.

Notable occasions when characters in fiction discuss *Hamlet* would have to include the long sequence set in the National Library in Dublin in James Joyce's *Ulysses* (1922), where Stephen Dedalus expounds his theory of the play, only to end by denying that he believes anything he has said. A comparable moment of *Hamlet*-related self-destruction occurs in Herman Melville's *Pierre* (1852, book 9), where the hero's reflections on *Hamlet* end in his tearing a copy of the play to pieces.

With the exception of *Tom Jones*, all the novels named so far do not merely mention *Hamlet* casually in passing but are, arguably, far more deeply influenced and informed by the play. *Wilhelm Meister* is the classic *Bildungsroman* in which the young hero's development is both implicitly and explicitly related to an interpretation of *Hamlet*. The novel contains what became a standard Romantic metaphor for Hamlet's character: 'An oak tree planted in a precious pot which should only have held delicate flowers. The roots spread out, the vessel is shattered' (Goethe, book 5, 11.146). These words, which occur in Wilhelm's instructions to the director of the production in which he is to star, are often cited as Goethe's own view of Hamlet. The actors also discuss the differences between drama and the novel, concluding that characters in a novel are less subject to the (usually malign) intervention of Fate, but allowing that *Hamlet* 'has something of the breadth of a novel' (11.186).

Apart from the visit to the theatre, *Hamlet* is less overt as an influence on *Great Expectations*, but the plot includes ghost-like characters in Magwitch and Miss Havisham, and it is driven by revenge actions and by Pip's guilt about his feelings for the man who so alarmingly reappears in the middle of the night and claims the role of a father. Alexander Welsh argues that in this novel 'The revenge play becomes a sort of *bildungsroman* with opportunity for therapy awaiting its interpretation' and that 'Dickens' novel anticipates psychoanalytic readings of *Hamlet* itself' (Welsh, 131). He points out further that, like *Wilhelm Meister, Great Expectations* has also been regarded as an autobiographical novel, though the element of the *Künstlerroman* (the novel showing the hero's development as an artist or poet) is less overt in the latter.[1]

Melville's *Pierre* and Joyce's *Ulysses* both centre on Hamlet-like heroes who are also trying to be writers in *Künstlerroman* style. The chapter on *Pierre* in F.O. Matthiessen's classic study of *The American Renaissance* (1941) is actually called 'An American *Hamlet*'; he sums up the parallels as follows:

> Lucy's pale innocence fails Pierre as Ophelia's did Hamlet; the well-named Reverend Falsgrave's cushioned view of worldly policy is not unlike the platitudinizing of Polonius; Charlie Milthorpe plays a kind of Horatio; Glen Stanly confronts Pierre's seemingly mad violence with the decisiveness of Laertes. But the crucial relation here as in *Hamlet* is that of son and mother.
>
> (Matthiesson, 477–8)

Melville, like Dickens, anticipates psychoanalytic readings of *Hamlet*. The dead father, represented significantly by two contrasting portraits, returns in the form of the illegitimate daughter with whom Pierre can pursue the quasi-incestuous relationship invited by his mother. Destroying his copy of the play in a symbolic gesture that asserts his ability to take action, Pierre nevertheless succumbs to failure, both as a man and as a writer.

---

1   See also John, 46–60, and Poole, 122–6. Welsh also discusses Walter Scott's *Redgauntlet* (1824) as an autobiographical *Hamlet* novel, influenced by *Wilhelm Meister*, but with an emphasis on the political dimension of *Hamlet* rather than on the hero's character. George Meredith's *The Tragic Comedians: A Study in a Well-Known Story* (1892) is a meditation on the indecisive, nineteenth-century Hamlet.

Joyce manages a more upbeat version of the *Hamlet* story in *Ulysses*, perhaps in part because he does not allow Stephen, his Hamlet figure, to be the sole focus of attention, and perhaps too because, as the very title demonstrates, *Hamlet* is only one of a number of mythical and literary influences operating in this novel. Whether or not the author seriously believed the reading of *Hamlet* through Shakespeare's own life that he puts into Stephen's mouth (unfortunately we do not know what Joyce said when he lectured on the play in Trieste in 1912–13), the parallels Stephen sees between himself and Hamlet are offset by Leopold Bloom's very different awareness of the play. Stephen's serious and troubled Hamlet-like alienation from his father and from patriarchal authorities is in part redeemed by his acceptance of the anti-heroic Bloom and the novel's representation of an adultery which does not lead to obsession and revenge.

Hamlet *and women novelists*

Edward Thomas wrote with some irony, 'I suppose most men think *Hamlet* was written for them, but I *know* he was written for me' (quoted in Scofield, 109). But what about most women? Studies such as those by Scofield and Welsh have almost nothing to say about women writers, and it is in fact difficult to nominate a major novel written by a woman that has the kind of strong and obvious relationship with *Hamlet* that can be claimed for *Wilhelm Meister, Great Expectations, Pierre* or *Ulysses*. Admittedly, it seems unlikely, on the face of it, that Jane Austen would have elected to rewrite *Hamlet*, but what about writers like George Eliot, Virginia Woolf, Angela Carter and Margaret Atwood? What has *Hamlet* been saying to them?

During the last decade of the twentieth century, feminist critics have certainly taken an interest in women writers' responses to Shakespeare and have investigated the ways in which women have appropriated and rewritten his plots, but it turns out that *Hamlet* has played a relatively small role in this drama. Marianne

Novy has been at the forefront of the relevant scholarship, both in her own book (*Engaging*) and in her edited collections (*Re-Visions* and *Differences*). Other significant contributions have been made by Kate Chedgzoy (*Shakespeare's Queer Children*) and Julie Sanders (*Novel Shakespeares*). Novy does find *Hamlet* in the novels of George Eliot, notably in *The Mill on the Floss* in Maggie Tulliver, who is explicitly compared with Hamlet, but 'in a way that demythologizes Hamlet by imagining him "with a reputation of sanity, notwithstanding many soliloquies, and some moody sarcasms towards the fair daughter of Polonius, to say nothing of the frankest incivility to his father-in-law"'. However, despite the Victorian feminizing of Hamlet (and the popularity of the role among female performers), elsewhere Eliot sees him in relation to her male characters, Felix Holt and Daniel Deronda. Both of these are extensions of Hamlet as student or philosopher, taking on the world's wrongs; Deronda even saves his Ophelia from drowning. Somewhat problematically, as Novy comments, Eliot makes Felix Holt criticize Esther in language borrowed from Hamlet's misogynistic attack on Ophelia (3.1.141–5), but given that Eliot may be copying the attitude of Mary Wollstonecraft, who cites the same passage in her *Vindication of the Rights of Women* as part of a critique of the trivialization of women in contemporary society, it is arguable that Hamlet's attack has been deflected from women on to the men who oppress them (Novy, *Engaging*, 62, 77–8).

Virginia Woolf, who famously wrote of the historical silencing of 'Shakespeare's sister' in *A Room of One's Own* (1927), nevertheless used the myth of the thwarted female to empower her own fiction and turned his Rosalind into *Orlando* (1928) in a dazzling fantasy of writing freed from the constraints of both time and gender. 'Shakespeare' becomes a kind of anonymous, invisible presence in her work that, far from inhibiting it, inspires creative emulation (see also Briggs). But she was nervous of any direct comparison, as Christine Froula demonstrates:

The Waves is the flower of Woolf's autobiographical involvement with Shakespeare in its most intense phase. Yet her book did not resemble Shakespeare, she told John Lehmann, who had written an essay suggesting that it did: 'if you print it, as I hope you will, leave out Shakespeare, because I don't think anyone in their senses can have mentioned him in that connection.'

(Froula, 140)

Julie Sanders suggests one reason for the comparative neglect of *Hamlet* by twentieth-century women writers when she remarks in the introduction to *Novel Shakespeares*:

Particular plays occur and recur in the appropriations studied here with greater frequency than others. The special pertinence to women writers of plays such as *King Lear* or *The Tempest*, with their obvious themes of fathers and daughters and patriarchal rule, is therefore explored.

(Sanders, 5)

Jane Smiley's rewriting of *King Lear* as *A Thousand Acres* (1992) and the rewritings of *The Tempest* by Margaret Laurence as *The Diviners* (1974) and by Marina Warner as *Indigo* (1992) would fall into this category, but, apart from *King Lear*, the tragedies have apparently not attracted women writers. It does seem to be the case that many of them are more drawn to the comedies, whose woman-centred courtship plots have obvious affinities with the modern novel: Sanders finds extensive use of the comedies in writers such as Angela Carter (especially *Wise Children*, 1992), Barbara Trapido (especially *Juggling*, 1994) and Kate Atkinson (especially *Human Croquet*, 1997), and she concludes that *The Tempest* is a more important influence on Gloria Naylor's novel *Mama Day* (1988) than *Hamlet*, despite the fact that a central character is called Ophelia (see also Traub).

Kate Chedgzoy argues that an Ophelia figure *is* central in *Wise Children*, and that the novel is in its way

> *Hamlet* without the prince, in that Carter takes the structures of desire and loss which characterise that play's representations of familial dynamics from the point of view of the son, and makes the daughter's experience central to them. So Hamlet himself figures only as Melchior's and Peregrine's dead mother, inheritor of the alternative female tradition of theatrical succession embodied by Sarah Siddons, Charlotte Cushman *et al.*[1]

Hamlet's most famous soliloquy is converted here into a song-and-dance routine performed by the young twins, Nora and Dora Chance, dressed as bellhops in a hotel, debating whether a parcel should be delivered to '2b or not 2b' (Chedgzoy, *Queer*, 90). Estella Hazard's dazzling career as a female Hamlet on the American stage is cut short by the birth of Melchior ('a female Hamlet is one thing but a pregnant prince is quite another', 16), and the traumatic issues around questions of paternity are reduced to comedy, as in Gorgeous George's story in which a father advises a son not to marry a girl on the grounds that she may be his half-sister, whereupon the mother defiantly intervenes, 'You just go ahead and marry who you like, son, . . .' *E*'s not your father' (65).

As it happens, the figure of the woman enacting the role of Hamlet recurs in two other *Hamlet*-based novels by women, Iris Murdoch's *The Black Prince* (1973) and Carole Corbeil's *In the Wings* (1997). In the former, the central character Bradley Pearson is fascinated by *Hamlet* and by a young woman called Julian; in the course of an informal and increasingly intimate 'tutorial' Bradley gives her on *Hamlet*, he expounds a theory of the play as a text in which 'Shakespeare is passionately exposing

---

1   Chedgzoy, *Queer*, 81. See also Chedgzoy, 'Prince'; and Howard.

himself to the ground and author of his being . . . [he] makes the crisis of his own identity into the very central stuff of his art.'[1] In a perhaps deliberately banal contrast to the response to Stephen's lecture on *Hamlet* in *Ulysses*, Julian reveals at this point that she had acted the part at school when she was sixteen, and this apparently causes Bradley to fall in love with her. Later, her appearance dressed as Hamlet provokes a violent sexual assault. Corbeil's *In the Wings* revolves around a production of *Hamlet* and the various relationships between the people involved: members of the cast and a theatre reviewer. Catastrophe strikes when the actor who is playing Hamlet refuses to go on during a preview and runs away, apparently to commit suicide. The production is postponed and his lover, who had been playing Gertrude and is pregnant with his child, eventually takes over the central role.

Shakespeare is a more diffuse presence in the novels of Margaret Atwood. Cordelia in *Cat's Eye* (1990), who has sisters called Perdita and Miranda, fails in her attempt to become a Shakespearean actress at Stratford, Ontario. Atwood does, however, engage directly with *Hamlet* in 'Gertrude Talks Back', a brisk four-page rewriting of the closet scene from the Queen's point of view in which she claims Claudius, unlike his brother, 'enjoys a laugh', expresses doubts about Óphelia ('there's something off about that girl'), and puts Hamlet right on the question of his father's murder: 'It wasn't Claudius, darling, it was me'.[2]

This takes us into the territory of overt sequels and prequels. While many of the most famous and respected of novelists, both male and female, have engaged with *Hamlet* in one way or another in their work, others have of course contributed more straightforward rewritings of this kind, imagining events both

---

1 Iris Murdoch, *The Black Prince* (Harmondsworth, England, 1975), 199–200. For the sexual assault, see 328–9; and see also Todd.

2 Margaret Atwood, 'Gertrude talks back', in *Good Bones* (1992), 16–18.

before and after the play and filling in gaps in the offstage lives of the characters.

Prequels and sequels

The silence of the longer texts on the question of the Queen's involvement in the murder of old Hamlet has provoked a number of investigations and justifications such as the quasi-judicial *'Hamlet': An Essay on the Murder of the King* (published anonymously in 1856), which has the explanatory subtitle: 'An Attempt to Ascertain whether the Queen were an Accessory, before the Fact, in the Murder of her First Husband'. The author defends her from the charge of murder (triumphantly quoting her denial in Q1, which had been rediscovered in 1823), but concedes that of adultery. Similar but more emotional defences are to be found in 'The Frailty Whose Name Was Gertrude' (one of a collection of stories published anonymously by 'An Actress' under the title *The True Ophelia and Other Studies of Shakespeare's Women* in 1913) and in *Gertrude of Denmark: An Interpretative Romance* by Lillie Buffum Chace Wyman (1924). Both these female authors champion the Queen; the 'Actress' deplores the standard stage practices of cutting some of her lines and having her die offstage, while Wyman goes so far as to attack Hamlet as 'a gigantic egoist'.[1]

In a radio talk called 'The Mysterious Affair at Elsinore' broadcast in 1949,[2] the academic J.I.M. Stewart (who had published many detective novels under the pseudonym Michael Innes, including one called *Hamlet, Revenge!* in 1937 centring on a country-house production of the play) treated the plot of *Hamlet* as a contemporary unsolved murder mystery: Fortinbras

---

1 Fictional explorations of characters from *Hamlet* are far more numerous and widespread than we can cover in this context. We are particularly grateful to Reiko Oya for providing us with translations of two short Japanese pieces, Naoya Shiga's *Claudius's Diary* (1912) and Hideo Kobayashi's *Ophelia's Testament* (1931).

2 Published in Heppenstall and Innes, 75–89.

is criticized for destroying evidence by moving the bodies; Ophelia was secretly married to Hamlet (and was pregnant when she died); and Rosencrantz and Guildenstern were bastard sons of Claudius and had to be killed in order to allow Fortinbras, the real villain, to succeed, aided by his co-conspirator Horatio, whose long-awaited six-volume *Life and Letters of Hamlet the Dane* had proved a disappointment on publication, merely obfuscating the truth. Horatio fares better in Alethea Hayter's 1972 novel, *Horatio's Version*, which is another quasi-judicial treatment, alternating between a court of inquiry headed by Judge Voltimand (*sic*) and Horatio's own thoughtful but puzzled diary of his experiences.

Fictional prequels range from Mary Cowden Clarke's 'Ophelia, the Rose of Elsinore' in *The Girlhood of Shakespeare's Heroines* (1852) to John Updike's *Gertrude and Claudius* (2000). While Cowden Clarke goes some way towards explaining the precarious state of Ophelia's mental health at the beginning of Shakespeare's play, Updike exonerates the Queen, who is presented as a lonely figure, unhappy in her arranged marriage to a stern and gloomy king, and ready for the light relief provided by his attractive and more sociable brother.[1]

THE CONTINUING MYSTERY OF *HAMLET*

The publishers of John Updike's *Gertrude and Claudius*, Alfred A. Knopf, claimed (on the dustjacket of the first American edition of 2000) that 'gaps and inconsistencies in the immortal play are . . . filled and explained by this prequel.' The many

---

1 Of course, *Hamlet* has attracted rewritings, prequels and sequels in other fictional forms. Apart from those mentioned in the previous section, notable dramatic versions include one very long prequel, Percy MacKaye's 1949 *The Mystery of Hamlet, King of Denmark, or What We Will: A Tetralogy in Prologue to Shakespeare's 'Hamlet'*; one very long sequel, Denton Jacques Snider's 1923 two-part *The Redemption of the Hamlets*; and one very short sequel, St John Hankin's 1901 *The New Wing at Elsinore* (see Thompson, *'New Wing'*).

rewritings of *Hamlet*, and the provision of sequels and prequels, do seem to demonstrate an ongoing need to explain the play, to tidy it up, to tie its loose ends and resolve its ambiguities and mysteries. And as editors and critics we are engaged in the same endeavour: we yearn after the (unachievable) 'definitive' text of the play, and we aspire, like the imaginary friend of Horace Howard Furness whom we quoted at the beginning of this Introduction, to divulge our conclusive and authoritative 'theory of *Hamlet*' before we die.

This process may have begun as early as 1603: commenting on the following exchange between Hamlet and his mother in the closet scene in Q2 and F

> HAMLET A bloody deed – almost as bad, good mother,
>   As kill a king and marry with his brother.
> QUEEN   As kill a king?
> HAMLET   Ay, lady, it was my word.
>
> (3.4.26–8)

Philip Edwards remarks,

> It is extraordinary that neither of them takes up this all-important matter again. Gertrude does not press for an explanation; Hamlet does not question further the queen's involvement. It is clear that this silence was felt to be a fault in the theatre. In Q1, Hamlet reiterates the fact that his father was murdered ('damnably murdred'), and the queen says 'I never knew of this most horride murder.'
>
> (Cam[2], 175)

The assumption here is that a text like Q2 or F preceded Q1 and that whoever was responsible for the 1603 text was consciously clarifying an ambiguity in the longer version. One might argue further that the absence of Horatio from Q1's Scene 13 (the equivalent of Q2's 4.5) could be a conscious attempt to avoid the question that arises in the longer texts where he witnesses Ophelia's madness but has apparently not mentioned it to Hamlet when they appear in 5.1. In their discussion of the earliest staging of *Hamlet*, Gurr and Ichikawa argue that Osric is one of the Lords who make up Ophelia's funeral procession in 5.1, even though he is not mentioned in the stage direction in any of the three texts:

> He must be on stage here, because he notes Hamlet's misleading claim to be king, a claim he makes much of in the next scene. His identity might be clarified by his wearing for this procession the elaborate hat that he was to flourish in that scene.
>
> (Gurr & Ichikawa, 152)

Again, the point seems to be driven by a desire to clarify what is felt to be a 'fault' or omission in the text.

Productions and films of the play frequently offer explanations of this kind: they transfer some of Horatio's lines in the opening scene to Barnardo to avoid the discrepancy between Horatio-as-knowledgeable-local in 1.1 and Horatio-as-visitor-from-Wittenberg in 1.2 (see 1.1.79–94n. and List of Roles, 10n.); they present the relationship between Hamlet and his mother as an overtly or covertly erotic one, they motivate Ophelia's madness by having her stumble upon the body of her father; they provide explanations of how she gets away despite the King's command to 'Give her good watch' (see 4.5.74n.). As we have seen, they move the soliloquies around (without necessarily invoking the authority of Q1) to provide a more logical 'journey' for the hero. They cannot avoid answering some of the questions that arise for the reader: simply by casting a particular actor, for example, they have to make a decision about Hamlet's age (see List of Roles, 1n.), and they have to decide whether Polonius' attitude to his daughter in 3.1 is kind or cruel (see 3.1.177–9n.).

Editors sometimes cannot refrain from providing answers themselves: we may feel it would be intrusive to add Osric to the stage direction at 5.1.205, but the proliferation of square brackets in our stage directions indicates the frequency with which we, like all editors, have felt the need to fill some of the gaps in the original texts. One of our predecessors, John Dover Wilson, interfered rather more: he describes in his Introduction how Hamlet's attitude to Ophelia is 'very perplexing to the ordinary reader and playgoer' and offers his solution:

> Something is lost, some clue to the relationship between them, some accidental misunderstanding which would explain Hamlet's conduct and render her fate even more pathetic. And what is lost is a very simple thing – a single stage-direction giving Hamlet an entry (on the inner Elizabethan stage) nine lines before his entry on the other stage at [2.2.164], an entry which enables him accidentally and unseen to overhear the eavesdropping plot hatched between Polonius and Claudius, and so implicates Ophelia beyond possibility of doubt as one of his uncle's minions.
>
> (Cam¹, lvi–lvii)

Yet it is surely arguable that part of the fascination of this play is precisely its refusal to give us all the answers and its resistance to yield to any 'theory'. It is remarkable how much information is withheld from the characters themselves, let alone the audience or reader. The longer texts do not give us any insight into whether the Queen was already erotically involved with her husband's brother before the former's death, or whether she was aware of the murder. Hamlet does not even focus on these questions. His attitude to Ophelia remains a mystery: his protestation over her grave that he loved her more than 'forty thousand brothers' seems extravagant (the Queen apparently takes it as evidence of his madness and it is toned down (deliberately perhaps) to 'twenty brothers' in Q1), and it is out of line with his treatment of her in 3.1 and 3.2. He does not mention her at all in 5.2, though she is presumably included in his somewhat conditional apology to Laertes at 5.2.204–21, where he attributes 'What I have done / That might your nature, honour and exception / Roughly awake' to his madness. The analogy he offers (in Q1 and Q2), 'I have shot my arrow o'er the house / And hurt my brother' (220–1), seems, to say the least, tactless in the context.

More surprisingly, he barely mentions his father after his soliloquy in 4.4 (in Q2, that is; his last substantial reference to him in F is in the closet scene), apart from telling Horatio how lucky it was that he had his father's signet with him so that he could seal the substituted document, and describing the present King as 'He that hath killed my King and whored my Mother', where the emphasis is on the role rather than the relationship. He seems by this stage to be thinking about his own potential death (see especially his musing on 'the readiness is all' at 5.2.190–202), reverting to the topic of his first two soliloquies, rather than about revenge; F does, however, give him a line about 'quitting' the King and the additional motivation of preventing him from committing further crimes (see Appendix 1). In none of the three texts does he ever confront the King with the murder of his father, even when he kills him; his cry of 'Treachery!' and his line 'thou incestuous, damned Dane!' would presumably be taken by the courtiers to refer to his uncle's marriage (this is the first time anyone has made the incest accusation publicly) and to his plots against Hamlet himself, just revealed by the dying Laertes (see 5.2.297–309 and nn.). F's version, 'thou incestuous, murderous, damned Dane', is no more explicit to those who do not know about the earlier crime.

Horatio, enigmatic throughout, becomes even more baffling in the last scene. It is difficult to judge the tone of his response to Hamlet's account of the events on the voyage: 'So Guildenstern and Rosencrantz go to't' (5.2.56); Hamlet's additional line in F, 'Why man, they did make love to this employment', may indicate that he receives it as a question or even a criticism, and in an additional passage, again found only in F, Horatio seems to refuse to give Hamlet the endorsement he seeks (see Appendix 1). His promise to tell 'th' yet unknowing world / How these things came about' is couched in very general terms (see 5.2.363–9 and nn.) and does not give any specific details about such matters as the murder of old Hamlet or the King's plots against young Hamlet. Scott Handy, who played Horatio in Peter Brook's 2000 production (which highlighted him by giving him both the opening and closing lines of the play), told us of his frustration in his attempts to understand the character until he injured himself and had to perform on crutches, which gave him an insight into Horatio as a kind of impotent bystander who wants to help Hamlet but is unable to do so. One could see this as a desperate and of course unintended example of a production offering an explanation of one of the play's many mysteries.

Theories that Shakespeare revised his play have recently played their part in the ongoing attempts to solve its problems (see pp. 83–6 and Appendix 2): to put it crudely, some of the problems are not of Shakespeare's making but can be attributed to the accidental but enormously influential emergence of the conflated text, which includes contradictory material that he may have intended to cut. Philip Edwards and George Hibbard both write eloquently in favour of the Folio as an authorial revision which resolves some of the difficulties present in Q2, but neither would go so far as to say that such a theory would answer all our questions: the roles of the Queen and Horatio are just as baffling in F as they are in Q2; Hamlet's relationship with Ophelia remains 'very perplexing', as does his behaviour in the last two scenes.

It is probably time to confess that we do not, after working on the play for about ten years, have a new or sensational 'theory of *Hamlet*' to offer our readers. We did not set out with one and we have not acquired one along the way. We suspect that any new or sensational theory would very probably be simply wrong, and in any case this is an edition, not a manifesto. We hope, however, that we have given our readers a clear sense of why it is still possible for people to disagree about almost every aspect of this play, why those disagreements continue to be interesting, and why they are likely to continue for the foreseeable future.

ADDITIONS AND RECONSIDERATIONS

2016 marks ten years since the first publication of our two-volume Arden 3 *Hamlet*, and of course four hundred years since the death of Shakespeare. Back in 2006 we began our Introduction by acknowledging the extraordinary size of 'the *Hamlet* phenomenon' and the challenge it represents to everyone who confronts it, whether actors, editors or critics. In just ten years that phenomenon has continued to grow and to diversify at an impressive rate. We very much welcome the opportunity to update this Introduction, to make some corrections and to supply some omissions, but mainly to concentrate on new contributions to the ongoing debate. Given limitations of space we cannot claim to be comprehensive, but hope to give an overview of the field, concentrating on four areas: biography, textual studies, criticism and afterlife.[1]

BIOGRAPHY

A phenomenon that has struck us over the last decade is the surprising increase in the publication of biographies of Shakespeare. James Shapiro's book, *1599: A Year in the Life of William Shakespeare*, appeared in 2005 just as our edition went to press, and we mentioned it only in a footnote (see p. 50 above), but since then there have been further offerings from, amongst others, Peter Ackroyd (2012), Jonathan Bate (*Soul*, 2008) Katherine Duncan-Jones (*Upstart*, 2011), Lois Potter (*Life*, 2012) and René Weis (2007), while Germaine Greer has

---

1 As in 2006, we have benefited while preparing these additions from consultations with numerous friends and colleagues. We would particularly like to mention the Arden General Editors, especially Richard Proudfoot; also Nick Clary, Tony Dawson, Gabriel Egan, Shehzana Mamujee and Eric Rasmussen.

contributed a biography of Shakespeare's wife (2007). In their various ways, some of these books have contributed to our understanding of the phenomenon that is *Hamlet*, by exploring (or speculating about) its topicality either in the personal life of its author or in relation to the social, political and cultural circumstances of its production.

Biographers have continued to speculate about the possible relevance to Shakespeare's writing of *Hamlet* of the death of his son Hamnet or Hamlet in 1596 and the death of his father John in 1601 (see 36–8 above), but they disagree on the specific nature of that relevance. Lois Potter and René Weis, for example, both point to the powerful depiction of a parent's grief for a child in Constance's (premature or predictive) mourning for Arthur in *King John* which is generally held to pre-date Hamnet's death, but Potter argues that these lines may have been added to the play at a later date (*Life*, 224), while Weis suggests that 'perhaps the Shakespeares were told in the spring of 1596 that their little boy was incurably sick' (183). We do not know the cause of the child's death: Potter comments that the bad harvests of 1594–6 'left children in particular susceptible to the illnesses spread by insects in warm, wet weather' (204–5), but Germaine Greer points out that there were only four other burials recorded in the Stratford parish register in August 1596, three of them newborns and the other an old man, so an infectious disease seems unlikely; her suggestion is that Hamnet may have been weak, even suffering from cerebral palsy, from birth (134, 194–5). Weis however speculates that, in a closer link to *Hamlet*, Shakespeare's son may perhaps have drowned (268). Potter thinks that the news of the child's illness may have reached Shakespeare 'too late for him to see the boy alive or even to attend the funeral' (205) and Greer agrees, pointing out that it would have taken at least four days for the news to reach him and another four for him to return home (197), whereas Weis says that on 11 August 1596 'Shakespeare almost certainly stood at his son's graveside' (200) and that he 'probably stayed on in Stratford for a while after the death of his son to comfort his family' (205). Potter and Weis agree that Shakespeare's writing must have been influenced by this death but Potter concentrates on the father–son relationships in *1 Henry IV* (205–7) while Weis suggests that *Romeo and Juliet* might have been inspired by reflections on the premature death of young people (200–205). Both make the point that the apparently miraculous revival from death of the male twin in *Twelfth Night* (probably but not certainly written soon after *Hamlet*) held a special poignancy for the playwright as well as for his character (Potter, 288; Weis, 391–2).

As for Shakespeare's father, Weis sees 'the glorious muddle over religion in *Hamlet*, whether that of the Catholic purgatory or the Wittenberg theses [of Martin Luther], echoes the divided allegiances of the nation – and perhaps of the Shakespeare family' (49) and goes on to suggest, dating the play 'after the summer of 1601', that perhaps 'Shakespeare used *Hamlet* as a way of coming to terms with his own spiritual betrayal of his father' by attempting to suppress his Catholicism (272). Biographers have continued to want to connect the ghost scenes in *Hamlet* with John Shakespeare or to speculate, as James Joyce did in *Ulysses*, that Shakespeare saw himself in the ghost and his son in the young prince, but the likely date of the play (before the death of the father) and the age of the son (the young prince is 30 in both Q2 and F, while Hamnet died at 11) militate against this. James J. Marino, on the other hand, argues that if we want a biographical reference for *Hamlet* we should be thinking rather about James Burbage and his son Richard who possibly played Hamlet at his father's Theatre and certainly played the role at the Globe when it had passed out of his father's hands. Thus Richard could be seen as 'literally displaced from his proper legacy'. However, 'The play proposes its hero's interiority as a defence against its star's celebrity' thereby 'freeing Richard Burbage's Hamlet from the expectation of unmediated autobiography' ('Ghost', 2014, 76–7).

Katherine Duncan-Jones adds to our knowledge of early references to *Hamlet* in her discussion of Edward Pudsey (1573–1612/13), one of 'three early readers' of Shakespeare. Pudsey noted fifty passages from the play in his commonplace book, sometimes seeming to agree with Q1 and sometimes with Q2 (*Upstart*, 72–83).[1] He may also have taken notes in the theatre: Duncan-Jones remarks that his substitution of 'witty worded' for Hamlet's puzzling 'picked' at 5.1.132 may in fact be the correct (heard) reading (82–3).

Perhaps not surprisingly, given his overall project to focus on 1599, Shapiro makes much of the play's political or social topicality. He sees *Hamlet* as being 'born at the crossroads of the death of chivalry and the birth of globalization' (309) and finds in it, as in *Troilus and Cressida*, a kind of nostalgia for heroic action which has now been consigned to the past: the rigged fencing match that ends the play can hardly be compared with the mortal combat between Old Hamlet and Old Fortinbras, described at some length by Horatio (1.1.79–94). In his view, *Hamlet* is indeed a *fin de siècle* play reflecting the epochal change when the old religion had been replaced by the new and the end of the Tudor dynasty was imminent: Shakespeare conveys 'what it means to live in the bewildering space between familiar past and murky future' (313). Potter finds more specific topical references, noting that the atmosphere of *Hamlet*'s first scene suggests the conspiratorial secrecy of the final years of Elizabeth's reign and that 'Two well-known public figures had mothers who were thought to have married the murderers of their fathers' (the Earl of Essex and James VI of Scotland) (278–9).

Shapiro is particularly interested in the literary context of the play and emphasizes the importance of Montaigne's *Essays*, while acknowledging, as we point out above (74), that Florio's translation was not published until 1603. Shapiro stresses the

---

1   E. A. J. Honigmann discussed this commonplace book in his Arden edition of *Othello* (1997), 388–9.

importance of the work of William Cornwallis who explicitly acknowledged his debt to Montaigne in his own *Essays*, the first set of which, published in 1600, was written before *Hamlet*. Without claiming that Cornwallis is, strictly speaking, a new 'source', but quoting him generously (329–32), he argues that the essays share with *Hamlet* an attempt to articulate a different kind of sensibility and that the new genre of the personal essay had much in common with the kind of soliloquies Shakespeare was beginning to write, first for Brutus and then for Hamlet. Bate also feels that '[Shakespeare's] mind and Montaigne's worked in such similar ways that Hamlet seems like a reader of Montaigne even though he could not have been one' (*Soul*, 410). Potter points out that John Marston knew Montaigne's essays and may have been the person who introduced Shakespeare to them. She comments that Marston's plays 'have an obvious, though puzzling, relationship to some of the ones that Shakespeare was writing in the period between 1599 and 1604, as if the two playwrights were deliberately choosing the same subjects or the same genres' (243). Duncan-Jones agrees that they were working 'simultaneously and in friendly emulation' (243).

Finally, Bate suggests that Thomas Pope, Shakespeare's fellow actor and one of the original sharers in the Chamberlain's Men in 1594, may have been his source for the names of Rosencrantz and Guildenstern as he had been (along with Will Kempe and George Bryan) among a group of English 'instrumentalists and tumblers' in the entourage of the Danish ambassador, Henrik Ramel, in 1586. They accompanied him back to Elsinore and worked there for several months, so Pope could have supplied Shakespeare with the names and with other local colour such as a description of the gun platforms at the castle (*Soul*, 372).

THE TEXT

The year before publication of our *Hamlet*, in the book we have already mentioned, James Shapiro wrote:

> Since the 18th century the play has existed in multiple, hybrid versions ... The long-awaited publication of the new Arden edition of *Hamlet* promises to change this situation. ... Soon – in a generation or two, I suspect – only scholars interested in the history of the play's reception will be reading a conflated *Hamlet*.
>
> (Shapiro, 357)

By 30 December 2006, Ron Rosenbaum, the author of *Explaining Hitler*, was looking back over the cultural events of the year for the *Washington Post* and concluding that 'the development that will have the most lasting significance – because it will force us to reconsider, re-argue, re-envision the supreme icon of English literature – is the publication of the three-text Arden edition of *Hamlet*'. More recently Janet Clare has written that 'It is now editorial orthodoxy that the three variant texts of *Hamlet* each have distinctive features, and it is difficult to imagine in the current bibliographical climate the production of a scholarly conflated edition' (Clare, 166). Time will tell, of course, and even if these predictions prove to be accurate, it will not necessarily have anything to do with the effect of our edition, but it is certainly the case that in the last ten years there has been a deal of reconsideration of the distinctive features of these three texts, and of the relationships of each to the others.

The one major scholarly edition of *Hamlet* to have been published since 2006 is the one which Jonathan Bate and Eric Rasmussen printed in their 2007 RSC *Complete Works*. Our edition prints three texts, but almost all previous editors of *Hamlet* have printed just one, basing it on either Q2 or F. (For example, Harold Jenkins in his 1982 Arden edition chose Q2, whereas G.R. Hibbard in his 1987 Oxford edition chose F.) On the face of it there was therefore nothing unusual about the fact that Bate and Rasmussen's *Hamlet* was based on F. However, as Bate explained in a 2007 online essay entitled 'The Case for the Folio', their reason for doing this was highly unusual. It was not because they believed F to be superior to or more authentic than Q2. They were not aspiring to get back to 'what Shakespeare originally wrote', neither were they aspiring (as Stanley Wells and Gary Taylor had been in the 1986 Oxford *Complete Works*) to get back to the 'putative first performance'. Instead, they had decided to base every play in their edition on the text established by the editors of the First Folio in 1623, 'as it went into the printing house' (Bate, 'Case'). Why did they choose the First Folio as the source for every play? Because its editors, the actors John Heminges and Henry Condell, 'were trying to present the most theatrically-inflected versions of Shakespeare that they could find' (ibid.), Bate and Rasmussen's edition was commissioned by an acting company, the Royal Shakespeare Company, and F provides a copy-text 'authorized by Shakespeare's own acting company' (Bate & Rasmussen, 55). In Heminges and Condell's case, this meant working largely from or with reference to the playbooks held by Shakespeare's acting company, the King's Men; in Bate and Rasmussen's case, it meant working from Heminges and Condell's edition of Shakespeare's plays. Thus, when it came to *Hamlet*, they were producing not so much an edition of the play as an edition of an edition.

In the year following publication of our edition, Brian Vickers wrote a review in which he expressed astonishment and exasperation that, by treating all three early texts, Q1, Q2 and F, as worthy of serious critical attention, we were prepared to upgrade Q1 and downgrade what he regarded as the authentic texts; Duthie, he protested, had demonstrated beyond reasonable doubt, and as long ago as 1941, that Q1 is a distorted memorial reconstruction of the play text lying behind Q2 and F (Vickers).

Q1 and its relationship to Q2 and F have come in for considerable scrutiny since our edition came out. Some scholars have not quarrelled with Vickers's belief that Duthie was right. Lene Petersen, for example, in her book on *Shakespeare's Errant Texts: Textual Form and Linguistic Style in*

149

Shakespearean 'Bad' Quartos and Co-authored Plays, adopts what became in the twentieth-century the conventional view of the temporal relationship between the texts – namely that the text behind Q1 comes later than those behind Q2 and F. Indeed, she attempts to demonstrate that as we move from Q2/F to Q1 and then on to *Der bestrafte Brudermord*, a process of streamlining of the narrative material takes place, a process akin to the concept of *Zielform* known to students of folk tale (originated by the Swiss folklorist, Max Lüthi) whereby 'a text submitted to oral-memorial transmission will eventually and inevitably move towards a stylistically predictable reduced form' (Petersen, xii).

But Charles Adams Kelly, in a series of publications issuing from the Triple Anvil Press since 2007 (assisted since 2009 by Dayna Leigh Plehn), has consistently argued that the text of Q1 could not have been derived by memorial reconstruction from either the Q2 or the F text. He is particularly struck by the absence from Q1 of ten Q2 passages which are not in F, and three F passages which are not in Q2. Together these passages total 259 lines, and Kelly calculates the statistical probability of the author of Q1 not remembering any of these lines if they had existed: he concludes that it is a statistical certainty that these lines could not have been in existence when Q1 was created. This and other evidence has persuaded him that Q1's text predates both Q2 and F, and he has also come to believe that the *Der bestrafte Brudermord* text derives from an even earlier version.

Kelly has not been alone in challenging the memorial reconstruction theory. Paul Menzer's study of *The 'Hamlets': Cues, Qs, and Remembered Texts* points out that Q2 and F have most of their cues in common, whereas Q1's are largely very different. Since actors were only supplied with their own parts along with the briefest of cues, this encourages Menzer to conclude that Q1 is not a memorial reconstruction of Shakespeare's play by one or more minor actors in the company.

While it involves the memory of earlier versions of the Hamlet tale (e.g. the so-called *Ur-Hamlet*) as well as Shakespeare's version, Q1 is nevertheless 'a separate Hamlet project – an independent act of creation by a person or persons unknown.' Menzer reckons that the manuscript behind Q1 'was solely intended for publication, making Q1, oddly enough, the most "literary" of the early *Hamlets*' (Menzer, 20–21). Zachary Lesser and Peter Stallybrass, in an essay written in the same year as Menzer's book (2008), also argued (but for different reasons) that Q1 could be regarded as 'literary'. They point out that, for all that it is usually regarded as recording an early moment in the performance history of Shakespeare's play, the inverted commas at the beginning of Corambis's sententious lines to Leartes at Q1 3.28–37 and 40 make Q1 the first of Shakespeare's plays to mark commonplaces, and such marking was 'a feature central to early seventeenth century attempts to forge a culture of literary drama or poesy in the vernacular' (Lesser & Stallybrass, 376). However, these marks were unlikely to have originated with Shakespeare but probably reflected an attempt by Nicholas Ling, the publisher, to satisfy his readers' taste for literary texts.

Another challenge to the theory that Q1 is a memorial reconstruction by actors who had performed in the play has come from Tiffany Stern, writing in 2013 on 'Sermons, plays and note-takers: *Hamlet* Q1 as a "noted" text'. She revives an earlier theory and argues that it may well be a record of an attempt by one or more members of the audience to reconstruct Shakespeare's play (possibly over more than one performance) by taking it down in a mixture of shorthand and longhand (Stern, 'Sermons').

In *Owning William Shakespeare: the King's Men and their Intellectual Property*, James J. Marino argues for a *Hamlet* that was evolving continuously from before Nashe's reference to it in 1589 to at least its publication in 1623. Shakespeare's acting company asserted ownership of *Hamlet* through intense rewriting combined with progressively insistent attribution to Shakespeare. The surviving texts show 'marks of incremental revision, and of revisions centered on the partial working texts used in the playhouse rather than on the master text' (Marino, *Owning*, 79), and the process of ongoing revision in the theatre did not necessarily begin with Shakespeare's original manuscript or end when he died. An ascription by the company of any play to 'Shakespeare' did not imply that it was following a fixed, authorial text; rather, it indicates an attempt to maintain exclusive control over a set of open-ended, theatrically revised scripts. Marino's discussion of Q1 is particularly interesting.

> More interesting perhaps than the "goodness" of Marcellus's part in the First Quarto is the "badness" of Hamlet's part, the one role in the 1603 text that is marred not only by pedestrian verse but by garbled syntax ... [So] somewhere behind the First Quarto may lie a text cobbled together from actors' parts of varying quality.
>
> (Marino, *Owning*, 93–4)

In the end Marino considers Q1 to be 'an unexplained and perhaps inexplicable text, full of useful information about stage practice but offering no easy key to its identity' (94).

However, in 2014, Margrethe Jolly's *The First Two Quartos of 'Hamlet': a New View of the Origins and Relationships of the Texts* and Terri Bourus's *Young Shakespeare's Young Hamlet: Print, Piracy and Performance* each argued that they could explain Q1: Shakespeare wrote it. Furthermore, they believe there is no need to imagine that there was any other *Ur-Hamlet*, since Shakespeare could well have written it as early as 1589, the year that Thomas Nashe referred to 'whole Hamlets, I should say handfuls, of tragical speeches'. Jolly has little to say about F, but argues that Q2 represents Shakespeare at some point between 1598 and 1604 revising the text behind Q1. Bourus goes further: her thesis is that Shakespeare revised his play twice, the text behind Q2 being a revision of the text behind F, while the text behind F, composed in about 1602 but not published until 1623, was a revision of the text underlying Q1. It is worth noting that Gary Taylor, who edited *Hamlet* for the Oxford *Collected Works*, dismissed the idea that Q1 was anything other than a memorial reconstruction (Wells & Taylor, *Companion*, 398). But he has written the General Editor's Preface to Bourus's book, and in it he confesses that she has persuaded him that he was 'wrong about the early texts of *Hamlet*, wrong about the 1589 reference to *Hamlet*, wrong about the date(s) of *Hamlet*, wrong about Shakespeare's changing relationship to the play' (Bourus, xii–xiii). This is tantalizing, since Taylor fails to define his new position on these issues. But no doubt it will become clear in the forthcoming new edition of the Oxford *Complete Works*.

More recently, Zachary Lesser in *'Hamlet' After Q1: An Uncanny History of the Shakespearean Text* discusses in considerable and fascinating detail the widespread influence of Q1's rediscovery in 1823. As Lesser demonstrates, that influence has shown up, not just in scholarly theories of the status of the other two texts, but (and most surprisingly) in mainstream interpretations of *Hamlet* by both literary critics and theatre directors. Lesser concludes with a detailed discussion of our edition, which, he says, 'crystallizes the dominant postmodern approach to the Shakespearean text' (Lesser, 207).

There has been less published about Q2 since 2006, but two features of our edition have been challenged. The first concerns the copy text. Whereas our conclusion was that the primary copy for Q2 was probably Shakespeare's foul papers (Appendix 2, p. 540), Paul Werstine finds evidence in the duplication of stage directions at 5.2.262, 263, 265, that 'Q2 *Hamlet* has picked up a bookkeeper's annotation and has therefore . . . been printed from a playhouse MS' (Werstine, *Scripts*, 233). The second issue is the variant readings in the seven extant copies of Q2. In an article on 'The editorial problem of press variants: Q2 *Hamlet* as a test case', Gabriel Egan questions our decision to label certain variants as 'uncorrected' (see our Appendix 2, Table 2). After observing that 'Instead of offering an obviously correct and an obviously incorrect reading, many press variants offer alternatives that are about equally acceptable' (Egan, 313), he examines each of the 26 variants in detail. Among other things, he notices that the supposed variants at 1.2.212 ('watch,'/'watch'/'watcl') are in fact an illusion, since all that has happened is that the type has not been consistently inked. More interesting is the use to which he puts Joseph A. Dane's 1996 article on 'Perfect order and perfected order: the evidence from press-variants of early seventeenth-century quartos' (Dane), which provides evidence that, in the process of assembling individual copies of quartos in the printing house, printers did not pick up printed sheets at random, but tended to work reasonably consistently through the pile and therefore maintain the order in which they had been printed. This leads Egan to conclude that each of the individual surviving copies of Q2 is likely to be either more corrected as a whole or less corrected as a whole. In light of this and other evidence, along with his belief that correction is likely to have been made by reference to the manuscript from which the compositor had been working, Egan's argument leads him to propose some different readings to those adopted by our edition (for example, 'braves' rather than 'brains' at 2.2.522, 'feelingly' rather than 'sellingly' at 5.2.95, and 'raw' rather than 'yaw' at 5.2.100).

CRITICISM

Psychological readings of Hamlet's behaviour continue to appear. Tom Macfaul's study of *Problem Fathers in Shakespeare and Renaissance Drama* wonders whether Hamlet's delay might be the result of his anxiety about whether his father was Claudius rather than Hamlet senior (an idea mooted earlier by Harold Bloom), and there is some psychoanalytic analysis within such studies as David Hillman's *Shakespeare's Entrails: Belief, Scepticism and the Interior of the Body* and Simon Critchley and Jamieson Webster's *The Shakespeare Doctrine*. But while Graham Holderness's essay, "'I covet your skull": death and desire in *Hamlet*', duly invokes Freud when it describes skulls as 'uncanny' (lifeless objects which nevertheless encourage the idea that they might be alive), he quickly moves beyond the psychoanalytic to argue that both Hamlet's impulse to converse with Yorick's skull and Victorian scholars' interest in disinterring Shakespeare are both expressions of a vision of the dead as 'alive, speaking, still accessible to inquiry, prayer and love' – a vision which he describes as 'early modern Catholic' (Holderness, 'Skull', 236).

Indeed, as David Scott Kastan wrote in 2014, 'Where the twentieth century, following Freud's student, Ernest Jones, tended to see the tragedy mainly in psychological terms, recently we have been more likely to see it in theological ones' (Kastan, *Religion*, 118). Brian Cummings's *Mortal Thoughts: Religion, Secularity and Identity in Shakespeare and Early Modern Culture*, published in the same year, challenges the view that Shakespeare's treatment of 'selfhood' in such devices and topics as soliloquy, conscience and suicide is to be seen as evidence of the increasing secularization of Elizabethan/Jacobean society rather than of exploratory thinking within a religious framework. He has a particularly illuminating chapter on the concept and major role of luck in *Hamlet*, arguing that the accidental does not have to be seen as being at odds with the providential.

Shakespeare's attitude towards Catholicism has been explored by both Richard Wilson and John E. Curran. Wilson concentrates on Shakespeare's use of Catholic and apocalyptic language and imagery in a play which is first published at the moment when the Protestant King James comes to the throne and Wilson can detect in it 'a rising apprehension, as the new age dawns, of the disaster of Stuart rule' (Wilson, 237). Curran is less concerned with the political environment in which the play was written and published, and more concerned with the philosophical implications of Shakespeare's portrayal of his hero's mental life. He argues that while Shakespeare was not necessarily a Catholic, he was a Catholic-minded person trying futilely to apply his world view to a deterministic, Protestant universe, and finally embracing that universe. Shakespeare 'endows no other play with the unmitigated determinism he infuses into *Hamlet*, and this because, I think, he could not reconcile himself to such an outlook' (Curran, 16). Ultimately, Curran believes that the play registers Shakespeare's disapproval of Protestantism.

Meanwhile, in his *Godless Shakespeare* of 2007, Eric S. Mallin asks a series of awkward questions about the religious / moral attitudes in the play – questions such as this:

> The play labours to suggest that its hero is redeemable. In religious terms, as far as Hamlet is concerned, the main threat to his salvation seems to lie in that troublesome desire for suicide – not in any of his countless acts and words of savagery and turpitude. If Hamlet can happily enough deal death to others, which he never seems to regard as a moral problem, then why should there be any difficulty with suicide . . .?'
>
> (Mallin, 63)

To take another example,

> '[in lines 5.1.240–43 and 269–72] Hamlet and Laertes wish to emulate the Titans, who tried to heap mountain on mountain until they reached heaven . . . Do they really think that the construction of a super-hill on the body of Ophelia will bring them closer to heaven? It is a monstrous vignette of shame, self-justification, and rampant bullshit'.
>
> (62)

Marguerite A. Tassi's *Women and Revenge in Shakespeare: Gender, Genre, and Ethics* also asks an awkward question, this time about Shakespeare's attitude to the revenge ethic. Early Modern drama appears to condemn revenge as unChristian, but 'the fundamental passion motivating revenge is, more often than not, a love of justice' (Tassi, 12) and, in Hamlet, not only the Ghost, but both Gertrude and Ophelia appear as unappeased grievants, compelled by an inward sense of injustice, as well as remorse. Gertrude's dying words at 5.2.295 ('The drink, the drink – I am poisoned') give Hamlet a motive and cue for killing the King. Similarly, Ophelia's call to Laertes to remember their father's wrongful death and burial feeds the play's other revenge cause.

In 2012, Ophelia gained a whole book to herself – *The Afterlife of Ophelia*, edited by Kaara L. Peterson and Deanne Williams. This is a diverse collection of essays on a wide range of different ways in which Ophelia has been and is currently represented (in painting, film, social media, photography, as well as in the theatre) and, as the editors explain in their Introduction, continues to be 'a screen on which a culture projects its preoccupations and reflects its values back onto itself' (Peterson & Williams, 2). But a more surprising character to edge into the limelight is Horatio. In our discussion of Casting (Appendix 5) we noted the peculiarity of Horatio's part, in that he is the only character who cannot be doubled. Two recent studies also identify Horatio as holding a special structural significance. Christopher Warley, in an essay on 'Specters of Horatio', explores the personal and political ambiguity of Horatio's role: he seems to Hamlet to be reliable because he is a disinterested outsider, whereas to Marcellus he is reliable because he is an interested insider. Meanwhile, Franco Moretti has conducted a visual analysis of the plot of *Hamlet*. He does this by drawing lines between any characters who at least once communicate orally with one another and thereby creating a set of nodes (the characters) and edges (representing the existence of speech acts between them) that records spatially the temporal flow of plot. What he discovers is that if Hamlet is removed from the network, two camps begin to emerge (the Court and the others) and only Horatio keeps them in touch, whereas if Horatio is also removed, not only does the Court split off completely but the network of 'others' disintegrates. Horatio is also peculiar within the play for being remarkably unmotivated (what does he actually want to do?) and for using remarkably flat and unfigurative language. Moretti characterizes Horatio's network of ambassadors, messengers and sentinels as being rather impersonal, almost bureaucratic: it is, he suggests, as if Horatio heralds the coming of a new political reality – the replacement of the Court by the State.

Inevitably, it is Hamlet himself who is the focus of attention for many scholars, and inevitably one of them has now written a whole book entitled, *To Be Or Not To Be*, published in 2007. In it Douglas Bruster skilfully analyses what he calls 'the central speech of the central character in the central play of the language's central author' (Bruster, 9). He notes that, while it is 'messy' (8), its disorder can produce a kind of trance, and while it may be 'all but useless to its speaker and story' (9), neither Hamlet nor *Hamlet* would be imaginable without it. Bruster devotes a whole chapter to Q1's version of the soliloquy, but not because he believes Q1 is the equal of the version that has come down to us via Q2 and F (in fact, he explicitly calls it 'inferior'), but because it further clarifies the nature of each of the Q2/F versions – by telling us 'things it is not' (90).

However, James Hirsh is unhappy with Bruster's readings of the speech. This is because he believes they misrepresent the plot. In an essay on '*Hamlet* and empiricism' in 2013, Hirsh attacks Bruster's acceptance of 'the conventional, sentimental post-Renaissance cliché that the "To be" speech is the sincere expression of Hamlet's sublime innermost thoughts' (Hirsh, *Hamlet*, 342). No, he says, it is a 'feigned soliloquy' and

Shakespeare 'intended playgoers to infer that Hamlet pretends to speak to himself but actually allows those he regards as agents of the King ... to hear the speech in order to mislead them' (341). Hirsh is angered that no edition of *Hamlet* – and in an earlier essay (Hirsh, 'To be') he had included ours – has ever corrected the false impression about the speech 'that is maintained by pervasive cultural indoctrination' (342).

Alan Stewart's *Shakespeare's Letters* has two valuable chapters on *Hamlet*, both of which concern the plot. In 'Letters to Ophelia', he argues that the letter Polonius shows Claudius and Gertrude in Q2 2.2 is evidence that Hamlet and Ophelia are to be married 'and the most disastrous proof of Ophelia's acquiescence to his sexual attentions' (Stewart, 237). In 'Rewriting Hamlet', Hamlet's decision at Q2 5.2.26 to give Horatio the letter which Claudius wrote to the King of England means that, were Horatio to tell Hamlet's story aright, were the letter in his possession to be produced in evidence, and were Hamlet's forged letter to the King of England (which the English ambassadors could produce in evidence) to be put alongside it, they would together suggest the moral equivalence of Claudius and Hamlet's acts. Stewart reckons Horatio should destroy his letter, so that only the audience's memory would survive to discredit Hamlet.

Crucial to the significance of this letter is the fact that Hamlet has sealed it with his father's signet ring. Hugh Grady discusses the idea that *Hamlet* is a collection of ambiguous 'signifying objects' in a melancholy world empty of intrinsic meaning – and one such object is the signet ring, which Grady describes as a 'sign that holds the power of life and death' – a sign 'that allows Hamlet to be at once his father, his father's usurper, and himself as dutiful son' (Grady, 181). However, the most emotionally powerful of these objects are the graveyard and the iconic skull within it. The clowns' gallows humour provides Hamlet with a context for coming to terms with death as a physical, corporeal reality, and we are forced to rethink everything as, momentarily, we suddenly find ourselves in a plebeian world where death is both commonplace and 'a moment of life which continues in the community as it is extinguished in the individual' (179).

Perhaps the most provocative book on *Hamlet* to emerge in this period (and in many ways the richest in ideas) is Margreta de Grazia's *'Hamlet' Without Hamlet* of 2007. Put simply, she sets out to demodernize Hamlet by resisting the post-Romantic emphasis on his inwardness and emphasizing instead the senses in which the play is history rather than tragedy. She reads the prince's supposed madness and delay as functions of a plot in which his behaviour is largely determined by his uncle and mother's conspiracy to dispossess him of his inheritance – his crown, his property, his land. Like de Grazia, Paul A. Kottman (writing about *Tragic Conditions in Shakespeare*) thinks the play is about Hamlet's inheritance. But he also thinks it is about emotional response. Claudius is king because of his sexual conquest of Gertrude, and the intensity of Hamlet's disgust at what he regards as this incestuous union derives from the fact that Hamlet would lose his inheritance if Claudius and Gertrude were to have a child. Indeed, 'in a total inversion of the Oedipal model – it is precisely because Hamlet did *not* have a child with his mother, and thereby insert himself between her and any further offspring, that he stands to lose everything' (Kottman, 46).

We might seem here to be revisiting the world of psychoanalytic discourse. But Kottman moves on to consider another kind of disgust. Noting Hamlet's physical revulsion at the smell of Yorick's skull (5.1.190), he recalls that the seventeenth/eighteenth century Italian philosopher Giambattista Vico traced the origins of societal life to the practice of stanching the stench of one's own dead by burying them. Kottman concludes that 'in order to inherit his own life as humanly livable', Hamlet must avenge his father's death and thereby 'adequately bury' him (57). This is a social act, both honouring and creating social bonds. And so, Kottman argues, is tragedy, because if it works it unites us all in a natural, spontaneous and shared emotional response. Just as Hamlet seeks Claudius's unfeigned and public reaction to *The Murder of Gonzago*, so Shakespeare's *Hamlet* is a formal attempt to close 'the diremption of nature from sociality' through the prompting in an audience of 'shared tears, a collective shiver of the spine' (77).

AFTERLIFE

As we write this in 2015, a company from Shakespeare's Globe in London is halfway through touring a small-scale production of *Hamlet* to every country in the world (see Fig. 19). The play opened on 23 April 2014, the 450th anniversary of Shakespeare's birth, and will close on 23 April 2016, the 400th anniversary of his death, after what Dominic Dromgoole, the director, describes as 'a brain-defying, logistics-confounding' tour of 205 countries 'at the last count' (Globe to Globe *Hamlet* programme note, unpaginated). A revival of the Globe's touring version from 2011, it features two actors alternating in the title role, Ladi Emeruwa (originally from Nigeria) and Naeem Hayat (whose family come from Pakistan), and the abbreviated text is mainly based on the Folio but includes Hamlet's last soliloquy from Q2 and his examples of clowning adlibs from Q1. This international, eclectic project seems an appropriate starting point for an attempt to sketch what has been happening to *Hamlet* on stage and screen since our Arden edition went to press in 2005. In our original Introduction we explored some topics which seemed to us significant in the 400 years since the play was first performed around 1600, and here we will re-examine some of those topics and add some new ones.

Directors have of course continued to dominate the stage tradition, even though star actors are relied on to bring in the punters. People who have seen *Hamlet* on the English stage in

19 Students from the Chobe Community School in Kasane, Botswana, arriving to see *Hamlet* in the Shakespeare's Globe world tour, 15 April 2015 (courtesy of Malcolm Cocks, photographer).

the last ten years will remember performances by, for example, David Tennant, Jude Law, Rory Kinnear, Michael Sheen, Maxine Peake and Benedict Cumberbatch rather than the fact that those actors were expressing the interpretations of, respectively, Gregory Doran (for the Royal Shakespeare Company in Stratford, 2008), Michael Grandage (for the Donmar at Wyndham's, 2009), Nicholas Hytner (for the National Theatre, 2010), Ian Rickson (for the Young Vic, 2011), Sarah Frankcom (for Manchester's Royal Exchange, 2014) and Lyndsey Turner (for the Barbican, 2015). Some of these directors have enthusiastically taken up the theme of political surveillance in the play, common, as we previously noted, in eastern European productions, but also present in the work of Peter Hall, Buzz Goodbody and Richard Eyre in England from the 1960s to the 1980s. One reviewer indeed remarked that 'In setting his production of *Hamlet* in the declining years of a late 20th-century Eastern European dictatorship, Nicholas Hytner does little more than revisit the *Hamlet* of Yuri Lyubimov for the Leicester Haymarket, or Alexandru Tocilescu's staging . . . in Bucharest', and queried 'the entitlement of a contemporary English director to appropriate and condemn the history of another time and place' (Smith, P., 45). But others felt that Hytner 'made brilliant use of his extras as an in-house army of wired-up goons, earpieces like implants, whispering into their lapels, shadowing every scene' (Rutter, '2010', 375). The 'goons' not only spied on everyone but eventually dragged Ophelia offstage, clearly indicating that her death was not accidental. Michael Grandage's set consisted of towering black walls and heavy wooden gates, and Ian Rickson's production took the familiar prison metaphor to an extreme by setting the entire play in the secure wing of a psychiatric unit, implicating the audience too in its apparent questioning of who was a patient, who was a doctor and who was a visitor. A more radical 'remix' of the play, *The Rest is Silence*, directed by Tristan Sharps for dreamthinkspeak and starring Edward Hogg as Hamlet, was presented at the Brighton Festival and at London's Riverside Theatre in 2012. All the action took place behind large glass panels acting as windows but also as mirrors and video screens. Again the audience was made to feel complicit in spying on the characters in both their onstage and offstage moments.

The prison metaphor also appeared in the production by the Baxter Theatre Centre from Cape Town, directed by Janet Suzman, which played briefly at the Royal Shakespeare Company's Swan Theatre in Stratford as part of the 2012 Complete Works Festival. The multiracial company had chosen an image of a prison cell to insert into the programme 'to give context to the work in this production', but one reviewer expressed puzzlement about how this image worked in practice.

What does it mean when a South African Asian Hamlet [Vaneshran Arumugam] adopts an antic disposition by donning what look like prison-camp clothes, wearing khaki shorts and carrying a blanket and an enamel cup and plate? Clearly he is reiterating in another register his sense that Denmark is a prison, and that he is being detained in Elsinore against his will, but what other connotations does this particular kit bring with it in South Africa?

(Dobson, '2006', 290)

The play was performed in English (with some brief snatches of, presumably, African languages), but many of us shared this desire for further information about the specific resonances of things like casting decisions and costume choices as we watched the abundance of 'foreign' Shakespeares made available as part of the 2012 Cultural Olympics, including the 37 plays in 37 languages offered by the Globe to Globe season. In the second decade of the 21st century, London audiences had the opportunity to see at least four 'classic' foreign (and foreign language) *Hamlet*s: one by the Schaubuhne ensemble from Berlin (directed by Thomas Ostermeier with Lars Eidinger as Hamlet), who brought their 2008 production to the Barbican in 2011; one by Meno Fortas from Lithuania (directed by Eimuntas Nekrosius with Andrius Mamontovas), whose 1997 production was Lithuania's contribution to the 2012 Globe to Globe festival; and one by the Yohangza Theatre Company from South Korea (directed by Yang Jung-Ung with Jun Jung-Yong), whose 2009 production for Myeondong theatre in Seoul played for just one performance at the Peacock Theatre in London in 2014. We also saw another version of the play directed by Yukio Ninagawa at the Barbican in 2015 starring Tatsuya Fujiwara, who had played Hamlet for the same director in the same theatre in 2003.

It is salutary for Anglophone audiences to be challenged by foreign interpretations, and to see productions that have become classics in their own countries, staying in the repertory for much longer than is usual for British productions. Ninagawa's interpretations over the years have been relatively conventional, even causing some reviewers to complain that they are insufficiently 'exotic', but each of the German, Lithuanian and Korean versions, while containing some striking images, also raised questions it was difficult to answer. In a programme note for the 2014 Globe to Globe season, Dennis Kennedy remarks that, 'In English, *Hamlet* is a series of well-known quotations, in Chinese it is a new play' (unpaginated). But what kind of new play does it become? Why was the comedy of both the German and the Lithuanian productions so aggressive? Were both of them deliberately offering a travesty of the play or were their rearrangements of the text more meaningful to international audiences than to British ones (both have toured extensively)? What should we make of the shamanic rituals and the percussive musical score of the Korean version? It is good that *Hamlet* apparently still 'works' for audiences worldwide, but what kind of work does it do? Does it matter if *Hamlet* means something completely different in Lithuania or Korea from what we think it means in England?

All the productions discussed so far have been fairly 'straight' (despite the somewhat kaleidoscopic approach to the text taken by dreamthinkspeak and by the foreign language versions), but *Hamlet* has continued to inspire adaptations, cut-up versions, spinoffs, prequels and sequels. Two further versions from overseas worthy of mention are *Kupenga Kwa Hamlet* (*The Madness of Hamlet*) directed by Arne Pohlmeier for Two Gents Productions, a company in which two actors from Zimbabwe, Denton Chikura and Tonderai Munyevu, literally play all the parts. They brought this production, loosely based on Q1, to the Oval House Theatre in London in 2010 and they managed to make the play fresh, imaginative, funny and moving. Teatro de los Andes from Bolivia used three extremely versatile and physical performers (plus one musician) for its much more free adaptation, *Hamlet de los Andes*, directed by Diego Aramburo, which played at the Barbican in 2013. Meanwhile, the National Theatre's Youth Theatre offered a prequel, Michael Leslie's *Prince of Denmark* (directed by Anthony Banks with Calum Finlay as Hamlet), which played briefly at the Cottesloe in 2010 while the Hytner/Kinnear *Hamlet* ran in the Olivier. The use of teenage actors for *Prince of Denmark* chimes with the perhaps surprising number of teen novels making use of the story: Jeremy Trafford's *Ophelia* (2001) is also a prequel, while Lisa Fiedler's *Dating Hamlet* (2002) and Lisa Klein's *Ophelia* (2006) both tell the story of the play from Ophelia's point of view, empowering her to save both herself and her prince. Ophelia is also saved from drowning in the adult novel, *The Prince of Denmark*, by Graham Holderness (*Prince*, 2002), only to die giving birth to Hamlet's son. Brought up by monks, this child is eventually tracked down by Horatio, returns to Elsinore and wins a battle against Fortinbras but refuses to kill him or to become king. To some extent, these fictions 'redeem' Hamlet from his tragedy rather as Denton Jacques Snider did back in 1923 (see above, 135).

In the United States, two quite remarkably self-conscious experiments with what one might call 'the *Hamlet* tradition' occurred in 2007 and 2013. In 2007 the Wooster Group in New York took as their starting point not Shakespeare's play but the 1964 film of John Gielgud's Broadway production starring Richard Burton. In 2013 The Hidden Room Theater of Austin, Texas, offered a version of *Der Bestrafte Brudermord* (*Fratricide Punished*), the German drama that may or may not derive from Q1, as a puppet play at the Blackfriars Theater in Staunton, Virginia. The Wooster Group, directed by Elizabeth LeCompte and starring Scott Shepherd as Hamlet, performed what was to some extent a re-enactment of the 1964 film, digitally re-edited on onstage screens, but also a more complicated layering with other films (Kozintsev, Branagh and Almereyda), putting the focus on *Hamlet*'s theatrical past and its constant remediation as much as on its present meaning (see Cartelli, Werner and Worthen, 'Wooster'). Hidden Room, directed by Beth Burns, built on current scholarly work by

Tiffany Stern ('Puppets') who argued that the eighteenth-century text that survives of *Der Bestrafte Brudermord* may be a text derived from the puppet theatre, or one that has been reworked for puppets. Certainly the audience of Shakespeare scholars for the performance in Staunton seemed to agree that it worked well in this medium, as did audiences who saw the same production in London, Oxford and Stratford-upon-Avon in 2015.

Given the frequent use of video screens on stage (by the Wooster Group, for example, as well as by dreamthinkspeak) and the ubiquity of various sorts of screens and tablets in everyday life, it is perhaps surprising that there has not been a major new film in the Anglo-American tradition since Almereyda's in 2000, though Mark Thornton Burnett discusses Steven Cavanagh's 2005 version, set and filmed in Londonderry, Northern Ireland in his book, *Filming Shakespeare in the Global Marketplace* (2007). Patrick Cook's book, *Cinematic 'Hamlet'* (2011) analyses the films by Olivier, Zeffirelli, Branagh and Almereyda. The Doran/Tennant production was however filmed for television and is available on video. Andrew Fleming's *Hamlet 2* (Momentum Pictures, 2008) stars Steve Coogan as a failed actor-turned-teacher who decides to stage a musical sequel to *Hamlet* involving time-travel (Hamlet goes back and saves Gertrude, Laertes and Ophelia) and some degree of blasphemy: it is also a sequel to the New Testament and contrives a happy ending in which both Jesus and Hamlet forgive their fathers. Elsewhere in the world, a Bollywood version called *Haider* set in Kashmir was released in 2014, directed by Vishal Bhardwaj, who had previously adapted *Macbeth* and *Othello* as *Maqbool* (2003) and *Omkara* (2006), and an Iranian adaptation called *Tardid*, directed by Varuzh Karim Masihi, was released in 2009. Two *Hamlet*-derived films have been produced in China: *The Banquet*, directed by Xioaogang Feng, and *Prince of the Himalayas*, directed by Sherwood Hu, both released in 2006. Both bore some resemblance to recent and internationally successful martial arts movies such as *Crouching Tiger, Hidden Dragon* (directed by Ang Lee, 2000) and reshaped the material in terms of an eastern code of chivalric heroism, carefully avoiding any overt reference to contemporary politics, as Mark Thornton Burnett notes (*Cinema*, 125–7; see also his forthcoming book, *Translating 'Hamlet': Travels in World Cinema*).

So *Hamlet* continues to fascinate and indeed obsess biographers, textual scholars, critics, actors and directors. New interpretations are still possible and old arguments have been revived with renewed vigour. People still disagree about it and will no doubt continue to do so, but we can at least say with certainty that it shows no likelihood of ceasing 'to be'.

THE TRAGICAL HISTORY OF HAMLET, PRINCE OF DENMARK

The Second Quarto (1604–5)

LIST OF ROLES

HAMLET	*Prince of Denmark*	
GHOST	*of Hamlet's father, the late King Hamlet of Denmark*	
KING Claudius	*of Denmark, brother of the late King*	
QUEEN Gertrude	*Hamlet's mother and his father's widow, now married to King Claudius*	
POLONIUS	*King Claudius' councillor*	5
LAERTES	*Polonius' son*	
OPHELIA	*Polonius' daughter*	
REYNALDO	*Polonius' man*	
FOLLOWERS	*of Laertes*	
HORATIO	*Hamlet's friend and fellow student*	10
ROSENCRANTZ ⎱ GUILDENSTERN ⎰	*other fellow students*	
VOLTEMAND ⎱ CORNELIUS ⎰	*Danish ambassadors to Norway*	
BARNARDO ⎫ FRANCISCO ⎬ MARCELLUS ⎭	*sentinels*	15
OSRIC	*a courtier*	
PLAYERS	*playing* Prologue, Player King, Player Queen *and* Lucianus	
GRAVEDIGGER	*a clown*	20
SECOND MAN	*another clown*	
PRIEST		
LORDS		
GENTLEMEN		
MESSENGERS		25
SAILORS		
FORTINBRAS	*Prince of Norway*	
CAPTAIN	*in Norwegian army*	
AMBASSADORS	*from England*	

Attendants, Courtiers, Trumpets, Kettledrums, Drums, Officers, Norwegian Soldiers   30

LIST OF ROLES not in Q1, Q2 or F; a list of 'The Persons Represented' is first provided in Q6 (1676), which also gives the names of the actors in Thomas Betterton's 1661 production. For the convenience of readers, we have in this text adopted the most familiar modern forms of the names of the characters, even when they are not the ones most frequently used in Q2 (see 4n., 11n., 12n., 18n. and 27n.).

1 HAMLET The hero is Amleth in Saxo Grammaticus and Hamblet in the 1608 English translation of Belleforest (see pp. 65–72), but references to 'Hamlet' precede Shakespeare's play and the name had significance in his immediate circle of family and friends (see pp. 37–8 and 42–4). In both Q2 and F we are informed in 5.1 that Hamlet is 30 years old (134–53) and he remembers Yorick who has been dead 'three and twenty years' (163–4); Q1 does not specify his age but informs us that Yorick has been dead 'this dozen year' (16.86), perhaps implying that Hamlet is about 18. Shakespeare (or the author of the *Ur-Hamlet*) presents Hamlet as a student, currently at the University of Wittenberg, and his youth is stressed, for example by Laertes and Polonius in 1.3 and by the Ghost, who addresses him as 'thou noble youth' at 1.5.38. Richard Burbage is generally presumed to have been the originator of the role (see 5.1.247 SDn.); he would have been in his mid-thirties at the time. Subsequent professional performers have ranged from 13 to 74, with most recent performers being in their thirties (see pp. 6–7).

2 GHOST 'The Persons Represented' in Q6 include 'Ghost of Hamlet's Father', and this designation has become standard, though it perhaps pre-empts any debate as to whether this is 'an honest ghost' (1.5.137) or not. Hamlet's father is called Horwendill in Saxo, Horvendile in Belleforest; Shakespeare (or the author of the *Ur-Hamlet*) takes the step of calling the father by the same name as the son. There is an unproven tradition that Shakespeare himself acted this role originally. Despite the contrast between the physical appearances of the two men stressed by Hamlet at 3.4.51–69, it is possible for the actor playing the Ghost to double in the role of the King; this has happened on stage occasionally since (at least) John Gielgud's production in 1939 (see Appendix 5).

3 KING **Claudius** Feng in Saxo, Fengon in Belleforest, the King is never given a personal name in the dialogue in any of the three texts of *Hamlet*, but is generally designated simply 'King'. He is named Claudius in Q2 only in the SD for his first entry and in the SP for his first speech (1.2.0 and 1.2.1); he is named Claudius in F only in the SD for his first entry; he is not named at all in Q1. From the fact that a messenger mentions a character called Claudio (who does not appear) at 4.7.40, we suppose that Shakespeare was not actively thinking of the King as Claudius, though the name has subsequently become common in critical discussion and is used as an SP by Edwards, Oxf and Hibbard. Jenkins argues that it was 'evidently suggested by that of the Roman emperor who married Agrippina, his niece and the mother of Nero, referred to at [3.2.384]'. But, if the analogies with an incestuous marriage and an uncle-stepfather are intended, they have never been available for audiences as opposed to readers.

4 QUEEN **Gertrude** Gerutha in Saxo, Geruth in Belleforest. Possibly, Shakespeare combines this name with that of Hermutrude or Hermetrude, Amleth's own second wife in the sources. The Queen is named 'Gertrard' 12 times in the dialogue in Q2 (first at 2.2.54) and twice in SDs, 'Gertrad' once in an SD. SPs call her 'Quee.'/'Queene' (40 times) or 'Ger.' (28 times). She is regularly 'Gertred' in Q1 but we have adopted F's 'Gertrude' as the most common modern form.

5 POLONIUS Q6 describes Polonius as 'Lord Chamberlain' in 'The Persons Represented' and he is given this title in *Fratricide Punished* (in the 'Persons Represented' and in the dialogue in 3.5: Bullough, 7.128, 145), but the play does not specify his office, although the King stresses his importance (1.2.47–9). The friend of Feng or Fengon who eavesdrops on the hero's encounter with his mother is not named in Saxo or Belleforest. Polonius is named first in the dialogue at 1.2.57. He is designated 'old Polonius' in the SD for his entry at 2.1.0 in Q2. Polonius is perhaps a surprising choice of name for a Danish councillor in a context in which the Poles or 'Polacks' are defined as Denmark's enemies (see 1.1.62). King John of France, however, welcomes the military support of both 'The stern Polonian and the warlike Dane' in *Edward III*, and the two supporting armies enter simultaneously from either side of the stage in that play (3.1.34); Shakespeare's involvement in *Edward III* is of course disputed. The name is given as Corambis in Q1 (where it does not appear in the dialogue until 8.30), Corambus in *Fratricide Punished*. Jenkins (LN) and Bullough (7.44–5) speculate on possible topical allusions and consequent theories about why the name was changed, though the associated change of his servant's name from Reynaldo to Montano makes the idea of direct personal satire unlikely (as well as uncharacteristic for Shakespeare); one might also note the comparable change of names between the Folio text of *TS* and the anonymous *Taming of a Shrew* (possibly a reported text) whereby Petruchio and his servant Grumio become Ferando and Sander. It is often assumed that John Heminges was the originator of the role of Polonius (see 3.2.99–102n.); he received a bequest in Shakespeare's will in 1616 and, with Henry Condell, collected and published most of Shakespeare's plays in the First Folio of 1623. The actor playing Polonius has, since 1730, often doubled in the role

of the Gravedigger (see Appendix 5). Perhaps because of this traditional doubling, the role was frequently interpreted as a comic one in the past (see 1.3.56n.).

6 LAERTES There is no equivalent of Laertes in Shakespeare's sources. Laertes is the name of the father of Odysseus in Homer's *Odyssey*, mentioned in *Tit* at 1.1.385. Like Hamlet, Laertes is presented as a student, in his case currently at university in Paris. The name is changed, perhaps mistakenly but consistently, to Leartes in Q1; he is Leonhardus in *Fratricide Punished*. It is possible for the actor playing Laertes to double in the role of Guildenstern (see Appendix 5).

7 OPHELIA described as 'in love with Hamlet' in Q6's list of 'The Persons Represented'. A nameless young woman who has been brought up with the hero is set up by his uncle as a temptation for him in the sources and his first wife, the equally nameless daughter of the King of England, is, like Ophelia, divided in her loyalties between the hero and her father. The name is consistently Ofelia in Q1.

8 REYNALDO Polonius' servant is identified by name three times in the dialogue at the beginning of his one scene (2.1.1, 3 and 15); he is 'Reynoldo' in F and 'Montano' in Q1. His Q2/F names are variants of 'Reynard', the name of the fox in Edmund Spenser's *Mother Hubbard's Tale*. In *AW* the Countess's Steward is apparently called Rynaldo, but the name is used only once (*AW* 3.4.29).

9 FOLLOWERS of Laertes enter briefly at 4.5.111; they just make a noise offstage at the equivalent moments in F and Q1, which is an obvious way to economize on costumes, if not on actors.

10 HORATIO The sources mention a nameless foster-brother (Saxo) or childhood friend (Belleforest) of the hero who helps him to avoid his uncle's first trap. Horatio is another name with classical connotations, but also that of the loyal friend and murdered son in Thomas Kyd's *The*

Spanish. Tragedy (c. 1587, revived in 1597). The role has many inconsistencies: apparently a citizen of Elsinore with local knowledge of Danish politics in 1.1, on friendly terms with the sentinels but seen by them as 'a scholar' who knows how to address the Ghost, Horatio is hailed by Hamlet as a fellow student who is visiting from Wittenberg in 1.2 (164, 176), although it seems odd that he has not encountered Hamlet in the two months since old Hamlet's death. His questions at 1.4.7 and 12 seem to confirm his role as a visitor, and Hamlet has to tell him who Laertes is at 5.1.213. Clearly established as Hamlet's confidant in 3.2, he nevertheless does not tell his friend about Ophelia's madness, which he witnesses in 4.5; the King seems to regard him as an ally both in 4.5 and 5.1. He has long periods of silence onstage and sometimes editors are unsure whether he is onstage or not (see 3.2.377 SDn. and 4.5.74 SDn.). In Q1 he is presented even more strongly as Hamlet's supporter in a unique scene with the Queen (Scene 14). His age is problematic in all three texts, since in 1.1 he seems to recognize the armour old Hamlet wore in a battle that we subsequently learn happened 30 years previously. It has been argued that these difficulties arise from Shakespeare's imposition of Horatio-as-student on to a Horatio-as-soldier figure in the *Ur-Hamlet* (see Newell, 143–56). The actor playing Horatio cannot easily double any other part (see Appendix 5). The importance of the role, and of the character's relationship with Hamlet, was stressed in Peter Brook's 2000 production, which allowed him both to begin and to end the play.

11 ROSENCRANTZ consistently named 'Rosencraus' in dialogue (four times) and SDs (eight times) in Q2, abbreviated to 'Ros' in three SDs and all SPs. As with our use of 'Gertrude', we have adopted this form (derived from F's 'Rosincrance') as the most familiar modern version of the name; it means 'wreath or crown of roses'. Q1 calls him 'Rossencraft'. Rosencrantz and Guildenstern are both Danish names. In 1588 Daniel Rogers was sent by Queen Elizabeth I to Elsinore to pay her respects to the new King of Denmark, Christian IV, and his report mentions among the members of Christian's court 'George Rosenkrantz of Rosenholm', 'Axel Guildenstern of Lyngbye, Viceroy of Norway' and 'Peter Guildenstern, Marshall of Denmark' (see Bullough, 7.184). Another possible source for Shakespeare is the portrait of the Danish astronomer Tycho Brahe which was published in the 1596 and 1601 editions of his collected astronomical letters: the family names 'Rosenkranz' and 'Guldensteren' appear under coats of arms representing Brahe's ancestors on the arch surrounding the likeness. (For a further possible link between *Hamlet* and Brahe, see 1.1.35n.) Rosencrantz and Guildenstern are introduced as having been brought up with Hamlet at 2.2.11; he addresses them as 'my excellent good friends' at 2.2.219 and calls them 'my two schoolfellows' at 3.4.200, but they do not seem to be acquainted with Horatio and never exchange any words with him. The King and Queen address them as 'Good gentlemen' (2.2.19, 3.1.26). They are often designated as 'Lords' in Q1's SDs and addressed as such by Q1's King (8.1, 11.116). There is a long-standing joke that the two are indistinguishable (see 2.2.33–4n.).

12 GUILDENSTERN consistently 'Guyldensterne' in dialogue (seven times) and SDs (five times) in Q2; abbreviated most often to 'Guyl' in SPs. Again we adopt the usual variant of F's 'Guildensterne' as the most familiar modern form. The name means 'golden star'. Q1 calls him 'Gilderstone'.

13 VOLTEMAND Q2 uses this form once in dialogue and 'Valtemand' once; F has 'Voltemand' and 'Voltumand'; Q1 has 'Voltemar', which is closer to 'Valdemar', the name of several Kings of Denmark. It has been argued by those who favour the 'memorial reconstruction' theory of Q1

that the actor who played Voltemand doubled in the role of Marcellus; Irace adds the Prologue and Lucianus to his workload ('Origins', 118–19; see Appendix 5).

14 CORNELIUS a Dutch name, according to Jenkins; 'Cornelia' (but probably not a woman) in Q1.

15, 16, 17 BARNARDO, FRANCISCO, MARCELLUS primarily defined as sentinels, but Hamlet addresses Barnardo and Marcellus, along with Horatio, as 'friends, scholars and soldiers' at 1.5.140. Marcellus has easily the most substantial role in all three texts and is distinguished as 'an Officer' in the list of 'The Persons Represented' in Q6. These characters do not appear in any of the three texts after Act 1, but in eighteenth- and nineteenth-century theatrical tradition Francisco (who is not named in Q1 and who disappears from Q2 and F at 1.1.16) returned the Gentleman who announces the arrival of the sailors to Horatio at 4.6.0, Marcellus returned as the Messenger who enters to announce the arrival of Laertes and his followers at 4.5.96, and Barnardo returned as the Messenger bearing letters to the King at 4.7.36. All three used to reappear among the courtiers at 5.2.202, with Francisco acting as the King's cup-bearer later in that scene. Our casting charts allow for the actors of all three roles to double in other roles after Act 1 (see Appendix 5). 'Barnardo' is the regular form in F and in Q2 except for 'Bernardo' at 1.2.159.1.

18 OSRIC first introduced as a *courtier* in Q2 at 5.2.66.1, named as 'young *Ostricke*' at 5.2.176 and again at 5.2.236, after which he becomes *Ostr.* or *Ostrick* in SPs. F calls him '*young Osricke*' in the SD at 5.2.80 and again in the dialogue at 5.2.206; in Q1 he is '*a Bragart Gentleman*' (17.4.1); in the Q6 list of 'The Persons Represented' he is 'a fantastical Courtier'; in *Fratricide Punished* his role is developed into that of Phantasmo, the clown, who appears earlier in the play. The insistence on 'young' in both Q2 and F may imply that this was

originally a role for a boy actor (perhaps, according to Gurr & Ichikawa (152), the boy who also played Ophelia), since elsewhere Shakespeare uses 'young' only to distinguish characters like 'young Fortinbras' (1.1.94), 'young Hamlet' (1.1.169) and 'young Siward' (*Mac* 5.7) from their fathers. Snyder (110–11) suggests that 'young' emphasizes the character's innocence or ignorance: he recalls Polonius ('That great baby', 2.2.319) as a child among adults. E.K. Chambers notes mention of a lost play by Heywood and Smith called *Marshal Osric* performed by Worcester's Men in November 1602 (Chambers, *Stage*, 2.227).

19 PLAYERS At least three are needed, assuming one actor can double the Prologue and Lucianus in 3.2. The First Player is addressed by Hamlet as 'old friend' (2.2.360, 473–4) and is often cast as an experienced, older performer, though this may be inconsistent with Hamlet's remarking on the fact that he has just grown a beard (2.2.361–2). One of the three is the boy who acts the Player Queen, who may be almost too old for women's parts (see 2.2.362–6).

20 GRAVEDIGGER The designation *clown* in all three texts indicates a rustic or lower-class character, not necessarily a comedian, though the Gravedigger does indulge in witty repartee with his companion and with Hamlet. Shakespeare's company may have lacked a professional clown at the time that *Hamlet* was first performed (see pp. 57–8 and 3.2.36–7n.), but Mahood (*Bit Parts*, 83) argues that this was one of Robert Armin's first roles for the Chamberlain's Men; certainly the Gravedigger's style of prevarication is comparable to that of Feste in *TN* or the Porter in *Mac*, both roles generally attributed to Armin.

21 SECOND MAN Despite Q6's listing of 'Two Grave-makers' and subsequent stage tradition, the Gravedigger's companion is not necessarily or even plausibly another Gravedigger, as Jenkins points out (5.1.0 n.); he may be just a passing acquaintance.

22 PRIEST 'Doct.' twice in SPs in Q2, presumably short for 'Doctor of Divinity', but addressed by Laertes as 'churlish priest' (5.1.229) and designated 'Priest' in SPs in F and Q1 (Q1 is the only text to mention him in a SD).

26 SAILORS Q2 calls for 'Sailors' to enter at 4.6.6.1 and Horatio says 'Let them come in' in both Q2 and F, but many productions assume one is enough.

27 FORTINBRAS son of old Fortinbras, the former King of Norway, and nephew of the present King (old Norway). Most often 'Fortinbrasse' in Q2 (eight times in dialogue and SDs), 'Fortenbrasse' four times, abbreviated to 'For' or (once) 'Fortin' in SPs. Again we adopt F's more familiar form (found 13 times in dialogue and SDs). There is no equivalent of Fortinbras in the sources. As with the Hamlets, father and son share the same name, which means 'strong in arm' in French.

28 CAPTAIN Mahood (*Bit Parts*, 40) suggests the man was a farmer in civilian life: see 4.4.19n.

HAMLET

1.1   *Enter* BARNARDO *and* FRANCISCO, *two sentinels.*

BARNARDO
   Who's there?
FRANCISCO
   Nay, answer me. Stand and unfold yourself.

1.1 Q2 has no act or scene divisions; F has them up to 1.3, then marks 2.1 and 2.2; subsequent divisions are from Q6 or from eighteenth-century editions. We have followed the traditional divisions in this text, but see Appendix 4. The three texts: this scene runs to 131 lines in Q1 (scene 1), 174 lines in Q2, 156 lines in F (line-counts throughout are from our edited texts). The most substantial difference, common to Q1 and F, is that the conversation immediately before the second appearance of the Ghost is shorter: only Q2 contains Horatio's analogy between the current state of Denmark and the state of Rome before the murder of Julius Caesar at this point (see 107–24 and n.). Because we are editing all three texts of *Hamlet* (in two volumes), our procedures in the textual notes vary somewhat from standard Arden series 3 format: see Appendix 3. Location and timing: these matters are indicated in Q2 (if at all) in the dialogue, never in the stage directions; Shakespeare's stage at the Globe was unlocalized and was lit by natural light. It is clear from 5 that the scene begins between midnight and 1.00 a.m., and from 165–6 that it ends at dawn. We learn from 139 that the sentries are

armed, from 1.2.212 that the setting is the battlements (*platform*) of the royal castle, and from 1.2.173 that the castle is in Elsinore. Although night-time scenes would have been a challenge in daylight performances at the Globe, Shakespeare used them frequently (see Jones, 'Sequences'); the actors would have carried lanterns or torches to indicate that it is supposed to be dark.

0.1 *sentinels* sentries, watchmen. It is revealed at 6 that Barnardo has come to relieve Francisco, and he should perhaps enter after him.

1 **Who's there?** This famous opening line was used by Peter Brook for the title of his 1996 *Hamlet*-derived play in French, *Qui est là?* His 2000 adaptation of *Hamlet* ended with it.

2 **Nay, answer me** Francisco, the watchman on guard, understandably disputes the right of Barnardo, the newcomer, to question him, creating an atmosphere of unease. Daniell points out the similarity to *JC* 1.3.41, where the newcomer, Cassius, challenges Caska (*sic*) with 'Who's there?' **unfold yourself** 'tell me who you are'; the first of the play's many metaphors from clothing.

TITLE (The Tragical History of Hamlet, Prince of Denmark)] *(title-page), Q1 (title-page and head title)*; The Tragedie of HAMLET *Prince of Denmarke. Q2 (head and running titles), F (head title); The Tragedy of Hamlet. Q1 (running title), F (running title and catalogue)* **1.1]** *F (Actus Primus. Scœna Prima.); not in Q21*

177

BARNARDO

Long live the King.   *Irony*

FRANCISCO   Barnardo?

BARNARDO   He.

FRANCISCO

You come most carefully upon your hour.

BARNARDO

'Tis now struck twelve. Get thee to bed, Francisco.   5

FRANCISCO

For this relief much thanks. 'Tis bitter cold

And I am sick at heart.   *metonymy*

BARNARDO

Have you had quiet guard?

FRANCISCO   Not a mouse stirring.

BARNARDO

Well, goodnight.

If you do meet Horatio and Marcellus,   10

The rivals of my watch, bid them make haste.

3   **Long . . . King** This statement (ironical in the context) is used as a kind of password. **Barnardo?** F's question mark seems appropriate here.

4   'You are very punctual.' This is sometimes spoken reprovingly, as if Barnardo is only just on time.

5   **'Tis . . . twelve** i.e. twelve has already struck. The fact that both here and in 1.4 (and indeed in a similar context in *MW* 5.1) the characters claim that the hour has already struck may indicate that these scenes began with a sound effect imitating a bell-tower clock.
   struck Here and at 1.4.4 Riv prints 'strook', a variant of Q2/F 'strooke', though Q1's 'strucke' would seem to challenge the implication that 'strook' preserves an authentic pronunciation.

6   **'Tis bitter cold** attempts to pin down the time of year when the play begins

have proved inconclusive. Guilfoyle, however, draws an analogy between this opening scene and the typical 'Shepherds' Play' in the medieval cycle plays where the shepherds, like *Hamlet*'s sentries, wait on a cold night for a supernatural event (see 157 and n. and pp. 72–3).

7   **I . . . heart** Francisco's 'sickness' is not explained, unless by the subsequent discussion of the Ghost.

8   **Not . . . stirring** proverbial (Dent, M1236.1)

11 **rivals** partners (which is Q1's reading). Both Horatio and Marcellus seem here to be members of the castle's guard, but it transpires from Marcellus' speech at 25–8 that Horatio is present by special invitation. Hamlet greets Horatio in the next scene as a *fellow student*, visiting from Wittenberg (1.2.164, 176), and he addresses

3 Barnardo?] *F; Barnardo. Q2*   9–11] *prose F*   11 rivals] *F; partners Q1*

Enter HORATIO *and* MARCELLUS.

FRANCISCO
I think I hear them. Stand ho, who is there?
HORATIO
Friends to this ground.
MARCELLUS   And liegemen to the Dane.
FRANCISCO
Give you goodnight.
MARCELLUS
O farewell, honest soldiers; who hath relieved you?   15
FRANCISCO
Barnardo hath my place. Give you goodnight.   *Exit.*
MARCELLUS
Holla, Barnardo!
BARNARDO
Say, what, is Horatio there?
HORATIO   A piece of him.

Horatio, Marcellus and Barnardo as 'friends, scholars and soldiers' at 1.5.140 (see List of Roles, 10n. and 15n.)
bid . . . haste The sense of tension and anxiety increases.
13 **liegemen . . . Dane** men who have sworn allegiance to the King of Denmark (in contrast to the *Switzers* at 4.5.97?)
14 **Give you goodnight** 'May God give you (i.e. I wish you) a good (quiet) night.'
15 **soldiers** The plural in Q2 perhaps indicates that someone (Marcellus, Shakespeare, the scribe or compositor) expected the two new arrivals to replace Barnardo and Francisco, rather than that one watchman, Francisco, should be replaced by the other three.

16 SD This is the last we see of Francisco in either Q2 or F; in eighteenth- and nineteenth-century theatrical tradition, however, he reappeared in 4.6 (see 4.6.0.1n.), Marcellus reappeared in 4.5 (see 4.5.96 SD2n.), Barnardo in 4.7 (see 4.7.36.1n.) and all three in 5.2 (see 5.2.202.3n.). The original actors of these parts would very likely have doubled in other roles: see Appendix 5.
17 **Holla** earlier form of hallo/hello: a greeting or a shout to attract attention
18 **Say . . . there** It is presumed that Barnardo cannot see Horatio in the darkness.
A . . . him Perhaps Horatio offers his hand as a literal *piece* or perhaps he implies that the cold night has reduced him to a shrunken fragment of his real self.

---

12 ho] *om. F*   who is] who's *F*   15 soldiers] souldier *Q1F*   16 hath] *Q1;* ha's *F*

BARNARDO

Welcome Horatio, welcome good Marcellus.

HORATIO

What, has this thing appeared again tonight?   20

BARNARDO

I have seen nothing.

MARCELLUS

Horatio says 'tis but our fantasy
And will not let belief take hold of him
Touching this dreaded sight twice seen of us.
Therefore I have entreated him along   25
With us to watch the minutes of this night
That, if again this apparition come,
He may approve our eyes and speak to it.

HORATIO

Tush, tush, 'twill not appear.

BARNARDO   Sit down awhile,
And let us once again assail your ears   30

---

20 SP Q1 agrees with F; MacDonald, who usually favours F, follows Q2 here, commenting: 'Better, I think; for the tone is scoffing, and Horatio is the incredulous one who has not seen it.'

20 **this thing** The lack of definition – see *this dreaded sight* (24), *this apparition* (27) and *it* (28) – serves to enhance the suspense, as does the alternation between *'a* and *it* from 42.

22 **fantasy** imagination

23 **will . . . him** 'will not allow himself to believe'

24 **Touching** concerning
twice . . . us which has been seen by us twice

26 **watch . . . night** stay awake or keep watch through the night

28 **approve our eyes** confirm or corroborate what we saw

29 **Tush** an expression of contempt

Sit down awhile Editors have worried that this behaviour is inappropriate for sentries (the request is repeated at 32 and 69, and it also occurs three times in both Q1 and F). It is possible that only Barnardo and Horatio sit, Marcellus remaining sentry-like. On stage, it raises the question of whether there is something for them to sit on or whether they just sit on the ground; in their study of the earliest staging of the play, Gurr and Ichikawa suggest that they 'hunch down' (126); a bench was used at the reconstructed London Globe in 2000. The words are deleted in the earliest promptbooks we have of *Hamlet*, those of John Ward dating from the 1740s (see Thompson, 'Ward', 144).

30 **assail** attack. The first of the play's many metaphorical references to assaults on ears, inspired presumably by the literal facts of the elder

20 SP] *Mar. Q1F*

That are so fortified against our story
What we have two nights seen.

HORATIO   Well, sit we down,
And let us hear Barnardo speak of this.

BARNARDO

Last night of all,
When yond same star that's westward from the pole   35
Had made his course t'illume that part of heaven
Where now it burns, Marcellus and myself,
The bell then beating one –

Enter GHOST.

Hamlet's murder: see 1.5.59–70. For further discussion of this motif, see Thompson & Thompson, 102–4, and P. Berry, 'Ear'.

31 **fortified** i.e. Horatio is incredulous.

32 **What** i.e. with what
Sit we down See 29n.

33 Perhaps the implication is that Horatio has previously heard Marcellus' version of the story.

34 **Last . . . all** i.e. the most recent night ('only last night')

35 **yond same star** Astronomers have recently argued that, if Shakespeare had a specific star in mind, he might be alluding to the supernova in Cassiopeia which was first seen in Wittenberg in 1572 and also discovered independently by the Danish astronomer Tycho Brahe: see Olson et al.; for a further possible link between *Hamlet* and Brahe, see List of Roles, 11n.
pole pole-star or northern star: the star in the constellation *Ursa Minor* (Latin: Little Bear) which lies so close to the northern pole of the heavens that it seems to remain still in the sky while the other stars revolve around it

36 **his** its
t'illume to illuminate, enlighten. This is Shakespeare's only use of *illume*, and the only usage cited by *OED*. Q1 has the more familiar 'Illumine' and Q6 'modernizes' to 'enlighten', but see the similar Shakespearean coinage 'relume' at *Oth* 5.2.13.

38 **beating** striking. Q1's 'towling' (tolling), as Staunton says, 'perhaps imparts additional solemnity'.

38.1 We learn from 59 that the Ghost is in armour; a fuller description of both its appearance and its behaviour is provided at 1.2.198–240. Foakes ('Ghost') points out that the costume, unusual if not unique for a ghost on the Elizabethan stage, might have emphasized the character's association with an obsolete kind of militarism, in contrast to the contemporary military uniforms worn by the sentinels; all the other characters in Shakespeare's plays who are associated with body armour appear in plays set in the past, whether the period of classical Greece and Rome or that of the War of the Roses. Modern productions usually make use of 'spectral' lighting, music and other 'special

32 have two nights] *Q1;* two Nights haue *F*   36 t'illume] *F;* to / Illumine *Q1*   38 beating] *F;* towling *Q1*   38.1] *after* of: *39 F*   GHOST] *Q1; the Ghost F*

MARCELLUS

Peace, break thee off, look where it comes again.

BARNARDO

In the same figure like the King that's dead.   40

MARCELLUS

Thou art a scholar – speak to it, Horatio.

BARNARDO

Looks 'a not like the King? Mark it, Horatio.

HORATIO

Most like. It harrows me with fear and wonder.

BARNARDO

It would be spoke to.

MARCELLUS   Speak to it, Horatio.

---

effects' to enhance the appearances and disappearances of the Ghost (see Hapgood). It is possible that the Ghost originally ascended through a trapdoor, like the spirits in George Chapman's *Bussy d'Ambois* (1604) and Ben Jonson's *Catiline* (1611*)*, but, as Jenkins says (LN), the dialogue suggests movement across the stage. Despite the arguments in favour of the trap advanced by Gurr and Ichikawa (126), the Ghost used one of the doors at the back of the stage at the London Globe in 2000.

40 **same figure** identical shape, appearance. *Same* could refer to the likeness to the King or to the previous appearances of the Ghost.

41 Marcellus makes the conventional assumptions that (a) a ghost cannot speak until spoken to, and (b) an educated man – perhaps one who speaks Latin – will be better equipped to make this attempt.

42 **'a** he. A colloquial form common in Middle English, especially in the south and west of England, which occurs frequently in Q2

but only once in F; Hope (1.3.2c) notes that Shakespeare's linguistic roots in this dialect area make him one of the final citations for the usage in *OED*, but that the form is 'highly unstable textually' and liable to be changed to 'he' by scribes and compositors.

Mark it observe it closely.

43 ***harrows** Q2's 'horrowes' is usually assumed to be an obsolete form of F's 'harrowes', a word which recurs in both texts at 1.5.16. The metaphor derives from the agricultural implement that breaks up the ground after ploughing, and *OED* records these as the earliest examples of the transferred use. *OED* also implies that there is no direct connection with 'the harrowing of Hell', where 'harrow' derives from 'to harry' (to raid or despoil), but, given the context of Shakespeare's usages, there might have been a link in his mind.

44 **Speak to it** Q2's reading picks up *speak to it* (41) and *It would be spoke to*; Q1/F 'Question it' implies a more formal interrogation.

39 off] *(of) F, Q1*   41 scholar –] *(scholler,) Q1, F (*Scholler;*)*   42 'a] it *Q1F*   43 harrows] *F;* horrowes *Q2;* horrors *Q1*   44 Speak to] Question *Q1F*

HORATIO

What art thou that usurp'st this time of night   45
Together with that fair and warlike form
In which the majesty of buried Denmark
Did sometimes march? By heaven, I charge thee speak.

MARCELLUS

It is offended.

BARNARDO   See, it stalks away.

HORATIO

Stay, speak, speak, I charge thee speak.   *Exit Ghost.*

MARCELLUS

'Tis gone and will not answer.   51

BARNARDO

How now, Horatio, you tremble and look pale.
Is not this something more than fantasy?
What think you on't?

HORATIO

Before my God, I might not this believe   55
Without the sensible and true avouch

45–7 **usurp'st ... Denmark** 'misappropriate both the time of night and the appearance of the dead King' (ironic, since it transpires that it is the present king who is in effect the usurper). At this point Horatio concedes that the Ghost looks like the former King, but not that it is him.

47 **majesty ... Denmark** i.e. dead King of Denmark (a synecdoche which identifies the fate of the country with that of its king)

48 **sometimes** formerly, i.e. when he was alive

49 **offended** Perhaps the Ghost is offended by Horatio's *usurp'st*, by his over-importunate use of *charge* (should a subject command a king?), or, as at 139–45, by an apparent threat

of violence.

stalks moves in a stiff or stately way; see 65, where Marcellus adds the notion that the Ghost's walk has a military style about it.

54 **on't** of it

55 **Before** i.e. I swear before
might not would not be able to

56–7 **sensible ... eyes** true testimony based on the evidence of my senses; 'to believe one's (own) eyes' was proverbial (Dent, E264.1; see also B268). (*Avouch* does not occur as a noun in Shakespeare other than in all three texts of *Hamlet*, which *OED* records as the first use of the word.)

56 **sensible** Hope (1.2.2b) points out that *sensible* is used objectively here, meaning 'able to be sensed or felt', and

---

50 SD *Ghost*] *Q1; the Ghost F*

183

Of mine own eyes.

MARCELLUS   Is it not like the King?

HORATIO

As thou art to thyself.
Such was the very armour he had on
When he the ambitious Norway combated.   60
So frowned he once, when in an angry parle
He smote the sledded Polacks on the ice.
'Tis strange.

MARCELLUS

Thus twice before, and jump at this dead hour,

compares Macbeth's use of the same word in relation to the visionary dagger (*Mac* 2.1.36); see also *dreadful* at 1.2.206 and 1.4.70.

59 **the very armour** The assumption here seems to be that Horatio recognizes the armour, which is mentioned again at 1.2.199, just as Hamlet later recognizes 'My father in his habit as he lived' (3.4.133), but this raises problems of chronology (and Horatio's age) when we learn that the event referred to happened 30 years previously (5.1.135–53); see 79–94n. and List of Roles, 10n.

60 **Norway** King of Norway
   combated The stress is on the first syllable.

61 **So . . . once** Again, the particularity of the memory is striking, if not unnerving.
   parle (one syllable) parley, usually a negotiation rather than a truce; here apparently a hostile encounter

62 ***sledded Polacks** a notoriously difficult phrase which is almost identical in all three early texts (see t.n.). Most recent editors emend 'pollax' to 'Polacks', i.e. Poles, and interpret 'sledded/sleaded' as 'using sleds

or sledges', since this makes sense of the reference to ice. The word *Polack* occurs again at 2.2.63 and 75, 4.4.22 and 5.2.360; it is not derogatory (as it has become in modern North American usage).

In favour of 'pole-axe' (the weapon), however, in Christopher Marlowe and Thomas Nashe's *Dido, Queen of Carthage* (*c.* 1585, printed in 1594), Aeneas describes the destruction of Troy: 'Old men with swords thrust through their aged sides, / Kneeling for mercie to a Greekish lad / Who with steele Pol-axes dasht out their braines' (*Dido*, 2.1.198–9). The 'Greekish lad' is Pyrrhus and Shakespeare drew on this scene for the Player's speech in 2.2. But it is not clear what 'sleaded' would mean: perhaps 'leaded' or 'studded' (as in modern 'sledgehammer'?: *OED* cites a 1495 reference to 'Slege hamers of yron').

64 **jump** precisely (the same meaning as F's 'iust')
   dead still, midnight (see 'the dead waste and middle of the night' at 1.2.197, and similar phrases ('dead of night', 'dead midnight', etc.)

60 he the] *Q1*; th' *F*   62 smote] *(smot) Q1F*   sledded] *F*; sleaded *Q21*   Polacks] *Malone*; pollax *Q21*; Pollax *F*; Poleaxe *F4*; Pole-axe *Rowe*; Polack *Pope*   64 jump] *Q1*; iust *F*

With martial stalk hath he gone by our watch. 65

HORATIO

In what particular thought to work, I know not,
But in the gross and scope of mine opinion
This bodes some strange eruption to our state.

MARCELLUS

Good now, sit down, and tell me he that knows
Why this same strict and most observant watch 70
So nightly toils the subject of the land,
And with such daily cost of brazen cannon
And foreign mart for implements of war,

65 **by our watch** past us as we stood on watch. Staunton adopts Q1's more graphic reading 'through our watch' – which was perhaps inspired by 109.

66 The phrasing is obscure. Horatio seems to mean either 'I don't know what particular theory about the Ghost to pursue' or perhaps 'I don't know what the specific object of the Ghost's return might be'.

67 **gross and scope** broad view, general drift. Noted by Wright as the first example of the play's 66 uses of the rhetorical figure of hendiadys.

mine Many editors emend Q2 in line with Q1/F, but *mine* is perfectly acceptable before a word beginning with a vowel; see 'Mine own, and not mine own', *MND* 4.1.192.

68 **eruption ... state** political revolt or disturbance. In Horatio's opinion here and in the ensuing conversation, including the analogy with the death of Julius Caesar (112–24), it is assumed that the Ghost's appearance relates to future rather than to past events. (In view of the Ghost's description of his disfigurement at 1.5.59–73, it is perhaps worth noting that *eruption* could also refer to a skin condition.)

69–124 It seems curious that the men, in all three texts, seem to recover from the shock of seeing the Ghost and move so quickly to the indirectly related topic of Denmark's preparations for war, though this preoccupation makes the Ghost's reappearance more effective.

69 **Good now** 'An expression of entreaty, *good* being a vocative with the omission of the noun' (Jenkins), i.e. 'good friends' or 'good Horatio'

sit down See 29 and n.

70 **watch** wakefulness, vigilance

71 **toils the subject** imposes toil on the inhabitants

72 **with** Most editors (including Jenkins, who usually favours Q2) adopt Q1/F 'why', assuming ellipsis of 'there is', but *with* makes acceptable sense.

cost The word makes good sense in parallel with *foreign mart* in 73: as Jennens explains, 'They might not have the art of casting cannon; if so, they consequently must buy it.' But many editors (again including Jenkins) prefer F's 'Cast', meaning casting or manufacturing (a unique usage, according to *OED*).

73 **foreign mart** expenditure abroad. Q1 and Q2 agree on the spelling 'forraine' here, and on 'ship-writes' at 74, suggesting that Q2 is following Q1.

65 by] *F;* through *Q1, Staunton*   67 mine] my *Q1F*   72 with] why *Q1F*   cost] *Q1;* Cast *F*   73 foreign] (forraine) *Q1, F* (Forraigne)

Why such impress of shipwrights, whose sore task
Does not divide the Sunday from the week.   75
What might be toward that this sweaty haste
Doth make the night joint labourer with the day?
Who is't that can inform me?

HORATIO   That can I.
At least the whisper goes so. Our last King,
Whose image even but now appeared to us,   80
Was as you know by Fortinbras of Norway –
Thereto pricked on by a most emulate pride –
Dared to the combat, in which our valiant Hamlet
(For so this side of our known world esteemed him)
Did slay this Fortinbras, who by a sealed compact   85
Well ratified by law and heraldry
Did forfeit with his life all these his lands
Which he stood seized of to the conqueror;

---

74 **impress** forced labour, conscription
75 i.e. they work all seven days without the traditional day of rest.
76 **toward** anticipated, in prospect
79 **whisper** rumour. This might suggest that Horatio is not after all speaking from personal knowledge.
79–94 **Our ... Hamlet** It becomes apparent at 5.1.135–53 that the events Horatio recounts happened 30 years before the play begins, though one might otherwise suppose that they were recent and that Horatio was old enough to remember them. His confident knowledge of Danish politics here might suggest he is a local, but in the next scene Hamlet greets him as a fellow student on a visit from Wittenberg (see List of Roles, 10n.). One recent production, directed by Trevor Nunn at London's Old Vic in 2004, avoided this problem by transferring these lines to Barnardo.
81 **Fortinbras** See List of Roles, 27n.

82 'incited to it by a competitive sense of honour or self-esteem' (*emulate* is a unique usage according to *OED*)
83 **the combat** i.e. that [famous] single combat
84 **this ... world** i.e. all Europe
85 **sealed compact** sworn agreement; the stress is on the second syllable of *compact*.
86 'thoroughly sanctioned by legal and chivalric conventions' (Q2's 'heraldy' is an obsolete form which also appears at 2.2.394; Dover Wilson and Spencer retain it). Malone quotes Puttenham on 'the Figure of Twinnes': Shakespeare expresses one thing by two substantives'; Wright notes *law and heraldry* as another example of hendiadys (see 67n.).
88 **stood seized of** held in legal possession. Editors regularly explain that this agreement refers to the personal estates of the two kings, not to their entire kingdoms; nevertheless it is a pact that would in some sense disinherit one of their sons.

---

74 shipwrights] *(ship-writes) Q1, F (Ship-wrights)*   83 combat,] *(combat;), Q1 (combate,); Combate.*
F   86 heraldry] *(heraldy), Q1F*   87 these] those *Q1F*   88 of] *Q1; on F*

Against the which a moiety competent
Was gaged by our King, which had return   90
To the inheritance of Fortinbras
Had he been vanquisher, as by the same co-mart
And carriage of the article design
His fell to Hamlet. Now, sir, young Fortinbras,
Of unimproved mettle, hot and full,   95
Hath in the skirts of Norway here and there
Sharked up a list of lawless resolutes
For food and diet to some enterprise

89 **moiety competent** equivalent portion (of land)

90 **gaged** gagèd (disyllabic); wagered
had return was to revert. *Return* (often emended to F's 'return'd') seems misleading if it implies that Fortinbras and his heirs would recover lands they had previously owned.

92 **co-mart** This Q2 reading (a unique word according to *OED*) is defended by Malone and by Caldecott, who offers the analogy of 'co-mates' at *AYL* 2.1.1. It is accepted by Dover Wilson and by Edwards, who usually favours F; the latter calls it 'a nonce-word having something to do with "bargain" '; White dismisses it as having 'a trading purpose not well suited to a royal combat for a province'; some editors (including Jenkins) prefer F's 'Cou'nant' (covenant); Q6 quite sensibly emends by repeating *compact* from 85.

93 **carriage ... design** an obscure phrase (identical in F) which must mean something like 'fulfilment of the agreed terms'. F2 and many editors emend *design* to 'designed'; RP suggests 'articled design' as another graphic possibility.

94 **His fell to** his (land) would be forfeit to

sir Perhaps Horatio directs his speech primarily to Marcellus, whose question he is answering.

95 **unimproved mettle** untried or perhaps undisciplined spirit; 'untried' allows for a pun on 'metal' (see 3.2.106n.), and the assumption may be that Fortinbras is eager to *prove* his *mettle*. Shakespeare does not use *unimproved* elsewhere and *OED* lists this as a unique usage; Q1's 'inapproved' gives the easier meaning 'unproven'.

96 **skirts** outskirts, distant parts (with a derogatory overtone)

97 **Sharked up** seized (in a predatory way). Klein points out that *Sharked* begins a series of metaphors from eating, being followed by *food and diet* in 98 and *stomach* in 99.
list quantity or troop
lawless F's 'Landlesse' indicates an army of younger sons rather than one of (potential) criminals. Jenkins points out that the followers of Fortinbras are not particularly *lawless* when they do appear and suggests that it is Laertes who, in 4.5, fulfils this idea of a revenging son accompanied by an unruly mob.
resolutes resolved (but desperate?) men

90 return] return'd *F*   92 co-mart] *(*comart*);* Cou'nant *F;* compact *Q6*   93 article design] *F;* articles deseign *Q3;* article design'd *F2;* articles design'd *Pope*   95 unimproved] *F;* inapproued *Q1*   97 lawless] *Q1;* Landlesse *F*

That hath a stomach in't, which is no other,
As it doth well appear unto our state,   100
But to recover of us by strong hand
And terms compulsatory those foresaid lands
So by his father lost. And this, I take it,
Is the main motive of our preparations,
The source of this our watch, and the chief head   105
Of this post-haste and rummage in the land.

BARNARDO

I think it be no other but e'en so.
Well may it sort that this portentous figure
Comes armed through our watch so like the King

99 **stomach** appetite (i.e. the *resolutes* will serve as fodder for the enterprise). Dowden suggests 'For food and diet' means 'paid only by what they eat', but notes that the lack of a comma after *diet* in Q2 and Q1 may mean the *resolutes* are *food* for the *enterprise*.

100 **our state** the Danish authorities

101 **of** from
strong hand close to the literal meaning of 'Fortinbras' (strong in arm)

102 **compulsatory** Both this and F's 'Compulsatiue' are recorded by *OED* as first uses of now obsolete forms of 'compulsory'; Shakespeare does not use the common modern form.

105 **head** source, origin

106 **post-haste** rapid activity, urgency
rummage disturbance, commotion. This word, originally used in the context of arranging or rearranging a ship's cargo, is now obsolete as a noun but still in use as a verb (to search or ransack) and as an adjective in 'rummage sale' (a sale of junk or odds and ends). The spellings in Q2 and F (see t.n.) may suggest a link with the description of events in Rome that follows.

107–24 These lines are printed only in Q2; F-favouring editors such as Edwards and Hibbard argue that Shakespeare intended to delete them, the former on the grounds that this 'is not a strong or necessary speech', the latter arguing that 'they do not advance the action in any way' and were merely intended as an advertisement for Shakespeare's own *Julius Caesar*. That play, probably written just before *Hamlet* in 1599, makes considerable use of the supernatural omens and occurrences related here (see 3.4.99.1n., and Daniell, 87–8). Gielgud, however, makes the point that if these lines are cut the second appearance of the Ghost follows too quickly after the first and fails to surprise the audience (see Gilder, 36).

107 **e'en** even (monosyllabic)

108 **sort** accord (with Horatio's explanation)
portentous in the literal sense: heralding or foreboding some calamity. Hibbard points out that Shakespeare's only other use of the word is at *JC* 1.3.31, where Caska describes the strange sights before the death of Caesar as 'portentous things'.

109 **armed** armèd
through See 65n.

100 As] And *F*   102 compulsatory] Compulsatiue *F*   106 post-haste] *(post hast)*, *F*   rummage] *Q2u (Romeage)*, *Q2c (Romadge)*, *F (Romage)*   107–24] *not in Q1F*   107 e'en so] *(enso)*

That was and is the question of these wars. 110

HORATIO

A mote it is to trouble the mind's eye.
In the most high and palmy state of Rome
A little ere the mightiest Julius fell   Allusion
The graves stood tenantless and the sheeted dead
Did squeak and gibber in the Roman streets; 115
At stars with trains of fire and dews of blood,

110 **question** cause, focus of the dispute
111 **mote** piece of grit or dust. Horatio presumably doesn't mean to underestimate the significance of the Ghost but to see it as a serious cause for concern. Shaheen cites the biblical parable, 'Let me pul out the mote that is in thine eye' (Luke, 6.42) and 'Why seest thou the mote, that is in thy brother's eye?' (Matthew, 7.3).
   mind's eye This instance and Hamlet's line at 1.2.184 are the first uses of this phrase recorded by *OED*, but the basic metaphor is a traditional one in classical, medieval and Renaissance texts.
112 **palmy** flourishing, worthy to 'bear the palm', a traditional symbol of triumph (a Shakespearean coinage, according to *OED*)
114–15 The portents described by Shakespeare's Caska and Cassius on the night before Caesar's death include 'gliding ghosts' and open graves; Calphurnia also recounts a report that 'graves have yawned and yielded up their dead' (*JC* 1.3.63, 74; 2.2.18); Shakespeare is using Plutarch ('Life of Julius Caesar' in North's translation; Bullough 5.83) as his source for this material, but see also note on *doomsday* at 119.
114 **sheeted** dressed in the winding sheets in which they had been buried
115 **Did . . . gibber** made inarticulate noises (perhaps evoking those made by bats).

Spencer asserts the 'g' in *gibber* is hard as in 'give', but *OED* admits 'jibber' as an alternative though more rare spelling and this has become the more common modern pronunciation.
116 *****At stars** Q2's 'As starres' seems to begin a grammatical construction which is never finished; it could be interpreted loosely as meaning 'people also observed stars . . .', but the Oxf emendation is neat and plausible. Jennens in 1773 was the first editor to print a row of asterisks between 115 and 116, suggesting that a line 'somewhat like *Tremendous prodigies in heav'n appeared*' had been mistakenly omitted. MacDonald suggests inserting line 121 between 115 and 116; Spencer suggests inserting 121–5 between 115 and 116; Rolfe suggests inserting a line from *JC* (2.2.19): 'Fierce fiery warriors fight upon the clouds.'
   trains . . . blood The stars are seen as having luminous tails like comets, and as being either spotted with blood or drizzling blood; see the 'fiery warriors' in the sky in Calphurnia's report which 'drizzled blood upon the Capitol' (*JC* 2.2.21). Dew was formerly regarded as something which fell from the sky and could be harmful: see Titinius' despairing cry 'Clouds, dews and dangers come; our deeds are done!' (*JC* 5.3.64).

111 mote] *(moth)* 114 tenantless] *(tennatlesse)* 116 At] *Oxf;* As *Q2*

Disasters in the sun; and the moist star
Upon whose influence Neptune's empire stands
Was sick almost to doomsday with eclipse.
And even the like precurse of feared events,   120
As harbingers preceding still the fates
And prologue to the omen coming on,
Have heaven and earth together demonstrated
Unto our climatures and countrymen.

Enter GHOST.

But soft, behold, lo where it comes again;   125
I'll cross it though it blast me. Stay, illusion.
It spreads his arms.
If thou hast any sound or use of voice,

---

117 **Disasters** in a literal sense: unfavourable aspects of a star or planet .

117–18 **the moist ... stands** i.e. the moon, controller of the tides, called 'governess of floods' at *MND* 2.1.103

118 **Neptune** Roman god of the sea

119 **almost to doomsday** almost as if it were the end of the world (the Day of Judgement when the prophesied second coming of Christ would be heralded or accompanied by eclipses. As Shaheen points out, the use of the word *doomsday* suggests biblical parallels for this speech in addition to the classical ones, notably Matthew, 27.52 ('And the graues did open themselues, and many bodies of the Saints which slept, arose'), and Acts, 2.19 ('Wonders in heaven above, and tokens in the earth beneath').

120 **precurse** precursor(s), warning signs; the sole example of this word given by *OED*
*feared Q2's 'feare' is generally thought to be a misreading of 'feard'. Tronch-Pérez, however, retains 'fear' as a noun modifying

events and cites *AC* 1.3.101–2, 'Upon your sword / Sit laurel victory', as a similar construction.

121 **harbingers** literally, those who go before to prepare the way
still always

122 **omen** strictly, 'sign of a terrible event', but it must mean the terrible event itself here

124 **climatures** climes, regions

124.1 The doubly disturbing effect of having a Ghost appear twice is something Shakespeare repeats effectively with Banquo in *Mac* 3.4.

125 **soft** enough, be quiet

126 **cross it** cross its path, impede its progress (also suggests 'make the sign of the cross', a traditional way of attempting to ward off the supernatural)
blast blight, destroy

126 SD Q2's version seems most likely to refer to the Ghost, though from Q6 onwards the question has been raised as to whether *It* refers to Horatio, who perhaps stretches out his arms in his attempt to *cross* the Ghost.

---

120 feared] *Parrott-Craig (Collier)*; feare *Q2*; fearce *Q3*   126 SD] *opp. 126–7; not in Q1F; He spreads his arms. Q6*   128–9] *Pope; one line Q2F*

Speak to me.
If there be any good thing to be done
That may to thee do ease and grace to me,   130
Speak to me.
If thou art privy to thy country's fate
Which happily foreknowing may avoid,
O, speak.
Or if thou hast uphoarded in thy life   135
Extorted treasure in the womb of earth –
For which they say your spirits oft walk in death –
Speak of it, stay and speak.   *The cock crows.*
                     Stop it, Marcellus!

MARCELLUS
Shall I strike it with my partisan?

HORATIO
Do, if it will not stand.

BARNARDO   'Tis here.

HORATIO   'Tis here.   [*Exit Ghost.*]

---

132 **art privy to** have private knowledge of
  fate destiny (implicitly ominous here)
133 **happily** (1) perhaps; (2) fortunately
  foreknowing advance knowledge
135 **uphoarded** hoarded up, accumulated
136 **Extorted** wrongfully obtained
  womb of earth The earth is seen
  (ironically) as a burying place as well as a
  place of origin: the fact that *womb* rhymes
  with 'tomb' is perhaps one reason why this
  figure is so familiar; see 'The earth that's
  nature's mother is her tomb: / What is her
  burying grave, that is her womb' (*RJ*
  2.3.9–10).
137 **your** an indefinite version of the possessive
  like *your philosophy* (see 1.5.166 and n.)
  and 'your water is a sore decayer of
  your whoreson dead body' (5.1.161–2);
  perhaps more informal than F's 'you' (see

Hope 1.3.2b).
138 SD John Ward's promptbook (see 29n.)
  has 'one Ready to Crow' as a 'warning
  entry' some 30 lines before this SD
  (Thompson, 'Ward', 144); modern
  productions normally use a recorded sound
  effect, but an actor was used to mimic the
  sound at the London Globe in 2000.
139 **partisan** long-handled spear or halberd.
  (The metaphorical sense of 'adherent' or
  'party member' also occurs in the sixteenth
  century, though not in Shakespeare.)
140 **stand** i.e. stay to be questioned
140–1 **'Tis ... gone** Many nineteenth- and
  twentieth-century productions have made
  use of sound effects or even multiple
  ghosts to enhance the impression that the
  Ghost is ubiquitous (see Rosenberg;
  Hapgood).

130–1] *Q1; one line F*   133–4] *one line Q1F*   137 your] you *Q1F*   138 SD] *opp. 137–8; not in Q1F*
139 it] at it *F*   140 SD] *Sisson; opp.* ¹heere *Q1; opp. 141 F*

MARCELLUS

'Tis gone.   141
We do it wrong being so majestical
To offer it the show of violence,
For it is as the air, invulnerable,
And our vain blows malicious mockery.   145

BARNARDO

It was about to speak when the cock crew.

HORATIO

And then it started like a guilty thing
Upon a fearful summons. I have heard
The cock that is the trumpet to the morn
Doth with his lofty and shrill-sounding throat   150
Awake the god of day and, at his warning,
Whether in sea or fire, in earth or air,
Th'extravagant and erring spirit hies
To his confine – and of the truth herein
This present object made probation.   155

---

142 **being so majestical** i.e. given that its (the Ghost's) behaviour is so much that of 'the majesty of buried Denmark'. Woudhuysen points out that Shakespeare uses the more archaic form *majestical* in his plays up to and including *Hamlet*, thereafter using 'majestic' (in *LLL* 5.1.11n.).

145 **malicious mockery** a derisory show, or mere imitation of hostility

147–8 **And . . . summons** a sort of retrospective stage direction for the Ghost's actions at 137

148–54 **I . . . confine** Puck expresses a similar belief at *MND* 3.2.378–87, distinguishing between ghosts of those who have been buried in churchyards and 'damned spirits' who have not received proper funerals (see Greenblatt's discussion of this distinction in *Purgatory*, 162).

149 **trumpet** trumpeter, herald

151 **god of day** the sun-god, Phoebus Apollo in classical mythology. In the next speech Shakespeare indicates that the characters are Christians; this mixture of classical and Christian allusions was common at the time (see 119n. and 1.5.33 and n.).

152 **sea . . . air** the four elements, according to contemporary science

153 **extravagant and erring** wandering beyond its proper bounds. *OED* lists this as the first use of *extravagant* in this sense.
hies hurries, hastens

154 **confine** (1) proper home; (2) place of confinement

154–5 **of . . . probation** (*probation* has four syllables); 'this recent sight proves the truth of that supposition'.

---

149 morn] day *F*; morning *Q1*   150 shrill-sounding] *(*shrill sounding*). F;* shrill crowing *Q1*

MARCELLUS

It faded on the crowing of the cock.
Some say that ever 'gainst that season comes
Wherein our Saviour's birth is celebrated
This bird of dawning singeth all night long,
And then, they say, no spirit dare stir abroad,   160
The nights are wholesome, then no planets strike,
No fairy takes, nor witch hath power to charm,
So hallowed and so gracious is that time.

HORATIO

So have I heard and do in part believe it.
But look, the morn in russet mantle clad   165

---

157 **gainst** just before, in anticipation of
    that season i.e. late December, in the Christian calendar (see 6n.). Despite the fact that Marcellus seems to be saying that ghosts cannot *walk abroad* at this time, earlier editors sometimes took his words as an indication that the play begins in midwinter; this, however, gave them a problem with the flowers Ophelia distributes in 4.5, and those she is said to pick in 4.7.

159 **This . . . dawning** the cock, as at 138 SD and 156

160 **dare stir abroad** i.e. dare move beyond its *confine* (154); Spencer finds F's 'walke' more appropriate, but Edwards follows Q2 and uses these variants to illustrate 'how Shakespeare's language was progressively weakened' in the process of textual transmission (Edwards, 29–30).

161 **wholesome** Night air was usually thought of as unhealthy: see *JC* 2.1.264–5, where Portia upbraids Brutus that he should 'steal out of his wholesome bed / To dare the vile contagion of the night'.
    strike exert evil or destructive influences

162 **No fairy takes** no supernatural being has

effective power. MacDonald asks, 'Does it mean "carries off any child, leaving a changeling" or "affect with evil", as a disease might infect or *take*?' He prints F's 'talkes' but, despite the fact that Q2's usage of *take* without an object is unique, almost all other editors prefer it.

163 **hallowed** made holy, sanctified

164 **and . . . it** Horatio continues to be characterized as slightly sceptical about ghost-lore in general, though he now believes in this one.

165–6 The cock has duly heralded the dawn which is visible 165 lines after the scene began around midnight. This would not have been a problem on the non-illusionist Elizabethan stage but raises questions for modern lighting designers. The movement from midnight to dawn is even swifter in *MA* 5.3, where there are only nine lines between the appeal to 'Midnight' to 'assist our moan' (16) and the observation that 'the gentle day . . . Dapples the drowsy east with spots of grey' (25–7). These two lines were transferred to Horatio's closing speech, after Hamlet's death, in Peter Brook's 2000 production.

---

157 say] *Q1;* sayes *F*   159 This] The *Q1F*   160 dare stir] dare walke *Q1;* can walke *F*   162 takes] *Q1;* talkes *F*   163 that] *Q1;* the *F*

Walks o'er the dew of yon high eastward hill.
Break we our watch up and by my advice
Let us impart what we have seen tonight
Unto young Hamlet, for upon my life
This spirit dumb to us will speak to him.   170
Do you consent we shall acquaint him with it
As needful in our loves, fitting our duty?

MARCELLUS

Let's do't, I pray, and I this morning know
Where we shall find him most convenient.   *Exeunt.*

1.2   *Flourish. Enter* Claudius, KING *of Denmark,*
Gertrude *the* QUEEN, *Council – as* POLONIUS *and his son*
LAERTES [*and*] HAMLET, *with others* [*including* VOLTEMAND
and CORNELIUS].

166 **eastward** Hibbard prefers F's 'Easterne'
which is found elsewhere in Shakespeare
(especially in relation to the dawn), but RP
points out that 'eastward ho' was common
currency in Thames boatmen's English.

167 **Break . . . up** let us bring our guard duty to
an end

by my advice i.e. I suggest

169 **young Hamlet** the first mention of the play's
hero, assumed to be the son of the deceased
king, *our valiant Hamlet* (83), as *young
Fortinbras* (94) is the son of the deceased
King of Norway (see List of Roles, 1n.).

174 **convenient** The adjectival form was
acceptable as an adverb at the time: see
Blake, 5.1.2.1.

1.2 The three texts: this scene runs to 169 lines
in Q1 (scene 2), 256 lines in Q2 and 255
lines in F. The King's opening speech in Q1
begins at what is line 27 in Q2/F, omitting
his announcement of his marriage to the

dead King's widow. Many subsequent
speeches are shorter in Q1, notably the
King's conversation with Leartes (*sic*) and
his father at 42–63, his speech to Hamlet at
87–117 and Hamlet's soliloquy at 129–59.
Location and timing: while there would
have been minimal changes of props on
stage at the Globe (perhaps two thrones
would have been brought on for the King
and Queen), the assumption is that this
scene takes place in a formal, indoor Court
setting. From the arrival of Horatio,
Marcellus and Barnardo at 159.1 we may
deduce that this is the day after the night
represented in 1.1, but time is moving
quickly: they say they will seek Hamlet
this morning (1.1.173), but at 166 he greets
them with *Good even* (see n.).

0.1 ***Flourish*** a fanfare of trumpets to announce
the entry of the King

CLAUDIUS This entry direction and the

166 eastward] Easterne *F*   173 Let's] *Q1;* Let *F*   174 convenient] conueniently *Q1F*   **1.2**] *F (Scena
Secunda.); not in Q21*   0.1 *Flourish] not in Q1F*   0.1–3 Claudius . . . HAMLET] *King, Queene, Hamlet,
Leartes, Corambis, and the two Ambassadors Q1; Claudius King of Denmarke, Gertrude the Queene,
Hamlet, Polonius, Laertes, and his Sister Ophelia F*   0.2 Gertrude] *F; Gertrad Q2*   Council – as]
(Counsaile: as)   0.3 *and] this edn*   with others] *(Cum Alijs); with Attendants Q1; Lords Attendant F*
0.3–4 including . . . CORNELIUS] *Riv; and the two Ambassadors Q1*

KING

> Though yet of Hamlet our dear brother's death
> The memory be green, and that it us befitted
> To bear our hearts in grief, and our whole kingdom
> To be contracted in one brow of woe,
> Yet so far hath discretion fought with nature   5
> That we with wisest sorrow think on him
> Together with remembrance of ourselves.

---

first speech prefix are the only times the King is named in Q2; his name is never used in the dialogue and he is simply *King* in all subsequent directions and prefixes: see List of Roles, 3n. (F is even more sparing with the name, using it only in this entry direction.)

0.2 GERTRUDE See List of Roles, 4n.

Council – **as** councillors – namely (though Dover Wilson argues Q2's 'Counsaile: as' is an error for 'Councillors')

0.3 HAMLET Q2's entry direction ends with '*Hamlet, Cum Alijs*', perhaps indicating that he is visibly separated from the King and Queen by this as well as by his mourning clothes; in F he is listed immediately after his mother and stepfather.

others Q2's '*Alijs*' must include the ambassadors, Cornelius and Voltemand (unless they are considered as part of the *Council*), since they are addressed at the end of the King's opening speech; F brings them on rather awkwardly after 25. Unlike F, Q2 does not include Ophelia in this entry: she does not speak in this scene in either text, but her silent presence is often significant in productions and films; in Michael Almereyda's 2000 film, for example, Ophelia is present and trying to pass a small package to Hamlet but is prevented by Laertes (Almereyda, 12). F

also specifies '*Lords Attendant*' and it is usual for this scene to be performed as a big public occasion with as many extras as the company can muster.

1–39 The King's opening speech has often been admired as a demonstration of his political skill in (a) putting a positive 'spin' on his own rather delicate position and (b) dealing firmly with the threat from Fortinbras (see Jenkins, LN). He is certainly masterly in his deployment of first person plural pronouns – *our*, *us*, *we* – which slide from the royal 'we' to include the whole Court in his discourse.

2 **that** i.e. consequently

us befitted would have been appropriate for us

3–4 **our ... woe** The King describes the kingdom as being like a person whose face is twisted or contorted in mourning – personifications and synecdoches of this kind are frequent in the play; see 'the majesty of buried Denmark' (1.1.47) and 9n.

5 **discretion ... nature** rational judgement competed with natural emotion

6–7 'our most intense mourning for him has led us to no foolish neglect of ourselves'. Dent (W532) cites 'He is not wise that is not wise for himself' as proverbial. Fortinbras strikes a similar note at 5.2.372: 'with sorrow I embrace my fortune.'

---

1 SP] *Q1F; Claud. Q2*

Therefore our sometime sister, now our Queen,
Th'imperial jointress to this warlike state,
Have we, as 'twere with a defeated joy,   10
With an auspicious and a dropping eye,
With mirth in funeral and with dirge in marriage,
In equal scale weighing delight and dole,
Taken to wife. Nor have we herein barred
Your better wisdoms, which have freely gone   15
With this affair along. For all, our thanks.
Now follows that you know: young Fortinbras,
Holding a weak supposal of our worth
Or thinking by our late dear brother's death
Our state to be disjoint and out of frame –   20

8 **sister** i.e. sister-in-law. The abbreviation was familiar, but the King's use of it at this point raises the suggestion of incest: see 157 and n., and the opening scene of *Cym*, where we are told of the King's desire to match his daughter with 'his wife's sole son' (*Cym* 1.1.5).

9 **jointress** legally, a widow who holds a jointure – a lifetime right in some property. This is not literally true here, but Gertrude was previously 'married to Denmark' in the person of her former husband and the present King is consolidating his position by marrying his predecessor's widow.
warlike See the *warlike form* of the deceased King at 1.1.46. His successor is presumably alluding to the preparations for war described by Marcellus and Horatio at 1.1.69–106.

10–14 **Have ... wife** The predicate of this sentence is separated from the subject by a lengthy parenthesis as the King builds to his climax.

10 **defeated** frustrated, disfigured

11 proverbial: 'To cry with one eye and laugh with the other' (Tilley, E248). See the description of Paulina at the end of *WT* having 'one eye declined for the loss of her

husband, another elevated that the Oracle was fulfilled' (5.2.75–7).

13 'balancing joy against an equivalent quantity of sorrow (*dole*)'

14–16 **Nor ... along** The King reminds his councillors that they have apparently approved of his marriage to his brother's widow and his accession to the throne.

14 **barred** excluded

17–25 The King summarizes the political situation. Editors' glossing of *that you know* in 17 as 'that which you should know', on the grounds that there is no point in the King telling the members of his Council what they know already, seems unnecessarily literal: the audience does need to be told. *That you know* could also be glossed 'a further piece of business which you know needs our attention'.

18 'supposing that our [military] position is weak'

19 **by** because of

20 **disjoint ... frame** The underlying metaphors are from carpentry, but Shakespeare applies them to social and political disruption elsewhere; see 'But let the frame of things disjoint (*Mac*

8 sometime] sometimes *F*   9 to] of *F*   11 an ... a] one ... one *F*   17 know:] *Ard¹ (Walker);* knowe *Q2F*

Co-leagued with this dream of his advantage –
He hath not failed to pester us with message
Importing the surrender of those lands
Lost by his father with all bands of law
To our most valiant brother. So much for him.   25
Now for ourself, and for this time of meeting,
Thus much the business is: we have here writ
To Norway, uncle of young Fortinbras –
Who impotent and bedrid scarcely hears
Of this his nephew's purpose – to suppress   30
His further gait herein, in that the levies,
The lists and full proportions are all made
Out of his subject; and we here dispatch
You, good Cornelius, and you, Voltemand,
For bearers of this greeting to old Norway,   35
Giving to you no further personal power

3.2.16). 'Joint' also picks up *jointress* in 9 above and anticipates Hamlet's 'The time is out of joint' (1.5.186).

21 Fortinbras's erroneous view of Denmark's weakness is accompanied by (*co-leagued with*) a fantasy of his own advancement.
Co-leagued co-leaguèd; Oxf adopts this spelling (which actually appears first in Capell) in order to avoid the suggestion of modern 'colleague' in the more usual 'colleagued'.

22 **He** Fortinbras: the King repeats the subject for the sake of clarity.
message possible as a general term or plural, meaning here 'demands'

23 **Importing . . . of** calling on us to give up

24 **bands** F's 'Bonds' means the same: 'binding agreements'.

28 **Norway . . . Fortinbras** In Norway as in Denmark, the brother of the dead king (*Fortinbras of Norway*, 1.1.81) has apparently succeeded to the throne rather than the son.

29 **impotent** incapable, helpless. The King of Norway refers to his 'sickness, age and impotence' in his message to the Danish King at 2.2.66.

31 **gait** proceeding

31–2 **levies . . . proportions** i.e. the men, money and other resources

32–3 **made / Out of** conscripted or requisitioned for the campaign from among

33 **his subject** those who are subject to him: the people of Norway (see 1.1.71 and n.)

35 **For bearers** as carriers or messengers

21 Co-leagued] *(Coleagued)*, *Capell*; Colleagued *F*   this] the *F*   24 bands] Bonds *F*   25 him.] him. / *Enter Voltemand and Cornelius. F*   29 bedrid] *(bedred)*   33 subject] *F*; subjects *Q5*   34 Voltemand] *F*; *Valtemand Q2*   35 bearers] bearing *F*

To business with the King more than the scope
Of these delated articles allow.
Farewell, and let your haste commend your duty.

CORNELIUS, VOLTEMAND

In that and all things will we show our duty.   40

KING

We doubt it nothing. Heartily farewell.

[*Exeunt Voltemand and Cornelius.*]

And now, Laertes, what's the news with you?
You told us of some suit – what is't, Laertes?
You cannot speak of reason to the Dane
And lose your voice. What wouldst thou beg, Laertes,   45
That shall not be my offer, not thy asking?

37 **To business** to do business, i.e. negotiate
than All three texts read 'then', a common
spelling of *than* in sixteenth-century usage.

38 **these delated articles** these terms or
conditions I am handing over to you. The
King presumably presents or gestures
towards some documents that lay down his
terms.
delated F reads 'dilated': 'Which of these
two is right, I cannot tell. *Dilated* means
expanded and would refer to *the scope*;
delated means *committed* – to them, to
limit them' (MacDonald). On the relation
between these two words in *Ham* and *Oth*,
see Parker, 'Dilation'.

39 **let** . . . **duty** i.e. prove your duty by the
speed with which you accomplish your
mission.

40 SP F attributes this line to Voltemand alone
and Q1 to 'Gent', but *we* occurs in all three
texts, perhaps indicating that both
ambassadors speak together, though this
usually seems awkward in performance
and *we* could merely be inclusive.

41 **We** . . . **nothing** 'We (I) have complete
confidence in you.'

42–50 **And** . . . **Laertes?** Sometimes in
performance Hamlet seems about to
address the King, who deliberately turns
away from him to Laertes; the King may
appear ingratiating by his repetition of
Laertes' name and flattery of his father;
alternatively he may be coaxing a shy
Laertes to speak up.

42, 45 **you, thou** The King mainly uses the
more formal *you* to Laertes and to Hamlet
at 66 and 87–117, while the Queen uses the
more familiar *thou* to Hamlet at 68–73; see
also 1.3.4n.

43 **suit** formal request (literally, what is
sought)

44 **speak of reason** make a reasonable request
the Dane the King of Denmark (see
Hamlet's later declaration that he is *Hamlet
the Dane* at 5.1.247)

45 **lose your voice** not have your request
granted

46 The King claims he will give Laertes what
he wants before he asks for it. Spencer
quotes Isaiah, 65.24: 'Whenever they call,
I will answer them; while they are yet but
thinking how to speak, I will hear them.'

37 than] *(*then*) Q1F*   38 these delated] these dilated *F*; those related *Q1*   40 SP] *(Cor. Vo.); Gent. Q1;
Volt. F*   41 SD] *F (Exit Voltemand and Cornelius.); not in Q21*

The head is not more native to the heart,
The hand more instrumental to the mouth,
Than is the throne of Denmark to thy father.
What wouldst thou have, Laertes?

LAERTES   My dread lord,   50
Your leave and favour to return to France,
From whence though willingly I came to Denmark
To show my duty in your coronation,
Yet now I must confess, that duty done,
My thoughts and wishes bend again toward France   55
And bow them to your gracious leave and pardon.

KING
Have you your father's leave? What says Polonius?

POLONIUS
He hath, my lord, wrung from me my slow leave
By laboursome petition, and at last
Upon his will I sealed my hard consent.   60
I do beseech you give him leave to go.

KING
Take thy fair hour, Laertes, time be thine

47–9 The King flatters Polonius by designating the *throne of Denmark* as merely *instrumental* or serviceable to his wishes.

47 **native** naturally connected with or obliged to

50 **dread** respected, feared

51 **leave and favour** another example of hendiadys which can be unpacked to mean 'the favour of your permission', though Wright is doubtful: see 1.1.67n.

53 Unlike Horatio at 175, Laertes does not mention the funeral of the old king as a motive for his visit in either Q2 or F, though he does in Q1.

55–6 'Although my desires turn towards France, I submit them to your permission.' See the similar association of verbs at *KL* 3.6.106: 'that which makes me bend makes the King bow.'

59 **laboursome petition** See 'Your laboursome and dainty trims' (*Cym* 3.4.164); Shakespeare does not use 'laborious', which has become the standard modern form, though it is recorded by *OED* from 1390.

60 'I gave my hard-won consent to his wishes.' The words *will* and *seal* suggest that Polonius sees his permission as comparable to a legal document.

---

50 My dread] My gratious *Q1;* Dread my *F*   55 toward] for *Q1;* towards *F*   58 He hath] *Q1F;* Hath *Q2*   58–60 wrung . . . consent] wrung from me a forced graunt *Q1; om. F*

And thy best graces spend it at thy will.
But now, my cousin Hamlet, and my son –
HAMLET
A little more than kin, and less than kind.   65
KING
How is it that the clouds still hang on you?
HAMLET
Not so much, my lord, I am too much in the 'son'.
QUEEN
Good Hamlet, cast thy nighted colour off

63 'and may your good qualities (help you to) use the time as you wish'. The King's words can be interpreted as a kind of dismissal and Q1 provides an exit for Leartes at this point; producers and editors of Q2/F have to decide whether to take him off here or leave him onstage until the general *Exeunt* at 128. In some productions (e.g. Gielgud 1936, as recorded in Gilder, 30), the King dismisses the entire Court at this point, rendering 64–128 a more 'private' sequence.

64 **cousin** used loosely in this period to denote a number of kinship relationships more distant than parent, child or sibling
son Hamlet's comment implies that he objects to this word, which the King repeats at 117 (and three more times in Q1).

65 Characteristically, Hamlet's first line is a play on words, indicating that the King is claiming an excess of kinship in designating himself father as well as uncle while acting in a way which could be construed as 'unkind' or unnatural. 'The nearer in kin, the less in kindness' was proverbial (Tilley, K38); Steevens quotes parallels in Thomas Sackville and Thomas Norton's *Gorboduc* (1561), where the Queen remarks to one of her sons, 'A

father? No. / In kind a father, not in kindliness' (1.1), and in Lyly's *Mother Bombie* (1591), where Maestius says to his supposed sister Serena, 'the greater the kindred is, the less the kindness must be' (3.1). Many editors mark this speech as an aside (like Cordelia's first words), and the fact that the King continues with his sentence structure supports this. But it could also be a deliberate piece of rudeness or confrontation – and was played as such by Colin Keith-Johnston in the first modern-dress *Hamlet* staged by Barry Jackson and H.K. Ayliff at the Kingsway theatre in London in 1925 (see Dawson, 88).

67 **'son'** *Eastward Ho* (1605) by George Chapman, Ben Jonson and John Marston, which contains several allusions to *Ham*, includes 'son/sun' puns at 3.2.122–5. See 179–80n. and pp. 58–9.

68 **nighted colour** (1) black (mourning) clothes (see 'Winter'd garments' in *AYL* 3.2.102), (2) mournful behaviour. F's 'nightly' could equally well mean 'night-like', but is rejected by most editors apart from MacDonald and Hibbard (whose commitment to F is greater than that of Edwards).

64] *Exit. Q1, opp. 64*   67 ¹*much] om. F*   in the 'son'] *Cam¹; in the sonne Q2; i'th'Sun F*   68 nighted] nightly *F*

And let thine eye look like a friend on Denmark.
Do not for ever with thy vailed lids   70
Seek for thy noble father in the dust.
Thou knowst 'tis common all that lives must die,
Passing through nature to eternity.

HAMLET
Ay, madam, it is common.

QUEEN   If it be
Why seems it so particular with thee?   75

HAMLET
'Seems', madam – nay it is, I know not 'seems'.
'Tis not alone my inky cloak, cold mother,
Nor customary suits of solemn black,
Nor windy suspiration of forced breath,

---

69 **Denmark** most obviously (1) the King, but possibly (2) the country
70 **vailed lids** vailèd; lowered eyelids. Q2's 'vailed' is more popular with editors than F's 'veyled' (veiled), though the latter is acceptable if we assume that the downcast lids 'veil' the eyes (see Thompson & Thompson, 99–100, 128). The Queen sees in Hamlet's metaphorically downcast (*dropping*, 11) eyes a literal attempt to find his father's body in the ground – the first of the play's many references to the physical facts of corporeal decay: see, for example, 2.2.178–9 and 273–4, 4.3.19–30 and 5.1.154–205.
72–4 **Thou ... common** proverbial: Dent, D142
74 **common** Hamlet again takes up the word and twists it against the speaker; he is sometimes quite aggressive in performance as he turns the Queen's banal statement into an accusation that she has acted in an all too predictable or commonplace way – perhaps even that she has been sexually promiscuous.

77 **not alone** not only. The subsequent list of four parallel items with *nor* between each is a classic example of the rhetorical device of syndeton.
cold mother Q2's reading is preserved in the Restoration and eighteenth-century 'players' quartos' and was presumably spoken by actors, although most editors prefer F's 'good Mother'. Hamlet could be accusing Gertrude of being *cold* in her failure to display grief. Andrews, following Q2, reads 'coold', arguing that Hamlet implies his mother's affection towards him and his father has 'cooled'. Oxf's 'good-mother' is a term for stepmother or mother-in-law, used sarcastically here (and perhaps at 3.2.106 and 3.4.26).
78 **customary suits** conventional garments
79 **suspiration** sighing, breathing deeply
forced This most obviously applies to the *breath* forcibly expelled in sighs, but it could also imply that the sighs are insincere.

---

70 vailed] veyled *F*   72 lives] *F;* live *F2*   77 cold mother] *(*coold mother*);* could smother *Q3, Q4;* good Mother *F;* good-mother *Oxf*

No, nor the fruitful river in the eye,   80
Nor the dejected haviour of the visage,
Together with all forms, moods, shapes of grief,
That can denote me truly. These indeed 'seem',
For they are actions that a man might play,
But I have that within which passes show,   85
These but the trappings and the suits of woe.

KING

'Tis sweet and commendable in your nature, Hamlet,
To give these mourning duties to your father,
But you must know your father lost a father,
That father lost lost his, and the survivor bound   90
In filial obligation for some term
To do obsequious sorrow; but to persever
In obstinate condolement is a course

---

80 **fruitful** copious
81 **dejected haviour** downcast, depressed demeanour
    visage face
82 **moods** This must mean something like shows or outward appearances.
83 ***denote** Q2's 'deuote' is an easy scribal or compositorial mistake – a minim misreading, 'foul case' or turned letter – and does not make sense in the context.
84 **might play** would be able to act
85 See the extended discussion of internal and external grief at *R2* 4.1.276–99.
    passes surpasses. F (unusually) has the more old-fashioned 'passeth'. As Edwards points out, *passes* is easier to say.
86 **trappings** superficial appearances, accoutrements
87–117 The King's speech against 'obstinate condolement' is echoed in a different vein in Feste's 'catechism' of Olivia in *TN* 1.5.63–9.
87 **commendable** The stress is on the first syllable.

90 **bound** was obliged, committed
92 **obsequious** dutiful in regard to the dead (*OED a.* 1b). The adjective, from 'obsequies' (as at 5.1.215), is now more common in its later meaning, 'flattering'.
    persever (stressed on second syllable) persist, continue
93 **condolement** grieving. *OED* cites this and a line in the final speech of John Marston's *Antonio's Revenge* (5.3.174) as the earliest uses of this word; it dates both plays to 1602 (but see p. 52). The case for a Shakespearean coinage is supported by the large number of words ending in '-ment' which appear for the first time in *Hamlet*: Elze noted a few of these in his edition, but a full list would include *blastment* (1.3.41), *entreatment* (1.3.121), *investment* (1.3.127), *impartment* (1.4.59), *distilment* (1.5.64), *encompassment* (2.1.10), *annexment* (3.3.21), *strewment* (5.1.222), *definement* (5.2.98) and *extolment* (5.2.101).

82 moods] *F;* modes *Q9*   shapes] *(chapes), Q3;* shewes *F*   83 denote] *F;* deuote *Q2*   85 passes] passeth *F*

Of impious stubbornness, 'tis unmanly grief,
It shows a will most incorrect to heaven,   95
A heart unfortified, or mind impatient,
An understanding simple and unschooled;
For what we know must be, and is as common
As any the most vulgar thing to sense –
Why should we in our peevish opposition   100
Take it to heart? Fie, 'tis a fault to heaven,
A fault against the dead, a fault to nature,
To reason most absurd, whose common theme
Is death of fathers, and who still hath cried
From the first corpse till he that died today   105
'This must be so.' We pray you throw to earth

94 **impious** irreligious, profane. Klein notes the growth of the King's displeasure in his chain of negative prefixes: *impious, unmanly, incorrect, unfortified, impatient, unschooled.*
   unmanly a prominent concern in the play and in its theatrical and critical history: see 2.2.520n.
95 The assumption is that people should accept death and the timing of it as the will of God. (The King has his own reasons for insisting that this particular death was a natural one, ordained by heaven.)
   incorrect disobedient
96 **unfortified** (with Christian counsel)
   or Jenkins emends to F's 'a' here, presumably on the grounds that 'or' was misread as 'a' (as in *sate/sort* at 1.5.56), but *or* also makes sense.
   impatient not capable of suffering
99 'as the most familiar and obvious thing in the world'
102 **fault to nature** refusal to accept a natural law
103 **whose** i.e. nature's
   theme topic

104 **still** always, incessantly
105 **first corpse** In Judaeo-Christian tradition, the first person to die was Abel, killed by his brother Cain (Genesis, 4.11–12): an unfortunate (and presumably unconscious) reference on the King's part here, but one he returns to consciously at 3.3.37–8 and which Hamlet mentions at 5.1.72–3. This archetypal murder was often in Shakespeare's mind while he was writing his English history plays where civil wars turn relatives against each other: see *1H6* 1.3.39–40, *R2* 1.1.104 and 5.6.43, *2H4* 1.1.155–60 and *KJ* 3.3.79.
106 'This ... so' In Peter Brook's 2000 production, the King repeated these words as he accepted his death-wound in the final scene.
   We ... earth perhaps a subjunctive ('we pray that you may throw to earth'), or more likely an imperative ('we require that you throw to earth')
   throw to earth Hibbard suggests a metaphor from wrestling, but, given the talk of *dust* at 71, the King may be saying 'bury your grief'. The phrase also evokes the Christian burial service 'earth to earth'.

96 or] a *F*   105 corpse] *Oxf;* course *Q2;* Coarse *F*

This unprevailing woe, and think of us
As of a father, for let the world take note
You are the most immediate to our throne,
And with no less nobility of love   110
Than that which dearest father bears his son
Do I impart toward you. For your intent
In going back to school in Wittenberg
It is most retrograde to our desire,
And we beseech you bend you to remain   115
Here in the cheer and comfort of our eye,
Our chiefest courtier, cousin, and our son.

QUEEN

Let not thy mother lose her prayers, Hamlet.

107 **unprevailing** ineffective (*OED*'s first usage)
us The King again uses the royal plural.

109 'you are my heir'. The King seems to be claiming publicly that he has been rightfully elected, but Hamlet implies at 3.4.97–9 and at 5.2.64 that he has *stolen* the crown and that he, Hamlet, should have been king by now rather than crown prince.

110–12 **And ... you**. The construction is awkward (*with* seems redundant), but the King clearly means to claim that he loves Hamlet like a son. Hibbard finds evidence of duplicity in the contorted syntax.

113 **school** university. The assumption is that, like Laertes, and like Horatio at 164–75, Hamlet wishes to continue with the overseas studies he interrupted to attend his father's funeral, his mother's marriage and the new King's coronation. We learn at 5.1.135–53 that Hamlet is 30 – which would make him an unusually mature student by Elizabethan standards. It is Shakespeare's addition to the story to designate all the young men as students – most obviously Hamlet, Horatio, Laertes, Rosencrantz and Guildenstern, but also implicitly Marcellus and Barnardo (see List of Roles).

Wittenberg city in Germany, home of a university founded in 1502 and attended in reality by Martin Luther (who became a member of its staff in 1509 and nailed his famous 95 theses to the door of the Schlosskirke in 1517) and in fiction by Dr Faustus: the town is mentioned several times in Marlowe's *Dr Faustus* (*c.* 1592).

114 **retrograde** contrary (literally, a step backwards; the word could also, in astronomy, refer to the movement of a planet, apparently against the zodiac)

115 **bend ... remain** subordinate your wishes to ours by staying (see the use of *bend* in 55)

117 **cousin** See 64 and n. In this line, *cousin* could be a direct address to Hamlet.

118 **lose her prayers** fail to achieve what she requests

112 toward] towards *F*   you. For] *F*; you for *Q2*   114 retrograde] *(*retrogard*)*, *F*

I pray thee stay with us, go not to Wittenberg.

HAMLET

I shall in all my best obey you, madam.   120

KING

Why, 'tis a loving and a fair reply.
Be as ourself in Denmark. Madam, come –
This gentle and unforced accord of Hamlet
Sits smiling to my heart, in grace whereof
No jocund health that Denmark drinks today   125
But the great cannon to the clouds shall tell
And the King's rouse the heaven shall bruit again,
Re-speaking earthly thunder. Come away.

Flourish. Exeunt all but Hamlet.

HAMLET

O that this too too sallied flesh would melt,

---

119 **pray thee** F has 'prythee' (consistently according to *TxC*, but see 176 and n.). Jackson notes that all the 'good' quartos published up to 1600 show an almost exclusive preference for 'pray thee' over the more colloquial 'prithee', but the latter becomes the norm from Q2 *Hamlet* on. Q2 actually has six 'prithees' to two 'pray thees'.

120 Hamlet pointedly responds to the entreaty of his mother, not that of the King, and employs the more formal *you* (see 42, 45n.).

122 **Be as ourself** behave as if you were king

124 **Sits smiling to** has a happy effect on, pleases

grace thanks, gratitude

125–8 **No … thunder** 'The king's intemperance is very strongly impressed; everything that happens to him gives him occasion to drink' (Johnson).

125 **jocund** joyful

126 **tell** announce, count (or enumerate: see 236n.), i.e. artillery will be fired to mark the occasions. In 1.4.6 SD–12 trumpets and kettledrums are specified as well as *pieces* or guns.

127 **rouse** toast, ceremonial drink, perhaps an abbreviated form of 'carouse'

bruit make a noise, echo

128 **Re-speaking** echoing (*OED*'s first usage)

129–59 Hamlet's first soliloquy reveals pent-up emotion through its exclamations, questions and expressions of pain. See our discussion of the soliloquies on pp. 18–25.

129 **sallied** assailed, besieged[?]. Q1 also reads 'sallied' – 'O that this too much griev'd and sallied flesh'. F's 'solid' provides a more specific sense for *melt* (and see *2H4* 3.1.47–9: 'and the continent, / Weary of solid firmness, melt itself / Into the sea') but which chimes unhappily for some readers with Gertrude's later statement that

---

119 pray thee] prythee *F*   127 heaven] Heauens *F*   128 Re-speaking] *(*Respeaking*)*   SD *Flourish*] *not in Q1F*   129 sallied] *Q1;* solid *F*

Thaw and resolve itself into a dew,   130
Or that the Everlasting had not fixed
His canon 'gainst self-slaughter. O God, God,
How weary, stale, flat and unprofitable
Seem to me all the uses of this world!
Fie on't, ah, fie, 'tis an unweeded garden   135
That grows to seed, things rank and gross in nature

Hamlet is *fat* (see 5.2.269n.). Many editors emend *sallied* to 'sullied', meaning 'contaminated': see the Princess's reference to her 'maiden honour' as an 'unsullied lily' in *LLL* 5.2.351–2, where both Q and F texts read 'unsallied'. MacDonald glosses *sallied* as 'sullied', which, despite his commitment to F, he thinks 'nearer the depth of Hamlet's mood' than *solid*.

melt The idea of annihilation by melting or dissolving also occurs in *R2* ('O that I were a mockery king of snow / ... To melt myself away in water-drops', 4.1.260–2) and in *AC* 'Here I am Antony, / Yet cannot hold this visible shape', 4.14.13–14).

130 **resolve** dissolve

132 **canon** divine law. Noting Pope's spelling 'cannon' here, and the correction to 'canon' in John Hughes's text of 1723, Theobald comments that Shakespeare 'intended the *Injunction*, rather than the *Artillery* of Heaven' (Theobald, *Restored*, 16–17). 'This is an unhappy word to use here. I fear the truth is that the noise of the cannon in the king's speech [126] was still ringing in the Poet's ears' (Hunter, 2.218). Caldecott observes that '*ordinance*, which has the same sense as *canon*, differs also from *ordnance*, or artillery in one letter only; and this difference in pronunciation is no way felt.' Booth picks up the canon/cannon echo as an example of the 'casual,

substantively inconsequential relationships among words and ideas in Shakespeare' whose 'undelivered meanings' contribute to the richness of the effect (Booth, 43).

*self-slaughter Q2's 'seale slaughter' is clearly erroneous. There is no specific biblical prohibition of suicide, although the sixth commandment, against murder, would cover it. Imogen also believes that 'Against self-slaughter / There is a prohibition so divine / That cravens my weak hand' (*Cym* 3.4.75–7). For Shakespeare, this was clearly a major difference between Christian and pagan belief systems: see 5.1.1–29, and Edgar's attempts to cure his father's despair in *KL*, and contrast the heroic suicides at the end of *JC* and *AC*.

134 **uses** doings, in the sense of opportunities or activities

135 **Fie** a strong exclamation of shock, reproach, disgust

135–7 **'tis . . . merely** Dent cites 'Weeds come forth on the fattest soil if it is untilled' as proverbial (W241). For other examples of the neglected garden as a metaphor for social disorder, see *R2* 3.4.29–47 and *H5* 5.2.31–67.

136 **rank** excessively (offensively) vigorous in growth; see other uses of *rank* and *ranker* at 2.1.20, 3.2.250, 3.3.36, 3.4.90 and 150 and 4.4.21.

in nature probably 'in their own beings' rather than 'as they occur in nature'

132 self-slaughter] *F;* seale slaughter *Q2*   God, God,] God, O God! *F*   133 weary] (wary*), F*   134 seem] Seemes *F*   135 ah, fie] Oh fie, fie *F*

Possess it merely. That it should come thus:
But two months dead – nay not so much, not two –
So excellent a king, that was to this
Hyperion to a satyr, so loving to my mother   140
That he might not beteem the winds of heaven
Visit her face too roughly. Heaven and earth,
Must I remember? Why, she should hang on him
As if increase of appetite had grown
By what it fed on. And yet within a month   145
(Let me not think on't – Frailty, thy name is Woman),

137 **merely** completely, absolutely
   come thus work out this way. Apart from
   Pope, most editors prefer F's 'come to
   this'.
138 **two months** Ophelia claims it is *twice two
   months* since the death of Hamlet's father
   at 3.2.121: in the light of Hamlet's
   reduction of the time to *A little month* at
   147, it is easier to suppose that he is being
   deliberately inaccurate here in order to
   exaggerate how quickly his father has been
   forgotten than to suppose that there is a
   two-month gap between these scenes.
139 **to this** compared to this (his uncle, the new
   king)
140 **Hyperion** Greek god of the sun. Spencer
   notes resignedly that, because of the
   influence of this line and Hamlet's later
   reference at 3.4.54, the customary English
   pronunciation has become 'high-peer-i-on'
   rather than the arguably more correct
   'hipper-eye-on' or 'highper-eye-on'.
   satyr grotesque creature, half human and
   half goat. Satyrs were companions of
   Bacchus/Dionysus in classical mythology
   and hence associated with drunkenness and
   lechery.
141 **might not** did not have the strength (*might*)
   to. Hope (2.1.2b) points out the shift from
   this sense of 'may' in Early Modern
   English to one meaning permission or

possibility in Present-day English, but it
still seems awkward with *beteem*.
   beteem allow, permit. 'The context insists
   on this meaning, but it is a strained usage
   of a rare word' (Edwards). Shakespeare's
   only other use of *beteem* is in *MND*, where
   Hermia says the roses in her cheeks lack
   rain 'which I could well / Beteem them
   from the tempest of my eyes' (1.1.130–1);
   in this case it has the more normal meaning
   of 'grant' or 'afford'.
143 **should** Q2's reading implies admonition,
   where F's implies habitual action.
144–5 **As . . . on** as if her desire for him had
   increased by being satisfied. 'Appetite
   comes with eating' was proverbial (Dent,
   A286). Sexual desire is frequently seen as
   'appetite' in Shakespeare (see *TN* 1.1.1–4
   and 2.4.94–102, *AC* 2.2.246–8), but in this
   context the metaphor may prefigure
   Hamlet's obsession with the literal
   consumption of the dead by worms (see
   2.2.178–9 and 4.3.19–30).
146 **Frailty . . . Woman** i.e. women embody or
   personify frailty or lack of constancy: a
   standard   misogynistic   attitude   of
   Shakespeare's time and proverbial (Dent,
   W700.1), but see *MM* 2.4.121–86, where
   Isabella, admitting that women are 'ten
   times frail', nevertheless rejects Angelo's
   advances.

137 merely.] *F;* meerely *Q2*   thus] to this *F*   141 beteem] beteene *F;* let e'en *Theobald*   143 should]
would *Q1F*

A little month, or e'er those shoes were old
With which she followed my poor father's body,
Like Niobe, all tears. Why, she –
O God, a beast that wants discourse of reason   150
Would have mourned longer – married with my uncle,
My father's brother (but no more like my father
Than I to Hercules). Within a month,
Ere yet the salt of most unrighteous tears
Had left the flushing in her galled eyes,   155
She married. O most wicked speed! To post

147 **or . . . old** The assumption must be that the Queen's shoes were made of cloth or perhaps very fine leather, as worn by Elizabethan Court ladies indoors, and consequently quite fragile; more substantial shoes worn outdoors by ordinary people would not have been considered *old* after *a month* or *two months*.

or e'er even before (literally, 'before ever'); see 182.

149 **Niobe** Greek mythical figure who mourned for the deaths of her children until she was turned into a weeping stone statue; see Ovid, *Metamorphoses*, 6.146–312 (Latin text); 6.184–395 (Golding).

she F follows *she* with *even she*, seen by Jenkins as an actor's interpolation, though it does make the line metrically regular (see 223n.).

150 **God** F's 'Heauen' may be expurgation (as at 194), following the 1606 'Act to Restrain Abuses of Players'; see Appendix 2 and Taylor, 'Swounds'.

discourse of reason process or faculty of reasoning. *OED* lists uses of this formulaic phrase from 1413.

153 **Hercules** At this point, Hamlet sees himself as quite unlike this mythical hero, famous for his twelve superhuman

'labours' which included killing the many-headed Hydra and relieving Atlas of his burden, the globe, while Atlas stole the golden apples of the Hesperides (see Appendix 1 for Hamlet's later reference to this in the Folio text). Later, he seems prepared to vie with Hercules (see 1.4.83). The story of Amleth as told by Saxo Grammaticus ends with a complimentary version of the same comparison: 'Had fortune been as kind to [Amleth] as nature, he would have equalled the gods in glory, and surpassed the labours of Hercules by his deeds of prowess' (Bullough 7.79); in his more prolix version, Belleforest compares Hamblet with Hercules twice (Bullough 7.118, 123). Miola (*Tragedy*) argues, however, that Shakespeare may be drawing on Seneca's *Hercules Furens* (see p. 72).

154 **unrighteous** false, wicked

155 **flushing** redness. *OED* gives this example under 'flushing' (*sb.* 2) meaning 'a sudden flowing of blood to the face', though the word can also mean 'a rushing of water', which perhaps goes better with F's 'flushing of'.

galled gallèd: irritated, sore

156 **post** move quickly, hurry

147 e'er] *(ere) F*   149 she –] *(she);* she, euen she. *F*   150 God] *Q1;* Heauen *F*   151 my] mine *F* 155 in] *Q1;* of *F*

With such dexterity to incestuous sheets,
It is not, nor it cannot come to good;
But break, my heart, for I must hold my tongue.

Enter HORATIO, MARCELLUS *and* BARNARDO.

HORATIO
Hail to your lordship.

HAMLET   I am glad to see you well –   160
Horatio, or I do forget myself.

HORATIO
The same, my lord, and your poor servant ever.

HAMLET
Sir, my good friend, I'll change that name with you.

---

157 **incestuous**] For a man to marry his
brother's wife was forbidden by Judaeo-
Christian tradition (Leviticus, 18.16 and
20.21; Book of Common Prayer, 'Table of
Kindred and Affinity'). The audience
would presumably be aware that Henry
VIII had gained papal permission to do
just this when he married Katherine of
Aragon (widow of his brother Arthur),
though he subsequently claimed it was a
sin after all when he wished to marry Anne
Boleyn (mother of Queen Elizabeth),
thereby precipitating the English
Reformation (Shakespeare and John
Fletcher were later to dramatize this event
in *Henry VIII*). Interestingly, the Queen in
Fratricide Punished (see pp. 46–7)
mentions a papal dispensation for her
second marriage in the equivalent of the
closet scene (3.6; Bullough, 7.145–6).
Within *Hamlet*, only Hamlet and the Ghost
seem concerned about the charge of incest
(see 1.5.42 and 83); the King himself, for

example, does not list it among his sins in
his attempt to pray in 3.3; the Queen sees
her second marriage as merely 'hasty'
(2.2.57) and the councillors have
apparently 'gone along' with it (15–16).

158 **nor it cannot** an emphatic double negative
(Hope, 2.1.9)

159 **break, my heart** See 5.2.343, 'Now cracks
a noble heart', and *R2* 2.1.228, 'My heart is
great, but it must break with silence.' The
metaphor is biblical: see instances
especially from the Psalms in Spencer, who
notes 'The modern use of the phrase as
referring sentimentally to amorous
disappointment came much later.'

159.1 BARNARDO This is the only time Q2
spells the name 'Bernardo'.

160–1 Hamlet at first offers an impersonal
general greeting, perhaps because he is still
preoccupied with his own thoughts, then he
recognizes Horatio.

163 **change . . . you** i.e. you are my friend, not
my servant.

160–1 I . . . myself] *F; one line Q2; prose Q1*   162–3] *prose Q1; F lines* Lord, / euer. / friend, / you: /

And what make you from Wittenberg, Horatio?
Marcellus!

MARCELLUS   My good lord.   165

HAMLET

  I am very glad to see you. [*to Barnardo*] Good even,
    sir. –

  But what in faith make you from Wittenberg?

HORATIO

  A truant disposition, good my lord.

HAMLET

  I would not hear your enemy say so,
  Nor shall you do my ear that violence   170
  To make it truster of your own report
  Against yourself. I know you are no truant;
  But what is your affair in Elsinore?
  We'll teach you for to drink ere you depart.

HORATIO

  My lord, I came to see your father's funeral.   175

---

164 **make you from** are you doing away from. Hamlet turns aside to greet Marcellus before receiving Horatio's response at 168. In all three texts it is slightly puzzling that Horatio, who seemed to have an insider's knowledge of Danish politics at 1.1.78–106, now seems to be on a brief and unsanctioned (*truant* in 168) visit from the university in Wittenberg. It is also surprising that Hamlet has not been aware of his presence before this moment if he has been at court since the funeral, two months or more ago (see List of Roles, 10n.).

166 **Good even, sir** presumably addressed to Barnardo, whom Hamlet does not recognize
    even evening/afternoon (used at any time after midday)

167 **in faith** in truth, really

168 **truant** time-wasting, delinquent

good my lord a particularly deferential form of address (Blake, 8.1.4) conveying apology in this case. See also 2.2.460; 3.1.89; 3.2.288, 300, 306 and 328; 5.1.254 and 5.2.91.

169 **hear** F's 'haue' avoids the *hear* / *ear* internal rhyme. The meaning is the same: 'I would not let even your enemy say such a thing without objecting.'

170–2 **Nor . . . yourself**. 'you won't make me believe your statement which slanders yourself.'

170 another *ear* metaphor: see 1.1.30 and n.

173 **Elsinore** modern Helsingor; the first mention of the play's specific location

174 Hamlet deplores the Danish custom of heavy drinking at 1.4.13–38, so perhaps this is spoken ironically.
    for to drink to drink deeply; editors (including Jenkins) prefer Q1/F's 'to drinke deepe'.

---

166 SD] *White*   169 hear] haue *F*   170 my] mine *F*   174 for to drink] to drinke deepe *Q1F*

HAMLET

I prithee do not mock me, fellow student,
I think it was to see my mother's wedding.

HORATIO

Indeed, my lord, it followed hard upon.

HAMLET

Thrift, thrift, Horatio, the funeral baked meats
Did coldly furnish forth the marriage tables.   180
Would I had met my dearest foe in heaven
Or ever I had seen that day, Horatio.
My father, methinks I see my father.

HORATIO

Where, my lord?

HAMLET   In my mind's eye, Horatio.

---

176 **prithee** F's 'pray thee' is unusual (see 119
and n.).
   student Jenkins sees in the shared spelling
   'student' evidence of Q2 following Q1,
   but Hibbard argues that 'student' was a
   common Elizabethan spelling. (They also
   disagree about 'gelly' at 204.)
177 *****see** omitted in Q2 but necessary for both
   sense and metre
178 **followed hard upon** happened very
   quickly afterwards
179 **Thrift** At 3.2.57–8 Hamlet expresses
   contempt for people who 'crook the
   pregnant hinges of the knee / Where thrift
   may follow fawning', and at 3.2.176–7 the
   Player Queen asserts that '*The instances
   that second marriage move / Are base
   respects of thrift, but none of love.*' In a
   highly political production performed in
   Bucharest in 1989, the Romanian
   translation of *thrift* as 'economia' was
   received as an attack on the Communist
   dictator Ceauşescu, who used this term for
   austerity measures imposed on the people
   while indulging in a lavish lifestyle himself

(see Stříbrný, 134).
179–80 **the . . . tables** i.e. the leftovers of the
   food cooked for the funeral were available
   to be served cold for the wedding (*meat*, as
   in Old English, could and still can mean
   'food' in a general sense). Hamlet again
   exaggerates to make his point, having
   already claimed that his father had been
   dead for *But two months* (138 and n.) and
   that (at least) *A little month* passed before
   the wedding (147). This statement is
   parodied twice in *Eastward Ho* (see 67n.
   and pp. 58–9).
181 **dearest** most significant, most bitter (see
   AYL 1.3.31, 'my father hated his father
   dearly'). This line is a curious way of
   intensifying 'I would rather have died'; it
   anticipates Hamlet's reluctance in 3.3 to
   send the King to heaven.
182 **Or ever** See 147 and n.
184 **Where, my lord** Horatio and Marcellus
   sometimes look around in alarm at this
   point, assuming Hamlet is literally seeing
   the Ghost.
   mind's eye see 1.1.111 and n.

---

176 prithee] *(*prethee*), Q1 (*pre thee*); pray thee *F*   student] *(*student*) Q1, F (*Student*)   177 see] *Q1F; not
in Q2*   182 Or . . . had] Ere euer I had *Q1;* Ere I had euer *F*   184 Where] *Q1;* Oh where *F*

HORATIO

I saw him once – 'a was a goodly king.   185

HAMLET

'A was a man, take him for all in all,
I shall not look upon his like again.

HORATIO

My lord, I think I saw him yesternight.

HAMLET

Saw, who?

HORATIO   My lord, the King your father.

HAMLET

The King my father?   190

HORATIO

Season your admiration for a while
With an attent ear till I may deliver
Upon the witness of these gentlemen
This marvel to you.

HAMLET   For God's love let me hear!

HORATIO

Two nights together had these gentlemen,   195

---

185 **I . . . once** This again raises the question of Horatio's age: see 1.1.79–94 and n., and 210 below.

186 **a man** Clearly Hamlet regards his father as an ideal of manhood; see Antony's eulogy of the dead Brutus: 'Nature might stand up / And say to all the world, "This was a man!" ' (*JC* 5.5.74–5).

188 **yesternight** last night. This and similar expressions – 'yestereve', 'yestermorn', 'yesteryear' – now survive only in poetic or archaic uses, unlike 'yesterday'.

189 **Saw, who?** For punctuation, see t.n. Modern performers usually make this a

question, as in Q6.

191 **Season** moderate, qualify
admiration wonder, astonishment

192 **attent** attentive. It is a little illogical that an *ear* should *season . . . admiration*, but Horatio is saying, 'Stop exclaiming at the wonder and listen to the full story.'
deliver communicate, express

195–8 **had . . . encountered** Blake notes that the formulation could be either active, 'these gentlemen had encountered something', or passive, 'something had appeared to these gentlemen' (Blake, 4.3.9a).

---

185 'a] he *Q1F*   goodly] *F*; gallant *Q1*   186 'A] He *Q1F*   189 Saw, who?] *Q1*; Saw? Who? *F*; Saw who? *Q6*   194 God's] *Q1*; Heauens *F*

Marcellus and Barnardo, on their watch
In the dead waste and middle of the night
Been thus encountered: a figure like your father
Armed at point, exactly cap-à-pie,
Appears before them and with solemn march   200
Goes slow and stately by them; thrice he walked
By their oppressed and fear-surprised eyes
Within his truncheon's length whilst they, distilled
Almost to jelly with the act of fear,
Stand dumb and speak not to him. This to me   205
In dreadful secrecy impart they did,

197 **dead waste** lifeless desolation. The Q1
reading (see t.n.) has been adopted by some
editors (Cam, Dowden, Kittredge) in place
of Q2 and F's 'wast'; they usually cite
Prospero's reference to 'that vast of night'
(*Tem* 1.2.328) to support their case. Other
editors who do not adopt 'vast' feel obliged
to discuss it (Jenkins, Edwards, Hibbard).
As Edwards notes, the meaning is much
the same (but *waste* allows a pun on 'waist'
= middle).

199 **at point** in readiness (as at *KL* 1.4.317)
cap-à-pie from head to foot (from Old
French *cap-a-pie*: in modern French *de
pied en cap*)

201 **slow** slowly; Blake (5.1.2.2v) cites other
instances where only the last of a group of
adverbs has the ending '-ly', e.g. 'he
demean'd himself rough, rude and wildly'
(*CE* 5.1.88).

202 **fear-surprised** fear-surprisèd; suddenly
attacked or affected by fear. For a similar
use of 'surprised' in a sense stronger than
the modern one, see *Tit* 1.1.288: 'Treason,
my lord – Lavinia is surprised.'

203 **truncheon's** A truncheon was a military
staff. This implies either that the Ghost was

a truncheon's length away from them, or
that he measured his pace with his
truncheon.
distilled dissolved, reduced. F has
'bestil'd' (bestilled), defended by Capell
and Caldecott. MacDonald argues: 'Either
word would do: the *distilling* off of the
animal spirits would leave the man a jelly;
the cold of fear would *bestil* them and him
to a jelly . . . But I judge *bestil'd* the better,
as the truer to the operation of fear.'
Edwards, Hibbard and Oxf, however,
follow Q2.

204 **jelly** Perhaps the assumption is that they
are quivering with fear, or that their bones
have given way (as in 'spineless').
act effect

205–6   **This . . . did** Horatio's sentence
structure is inverted with the object *This*
and the adverbial phrase 'to me / In
dreadful secrecy' both preceding the verb
and subject *impart they did*.

206 **dreadful** As Hope points out (1.2.2b), this
carries an objective rather than a subjective
sense: the secrecy was laden with dread
(see *dreadful* used subjectively at 1.4.70
and *sensible* used objectively at 1.1.56).

197 waste] *(wast) F;* vast *Q1, Q4;* waist *Malone*   199 Armed at point] Armed to poynt *Q1;* Arm'd at all
points *F* cap-à-pie] *(Capapea) Q1,* F *(Cap a Pe)*   202 fear-surprised] *(feare surprised), F;* feare
oppressed *Q1*   203 distilled] *Q1;* bestil'd *F*   204 jelly] *(gelly) Q1,* F *(Ielly)*

And I with them the third night kept the watch
Where, as they had delivered, both in time,
Form of the thing, each word made true and good,
The apparition comes. I knew your father,   210
These hands are not more like.

HAMLET   But where was this?

MARCELLUS

My lord, upon the platform where we watch.

HAMLET

Did you not speak to it?

HORATIO   My lord, I did,
But answer made it none. Yet once methought
It lifted up it head and did address   215
Itself to motion like as it would speak.
But even then the morning cock crew loud
And at the sound it shrunk in haste away
And vanished from our sight.

HAMLET   'Tis very strange.

HORATIO

As I do live, my honoured lord, 'tis true,   220
And we did think it writ down in our duty
To let you know of it.

208–10 **as . . . comes** The phrasing is awkward though the meaning is clear, i.e. that the Ghost appeared exactly at the time and in the shape that they had described.

211 **These . . . like** 'my hands are not more like each other than the Ghost was like your father.'

212 **platform** battlements or terrace (of a castle)
watch keep the watch. Q2's present tense implies a habitual pattern ('where we usually watch'); Q1/F's 'watcht'/'watched' implies a reference to this specific occasion.

215 **it head** The more usual possessives would have been 'its' or 'his', but Shakespeare sometimes uses the older, uninflected genitive *it* as in 'The hedge-sparrow fed the cuckoo so long / That it's had it head bit off by it young' (*KL* 1.4.206–7); see Hope, 1.3.2c. The oscillation between *it* and *he* for the Ghost throughout this conversation is both understandable and unsettling.

215–16 **address . . . speak** 'begin to make motions as if it was about to speak'

221 **writ . . . duty** required by the loyalty we owe you

208 Where, as] *Q5;* Whereas *Q2F;* Where as *Q1*   212 watch] watched *Q1F*   215 it] *F;* his *Q1;* its *Q4*

HAMLET

Indeed, sirs, but this troubles me.
Hold you the watch tonight?

HORATIO, MARCELLUS, BARNARDO

We do, my lord.

HAMLET

Armed, say you?

HORATIO, MARCELLUS, BARNARDO

Armed, my lord.   225

HAMLET

From top to toe?

HORATIO, MARCELLUS, BARNARDO

My lord, from head to foot.

HAMLET

Then saw you not his face.

HORATIO

O yes, my lord, he wore his beaver up.

HAMLET

What looked he – frowningly?

HORATIO

A countenance more in sorrow than in anger.   230

HAMLET

Pale, or red?

223 **Indeed** Q1/F's repetition is seen as an actor's interpolation by Jenkins, but again it regularizes the metre (see 149n.).
224 SP *F's 'Both', here and at 225 and 226, perhaps implies that Marcellus and Barnardo, the official watchmen, reply, but not Horatio, who was there by invitation (see 1.1.25); again, the role of Horatio seems inconsistent (see List of Roles, 10n.). Barnardo does not, in any case,

appear in 1.4 or 1.5, possibly because the actor is doubling Reynaldo in 2.1 (see doubling chart in Appendix 5).
227 This is a statement in Q2 (but not in Q1/F) implying that Hamlet has deduced this fact from what he has been told.
228 **beaver** visor (of a helmet)
229 **What** how (as in Q1)
   frowningly See 1.1.61: *So frowned he.*
230 **countenance** face, expression

223 Indeed] Indeed, indeed *Q1F*   224 SP, 225 SP2, 226 SP2] *this edn; All. Q21; Both. F*   227 face.]
face? *Q1F*   229 What] How *Q1;* What, *F*

HORATIO
Nay, very pale.

HAMLET   And fixed his eyes upon you?

HORATIO
Most constantly.

HAMLET   I would I had been there.

HORATIO
It would have much amazed you.

HAMLET   Very like.
Stayed it long?   235

HORATIO
While one with moderate haste might tell a hundred.

MARCELLUS, BARNARDO
Longer, longer.

HORATIO
Not when I saw't.

HAMLET   His beard was grizzled, no?

HORATIO
It was as I have seen it in his life:
A sable silvered.

HAMLET   I will watch tonight.   240

---

232 **Nay** emphatic: Horatio rejects the alternative *red*.
234 **Very like** perhaps, possibly (as at 2.2.149, where this phrase occurs in apposition to *It may be*). Q1/F's repetition is another actor's interpolation for Jenkins. Some actors of Hamlet use the words to express impatience, some scepticism.
236 **one . . . tell** a person . . . count (see *R3* 1.4.116–18: 'this passionate humour . . . was wont to hold me but while one tells twenty')
237 SP Q2's '*Both*' (i.e. Marcellus and

Barnardo) seems definitely preferable to F's '*All*' here, given that Horatio disagrees.
238 **grizzled** grey or mixed with grey. Most editors read 'grizzled', though Hibbard makes a case for F's 'grisly' as an alternative spelling of 'grizzly' which is what he prints. **no** i.e. 'wasn't it?'; a negative tag expecting an affirmative answer (Blake, 6.2.3.4a)
240 **A sable silvered** a mixture of black and silver-grey (see *Son* 12.4, 'sable curls all silvered o'er with white'). Sable is literally a fur derived from the small animal of the same name. In Q1

---

234 like] like, very like *Q1F*   236 hundred] *(hundreth)*   237 SP] *(Both.); Mar. Q1; All. F*   238 grizzled] *(grissl'd), Q1 (grisleld); grisly F*   240–1 I . . . again] *one line Q1F*   240 I will] *Q1;* Ile *F*   tonight] *(to nigh), Q1F*

Perchance 'twill walk again.

HORATIO   I warrant it will.

HAMLET

If it assume my noble father's person
I'll speak to it, though hell itself should gape
And bid me hold my peace. I pray you all,
If you have hitherto concealed this sight   245
Let it be tenable in your silence still
And whatsomever else shall hap tonight

Hamlet refers to his 'sable suit' at the equivalent of 77, rather than to his *inky cloak*; later, during the play scene in all three texts, he says, 'let the devil wear black, for I'll have a suit of sables', making the point that sable, while black, is also luxurious (see below 3.2.122–3 and n.)

241 **walk** generally preferred to F's 'wake', though either seems acceptable
warrant guarantee; monosyllabic, as Q2's 'warn't' indicates (see 3.4.5 and e.g. *Oth* 3.3.3)

242 **assume . . . person** take on or enact my father's role. Hamlet seems cautious about the Ghost's relationship to his father here, using a theatrical analogy, but he refers to it as *My father's spirit* at 253.

243 **though . . . gape** Hamlet's personification evokes hellmouth (a familiar stage property from medieval and Renaissance drama – one is listed in the Admiral's Men's effects in 1598). Christopher Marlowe has two similar lines at climactic moments, Zabina's 'Gape earth and let the fiends infernal view / A hell as hopeless and as full of fear / As are the blasted banks of Erebus' (*1 Tamburlaine* (1587), 5.1.241–3), and Faustus' final cry, 'Ugly hell gape not' (*Dr Faustus* (*c.* 1592), 5.3.183). Shaheen argues that the biblical parallel here is with the Bishops' Bible, since its

translation of Isaiah, 5.14, reads, 'Therefore gapeth hell', where the Geneva Bible has 'Hell hath inlarged itself'. Hamlet may also be indicating that he is prepared to risk damnation by conversing with a spirit who could be a devil.

244 **hold my peace** be silent

246 **tenable** capable of being held (maintained as a secret). This is Shakespeare's only use of the word (though Helena mentions an 'intemible' (F) or 'intenible' (F2) – i.e. bottomless – sieve at *AW* 1.3.199), but F's 'treble' is usually assumed to be an error, though it is defended by Caldecott – 'a threefold obligation of silence' – and MacDonald, who suggests Hamlet points to each of the three men in turn and cites *Cym*, 'your three motives to the battle' (5.5.389) – meaning 'the motives of you three' – as a comparable usage. 'Treble' might also mean 'conceal it trebly'.

247–9 *And* introduces a further conditional clause, following on from *If* in 245 ('If you have concealed . . . and if you continue to do so . . . I will requite you').

247 **whatsomever** F's 'whatsoeuer' has sometimes been regarded as a modernization but is actually more common in Shakespeare, as *TxC* notes. See also *howsomever* at 1.5.84 and *some'er* at 1.5.168.

241 walk] *Q1;* wake *F*   warrant] *(warn't), Q1;* warrant you *F*   246 tenable] *Q1;* treble *F*   247 whatsomever] whatsoeuer *Q1F*

Give it an understanding but no tongue,
I will requite your loves. So, fare you well.
Upon the platform 'twixt eleven and twelve   250
I'll visit you.

HORATIO, MARCELLUS, BARNARDO
                    Our duty to your honour.

HAMLET
Your loves, as mine to you, farewell.

                              Exeunt [all but Hamlet].

My father's spirit – in arms! All is not well;
I doubt some foul play. Would the night were come.
Till then sit still my soul – foul deeds will rise   255
Though all the earth o'erwhelm them to men's eyes.   *Exit.*

1.3   *Enter* LAERTES *and* OPHELIA *his sister.*
            rhyming couplets

248 Hamlet has moved from imagining hell bidding him be silent to urging the others to keep quiet about the Ghost
249 **requite** repay, reward
252 Hamlet rejects the colder *duty*, as he rejected Horatio's *servant* at 163. This note at the end of the scene is comparable to the moment after the quarrel between Brutus and Cassius in *JC*, when Cassius takes his leave with 'Good night, my lord', but Brutus insists 'Good night, good brother' (4.3.235).
254 **doubt** suspect, fear
255–6 **foul . . . eyes** i.e. crimes will eventually be revealed, even though the whole world attempts to submerge or bury them. See 2.2.528–9: 'For murder, though it have no tongue, will speak / With most miraculous organ', and the proverbial 'Murder will out' (Dent, M1315). The others have not mentioned their theory about the

connection between the Ghost's appearance and Denmark's preparations for war; Hamlet's notion of *foul play* seems immediately a more personal one, following on from his first soliloquy.
255 *****foul** Q2's 'fonde' is plausibly explained as a misreading. Andrews, however, retains it and glosses 'foolish or mad'. The repetition of *foul* from 254 makes 'fonde' attractive, but this sense seems strained (and misleading to a modern auditor or reader).
1.3 The three texts: this scene runs to 71 lines in Q1 (scene 3), 135 lines in Q2 and 136 lines in F. Laertes' advice to Ofelia is much briefer in Q1, as is the closing dialogue between Corambis (Q1's name for Polonius) and Ofelia. Location and timing: this scene takes place later on the same day as 1.2, where Laertes' departure was discussed, and before the night appointed

249 So, fare] *(so farre), Q1F*   you] *Q1;* ye *F*   250 eleven] *(a leauen), Q1F*   251 SP] *this edn; All. Q21F*   duty] *F;* duties *Q1*   252 loves] *Q1;* loue *F*   SD] *Q6 (Exeunt. / Manet* Hamlet. *opp. 251–2); Exeunt. Q21F, opp. 251*   255 foul] *Q1F;* fonde *Q2*   256 o'erwhelm] *(ore-whelme), Q1F*   **1.3**] *F (Scena Tertia.); not in Q21*   0.1 *his sister*] *not in Q1F*

LAERTES

My necessaries are embarked; farewell.
And sister, as the winds give benefit
And convey is assistant, do not sleep
But let me hear from you.

OPHELIA   Do you doubt that?

LAERTES

For Hamlet and the trifling of his favour,   5
Hold it a fashion and a toy in blood,
A violet in the youth of primy nature,
Forward, not permanent, sweet, not lasting,
The perfume and suppliance of a minute,

for Hamlet's encounter with the Ghost. Unlike 1.1 and 1.2, it is a relatively intimate domestic scene that is assumed to take place in the home of Polonius.

0.1 **his sister** The relationship is established in Laertes' opening speech in all three texts. If she has not been a silent presence in 1.2 (see 1.2.0.3n.), this is Ophelia's first appearance. Some productions anticipate her appearance in 4.5 by having her practise the lute in this scene.

1 **necessaries are embarked** luggage is on board ship; see *Oth* 2.1.281: 'I must fetch his necessaries ashore.'

2 **as** at such times as, whenever

3 ***convey is assistant** means of conveyance or communication are available. Q2's 'conuay, in assistant' seems erroneous.

4 **But let** without letting

you . . . you Laertes and Ophelia consistently use the more formal pronouns to each other in this scene; Polonius uses *thee* and *thou* to Laertes from 56 to 80 (see 56n.), and in Q1 Laertes uses 'thee' to his sister. During Shakespeare's lifetime the former plural form 'you' was usurping many of the functions of the singular 'thou'

and the distinctions between the two forms were not always marked, either by Shakespeare or by his printers (see Blake, 3.3.2.1.1, and Hope, 1.3.2b).

5 **For Hamlet** as regarding Hamlet
trifling . . . favour playful level of his attention to you

6 **fashion** passing fancy
toy in blood superficial sensual attraction

7 **primy** a Shakespearean coinage meaning 'in its prime' or perhaps 'spring-like'; see 'For love is crowned with the prime / In spring-time' (*AYL* 5.3.35–6) and 'When I behold the violet past prime' (*Son* 12.3). It may carry a sense of 'lustful' here (see *Oth* 3.3.406, 'as prime as goats') and also implies that Hamlet is younger than the 30 years insisted upon at 5.1.135–53 (see List of Roles, 1n.).

8 **Forward** premature (and therefore, as in a flower, fragile and unlikely to last long)

9 'that which supplies the volatile sensory pleasure of a moment'. Shakespeare uses *perfume* to stand in for the fleeting pleasures of spring in *Son* 104.7: 'Three April perfumes in three hot Junes burned.' *Perfume and suppliance*

3 convey] *(conuay); Conuoy F   is] F; in Q2   5 favour] fauours F   8 Forward] Froward F   9–10 The . . . No more.] one line F   9 perfume and] om. F*

No more.

OPHELIA   No more but so.

LAERTES   Think it no more.   10
For nature crescent does not grow alone
In thews and bulks, but as this temple waxes
The inward service of the mind and soul
Grows wide withal. Perhaps he loves you now,
And now no soil nor cautel doth besmirch   15
The virtue of his will; but you must fear,
His greatness weighed, his will is not his own.
He may not, as unvalued persons do,

is another example of hendiadys: Wright points out that Laertes uses the figure seven times in this speech, which he sees as revealing 'his own uncertain and divided sensibility' which perceives 'doubleness in everything' (Wright, 176–7).

suppliance Jenkins glosses 'something which fills up (a vacancy); pastime'; Spencer glosses simply 'pastime'.

10 **No . . . so** 'No more than that.' Ophelia's four words are a statement in all three texts but many editors and performers make them a question. The phrase *no more*, repeated three times in this line, reverberates through the play until Laertes' 'I can no more' (5.2.305).

11–14 **For . . . withal** Laertes' general meaning is that the mind and soul change and mature as well as the body.

11 **crescent** growing, as it grows

12 **thews and bulks** physical sinews and strength. F has 'Bulke', and it is possible an extra 's' may have been picked up from one of the other words ending in 's' in this line, or from confusion about an attached comma in some hands; Shakespeare does not use 'bulks' elsewhere.

this temple the body (seen as the temple of the soul)

waxes grows larger

13 **inward service** inner life (continuing the religious metaphor)

14 **Grows wide withal** becomes enlarged or developed at the same time. Again, the focus is on Hamlet's immaturity.

15 **soil** impurity, stain

cautel craft or deceit. Shakespeare also uses the adjective, as in Brutus' reference to 'men cautelous' (*JC* 2.1.129).

besmirch deface, contaminate (*OED*'s first usage; see also *unsmirched* at 4.5.119).

16 **The . . . will** the sincerity or purity of his intentions (though *will* may also carry a sexual sense)

17 **His greatness weighed** when you consider his high position (as crown prince). F has another line after *own* (see t.n.); this is included by Jenkins, presumably on the grounds that Q2 omitted it in error, though the syntax makes sense without it.

18 **unvalued** i.e. unimportant or ordinary

11 crescent] *(*cressant*)* *F*   12 bulks] Bulke *F*   this] his *F*   16 will] feare *F*   17–18 own. / He] owne; / For hee himselfe is subiect to his Birth: / Hee *F*

Carve for himself, for on his choice depends
The safety and health of this whole state,   20
And therefore must his choice be circumscribed
Unto the voice and yielding of that body
Whereof he is the head. Then if he says he loves you
It fits your wisdom so far to believe it
As he in his particular act and place   25
May give his saying deed, which is no further
Than the main voice of Denmark goes withal.
Then weigh what loss your honour may sustain
If with too credent ear you list his songs
Or lose your heart, or your chaste treasure open   30

19 **Carve for himself** i.e. make his own choice (the metaphor is from serving or helping oneself at table and had become proverbial: see Dent, C100). The belief that Ophelia would be an inappropriate partner for Hamlet which is reiterated by Polonius later in this scene is not shared by the Queen: see 3.1.37–41 and 5.1.233–5.

20 **safety** F's 'sanctity' is retained by Edwards; Theobald (*Restored*) suggested 'sanity' on the analogy of 'Reason and Sanitie' in F at 2.2.207 (where Q2 has 'reason and sanctity'). It goes better with *health* and is adopted by Jenkins and Hibbard, but *safety* makes acceptable sense. Dowden points to a trisyllabic pronunciation of *safety* in Spenser's *FQ* (5.4.46), but acknowledges that it is usually disyllabic in Shakespeare, as at 42. Warburton's suggestion (see t.n.) improves the metre.

21–2 **circumscribed / Unto** The idiom is rare compared with 'circumscribed by'; *OED* cites no other examples.

22 **voice and yielding** vote and consent

23 **he ... head** Laertes assumes that Hamlet is indeed heir to the throne (see 1.2.109 and n.).

24 'you would be wise to believe it only so far'

25 **his ... place** i.e. his specific role and situation

26 **May ... deed** 'Saying and doing are two things' was proverbial (Dent, S119); this is the first of the play's many oppositions of actions and words.

27 'than he has the general agreement (*main voice*) of the country'
   withal in addition (to his own choice)

29 **credent** credulous (*OED*'s first usage)
   list listen to. The Hamlet we actually encounter in the play seems unlikely to serenade Ophelia, but see his letter to her read out by Polonius at 2.2.108–21.

30 **lose** Q2's 'loose' is probably just a variant spelling, though it could mean 'open up' or 'unlock'.
   chaste treasure i.e. the treasure of your chastity. Laertes assumes, as does Polonius later in this scene (see *maiden presence* at 120), that Ophelia is still a virgin; some productions and films indicate, contrary to any evidence in the text, that her relationship with Hamlet is already a sexual one – which they may perhaps deduce from the songs she sings in 4.5 (see 4.5.23–40 and n.).

20 safety and] sanctity and *F*; sanity and *Hanmer (Theobald)*; safety and the *Warburton*   this whole] the weole *F*   25 particular ... place] peculiar Sect and force *F*   30 lose] *(loose), F*

To his unmastered importunity.
Fear it, Ophelia, fear it, my dear sister,
And keep you in the rear of your affection
Out of the shot and danger of desire.
The chariest maid is prodigal enough   35
If she unmask her beauty to the moon.
Virtue itself scapes not calumnious strokes.
The canker galls the infants of the spring
Too oft before their buttons be disclosed,
And in the morn and liquid dew of youth   40
Contagious blastments are most imminent.
Be wary then: best safety lies in fear,
Youth to itself rebels, though none else near.

---

31 **unmastered importunity** undisciplined
persistence. Perhaps Laertes tells us as
much about himself as about Hamlet in
these lines.
33–4   The metaphor is from military
action, as if Hamlet is besieging Ophelia.
34 **shot** range of a bow or gun
35, 37, 38 These lines are prefaced with
double quotation marks in Q2, indicating
that they are sententious or quasi-
proverbial. Dent cites 'Envy (calumny)
shoots at the fairest mark' (E175) and 'The
canker soonest eats the fairest rose' (C56).
35 **chariest** most cautious, shy
prodigal extravagant, wasteful (also at
115)
36 **unmask . . . moon** the moon is an emblem
of chastity. Laertes exaggerates here; an
Elizabethan Court lady would, however,
have literally masked her face and hands
from the sun; see Rosalind's horror at
Phoebe's tanned skin at *AYL* 4.3.24–7. In
this context, a fuller 'unmasking' in the
bedchamber is probably implied.
37 **scapes** avoids. This aphetic variant of
'escapes' was common up to the end of the
seventeenth century.
calumnious slanderous, defamatory (see

Hamlet's use of 'calumny' at 3.1.136)
38 **canker** caterpillar or other insect pest. The
word is also used by Shakespeare to mean
a disease that consumes people – 'cancer'
in modern spelling. In F, but not in Q2,
Hamlet later refers to the King as 'this
canker' (see 5.2.69 and n.).
galls damages
infants i.e. young flowers, as at *LLL*
1.1.101, 'the first-born infants of the
spring'
39 **buttons be disclosed** buds are open
40 **in . . . youth** in their earliest state, which is
like a dew-sprinkled morning (hendiadys
again). The metaphor works both ways
here: the flower buds, standing in for
vulnerable   youthful   affections,   are
themselves seen as young people.
41 **Contagious   blastments**   infectious
blightings (*blastments* is a Shakespearean
coinage: see 1.2.93n.)
imminent immediately threatening
43 'Young people can betray themselves
without need of outside provocation.'
Laertes seems to be saying that the passions
of youth are so volatile that they chafe
against self-restraint even when no
temptation is present.

---

33 you in] within *F*   39 their] the *F*

OPHELIA

I shall the effect of this good lesson keep
As watchman to my heart. But, good my brother, 45
Do not as some ungracious pastors do
Show me the steep and thorny way to heaven
Whiles, a puffed and reckless libertine,
Himself the primrose path of dalliance treads
And recks not his own rede.

LAERTES O fear me not. 50
I stay too long.

Enter POLONIUS.

But here my father comes.

44–5 **I . . . heart** In performance, Ophelia may begin by mocking the solemnity of Laertes' *lesson* or lecture.

44 **effect** meaning, moral

45 **watchman** . . . **heart** guardian to my affections

46–50 **Do . . . rede** 'Practise what you preach' was proverbial (Dent, P537a).

46 **ungracious** irreligious (lacking divine grace)
   pastors priests (literally, shepherds)

48 **Whiles** F's 'Whilst like' improves the metre; 'whilst' has been claimed as a modernization but *TxC* notes that both texts agree on *while* 17 times but on *whilst* only three times.
   puffed swollen or bloated (presumably as the result of a dissipated lifestyle; Falstaff is described as 'a puffed man' at *MW* 5.5.151); Jenkins and Hibbard gloss 'inflated with pride'.
   libertine a dissolute or licentious man (as *OED* notes, 'rarely applied to a woman')

49 **Himself** We might expect 'Yourself', following on from *Do not* in 46, or

'Themselves' if the reference is to the *ungracious pastors* (also in 46); perhaps *Himself* includes both. Blake (3.3.2.3a) classifies this as a non-reflexive emphatic pronoun.
   primrose . . . **dalliance** flower-strewn road of pleasure, often seen as the way to hell: see the Porter's reference in *Mac* 2.3.18–19 to 'the primrose way to th'everlasting bonfire' and that of the Clown in *AW* to 'the flow'ry way that leads to the broad gate and the great fire' (4.5.52–4).

50 **recks . . . rede** pays no attention to his own teaching
   fear me not do not be afraid on my account, don't worry about me. Laertes picks up the notion of *fear* from his speech to Ophelia: see 16 and 32.

51 **stay too long** linger, delay too long. Laertes is sometimes represented as being impatient with what he sees as the beginning of a moral lecture: Ophelia has listened to him but he is not prepared to listen to her.

44 the effect] th'effect *F*   45 watchmen] watchmen *F*   47 steep] *Q2cF;* step *Q2u*   48 Whiles,] *(*Whiles*);* Whilst like *F;* While *Q1*   51 SD] *Sisson; opp.* reed *50 Q2; after 53 Q1; after 50 F; after* comes *51 Capell*

A double blessing is a double grace:
Occasion smiles upon a second leave.

POLONIUS

Yet here, Laertes? Aboard, aboard for shame!
The wind sits in the shoulder of your sail   55
And you are stayed for. There, my blessing with thee,
And these few precepts in thy memory
Look thou character: give thy thoughts no tongue
Nor any unproportioned thought his act.
Be thou familiar but by no means vulgar;   60

53 i.e. I am fortunate in having a second opportunity of saying goodbye to my father. *Occasion* (Opportunity) is often personified in Shakespeare. The whole line sounds quasi-proverbial and is perhaps intended to counter the more natural assumption that it is unlucky (or at least embarrassing) to meet someone again just after you have bidden them farewell.

54 **for shame** ' "For shame" attached to an imperative (or a word of injunction) creates an admonition' (Edwards).

55 i.e. you have a following wind

56 **stayed for** awaited

There Some gesture probably accompanies this word: an embrace, a shake of the hand, a pat on the back or head. Theobald provides an explicit SD, '*Laying his hand on Laertes's head*', and comments, 'The Manner, in which a Comic Actor behav'd upon this Occasion, was sure to raise a Laugh of Pleasure in the Audience; and the oldest *Quarto*'s, in the Pointing [punctuation], are a confirmation that thus the Poet intended it, and thus the Stage express'd it.' It is rare, however, to see a comic Polonius on the modern stage.

thee The shift in pronoun may reflect a change to a more intimate tone (see 4n.).

57 **these few precepts** Sometimes in performance Polonius reads the *precepts* from a paper which he gives to Laertes at the end of the speech. Perhaps surprisingly, Q2 does not mark 58–79 as 'sentences' (see 35, 37, 38n.), though Q1 does. Dent points out that 'every idea in the speech is a commonplace' (28) and that as many as 20 proverbs may be relevant (xxvi, n. 29); he cites such examples as 'Keep well thy friends when thou hast gotten them' (F752), 'Try (your friend) before you trust' (T595), 'Give not your (right) hand to every man' (H68), 'Hear much but speak little' (M1277), 'A man should hear all parts ere he judge any' (M299), 'Apparel makes the man' (A283) and 'Who lends to a friend loses double' (F725). Shakespeare stages a similar occasion in the opening scene of *AW* when the Countess gives some parting advice to her son Bertram (1.1.60–9).

58 **character** (stressed on second syllable) inscribe, write (see *Hamlet's character* at 4.7.49)

59 'Do not act on any thought that is not properly developed or controlled.'

his its

60 **familiar ... vulgar** friendly but not promiscuous

54 aboard for] *F*; aboord, for *Q1*   56 for. There,] *Theobald subst.*; for, there *Q21*; for there: *F*   thee] *Q1*; you *F*   58 Look] See *F*

Those friends thou hast, and their adoption tried,
Grapple them unto thy soul with hoops of steel,
But do not dull thy palm with entertainment
Of each new-hatched, unfledged courage. Beware
Of entrance to a quarrel but, being in,   65
Bear't that th'opposed may beware of thee.
Give every man thy ear but few thy voice;
Take each man's censure but reserve thy judgement.
Costly thy habit as thy purse can buy
But not expressed in fancy – rich, not gaudy;   70
For the apparel oft proclaims the man
And they in France of the best rank and station

61 **their adoption tried** their suitability for adoption as friends proven
62 The metaphor moves from boarding an enemy ship (*Grapple*, used literally at 4.6.17–18) to manufacturing a barrel (strengthening the wood with *hoops of steel*). Iago uses similar metaphors to describe his (false) friendship with Roderigo: 'I confess me knit to thy deserving with cables of perdurable toughness' (*Oth* 1.3.339–40).
63 **dull thy palm** literally, desensitize your hand (by shaking hands with everyone), or perhaps more broadly, make your gesture meaningless
64 **new-hatched** newly born (as a bird just hatched from an egg)
   unfledged untried (unable to fly)
   courage gallant or dashing fellow (*OED* 1b). Thus Q2 and Q1; F's 'Comrade' is easier, but *m/u* is a possible minim misreading. RP points out that the word intended may have been 'comrague' or 'comrogue', a term meaning 'fellow rogue'

('often jocularly confused with *comrade*' – *OED*) which occurs in John Webster's *Appius and Virginia* (1624; 4.2.8), Ben Jonson's *Masque of Augurs* (1622; 49) and in Thomas Dekker and John Ford's *The Welsh Ambassador* (1623; 3.2.110, 4.2.76 and 5.2.73).
66 **Bear't that** manage it so that
   th'opposed your opponent
68 **censure** opinion (not necessarily negative)
69 **habit** dress, clothing
70 **fancy** frivolous fashion
   rich, not gaudy expensive but not ostentatious. Sometimes in performance Polonius draws a contrast between his own garments and those of Laertes, but this makes nonsense of the context in which Laertes is dressed for sea travel, presumably wearing a *sea-gown* of the kind Hamlet refers to at 5.2.13 and may himself be wearing in 5.1 (see 5.1.246–7n.).
71 'a man's true nature is often shown by his clothes'

61 Those] *Q1; The F*   62 unto] to *Q1F*   64 new-hatched] *(*new hatcht*); new Q1;* vnhatch't *F* courage] *Q1;* Comrade *F*   67'thy] thine *F*   69 buy] *Q2cIF;* by *Q2u*

Are of all most select and generous chief in that.
Neither a borrower nor a lender, boy,
For loan oft loses both itself and friend   75
And borrowing dulleth th'edge of husbandry.
This above all, to thine own self be true
And it must follow as the night the day
Thou canst not then be false to any man.
Farewell, my blessing season this in thee.   80

LAERTES

Most humbly do I take my leave, my lord.

POLONIUS

The time invests you. Go, your servants tend.

LAERTES

Farewell, Ophelia, and remember well
What I have said to you.

73 ***Are ... that** A difficult line, problematic in both Q2 and F, which must mean something like '[the French] are particularly distinguished in this respect [i.e. their choice of dress].' We adopt Q1/F's 'Are' for Q2's 'Or' and emend 'a' to *all* in both Q2 and F, an emendation suggested in 1938 and printed by Oxf; *TxC* speculates that the compositor may have been misled by something that looked like 'are/or of almost' and compares 4.7.133, 'Most generous and free from all contriving'.

74 **boy** F's 'be' is an easier reading, but Polonius could be addressing his son as *boy* and suppressing the obvious verb.

75 ***loan** Q2's 'loue', a fairly obvious reversed letter or minim error, had a surprisingly long history of being uncorrected through the seventeenth-century quartos until Q8 in 1683.

76 ***dulleth th'edge** Most editors (including Jenkins) prefer F's 'duls the edge' as better grammar; RP suggests 'dulleth'edge', which is probably how the Parrott–Craig conjecture would be heard.
edge blade (as of a knife)
husbandry thrift, good household management

80 **season** ripen, mature
this my advice

82 **invests** If this Q2 reading is correct, it could mean something like 'vests power in you' or 'makes an investment in you' (as at *KL* 1.1.131: 'I do invest you jointly with my power'); Jenkins retains and glosses 'besieges, presses upon', noting that this is a unique usage but one which 'has the character of a Shakespearean metaphor'. F's easier reading (see t.n.) is often preferred.
tend attend, are waiting

73 Are] *Q1F;* Or *Q2* of . . . chief] *Oxf (Cripps);* of a most select and generous, chiefe *Q2;* of a most select and generall chiefe *Q1;* of a most select and generous cheff *F;* most select and generous, chief *Rowe;* most select and generous *White;* of a most select and generous choice *Collier²* (choice *(Steevens))*   74 boy] be *F*   75 loan] *F (*lone*);* loue *Q2*   76 dulleth th'edge] *(Parrott–Craig);* dulleth edge *Q2;* dulleth the edge *Q3;* duls the edge *F;* dulleth'edge *(RP)*   82 invests] inuites *F*

OPHELIA   'Tis in my memory locked

  And you yourself shall keep the key of it.   85

LAERTES

  Farewell.   *Exit.*

POLONIUS

  What is't, Ophelia, he hath said to you?

OPHELIA

  So please you, something touching the Lord Hamlet.

POLONIUS

  Marry, well bethought:

  'Tis told me he hath very oft of late   90

  Given private time to you, and you yourself

  Have of your audience been most free and bounteous.

  If it be so – as so 'tis put on me,

  And that in way of caution – I must tell you

  You do not understand yourself so clearly   95

  As it behoves my daughter and your honour.

  What is between you? Give me up the truth.

---

87 Polonius' question puts Ophelia in a difficult position: she has just promised to keep Laertes' advice secret, but this was her offer rather than his request and would presumably give way to filial duty.

88 **touching** concerning

89, 104 **Marry** by (the Virgin) Mary – a mild oath

89 **bethought** thought of

90–2 Polonius puts the meetings into a highly formal context, implying that it is improper (or at least unusual) for a prince to give an unmarried girl *private time* and for her to grant him 'free and bounteous audience'.

90, 98 **of late** recently. The implication would seem to be that Hamlet and Ophelia have been spending time together quite recently, that is since his return from Wittenberg, but this is not very compatible with his preoccupation with his father's death. The inconsistency is comparable with the contradictions in the role of Horatio (see 1.2.164n.).

92 **audience** hearing, attention

93–4 Rather a loose construction: Polonius may be saying, 'those who suggested this to me did so to warn me' (implied by the dashes after *so* and *caution* in Jenkins's and Hibbard's punctuation), or he may be saying, 'I'm telling you this to warn you.'

93 **put on me** suggested to me

95 **understand yourself** appreciate your position

96 **behoves** is appropriate for
honour reputation. Q1's reading (see t.n.) reflects the father's self-interest more directly.

---

96 behoves . . . honour] *F;* befits my honor, and your credite *Q1*

OPHELIA

He hath, my lord, of late made many tenders
Of his affection to me.

POLONIUS

Affection? Pooh, you speak like a green girl   100
Unsifted in such perilous circumstance.
Do you believe his 'tenders', as you call them?

OPHELIA

I do not know, my lord, what I should think.

POLONIUS

Marry, I will teach you; think yourself a baby
That you have ta'en these tenders for true pay   105
Which are not sterling. Tender yourself more dearly
Or – not to crack the wind of the poor phrase,
Wronging it thus – you'll tender me a fool.

---

98 **tenders** offers. Polonius picks the word up
and mocks it at 102 and 105–8, apparently
questioning whether Hamlet's offers have
any legal or financial backing. There may
be a suppressed pun on 'tender' as a
synonym of *green* in 100: see *R2* 2.3.41–2,
'My gracious lord, I tender you my service,
/ Such as it is, being tender, raw and
young.'

99 **affection** passion (stronger than the
modern sense, as in 'I heard him swear his
affection' (*MA* 2.1.159)

100 **green** inexperienced

101 **Unsifted** untried, untested (*OED* sift *v.* 2)
circumstance matters, circumstances.
Shakespeare often uses the singular where
modern usage would dictate the plural.

105 **ta'en** taken; monosyllabic, as 'tane', the
regular spelling in Q2 and the other texts,
implies

106 **sterling** real, lawful (English) money

Tender . . . dearly (1) take better care of
yourself; (2) offer yourself at a higher rate

107 Polonius' metaphor sees the phrase as a
broken-winded horse.

108 *****Wronging** We follow Johnson and
Jennens in adopting Pope's emendation of
Q2's 'Wrong' as making better sense with
the least disturbance of the text, although
'Wringing' is an attractive conjecture; most
editors (including Jennens) adopt
'Running', an emendation of F's 'Roaming'
(see t.n.). Blake suggests 'Wrong' could be
taken with what follows rather than with
what precedes it, so that line 108 would
mean 'If you corrupt your conduct in this
way, you will make a fool of me" (Blake,
4.3.3c).

tender . . . fool (1) make a fool of me; (2)
present yourself to me as a fool. Ophelia
defends herself against the latter accusation
in her reply.

---

104 I will] Ile *F*   105 these] his *F*   108 Wronging] *Pope;* Wrong *Q2;* Roaming *F;* Wringing *Theobald
(Warburton);* Running *Collier²*

OPHELIA

My lord, he hath importuned me with love
In honourable fashion.   110

POLONIUS

Ay, 'fashion' you may call it. Go to, go to.

OPHELIA

And hath given countenance to his speech, my lord,
With almost all the holy vows of heaven.

POLONIUS

Ay, springes to catch woodcocks – I do know
When the blood burns how prodigal the soul   115
Lends the tongue vows. These blazes, daughter,
Giving more light than heat, extinct in both
Even in their promise as it is a-making,
You must not take for fire. From this time
Be something scanter of your maiden presence;   120

---

109 **importuned** (accented on second syllable)
persistently solicited (see 31 and n.)
111 **'fashion'** Polonius seizes on the word, as he
did on her *affections* and *tenders*, and twists
it from a neutral meaning (manner or style)
to a negative one (passing fancy, as at 6).
Go to a contemptuous or dismissive
expression: what nonsense, don't be silly
112 **countenance** (probably disyllabic:
count'nance) support, credit
114 **springes** (pronounced to rhyme with
'hinges') snares, traps
woodcocks These birds were proverbially
thought to be easy to catch (Tilley has 'A
springe to catch a woodcock', S788):
characters in Shakespeare use the word
derogatively of other people they are
tricking at *TN* 2.5.82, and *AW* 4.1.89. See
also Laertes' reference to himself as 'a

woodcock to mine own springe' at 5.2.291.
115 **When … burns** when sexual desire is
aroused
115–16 **how … vows** how generous the soul is
in lending the tongue promises. Curiously,
the interchange of terms in Q1/F (see t.n.)
seems to make little difference to the
meaning: Polonius/Corambis assumes that
vows arising from desire are insincere –
that the words come from the tongue only,
not from the heart or soul.
116 **blazes** flashes of rhetoric (Hamlet's vows)
117–18 **extinct … a-making** the promise of
both light and heat vanishes even as it is
being made.
119 **take** mistake
fire disyllabic: 'fi-er'
120 **something scanter** somewhat more
sparing (less generous)

112–13] *Rowe; Q2F line* speech / heauen. /   113 almost all the holy] all the *F*   114 springes] *Q1F;*
springs *Q2*   115–16 soul … tongue] tongue lends the heart *Q1;* Soule / Giues the tongue *F*   118 a-making]
(a making) *F*   119 From] For *F*   time] time Daughter *F*   120 something] somewhat *F*

Set your entreatments at a higher rate
Than a command to parle. For Lord Hamlet,
Believe so much in him that he is young
And with a larger tether may he walk
Than may be given you. In few, Ophelia,   125
Do not believe his vows, for they are brokers
Not of that dye which their investments show
But mere implorators of unholy suits
Breathing like sanctified and pious bonds

121 **entreatments** negotiations, perhaps also suggesting 'entreaties' = solicitations. The word is a Shakespearean coinage: see 1.2.93n.

122 **command to parle** literally, 'call to discuss terms': to call for a parley can imply a willingness to capitulate. Polonius is saying, 'Don't let him see you whenever he wants to.'

123 **in** of

young See 7 and n.

124 **larger** longer, wider (implying the area of grazing within range of a tethered animal)

125 **In few** in brief

126–30 **Do . . . beguile** a dense and highly figurative passage whose interpretation is rendered even more difficult by textual variants and emendations. In the Q2 text we have emended only 'imploratotors' to *implorators* (assuming 'to' is repeated erroneously, but see 128n.) and 'beguide' (not found in *OED*) to *beguile*. Hamlet's vows are personified as *brokers* acting on behalf of his *suits* – his requests for sexual favours. The vows act like (breathe like) another set of personified verbal or written promises, *bonds*, which are pretending to be *sanctified and pious* in order to *beguile* Ophelia. In this reading the focus is on the near-synonymous triplet of *vows – suits – bonds* as the main focus of the passage (see

longer discussion in Thompson & Thompson, 115–16).

126 **brokers** go-betweens, especially in financial and sexual matters. See *Luc* 173, where the speaker admits that she knew her seducer's 'vows were ever brokers to defiling'.

127 **that dye** that colour

their investments their garments. The assumption is that the clothes worn by the personified *vows* are deceptive: perhaps, using traditional terms, we should imagine white garments concealing black intentions? *Investments* in this sense seems to be a Shakespearean coinage, first occurring in *2H4* 4.1.45: 'Whose white investments figure innocence' (see also 1.2.93n.)

128 **implorators** intercessors, solicitors. *TxC* argues for 'imploratators', a version of Q2's 'imploratotors', on the grounds that it is hard to be dogmatic in emending a unique Shakespearean coinage and that the resulting line forms an acceptable hexameter. We think, however, that *implorators* would be easier for an actor to say and for an audience to understand.

unholy suits immoral or wicked requests

129 **bonds** Theobald's popular emendation to 'bawds' destroys the *vows – suits – bonds* triplet (see 126–30n.), but 'bawds' does go nicely with *brokers* (see 126n.).

122 parle] parley *F*   124 tether] *F; tider Q2*   127 that dye] the eye *F*   128 implorators] *F, Q4;* imploratotors *Q2;* imploratators *Oxf*   129 bonds] *F;* bawds *Pope² (Theobald)*

230

The better to beguile. This is for all; 130
I would not in plain terms from this time forth
Have you so slander any moment leisure
As to give words or talk with the Lord Hamlet.
Look to't, I charge you. Come your ways. 134

OPHELIA

I shall obey, my lord. *Exeunt.*

[**1.4**] *Enter* HAMLET, HORATIO *and* MARCELLUS.

HAMLET

The air bites shrewdly; it is very cold.

HORATIO

It is nipping, and an eager air.

---

130 **This . . . all** 'this is once for all', i.e. this is the first and last time I am going to tell you this.

132 **slander** bring into disrepute, abuse
moment leisure moment's leisure (which is the modernized Q3 reading, as compared with Q2's 'zero genitive': see Hope, 1.1.4f)

133 **words or talk** The terms seem synonymous, but Polonius may mean to cover both direct face-to-face contact and indirect contact through letters and messages. He has concentrated on the former here, but at 2.1.105–7 Ophelia clearly believes that she has been told to *repel* Hamlet's *letters*.

134 **Look to't** pay attention to this
Come your ways come away, i.e. let us go

1.4 There is no scene division at this point in Q1, Q2 or F, but Capell's introduction of one is justified by the *Exeunt* of the Polonius family, the entry of a different group of characters and the evident change of location. The three texts: this scene

consists of 61 lines in Q1 (scene 4), 91 lines in Q2 and 66 lines in F. The most significant differences are that 22 lines from Hamlet's speech (17–38) and four lines from Horatio's speech (75–8) are not present in Q1 or F. Location and timing: this is the same location, the *platform* or battlements of the castle, as in 1.1, and it is again midnight, exactly 24 hours later.

0.1 Although Barnardo has featured in 1.1 and has confirmed that he is a member of the watch *tonight* in 1.2, he is absent from this scene in all three texts, leaving a group of three characters to encounter the Ghost, as in 1.1 (see also 1.2.224 SPn.).

1 *****shrewdly** severely, bitterly. Q2's spelling 'shroudly' is attractive for its (fortuitous) association with 'shroud', but it does not occur elsewhere, whereas 'shrodly' is recorded as an obsolete spelling of *shrewdly*.

2 **nipping** All editors prefer F's 'a nipping' to Q2's *nipping*, but the latter could make sense, referring to the temperature, i.e. 'it is

---

130 beguile] *F;* beguide *Q2* 132 moment] *F;* moments *Q3;* moment's *Pope* **1.4**] *Capell* 1 shrewdly] (shroudly), *F;* shrewd *Q1* it . . . cold] is it very cold? *F* 2 nipping] An nipping *Q1;* a nipping *F*

HAMLET

What hour now?

HORATIO   I think it lacks of twelve.

MARCELLUS

No, it is struck.

HORATIO   Indeed, I heard it not.
It then draws near the season   5
Wherein the spirit held his wont to walk.

                A flourish of trumpets and two pieces goes off.

What does this mean, my lord?

HAMLET

The King doth wake tonight and takes his rouse,
Keeps wassail and the swaggering upspring reels,

---

bitter (cold)'.
eager keen, sharp. From Old French *aigre*
= sour.

3   **hour** disyllabic: 'how-er'
     lacks of is just short of, i.e. is just before
4   **struck** Again Riv prints 'strook' (see
     1.1.5n.).
     Indeed, Q2's semicolon after 'Indeede'
     could be replaced by a question mark.
5   **season** time
6   **held his wont** observed his (its) custom or
     habit
6   SD Q2's SD indicates a fanfare and the
     discharging of two *pieces* (of artillery).
     This SD and its careful placing are unique
     to Q2, though Q1 has '*Sound Trumpets*'
     at 3. The noise confirms the King's promise
     at 1.2.123–8 to have the cannon sound at
     every *jocund health* he drinks in celebration
     of Hamlet's obedience in staying in
     Denmark. As we learn at 11 below,
     kettledrums are also used.
7   Horatio's questions, here and at 12, seem to
     confirm his role as a visitor rather than a
     native as he appeared by his knowledge of

Danish politics in 1.1 (see 1.1.79–94n.,
1.2.164n. and List of Roles, 10n.).
8   **wake** stay up late
     takes his rouse drinks deeply, carouses
9   **Keeps wassail** To 'keep wassail' was a
     formulaic or idiomatic expression meaning
     to drink numerous toasts (and hence often
     to become disorderly).
     the . . . reels a difficult expression found in
     virtually identical form in all three texts.
     The general meaning is that a riotous form
     of dancing accompanies the drinking. Most
     editors take *reels* to be a verb, with *The
     King* as the subject and *the . . . upspring* as
     the name of a lively dance (Elze says the
     word literally translates the German
     Hupfauf, which was 'the last and
     consequently the wildest dance at the old
     German merrymakings', and Klein
     considers this plausible), but Hibbard takes
     upspring as an adjective qualifying *reels*
     (= revels) and reads the whole line to
     follow on from *Keeps* (i.e. holds)
     'blustering new-fangled revels'. See also
     Jenkins (LN).

4–5] *Ard²; Q2F line* strooke. / season, /   5 It then] then it *F*   6 SD] *opp. 6–7; not in Q1F*   9 wassail]
*(*wassell*) Q1;* wassels *F*   swaggering] *(*swaggring*), Q1F*

And as he drains his draughts of Rhenish down   10
The kettledrum and trumpet thus bray out
The triumph of his pledge.

HORATIO   Is it a custom?

HAMLET
Ay, marry is't,
But to my mind, though I am native here
And to the manner born, it is a custom   15
More honoured in the breach than the observance.
This heavy-headed revel east and west
Makes us traduced and taxed of other nations:

---

10 **Rhenish** wine from the Rhine region of
Germany
11 **kettledrum and trumpet** instruments
associated with Denmark. As RP points
out, these would be safer and cheaper than
the repeated discharge of *pieces*.
  bray out make a loud, harsh noise. The
choice of verb and its associations with
animals, especially donkeys, is not
complimentary to the instruments.
12 **triumph ... pledge** public celebration of
his promise (presumably as made at
1.2.125–8, though Hibbard suggests 'his
promise to drain the cup in one draught')
13 **marry** by (the Virgin) Mary – a mild oath
14 **But** perhaps more emphatic than F's 'And'
which could be a mistaken anticipation
of 15.
15 **to ... born** accustomed to this tradition
from birth. Hamlet clearly disapproves of
the custom and expects Horatio to agree
with him. (The phrase, heard as 'to the
manor born', has curiously become
familiar in a different sense – born to a life
of privilege.)
16 **More ... observance** 'which it is more
honourable to break than to observe'
17–38 **This ... scandal** These 22 lines on
Danish drunkenness are unique to Q2. It was

formerly argued that they might have been
deemed offensive after 1603 when James I
acceded to the throne, since his wife was
Anne of Denmark, but this would make for
rather inconsistent expurgation, because it is
only in F that Hamlet calls Denmark a prison
(see p. 53 and Appendix 1). Recent editors
(e.g. Edwards, Hibbard) argue that the lines
were omitted from both Q1 and F as
'undramatic' ones that 'slow the action
down'. The syntax is complex, but Elze
claims this is deliberate to show Hamlet
'absorbed in thought ... He is continually
losing the thread of his speech and does not
finish a single sentence.' RP points out an
analogy with a similarly convoluted speech
about motivation and personality in *Cor*
4.7.37–49. The cut (if it is one) is comparable
to that in 1.1 where Horatio's leisurely
analogy of 'the most high and palmy state of
Rome' is similarly interrupted by the
appearance of the Ghost (see 1.1.107–24
and n.). Again the effect of the longer
version may be to increase the impact.
17 **This ... revel** this drunken revelling
  east and west i.e. universally (modifying
traduced and taxed)
18 **traduced and taxed of** defamed and
censored by

---

14 But] And *F*   17–38 This ... scandal –] *not in Q1F*   17 heavy-headed] *(heauy headed)*   17 revel]
(reueale)

233

They clepe us drunkards and with swinish phrase
Soil our addition, and indeed it takes   20
From our achievements, though performed at height,
The pith and marrow of our attribute.
So oft it chances in particular men
That, for some vicious mole of nature in them,
As in their birth wherein they are not guilty   25
(Since nature cannot choose his origin),
By their o'ergrowth óf some complexion
Oft breaking down the pales and forts of reason,
Or by some habit that too much o'erleavens

19   **clepe** call
19–20 **with . . . addition** tarnish our reputation
by calling us pigs. 'As drunk as a swine'
was proverbial (Dent, S1042).
20   **addition** name, reputation; see similar uses
at *Mac* 1.3.106 and 3.1.99 and *Cor* 1.9.65.
takes detracts
21   **though . . . height** although these may be
outstanding
22   **The . . . attribute** the very essence or heart
of our good name
23–38 This is a difficult section of the speech
which comes to a climax with one of the
most notoriously obscure passages in the
entire canon. The general drift is clear
enough and even proverbial: 'One ill
condition mars all the good' (Dent, C585).
Hamlet is elaborating on the idea that a
single fault (*some vicious mole*, *the stamp
of one defect* or finally *that particular
fault*) can corrupt or destroy the reputation
of an individual person as the fault of
drunkenness destroys the reputation of the
Danes as a nation. But the long sentence
from 23 to 38 is convoluted and some
details of the expression are complex. It
has been argued, especially by those who
think Shakespeare intended to delete these
lines, that he gave up on the speech,
leaving it unfinished (see Nosworthy,
Occasional, 141). If so, it deserves
attention as an example of an unrevised

draft, illustrating perhaps that Shakespeare
wrote in phrases and metre first and left
sorting out the structure and syntax until
later.
23   **So** in the same way
24   **mole of nature** (1) natural mark
(birthmark) or blemish, (2) hidden
undermining presence (as literally at
1.5.161)
25   **As** for example
26   **his** its (the regular neuter form in this
period; see Hope 1.3.2c)
27   **their . . . complexion** the over-
development of some element in their
natural constitution. *Complexion* is a quasi-
technical term referring to the combination
of the four 'humours', the sanguine,
phlegmatic, choleric and melancholic,
which were supposed to be maintained in
harmony.
28   **pales and forts** defences (palisades) and
fortifications
29–30 **o'er-leavens . . . manners** causes an
excess in what would otherwise be
acceptable behaviour (over-leavened bread
rises or swells too much). Imogen uses a
similar metaphor at *Cym* 3.4.60–3: 'So
thou, Posthumus / Wilt lay the leaven on all
proper men; / Goodly and gallant shall be
false and perjur'd / From thy great fail.'
Shaheen cites a biblical analogy in 1
Corinthians, 5.6–8.

19 clepe] *(clip), Q5*   27 their] *the Pope*

The form of plausive manners – that these men,   30
Carrying, I say, the stamp of one defect
(Being Nature's livery or Fortune's star),
His virtues else, be they as pure as grace,
As infinite as man may undergo,
Shall in the general censure take corruption   35
From that particular fault: the dram of eale
Doth all the noble substance of a doubt
To his own scandal –

Enter GHOST.

HORATIO   Look, my lord, it comes.
HAMLET
Angels and ministers of grace defend us!

---

30 **plausive** applauded, approved
32 **Nature's ... Fortune's** The stock opposition of heredity and environment; see Rosalind and Celia's debate on this topic in *AYL* 1.2.30–54.
   livery dress or uniform (perhaps picking up *habit* in 29, since *habit* usually means 'dress' rather than 'custom' in Shakespeare)
   star in a transferred sense: something supposedly caused by astrological influence
33 **else** in other respects
34 **undergo** sustain, enjoy
35–6 **take corruption / From** become infected or misconstrued because of
36–8 **the dram ... scandal** a famously obscure passage (see 23–38n.). Theobald comments: 'In reality, I do not know a Passage, throughout all our Poet's Works, more intricate and deprav'd in the Text, of less Meaning to outward Appearance, or more likely to baffle the Attempts of Criticism in its Aid. It is certain, there is neither *Sense*, *Grammar*, nor *English*, as it now stands'

(*Restored*, 35). The general meaning is clear (see 23–38n.): a very small quantity (*dram*) of badness can damage a good thing or person (*noble substance*) to the extent of bringing it or them into disrepute (*scandal*). But it is difficult to derive this meaning very precisely from the words on the Q2 page because of (a) the absence of a verb apart from the unsatisfactory *Doth*, (b) the otherwise unknown word *eale*, much emended (see t.n.), usually to 'evil' on the analogy of Q2's spelling 'deale' for *devil* at 2.2.534, (c) the phrase *of a doubt*, also much emended (see t.n.). The sentence may be left unfinished because of the appearance of the Ghost, and this is an attractive option in performance.
38.1 Gurr and Ichikawa (131) again suggest that the Ghost enters and leaves by the centre trap (see 1.1.38.1n.).
39 **ministers** agents, messengers. 'Angels and ministers of grace' is another example of hendiadys, i.e. 'Angels who minister grace' (Wright, 186).

---

33 His] Their *Pope*   36 eale] ease *Q3;* Base *Theobald;* ill *Jennens;* evil *Keightley;* e'il *Kittredge;* ev'l *Riv*   37 of a doubt] of worth out *Theobald;* of a worth dout *Malone;* often dout *Steevens³;* to a doubt *Sisson;* over-daub *Oxf*   38 To] Of *Sisson*

Be thou a spirit of health or goblin damned,   40
Bring with thee airs from heaven or blasts from hell,
Be thy intents wicked or charitable,
Thou com'st in such a questionable shape
That I will speak to thee. I'll call thee Hamlet,
King, father, royal Dane. O answer me,   45
Let me not burst in ignorance but tell
Why thy canonized bones hearsed in death
Have burst their cerements, why the sepulchre
Wherein we saw thee quietly interred
Hath oped his ponderous and marble jaws   50

40 **thou** Hamlet's immediate use of the familiar *thou* rather than the more formal 'you' is surprising, especially as his speech otherwise implies an element of conscious distancing or even incredulity. Perhaps *thou* indicates a dismissive scepticism, whereas 'you' would indicate his acceptance that the Ghost is indeed his father, as it seems to at 3.4.101–5. See also 1.3.4n.

goblin demon (a stronger meaning than the modern one; see *Paradise Lost*, 2.688, where Milton refers to Death as 'the Goblin')

41 **airs ... blasts** The contrast is between gentle breezes and violent blighting gusts.

43 **questionable** inviting questions; see the opposite in *AYL* where Rosalind denies that Orlando has 'an unquestionable spirit' (3.2.365–6). Editors point out that *questionable* was not used to mean 'uncertain' or 'baffling' until the eighteenth century, but it is difficult for a modern audience or reader not to take it in this sense and Mahood identifies *questionable* as a pun here (*Wordplay*, 123).

47 **canonized** (three syllables, with stress on the second) blessed, consecrated (by Christian burial rites). Pursuing the *cannon/canon* pun noted at 1.2.132, Booth

(49–50) points out that we have recently heard the cannon (see 6 SD and n.) and that the bones themselves seem to become projectiles here, bursting out of the grave. The repetition of *burst* (46, 48) is slightly awkward, an effect exaggerated in Q1, where it occurs three times in five lines.

hearsed hearsèd: enclosed in a hearse or coffin

48 **cerements** grave-clothes (pronounced 'seerments'); apparently a Shakespearean coinage from the more familiar 'cerecloth', meaning literally 'waxed cloth'. The word is not connected with 'ceremonies', the Q1 reading, which could be an aural or visual error.

49 **interred** buried. Most editors (including Jenkins) prefer F's 'enurn'd'; Jennens, however, comments: '*Interred* is certainly the most proper when spoken of a body buried without burning; though the other may be allowed as alluding to the *Roman* custom.' *Interred* also seems more consistent with the metaphor of the *sepulchre* opening its *jaws*.

50 **ponderous and marble** another example of hendiadys: 'ponderous (heavy) *because* marble'. Wright (171) points out that Edgar Allen Poe imitated

42 intents] *Q1;* euents *F*   45 O] *(ô), Q1;* Oh, oh *F*   48 cerements] *(cerements), F (cerments);* ceremonies *Q1*   49 interred] *Q1;* enurn'd *F*

To cast thee up again. What may this mean
That thou, dead corpse, again in complete steel,
Revisits thus the glimpses of the moon,
Making night hideous, and we fools of nature
So horridly to shake our disposition   55
With thoughts beyond the reaches of our souls?
Say why is this? Wherefore? What should we do?
[*Ghost*] *beckons.*

HORATIO

It beckons you to go away with it
As if it some impartment did desire
To you alone.

MARCELLUS   Look with what courteous action   60
It waves you to a more removed ground,

---

this line when he wrote of 'ponderous and ebony jaws' in the penultimate paragraph of 'The Fall of the House of Usher'.

51 **cast thee up** The tomb is personified (animalified?) as vomiting the Ghost from its mouth; perhaps a remote allusion to the story of Jonah and the whale.

52 **in complete steel** dressed entirely in steel, i.e. in full armour (presumably the same suit of armour recognized by Horatio at 1.1.59–60)

53 **Revisits** This should strictly read 'revisitest' or 'revisit'st', but the final 't' of the second person form could be dropped when the verb ended in 't' (see Blake, 4.2.2b, and Hope, 2.1.8a).

glimpses pale or perhaps fitful gleams. The line seems to alleviate the horror with a more romantic touch. (*The Glimpses of the Moon* was used by Edith Wharton as the title of her 1922 novel which otherwise has nothing to do with *Hamlet*.) (Jenkins and

Hibbard see in the shared spelling 'glimses' evidence of Q2 following Q1.)

54 **we . . . nature** i.e. turning us into ignorant or weak creatures limited by or victims of nature. For this use of *we* where we might expect 'us' before an infinitive, see Blake, 6.1.2.2.

55 **horridly** horrendously (a stronger meaning than modern 'horrid', possibly with a glance at the literal meaning of Latin *horridus*, bristling or with hair standing on end: see 1.5.19–20)

disposition equanimity, composure

56 **reaches** capacities

57 **What . . . do** what must we do (i.e. to help you or ourselves); see 1.1.127–38.

59 **impartment** communication (a Shakespearean coinage: see 1.2.93n.)

61, 79 **waves** gestures by waving its hand or arm. 'Shakespeare is thinking in terms of the theatre. The *platform* is out of doors in Elsinore, but at the Globe the Ghost stands by one of the

---

53 Revisits] *Q1F*; Reuisitst *F2*   glimpses] *(*glimses*) Q1, F(*glimpses*)*   56 the] *Q1*; thee; *F*   57 SD] *F*
(Ghost beckens Hamlet.); Beckins. Q2; not in Q1   61 waves] *Q1*; wafts *F*

237

But do not go with it.

HORATIO   No, by no means.

HAMLET

It will not speak: then I will follow it.

HORATIO

Do not, my lord.

HAMLET   Why, what should be the fear?
I do not set my life at a pin's fee,   65
And for my soul – what can it do to that,
Being a thing immortal as itself?
It waves me forth again. I'll follow it.

HORATIO

What if it tempt you toward the flood, my lord,
Or to the dreadful summit of the cliff   70
That beetles o'er his base into the sea,
And there assume some other horrible form

stage exits and *waves forth* [68]' (Dover Wilson).

removed removèd; secluded

64 **what . . . fear** what is there to fear? For similar (and, judging from the absence of this usage in the *OED*, similarly rare) examples of *the fear* as a noun, see *Luc* 229, 'The guilt being great, the fear doth still exceed', and *Mac* 4.2.12, 'All is the fear, and nothing is the love.'

65 'I do not value my life at the worth of a pin' (proverbial: Dent, P334)

69–71 The notion of an evil spirit luring someone to the top of a cliff is evoked again at 4.6.67–72 of *KL*. Many film versions of *Hamlet* (Plumb, Rodolfi, Olivier, but most notably Kozintsev) make use of this suggestion and set the next scene literally overlooking the sea

69 **flood** sea

70 **dreadful** The usage here is subjective

(unlike the objective use at 1.2.206): the *dread* is felt by the speaker rather than being an attribute of the cliff.

*summit** The word derives from Old French *sommette*, hence perhaps the Q2/F spellings (see t.n.). Q2/F have 'somnet' at 3.3.18, and this is the spelling at *KL* 4.6.57 (Q only), the only other occurrence of the word in the canon; both lines are omitted in Q1.

71 *beetles . . . base** overhangs its bottom or foot. *Beetles* perhaps personifies the cliff, since it occurs otherwise only in the expression 'beetle-browed', meaning 'having bushy eyebrows'. A similar but more benign picture is evoked in *Tem* when Francisco describes Ferdinand swimming 'To th' shore, that o'er his wave-worn basis bowed, / As stooping to relieve him' (2.1.121–2).

72 **assume** subjunctive mood following *if* in 69 ('what if it should assume')

63 I will] will I *Q1F*   69 my lord] *Q2c1F;* my *Q2u*   70 summit] *Rowe;* somnet *Q2;* Sonnet *F*   70 cliff] *(cleefe)*   71 beetles] *F;* beckles *Q1;* bettles *Q2*   72 assume] *Q1;* assumes *F*

Which might deprive your sovereignty of reason
And draw you into madness? Think of it:
The very place puts toys of desperation   75
Without more motive into every brain
That looks so many fathoms to the sea
And hears it roar beneath.

HAMLET

It waves me still. Go on, I'll follow thee.

MARCELLUS

You shall not go, my lord.

HAMLET   Hold off your hands.   80

HORATIO

Be ruled, you shall not go.

HAMLET   My fate cries out
And makes each petty artery in this body

---

73 **deprive . . . reason** Editors gloss 'deprive
you of the rule or supremacy of reason',
but a modern ear or eye also understands
'deprive your highness of your reason'.

74 **madness** This is the first mention of a
threat to Hamlet's sanity. It is reinforced in
the next scene in three different ways: the
Ghost's threat to 'harrow up thy soul'
(1.5.16), the conjuration 'Taint not thy
mind' (1.5.85), and Hamlet's hint that he
may 'put an antic disposition on' (1.5.170).

75–8 **The . . . beneath** These lines are unique
to Q2. Edwards argues that Shakespeare
intended to delete them 'as confusing
Horatio's main point' (Edwards 13–14),
while Hibbard argues that they must be a
deliberate cut because 'they have left no
mark whatever on Q1' and 'the excision is
a neat one, affecting neither sense nor
metre'. A similar thought is expressed by

Edgar in *KL*: 'I'll look no more/Lest my
brain turn' (4.6.22–3).

75 **toys of desperation** not just vertigo, but
whims to behave desperately (in the
context, these are impulses to suicide
which are in fact frivolous or unjustified)

77 **fathoms** A fathom is (appropriately) a
nautical unit of measurement equivalent to
about six feet or just under two metres.

80 **hands** Q2's plural accords with *unhand
me, gentlemen* at 84.

81 **My . . . out** my destiny calls (i.e. I must do
this)

82 **each petty** i.e. even the most insignificant
*artery The spellings in all three texts (see
t.n.) suggest disyllabic pronunciation,
probably 'arter', but the modern form
would have to be 'art'ry'. MacDonald
defends 'arture', deriving it from Latin
artus (= joint).

75–8] *not in Q1F* 79] *F; Q2 lines* still, / thee. / waves] wafts *F* 80 hands] hand *F* 82 artery] *Q5;*
arture Q2; Artiue *Q1;* artyre *Q3, F;* attire *Q4*

As hardy as the Nemean lion's nerve.
Still am I called – unhand me, gentlemen –
By heaven I'll make a ghost of him that lets me!   85
I say away! – Go on! I'll follow thee.

Exeunt Ghost and Hamlet.

HORATIO

He waxes desperate with imagination.

MARCELLUS

Let's follow. 'Tis not fit thus to obey him.

HORATIO

Have after. To what issue will this come?

MARCELLUS

Something is rotten in the state of Denmark.   90

HORATIO

Heaven will direct it.

MARCELLUS   Nay, let's follow him.   *Exeunt.*

[1.5]   *Enter* GHOST *and* HAMLET.

83 **Nemean lion** (stress on first syllable of *Nemean*, an anglicized pronunciation also found at *LLL* 4.1.86 and *TNK* 1.1.68); a supposedly invulnerable beast strangled by Hercules as the first of his twelve labours. In contrast to his earlier reference to Hercules at 1.2.153, Hamlet is now prepared to vie with the mythical hero.

84 **called** summoned (not necessarily verbally)
   unhand take your hands off (*OED*'s first usage)

85 **make a ghost** Hamlet speaks as if he or someone else has just used the word *ghost*: see *R3* 1.2.36–7: 'Villains! set down the corse or by Saint Paul / I'll make a corse of him that disobeys!'
   lets prevents. This otherwise obsolete sense survives in the formulaic phrase 'let or hindrance'.

87 **waxes** grows

*imagination Q2's 'imagion' is not found elsewhere and could easily be a careless transcription/setting of 'imagination' as found in Q1 and F.

89 **Have after** Let us go after him.
   issue outcome

90 **state** polity, kingdom (as opposed to 'condition')

91 **Heaven . . . him** Horatio seems at first to move away from his more interventionist position at 89, but his fatalism is presumably rejected by Marcellus (*Nay*) and they follow Hamlet.
   it i.e. *the issue* of 89

1.5 There is no scene division at this point in Q1, Q2 or F, and the Ghost at the Globe may have re-entered by one door as Horatio left by another, but the change of both speakers and location justifies the division introduced by

87 imagination] *Q1F;* imagion *Q2*   **1.5**] *Capell*

HAMLET

Whither wilt thou lead me? Speak! I'll go no further.

GHOST

Mark me.

HAMLET   I will.

GHOST   My hour is almost come

When I to sulphurous and tormenting flames

Must render up myself.

HAMLET   Alas, poor ghost.

GHOST

Pity me not, but lend thy serious hearing   5

To what I shall unfold.

HAMLET   Speak, I am bound to hear.

GHOST

So art thou to revenge when thou shalt hear.

HAMLET

What?

GHOST

I am thy father's spirit,

Doomed for a certain term to walk the night   10

Capell. The three texts: this scene runs to 158 lines in Q1 (scene 5), 188 in Q2 and 190 in F. The Ghost's speeches are shorter in Q1 as is Hamlet's speech after the Ghost's exit and his contributions to the conversation after the return of Horatio and Marcellus. Location and timing: the action is continuous with 1.4 but Hamlet's opening words imply that the location is supposed to have shifted to a different area of the battlements (see also 1.4.69–71n.).

2   **Mark me** pay attention to me
    My . . . come i.e. it is nearly dawn. As in 1.1, the movement from midnight to dawn is rapid.

3   **sulphurous . . . flames** i.e. the flames of the Catholic purgatory, a place of spiritual purging preparatory to entry into heaven
    sulphurous dissyllabic: sulph'rous

6, 15   **unfold** reveal (see 1.1.2), narrate

6–7   **Speak . . . hear** This exchange is quoted and parodied in Beaumont and Fletcher's *The Woman Hater* (1606) when Lazarello says, 'speake I am bound to heare', and the Count replies, 'So art thou to revenge, when thou shalt heare. / The fish head is gone, and we know not whither' (2.1.344–7): see pp. 58–9 for early parodic citations of *Hamlet*.

6   **bound** (1) destined, (2) committed, obliged

10   **walk the night** walk throughout the night

---

1 Whither] *Q1;* Where *F*

And for the day confined to fast in fires
Till the foul crimes done in my days of nature
Are burnt and purged away. But that I am forbid
To tell the secrets of my prison-house
I could a tale unfold whose lightest word   15
Would harrow up thy soul, freeze thy young blood,
Make thy two eyes like stars start from their spheres,
Thy knotted and combined locks to part
And each particular hair to stand on end
Like quills upon the fearful porpentine –   20
But this eternal blazon must not be
To ears of flesh and blood. List, list, O list,

11 **fast in fires** a traditional punishment in purgatory, perhaps implying that old Hamlet was literally *full of bread* (3.3.80), since punishments were thought, as in the classical Hades, to fit the sins or crimes

12 **foul crimes** As at 76–9 and at 3.3.80–4, the degree of the former King's sinfulness is perhaps exaggerated to intensify the horror of his dying without the opportunity for confession and absolution.

13 **purged** This word again evokes the notion of purgatory.

16 **harrow up** tear up, uproot. The metaphor of digging something up (as with a harrow) picks up the idea of *foul deeds* being buried at the end of 1.2. See also 1.1.43n.

17 **spheres** sockets. Eyes are seen as being enclosed in their sockets as stars were thought to be enclosed in their spheres or orbits.

18 **knotted and combined** combinèd, i.e. combed and wound together. Hibbard argues that this means elaborately coiffed – 'During the first act Hamlet should be *the glass of fashion* [see 3.1.152]' – but this may not be compatible with his mourning garb.

19 *****on end** Jenkins argues that Q2's 'an' is not a variant of 'on' but the preposition 'a' (as in 'afoot' or 'awork') which takes an 'n' before a vowel.

20 **fearful** fear-inducing, terrifying. Edwards argues that F's 'fretfull' is stronger, reading *fearful* in the more common modern sense as 'frightened'.
porpentine porcupine (*porpentine* is Shakespeare's usual form) – assumed by the Elizabethans to be an aggressive animal which could shoot its quills out like darts

21 **eternal** relating to the realm of the supernatural. Shakespeare often associates the word with 'infernal', as in Cassius' reference to 'Th'eternal devil' (*JC* 1.2.158) and Emilia's evocation of 'some eternal villain' (*Oth* 4.2.132). See also 5.2.349.
blazon (1) itemized description, (2) public announcement
be be delivered

22 **List** listen. In Q1/F, the Ghost addresses Hamlet by name for the first time at this point (5.17).

18 knotted] *Q1;* knotty *F*   19 on] *(an)*   20 fearful] fretfull *Q1F*   porpentine –] Porpentine, *Q21;* Porpentine: *F*   22 List, list, O list] Hamlet *Q1;* list *Hamlet*, oh list *F*

If thou didst ever thy dear father love –

HAMLET

O God!

GHOST

– Revenge his foul and most unnatural murder!   25

HAMLET

Murder!

GHOST

Murder most foul – as in the best it is –
But this most foul, strange and unnatural.

HAMLET

Haste me to know't that I with wings as swift
As meditation or the thoughts of love   30
May sweep to my revenge.

GHOST   I find thee apt.
And duller shouldst thou be than the fat weed
That roots itself in ease on Lethe wharf
Wouldst thou not stir in this. Now, Hamlet, hear:
'Tis given out that, sleeping in my orchard,   35

---

24 **God** F's 'Heauen' is a likely expurgation. *TxC* notes a 'clear preponderance' of 'O God' in Shakespeare.

27 **as . . . is** i.e. all murders are bad (but mine was especially bad).

29–30 'As swift as thought' was proverbial (Dent, T240).

31 **apt** responsive

32 **fat weed** Commentators have failed to identify any particular plant; *fat* seems to connote bloated or perhaps torpid.

33 **roots** Q2's reading (supported by Q1) suggests moral inactivity ('not stirring') whereas F's 'rots' which suggests moral decay. Hibbard, unusually, adopts *roots*, because it 'offers a strong antithesis to *stir* [34], and it fits perfectly with the other instances of "things rank and gross in

nature" which are so frequent in the play.'
Lethe wharf the banks of the river Lethe, a river in the classical underworld from whose name we derive 'lethargic'; drinking its water induced forgetfulness and drowsiness. The *wharf* suggests a suppressed reference to Charon, who ferried souls across Lethe; the afterlife evoked here combines pagan and Christian elements, as does that evoked in Clarence's dream in *R3* 1.4.

35 **'Tis** *TxC* notes 1526 instances of ''Tis' in the canon as against 35 instances of 'It's' (the F reading).
given out announced publicly (presumably by the King and supporters)
sleeping . . . orchard while I was sleeping in my orchard. The qualifying

---

24 God] *Q1*; Heauen *F*   26 Murder!] *F (*Murther?*)*; Murther. *Q21*   29 Haste] *Q1*; Hast, hast *F* know't] knowe it *Q1F*   that I] that *Q1F*   33 roots] *Q1*; rots *F*   35 'Tis] *Q1*; It's *F*   my] *Q1*; mine *F*

A serpent stung me. So the whole ear of Denmark
Is by a forged process of my death
Rankly abused. But know, thou noble youth,
The serpent that did sting thy father's life
Now wears his crown.

HAMLET   O my prophetic soul!   40
My uncle!

GHOST

Ay, that incestuous, that adulterate beast,
With witchcraft of his wits, with traitorous gifts –
O wicked wit and gifts that have the power
So to seduce – won to his shameful lust   45

phrase refers forward to *me* in 36 (see
Blake, 3.3.6.3). The murder victim is not
asleep in either Saxo or Belleforest (see
Bullough 7.62 and 87).

orchard garden; the term was formerly
used in a general sense, not necessarily
implying the cultivation of fruit trees as it
does today.

36–8 **ear . . . abused** See 59–73 and 1.1.30n.
37 **forged process** forgèd; false account
38 **Rankly** grossly, offensively
   youth Again there is an insistence that
   Hamlet is young (see 1.3.7n. and List of
   Roles, 1n.).
39 **sting . . . life** poisoned your father (the
   Ghost continues the serpent metaphor from
   36); *sting*, not 'bite', because of the
   Elizabethan belief that the tongue was
   the source of a snake's poison rather than
   the teeth
40 **prophetic** foreknowing, speculative;
   Hamlet has not expressed a specific
   suspicion that the present King murdered
   his father, though this confirms and justifies
   his hostile attitude in 1.2.
42 **incestuous** see 1.2.157n.

adulterate literally, defiled or stained by
adultery. The word can also mean
'corrupted' in a more general way;
Shakespeare uses it in its literal sense in *Luc*
1645, *CE* 2.2.139 and *R3* 4.4.69, and in a
more general sense in *Son* 121.5 and *LC*
175. It is notoriously unclear whether the
Ghost means to say that his wife embarked
on an adulterous relationship with his
brother before his death: the strength of his
feeling in this speech seems to imply that
she did, but his relative lenience towards
her at 84–8 and at 3.4.108–11 might
indicate otherwise, as does the behaviour of
the Queen in the dumb-show and *The
Murder of Gonzago* in 3.2.

43 **wits** Most editors emend to 'wit' to match
   the singular in 44.
   gifts often glossed as 'natural gifts', i.e.
   personal qualities or talents, which is
   clearly what it means at 51, but the more
   obvious meaning of 'presents' could also
   be acceptable here and is supported by
   TGV 3.1.89 ('Win her with gifts, if she
   respect not words') and indeed by the SD
   for the dumb-show at 3.2.128.9–10.

40–1] *Riv; Q2F line* Crowne. / Vncle? /   41 My] *Q1; mine F   uncle!] Q1; Vncle? Q2F   43 wits] F; wit
*Pope   with] Q1; hath F   45 to his] to to this F

The will of my most seeming-virtuous Queen.
O Hamlet, what falling off was there,
From me whose love was of that dignity
That it went hand in hand even with the vow
I made to her in marriage, and to decline   50
Upon a wretch whose natural gifts were poor
To those of mine.
But Virtue, as it never will be moved
Though Lewdness court it in a shape of heaven,
So Lust, though to a radiant angel linked,   55
Will sate itself in a celestial bed
And prey on garbage.
But soft, methinks I scent the morning air.
Brief let me be. Sleeping within my orchard –

46 **will** sexual desire. The word carries a stronger meaning than the modern 'inclination'; see *Son* 135 and 136, where Shakespeare puns on this meaning and his own first name.

47 **what falling off** what a desertion or decline in standards. F's 'what a falling' improves both grammar and metre, but Jenkins, while printing 'what a falling', compares Q2's 'what piece of work is a man' at 2.2.269.

48 **dignity** worth

49 **even . . . vow** with the very vow (i.e. I took my marriage vows seriously)

50–1 **and . . . Upon** i.e. and that she should descend to

53–7 'While Virtue could not be seduced even if Lewdness wooed it in the guise of an angel, Lust is capable of glutting its appetite in a heavenly bed and then turning to prey on filth.' Iachimo uses similar metaphors when he is accusing Posthumus of deserting Imogen for prostitutes: 'The

cloyed will – / That satiate yet unsatisfied desire . . . – ravening first the lamb, / Longs after for the garbage' (*Cym* 1.7.47–50).

55 *****Lust** Q2's 'but' is a plausible misreading, but not a plausible word in this context.
angel Jenkins sees the influence of Q1 on Q2's spelling ('Angle').

56 *****sate** satiate. This F reading is supported by Q1's 'fate', a possible misreading of long *s*, and by the use of 'satiate' in the *Cym* example quoted above; Q2's 'sort' is difficult to justify (though Andrews retains, glossing it as 'situate, place') and is an easy misreading of 'a' as 'or' (see 1.2.96).

57 **garbage** entrails, foul remains (a stronger meaning than the modern 'rubbish')

58 **soft** wait (see, listen). The Ghost interrupts himself, remembering the need for haste.
scent . . . air The assumption is that the Ghost must return to hell or purgatory at dawn; see 1.1.146–55.

47 what] what a *F*   52–3] *Pope; one line Q2F*   55 Lust] *Q1F;* but *Q2*   angel] *(Angle), Q1 (angle),*
F (Angell)   56 sate] *F;* sort *Q2;* fate *Q1*   56–7] *one line F*   58 morning] mornings *Q1F*   59 my] *Q1;*
mine *F*

My custom always of the afternoon –   60
Upon my secure hour thy uncle stole
With juice of cursed hebona in a vial
And in the porches of my ears did pour
The leperous distilment whose effect
Holds such an enmity with blood of man   65
That swift as quicksilver it courses through
The natural gates and alleys of the body
And with a sudden vigour it doth possess
And curd like eager droppings into milk
The thin and wholesome blood. So did it mine   70

60 Caliban tells of Prospero's similar habit: ' 'tis a custom with him / I'th' afternoon to sleep' (*Tem* 3.2.89–90).

61 **secure** free from care, relaxed. The implication is that this was a time when there was no need to take any precautions.

62 **juice ... hebona** poison. Marlowe mentions 'the jouyce of Hebon' as a poison in *The Jew of Malta* (1589; 3.4.101), but the specific nature of this poison has not been identified; these names may be just exotic variants of the more homely 'henbane', the plant *hyoscamus niger*, whose Latin name also suggests ebony (*niger* = black).

vial (phial) small container for liquid

63–70 The King's body becomes first a house, then a town or city. Perhaps the sack of Troy is already present behind these lines.

63 **porches . . . ears** i.e. my ears, viewed as the porches of the house which is my head/ body. Modern medicine tells us that such a method of poisoning would not actually be effective, but Bullough suggests that Shakespeare took the idea from accounts of the murder of the Duke of Urbino in 1538, allegedly done in this way (Bullough 7:29– 33; see p. 62). Another source might be

Marlowe's villain Lightborn in *Edward II* (1592) who describes a method of killing he claims to have learned in Naples: 'whilst one is a sleepe, to take a quill, / And blowe a little powder in his eares' (5.4.34–5).

64 **leperous distilment** distillation or essence causing (the appearance of) leprosy, i.e. scales and discoloration of the skin. Q2 has 'leaprous', a spelling it shares with Q1. *Distilment* is a Shakespearean coinage (see 1.2.93n.); curiously, Johnson's 1773 error, 'instilment', became an attested word in the nineteenth century.

65 **with blood** Thus in all three texts; one might be tempted to print 'wi'th' blood'.

66 **quicksilver** the liquid metal mercury

68 **possess** This must mean something like 'take control of' or 'overpower'; Shakespeare uses the verb elsewhere in relation to sickness or disease, as in 'I will possess him with yellowness' (*MW* 1.3.97). F's 'posset' means the same thing as *curd*: the idea is that the poison causes the blood to curdle or clot like sour milk.

69 **eager droppings** sour or bitter drops

70 **thin and wholesome** hendiadys: 'thin because wholesome (or vice versa?)' (Wright, 186)

62 hebona] *Q1;* Hebenon *F*   63 my] *Q1;* mine *F*   64 leperous] *(*leaprous*) Q1, F (*leaperous*)* 68 possess] posset *F*   69 eager] *Q1;* Aygre *F*

And a most instant tetter barked about
Most lazar-like with vile and loathsome crust
All my smooth body.
Thus was I sleeping by a brother's hand
Of life, of crown, of queen at once dispatched,   75
Cut off even in the blossoms of my sin,
Unhouseled, disappointed, unaneled,
No reckoning made but sent to my account
With all my imperfections on my head.
O horrible, O horrible, most horrible!   80
If thou hast nature in thee bear it not,
Let not the royal bed of Denmark be

71–3 'an immediate blistering (*tetter*) resembling leprosy (*lazar-like*) encrusted my smooth skin like the bark of a tree.' The metaphor suggests an Ovidian metamorphosis, as when Daphne is transformed into a tree (Book 1), but it also anticipates the decomposition of the body after death.

75 **dispatched** deprived

76 **in . . . sin** 'in the height of my sinful state' (see 12n. and the similar metaphor at 3.3.81)

77 **Unhouseled** without having taken the sacrament ('housel' is an old name for the 'host' or consecrated element of Christian mass or communion)
disappointed improperly appointed, unprepared
unaneled not anointed, i.e. without having taken extreme unction – the special sacrament for the dying. (The syllable *nel* is pronounced like 'kneel'.) Taken together, these three adjectives emphasize that the Ghost has been deprived of the 'last rites' due to a dying Christian.

78 **No reckoning made** given no chance to settle my affairs (with God, by confessing my sins)

80 Johnson, who claimed to be following the hint of 'a learned lady', notes in an appendix that this line might be spoken by Hamlet; Rann's edition was the first to reassign it (though Q1 has Hamlet interject 'O God' at this point). Editors have conjectured that Johnson's lady was either Elizabeth Montagu or Elizabeth Carter, but Oya (23) points out that in fact the suggestion had been made to Garrick in a letter from P[eter] W[halley] dated 20 February 1744 (see Boaden, 23) and he spoke the line on stage. Subsequent Hamlets, including Kemble, Kean, Irving, Gielgud, Olivier (in the 1948 film) and Jacobi (in the 1980 BBC television version) have also used it effectively to break the Ghost's monologue. Kiasashvili (186) records that, without having access to any of these sources, Ivane Machabeli independently gave the line to Hamlet, the only significant change in his otherwise faithful Georgian translation of 1886.

81 **nature** natural feeling

71 barked] *Q1;* bak'd *F*   72 lazar-like] *(Lazerlike), F*   75 of queen] *Q1;* and Queene *F*   77 Unhouseled] *(Vnhuzled), F (Vnhouzzled)* unaneled] *(vnanueld), F (vnnaneld)* 78 reckoning] *(reckning), Q1F* 80–1 O . . . If] *F;* HAMLET O . . . GHOST If *Rann (Johnson)*

A couch for luxury and damned incest.
But howsomever thou pursues this act
Taint not thy mind nor let thy soul contrive   85
Against thy mother aught; leave her to heaven
And to those thorns that in her bosom lodge
To prick and sting her. Fare thee well at once:
The glow-worm shows the matin to be near
And 'gins to pale his uneffectual fire.   90
Adieu, adieu, adieu, remember me.   [*Exit.*]

HAMLET

O all you host of heaven, O earth – what else? –
And shall I couple hell? O fie! Hold, hold, my heart,
And you, my sinews, grow not instant old

---

83 **luxury** lust, lechery (as always in Shakespeare)

  damned Some editors (including Edwards and Hibbard) suggest that this is pronounced damnèd, but the standard modern monosyllable is acceptable.

  incest See 1.2.157n.

84 **howsomever** howsoever (see 1.2.247n.)

  pursues F's 'pursuest' is strictly grammatical but *pursues* is easier to say (see *Revisits* at 1.4.53 and n.).

85 **Taint . . . mind** do not let your mind become contaminated. It is of course a major point of discussion whether Hamlet's *mind* does become *tainted* in the course of the play; see pp. 26–32.

86 **aught** anything (as at 177)

  leave . . . heaven i.e. let God judge and punish her. Again, the Ghost seems to assume that she is not equally guilty.

87–8 **thorns . . . her** There is possibly a suppressed reference to the supposed source of the nightingale's wakefulness: 'Everything did banish moan, / Save the nightingale alone: / She, poor bird, as all forlorn, / Lean'd her breast up-till a thorn' (*PP* 20.7–11).

88 **at once** immediately

89–90 i.e. the fact that the faint light of the glow-worm is diminishing shows that morning (*matin*) is approaching. This is Shakespeare's only use of the word *matin* and it may be chosen for its religious connotations, 'matins' being a church service that takes place in the morning.

91 **Adieu** farewell (literally '[I commend you] to God' in French)

91 SD *It seems possible that at the Globe the Ghost would have descended through a trap-door, especially in the light of his voice coming from *under the stage* at 149 (see Gurr & Ichikawa, 131). John Ward's prompt-book has 'Ring for Trap to be ready' and 'Ghost Ready below' at the appropriate points (see Thompson, 'Ward', 144), but at the London Globe in 2000 the Ghost used one of the stage doors.

93 **couple** join, link (not necessarily just two things)

  fie an expression of disgust or reproach

94 **sinews** tendons, muscles

  grow . . . old don't become feeble as if with sudden ageing

---

84 howsomever] howsoeuer *Q1F*   pursues] pursuest *F*   85 Taint] *(Tain't)*, *F*   90 'gins] *Q2u (*gines)*, *Q2cF (*gins)   91 Adieu, adieu, adieu] Hamlet adue, adue, adue *Q1;* Adue, adue, *Hamlet F* SD] *Q1F* 93 Hold, hold] hold *F*

But bear me swiftly up. Remember thee?   95
Ay, thou poor ghost, whiles memory holds a seat
In this distracted globe. Remember thee?
Yea, from the table of my memory
I'll wipe away all trivial fond records,
All saws of books, all forms, all pressures past   100
That youth and observation copied there
And thy commandment all alone shall live
Within the book and volume of my brain
Unmixed with baser matter. Yes, by heaven,
O most pernicious woman,   105
O villain, villain, smiling damnèd villain,
My tables! Meet it is I set it down
That one may smile and smile and be a villain –

95 **swiftly** Presumably the implication is that Hamlet will move quickly to his revenge (see 29–31), but most editors prefer F's 'stiffely' meaning 'strongly', which is supported by *H5* 3.1.7: 'Stiffen the sinews.'

96–7 **whiles ... globe** (1) while [my] memory has any power over my shattered frame; (2) while memory [in general] is a force in this disordered world. Yet a third meaning may have occurred to the earliest auditors at the Globe.

98 **table** Hamlet envisages his memory as a wax writing tablet on which items can be inscribed or erased (see 107 and *Son* 122).

99 **fond** foolish
records (stressed on second syllable) recollections

100 **saws of books** commonplaces or maxims copied from books
forms ... pressures familiar formulas and impressions: literally shapes drawn on the tablet. See 'to show ... the very age and body of the time his form and pressure' (3.2.22–4).

101 'that I noted in my youth through observation'

103 Hamlet's mind is now a book – a familiar metaphor, as when Orsino tells Cesario/ Viola, 'I have unclasp'd / To thee the book even of my secret soul' (*TN* 1.4.13–14); for further discussion of this metaphor, see Thompson & Thompson, 165–70.
volume in one sense synonymous with *book*, but also carrying the sense of size or spaciousness

104 **baser** less valuable

106 **damned** damnèd

107 **tables** Hamlet now produces a literal writing tablet or notebook (see *1H6* 2.4.100, 'I'll note you in my book of memory'). Earlier editors used to worry about Hamlet's apparent naïvety in feeling this trite observation was worth recording (see Var for examples).
Meet fitting, appropriate (as at 169)

108 The idea is traditional: see Chaucer's 'smylere with the knyf under the cloke' (*Knight's Tale*, 1999) and also clearly a possibility in England: see Richard of Gloucester's 'I can smile, and murder whiles I smile' (*3H6* 3.2.182).

95 swiftly] stiffely *F*   96 whiles] while *F*   104 Yes] Yes, yes *Q1F*   107 tables] *Q1;* Tables, my Tables *F*

At least I am sure it may be so in Denmark.
So, uncle, there you are. Now to my word. 110
It is 'Adieu, adieu, remember me.'
I have sworn't.

Enter HORATIO *and* MARCELLUS.

HORATIO
My lord, my lord!
MARCELLUS   Lord Hamlet!
HORATIO   Heavens secure him!
HAMLET
So be it.
MARCELLUS   Illo, ho, ho, my lord!
HAMLET
Hillo, ho, ho, boy, come and come! 115

---

110 **So ... are** Hamlet perhaps contemplates with satisfaction the note in which he has summed up his uncle's villainy. From here on the lines invite the actor to exhibit a kind of manic exhilaration (see Horatio's comment at 132). The shift from fear or horror to jocularity contrasts strangely with Brutus' response to the ghost of Caesar where he moves in 10 lines from horror at the 'monstrous apparition' which 'mak'st my blood cold and my hair to stare' to the stoical 'Well, I will see thee at Philippi then' (*JC* 4.3.275–85).

    to my word i.e. I must keep my promise to the Ghost (but Hibbard and Jenkins read *word* as 'watchword' or 'motto'). Between here and 115 Hamlet may perform some private ritual of swearing before the others enter: see 114 and n.

112 F's placing of the SD indicates that we hear Horatio and Marcellus calling before they appear. In the supposed darkness of the stage, they do not see Hamlet until he answers them at 115.

113 **secure** safeguard, save (from the possibly malign influence of the Ghost)

114 **So be it** Spoken by Hamlet in Q2 where it seems to conclude his private pact with the Ghost (or perhaps just his act of writing); spoken by Marcellus in F where it is an assent to Horatio's *Heavens secure him.*

114–15 **Illo ... Hillo** listed by *OED* as variants of holla/hallo. In all three texts the others enter hallooing or calling for Hamlet. His reply, 'ho, boy, come and come', compares their cries (perhaps mockingly) to those of a falconer calling to his preying bird to return. (F's reading makes this more obvious.)

---

109 I am] *Q1;* I'm *F*   111–12] *one line F*   112.1] *opp.* lord. / Hamlet. *113 Q1; after* Lord, my Lord. *113 F*   113 SP1] *Q1; Hor. & Mar. within. F*   Heavens] *Q1;* Heauen *F*   114 SP1] *Mar. F*   SP2] *Hor. Q1F*   115 SP] *F; Mar. Q1*   and] boy *Q1;* bird *F*

MARCELLUS

How is't, my noble lord?

HORATIO   What news, my lord?

HAMLET

O, wonderful.

HORATIO   Good my lord, tell it.

HAMLET

No, you will reveal it.

HORATIO

Not I, my lord, by heaven.

MARCELLUS   Nor I, my lord.

HAMLET

How say you then – would heart of man once think

   it? –   120

But you'll be secret?

HORATIO, MARCELLUS   Ay, by heaven.

HAMLET

There's never a villain dwelling in all Denmark

But he's an arrant knave.

HORATIO

There needs no ghost, my lord, come from the grave

To tell us this.

HAMLET   Why, right, you are in the right!   125

And so without more circumstance at all

---

116 **How is't** How is it (with you), i.e. are you all right?

117–18 **Good . . . reveal it** It becomes clear at 3.2.72–3 that Hamlet does subsequently confide in Horatio, though not, presumably, in Marcellus. Beginning with Kemble, many Hamlets have seemed distrustful of Marcellus at this point, anticipating the later distrust of Rosencrantz and Guildenstern (see Hapgood). The banality or tautology of 122–3 may indicate that Hamlet deflects what might have begun as a serious response.

120 **once** i.e. ever

123 **arrant** veritable, downright (an 'opprobrious intensive' (*OED*) always used by Shakespeare with nouns like knave, traitor, thief, whore)

124–5 **There . . . this** Horatio is disappointed by the banality of Hamlet's revelation.

124 **come** to come

126 **circumstance** elaboration of detail

---

118 you will] you'l *Q1F*   121 SP] *(Booth.)*   heaven] heauen, my lord *Q1F*   122] *Q1F; Q2 lines* villaine, / Denmarke /   never] *Q1*; nere *F*   124–5 There . . . this] *prose Q1F*   125 in the] *Q1*; i'th' *F*

I hold it fit that we shake hands and part –
You as your business and desire shall point you
(For every man hath business and desire
Such as it is) and for my own poor part   130
I will go pray.

HORATIO

These are but wild and whirling words, my lord.

HAMLET

I am sorry they offend you – heartily,
Yes, faith, heartily.

HORATIO   There's no offence, my lord.

HAMLET

Yes, by Saint Patrick, but there is, Horatio,   135
And much offence too. Touching this vision here
It is an honest ghost – that let me tell you.
For your desire to know what is between us
O'ermaster it as you may. And now, good friends,

---

127 **shake hands** a gesture (or metaphor) of parting rather than of meeting, most strikingly at *AC* 4.12.19–20: 'Fortune and Antony part here; even here / Do we shake hands.'

128 **point** direct

130 **poor** Hamlet uses this word three times from here to the end of the scene in all three texts (see 141 and 182), apparently emphasizing his relatively powerless position; unlike the experience of *every man*, his *business and desire* have been diverted by his uncle's actions.

131 **I ... pray** Hamlet continues with the parting formulas begun at 127.

132 Horatio's response indicates that he does not approve of Hamlet's desire to put an end to the conversation.
   whirling excited, extravagant

135 **Saint Patrick** Editors suggest he is appropriate, either as a saint associated with purgatory (see also Greenblatt, *Purgatory*, 233–4), or because he is supposed to have banished snakes from Ireland (see *serpent* in 39). This line (present in all three texts) is Shakespeare's only reference to the saint or the name apart from references to Friar Patrick in *TGV*.

136 **Touching** concerning

137 **honest** Hamlet claims (jocularly? certainly temporarily) to have resolved the issue he raised at 1.4.40 as to whether the Ghost is a *spirit of health* or a *goblin damned*, though its status in purgatory renders it neither angel nor devil. Perhaps *honest* just means 'genuine' or 'truthful'.

138 **what ... us** i.e. what has passed (or been agreed) between me and the Ghost

---

128 desire] desiers *Q1F*   129 hath] *Q1;* ha's *F*   130 my] *Q1;* mine *F*   131 I will] ile *Q1;* Looke you, Ile *F*   132 whirling] *Q1;* hurling *F*   133 I am] *Q1;* I'm *F*   135 Horatio] *Q1;* my Lord *F*   136 too.] *Rowe;* to, *Q2, (*too,) *Q1F*   139 O'ermaster it] *Q1,* Oremastret *Q2,* O'remaster't *F*

As you are friends, scholars and soldiers,   140
Give me one poor request.

HORATIO

What is't, my lord? We will.

HAMLET

Never make known what you have seen tonight.

HORATIO, MARCELLUS

My lord, we will not.

HAMLET

Nay, but swear't.

HORATIO   In faith, my lord, not I.   145

MARCELLUS

Nor I, my lord, in faith.

HAMLET   Upon my sword.

MARCELLUS

We have sworn, my lord, already.

HAMLET

Indeed, upon my sword, indeed.

GHOST   (*Cries under the stage.*)
Swear.

---

140 **friends ... soldiers** See 1.1.11n. and
Ophelia's lament at 3.1.150.
145–6 **not I ... Nor I** Horatio and Marcellus
are probably saying 'we will not make it
known', not 'we will not swear', despite
Hamlet's insistence at 152.
146 **Upon my sword** The hilt of a sword could
be used to stand in for a crucifix, as at *R2*
1.3.179.
149 SD *under the stage* In the Elizabethan
theatre the space under the stage was
associated with hell, as for example in the
dumb-show before Act 4 of Thomas
Sackville and Thomas Norton's *Gorboduc*
(1561): 'there came from under the stage,
as though out of hell, three furies.' There
are several references in plays of the period

to properties or characters ascending or
descending through a trapdoor and to
noises emanating from below (see Dessen
& Thomson, 'under the stage'), though the
only other example of Shakespeare's use of
the latter effect is the SD '*Music of the
Hoboys is under the Stage*' for the
unearthly music signifying Hercules'
desertion of Antony at *AC* 4.3.12. It turned
out, however, not to be practicable to have
the Ghost speak from under the stage at the
London Globe in 2000: the actor could not
be heard by the audience; nor could he hear
his cues. Wherever the voice comes from,
the Ghost seems to add to or even
participate in Hamlet's wildness (see
110n.).

149 SD] *Ghost cries vnder the Stage. after 148; after 149 Q1; opp. 149 F*

HAMLET

Ha, ha, boy, sayst thou so? Art thou there, truepenny?   150
Come on, you hear this fellow in the cellarage?
Consent to swear.

HORATIO   Propose the oath, my lord.

HAMLET

Never to speak of this that you have seen,
Swear by my sword.

GHOST

Swear.   155

HAMLET

Hic et ubique? Then we'll shift our ground.
Come hither, gentlemen, and lay your hands
Again upon my sword. Swear by my sword

---

150 **truepenny** honest fellow; Tom Truepenny
   is the name of a character in Nicholas
   Udall's play *Ralph Roister Doister* (*c.*
   1553).
151 **Come on** Hamlet presumably gestures the
   others to move away from the sound of the
   Ghost's voice.
   you … fellow It is not clear from the
   dialogue whether anyone other than
   Hamlet does hear the Ghost, though it
   might be argued that if his companions can
   see the Ghost they can also hear him,
   unlike the Queen in 3.4. Q1's version of
   this line, 'come you here, this fellow in the
   selleridge', could be interpreted as an aural
   error ('here' for 'hear'), or it could be taken
   to imply that Horatio and Marcellus do not
   in fact hear anything.
   cellarage cellars (plural), a term more
   appropriate to the stage than to the *platform*
   setting of the fiction. Hibbard suggests
   cellarage might have been a technical term
   for the space under the stage, though *OED*
   does not have any examples of such a

usage; nor does it occur in Dessen &
Thomson.
152 **Propose the oath** Horatio and Marcellus
   may be puzzled as to what exactly they are
   being asked to swear to, or they may
   merely be signalling their readiness to
   swear.
156 *Hic et ubique* here and everywhere (Latin).
   All three texts use an ampersand at this
   point, and they also agree on the spelling
   'can'st' at 161, and the initial capitals in
   'Gentleman' at 157, 'Mole' at 161 and
   'Pioner' at 162. Ubiquity is traditionally a
   property shared by God and the devil.
   Sebastian evokes the same idea when
   confronted by his twin at the end of *TN*: 'I
   never had a brother; / Nor can there be that
   deity in my nature / Of here and
   everywhere' (5.1.222–4).
158 **Again** Jenkins, who argues that Horatio
   and Marcellus swear three times during
   this sequence, takes this as meaning that
   Hamlet repeats the ritual rather than that he
   begins again, but see 180 and n.

---

150 Ha, ha] *Q1;* Ah ha *F*   150–1] *prose F*   151 cellarage] *(Sellerige) Q1, F (*selleredge*)*   153 seen,]
*(seene); *seene. *F*   156 *et*] *(&) Q1F*   our] *Q1;* for *F*   157–9] *this edn; Q2 lines* Gentlemen / sword, /
sword / heard. / ; *F lines* Gentlemen, / sword, / heard: /   157 gentlemen] *(Gentlemen) Q1F* 158–9 Swear
. . . heard] Neuer to speake of this that you haue heard: / Sweare by my Sword *F*

Never to speak of this that you have heard.

GHOST

Swear by his sword. 160

HAMLET

Well said, old mole, canst work i'th' earth so fast?
A worthy pioner! Once more remove, good friends.

HORATIO

O day and night, but this is wondrous strange.

HAMLET

And therefore as a stranger give it welcome:
There are more things in heaven and earth, Horatio, 165
Than are dreamt of in your philosophy. But come,
Here as before: never – so help you mercy,
How strange or odd some'er I bear myself
(As I perchance hereafter shall think meet
To put an antic disposition on) – 170

159 **heard** Q1's 'seene' (as at 153) is more logical, since Horatio and Marcellus have seen the Ghost but perhaps not heard it speak unless they have heard the repeated *Swear* from 149 (see 151n.).

161–2 **mole . . . pioner** Hamlet compares the Ghost to a burrowing animal or to a soldier who digs to lay mines. De Grazia demonstrates how Hegel and Marx used Hamlet's metaphor of the mole to represent the emergence of modern consciousness (de Grazia, 'Teleology'; and see pp. 26–9).

162 **pioner** We preserve this Q2 spelling to distinguish the military sense (see 161–2n.) from the modern 'pioneer' (see also *enginer* at 3.4.204).

164 Hamlet alludes to the proverb 'Give the stranger welcome' (Dent, S914). He predicts his own *strange* behaviour at 168.

166 **your** Probably used colloquially (Blake, 3.3.4.5c) in a general rather than a personal sense (see *Your worm* at 4.3.21 and *your*

water at 5.1.161–2), though actors sometimes stress *your*, implying an attack on Horatio's (limited) beliefs about the natural world. (F's 'our' is assumed to be an error by Edwards but not by Hibbard.)

166–77 **But . . . me** The syntax is disjointed in all three texts, perhaps reflecting Hamlet's distraction as he both interrupts and repeats himself.

167 **never . . . mercy** 'never, as you hope to obtain [God's] mercy'

168 **How . . . some'er** howsoever, however (see 1.2.247n.)

169 **think meet** decide, see fit

170 **antic disposition** wild, fantastic or clownish manner or behaviour. *OED* records this as its second instance of *antic* in this sense, the first being in Marlowe's *Edward II* where Gaveston imagines that 'My men like Satyres grazing on the lawnes, / Shall with their Goate feete daunce an antic hay' (1.1.59–60).

159 heard] *F*; seene *Q1* 160] Sweare. *Q1F* 161 mole] *(*Mole*) Q1F* canst] *(*can'st*) Q1F* earth] *Q1*; ground *F* 162 pioner] *(*Pioner*) Q1F* 166 your] *Q1*; our *F* 168 some'er] *(*so mere*)*; soere *Q1*; so ere *F*

That you at such times seeing me never shall
With arms encumbered thus, or this headshake,
Or by pronouncing of some doubtful phrase
As 'Well, well, we know', or 'We could an if we
　　would',
Or 'If we list to speak', or 'There be an if they might', 175
Or such ambiguous giving out to note
That you know aught of me. This do swear,
So grace and mercy at your most need help you.

GHOST

　Swear.

HAMLET

　Rest, rest, perturbed spirit. So, gentlemen,　　　　　　180
　With all my love I do commend me to you,
　And what so poor a man as Hamlet is
　May do t'express his love and friending to you

172 Hamlet enacts gestures which would characterize one who has a secret s/he is prepared to reveal.
　　encumbered folded (?), a unique usage of the word (which occurs in all three texts). The following *thus* calls for a gesture that will clarify the meaning.
173 **doubtful** ambiguous
174 **Well, well** Jenkins sees this duplication in Q2 and Q1 as having 'all the air of an actor's repetition'.
　　could . . . would could [tell] if we wanted to
174, 175 **an if** if (intensive). All three texts have 'and if' but editorial convention prefers *an* in contexts where 'and' could be misleading: see *OED conj.* 2c.
175 **list** wished
　　There . . . might 'There are those (namely ourselves) who could explain if they chose to'

176 **giving out** pronouncement (as at 35)
　　to note to indicate. *To* is redundant, since *note* is governed by *never shall* in 171.
177 **This do swear** Hamlet cuts through the syntactical confusion (see 166–77n.) by starting again. Q1 and F resolve this problem differently by substituting 'this not to doe' for Q2's 'this doe sweare'.
178 'as you hope for grace and mercy to help you when you need them most'
180 **Rest . . . spirit** The Ghost is able to rest once revenge has been sworn (or, ideally, accomplished: see Brutus' dying words, 'Caesar, now be still', at *JC* 5.5.50). The implication is that Horatio and Marcellus have taken an oath by now, though none of the three texts indicates precisely when this happens.
183 **friending** friendship; Shakespeare's only usage of this word (also in F)

171 times] *Q1;* time *F*　172 this] *Q1;* thus, *F*　174 Well, well] *Q1;* well *F*　175 they] *Q1;* there *F* 177–8 do swear, . . . you.] not to doe, so grace, and mercie / At your most need helpe you, sweare / *Q1;* not to doe: / So grace and mercy at your most neede helpe you: / Sweare. *F*　181 With all] *(*Withall*), F;* In all *Q1*

God willing shall not lack. Let us go in together
And still your fingers on your lips, I pray.　　　　　185
The time is out of joint; O cursed spite
That ever I was born to set it right!
Nay, come, let's go together.　　　　　　　　　　*Exeunt*.

[**2.1**]　　　*Enter old* POLONIUS *with his man* [REYNALDO]
or two.

POLONIUS
Give him this money and these notes, Reynaldo.

185 **still** always
　　fingers . . . lips as a sign of secrecy
186–7 Some performers make this a kind of
　　aside in which Hamlet speaks to himself
　　(see Hapgood). The metaphor is from
　　the practice of setting broken bones to
　　mend.
186 **The time** the age, i.e. things in general
　　cursed cursèd
　　spite ill or outrageous fortune
188 **Nay, come** Presumably the others wait for
　　Hamlet to precede them off-stage but he
　　insists on their going together. See his
　　previous insistence that Horatio is his
　　friend, not his servant, and that the
　　relationship between them all is one of
　　love, not duty (1.2.163, 252).
2.1 The three texts: this scene runs to 64 lines
　　in Q1 (scene 6) and 117 lines in Q2 and F.
　　The general gist of it is much the same in
　　each but virtually all the speeches are
　　shorter in Q1, whose verse before Ofelia's
　　entry is very irregular. Location and
　　timing: presumably the scene, like 1.3,
　　takes place in the house of Polonius.
　　'Shakespeare gives several indications of a
　　lapse of time between Acts 1 and 2. Laertes

is settled in Paris, Ophelia has refused to
see Hamlet or receive his letters (Scene 1).
The King and Queen have been alarmed by
Hamlet's behaviour and have sent for
Rosencrantz and Guildenstern, who have
reached Elsinore. The ambassadors have
been to Norway and have returned (Scene
2)' (Edwards). On a literalist interpretation,
it may be that two months have elapsed,
given that at 3.2.121 Ophelia claims it is
twice two months since the death of
Hamlet's father, but Hamlet's *two months*
at 1.2.138 could be merely rhetorical.
0.1–2 Q2's entry direction has been taken as
　　evidence that the text derives from an
　　authorial　manuscript:　'*old　Polonius*'
　　elaborates on his first appearance in 1.2
　　and '*his man or two*' indicates uncertainty
　　at the time of composition but, as the scene
　　stands, only one *man* is needed.
　　*REYNALDO See List of Roles, 8n.
1　**him** The audience or reader's guess that
　　Polonius is talking about his son Laertes is
　　confirmed in his speech at 6–15.
　　notes messages, letters (perhaps letters of
　　introduction?); not 'banknotes', which is a
　　later usage

2.1] *Q6; Actus Secundus. F; not in Q21*　0.1–2] *Enter Corambis, and Montano. Q1; Enter Polonius, and Reynaldo. F*　0.1 REYNALDO] *this edn*　1 this] *Q1*; his *F*

REYNALDO   I will, my lord.

POLONIUS

You shall do marvellous wisely, good Reynaldo,
Before you visit him to make inquire
Of his behaviour.

REYNALDO   My lord, I did intend it.   5

POLONIUS

Marry, well said, very well said. Look you, sir,
Inquire me first what Danskers are in Paris,
And how, and who, what means, and where they keep,
What company, at what expense, and finding
By this encompassment and drift of question   10

---

2   **my lord** Reynaldo's use of this mode of
     address in all but one of his 13 one-line
     speeches might seem to indicate a
     sycophantic attitude, but Gérard Depardieu
     made him a sinister, powerful character in
     his memorable cameo in Branagh's 1996
     film. On stage, Alec Guinness is credited
     with 'discovering' the role in the London
     Old Vic production directed by Tyrone
     Guthrie in 1937 with Laurence Olivier as
     Hamlet (see Trewin, xii and 47).

3   **shall do** should be sure to do
     marvellous   used   adverbially:
     marvellously, wonderfully. The Q2 and F
     spellings (see t.n.) probably reflect
     disyllabic pronunciation: the word appears
     as 'maruel's' in both texts of *TC* at 1.2.133;
     see also 'trauells' for 'travailous' at Q1622
     Oth (1.3.140).

4   **inquire** an example of a verb used as a
     noun without the usual *-y* suffix, a frequent
     phenomenon in Early Modern English
     defined by modern linguists as 'zero-
     morpheme derivation' (see Hope, 1.2.8 and
     Glossary).

6   **Look you, sir** i.e. take care you do this.
     Polonius seems anxious to insist on

Reynaldo's attention, as at 15.

7   **me** for me (ethical dative: see Hope, 1.3.2i)
     Danskers Danes. Spencer calls this an
     'unusually correct' form, though some
     have argued that it really means 'citizens of
     Gdansk or Danzig' (a city now in Poland,
     well known to travelling English actors in
     Shakespeare's time); this is the only
     example listed in *OED*, though there
     is a cross-reference to Spenser's
     description of Concord in the Temple of
     Venus: 'for on her head a crowne / She
     wore much like vnto a Danisk hood' (*FQ*,
     4.10.31), where 'Danisk' apparently means
     Danish.

8   **how** i.e. how they live
     what means what are their resources
     keep live, frequent

10   **encompassment and drift** 'perhaps two
     techniques, but not really parallel' (Wright,
     176, who identifies this as hendiadys and
     notes that Polonius over-uses the device, as
     does Laertes at 1.3.11–43).
     encompassment act of encompassing, i.e.
     of talking around the topic (a
     Shakespearean coinage: see 1.2.93n.)
     drift general direction (as at 37)

---

3 marvellous] *(meruiles)*, Q3; maruels *F;* marv'lous *Oxf*   4 to make inquire] you make inquiry *F*

That they do know my son, come you more nearer
Than your particular demands will touch it;
Take you as 'twere some distant knowledge of him,
As thus, 'I know his father and his friends
And in part him' – do you mark this, Reynaldo?   15

REYNALDO   Ay, very well, my lord.

POLONIUS

'And in part him, but', you may say, 'not well.
But if 't be he I mean he's very wild,
Addicted so and so', and there put on him
What forgeries you please. Marry, none so rank   20
As may dishonour him – take heed of that –
But, sir, such wanton, wild and usual slips
As are companions noted and most known
To youth and liberty.

REYNALDO   As gaming, my lord?

POLONIUS

Ay, or drinking, fencing, swearing,   25
Quarrelling, drabbing – you may go so far.

11–12 **come . . . demands** 'approach the topic more closely than these particular questions'
   more nearer an emphatic double comparative: see Hope, 1.2.3.
13 **Take you** you may assume
15 **do . . . this** are you paying attention to this
19 **Addicted . . . so** devoted to such and such pursuits or pastimes. *Addicted* has no pejorative implication.
20 **forgeries** fabrications, inventions
   rank offensive; see other uses of *rank* and *ranker* at 1.2.136, 3.2.250, 3.3.36, 3.4.90 and 150 and 4.4.21.
22 **usual slips** common flaws or failings
23 **noted** well known, notorious
24 **youth and liberty** the unrestrained behaviour of young men (hendiadys)

gaming gambling
25 **fencing** While the ability to fence was valued in young aristocrats in Elizabethan England, fencing schools were seen as a typical resort of the wilder kind of young men; see Sir Andrew Aguecheek's regret: 'I would I had bestowed that time in the tongues [languages] that I have in fencing, dancing and bearbaiting' (*TN* 1.3.90–2).
26 **Quarrelling** For satirical accounts of the elaborate codes of quarrelling practised by young men of Shakespeare's time, see Touchstone's account of a quarrel 'upon the seventh cause' (*AYL* 5.4.45–101) and Ben Jonson's *The Alchemist* (1610), 3.3, where young Kastril arrives in London to learn how to quarrel.
   drabbing patronizing prostitutes

14 As] *Q1;* And *F*

REYNALDO My lord, that would dishonour him.

POLONIUS

Faith, as you may season it in the charge.
You must not put another scandal on him
That he is open to incontinency –   30
That's not my meaning – but breathe his faults so
 quaintly
That they may seem the taints of liberty,
The flash and outbreak of a fiery mind,
A savageness in unreclaimed blood
Of general assault.

REYNALDO   But my good lord –   35

POLONIUS

Wherefore should you do this?

REYNALDO   Ay, my lord,
I would know that.

POLONIUS   Marry, sir, here's my drift –
And I believe it is a fetch of wit –

(drabs). Polonius' assumption that this last accusation in particular will not harm his son's reputation is in stark contrast to the attitude both he and Laertes have shown towards Ophelia's *honour* in 1.3: an example of the 'double standard' whereby men are granted a sexual licence denied to women.

28 'not necessarily, that depends on how you can modify (make light of) the accusation'

30 **incontinency** Polonius seems to be drawing a distinction between acceptable and unacceptable levels of sexual licence (Edwards argues that he thinks naïvely that Laertes may visit prostitutes without actually having sex with them).

31 **quaintly** artfully ('quaint' does not come to mean 'old-fashioned' until late in the eighteenth century)

32 **taints of liberty** faults of too much freedom

33 This indulgent view of Laertes' misdemeanours is expressed in the same terms as Lepidus' excuses for Antony: 'His faults, in him, seem as the spots of heaven, / More fiery by night's blackness' (*AC* 1.4.12–13). See also 5.2.234n.

34 a wildness typical of immature spirits
unreclaimed unreclaimèd; untamed, wild. (See *RJ* 4.2.47, where Capulet rejoices that 'this same wayward girl is so reclaimed'.)

35 **Of general assault** which assails or affects most men

38 **fetch of wit** witty stratagem. Jenkins suggests that Q2's *wit* is a misreading of an abbreviation for F's 'warrant' (meaning 'approved'), as 'wait' is at 3.4.5.

28 Faith] Faith no *F* 34–5 A . . . assault] *one line F* 36–7 Ay . . . that] *Steevens²; one line Q2F* 38 wit] warrant *F*

You laying these slight sallies on my son
As 'twere a thing a little soiled with working, 40
Mark you, your party in converse (him you would
      sound)
Having ever seen in the prenominate crimes
The youth you breathe of guilty, be assured
He closes with you in this consequence:
'Good sir' (or so), or 'friend' or 'gentleman', 45
According to the phrase or the addition
Of man and country.

REYNALDO   Very good, my lord.

POLONIUS

And then, sir, does 'a this, 'a does –
What was I about to say? By the mass, I was about to
say something! Where did I leave? 50

39 **sallies** attacks, criticisms; F's 'sulleyes' means blemishes; either seems acceptable (see also 1.2.129n.).
40 'as if he were an object that had become somewhat dirtied with handling'. Jenkins adopts F's 'i'th' working'.
41 **Mark you** an extrametrical interjection, like *See you now* at 59; some editors print it as a separate line.
your . . . converse the person with whom you are conversing (*converse* is stressed on the second syllable)
him . . . sound he whom you wish to probe
42–3 Polonius' word order is convoluted: 'in the prenominate crimes' depends on 'guilty'.
42 **Having ever** if he has ever
prenominate aforementioned
43 **breathe of** speak about
44 **closes . . . consequence** confides in you as follows
45 **or so** or whatever

46 **phrase** form of words
addition form of address or title. *TxC* speculates that Q2's 'addistion' may have meant 'addiction', used in the sense of 'inclination' at *H5* 1.1.54 and *Oth* 2.2.6.
48–50 Most recent editors (including Jenkins, Edwards, Hibbard) treat this entire speech as prose. We assume rather that Polonius begins in verse, consistently with the preceding dialogue, then lapses into prose when he realizes he has lost his thread.
48 **'a** he (as at 56). See 3.3.73
49–50 **What . . . leave** Some performers of Polonius tease the audience by seeming genuinely to forget their lines here. (See 2.2.349n.; and pp. 43–4 on the play's self-consciousness about issues of memory.)
49 **By the mass** a mild oath, not unusual in a play with a Protestant setting, like *By'r Lady* at 2.2.363 (though this one is expurgated in F)

39 sallies] sulleyes *Q3, F* 40 with] i'th' *F;* wi' th' *Alexander* 46 or] and *F* addition] *F;* addistion *Q2* 48–50] *this edn; Q2 lines* say? / something, / leaue? /; *F lines* this? / say? / leaue? / 48'a this,] he this? *F* 'a does –] He does: *F* 49 By the mass] *om. F*

REYNALDO   At 'closes in the consequence'.

POLONIUS

    At 'closes in the consequence', ay, marry.
    He closes thus: 'I know the gentleman,
    I saw him yesterday, or th'other day,
    Or then, or then, with such or such, and as you say   55
    There was 'a gaming, there o'ertook in's rouse,
    There falling out at tennis', or perchance
    'I saw him enter such a house of sale',
    Videlicet a brothel, or so forth. See you now
    Your bait of falsehood take this carp of truth,   60
    And thus do we of wisdom and of reach,
    With windlasses and with assays of bias,
    By indirections find directions out:
    So by my former lecture and advice

---

51 Some performers of Reynaldo have been taking notes and read back from them here. Jenkins argues that F's additional line (see t.n.) is an actor's interpolation and Polonius ignores it.

56 *o'ertook in's rouse** overcome while carousing (i.e. drunk); F's reading and punctuation seem more idiomatic than Q2's.

57 **tennis** like fencing (see 25 and n.), notorious for attracting the wilder young men; see Prince Hal's claim that the tennis-court keeper will be familiar with the minimal supply of shirts owned by Poins (*2H4* 2.2.16–19).

59 **Videlicet** namely, that is to say (Latin); Q1's 'viz'. may indicate that the word was shortened to the standard abbreviation in performance.

60 **carp** a freshwater fish, often attaining considerable age and size. Q2's *take* follows on from *See* in 59: 'watch your bait catch'.

61 **we . . . reach** we who are wise and have wide-ranging comprehension

62 **windlasses** Literally, a windlass is a winching mechanism; metaphorically, 'to windlass' could mean to decoy or snare an animal by making a circuitous leeward approach. MacDonald asks 'Would it be absurd to suggest that, so-doing, the hunter "laces the wind"? Shakspere [*sic*] . . . speaks of "threading [dark-eyed] night" [*KL* 2.1.119].' Golding uses 'windlass' in a simile comparing a man's movements with those of a fox (7.1015; he also uses it of Mercury at 2.891).
    assays of bias indirect attempts; the metaphor is from lawn bowls, where the *bias* is a weight which causes the bowl to take a curved path towards its target.

63 'by indirect methods find out the way things are going'. Dent cites 'Tell a lie and find a truth' as proverbial (L237).

64 **lecture** lesson, teaching

---

51 At 'closes] *F*; He closeth with him *Q1*   consequence'.] consequence: / At friend, or so, and Gentleman. *F* 53 closes] closeth with him *Q1*; closes with you *F* 54 th'other] tother *Q1F* 55 such or] such and *F* 56 'a] he *F* gaming, there] *F*; gaming there, *Q2* o'ertook] *F* (o'retooke); or tooke *Q2* 59 *Videlicet*] (Videlizet), *F*; viz. *Q1* 60 take] takes *F* carp] Cape *F* 62 windlasses] *(windlesses)*

Shall you my son. You have me, have you not? 65

REYNALDO

My lord, I have.

POLONIUS   God buy ye, fare ye well.

REYNALDO   Good my lord.

POLONIUS

Observe his inclination in yourself.

REYNALDO

I shall, my lord.

POLONIUS   And let him ply his music.

REYNALDO   Well, my lord. 70

POLONIUS

Farewell.   *Exit Reynaldo.*

Enter OPHELIA.

How now, Ophelia, what's the matter?

OPHELIA

O my lord, my lord, I have been so affrighted.

POLONIUS

With what, i'th' name of God?

OPHELIA

My lord, as I was sewing in my closet

---

65 **have me** comprehend me

66 **God buy ye** a not uncommon abbreviation of 'God be with you' ('goodbye') found in both Q2 (see 2.2.484 and 4.5.192) and F; Hibbard points out the potential for confusion with the meaning 'God redeem you'.

68 Variously interpreted: 'accommodate yourself to his bent' (Jenkins); 'do yourself as he is inclined' (Hibbard); 'observe [his habits] personally' (Edwards). The last seems most likely.

69 **ply his music** attend to his study of music – another gentlemanly skill

71 SD1 Jenkins defends the placing of Reynaldo's '*Exit*' before Polonius' *Farewell* (in all three texts) on the grounds that characteristically the latter is thinking of further things to say.

74–97 This encounter is described, not staged, in all three texts, but some productions (and films) presented it in dumb-show, and it became a popular subject for illustration. Its attraction may be the opportunity to present Hamlet in disordered dress (see 2.2.164.1n.).

74 **closet** as in 3.4, a private chamber

---

66 ye . . . ye] you . . . you *F*   71 SD1] Dyce (after Singer); opp. 70 Q21F   SD2] Singer; after 70 Q21F
72 O my lord,] Alas *F*   73 i'th'] in the *F*   God] Heauen *F*   74 closet] Chamber *F*

Lord Hamlet, with his doublet all unbraced,   75
No hat upon his head, his stockings fouled,
Ungartered and down-gyved to his ankle,
Pale as his shirt, his knees knocking each other,
And with a look so piteous in purport
As if he had been loosed out of hell   80
To speak of horrors, he comes before me.

POLONIUS
Mad for thy love?

OPHELIA   My lord, I do not know,
But truly I do fear it.

POLONIUS   What said he?

OPHELIA
He took me by the wrist and held me hard,
Then goes he to the length of all his arm   85

---

used for prayer, reading, etc.; not necessarily a bedroom. F's 'Chamber' evokes a similar location, but Q1's 'gallery' (6.42) would be a more public space. (See 3.2.323n. and Jardine, Orlin and Stewart on the meaning of *closet* in Elizabethan England.)

75–7 **doublet ... ankle** See Rosalind's taunting of Orlando on how a genuine lover should appear: 'your hose should be ungartered, your bonnet unbanded, your sleeve unbuttoned, your shoe untied, and every thing about you demonstrating a careless desolation' (*AYL* 3.2.369–72).

75 **doublet** jacket. Shakespeare here as elsewhere imagines his characters as being dressed in English Elizabethan clothes; see, for example, Caska's description of Caesar's action: 'he pluck'd me ope his doublet and offer'd them his throat to cut' (*JC* 1.2.260–2).
unbraced unfastened, expressing

vulnerability as well as carelessness (see Cassius' claim to have 'thus unbraced ... bared my bosom to the thunder-stone', *JC* 1.3.48–9)

76 **No ... head** Elizabethans normally wore hats indoors; see some play on this at 5.2.79–90.
fouled unwashed

77 Garters are bands, worn above or below the knee, to hold stockings up, and it is the stockings that would be *down-gyved* – falling down and resembling *gyves* or fetters.
down-gyved down-gyvèd (a Shakespearean coinage)

79–81 At this point the otherwise slightly comic picture of the melodramatic lover becomes frightening: Hamlet, for the audience, if not for Ophelia, resembles his father's Ghost.

79 **in purport** in its implications

80 **loosed** loosèd; released

85 'then he stepped back an arm's length'

---

77   down-gyved] *F2;* downe gyved *Q2F;* downe gyred *Q3*   82–3 My ... it] *one line F*

And with his other hand thus o'er his brow
He falls to such perusal of my face
As 'a would draw it. Long stayed he so;
At last, a little shaking of mine arm
And thrice his head thus waving up and down,   90
He raised a sigh so piteous and profound
As it did seem to shatter all his bulk
And end his being. That done, he lets me go
And with his head over his shoulder turned
He seemed to find his way without his eyes   95
(For out o'doors he went without their helps)
And to the last bended their light on me.

POLONIUS

Come, go with me: I will go seek the King.
This is the very ecstasy of love,
Whose violent property fordoes itself   100
And leads the will to desperate undertakings
As oft as any passions under heaven
That does afflict our natures. I am sorry –
What, have you given him any hard words of late?

86, 90 **thus** Presumably Ophelia imitates Hamlet's gestures.

87 **perusal** detailed examination

88 **As** as if

92 **bulk** frame, body; see 1.3.12 and *R3* 1.4.40, where Clarence imagines the sea smothering his soul 'within my panting bulk'.

97 **bended their light** i.e. focused their attention

98 **Come . . . me** Ophelia does not appear in the next scene in Q2 and F when Polonius relates this matter to the King; she is given an entry direction but no dialogue until

much later in the equivalent scene in Q1. See also 114.

99 **ecstasy** madness

100 'whose capacity for violence causes self-destruction'

101 **desperate** despairing (perhaps suicidal)

102 **passions** Jenkins adopts F's 'passion'.

103, 108 **I am sorry** Ophelia's account has given her the temporary solace that her father now believes in the sincerity of Hamlet's affection and regrets the scepticism he displayed in 1.3; some performers of Polonius display affection here.

---

88 'a] he *F*   92 As] That *F*   94 shoulder] *Q1;* shoulders *Q3, F*   96 helps] helpe *Q1F*   98 Come] *om. F*   102 passions] passion *F*

OPHELIA

No, my good lord, but as you did command   105
I did repel his letters and denied
His access to me.

POLONIUS   That hath made him mad.

I am sorry that with better heed and judgement
I had not quoted him. I feared he did but trifle
And meant to wrack thee – but beshrew my
   jealousy –   110
By heaven it is as proper to our age
To cast beyond ourselves in our opinions
As it is common for the younger sort
To lack discretion. Come, go we to the King:
This must be known which, being kept close, might
   move   115
More grief to hide than hate to utter love.
Come.   *Exeunt.*

106–7 **denied / His access** Modern English would say 'denied him access'.

107 **That . . . mad** Polonius is confident of the cause of Hamlet's behaviour but an audience or reader may wonder whether it is a manifestation of the *antic disposition* he promised to adopt (1.5.170) – in which case it might seem a cruel experiment.

109 *****quoted** Q2's 'coted' may mean 'outstripped', i.e. outmanoeuvred, as at 2.2.283, which is just about acceptable. But 'coted' is a frequent Shakespearean spelling of 'quoted', the F reading, which means 'observed' or 'judged' and makes better sense in the context.

trifle play (with your affection)

110 **wrack** ruin (by seducing)

beshrew my jealousy shame upon (i.e. I now regret) my suspicions

111 **proper to** appropriate to, characteristic of

112 **cast beyond ourselves** overreach ourselves, i.e. read too much into things. Johnson comments, 'This is not the remark of a weak man'; Polonius shows more self-awareness and humility here than some performers and critics allow him.

114 **Come . . . King** See 98n.

115 **known** i.e. made known (to the King)

close secret

115–16 **might . . . love** i.e. it might cause more pain to hide this love than distress to reveal it.

---

108   heed] speed *F*   109 quoted] *(*coted*)*, *F*   feared] feare *F*   111 By heaven] *Q1;* It seemes *F*   117 Come] *om. F*

[2.2]   *Flourish. Enter* KING *and* QUEEN, ROSENCRANTZ
          and GUILDENSTERN [*and other Courtiers*].

KING

Welcome, dear Rosencrantz and Guildenstern.
Moreover that we much did long to see you
The need we have to use you did provoke
Our hasty sending. Something have you heard
Of Hamlet's transformation – so call it   5
Sith nor th'exterior nor the inward man
Resembles that it was. What it should be
More than his father's death, that thus hath put him
So much from th'understanding of himself
I cannot dream of. I entreat you both   10

2.2 The three texts: this scene runs to 435 lines in Q1 (scene 7), 540 lines in Q2 and 600 lines in F, making it the longest scene in the play in all three texts, though Q1's versions of the various segments of the scene are all abbreviated. F extends Hamlet's conversation with Rosencrantz and Guildenstern (see 234–5n., 299n. and Appendix 1). Q1 differs radically from the other texts in containing in this scene, between Hamlet's *fishmonger* conversation with Polonius/Corambis and his first meeting with Rosencrantz and Guildenstern, his 'To be or not to be' soliloquy and his encounter with Ophelia, which are delayed until the next scene in Q2 and F (see 164.1n.). Location and timing: like 1.2, this scene is assumed to take place in a formal, indoor Court setting, referred to as *the lobby* at 158, though some references later suggest ·an outdoor setting (see 158n.). From the arrival of Polonius with his offer of news about

Hamlet at 46–9, we may deduce that it takes place very soon after 2.1; the announcement of the return of the ambassadors at 40 marks the passage of time since their departure at 1.2.41.

0.1–2   ROSENCRANTZ, GUILDENSTERN See List of Roles, 11n. and 12n.

0.2   *other Courtiers* Although Q2 mentions only Rosencrantz and Guildenstern, the presence of at least one other is implied by the Queen's addressing *some of you* at 36.

2   **Moreover** in addition to the fact

4   **sending** sending for you, summoning of you

5   **transformation** Polonius more bluntly calls it *lunacy* at 49.
     so call it i.e. so we may call it

6   **Sith nor** because neither

7–10 **What ... of** The King seems here completely confident that his own crime has not been discovered.

10   **dream** F's 'deeme' is defended by Hibbard as meaning 'judge, decide'.

2.2] *F (Scena Secunda.); not in Q21*   0.1 *Flourish.*] *not in Q1F*   ROSENCRANTZ] *throughout play, Malone; Rosencraus Q2; Rossencraft Q1; Rosincran[c]e F   and*] *om. F*   0.2 GUILDENSTERN] *throughout play Q6, Q2 (Guyldensterne), F (Guildensterne); Gilderstone Q1*   0.2 *and other Courtiers*] *this edn; not in Q21; Cum alijs F*   5 so] so 1 *F*   6 Sith nor] Since not *F*   10 dream] deeme *F*

That, being of so young days brought up with him
And sith so neighboured to his youth and haviour,
That you vouchsafe your rest here in our Court
Some little time, so by your companies
To draw him on to pleasures and to gather   15
So much as from occasion you may glean,
Whether aught to us unknown afflicts him thus
That opened lies within our remedy.

QUEEN

Good gentlemen, he hath much talked of you
And sure I am two men there is not living   20
To whom he more adheres. If it will please you
To show us so much gentry and good will
As to expend your time with us awhile
For the supply and profit of our hope,
Your visitation shall receive such thanks   25
As fits a king's remembrance.

ROSENCRANTZ   Both your majesties
Might by the sovereign power you have of us

---

11 **of** from
12 **sith** possibly temporal (= 'since'), but also
causal (= 'because')
neighboured to familiar with. Q2's
spelling (see t.n.) probably reflects
pronunciation: see Holofernes' discussion
of this point in *LLL* 5.1.22–3.
youth and haviour youthful behaviour
(hendiadys)
13 **That** The King repeats *That* from 11.
vouchsafe your rest consent to remain
14 **your companies** the company of both of
you (like *your modesties* at 246)
15 **draw . . . to** encourage him to participate
in
16 **occasion** opportunity
glean pick up (the metaphor is from

collecting the remains of grain from a
recently reaped field)
18 **opened** revealed
20 **is** Verb endings in *-s* or *-es* for plural
subjects are common in Shakespeare: see
Hope, 2.1.8.
21 **more adheres** is more closely bound (by
friendship). The Queen seems to share the
King's confidence that Rosencrantz and
Guildenstern are Hamlet's closest friends,
raising another question about the role of
Horatio (List of Roles, 10n., 11n. and 12n.).
22 **gentry** courtesy
24 **supply . . . hope** help and advancement of
what we hope for
27 **of us** over us, concerning us; see Blake,
5.4.2, *of*.

---

12   sith] since *F*   neighboured] *(*nabored*), F*   haviour] humour *F*   16 occasion] Occasions *F* 17] *om.*
F   20 is] are *F*

Put your dread pleasures more into command
Than to entreaty.

GUILDENSTERN   But we both obey
And here give up ourselves in the full bent   30
To lay our service freely at your feet
To be commanded.

KING

Thanks, Rosencrantz, and gentle Guildenstern.

QUEEN

Thanks, Guildenstern, and gentle Rosencrantz.
And I beseech you instantly to visit   35
My too much changed son. Go some of you
And bring these gentlemen where Hamlet is.

GUILDENSTERN

Heavens make our presence and our practices
Pleasant and helpful to him.

QUEEN   Ay, amen.

Exeunt Rosencrantz, Guildenstern [and one or more Courtiers].

---

28 **your dread pleasures** i.e. the desires of you who can cause dread or fear. Edwards notes this as a comic extension of the common phrase 'my dread lord'.
into into the form of

29 **both** This could relate either to the courtiers ('we both obey you') or to the King and Queen ('we obey you both').

30 **in . . . bent** completely, to the full extent; the metaphor is from bending a bow.

33–4 In all three texts the Queen repeats the King's thanks, reversing the order of the names. In performance her line was frequently omitted from 1676 onwards. The reversal can be played simply as an example of courtesy, giving the two courtiers equal priority, or as a correction of the King, who has got the names wrong. In Tom Stoppard's play *Rosencrantz and Guildenstern Are*

Dead (1967) it is Rosencrantz himself who first confuses the names when the two men introduce themselves to the Players and the confusion continues throughout the play. (In a talk given in Bochum in 2000, the dramatist Peter Whelan recalled playing 'either Rosencrantz or Guildenstern' in an early one-act version of Stoppard's play which was then called *Guildenstern and Rosencrantz Are Dead*.)

36 **changed** changèd
some of you one of you; *some* can be used as an indefinite singular pronoun (Blake, 3.3.2.7j); see *R2* 4.1.268: 'Go some of you, and fetch a looking-glass.'

38 **practices** activities (but, as Edwards points out, the word could also mean 'stratagems', as at 4.7.65)

39 SD One additional courtier would be

---

29 But] *om. F*   31 service] Seruices *F*   36] *F lines* Sonne. / ye, / you] ye *F*   37 these] the *F* 39 Ay] *om. F*   SD *Exeunt . . . Guildenstern] (Exeunt Ros. and Guyld.); Exit. F, after* him *and . . . Courtiers] this edn; Attendants with them / Capell*

Enter POLONIUS.

POLONIUS

    Th'ambassadors from Norway, my good lord,   40
    Are joyfully returned.

KING

    Thou still hast been the father of good news.

POLONIUS

    Have I, my lord? I assure my good liege
    I hold my duty as I hold my soul,
    Both to my God and to my gracious King;   45
    And I do think, or else this brain of mine
    Hunts not the trail of policy so sure
    As it hath used to do, that I have found
    The very cause of Hamlet's lunacy.

KING

    O, speak of that, that do I long to hear.   50

POLONIUS

    Give first admittance to th'ambassadors.
    My news shall be the fruit to that great feast.

---

enough – see 36n. – but since Capell 'Attendants' have often been specified (perhaps because *some* at 36 has been misunderstood).

39.1 In Q1 Polonius/Corambis is accompanied by Ofelia, as we might expect from the end of the previous scene, but she does not speak until Hamlet addresses her after 'To be or not to be'.

41 **joyfully** i.e. bearing a positive report

42 **still** always

43 F's reading (see t.n.) is preferable metrically (see Hibbard, who prints 'I assure you my good liege' on the grounds that Q2 omits 'you' while F omits 'I').

45 **and to** Citing F's 'one to', MacDonald writes: 'I cannot tell which is the right reading: if the [second] Quarto's, it means "I hold my duty precious as my soul,

whether to my God or my king"; if the Folio's, it is a little confused by the attempt of Polonius to make a fine euphuistic speech: – "I hold my duty as I hold my soul – both at the command of my God, one at the command of my king".' The F reading is not popular, though it would provide editors with a differentiation they are keen to make between worldly and divine devotion.

47 **Hunts ... policy** follows the track of the (political) investigation (the analogy is that of a man or dog tracking prey). *Policy*, like *practices* at 38, was often used with negative connotations; see Mowbray's statement in *2H4* that the King's offer of terms to the rebels 'proceeds from policy, not love' (4.1.148).

52 **fruit** sweet conclusion, dessert

---

43 ²I . . . liege] I assure your grace *Q1;* Assure you, my good Liege *F*   45 and] *Q1;* one *F*   48 it hath] it had *Q1;* I haue *F*   50 do I] I do *F*   52 fruit] Newes *F*

KING

Thyself do grace to them and bring them in.
He tells me, my dear Gertrude, he hath found
The head and source of all your son's distemper.   55

QUEEN

I doubt it is no other but the main –
His father's death and our hasty marriage.

KING

Well, we shall sift him.

Enter VOLTEMAND *and* CORNELIUS.

Welcome, my good friends.
Say, Voltemand, what from our brother Norway?

VOLTEMAND

Most fair return of greetings and desires.   60

---

53 **do grace to them** give them a courtly welcome. Polonius may exit here, or he may just go to one of the stage doors to summon the ambassadors.

54 **dear Gertrude** Edwards prefers this Q2 reading to F's 'sweet Queene', which he sees as an example of a playhouse scribe attempting to maintain the decorum of royalty at the expense of domestic intimacy.

55 **head** origin (as in 'well-head')
distemper illness, being 'out of temper'

56–7 The Queen's straightforward analysis contrasts with the King's claims at 7–10 and 17 that he is completely mystified. It may be significant that in this private moment she says nothing of the murder, perhaps because she is unaware of it.

56 **doubt** suspect
main major cause

57 F's 'our o're-hasty' is generally adopted (e.g. by Jenkins), but Jennens retains Q2,

which requires *our* to be disyllabic (see *hour* at 1.4.3).

58 **sift him** examine him (Polonius) closely

58 SD The King addresses Voltemand by name immediately; he is the only one to speak in this scene in all three texts, but we may assume his companion is Cornelius as in 1.2. If Polonius left the stage at 53 he returns here.

59 **brother** because king (like the King of France's references to 'our brother England' at *H5* 2.4.75 and 115)

60–80 The fact that this speech is very similar in all three texts caused White ('Two *Hamlet*s', 478) and others who espouse the 'reported text' theory of Q1 to argue that the actor playing Voltemand/ Voltemar was involved in the reporting, or that his part was available to the reporters (see Appendix 2).

60 **return** reciprocation
desires good wishes

---

54 dear Gertrude] *(deere Gertrard); sweet Queene, that F*   57 hasty] o're-hasty *F*   58 SD] *Dyce subst.; Enter Embassadors. after 57 Q2; Enter the Ambassadors. Q1; Enter Polonius, Voltumand, and Cornelius. F*   my] *om. F*

Upon our first he sent out to suppress
His nephew's levies, which to him appeared
To be a preparation 'gainst the Polack;
But, better looked into, he truly found
It was against your highness; whereat, grieved   65
That so his sickness, age and impotence
Was falsely borne in hand, sends out arrests
On Fortinbras, which he in brief obeys,
Receives rebuke from Norway and, in fine,
Makes vow before his uncle never more   70
To give th'assay of arms against your majesty.
Whereon old Norway, overcome with joy,
Gives him threescore thousand crowns in annual fee
And his commission to employ those soldiers
So levied (as before) against the Polack,   75
With an entreaty herein further shown
That it might please you to give quiet pass

61 **Upon our first** i.e. at our first meeting, or in response to our first representation of the problem

62 **His nephew's levies** the actions taken by his nephew to levy forces, or the forces levied by his nephew (i.e. the *lawless resolutes* of 1.1.97)

63 **the Polack** Poland or the King of Poland (see 1.1.62n.)

64 **truly** This adverb modifies *was* in 65.

65 **whereat** whereupon, because of this

66 **impotence** helplessness

67 **Was** The combination of illness, age and disability is treated as a single phenomenon.
Falsely . . . hand abused or deluded with incorrect information
arrests orders to cease activities

69 **in fine** finally. The phrase could also mean 'in short'.

71 **give . . . arms** make trial (*assay*) of armed combat

73 **threescore thousand crowns** The 'three thousand' of Q1/F may make more sense

financially, depending on how we interpret the *twenty thousand ducats* Hamlet estimates as the cost of Fortinbras's campaign at 4.4.24. (The discrepancy is analogous to the numbers of 'talents' mentioned at different points in *Tim.*) Pope omitted *score* on metrical grounds, but Theobald responded that '2 Syllables may, by Pronounciation, be *resolv'd* and *melted* into one, as two Notes are *slur'd* in *Musick*.' (Dover Wilson assumes *him* should have been deleted; Edwards assumes *score* should have been deleted.)
fee payment, income

74 **commission** authorization

75 **as before** 'as previously [levied]', or perhaps 'as previously described'

76, 80 **herein . . . therein** Voltemand presumably produces a document detailing this request.

77 **quiet pass** peaceful (i.e. unopposed) passage

73 threescore] three *Q1/F*

Through your dominions for this enterprise
On such regards of safety and allowance
As therein are set down.

KING   It likes us well,   80
And at our more considered time we'll read,
Answer and think upon this business;
Meantime, we thank you for your well-took labour.
Go to your rest, at night we'll feast together.
Most welcome home.

Exeunt Voltemand, Cornelius [and Courtiers].

POLONIUS   This business is well ended.   85
My liege and madam, to expostulate
What majesty should be, what duty is,
Why day is day, night night, and time is time,
Were nothing but to waste night, day and time;
Therefore, brevity is the soul of wit   90

77–8 **pass . . . dominions** Fortinbras is taking
advantage of this permission when he
appears at 4.4.1 below; it is assumed that
he has to go through Denmark on his route
from Norway to Poland (Jenkins, LN).
Eventually he is poised to take over
Denmark without any fighting.
79 'with such conditions for our safety and for
the permission granted'
80 **likes** pleases
81 **at . . . time** when we have more time to
consider
81–2 **read . . . think** The order of the verbs
seems illogical (*Answer* before *think*), but
see 3.1.150 and n. Fortinbras' reference to
licence at 4.4.2 indicates that the King does
indeed *answer*.
82 **business** trisyllabic
83–4 The nearly rhyming couplet (*labour/*
together) signals the King's dismissal of
the ambassadors.
83 **well-took** well-undertaken

84 **at night** tonight
85 SD Hibbard argues that the attendants or
Courtiers should also leave at this point;
Jenkins keeps them on until 167, but it
seems unlikely that the King, Queen
and Polonius would want to discuss the
state of Hamlet's mind and emotions in
public.
86–104 Polonius' verbosity is usually
played for laughs but it could also reflect
genuine embarrassment about both
Hamlet's madness and its supposed cause.
86 **expostulate** discourse upon, dilate at
length; see Exeter urging the King and
Queen to flee in *3H6*: 'Nay, stay not to
expostulate; make speed' (2.5.135).
90 **Therefore, brevity** F's reading (see t.n.) is
generally preferred (e.g. by Jenkins) as an
improvement to syntax and logic. Polonius
may, however, hesitate after *Therefore* as if
he had meant to say something else.
wit wisdom

78 this] that *Q1;* his *F*   83 thank] *Q1Fc;* take *Fu*   well-took] *(well tooke), F, Q1 (well / Tooke)* 85 SD
Exeunt . . . Cornelius] (Exeunt Embassadors) Q1, Exit Ambass. F   and Courtiers] Alexander subst. well
ended] very well dispatched *Q1;* very well ended *F*   90 Therefore] Therefore, since *F*

And tediousness the limbs and outward flourishes.
I will be brief: your noble son is mad.
Mad call I it, for to define true madness,
What is't but to be nothing else but mad?
But let that go.

QUEEN More matter with less art. 95

POLONIUS

Madam, I swear I use no art at all.
That he's mad, 'tis true, 'tis true 'tis pity,
And pity 'tis 'tis true: a foolish figure!
But farewell it, for I will use no art.
Mad let us grant him then, and now remains 100
That we find out the cause of this effect –
Or rather say the cause of this defect,
For this effect defective comes by cause.
Thus it remains, and the remainder thus. Perpend,
I have a daughter – have while she is mine – 105
Who in her duty and obedience, mark,
Hath given me this. Now gather and surmise.

91 **tediousness** long-windedness
93–4 **Perhaps** Polonius means that it would be mad to try to define madness, rather than simply label (*call*) it.
95 **matter** substance
 art artfulness. Despite his denial (*let that go*), the Queen picks up on Polonius' elaborate style of speech.
97 **he's** Jenkins prefers F's 'he is', presumably on metrical grounds.
98 **figure** figure of speech. 'It is no figure at all. It is hardly even a play with the words' (MacDonald).
102 **defect** disability
103 'because this effect in Hamlet, which is a defect, does have a cause'. This play on *effect/defect* is echoed in *Eastward Ho*, 1.2.61–3: see pp. 58–9.

104 **Thus ... thus** Picking up *remains* in 100, Polonius seems to mean something like 'This is the situation, and here is how we can explore the cause.' Jenkins comments: 'He loses the thread of his argument and nonsensically repeats himself.'
104 **Perpend** consider, pay attention (like *mark* in 106). Extrametrical; some editors give *Perpend* a separate line.
105 **while ... mine** i.e. until she marries
107 **gather and surmise** 'understand what I am about to say and draw your own conclusion'. Some productions take *gather* literally as an invitation to the King and Queen to come closer to Polonius and look at the letter with him.

97 he's] he is *F* 98 'tis 'tis] it is *F* 104] *F; Q2 lines* thus / Perpend, / 105 while] *Q1;* whil'st *F*

[*Reads.*] *To the celestial and my soul's idol, the most
beautified Ophelia* – that's an ill phrase, a vile phrase,
'beautified' is a vile phrase, but you shall hear – *thus in*   110
her excellent white bosom, these, etc.

QUEEN

Came this from Hamlet to her?

POLONIUS

Good madam, stay awhile: I will be faithful.

108–21 This is the first of three letters from Hamlet to be read aloud during the play; see 4.6.13–28 and 4.7.43–6. Editors and critics have been troubled by the literary quality of this letter, which they see as unworthy of Hamlet; some attribute it to his *antic disposition*, though again this would seem cruel (see 2.1.107n.) and moreover it has been emphasized that Ophelia has refused to receive recent letters. In Branagh's 1996 film, and in the 1999 London Young Vic production, Ophelia, who was present in this scene (see 2.1.114n.), was required to read the letter herself. Her presence might lead some viewers to expect the Q1 placing of 'To be or not to be' (see 164.1n.). Roffe lists nine metrical and musical adaptations of this letter from 1786 to 1861 (see Appendix 6).

108–11 *To* . . . **etc.** Q2 indents this and prints all of it in italics, not distinguishing between what Polonius reads and his comments on it. This is clearly the superscription; the letter itself begins at 114, where Q2 has the heading 'Letter'.

109–10 **that's** . . . **phrase** It is not clear why Polonius finds the word *beautified* objectionable, though Hibbard suggests he may understand it as meaning 'made beautiful with cosmetics'; Shakespeare uses it straightforwardly in *TGV* when the

First Outlaw describes Valentine as 'beautified / With goodly shape' (4.1.55–6), and it occurs twice in *E3*: 'Our house, my liege, is like a country swain . . . yet inly beautified' (1.2.145–7) and 'Like as the wind doth beautify a sail' (2.1.280). It has been proposed that Shakespeare here recalls his offence at the description of him in Greene's *Groats-worth of Wit* (1592) as 'an upstart Crow, beautified with our feathers' (Chambers, *Shakespeare*, 2.188). Q1 gives the superscription '*To the beautifull Ofelia*' after the contents of the letter.

110–11 *thus* . . . *these* Presumably Polonius summarizes something like 'thus I commend these words to your exceptionally white bosom'; see Proteus' (false) promise to deliver Valentine's letters 'Even in the milk-white bosom of thy love' (*TGV* 3.1.250). Jenkins, however, prefers F's 'These . . . these', arguing that both pronouns refer to the letters, and Blake gives F's reading as an example of emphatic repetition (3.3.2.4f).

etc. Either Hamlet, in writing the superscription, or, more likely, Polonius, in reading it, abbreviates the commendations.

113 **stay** wait

I . . . **faithful** 'I will keep my word (to tell you everything)', or perhaps 'I will

---

108 SD] *Q6; The Letter. F*   109–10 that's . . . hear] *roman F; italic Q2*   110 hear – *thus in*] these in *F;* hear – *These to / Rowe;* hear; – *These in / Capell;* hear. Thus: *In / Malone;* hear – *these; in Ard²*   111 etc.] *(&c.); om. F; roman Q6*

[Reads.] Doubt thou the stars are fire,
Doubt that the sun doth move, 115
Doubt truth to be a liar,
But never doubt I love.
O dear Ophelia, I am ill at these numbers. I have not art
to reckon my groans, but that I love thee best, O most
best, believe it. Adieu. Thine evermore, most dear lady, 120
whilst this machine is to him. Hamlet.
This in obedience hath my daughter shown me;
And more about hath his solicitings
As they fell out, by time, by means and place,
All given to my ear.

KING   But how hath she 125
Received his love?

POLONIUS   What do you think of me?

KING

As of a man faithful and honourable.

---

read the entire letter'

114–17 The gist of this stanza is: 'You may
question the unquestionable, but do not
question that I love you.' The second line
has given editors trouble, since it refers to
the Ptolemaic belief that the sun moved
around the earth – a belief that Shakespeare
(if not Hamlet) knew to be outmoded.

116 **Doubt** The meaning of '*Doubt*' shifts from
'question' to 'suspect' here.

118 **ill ... numbers** incompetent at writing
these verses; Hamlet's self-doubt in this
context contrasts with his confidence later
in this scene that he can 'set down' 'a
speech of some dozen lines, or sixteen
lines' to be inserted into *The Murder of
Gonzago* (477–8).

119 **reckon** count up, enumerate; express in
verse

most best very best, absolutely best.
This could be read as an intensive of

the previous '*best*', or as a mode of address
(apostrophe) to Ophelia herself, as F's
capitalized '*Best*' might imply. 'Most'
without any degree of comparison has
become obsolete (Blake, 5.1.3.1v; Hope,
1.2.3).

120 **Adieu** farewell: the word used by the Ghost
at 1.5.91 and repeated by Hamlet at 1.5.111

121 **machine** physical frame: the body seen as
a combination of parts (as in Hamlet's
speech at 269–73). This is Shakespeare's
only use of the word *machine* (and *OED*'s
first use of the word in a metaphorical
sense); it perhaps prompted the title of
Heiner Muller's 1979 adaptation, *Hamletmachine* (see p. 123).

is to belongs to (i.e. while he is alive)

123 **more about** furthermore, in addition; F's
'more aboue' is often preferred (e.g. by
Jenkins).

124 **fell out** happened, took place

114 SD] *Rowe; 'Letter.' Q2, opp. 114; not in Q1F* 122 This] *F; Pol.* This *Q2* shown] shew'd *F*
123 about] aboue *F* solicitings] soliciting *F* 125–6] *Capell; Q2F line* eare. / loue? / me? /

POLONIUS

I would fain prove so. But what might you think
When I had seen this hot love on the wing –
As I perceived it (I must tell you that)   130
Before my daughter told me – what might you,
Or my dear majesty your Queen here, think
If I had played the desk or table-book,
Or given my heart a working mute and dumb,
Or looked upon this love with idle sight,   135
What might you think? No, I went round to work
And my young mistress thus I did bespeak:
'Lord Hamlet is a prince out of thy star.
This must not be.' And then I prescripts gave her
That she should lock herself from his resort,   140
Admit no messengers, receive no tokens;
Which done, she took the fruits of my advice,

128 **fain** willingly (as at 150)
129 **hot** impetuous, urgent
  on the wing i.e. developing very quickly
130 **As** because
  perceived Polonius seems here to take credit for having observed *this hot love* for himself, whereas at 1.3.90 he says to Ophelia that he has been *told* about it before she confirms it herself.
133 **played** ... **table-book** 'conveyed intelligence between them' (Warburton, cited by Hibbard) or 'taken note and said nothing' (Edwards); Polonius seems to be making a distinction between some kind of active collaboration in this line and a more passive pretence of ignorance in 134–5.
  desk In the Elizabethan sense, a *desk* was usually a box with a sloping top which would be placed on a table for writing rather than the item of furniture we would mean today.

134 **i.e.** forced my heart to remain silent (?). Dover Wilson defends Q2's *working* as referring to any kind of mental operation and cites *LLL* 4.1.33, 'the working of the heart', and *Son* 93.11, 'thy heart's workings', but most editors including Jenkins prefer F's 'winking' meaning a deliberate closing of the eyes.
135 **with idle sight** i.e. seeing it but doing nothing about it
136 **round** wholeheartedly
137 **bespeak** address, speak to
138 **out ... star** outside your destiny, beyond your (social) sphere, i.e. out of the question as a marriage partner
139 **prescripts** instructions
140 ***his resort** access by him. Q2's 'her resort' seems an error caused by misreading 'his' as 'hir', or by picking up 'her' either from earlier in the line or from 139.
142 **fruits** benefits

134 working] winking *F*   138 star] *Q1F;* Sphere *F2*   139 prescripts] Precepts *F*   140 his] *F;* her *Q2*

And he, repelled, a short tale to make,
Fell into a sadness, then into a fast,
Thence to a watch, thence into a weakness,   145
Thence to lightness, and by this declension
Into the madness wherein now he raves,
And all we mourn for.

KING

Do you think this?

QUEEN   It may be, very like.

POLONIUS

Hath there been such a time – I would fain know that –   150
That I have positively said 'tis so
When it proved otherwise?

KING   Not that I know.

POLONIUS

Take this from this if this be otherwise.

---

143 **repelled** repellèd; Jenkins supports *repelled* (against F's 'repulsed') by reference to Ophelia's use of *repel* at 2.1.106.

144–7 Polonius describes the classic symptoms of love-melancholy; see the description of Romeo (*RJ* 1.1.131–40). 'Into' and 'to' are interchangeable here.

145 ***watch** sleeplessness. Q2's 'wath' is erroneous.

146 **lightness** lightheadedness
declension deterioration (see 162n.). Polonius may also glance at the grammatical sense (the diagrammatic arrangement of the forms of a noun), given his obsession with word-play in this sequence.

148 **all ... for** all of us mourn for. Hibbard prints F's 'waile for' though he says it is more absurd than *mourn for* (perhaps because of the awkward alliteration with

we); Edwards prints *mourn*, though he says 'wail' is stronger.

149 **It ... like** The Queen's reply indicates that the King's question is addressed to her, but some performers play the line as if he is asking Polonius if he really believes what he has said.
very like probably, possibly (as at 1.2.234)

150–2 **Hath ... otherwise** 'I would very much like to know if there has ever been a time when I have said positively that something is the case and it has turned out not to be (true).'

153 **Take this from this** Polonius presumably illustrates by gesture that he means 'take my head from my body' or possibly 'take my staff of office from my hand' (Dowden) 'if what I have said is not true.' (Compare Poins in *1H4* 1.2.156–8: 'If you and I do not rob them, cut this head off from my shoulders.')

---

143 repelled] *(*repell'd*); repulsed *F*   145 watch] *Q3, F*; wath *Q2*   146 to] to a *F*   147 wherein] whereon *F*   148 mourn] waile *F*   149 Do ... this?] Thinke you t'is so? *Q1*; Do you thinke 'tis this? *F*   like] likely *F*   150 I would] I would very *Q1*; I'de *F*

If circumstances lead me I will find
Where truth is hid, though it were hid indeed   155
Within the centre.

KING   How may we try it further?

POLONIUS

You know sometimes he walks four hours together
Here in the lobby?

QUEEN   So he does, indeed.

POLONIUS

At such a time I'll loose my daughter to him.
Be you and I behind an arras then,   160
Mark the encounter: if he love her not
And be not from his reason fallen thereon
Let me be no assistant for a state
But keep a farm and carters.

KING   We will try it.

154 **circumstances** relevant (circumstantial) evidence
156 **the centre** i.e. the centre of the earth, traditionally supposed to be inaccessible
try test
157 **four** not necessarily a precise figure: *four* could be used to mean 'several' (see Elze, 'Four hours').
together at a time
158 **lobby** ante-room or corridor, used as a waiting-room by visitors to the Court. At 203, however, Polonius implies that they are out of doors, as does Hamlet in his talk of 'this brave o'erhanging firmament' at 266. The open stage at the Globe allowed for such flexibility.
159 **loose** let loose; the word reminds us that Polonius has restrained Ophelia from seeing Hamlet. There might also be a sexual overtone to it, as when Page comments of the amorous Falstaff, 'If he should intend this voyage toward my wife, I would turn her loose to him'

(*MW* 2.1.170–2).
160 **arras** tapestry or woven wall-hanging, used both for decoration and to exclude draughts. Polonius' assumption is that there is sufficient space between the *arras* and the wall for eavesdroppers to hide; at *1H4* 2.4.522 Falstaff is discovered asleep behind an arras. (The town of Arras, now in France, was a major centre for the manufacture of such tapestries, hence the name.)
162 **from . . . fallen** declined from rationality, descended into madness. Polonius has used the same metaphor of madness as a kind of falling at 144–7; it occurs again in Ophelia's lament for Hamlet at 3.1.149–53.
thereon because of it
163 **assistant . . . state** councillor with a role in government
164 **carters** men who drive carts; *OED* also notes (2b) that 'carter' was used 'as a type of low birth or breeding', citing George Puttenham's *The Art of*

157–8 You . . . lobby?] *F lines* sometimes / heere / Lobby. /   158 does] ha's *F*   164 But] And *F*

Enter HAMLET.

QUEEN

But look where sadly the poor wretch comes reading. 165

POLONIUS

Away, I do beseech you both, away.

I'll board him presently. O, give me leave.

Exeunt King and Queen.

How does my good lord Hamlet?

HAMLET   Well, God-a-mercy.

POLONIUS   Do you know me, my lord?   170

HAMLET   Excellent well, you are a fishmonger.

English Poesie (1589): 'Continence in a king is of greater merit than in a carter.'

164.1 This is Hamlet's first appearance since he spoke of putting on *an antic disposition* (1.5.170), though of course Ophelia has described his appearance and behaviour in 2.1. Eighteenth- and nineteenth-century performers often literalized her words, but this is no longer common (see Hapgood). In Q1 Hamlet's entry at this point 'poring upon a book' leads directly into 'To be or not to be', which is followed by the *fishmonger* dialogue. Dover Wilson brought him on at 156 so that he overheard the plot to use Ophelia against him, feeling that this was necessary in order to justify his behaviour to her in 3.1; this direction was followed by Olivier in his 1948 film and is noted by Norton.

165 **wretch** a term of endearment, as at 4.7.180

reading A number of suggestions have been made as to the identity of the book, often by commentators who wish to demonstrate that 'To be or not to be' is to be taken as a general reflection, inspired by Hamlet's reading, rather than a personal statement (see Var for examples), but

Jenkins comments: 'Attempts to identify the book are pointless.' Similar arguments have focused on what book Ulysses is reading in *TC* 3.3; like Hamlet at 193–201, he claims to find material in his reading which is surprisingly relevant to his interlocutor – in itself enough to make one doubt that Shakespeare had a specific book in mind.

167 **board** accost, address

presently instantly

give me leave (please) excuse me. Capell suggests this is addressed to the King and Queen; Cam and Dowden suggest it is addressed to Hamlet; Jenkins suggests it is addressed to the attendants who are still onstage in his text and are slow to leave.

169 **God-a-mercy** God have mercy on you – a polite response to a greeting from a social inferior

171 **fishmonger** a comic mistake and presumably a deliberate one, establishing that Hamlet is feigning madness at this point. Since Malone, editors have argued about whether *fishmonger* carries connotations of 'fleshmonger' or bawd (see Jenkins, LN).

164.1 HAMLET] *Q1; Hamlet reading on a Booke F*   167 SD *Exeunt . . . Queen*] *Capell; Exit . . . Queene opp.*   *166 Q2, after* presently *167 F*   171 Excellent] Excellent, excellent *F*   you are] y'are *Q1F*

POLONIUS   Not I, my lord.

HAMLET   Then I would you were so honest a man.

POLONIUS   Honest, my lord?

HAMLET   Ay, sir, to be honest as this world goes is to be   175
one man picked out of ten thousand.

POLONIUS   That's very true, my lord.

HAMLET   For if the sun breed maggots in a dead dog,
being a good kissing carrion – have you a daughter?

POLONIUS   I have, my lord.   180

HAMLET   Let her not walk i'th' sun: conception is
a blessing but as your daughter may conceive, friend
– look to't.

POLONIUS [*aside*]   How say you by that? Still harping on
my daughter. Yet he knew me not at first, 'a said I was   185
a fishmonger! 'A is far gone; and truly, in my youth I
suffered much extremity for love, very near this. I'll
speak to him again. – What do you read, my lord?

HAMLET   Words, words, words.

POLONIUS   What is the matter, my lord?   190

---

176 **ten thousand** 'A man among a thousand'
was proverbial (Tilley, M217).

178–9 **For ... carrion** Some performers
appear to be reading these words.

179 **good kissing carrion** good piece of
decaying flesh (carcass) to kiss;
Shakespeare often uses *carrion* to mean
sexual corruption, as in Diomede's
reference to Helen's 'contaminated
carrion weight' (*TC* 4.1.72). (Hanmer and
Warburton read 'God' for 'good', approved
but not followed by Spencer.)

181 **i'th' sun** The suggestion is that the sun will
cause her to breed, as it encourages the
breeding of maggots in a dead dog. Hamlet
may also allude to the sun/son pun (see
1.2.67), indicating that a son(-in-law) will
make Ophelia pregnant.

182 **but as** Jenkins finds Q2's uncompleted
thought more 'artful' than F's 'but not as',
suggesting it implies 'but to your daughter
it may be a blessing or otherwise according
as she may conceive'.

184 **How ... that?** 'What do you say to that?'
Polonius in effect addresses the audience
here.
Still harping on constantly dwelling on;
'to harp on one string' was proverbial
(Tilley, S936).

186 **far gone** seriously affected

187 **much extremity** inordinate stress

190–2 Polonius means 'What is the subject
matter of the book?' Hamlet pretends he
means 'What is the quarrel?'

175–6] *F; Q2 1 line* goes, / thousand. /   176 ten] *Q1;* two *F*   181–3] *F; Q2 lines* blessing, / to't. /
182 but] but not *F*   184 SD] *Capell*   185–6 'a said ... 'A] he said ... he *F*   186 gone] gone, farre
gone *F*

HAMLET   Between who?

POLONIUS   I mean the matter that you read, my lord.

HAMLET   Slanders, sir. For the satirical rogue says here
that old men have grey beards, that their faces are
wrinkled, their eyes purging thick amber and plumtree   195
gum, and that they have a plentiful lack of wit together
with most weak hams – all which, sir, though I most
powerfully and potently believe, yet I hold it not
honesty to have it thus set down. For yourself, sir,
shall grow old as I am – if, like a crab, you could go   200
backward.

POLONIUS [*aside*]   Though this be madness yet there is
method in't. — Will you walk out of the air, my lord?

HAMLET   Into my grave.

POLONIUS [*aside*]   Indeed, that's out of the air. How   205

---

193 **Slanders** malicious statements, deliberate defamations (which might in fact
be true or, as here, commonplace)
rogue Both *rogue* and F's variant 'slaue'
occur in 485.

195 **purging** discharging

195–6 **amber ... gum** both resins from
trees

196 **wit** wisdom

197 **hams** thighs

198 **potently** mightily (virtually synonymous
with *powerfully*, a redundant expression
perhaps mocking Polonius)

199 **honesty** honest or honourable behaviour

199–201 **For ... backward** Hamlet reverses
their roles, pretending that he is old,
Polonius young; crabs can move in any
direction and are frequently seen to go
backwards or sideways.

200 **old** as old

202–3 **Though ... in't** See Laertes' comment

on Ophelia, 'This nothing's more than
matter' (4.5.168 and n.), and Edgar's
comment on Lear, 'O matter and
impertinency mixed, / Reason in madness'
(*KL* 4.6.170–1). Whether characters are
really mad (like Ophelia and Lear) or just
pretending (like Hamlet at this point and
Edgar elsewhere in *KL*), their speech can
hardly descend into gibberish if they are to
retain the interest and attention of the
audience.

203, 205 **out ... air** Polonius implies
'indoors' – fresh air being thought
harmful to sick people – despite the fact
that this encounter supposedly takes place
in the indoor *lobby* (see 158n.), but Hamlet
puts a grimly literal interpretation on his
words. Dowden points out that the passage
echoes a scene in Jonson's *Everyman
In His Humour* (acted by Shakespeare,
among others, in 1598) where Dame

---

192 that] *not in Q1F*   read] *Q1;* meane *F*   193 rogue] Satyre *Q1;* slaue *F*   195 amber and] Amber,
or *F*   196 lack] locke *F*   197 ¹most] *om. F*   199 yourself] you your selfe *F*   199–200 shall grow]
shalbe *Q1;* should be *F*   202 SD] *Johnson*   202–3] *F lines* madnesse, / walke / Lord? /   205 SD]
Staunton   205–9] *F lines* Ayre: / are? / happinesse, / on, / not / of. / him, / meeting / daughter. /
humbly / you. /   205 that's] *Q1;* that is *F*   of the] *Q1;* o'th' *F*

pregnant sometimes his replies are – a happiness that often madness hits on, which reason and sanity could not so prosperously be delivered of. I will leave him and my daughter. – My lord, I will take my leave of you.

HAMLET   You cannot take from me anything that I will   210
not more willingly part withal – except my life, except my life, except my life.

POLONIUS   Fare you well, my lord.

HAMLET   These tedious old fools.

Enter GUILDENSTERN *and* ROSENCRANTZ.

POLONIUS   You go to seek the Lord Hamlet? There he is.   215
ROSENCRANTZ [*to Polonius*]   God save you, sir.   [*Exit Polonius.*]
GUILDENSTERN   My honoured lord.
ROSENCRANTZ   My most dear lord.
HAMLET   My excellent good friends. How dost thou,

Kitely asks her husband to 'come in, out of the air . . . the air will do you harm', and Kitely exclaims, 'The air!' (*Everyman In*, 3.2.46–52).

206 **pregnant** cogent, forcible; but Polonius also carries through the metaphorical train from *breed* (178) and *conception* (181) to *delivered of* (208)

happiness aptness, fortuitous relevance

207 ***sanity** Q2's 'sanctity' seems erroneous (though Andrews retains and glosses 'virtue, holiness of life').

208 **prosperously** effectively

208–9 **I . . . daughter** Q2 may have omitted the additional words in F (see t.n.), or this difference could be a sign that Shakespeare once intended the encounter with Ophelia to take place in this scene, as it does in Q1.

Jenkins remarks that 'honourable' and 'most humbly' are out of character for Polonius and argues that they are 'fillups' in F by Compositor B.

210–11   **cannot . . . not** Hibbard accepts F's version as an authorial revision to avoid Q2's double negative, but the same difference is present in Q1 and Jenkins defends Q2's usage as Shakespearean (see also Hope, 2.1.9).

214 i.e. How tedious these old men are. In performance Hamlet sometimes pretends he is reading this line from his book.

219 ***excellent** Q2's 'extent' is generally dismissed as an error, probably a misreading of 'exlent', a common spelling at this time.

---

207 sanity] *F;* sanctity *Q2*   208 and] And sodainely contriue the meanes of meeting / Betweene him, and *F*   209 My] *Q1;* My Honourable *F*   will] *Q1;* will most humbly *F*   210 cannot] cannot Sir *F*   211 not] *om. Q1F*   211–12 life . . . ³life] life, my life *F*   214.1] *Capell; opp.* 212 *Q2; after* 209 *Q1; after* 215 *F*   215 the] my *F*   216 SD1] *Malone*   SD2 *Exit*] *Q1, opp.* 215; *not in Q2F*   Polonius] *Capell*   217 My] Mine *F*   219–21] *F; Q2 lines* Guyldersterne? / both? /   219 excellent] *Q3, F;* extent *Q2*

Guildenstern? Ah, Rosencrantz! Good lads, how do   220
you both?

ROSENCRANTZ   As the indifferent children of the earth.

GUILDENSTERN   Happy, in that we are not ever happy.
On Fortune's cap we are not the very button.

HAMLET   Nor the soles of her shoe.   225

ROSENCRANTZ   Neither, my lord.

HAMLET   Then you live about her waist, or in the middle
of her favours.

GUILDENSTERN   Faith, her privates we.

HAMLET   In the secret parts of Fortune? O, most true –   230
she is a strumpet. What news?

ROSENCRANTZ   None, my lord, but the world's grown
honest.

HAMLET   Then is doomsday near – but your news is not

---

222 **indifferent** ordinary, at neither extreme

223 **ever happy** always happy. F's 'ouer-happy' is generally preferred.

224 ***Fortune's cap** Shakespeare does not use the expression 'Fortune's lap' elsewhere, and 'l' is an easy misreading of majuscule 'C'. In any case the contrast between *cap* and *shoe* establishes F's reading as correct. Richard Dutton points out that Fortune was usually depicted naked (certainly without cap or shoes), but that this may be a reference to the sign of the Fortune theatre that probably depicted 'Dame Fortune'. If so, it begins a series of extra- or subtextual references to contemporary theatres and acting companies which runs through Hamlet's mention of 'this majestical roof fretted with golden fire' (see 266–7 and 267n.) and the conversation about 'the tragedians of the city' and climaxes (but only in F: see Appendix 1) with a reference to the sign of the Globe.

button The assumption is that the *cap* would be topped by a button.

229 **privates** private (sexual) parts of the body, with perhaps also a sense of 'private individuals', holding no rank or office. (This is another example of a line from *Hamlet* used as a title: Frederic Manning's 1929 novel about the First World War was originally called *The Middle Parts of Fortune*; it was later reprinted as *Her Privates We*.)

231 **strumpet** prostitute (who bestows her favours indiscriminately) as at 431. This slightly edgy conversation may hint at Hamlet's suspicion, voiced at 240–2, that his friends have in effect 'prostituted' themselves to the King.

234 **Then ... near** 'Because honesty is incompatible with the world's nature and hence must be destructive of it' (Jenkins); 'because nothing but the threat of doomsday could convert this world to honesty' (Hibbard).

---

220 Ah] *(A);* Oh *F*   221 you] ye *F*   223–4] *F; Q2 lines* lap, / button. /   223 ever] ouer- *F*   happy.] *F (*happy:*);* happy *Q2*   224 cap] *F;* lap *Q2*   228 favours] fauour *F*   231 What] What's the *F*   232 but] but that *F*

284

true. But, in the beaten way of friendship, what make 235
you at Elsinore?

ROSENCRANTZ   To visit you, my lord, no other occasion.

HAMLET   Beggar that I am, I am ever poor in thanks, but
I thank you, and sure, dear friends, my thanks are too
dear a halfpenny. Were you not sent for? Is it your own 240
inclining? Is it a free visitation? Come, come, deal
justly with me. Come, come, nay speak.

GUILDENSTERN   What should we say, my lord?

HAMLET   Anything but to th' purpose. You were sent for,
and there is a kind of confession in your looks, which 245
your modesties have not craft enough to colour.
I know the good King and Queen have sent for you.

ROSENCRANTZ   To what end, my lord?

HAMLET   That you must teach me. But let me conjure

234–5 **but ... true** Hamlet denies that the world has grown honest. After *true*, F has a passage of some 30 lines in which Hamlet claims that 'Denmark's a Prison' and the three men discuss ambition; see Appendix 1. It is generally supposed that these lines were omitted from Q2 because of the offence they might cause to Anne of Denmark, wife of James I. There is no trace of the *prison* lines in Q1 but Hamlet does claim that he 'wants preferment'.

235 **beaten way** well-trodden track. Jenkins and Hibbard say this means Hamlet switches to 'plain words'; Edwards that he has neglected ordinary politeness.

235–6 **what make you** what are you doing

238 **Beggar ... am** As before, Hamlet emphasizes his relatively powerless position (see 1.5.130n.).
ever Jenkins prefers F's 'euen' which makes a sharper point, and 'ever' for 'even' is an easy error, but Hamlet could

be saying that he habitually fails to express gratitude.

239–40 **too ... halfpenny** too expensive at (i.e. not worth) a halfpenny, but possibly too expensive *by* a halfpenny – if his friends are the King's agents and don't deserve them

244 **Anything ... th'purpose** anything, so long as it is not to the point (sarcastic). F's reading was formerly favoured by editors as meaning 'Anything, so long as it is to the purpose'. In Q1 this conversation is much abbreviated when the two visitors remark immediately that 'We ... would be very glad / You were as when we were at *Wittenberg*' (7.238–9).

246 **modesties** modest or decent natures
colour present deceptively, disguise

249–54 After briefly flattering his visitors by implying that they are not capable of deception, Hamlet resorts to sarcasm again: at least his phrasing suggests self-conscious inflation.

249 **conjure** earnestly entreat

---

235 true.] *F follows this sentence with 30 lines of additional dialogue (238–67)*   238 ever] euen *F*
241 come, deal] deale *F*   244 Anything but] Why any thing. But *F*   to th'] to the *F*   245 of] *Q1; om. F*

you, by the rights of our fellowship, by the consonancy 250
of our youth, by the obligation of our ever-preserved
love, and by what more dear a better proposer can
charge you withal, be even and direct with me whether
you were sent for or no.

ROSENCRANTZ   What say you?   255

HAMLET   Nay then, I have an eye of you. If you love me,
hold not off.

GUILDENSTERN   My lord, we were sent for.

HAMLET   I will tell you why. So shall my anticipation
prevent your discovery and your secrecy to the King 260
and Queen moult no feather. I have of late, but
wherefore I know not, lost all my mirth, forgone all
custom of exercises and, indeed, it goes so heavily with
my disposition that this goodly frame the earth seems

250–1 **consonancy . . . youth** our childhood or youthful friendship

252–3 **by . . . withal** i.e. by whatever more significant exhortation a more skilful proposer of oaths than myself could put to you

253 **charge** exhort
even straightforward, 'on the level'

255 Rosencrantz presumably consults Guildenstern. (The line could conceivably be addressed to Hamlet, meaning 'What did you say?' or 'What do you mean?' but it would be inappropriately informal or even rude, and it wouldn't cue Hamlet's response.)

256 **Nay . . . you** Edwards and Hibbard mark this as an aside.
of on

257 **hold not off** do not hesitate to tell me

259–60 **my . . . discovery** my saying it first will save you from having to tell me your secret

261 **moult no feather** i.e. sustain no loss

261–74 **I have . . . dust** Edwards calls this speech 'a parade of fashionable melancholy'

intended to mislead Hamlet's interlocutors; he may, however, be describing his real feelings while concealing the cause. The speech was transferred to Hamlet's first appearance, at the very beginning of the film, in Almereyda's 2000 version, possibly in part as a tribute to Bruce Robinson's 1987 film *Withnail and I* which ends with it.

263 **custom of exercises** customary activities (such as the fencing and tennis mentioned in relation to Laertes in 2.1). 'Exercise' could also refer to religious observance, as at 3.1.44. Hamlet's position here is contradicted by his words at 5.2.188–9.

263–4 **it . . . disposition** my spirits in general are so depressed

264 **frame** structure; *this goodly frame* might also be a reference to the Globe playhouse. See also Marlowe and Nashe's *Dido*, where in her last speech before she throws herself into the flames Dido calls on 'ye gods that guide the starrie frame' (5.1.302).

252 can] could *F*   260 and] of *F*   263 exercises] exercise *F*   heavily] heauenly *F*

to me a sterile promontory, this most excellent canopy   265
the air, look you, this brave o'erhanging firmament, this
majestical roof fretted with golden fire, why it
appeareth nothing to me but a foul and pestilent
congregation of vapours. What piece of work is a man
– how noble in reason; how infinite in faculties, in form   270
and moving; how express and admirable in action; how
like an angel in apprehension; how like a god; the
beauty of the world; the paragon of animals. And yet to
me what is this quintessence of dust? Man delights not

265 **sterile promontory** barren headland.
Edwards quotes Kittredge: 'a barren rocky
point jutting out into the sea of eternity'.
canopy sky; see 'Where dwell'st thou? /
Under the canopy' (*Cor* 4.5.39–40).
266 **look you** an intensive expression (see
Blake, 8.3.2, 8.4.1), not necessarily
denoting a Welsh speaker, as it might
today, and as it clearly does in the speeches
of Fluellen in *H5* and those of Hugh Evans
in *MW*. (The phrase occurs earlier in
Hamlet's speech in F: see t.n. at 1.5.131.)
brave fine, magnificent
firmament sky
267 **fretted** inlaid, decorated. For early
audiences, Hamlet might be indicating the
overhanging roof of the Globe playhouse
(referred to as 'the heavens') as well as the
sky above it.
268 **appeareth . . . but** Edwards conflates here:
'appeareth no other thing to me but'.
269–73 **What . . . animals** Dover Wilson
explicitly defends Q2's punctuation (which
we largely follow) here, as conveying 'the
brooding Hamlet' through its semicolons

and commas, as compared with the more
declamatory style implied by the
exclamations and question marks in F (see
t.n. at 271–2).
269 **What . . . work** what a masterpiece of
creation. Jenkins defends Q2 as idiomatic,
and Kemble and Macready followed it
onstage (see Hapgood).
270 **faculties** capabilities
270–1 **form and moving** shape and motion
271 **express** well-framed or well-modelled
(listed by *OED* I 1b as a 'nonce-use')
272 **apprehension** understanding; see 4.1.11,
where it means 'misunderstanding'.
273 **paragon** supreme example
274 **quintessence of dust** an oxymoron,
like *paragon of animals* (see also the
religious connotations of *dust* at
1.2.71) *Quintessence* means concentration', literally, the 'fifth essence', the
substance of which heavenly bodies were
thought to be composed, and which,
according to alchemy, could be extracted
from earthly elements by a process of
distillation.

266 firmament] *om. F*   268 appeareth] appeares *F*   nothing . . . but] no other thing . . . then *F*
269 What] What a *F*   270 faculties,] faculty? *F*   271 moving;] *(*moouing,*); mouing *F*
271–2 admirable in action; how] *(*admirable in action, how*); admirable? in Action, how *F*   272 angel
in apprehension; . . . god;] *(*Angell in apprehension, how like a God:*); Angel? in apprehension, how
like a God? *F*

me – nor women neither, though by your smiling you 275
seem to say so.

ROSENCRANTZ   My lord, there was no such stuff in my
thoughts.

HAMLET   Why did ye laugh then, when I said man
delights not me?   280

ROSENCRANTZ   To think, my lord, if you delight not in
man what lenten entertainment the players shall
receive from you; we coted them on the way and
hither are they coming to offer you service.

HAMLET   He that plays the King shall be welcome – his 285
majesty shall have tribute on me – the Adventurous
Knight shall use his foil and target, the Lover shall
not sigh gratis, the Humorous Man shall end his part
in peace, and the Lady shall say her mind freely or the

---

275 **nor women neither** Hamlet presumably used *man* in the general sense of 'humankind' but his companions understood him to mean 'the male sex'. Jenkins prefers F's singular 'woman'.

282 **lenten** niggardly (the Christian season of Lent being a time of fasting and denial). In Elizabethan England theatres were closed altogether during Lent.
entertainment reception, welcome (as at 312)
players actors. In the ensuing conversation it is assumed that the situation in Denmark is analogous to that in London around 1600, with the acting companies undertaking provincial tours (sometimes reluctantly) to recoup their finances.

283 **coted** caught up with and passed

285 **He ... King** The King, like the other characters Hamlet names, is a stereotype of

the stage. Unlike his uncle, this man pretending to be a king is welcome.

286 **tribute** payment; praise
on of; Jenkins defends Q2's reading as idiomatic (see also Blake, 5.4.2, *Of* and *On*).

287 **foil and target** sword and shield

288 **gratis** for nothing, without reward (i.e. unrequited). Q1 omits *not* in 287, and Hubbard argues that this version makes better sense.

288–9 **the Humorous ... peace** i.e. the comic actor will not be interrupted. *Humorous* could, however, mean 'showing a particular humour, or psychological type', as it does in Le Beau's reference to the 'humorous' Duke in *AYL* (1.2.256) and in the 'humours' plays written by Jonson, Chapman and others. Both Q1 and F follow this with a separate reference to 'the Clowne'.

---

275 nor] no nor *Q1F*   women] woman *Q1, Q3, F*   279 ye] you *Q1F*   then] *Q1; om. F*   286 on] of *Q1F*   287 not] *F; not in Q1*   289 and] The clowne shall make them laugh / That are tickled in the lungs, or the blank verse shall halt for't / And *Q1;* the Clowne shall make those laugh whose lungs are tickled a'th'sere: and *F*

blank verse shall halt for't. What players are they?   290
ROSENCRANTZ   Even those you were wont to take such
delight in, the tragedians of the city.
HAMLET   How chances it they travel? Their residence,
both in reputation and profit, was better both ways.
ROSENCRANTZ   I think their inhibition comes by the   295
means of the late innovation.
HAMLET   Do they hold the same estimation they did
when I was in the city? Are they so followed?
ROSENCRANTZ   No, indeed are they not.
HAMLET   It is not very strange, for my uncle is King of   300

---

290 *blank ... it Q2's 'black' seems a likely
misreading. The general sense seems to be
that the Lady, like the Humorous Man, will
not be interrupted, 'or her delivery of blank
verse will lose its rhythm'. Hibbard
suggests that 'the boys playing female
roles were more likely to be put out by
comments from the audience than the more
experienced adult players.'
291 **were wont** used
292 **tragedians** actors (not exclusively of
tragedies)
293 **travel** tour (outside the city); see t.n. for
travail/travel spellings; either could be
used in Shakespeare's time for either
meaning.
residence usual residence (i.e. in the city)
294 **both ways** i.e. both for their reputation and
for their financial advantage
295–6 **their ... innovation** i.e. the restriction
on their performances (in the city) is
because of recent and unusual events.
Editors have interpreted *the late innovation*
as a reference to political disturbances –
perhaps the death of the elder Hamlet and
the preparations for war in the Danish
context, or the Essex rebellion in 1601 if an
English topical allusion is intended. In the
other texts the *innovation* could mean the

revived fashion for children's companies:
see 299n. (See pp. 52–4, Jenkins, LN, and
Bednarz.)
297 **estimation** reputation, esteem
298 **the city** It is not clear which Danish city
Hamlet might mean; again reference to
London makes more sense.
Are ... followed? Do they still retain their
power to attract audiences?
299 F has a further passage of some 25 lines
after *not* in which Hamlet asks why the
players travel and Rosencrantz explains
that it is because of the competition from
the children's companies: see Appendix 1.
It has been supposed that the lines were
omitted from Q2 because this was no
longer a topical issue in 1604, though it
would have been even less topical in 1623.
It is also strange that the reference to
'Hercules and his load' (the sign of the
Globe theatre) should occur only in the
1623 text and not in the earlier ones that
were printed closer to the time of the first
performances.
300–3 **It ... little** Hamlet compares the
fickleness of the theatre audience with
the behaviour of the Danish people in
transferring their allegiance from his
father to his uncle. (The logic of his

---

290 blank] *Q1F;* black *Q2*   291 such] *not in Q1F*   293 travel] *(trauaile)* F, trauell *Q1*   299 are they]
they are *F*   299–300 not. / HAMLET It] *In F the two speeches are separated by 25 lines of dialogue not in
Q2*   300 very] *om. F*   my] mine *F*

Denmark, and those that would make mouths at him
while my father lived give twenty, forty, fifty, a
hundred ducats apiece for his picture in little. 'Sblood,
there is something in this more than natural if
philosophy could find it out.   *A flourish*

GUILDENSTERN   There are the players!   306

HAMLET   Gentlemen, you are welcome to Elsinore. Your
hands, come, then! Th'appurtenance of welcome is
fashion and ceremony. Let me comply with you in
this garb lest my extent to the players, which I tell you 310
must show fairly outwards, should more appear like

argument is perhaps more obvious in F's
version, where the rise of the children's
companies (rather than the demise of the
adult companies) is compared with the rise
of the King.)

301 **make mouths** make derisive grimaces,
pull faces

302–3 **twenty ... ducats** Clearly the point is
that Hamlet is naming extravagant sums.
Shakespeare uses *ducat* in six plays as a
monetary unit for continental Europe,
especially Italy, as in *MV*; there does not
seem to be a precise relation to the *crowns*
of 73.

303 **picture in little** miniature portrait (an art
highly prized in Elizabethan England). In
F's version there is a more obvious
reference to the child actors as 'miniatures'.
A possible piece of stage business is for
Hamlet to grab a locket with a picture of
the King from one of his companions here
and produce it at 3.4.51, but more often he
grabs it from the Queen in that scene.
'Sblood abbreviation of 'God's blood'. F's
omission is a likely expurgation.

304 **more than natural** outside natural laws,
abnormal
philosophy science

305 SD This kind of fanfare (usually played
'within' on a trumpet or cornet) is most
frequently used when important figures
(such as royalty) enter or exit: see 'flourish'
in Dessen & Thomson. The Players'
offstage arrival is marked here, though
they do not enter for another 50 lines in Q2
and F, 30 lines in Q1.

307–8 **Your hands** i.e. give me your
hands. After the rather edgy preceding
conversation, Hamlet reaffirms the
greeting he gave Rosencrantz and
Guildenstern at 219–21.

308 **Th'appurtenance** the proper
accompaniment (that which appertains
to)

309 **comply with you** exchange courtesies with
you. *Comply* recalls the inflated tone of
249–54; in F, Hamlet also uses the word in
relation to Osric at 5.2.150 (see Appendix
1).

310 **garb** manner (i.e. by shaking hands)
*lest my extent Caldecott suggested
emending *extent* to 'ostent', meaning
'ostentatious welcome', but F's reading is
usually adopted. The scribe or compositor
may have been misled by 'let mee' in 309.
extent extension of welcome

301 mouths] mops and moes *Q1;* mowes *F*   302 fifty] *om. F*   a] an *F*   303 'Sblood] *om. F*   305 SD]
The Trumpets sound, Q1; Flourish for the Players. F   308 then] *om. F*   Th'appurtenance] The
appurtenance *F*   309 this] the *F*   310 lest my] *F;* let me *Q2*   311 outwards] outward *F*

entertainment than yours. You are welcome. But my
uncle-father and aunt-mother are deceived.

GUILDENSTERN   In what, my dear lord?

HAMLET   I am but mad north-north-west. When the   315
wind is southerly I know a hawk from a handsaw.

Enter POLONIUS.

POLONIUS   Well be with you, gentlemen.

HAMLET   Hark you, Guildenstern, and you too – at each
ear a hearer. That great baby you see there is not yet
out of his swaddling clouts.   320

ROSENCRANTZ   Happily he is the second time come to
them, for they say an old man is twice a child.

HAMLET   I will prophesy he comes to tell me of the

---

312 **entertainment** See 282n.
    yours i.e. the welcome Hamlet has given
Rosencrantz and Guildenstern

313 **uncle-father and aunt-mother** While the
King is Hamlet's uncle and has also
become his stepfather, his mother the
Queen has by the same marriage also
become his aunt.

315 **I . . . north-north-west** either 'I am mad
only when the wind is in the north-north-
west', or 'I am only one point of the
compass away from true sanity'. There is
an allusion to this line in *Eastward Ho* (see
pp. 58–9). (Stanley Cavell argues with
some ingenuity that *Hamlet* is alluded to in
Alfred Hitchcock's 1959 film *North by
Northwest*.)

316 **handsaw** emended to 'hernshaw' (a kind
of heron) by Hanmer in 1744 on the
grounds that the two things mentioned
should have a greater degree of similarity.
John Ward also made this change in his
prompt copy of Q6 which he annotated
some time in the 1740s, and Phelps

(99–100) records that 'When Mr. Barry
Sullivan came out as Hamlet [London,
1861], many persons attended the
Haymarket for the mere purpose of hearing
him say "I know a hawk from a heron –
pshaw!" instead of the ordinary reading.'
More recent editors and producers have
argued that the point of the remark is the
complete dissimilarity between a hawk and
a saw, and Dowden suggests *hawk*
indicates Hamlet's awareness that
Rosencrantz and Guildenstern are spying
on him.

317 **Well . . . you** i.e. I wish you well; an
archaic impersonal construction, rare in
Shakespeare (Blake, 4.4.1d)

318–19 **at . . . hearer** Hamlet encourages his
companions to stand close to him on each
side.

320 **swaddling clouts** swathing clothes, narrow
strips of cloth wrapped around a baby to
restrict its movement

321 **Happily** perhaps

322 **old . . . child** proverbial (Dent, M570)

---

320 swaddling] *Q1;* swathing *F*   321 he is] he's *F*   323 prophesy] *(prophecy,);* Prophesie. *F*

players. Mark it. – You say right, sir, o'Monday
morning, 'twas then indeed.   325

POLONIUS   My lord, I have news to tell you.

HAMLET   My lord, I have news to tell you. When Roscius
was an actor in Rome –

POLONIUS   The actors are come hither, my lord.

HAMLET   Buzz, buzz.   330

POLONIUS   Upon my honour.

HAMLET

– Then came each actor on his ass.

POLONIUS   The best actors in the world, either for
tragedy, comedy, history, pastoral, pastoral-comical,
historical-pastoral, scene individable or poem   335
unlimited. Seneca cannot be too heavy nor Plautus too

---

324 **Mark it** observe the outcome
324–5 **You . . . indeed** Hamlet teases Polonius
by pretending to be in the midst of a
conversation about a recent event.
327 **Roscius** Quintus Roscius, a famous actor
in classical Rome, also mentioned by
Shakespeare in *3H6* 5.6.10. Hamlet aims to
disconcert Polonius by talking about acting
before he announces the players. (William
Betty, who played Hamlet in the early
nineteenth century at the age of 13, was
known as 'the infant Roscius': see p. 3 and
Fig. 1.)
330 **Buzz, buzz** a contemptuous expression
(Blake, 6.4.1), here indicating that Hamlet
already knows Polonius' news.
332 Possibly a line from a ballad: *ass* rhymes
with *pass* and *was* (see 355–6), but also
suggests 'arse'.
334–5 **pastoral-comical, historical-pastoral**
Polonius elaborates still further on the
possible combinations of the classical
genres in F (see t.n.). Some neoclassical

critics, such as Philip Sidney in his *Apology
for Poetry*, deplored the mixture of genres,
but Shakespeare's own plays often broke
these rules and both Q1 and Q2 are called
The Tragicall Historie of Hamlet on their
title-pages.
335–6 **scene . . . unlimited** Both phrases
are obscure: *scene individable* may
mean 'plays without scene-breaks' and
poem unlimited may mean 'poetic
drama unrestricted by rules', but Jenkins
suggests they simply intensify the
catalogue of absurd categories and
convey 'all-inclusive' and 'unclassifiable'
respectively.
336 **Seneca . . . Plautus** 'Plautus and Seneca
are accounted the best for Comedy and
Tragedy among the Latins' (Francis Meres,
Palladis Tamia, 1598); Shakespeare's *Tit* is
particularly influenced by the former and
his *CE* by the latter. *TxC* suggests Q2's
spelling 'Sceneca' may contain a pun on
'scena'.

---

324 o'] *(a) Q1;* for a *F*   325 then] so *Q1F*   328 was] *Q1; om. F*   331 my] mine *F*   332 came] can *F*
334–5 pastoral-comical, historical-pastoral] *(*Pastorall Comicall, Historicall Pastorall*);* Pastorall,
Historicall, Historicall, Comicall, / Comicall historicall, Pastorall, Tragedy historicall: / *Q1;*
Pastoricall-Comicall-Historicall-Pastorall: Tragicall-Historicall: Tragicall-Comicall-Historicall-Pastorall
F   336 Seneca] *(Sceneca);* Seneca *Q1F*

light for the law of writ and the liberty. These are the
only men.

HAMLET   *O Jephthah, judge of Israel, what a treasure*
hadst thou?   340

POLONIUS   What a treasure had he, my lord?

HAMLET   Why,

One fair daughter and no more,
The which he loved passing well.

POLONIUS [*aside*]   Still on my daughter.   345

HAMLET   Am I not i'th' right, old Jephthah?

POLONIUS   If you call me Jephthah, my lord, I have a
daughter that I love passing well.

HAMLET   Nay, that follows not.

POLONIUS   What follows then, my lord?   350

HAMLET   Why,

As by lot,

---

337 **for . . . liberty** for either strictly regulated
or nonconforming drama (?). This is an
obscure phrase which is often taken as
modifying what follows, although neither
Q2 nor F has a full stop after *light*. Q1's
'For the law hath writ those are the onely
men' may indicate that it puzzled the
reporter(s) if it is a reported text.

337–8 **These . . . men** probably 'these [actors]
are the best available', though he could be
referring to Seneca and Plautus as 'the only
great dramatists'.

339 *Jephthah* An Old Testament figure, he
sacrificed his virgin daughter (Judges,
11.30–40); Shakespeare also alludes to
this story in *3H6* 5.1.93–4. Hibbard
notes that this line is a fourteener and
possibly a quotation on Shakespeare's
part. (Fourteeners were lines with 14
syllables, an old-fashioned metre in 1600,
though it was used by Chapman for his
translation of Homer's *Iliad* which began

appearing in 1598.)

343–4 Hamlet quotes from a ballad about
Jephthah which survives in a seventeenth-
century version (see Jenkins, LN, and
Edwards).

344 **loved** lovèd

passing surpassingly, extremely

349 (1) Your analogy between yourself and
Jephthah is false; (2) That isn't the next
line in the ballad. The brief representation
of Hamlet and Polonius reconstructing the
ballad, followed at 385ff. by the much
longer representation of Hamlet and the
First Player reconstructing the Pyrrhus
speech, has an odd resonance in the context
of Q1 as a reported text, reconstructed by
actors from memory (see pp. 82–8 and
Appendix 2).

352–3, 355–6 Hamlet continues to quote from
the ballad.

352–3 'as by chance (*lot*), God knows
(*wot*)'

---

337 light for . . . liberty.] *F subst.*; light. For . . . liberty, *Johnson*   writ] *F;* wit *Q6*   339, 346, 347
Jephthah, Jephthah] *F (Iephta); Ieptha Q2; Iepha Q1*   342–4] *Capell subst., distinguishing between*
Why *and verse lines; Q1F line* more, / well. / ; *prose Q2*   345 SD] *Capell*   352–3] *Malone; prose
Q21F*

293

> God wot,
> and then, you know,
>   It came to pass,   355
>   As most like it was.
> The first row of the pious chanson will show you more,
> for look where my abridgement comes.

Enter the Players.

> You are welcome, masters, welcome all. I am glad to see
> thee well. Welcome, good friends. O old friend, why,   360
> thy face is valanced since I saw thee last! Com'st thou to
> beard me in Denmark? What, my young lady and
> mistress! By'r Lady, your ladyship is nearer to heaven

355–6 'it happened, as was most likely'

357 **first . . . chanson** first line of the religious song; Q1's version (see t.n.) leads editors to interpret *row* as meaning 'verse'. F's reading, interpreted by Pope and other editors as meaning 'songs sung on bridges' or '*chansons de Pont Neuf*', is supported by Hunter, despite his general advocacy of Q1. Jenkins dismisses this as 'a cautionary tale' of unnecessary ingenuity.

358 **my abridgement** (1) that which will cut me off; (2) my entertainment (as at *MND* 5.1.39). Either way, Hamlet is referring to the arrival of the players.

358.1 Q2 does not specify how many players at this point; a minimum of three are needed for the play in 3.2, if the Prologue and Lucianus are doubled and a way is found of dispensing with the mutes. Two of them are addressed here by Hamlet, the First Player (assuming it is he who has grown the beard) and the boy, and he welcomes them as *all* at 359 and 366. RP points out that companies of four or five

were characteristic of the first half of the sixteenth century and that Shakespeare may be evoking an earlier period of acting (and play-writing) here (see also 461n.). As was the case with Elizabethan professional companies, all the players are male, with a boy to play the women's parts.

360 **thee** Hamlet usually addresses this speech to the First Player (but see next note).

361 **valanced** curtained, draped (i.e. bearded). The assumption may be that the First Player is quite young (if he has only just grown his first beard), but he is often cast as an older, experienced actor, a decision which may stem in part from Hamlet's phrase *old friend* (360, repeated at 473–4), and from the assumption that his style of acting is old-fashioned (see 403n.).

362 **beard** show me your beard; defy me
    my young lady i.e. the boy

363 *By'r Lady** by Our Lady (i.e. the Virgin Mary); Jenkins argues Q2's 'by lady' may have been the Shakespearean

355–6] *Pope; prose Q21F*   357 row] *F;* verse *Q1*   pious chanson] *Pons Chanson F;* godly Ballet *Q1*
358 abridgement comes] *Q1;* Abridgements come *F*   358.1 the] *not in Q1;* foure or fiue *F*   359 You
are] Y'are *F*   360 old] my olde *Q1F*   why] *not in Q1F*   361 valanced] *Q1;* valiant *F*
363 By'r Lady] *F;* by lady *Q2;* burlady *Q1*   to] *om. F*

than when I saw you last by the altitude of a chopine.
Pray God your voice, like a piece of uncurrent gold, be 365
not cracked within the ring. Masters, you are all
welcome. We'll e'en to't like French falconers – fly at
anything we see. We'll have a speech straight. Come,
give us a taste of your quality. Come, a passionate
speech.   370

1 PLAYER   What speech, my good lord?

HAMLET   I heard thee speak me a speech once – but it was
never acted, or, if it was, not above once, for the play I
remember pleased not the million, 'twas caviare to the
general. But it was, as I received it, and others whose 375
judgements in such matters cried in the top of mine, an
excellent play, well digested in the scenes, set down

form. This was a mild oath and it is not
unusual to find it in plays with a Protestant
setting (like *By the mass* at 2.1.49).

nearer to heaven (1) taller (nearer to the
sky); (2) older (nearer to death)

364 **chopine** shoe with a high platform sole

365–6 **uncurrent . . . ring** A gold coin clipped
or cracked inside the ring surrounding the
sovereign's head was no longer legal
tender. Editors sometimes suggest a sexual
meaning for *cracked* whereby Hamlet is
saying that the breaking of his voice for a
boy is like the losing of her virginity for a
girl.

367 **We'll . . . to't** let's go straight into it
*French falconers Q2's reading has not
been satisfactorily explained, while Q1 and
F agree. The assumption is that the French
are enthusiastic at this sport.
fly launch our birds (i.e., in this context, try
a speech). The implication is that the
speech will be chosen at random, but in
fact Hamlet makes a very specific request.

368 **straight** immediately

369 **quality** acting ability, skill

371 SP *F distinguishes this speech, and
those beginning at 406, 440 and 443, with
the SP '1. *Play*.' or '1. *Player*', whereas
Q2 uses the ambiguous '*Play*.' or '*Player*'
throughout this scene. It is generally
assumed that the only player to speak in
this scene is the leading actor of the
company.

372 **me** for me
it i.e. the play containing the speech

374–5 **caviare . . . general** a delicacy not
appreciated by the majority of people. (The
spellings, 'cauiary' in Q1/2 and 'Cauiarie'
in F, probably indicate four syllables in
pronunciation.)

376 **cried . . . mine** excelled mine (*?*).
Q1's 'Cried in the toppe of their
iudgements' perhaps indicates that this
slightly obscure expression might be
understood as 'proclaimed in their
authoritative opinions'.

377 **well digested . . . scenes** well organized
into scenes

367 French] *Q1F;* friendly *Q2*   falconers] *Q1F;* Fankners *Q2*   371 SP] *F (*1.*Play.*); *Player. Q2;*
Players Q1   good] *Q1;* om. *F*   376 judgements] *Q1;* iudgement *F*

with as much modesty as cunning. I remember one said
there were no sallets in the lines to make the matter
savoury nor no matter in the phrase that might indict   380
the author of affection, but called it an honest method,
as wholesome as sweet, and by very much more
handsome than fine. One speech in't I chiefly loved –
'twas Aeneas' talk to Dido, and thereabout of it
especially when he speaks of Priam's slaughter. If it live   385
in your memory begin at this line – let me see, let me
see –

378 **modesty** restraint
cunning skill
379–80 **sallets ... savoury** salads (usually
glossed as 'spicy bits' but perhaps just a
variety of ingredients) in the dialogue to
make it well seasoned
380 **no ... phrase** nothing in the manner of
expression
indict accuse
381 **affection** affectation: *OED* V, which cites
LLL, 'Three-piled hyperboles, spruce
affection, / Figures pedantical' (5.2.407–
8); both the 1598 quarto and the 1623
Folio texts of *LLL* read 'affection', but
the two words were often confused in the
late sixteenth century.
honest   method   straightforward
(unpretentious) effort of composition
382–3 **more ... fine** 'with more natural
grace than artful workmanship' (Jenkins);
the distinction recalls Polonius' advice
to Laertes about richness and ornament
in 1.3.
384 **Aeneas' ... Dido** Aeneas tells Dido the
story of the fall of Troy in Virgil's *Aeneid*
2, 506–58 (Jenkins, LN); Marlowe and
Nashe had dramatized this in *Dido Queen
of Carthage* (c. 1585). As Berry notes,
Hamlet casts himself in Dido's role as

choric listener (*Endings*, 60–1). Dryden
attacks the ensuing speech in 'The grounds
of criticism in Tragedy', prefaced to his
1679 adaptation of *Troilus and Cressida*,
where he gives it as an example of 'the
blown puffy style', not written by
Shakespeare but quoted from 'some other
poet': Dover Wilson points out, however,
that Dryden drew on this speech when
translating Virgil's account of Pyrrhus.
Theobald claims it is authentic 'from
its Subject ... there is scarce a Play
throughout all his Works, in which it
was possible to introduce the Mention
of them, where he has not by *Simile,
Allusion*, or otherwise, hinted at the
Trojan affairs, so fond was he of that
story' (Theobald, *Restored*, 72–3). The
most closely comparable passage in
Shakespeare's previous work is at *Luc*
1366–1568, where after her rape the
heroine looks at a painting of the fall of
Troy which includes a representation
of Pyrrhus killing Priam and the grief
of Hecuba (1443–70).
talk Most editors, including Jenkins, prefer
F's 'tale' = narration.
thereabout of it around that part of it
385 **Priam** the King of Troy

379 were] was *Q1F*   381 affection] affectation *F*   382–3 as wholesome ... fine] as wholesome as
sweete *Q1; om. F*   383 One] Come, a *Q1;* One cheefe *F* in't] in it *Q1F*   384 talk] tale *Q1F*
385 when] where *Q1F*

The rugged Pyrrhus like th' Hyrcanian beast . . .
– 'Tis not so. It begins with Pyrrhus.
The rugged Pyrrhus, he whose sable arms, 390
Black as his purpose, did the night resemble
When he lay couched in th'ominous horse,
Hath now this dread and black complexion smeared
With heraldry more dismal, head to foot.
Now is he total gules, horridly tricked 395
With blood of fathers, mothers, daughters, sons,
Baked and impasted with the parching streets

---

388 *rugged* fierce, savage
  Pyrrhus the son of the Greek Achilles, who went to Troy to avenge his father's death on Priam and his family
  th'Hyrcanian beast Hyrcania, near the Caspian Sea, was famous for its tigers; see York's accusation of Margaret: 'you are more inhuman, more inexorable – / O, ten times more – than tigers of Hyrcania' (*3H6* 1.4.154–5). Towards the end of Marlowe and Nashe's *Dido* the heroine upbraids Aeneas as unfeeling: 'Tygers of *Hircania* gave thee sucke' (5.1.159). In this context, the comparison with the *beast* associates Pyrrhus with savage or even heroic action, unlike the negative connotations of *beast* at 1.2.150, 1.5.42, 4.4.34 and 4.5.86.
389 *'Tis not so* See 349n. Hamlet's misremembering might be seen as an allusion to (and dismissal of?) the famous insult in Robert Greene's (posthumous) 1592 *Groatsworth of Wit*, where 'Shake-scene' is derided as 'an upstart Crow . . . with his Tiger's heart wrapped in a Player's hide'. Loewenstein argues that in this passage Shakespeare 'canonizes' *Hamlet* in relation to classical precedents (especially Virgil), rejecting Marlowe, Greene and Kyd in a context in which the supposedly Danish players are firmly

associated with English theatrical rivalries, as at 295–303.
390 *sable arms* black armour. See 1.2.240n. and 3.2.123n.
392 *couched* couchèd; crouched, hidden
  th'ominous horse the unlucky or ill-omened giant wooden statue of a horse inside which the Greeks smuggled themselves into Troy. The version of the story told by Aeneas in Marlowe and Nashe's *Dido* (2.1.121–288) makes more of 'Epeus' pine-tree horse' (and of Sinon's treachery, which Shakespeare had stressed in *Luc* 1366–1568).
393 *this . . . complexion* this (already) terrifying and dark general appearance
394 *heraldry more dismal* The blood Pyrrhus has smeared on his face is seen as the equivalent of the heraldic markings on his armour.
  dismal grim, dreadful
395 *total gules* red all over; *gules* is the heraldic term for 'red'. Marlowe and Nashe's Aeneas says, 'At last came Pyrrhus, fell and full of fire, / His harness dropping blood' (2.1.213–14).
  tricked decorated (another heraldic term referring to the patterning of markings)
397 *Baked . . . with* (as if) cooked (by the heat of the streets) and made into a pastry or crust

---

388] *as verse line Q1; prose Q2F Hyrcanian*] *(ircanian), F; arganian Q1* 389 'Tis] *Q1;* It is *F*
390] *as verse Q1F; prose Q2* 392 *th'ominous*] the ominous *Q1F* 393 *this*] *F;* his *Q1* 394 *heraldry*] *(heraldy), Q1F dismal, . . . foot.*] *(dismall . . . foote,); dismall, . . . foote, Q1; dismall: . . . foote F*
395 *total*] *Q1;* to take *F gules*] guise *Q1;* Geulles *F*

That lend a tyrannous and a damned light
To their lord's murder; roasted in wrath and fire,
And thus o'ersized with coagulate gore,   400
With eyes like carbuncles, the hellish Pyrrhus
Old grandsire Priam seeks.
So proceed you.

POLONIUS   'Fore God, my lord, well spoken – with good
accent and good discretion.   405

1 PLAYER   *Anon he finds him,*
Striking too short at Greeks. His antique sword,
Rebellious to his arm, lies where it falls,
Repugnant to command. Unequal matched,

---

parching streets The streets are supposed to be scorching because the houses are on fire.
398 *tyrannous* fierce
    damned damnèd
399 *their lord's murder* i.e. the imminent murder of Priam
    roasted . . . fire This is presumably part of the description of *the hellish Pyrrhus* (401), in parallel with *tricked* (395), *Baked and impasted* (397) and *o'ersized* (400), though it could conceivably relate to *the parching streets* (397). Q1's reading (see t.n.) perhaps indicates that the reporter was confused here.
400 *o'ersized* o'ersizèd; covered over as with size, 'a glutinous or viscid wash applied to paper . . . to provide a suitable ground for painting' (*OED sb.* 21). Hibbard, however, suggests: 'looking even bigger than his true size because of the clotted blood adhering to him'.
    coagulate gore congealed or clotted blood
401 *carbuncles* large red gems, thought to glow in the dark
402 *grandsire* Priam was supposed to have 50 sons and numerous grandchildren.
403 *So proceed you* In some productions the

Player displays impatience with the length of Hamlet's quotation and seems about to take over several times before he is invited to do so. The style in which he proceeds is often melodramatic, raising a problem of inconsistency with Hamlet's praise of naturalistic acting at the beginning of 3.1, but Bob Peck gave a memorably quiet and serious rendering of the speech in Buzz Goodbody's 1975 RSC production after Ben Kingsley as Hamlet had overplayed the first part (see Maher, 78, and Callaghan, 175). Some Hamlets continue to mouth or whisper the rest of the speech along with the Player.
404–5 **with   . . .   discretion** with good pronunciation and judgement
406 *Anon* soon (as at 424)
407 *Striking too short* The assumption is that Priam is too old to use his sword effectively and his thrusts fall short. Shakespeare makes fun of old men wielding swords at *2H6* 2.1.49, *RJ* 1.1.75 and *MW* 2.1.204–6.
    antique (stress on first syllable) ancient (perhaps Q2/F's 'anticke' also suggests 'antic' = comic)
409 *Repugnant to command* refusing to do his bidding

---

398 *a damned*] damned *F*   399 *lord's murder*] vilde Murthers *F*   *roasted in wrath*] *F;* Rifted in earth *Q1*   400 *o'ersized*] (ore-cised), *F* (o're-sized) *coagulate*] *F;* calagulate *Q1*   403] So goe on. *Q1; om. F*   406 SP] *F; Play. Q21*   407 *antique*] (anticke) *F, Q1* (antike)   409 *matched*] match *F*

> *Pyrrhus at Priam drives, in rage strikes wide,*   410
> *But with the whiff and wind of his fell sword*
> *Th'unnerved father falls. Then senseless Ilium*
> *Seeming to feel this blow, with flaming top*
> *Stoops to his base and with a hideous crash*
> *Takes prisoner Pyrrhus' ear. For lo, his sword*   415
> *Which was declining on the milky head*
> *Of reverend Priam seemed i'th' air to stick.*
> *So as a painted tyrant Pyrrhus stood*
> *Like a neutral to his will and matter,*

410 ***drives*** aims the thrusts of his sword

411 ***whiff and wind*** mere disturbance of the air. In Marlowe and Nashe's *Dido*, Achilles' son 'whiskt his sword about, / And with the wound thereof the King fell down' (2.1.253–4); most editors accept Collier's emendation of the 1594 Quarto 'wound' to 'wind' on the analogy of the present passage and the assumption that the idea is a commonplace: see *FQ*, 1.7.12, where the Red Cross Knight avoids a blow from a giant: '[he] lightly lept from vnderneath the blow: / Yet so exceeding was the villains power, / That with the wind it did him overthrow', and *TC* 5.3.41, where Troilus tells Hector that Greeks fall 'Even in the fan and wind of your fair sword'.
  fell cruel

412 ***unnerved*** unnervèd; enfeebled
  ****Then senseless Ilium*** These words from F seem necessary for the sense. There is no version of 412–35 in Q1, perhaps indicating, as Jenkins argues, that this passage was cut or marked for cutting – though it would be odd for Polonius to complain about the length after just six lines. *Ilium*, another name for Troy, is used by Shakespeare to mean the royal castle or citadel rather than the whole city, here and in *TC*.
  senseless insensible (but *Seeming to feel*)

414 ***his*** its

415 ***Takes . . . ear*** By metonymy the ear stands for the man: Pyrrhus' action is arrested by the noise.

416 ***declining*** descending. Nestor uses the same verb to describe how he has seen Hector in a similar posture: 'When thou hast hung thy advanced sword i'th' air, / Not letting it decline on the declin'd' (*TC* 4.5.187–8).
  milky i.e. white-haired

417 ***reverend*** The spellings 'reuerent' (Q2) and 'Reuerend' (F) were interchangeable at this time.
  seemed . . . stick possibly a recollection of two moments in Marlowe and Nashe's *Dido*: Pyrrhus is described as standing 'with his faulchion's poynt raisde up at once' while Priam and Hecuba plead for their lives (2.1.229) and later 'leaning on his sword, he stood stone still, / Viewing the fire wherewith rich *Ilion* burnt' (2.1.263–4). Bevington (372) points out that Troilus similarly imagines his sword hovering in the air before descending on Diomedes at *TC* 5.2.178–83; there too the action is compared to the approach of a storm.

418 ***painted*** (1) as if in a painting; (2) coated in blood

419 'like one who is unable to act in spite of his desire and duty'

412 *Then . . . Ilium*] F; *not in Q21*   413 *this*] his F   417 reverend] *(reuerent), F (Reuerend)*
419–20] *one line F*   419 *Like*] And like F

> *Did nothing.*   420
> *But as we often see against some storm*
> *A silence in the heavens, the rack stand still,*
> *The bold winds speechless and the orb below*
> *As hush as death, anon the dreadful thunder*
> *Doth rend the region, so after Pyrrhus' pause*   425
> *A roused vengeance sets him new a-work*
> *And never did the Cyclops' hammers fall*
> *On Mars's armour, forged for proof eterne,*
> *With less remorse than Pyrrhus' bleeding sword*
> *Now falls on Priam.*   430
> *Out, out, thou strumpet Fortune! All you gods*
> *In general synod take away her power,*
> *Break all the spokes and fellies from her wheel*
> *And bowl the round nave down the hill of heaven*
> *As low as to the fiends.*   435

421 **see** i.e. experience (in this case, hear)
against in advance of

422 **rack** cloud formation (as at *AC* 4.14.10)

423 **orb** globe, i.e. earth

424 **As . . . death** proverbial (Dent, 133.1)
hush silent; either an adjectival use of the verb (Hope, 1.2.8) or a past participle = hushed

425 **rend the region** tear through the sky. For *region* in this sense, see 514n., and Romeo's reference to 'the airy region' (*RJ* 2.2.21).

426 **A roused vengeance** rousèd. Since Collier (1843) many editors have printed 'Aroused vengeance', but both Q2 and F have 'A rowsed vengeance' which seems perfectly acceptable in the sense of 'an awakened desire for revenge'.

427 **Cyclops** The Cyclopes were three one-eyed giants who worked for Vulcan, the blacksmith-god; they are said to have made Achilles' armour in the *Iliad* and Aeneas' armour in the *Aeneid*.

428 **Mars's** This form of the possessive is necessary for the metre, which requires two syllables. Mars was the Roman god of war; it is assumed that the Cylops also made armour for him.
for proof eterne to be impenetrable for ever

429 **bleeding** i.e. dripping with blood

431 **strumpet** prostitute (as at 231)

432 **synod** general assembly, council; with one exception (*CE* 1.1.13), Shakespeare confines this word to meetings of gods.

433 ***fellies** the bent pieces of wood forming the outside or rim of a wheel
her wheel Fortune is often depicted standing on a wheel; 'Fortune's wheel is ever turning' was proverbial (Tilley, F617).

434 **nave** central part or hub of a wheel; in this case, what is left when the spokes and rim have been broken off
hill of heaven presumably Mount Olympus, home of the gods (see 5.1.243)

426 *A roused*] *F*; Aroused *Collier a-work*] (a worke) *F*   428 *Mars's armour*] Mars his Armours *F*
433 *fellies*] *F4*; follies *Q2*; Fallies *F*; felloes *Q5*

POLONIUS   This is too long.

HAMLET   It shall to the barber's with your beard. Prithee
say on – he's for a jig, or a tale of bawdry, or he sleeps.
Say on, come to Hecuba.

1 PLAYER
　　But who – ah woe – had seen the mobled queen –　　　440

HAMLET   'The mobled queen'!

POLONIUS   That's good.

1 PLAYER
　　– Run barefoot up and down, threatening the flames
　　With bisson rheum, a clout upon that head
　　Where late the diadem stood and, for a robe,　　　445

436 The comparable speech in Marlowe and
　　Nashe's *Dido* (2.1.121–288) is 167 lines,
　　with four one-line interjections by Dido
　　(see 384n.). Will Keen delivered it with
　　considerable tragic power in the London
　　Globe's production in 2003.

437 **It ... beard** This does not necessarily
　　imply that Polonius has a long beard;
　　perhaps just that he is old (or that he is in
　　need of a shave). DSK, however, suggests
　　that *your* could refer to the *valanced* First
　　Player and that Hamlet shares Polonius'
　　impatience.

438 **jig** comic entertainment including dancing,
　　often performed as an after-piece to a
　　tragedy
　　tale of bawdry dirty story

439 **Hecuba** Priam's wife, whose grief came to
　　epitomize tragic sorrow; significantly, she
　　does not appear in *TC* where these events
　　are depicted satirically. However, after her
　　rape, Shakespeare's Lucrece studies 'a
　　piece / Of skilful painting, made for
　　Priam's Troy' in which she sees Hecuba's

grief: 'Lo here weeps Hecuba, here Priam
dies' (*Luc* 1366–7, 1485).

440 *who ... had seen* whoever might have seen
　　mobled That this (also found in Q1) was an
　　unusual word is confirmed by F's 'inobled'
　　(repeated three times) as well as by Polonius'
　　comment. It is usually glossed as
　　meaning 'muffled' or 'veiled' (and hence
　　the phrase may evoke the figure of Nature,
　　who was also represented as veiled, as in
　　the 'Mutabilitie' cantos of *FQ*, 7.7.5–6),
　　but generations of playgoers must have
　　found it a vaguely impressive word without
　　knowing what it meant. Edwards argues
　　that the spelling 'mobbled', found in 1655,
　　indicates the pronunciation. The F reading,
　　'inobled', appears also as a correction in
　　Q8; it has subsequently been supported by
　　some editors (e.g. Caldecott, MacDonald)
　　as meaning either 'made noble' or its
　　opposite, 'ignobled' (degraded).

444 *bisson rheum* blinding tears
　　clout cloth

445 *diadem* crown

437 to the] *Q1;* to'th *F*　440, 443 SP] *F (1. Play.); Play. Q21*　440 *ah woe*] *(*a woe*);* O who *Q1F*
440–1 *mobled ...* mobled] *Q1;* inobled *...* Inobled *F;* ignobled *MacDonald (Tschischwitz)*
442 That's good.] Mobled Queene is good, faith very good. *Q1;* That's good: Inobled Queene is good. *F*
443] *F lines* downe, / flame / *flames*] flame *F*　444 *upon*] on *Q1;* about *F*

About her lank and all-o'erteemed loins,
A blanket in the alarm of fear caught up.
Who this had seen, with tongue in venom steeped,
'Gainst Fortune's state would treason have pronounced.
But if the gods themselves did see her then, 450
When she saw Pyrrhus make malicious sport
In mincing with his sword her husband limbs,
The instant burst of clamour that she made
(Unless things mortal move them not at all)
Would have made milch the burning eyes of heaven 455
And passion in the gods.

POLONIUS   Look where he has not turned his colour and
has tears in's eyes. – Prithee no more!

HAMLET   'Tis well. I'll have thee speak out the rest of this
soon. [*to Polonius*] Good my lord, will you see the 460
players well bestowed? Do you hear, let them be well

446 **lank ... loins** gaunt or withered loins which had borne (teemed with) an excessive number of children. (Not all of Priam's sons were also Hecuba's, but she was said to have given birth to as many as 20.)
o'erteemed o'erteemèd
447 **alarm** F's 'Alarum' carries the more specific meaning of a military emergency.
448 **Who this had seen** whoever had seen this
with ... steeped with a tongue steeped in poison
449 'would have spoken treason against the rule of Fortune'
450–6 The construction of this conditional sentence changes somewhat so that *the gods* as subject gives way to 'the instant burst of clamour'.
452 **mincing** cutting into small pieces
husband Q2's form is an archaic uninflected form of the genitive (see Hope, 1.1.4–5).

455 would have made the sun and stars weep
456 **And passion** i.e. and aroused passion
457–8 **Look ... more** Polonius is presumably close enough to the Player to claim to see the *tears* the audience cannot (and which may not, of course, exist). It may be that his impatience expressed at 436 ('This is too long') has turned to admiration, and that *Prithee no more* is spoken kindly. His addressing the Player as 'good heart' at this point in Q1 would support such an interpretation.
457 **Look where** see whether (how)
turned changed (i.e. gone pale)
461 **well bestowed** appropriately accommodated. As in *TS* Induction 1.101–3, a stress is placed on the quality of the hospitality offered to the visiting players, suggesting a nostalgic, almost feudal relationship between the players and their aristocratic patrons, unlike the more commercial or professional

446 *lank ... o'erteemed*] F; weake and all ore-teeming *Q1*   447 *the alarm*] th'Alarum *F*   452 *husband*] husbandes *Q1F*   458 Prithee] Pray you *F*   459–60 'Tis ... soon.] *prose F; one verse line Q2*   459 of this] *om. F*   460 SD] *Oxf*   461 you] ye *F*

used, for they are the abstract and brief chronicles of the time: after your death you were better have a bad epitaph than their ill report while you live.

POLONIUS   My lord, I will use them according to their 465 desert.

HAMLET   God's bodkin, man, much better! Use every man after his desert and who shall scape whipping? Use them after your own honour and dignity – the less they deserve the more merit is in your bounty. Take them in. 470

POLONIUS   Come, sirs.

HAMLET   Follow him, friends. We'll hear a play tomorrow. [*aside to First Player*] Dost thou hear me, old friend? Can you play *The Murder of Gonzago*?

1 PLAYER   Ay, my lord. 475

HAMLET   We'll ha't tomorrow night. You could for need study a speech of some dozen lines, or sixteen lines,

one evoked by the earlier references to the contemporary London theatres (see 358.1n.).
  Do you hear an intensive, meaning 'please pay attention to this' (like 'Dost thou hear me' at 473)
462–3 **abstract . . . time** i.e. they summarize or epitomize the age in which they live (but Jenkins defends Q2's combination of singular *abstract* with plural *chronicles*).
463 **you . . . have** it would be better for you if you had
465 **use** treat
467 **bodkin** an abbreviation of 'bodykin' = small (or dear) body.
468, 469 **after** according to
468 **scape** escape
  whipping the standard punishment for vagabonds, a category which could include unlicensed players
473 **Dost . . . me** please listen (as at 461), here meaning 'can I have a word with you before you go?'

474 ***The . . . Gonzago*** Hamlet claims at 3.2.256 that this is an Italian play, and it is clearly known to the players, but attempts to identify a literary source have proved fruitless (see 3.2.232–3n. and pp. 62–4). In performance, the First Player sometimes riffles through a few playbooks in his pack before producing the right title.
476–8 **You . . . not** It was not uncommon on the Elizabethan stage for old plays to be revived with 'additions' or insertions; Thomas Kyd's *The Spanish Tragedy* is perhaps the most famous example; first published in 1592, it was reprinted with additions in 1602.
476 **for need** as required
477 **study** learn
  speech . . . lines No one has convincingly identified this speech in the play in 3.2; the most popular choices are the lines in the Player King's speech from '*Purpose is but the slave to memory*' to '*their ends none of our own*'

462 abstract] Abstracts *F*   464 live] *Q1;* liued *F*   467 bodkin] bodykins *F*   much] farre *Q1;* om. *F*
468 shall] should *Q1F*   473 SD] *White subst.*   475, 479 SP] *Capell; Play.* Q2F; players *Q1*   476 for] for a *Q1F*   477 dozen lines] dozen *Q1F*

which I would set down and insert in't, could you not?
1 PLAYER   Ay, my lord.
HAMLET   Very well. Follow that lord – and look you mock   480
him not. [*to other Players*] My good friends, I'll leave
you till night. You are welcome to Elsinore.
ROSENCRANTZ   Good my lord.
HAMLET

    Ay so, God buy to you.   *Exeunt [all but Hamlet].*
              Now I am alone.
    O, what a rogue and peasant slave am I!   485
    Is it not monstrous that this player here,

(3.2, 182–207) and Lucianus' speech from '*Thoughts black*' to '*usurps immediately*' (248–53), the first speech being too long and the second too short. It is possible that Hamlet's speech may not be in *The Murder of Gonzago* at all – that the actors don't reach it before the play is disrupted. In any case the insertion seems redundant, since the plot alone is self-evidently relevant. (Edwards sees *some dozen* as a false start in the manuscript that he associates with the confusion over the number of crowns at 73.)

480–1 **and ... not** Perhaps Hamlet is regretting his own behaviour and discouraging the players from imitating him. Or perhaps he is warning them not to compete with him in this respect.

482 *****till** Q2's 'tell' seems erroneous (as at 4.5.156).

483 **Good my lord** a parting formula = farewell

484 **Ay ... you** Dover Wilson suggests he speaks 'in a tone of sarcastic relief after [Rosencrantz and Guildenstern] have gone'.
    God buy goodbye. See 2.1.66n. and 4.5.192.

484 SD Q1 and F take Polonius/Corambis off at the equivalent of 471 and the others at this point, while Q2 has the explicit

'*Exeunt Pol. and Players*' after '*Elsonoure*' at 482. It would seem from Hamlet's repetition of *Follow that lord* at 480 that the other players do not leave before then. Hibbard has Polonius and the players leave after *mock him not* (480–1), leaving Hamlet's 'You ... Elsinore' to be addressed to Rosencrantz and Guildenstern, who leave after the former's line. Some productions make it clear that Rosencrantz and Guildenstern are suspicious of what Hamlet may be saying to the First Player and reluctant to leave him alone; thus his 'Ay so, God buy to you' urges them offstage. In any case neither they nor Polonius should hear Hamlet's request at 473–8.

485–540 This soliloquy, in which Hamlet shares with the audience his amazement at what we have just witnessed, is, as Emrys Jones points out, somewhat in the melodramatic style of Richard III, especially his 'Was ever woman in this humour wooed?' speech at 1.2.232–68 (Jones, *Scenic Form*, 104–5). For further discussion of Hamlet's soliloquies, see pp. 18–25.

485 **peasant slave** Q1's 'dunghill idiote slave' carries the same class-based selfinsult.

486 **monstrous** unnatural, shocking

478 you] ye *F*   481 SD] *this edn*   482 till] *F;* tell *Q2*   484 God ... you] God buy'ye *F*   SD] *Q1;*
*Exeunt Pol. and Players. (opp. 482), Exeunt. (opp. 483) Q2; Exeunt. (opp. 483), Manet Hamlet. (after
483) F*   485 rogue and peasant] *F;* dunghill idiote *Q1*

But in a fiction, in a dream of passion,
Could force his soul so to his own conceit
That from her working all the visage wanned
– Tears in his eyes, distraction in his aspect,   490
A broken voice, and his whole function suiting
With forms to his conceit – and all for nothing –
For Hecuba?
What's Hecuba to him, or he to her,
That he should weep for her? What would he do   495
Had he the motive and that for passion
That I have? He would drown the stage with tears
And cleave the general ear with horrid speech,
Make mad the guilty and appal the free,
Confound the ignorant and amaze indeed   500

487 **But** merely

488 **force ... conceit** 'i.e. bring his innermost being into such consonance with his conception of the part' (Hibbard, who adopts F's reading)

489 **from her working** because of her (his conceit's) activity or influence

all ... wanned his whole face turned pale. Apparently the opposite of F (see t.n.), but either a sudden pallor or a sudden flush could be a sign of emotion. An oddly similar textual difference occurs at 3.4.48, where Q2 has 'heated visage' and F has 'tristfull visage'.

490 **distraction ... aspect** frenzy, intensity of feeling, in his general appearance. F's elision emphasizes the usual Shakespearean pronunciation of *aspect* with the accent on the second syllable.

491–2 **his ... conceit** everything about him completely matching in expression to what he is imagining (*whole function* means all his actions and emotions)

494 **to her** Jenkins dismisses F's reading as 'obviously an actor's (over-)emphasis',

while Hibbard defends it as 'a case of authorial revision, made to eliminate the repetition of *her* in the Q2 version'.

496 **and ... passion** Unemended, Q2 is defective in both sense and metre. It may be understood as meaning something like 'and that much cause for passion'; John Ward emended to 'and that cause for passion' in his prompt-books (see Thompson, 'Ward', 147), although he had access to the F reading, which is usually preferred (e.g. by Jenkins).

498 **general** universal

horrid causing horror (a stronger meaning than the modern one; see *horrible* at 1.5.80)

499 **appal the free** horrify the innocent (those free of guilt), or make them turn pale with fear: *OED* cites this line under *appale v.* 6.

500 **Confound the ignorant** discomfit, devastate those who are unaware (of the crime)

amaze stupefy, paralyse (again, a stronger meaning than the modern one)

488 own] whole *F*   489 the] his *F*   wanned] warm'd *F*   490 in his aspect] in's Aspect *F*   494 her] Hecuba *Q1F*   496 that] the Cue *F*

The very faculties of eyes and ears. Yet I,
A dull and muddy-mettled rascal, peak
Like John-a-dreams, unpregnant of my cause,
And can say nothing. No, not for a king
Upon whose property and most dear life   505
A damned defeat was made. Am I a coward?
Who calls me villain, breaks my pate across,
Plucks off my beard and blows it in my face,
Tweaks me by the nose, gives me the lie i'th' throat
As deep as to the lungs? Who does me this,   510
Ha? 'Swounds, I should take it. For it cannot be
But I am pigeon-livered and lack gall

---

501 **very faculties** proper functions
502 **muddy-mettled** poor-spirited; *muddy* has the sense both of being inert and of lacking clarity, while *mettled* may suggest a pun on 'metal' – in this case tarnished metal.

    peak mope or sneak about
503 **John-a-dreams** a stereotype of a dreamy, inactive man, comparable to the use of 'John-a-nokes' and 'John-a-stiles' as fictitious names for parties in a legal action

    unpregnant of not properly stimulated by; see *pregnant* in the sense of 'cogent' at 206.
504 **say nothing** can't speak out. Hamlet must mean 'do nothing', since he goes on to chide himself for talking rather than acting, but it is perhaps ironic that he wants to imitate the Player rather than Pyrrhus.
505 **property** possibly literal (i.e. the kingdom of Denmark) or possibly 'that which was properly his' – his identity as king. Hibbard reads 'property and most dear life' as 'a kind of hendiadys' meaning 'the dearest thing he owned – his life'. In Q1, Hamlet mentions that he has 'a Crowne bereft him' as an additional motive at this point.

506 **damned defeat** accursed destruction

    Am I a coward? This and the following rhetorical questions have sometimes provoked responses from the audience, notably in the case of David Warner's 1965 performance (see Hapgood, and p. 24).
507 **pate** head
508 **Plucks . . . beard** It is rare to see a bearded Hamlet (though a man of 30 might well have a beard) so this line is generally interpreted metaphorically (see Hamlet's words to Polonius at 437 and the King's reference to having his beard shaken at 4.7.33).
509 **gives . . . lie** accuses me of lying
509–10 **i'th' throat . . . lungs** 'To lie in one's throat' was proverbial (Tilley, T268); Hamlet intensifies it.
510 **Who . . . this** who does this to me
511 **'Swounds** by God's wounds

    I . . . it 'I would accept this lying down'
511–12 **it . . . am** I must surely be
512 **pigeon-livered . . . gall** Pigeons were thought to be mild and gentle because their livers lacked *gall* or bile, the supposed source of anger.

---

501 faculties] faculty *F*   502 muddy-mettled] *(muddy metteld), F*   509 by the] by'th' *F*   511 'Swounds] Sure *Q1;* Why *F*   512 pigeon-livered] *(pidgion liuerd), F*

To make oppression bitter, or ere this
I should ha' fatted all the region kites
With this slave's offal – bloody, bawdy villain,   515
Remorseless, treacherous, lecherous, kindless villain.
Why, what an ass am I: this is most brave,
That I, the son of a dear murdered,
Prompted to my revenge by heaven and hell,
Must like a whore unpack my heart with words   520
And fall a-cursing like a very drab,

513 **To ... bitter** Edwards glosses, 'to make Claudius's oppression bitter to himself', but Hamlet might mean 'to make my own oppression bitter enough for me to take action'.

ere before

514 **ha'** have

region kites the sky's birds of prey; Hope (1.1.4f) gives this as an example of 'zero genetive' (see also 1.3.132n.). For *region* meaning 'sky', see 425n. and compare 'region cloud' in *Son* 33.12.

515 **offal** literally, what falls off and is discarded – in the case of animal carcasses the entrails

bawdy lewd, immoral (see *bawdry* at 438)

516 **kindless** lacking natural feeling (see 1.2.65 and n.). Jenkins rejects F's 'Oh Vengeance!' after *villain* as an actor's addition, and Simon Russell Beale's gentle Hamlet could not bring himself to say it (Maher, 240); Edwards, however, argues that it is the turning-point of the speech.

517 **brave** admirable (sarcastic)

518 **a dear murdered** murderèd. Unemended, this must mean 'a person dear to me who has been murdered'. Many editors prefer the Q3 reading 'a deere father murthered' and justify this by pointing out that in Q1

Hamlet calls himself 'the sonne of my deare father' at this point. Halliwell defends Q2's phrase by analogy with 'the dear departed'; *TxC* suggests a pun on 'deer'.

519 **by ... hell** Hamlet is either going for rhetorical inclusiveness, invoking the entire universe in his cause as he did when he asked whether he should *couple hell* to heaven and earth (1.5.92–3), or he is concerned whether the Ghost is 'a spirit of health or goblin damned' (1.4.40) – a topic to which he returns at 533–8. To be *Prompted by hell* would undercut the moral authority of his revenge.

520, 521 **whore, drab** Both words mean 'prostitute'. 'In the traditional opposition of genders in which "Women are words, men deeds", Hamlet's comparison of his verbal and deedless delay to the impotent anger of a *drab* sets up a link between his entire period of inactivity and delay and womanish wordiness, in contrast to such one-dimensional emblems of masculinity as Laertes and the aptly named Fort-in-bras' (Parker, *Fat Ladies*, 23). For a further discussion of gender issues in *Hamlet*, see pp. 26–32.

520 **unpack** unload, relieve

514 ha'] *(a)Q1;* haue *F*   515 offal – bloody, bawdy] Offall, bloudy: a Bawdy *F*   516 villain.] villaine! / Oh Vengeance! *F*   517 Why] *Q1;* Who? *F*   this] *Q1;* I sure, this *F*   518 a dear murdered] my deare father *Q1;* a deere father murthered *Q3;* the Deere murthered *F*

A stallion! Fie upon't, foh! About, my brains!
Hum, I have heard
That guilty creatures sitting at a play
Have by the very cunning of the scene   525
Been struck so to the soul that presently
They have proclaimed their malefactions.
For murder, though it have no tongue, will speak
With most miraculous organ. I'll have these players
Play something like the murder of my father   530
Before mine uncle. I'll observe his looks,
I'll tent him to the quick. If 'a do blench
I know my course. The spirit that I have seen
May be a de'il, and the de'il hath power
T'assume a pleasing shape. Yea, and perhaps   535
Out of my weakness and my melancholy,

---

522 stallion male prostitute (a meaning attested by *OED* from 1553); Q1/F's 'scalion'/'Scullion' means a kitchen-boy or low-level domestic servant.
Fie a strong expression of disgust
About get to work

523 Hum Hamlet presumably muses – but Hunter (2.235) argues against those who interpret *Hum* as indicating a pause for thought, pointing out that this is not, after all, Hamlet's first conception of his plan; see 529–31n.

523–9 I . . . organ A widow confesses in this way to having murdered her husband in the anonymous play *A Warning for Fair Women* which was acted by Shakespeare's company in 1599 (see p. 61).

524 creatures people

525 very . . . scene sheer ingenuity of the performance

526 presently immediately

528 'Murder will out' was proverbial (Dent, M1315).

529 miraculous organ unnatural or supernatural instrument

529–31 I'll . . . uncle Hamlet made this decision at 473–4; he explains it further here.

532 tent . . . quick probe him to his most sensitive point; the metaphor is from probing a wound.
'a he
blench usually glossed 'flinch', but it could also (*pace* Jenkins) be a variant of 'blanch' = turn pale; either would make sense.

534 de'il devil. Q2's spelling may suggest the Scots and Middle English monosyllabic form 'deil' (pronounced like 'deal'). Words for 'devil' occur nine times in Q2 (including the possibly erroneous instance at 3.4.160), six times as 'deuill' and once as 'deule' (the spelling found twice in the first 'Hand D' passage in *Sir Thomas More* which has been ascribed to Shakespeare).

536 Out of by exploiting

522–4] *Johnson; Q2 lines* foh. / heard, / play, /; *F lines* Braine. / Play, /   522 stallion] scalion *Q1;* Scullion *F*   brains] *Q2c;* braues *Q2u;* braine *Q1F*   523 Hum] *not in Q1F*   532 'a do] he but *F* 534 a] the *Q1F*   de'il . . . de'il] *(deale . . . deale);* Diuell . . . Diuel *F*

As he is very potent with such spirits,
Abuses me to damn me! I'll have grounds
More relative than this. The play's the thing   539
Wherein I'll catch the conscience of the King.   *Exit.*

[**3.1**]   *Enter* KING, QUEEN, POLONIUS, OPHELIA,
        ROSENCRANTZ, GUILDENSTERN [*and*] *Lords.*

KING
And can you by no drift of conference
Get from him why he puts on this confusion,
Grating so harshly all his days of quiet

---

537 **potent ... spirits** influential with people who are melancholy. It was believed that such people were particularly susceptible to demonic powers.

538 **Abuses** deceives

539 **More relative** more relevant, more convincing or conclusive
this i.e. the word of the Ghost (and my own suspicions)

3.1 The three texts: this scene runs to 40 lines in Q1 (scene 8), 187 lines in Q2 and 189 lines in F. It is so much shorter in Q1 because it covers only the material up to 41; Hamlet's 'To be or not to be' soliloquy, his encounter with Ofelia and the reactions of the King and Corambis to what they have observed have already been staged in the previous scene (see headnote to 2.2). Location and timing: this scene takes place in the same location as 2.2 – *the lobby* mentioned at 2.2.158. It is now the following day: *tomorrow night* of 2.2.476 has become *This night* (21); Rosencrantz and Guildenstern are reporting on their first meeting with Hamlet and the plan to *loose* Ophelia to him (2.2.159) is put into effect.

0.2 The '*Lords*' specified in Q2 and F have no function other than to serve as silent attendants; neither text specifies an exit

for them. If they come on at all they need to be taken off either at 28 or at 41. Their presence might imply a relatively public occasion, but Spencer notes the absence of a *Flourish* for the royal entry in Q2, as compared with the openings of 1.2 and 2.2, and suggests that this may indicate a more private interview (which would be more appropriate for the report on the spying activities of Rosencrantz and Guildenstern).

1 **And** As often in Shakespeare's plays, the characters enter in the midst of a conversation which is supposed to have begun offstage. This could be another explanation for the lack of a *Flourish.*
drift of conference direction of the conversation

2 **puts on** assumes; see Hamlet's warning that he may 'put an antic disposition on' (1.5.170). The King seems to suspect that Hamlet's madness is faked, that his behaviour is wilful rather than involuntary, but *put on* could be used in a more neutral sense, as at *AYL* 5.4.179: 'The Duke hath put on a religious life.'
confusion mental perturbation

3 **Grating** literally 'roughening', i.e. disturbing, troubling

---

3.1] *Q6*   0.2 *and*] *Q1F*   1 conference] circumstance *F*

With turbulent and dangerous lunacy?

ROSENCRANTZ

He does confess he feels himself distracted 5
But from what cause 'a will by no means speak.

GUILDENSTERN

Nor do we find him forward to be sounded
But with a crafty madness keeps aloof
When we would bring him on to some confession
Of his true state.

QUEEN   Did he receive you well? 10

ROSENCRANTZ

Most like a gentleman.

GUILDENSTERN

But with much forcing of his disposition.

ROSENCRANTZ

Niggard of question, but of our demands
Most free in his reply.

QUEEN

Did you assay him to any pastime? 15

---

5   **distracted** seriously disturbed; see 1.5.97
     (a stronger meaning than the modern one)
6   **'a** he
7   **forward** readily disposed
     sounded probed, questioned (see 2.1.41)
8   **crafty madness** Guildenstern may make
     the common assumption that madness
     imparts cunning, or he may think it is a
     cunning disguise of Hamlet's *true state*
     (10). Hamlet himself speaks of being *mad
     in craft* at 3.4.186.
     keeps aloof keeps himself at a distance
12   **disposition** real inclination
13–14 **Niggard ... reply** Rosencrantz
     seems to mean 'reluctant to initiate
     conversation, but generous in his responses
     to our questions'. Warburton advocated
     emending to 'Most free of question, but of

our demands / Niggard in his reply',
which would certainly yield an easier
meaning, and which is closer to the Q1
version: 'But still he puts us off and by
no means / Would make an answer to that
we exposed' (8.7–8). As it stands, this
statement modifies Guildenstern's report
of Hamlet's aloofness, but is hardly
accurate as a report of what happened in
2.2.219–305: as Stoppard's Rosencrantz
puts it: 'Twenty-seven questions he got
out in ten minutes, and answered three'
(Stoppard, 40). It is notable that the pair do
not mention Hamlet's suspicion – and their
confession – that they were sent for.
15   **assay him to** encourage him to try
     pastime recreation, (pleasant) way of
     passing the time

---

6 'a] he *F*

310

ROSENCRANTZ

Madam, it so fell out that certain players
We o'erraught on the way. Of these we told him
And there did seem in him a kind of joy
To hear of it. They are here about the Court
And, as I think, they have already order   20
This night to play before him.

POLONIUS   'Tis most true,
And he beseeched me to entreat your majesties
To hear and see the matter.

KING

With all my heart, and it doth much content me
To hear him so inclined.   25
Good gentlemen, give him a further edge
And drive his purpose into these delights.

ROSENCRANTZ

We shall, my lord.
                Exeunt Rosencrantz and Guildenstern [and Lords].

KING   Sweet Gertrude, leave us two.
For we have closely sent for Hamlet hither
That he, as 'twere by accident, may here   30

---

17 **o'erraught** overtook (the past tense of 'to
    overreach')
20 **have already order** have already been
    given the commission
23 **hear and see** This formulation may alert
    audiences and readers to the importance of
    the dumb-show.
26 **give . . . edge** incite him more forcefully
27 **drive . . . delights** encourage his intention
    to undertake these pleasures
28 **two** F's 'too' is adopted by most editors
    (including Jenkins), but *leave us two*
    provides a perfectly acceptable meaning:

'leave the two of us alone' (assuming that
the King simply ignores Ophelia).
29 **closely** privately – or even 'secretly', i.e.
    without Hamlet realizing he is being
    manipulated. When he appears he does not
    make any mention of the fact that he is
    responding to a message from the King,
    though some performers make a show of
    looking carefully around them (see, for
    example, Branagh, 76). This slight
    awkwardness may relate to the larger
    problem of the placing of 'To be or not to
    be' (see pp. 18–19).

---

19 here] *om. F*   24] *F; Q2 lines* hart, / me /   25–7] *F lines* Gentlemen, / purpose on / delights. /
27 into] on / To *F*   28 SD *and Lords*] *this edn*   two] too *F*   30 here] there *F*

Affront Ophelia. Her father and myself –
We'll so bestow ourselves that, seeing unseen,
We may of their encounter frankly judge
And gather by him as he is behaved
If't be th'affliction of his love or no   35
That thus he suffers for.

QUEEN   I shall obey you.
And for your part, Ophelia, I do wish
That your good beauties be the happy cause
Of Hamlet's wildness. So shall I hope your virtues
Will bring him to his wonted way again   40
To both your honours.

OPHELIA   Madam, I wish it may. [*Exit Queen.*]
POLONIUS
Ophelia, walk you here. (Gracious, so please you,
We will bestow ourselves.) Read on this book

---

31 **Affront** confront, encounter (*OED*'s first usage)
   myself – Some editors argue that F's 'lawful espials' was inserted in Shakespeare's manuscript but overlooked by the Q2 compositor; they print either *Affront Ophelia* or 'Lawful espials' as a separate short line.
32 **We'll** F's 'Will' makes slightly smoother syntax in this awkward sentence. Q2's *We* may be an anticipation of the next line.
   bestow position
34 **And . . . behaved** and ascertain from his behaviour
37–41 **I . . . honours** The Queen makes it clear that, unlike Laertes and Polonius in 1.3, she has no objection to Ophelia's relationship with Hamlet.
38, 39 **beauties, virtues** The contrast suggested by the Queen anticipates (in a more optimistic vein) the opening of

Hamlet's tirade against Ophelia at 102–14.
38 **happy** fortuitous
40 **wonted way** normal behaviour
41 **To . . . honours** to the honour and credit of you both (*honours* may hint at marriage: see *honourable fashion* at 1.3.110).
   I . . . may i.e. I hope you are right.
41 SD *There is no SD in Q2 or F, but the Queen must leave at this point, having been asked to go at 28 and agreed that she will at 36. Edwards takes the *Lords* off with the Queen here (see 28 SD).
42 **Gracious** your grace (addressed to the King); unique as a form of address in Shakespeare, though phrases like 'gracious lord' and 'gracious sovereign' are common
43 **this book** presumably a prayer-book, from the references to *devotion* in 46 and *orisons* in 88

---

31 myself –] *(*my selfe*,); my selfe (lawful espials) *F*   32 We'll] Will *F*   37 your] *F*; my *Q3*   41 SD] *Theobald*   42 ²you] ye *F*

That show of such an exercise may colour
Your loneliness. We are oft too blame in this –   45
'Tis too much proved that with devotion's visage
And pious action we do sugar o'er
The devil himself.

KING   O, 'tis too true.

[*aside*] How smart a lash that speech doth give my
      conscience!
The harlot's cheek beautied with plastering art   50
Is not more ugly to the thing that helps it
Than is my deed to my most painted word.
O heavy burden!

44 **exercise** act of private devotion
    colour provide an excuse for, camouflage
45 ***loneliness** solitariness. Q2's 'lowlines'
    does not seem appropriate and is an easy
    misreading. Andrews, however, retains,
    glossing it as 'pious humility'.
    too blame Thus both Q2 and F; editors
    usually print 'to blame', but *OED* notes that
    'In the 16–17th c. the *to* was misunderstood
    as *too* and *blame* taken as an adjective =
    blameworthy, culpable' (*v.* 6). See a possible
    similar usage at 5.2.305 and see F *Oth*
    3.3.214, 'I am much too blame'; *MV*
    5.1.166, 'You were too blame'; and *1H4*
    3.1.171, 'you are too wilful-blame'. See
    also Blake, 4.3.1.5a where this phrase is
    glossed 'to be blamed'.
46 **'Tis . . . proved** it is too often demonstrated
    devotion's visage pretence (face) of
    religion
47 **sugar o'er** cover with sugar, i.e. render
    superficially attractive
48 **O . . . true** The King's whole speech is
    often marked '*aside*' (e.g. by Jenkins,
    Edwards and Hibbard), but Klein points
    out that it would be odd for him simply to
    turn away and that these four words are
    more likely a controlled response to
    Polonius before the private revelation.

49–53 The King's first direct confession of
    guilt to the audience is absent from Q1 and
    has often been omitted in performance
    (since at least 1676). It confirms the
    Ghost's story while lacking any specific
    reference to what *deed* is on the King's
    conscience.
49 **smart** sharp, stinging
50–2 The King takes up Polonius' notion
    of 'sugar[ing] o'er / The devil himself'
    and his suggestion of a deceptively
    attractive *visage* in reflecting on the
    contrast between his own words and
    deeds: he sets up a simile whereby the
    prostitute's (*harlot's*) cheek is as ugly
    compared with its covering layer of make-
    up as his actions are compared with his
    deceiving language.
50 **beautied** made beautiful
    plastering art The disparagement of
    make-up is typical of Elizabethan satires
    on women and is taken up again by Hamlet
    at 141–3 (see Jenkins, LN).
51 **to . . . it** in comparison with the makeup
    which enhances it (but Spencer suggests
    that *the thing* refers to the servant who
    helps the prostitute with her make-up, in
    which case *to* means 'from the point of
    view of')

45 loneliness] *F;* lowlines *Q2*   47 sugar] surge *F*   48 too] *om. F*   49 SD] *Pope*

POLONIUS

I hear him coming – withdraw, my lord.
[*King and Polonius hide behind an arras.*]

Enter HAMLET.

HAMLET

To be, or not to be – that is the question;   55
Whether 'tis nobler in the mind to suffer
The slings and arrows of outrageous fortune

54 **withdraw** Jenkins adopts F's 'let's withdraw', either on metrical grounds or because it is more deferential to the King. Dessen & Thomson give examples of plays where characters are instructed to 'withdraw behind the Arras' or 'withdraw behind the hangings' (under 'withdraw').

54 SD *No exit SD in Q2; F's '*Exeunt*' could be misleading, since it is clear in all three texts that they remain within earshot – and that the most famous of all soliloquies is not, strictly speaking, a soliloquy at all: three other characters are present, although Hamlet speaks as if he is alone. Derek Jacobi aroused considerable controversy by speaking the speech directly to Ophelia in Toby Robertson's production at the London Old Vic in 1977; Jonathan Pryce did the same at the Royal Court in 1980 (see Dawson, 219). *TxC* points out that this scene is unusual in having a re-entry direction for the characters who have been hiding in both Q2 and F.

54.1 Q2's placing of Hamlet's entry before 54 rather than after it has allowed editors to argue that he sees the King and Polonius 'withdrawing' and that this motivates his suspicion at 129. It would be very unusual for Shakespeare, or any dramatist of this period, not to clarify the situation if Hamlet is consciously directing his soliloquy or his

subsequent speeches at listeners; compare, for example, the moment in George Chapman's *The Conspiracy of Charles Duke of Byron* (1608), where La Fin signals his 'fake soliloquy' by beginning with the words 'A fained passion in his [Byron's] hearing now / Which he thinks I perceaue not . . . Would sound / How deepe he stands affected with that scruple', and later pretends shock: 'What! Did your highness hear?' (2.1.1–5, 24).

55–187 For Q1's earlier placing of this soliloquy and the remainder of the scene, see pp. 18–25.

55 **the question** Perhaps surprisingly after so much debate, editors and critics still disagree as to whether *the question* for Hamlet is (a) whether life in general is worth living, (b) whether he should take his own life, (c) whether he should act against the King. One reason for this, as Hibbard notes, is that the speech is cast in very general terms.

57 **slings and arrows** The sling is that which propels the missile (a hand-sling or catapult), so 'slings and bows' would be a more symmetrical formulation, but 'sling' can be read as a metonymy for 'missile'. Jenkins suggests *slings* might be a misprint for 'stings' (like 'extent'/'exlent' at 2.2.219), but he also notes that John

54 withdraw] let's withdraw *F*   54 SD] *Oxf¹ subst.; Exeunt. F*   54.1] *F; after 53 Q2*

Or to take arms against a sea of troubles
And by opposing end them; to die: to sleep –
No more, and by a sleep to say we end   60
The heartache and the thousand natural shocks
That flesh is heir to: 'tis a consummation
Devoutly to be wished – to die: to sleep –
To sleep, perchance to dream – ay, there's the rub,
For in that sleep of death what dreams may come   65
When we have shuffled off this mortal coil
Must give us pause: there's the respect
That makes calamity of so long life.
For who would bear the whips and scorns of time,

Fletcher has *slings and arrows* in his *Valentinian* (1614; 1.3.230), presumably echoing *Hamlet*.
outrageous excessively or grossly offensive
58 **take ... troubles** A *sea of troubles* was proverbial (Dent, S177.1); the notion of taking arms against a sea has been (a) deplored as a mixed metaphor, (b) commended as expressing Hamlet's sense of futility.
59 **by ... them** 'bring them to an end by actively taking them on'. Hamlet implies either that suicide is the only alternative to suffering (he would end his troubles by ending himself) or that action against the King would result in his own death (as indeed eventually it does).
60 **No more** i.e. to die is no more than to sleep. The line is parodied in Beaumont and Fletcher's *The Scornful Lady* (1613), when Sir Roger says to Welford, 'Have patience Sir, until our fellowe *Nicholas* bee deceast, that is, a sleepe: for so the word is taken; to sleepe to die, to die to sleepe: a very Figure Sir' (2.1.39–41; see pp. 58–9 for early parodic references to *Hamlet*).
62 **That ... to** that are the normal heritage of humanity
consummation completion, climax

64 **rub** impediment, disincentive (from the game of bowls, where a *rub* is an obstacle of some kind which diverts the bowl from its proper course, as at *R2* 3.3.3–4: 'Madam, we'll play at bowls. / 'Twill make me think the world is full of rubs')
66 **this mortal coil** '(1) this turmoil and trouble of living, (2) this mortal flesh ... which encloses within its coils or folds our essential being and has to be *shuffled off* at death as a snake sloughs its old skin' (Hibbard). The phrase seems to have been coined by Shakespeare: see *OED* coil *sb.* 2.4b.
67 **give us pause** cause us to hesitate
respect consideration
68 that allows calamitous experiences to last so long. But 'it is not easy to exclude the feeling that *long life* is itself being regarded as a *calamity*' (Jenkins).
69–75 The catalogue of complaints is similar to that given in *Son* 66 which begins: 'Tired with all these for restful death I cry.' It is easier to imagine the persona of *Son* being troubled by such things than a prince like Hamlet.
69 **time** Hamlet seems to mean 'the time or world we live in' rather than a personified Time; see 'The time is out of joint' (1.5.186).

59 die: to] *Q1 (*Die, to*), F (*dye, to*); die to *Q2*   sleep –] *Q1 (*sleepe,*); sleepe *Q2F*   61 heartache] *(*hart-ake*), F (*Heart-ake*)   63 wished – to] *F (*wish'd. To*); wisht to *Q2*

Th'oppressor's wrong, the proud man's contumely,   70
The pangs of despised love, the law's delay,
The insolence of office and the spurns
That patient merit of th'unworthy takes,
When he himself might his quietus make
With a bare bodkin. Who would fardels bear   75
To grunt and sweat under a weary life
But that the dread of something after death
(The undiscovered country from whose bourn
No traveller returns) puzzles the will

70 **contumely** insolence, insulting behaviour or treatment
71 **despised** F's 'dispriz'd' (un- or undervalued) is generally preferred, e.g. by Jenkins, who argues for it on the grounds that it is the more difficult reading and therefore less likely to be a scribal or compositorial error. Q2's 'despiz'd' also makes acceptable sense, though Shakespeare usually puts the stress on the second syllable.
72–3 **the spurns ... takes** the rejections or setbacks that a patient and deserving person receives from worthless or despicable (*unworthy*) people. Some translators of this speech have substituted their own topical references, for example Boris Pasternak's early version, which included complaints about 'red tape', 'foul-mouthed petty officials, and the kicks of the worthless kicking the worthy' (see Stříbrný, 98).
74 **his quietus make** pay his complete account (i.e. end his life); *quietus est* (Latin) was a phrase used to confirm that a bill or debt had been paid. The financial metaphor picks up the Ghost's reference to his *reckoning* and *account* at 1.5.78.
75 **bare** unsheathed, or perhaps puny
bodkin stiletto or dagger. Shakespeare does not use this word often: he may be

remembering Chaucer's description of the murder of Caesar in 'The Monk's Tale', where the conspirators 'caste the place in which he sholde dye, / With boydekyns, as I shal yow devyse' (2701–2) and then 'This false Brutus and his othere foon hym hente, / And striked hym with boydekyns anon' (2705–7). Dessen & Thomson (under 'bodkin') note that the word is used twice in SDs in plays of the period to indicate 'a small instrument used by women'.
fardels burdens
76 **To grunt** so as to grunt; eighteenth-century editors deplored *grunt* as vulgar and inappropriate (as they did *guts* at 3.4.210 and *hugger-mugger* at 4.5.84).
78 **bourn** boundary
79 **No traveller returns** The Ghost has made a rather notable return, but Hamlet presumably means that under normal circumstances death is irreversible; he seems to be speculating about a mortal making a brief visit to the *undiscovered country* of death and then returning to ordinary life, rather than the contrary. Famous counter-examples would include Alcestis and Lazarus, in classical and Christian legend respectively.
puzzles bewilders, paralyses (a stronger sense than the modern one)

70 Th'oppressor's] The Oppressors *F* proud] poore *F*   71 despised] dispriz'd *F*   73 th'unworthy] the vnworthy *F*   75 would] would these *F*

And makes us rather bear those ills we have   80
Than fly to others that we know not of.
Thus conscience does make cowards –
And thus the native hue of resolution
Is sicklied o'er with the pale cast of thought,
And enterprises of great pitch and moment   85
With this regard their currents turn awry
And lose the name of action. Soft you now,
The fair Ophelia! Nymph, in thy orisons
Be all my sins remembered.

OPHELIA   Good my lord,
How does your honour for this many a day?   90

82 **conscience** Some commentators argue that *conscience* means 'introspection' here rather than a sense of morality (see Jenkins, LN). Certainly the context indicates that Hamlet means 'fear of punishment after death' rather than 'innate sense of good and bad'.
   make cowards – cause us to be cowards. Q1/F's 'of vs all' is included by Jenkins, presumably on metrical grounds; the Q2 reading requires the actor to pause.

83 **native hue** natural colour. Hamlet perhaps suggests a personification of Resolution as a person whose normally healthy complexion is disguised by pallor.

84 ***sicklied o'er** unhealthily covered. (The first recorded use of the verb 'to sickly' in *OED*; subsequent uses show the influence of F's 'sicklied' rather than Q2's 'sickled'.) The relation between a covering or painting and the substance under it is taken up again (as at 46–8 and 50–2), though here it is the covering that is problematic.
   pale . . . thought pallid tinge of contemplation

85 **pitch** height, scope. Jenkins quotes 'How high a pitch his resolution soars!' (*R2* 1.1.109) for the association of *pitch* with *resolution* (83). Clark, Glover and Wright

point out that the 1676, 1683, 1695 and 1703 Quartos 'have, contrary to their custom' followed F in reading 'pith' (meaning importance, gravity) here, 'which may possibly indicate that "pith" was the reading according to the stage tradition'.
   moment significance, importance

87 **Soft you** be quiet, wait a moment (Hamlet sees Ophelia for the first time and breaks off his speech)

88–9 **Nymph . . . remembered** '*Hamlet*, at the sight of *Ophelia*, does not immediately recollect, that he is to personate madness, but makes her an address grave and solemn, such as the forgoing meditation excited in his thoughts' (Johnson). Others, however, find his tone ironic or even sarcastic. In Q2, this is the first time that Hamlet and Ophelia encounter each other onstage, though some productions and films anticipate their meeting by including a silent Ophelia in 1.2 or miming the encounter in her closet (see 1.2.0.3n. and 2.1.74–97n.).

88 **orisons** prayers

90 Ophelia implies here and at 93 that she has not seen Hamlet for a long time, although strictly speaking she saw him yesterday, as she reported at 2.1.74–97. The *many a day* may refer to the lapse

82 cowards] cowardes of vs all *Q1F*   84 sicklied] *F;* sickled *Q2*   85 pitch] pith *F*   86 awry] away *F*

HAMLET

I humbly thank you, well.

OPHELIA

My lord, I have remembrances of yours
That I have longed long to redeliver.
I pray you now receive them.

HAMLET

No, not I. I never gave you aught.   95

OPHELIA

My honoured lord, you know right well you did,
And with them words of so sweet breath composed
As made these things more rich. Their perfume lost,
Take these again, for to the noble mind
Rich gifts wax poor when givers prove unkind.   100
There, my lord.

in time between Act 1 and Act 2 (see headnote to 2.1), or, as Edwards suggests, Ophelia may be represented as nervous or embarrassed by her role in this scene and hence too flustered to be accurate.

91 **well** 'The F repetition [see t.n.] – variously interpreted as showing impatience, boredom, depression, or irony – appears to be no more than an actor's elaboration' (Jenkins).

92 **remembrances** gifts, mementoes, love-tokens, as at *Oth* 3.3.295: 'This was her first remembrance from the Moor.' Hamlet's hostile attitude to Ophelia in this scene has troubled commentators (see 54.1n.); the fact that she clearly has these *remembrances* with her for what is supposedly a chance encounter may arouse his suspicion.

93 **longed** longèd

95 Hamlet's lie may be motivated by hurt pride: she has refused to see him and tried to return his gifts so he pretends he

never gave her anything. Some performers, from Junius Brutus Booth in the 1820s, have made it clear at this point that Hamlet is aware of the eavesdroppers (see Hapgood). See 54.1, 129 and nn.
aught anything

96 **you know** Tronch-Pérez argues that F's 'I know' makes Ophelia 'a more determined character', but this seems arguable, since in Q2 she is directly accusing Hamlet of lying. See also 3.2.238n.

97 **of . . . composed** Ophelia means that the words or messages with the gifts were eloquent and charming.

98 **Their perfume lost** now that their attraction has gone (because of your unkindness)

99–100 **for . . . unkind** Dent records 'A gift is valued by the mind of the giver' as proverbial (G97).

100 **wax** become (in estimation)

101 **There, my lord** Ophelia presumably hands over (or tries to hand over) the gifts.

91 you, well] you: well, well, well *F*   95 not I] no *F*   96 ¹you] I *F*   98 these] the *F*   Their] then *F*
lost] left *F*

HAMLET Ha! Ha! Are you honest?

OPHELIA My lord?

HAMLET Are you fair?

OPHELIA What means your lordship?   105

HAMLET That if you be honest and fair you should admit
no discourse to your beauty.

OPHELIA Could Beauty, my lord, have better commerce
than with Honesty?

HAMLET Ay, truly. For the power of Beauty will sooner 110
transform Honesty from what it is to a bawd than the
force of Honesty can translate Beauty into his likeness.
This was sometime a paradox, but now the time gives it
proof. I did love you once.

OPHELIA Indeed, my lord, you made me believe so.   115

HAMLET You should not have believed me. For virtue

102–48 Hamlet responds to Ophelia's couplet
with a shift into prose which allows
for a more rapid question-and-answer
dialogue.

102 Hamlet's uneasy (perhaps aggressive)
response, like his lie at 95, may be
motivated by his sense that Ophelia has
rejected him – and is continuing to do so by
returning the gifts.

102–4 **honest . . . fair** Beauty and chastity (or
'honesty') were conventionally valued as
the most important qualities for women,
though they were often seen as being
incompatible or difficult to reconcile, as in
the proverb 'Beauty and honesty seldom
meet' (Tilley, B163), Celia's cynical
remark about Nature's gifts to women,
'those that she makes fair, she scarce
makes honest; and those that she makes
honest, she makes very ill-favouredly'
(*AYL* 1.2.36–8), and Nestor's retort to
Hector, 'tell him that my lady / Was fairer

than his grandam, and as chaste / As may
be in the world' (*TC* 1.3.297–9).

106–7 **you . . . beauty** i.e. your honesty ought to
permit no one to have converse with your
beauty. Although the terms vary (see t.n.), the
meaning is much the same in all three texts
– that beauty is a potential threat to chastity.

108–9 **Beauty . . . Honesty** Ophelia perhaps
attempts to move the focus away from
herself by using abstract personifications.

108 **commerce** relationships, dealings. Hamlet
seizes on the implication of sex as a
commercial transaction in his response.

111 **bawd** pander, pimp; the word could be
used of a person of either sex.

112 **translate** transform, change

113 **sometime** formerly, once
paradox utterance contrary to received
opinion

116 **You . . . me** Ironically, Hamlet echoes
Polonius' advice, 'Do not believe his vows'
(1.3.126).

106–7 you should . . . beauty] Your beauty should admit no discourse to your honesty *Q1;* your
Honesty should admit no discourse to your Beautie *F*   108–9] *F; Q2 lines* comerse / honestie? /
109 with] *Q1;* your *F*

cannot so inoculate our old stock but we shall relish of it. I loved you not.

OPHELIA   I was the more deceived.

HAMLET   Get thee to a nunnery! Why wouldst thou be a 120
breeder of sinners? I am myself indifferent honest but
yet I could accuse me of such things that it were better
my mother had not borne me. I am very proud,
revengeful, ambitious, with more offences at my beck
than I have thoughts to put them in, imagination to give 125
them shape, or time to act them in. What should such
fellows as I do crawling between earth and heaven? We
are arrant knaves – believe none of us. Go thy ways to
a nunnery. Where's your father?

OPHELIA   At home, my lord.   130

HAMLET   Let the doors be shut upon him that he may
play the fool nowhere but in's own house. Farewell.

116–18 **For virtue . . . it** The metaphor is from grafting plants: a trace of sinfulness will linger in the old stem even after virtue is grafted on to it.

117 ***inoculate** engraft. From F; Q2's 'euocutat' is a likely misreading, combining a minim error and *t/l* confusion. (Jennens follows Q3's 'euacuate' but this makes less sense of the grafting metaphor.)
relish retain a taste or trace

120 ***to** omitted in Q2 but necessary for the sense
nunnery convent, i.e. a religious community vowed to chastity. It has been suggested that *nunnery* is used here in a slang sense meaning 'brothel' (see Jenkins, LN); Folg and Norton record this meaning, though it does not seem very relevant, given that Hamlet is trying to deter Ophelia from 'breeding'. In Q1 Hamlet tells Ofelia to go to a nunnery eight times, compared with five times in Q2 and F.

121–8 **I . . . us** Hamlet's self-accusations are presumably rhetorical exaggeration.

121 **indifferent honest** reasonably or moderately virtuous

122 **accuse me** accuse myself

124 **beck** summons (as in modern 'beck and call'). Hamlet means that the *offences* are familiar ones in his repertory.

127 **We** humanity, or perhaps more specifically men, in general

128 **arrant** downright; see 1.5.123 and n.
knaves Jenkins adopts F's 'Knaves all', noting that it is supported by Q1.
Go thy ways be on your way, go away

129 **Where's your father** Some commentators and producers indicate that Hamlet's question is motivated by the suspicion that he is being spied on. (See Dover Wilson, who has Hamlet enter at 2.2.156 so that he overhears the plot.) See also 54.1, 147 and nn.

132 **in's** in his

---

117 inoculate] *F;* euocutat *Q2;* euacuate *Q3*   120 to] *F; not in Q2*   125 in, imagination] in imagination *F*   127 earth and heaven] heauen and earth *Q1F*   128 knaves] knaues all *Q1F*   131–2] *F; Q2 lines* him, / house, / Farewell. /   132 nowhere] *(*no where*) Q1;* no way *F*

OPHELIA [*aside*]   O help him, you sweet heavens!

HAMLET   If thou dost marry, I'll give thee this plague for
   thy dowry: be thou as chaste as ice, as pure as snow,   135
   thou shalt not escape calumny. Get thee to a nunnery.
   Farewell. Or, if thou wilt needs marry, marry a fool, for
   wise men know well enough what monsters you make
   of them. To a nunnery go, and quickly too. Farewell.

OPHELIA [*aside*]   Heavenly powers restore him.   140

HAMLET   I have heard of your paintings well enough.
   God hath given you one face and you make yourselves
   another. You jig and amble and you lisp, you
   nickname God's creatures and make your wantonness

132, 137, 139 **Farewell** Hamlet keeps
turning to go but then thinks of something further to say; he behaves in a
similar way in his encounter with
his mother in the 'closet scene' (see
3.4.178n.).

133, 140 Ophelia assumes Hamlet is genuinely
mad.

134–5 **this ... dowry** this curse in place of a
dowry or marriage portion (usually
provided by the woman's father)

136 **calumny** slander

138 **monsters** i.e. cuckolds (victims of marital
infidelity), who were depicted as men with
horns

138, 141–4 **you ... your ... you** Hamlet
shifts from his specific castigation of
Ophelia to attacking women in general.
His formulation *I have heard* signals the
conventional nature of his charges:
criticism of make-up is a standard element
in Elizabethan/Jacobean misogyny (see
e.g. John Webster's *Duchess of Malfi*
(1614), 2.1.21–60, where Bosola berates
an old woman for her 'scurvy face-physic',
and, for a discussion of cosmetics in real

life as well as onstage, see Garner).

143 **You ... amble** The criticism is directed
towards the way women move or hold their
bodies.

***lisp** speak in an affected way (see
Rosalind's satirical advice to Jacques at
AYL 4.1.31–2: 'Look you lisp, and wear
strange suits'). Q2's 'list' has no relevant
meaning.

144 **nickname God's creatures** It is not clear
why this (found in all three texts) is so
offensive, unless it is on the analogy of
making a new face, i.e. presuming to reject
what God has determined; or the
implication may be that the names are
obscene or *gross* as at 4.7.168. See,
however, the comparably odd inclusion of
fishing in Octavius Caesar's list of
Antony's vices: 'he fishes, drinks, and
wastes / The lamps of night in revel' (*AC*
1.4.4–5): perhaps in both cases the speaker
is made slightly absurd by his inclusion of
a relatively trivial charge.

144–5 **make ... ignorance** i.e. use *ignorance*
as an excuse for foolish or immoral
behaviour (*wantonness*).

133 SD] *this edn*   136–7 nunnery. Farewell] (Nunry, farewell); Nunnery. Go, Farewell *F*   140 SD]
this edn   Heavenly] O heauenly *F*   141 paintings] paintings too *Q1;* pratlings too *F*   142 hath] *Q1;*
has *F*   face] *Q1;* pace *F*   yourselves] *Q1;* your selfe *F*   143 jig and] *(*gig &); fig, and you *Q1;* gidge,
you *F*   lisp,] *F;* list *Q2*   143–4 you nickname] and you nickname *Q1;* and nickname *F*   144 wantonness]
wantonnesse, your *Q1F*

ignorance. Go to, I'll no more on't. It hath made me   145
mad. I say we will have no more marriage. Those that
are married already – all but one – shall live. The rest
shall keep as they are. To a nunnery, go!   *Exit.*

OPHELIA

O, what a noble mind is here o'erthrown!
The courtier's, soldier's, scholar's eye, tongue, sword,   150
Th'expectation and rose of the fair state,
The glass of fashion and the mould of form,
Th'observed of all observers, quite, quite down.
And I, of ladies most deject and wretched,
That sucked the honey of his musicked vows,   155

---

145 **I'll ... on't** I won't put up with it any
  longer
145–6 **It ... mad** Unless he is just saying, 'It
  has made me angry', this claim raises the
  question of Hamlet's level of self-
  awareness: is he sincerely claiming mental
  disturbance or is this his *antic disposition*?
146 **more** Q2's 'mo' (its only use of the word)
  is an archaic form (see Blake, 3.2.3.4).
147 **one** Hamlet presumably means the King.
  Performers who know they are being spied
  on (see 129n.) sometimes shout this line
  provocatively.
150 Ophelia gives Hamlet some of the
  attributes of the ideal Renaissance prince:
  sword presumably goes with *soldier* but
  eye and *tongue* could go with either
  courtier or *scholar*. The order of the terms
  owes more to rhetoric than to logic (see
  2.2.81–2n.).
151 **expectation and rose** rose-like expectation
  or hope (hendiadys). *Rose* is used to
  symbolize youth and beauty, as in
  Hotspur's description of Richard II as 'that
  sweet lovely rose' (*1H4* 1.3.173) or in the
  poet addressing the young man of *Son*
  109.14 as 'my rose'. The terms imply that
  Ophelia sees Hamlet as the heir to the

throne. Jenkins adopts F's 'expectansie',
perhaps on metrical grounds.
152 **glass of fashion** mirror or model of style.
  See Hotspur's widow on her husband: 'He
  was indeed the glass / Wherein the noble
  youth did dress themselves . . . He was the
  mark and glass, copy and book, / That
  fashion'd others' (*2H4* 2.3.21–2, 31–2).
  mould of form pattern of behaviour
153 **Th'observed ... observers** the admired
  object of all eyes; the object of general
  scrutiny
  down destroyed, ruined
154 **deject** cast down (picking up *down* in 153).
  The usual *-ed* ending of a preterite or past
  participle may be omitted when the word
  ends in *-t* (Blake, 4.2.4.1b); Hope (2.1.8c)
  cites an analogous use of 'twit' for 'twitted'
  at *2H6* 3.1.178.
155 **musicked** Jenkins prefers F's 'Musicke',
  arguing that Q2's 'musickt' could be an
  error induced by 'suckt' or by a final *e*
  being read as *d. OED* has no citations of
  'music' as a verb before 1713, whereas
  nouns are commonly used as modifiers.
  The meaning either way is that Hamlet's
  promises were like honey or music to
  Ophelia.

---

146 more] *(mo), Q1F*   marriage] marriages *Q1F*   151 expectation] expectansie *F*   154 And] Haue *F*
155 musicked] *(musickt);* Musicke *F*

Now see what noble and most sovereign reason
Like sweet bells jangled out of time and harsh –
That unmatched form and stature of blown youth
Blasted with ecstasy. O woe is me
T'have seen what I have seen, see what I see.   160
[*King and Polonius step forward from behind the arras.*]

KING

Love! His affections do not that way tend.
Nor what he spake, though it lacked form a little,
Was not like madness. There's something in his soul
O'er which his melancholy sits on brood
And I do doubt the hatch and the disclose   165

---

156 **what** Jenkins prefers F's 'that', which is in parallel with *That* in 158, but Ophelia's syntax may be more disjointed here.
  sovereign reason The reason is seen as ruling the other faculties (see 1.4.73 and n.).

157 **time** Jenkins after some debate (LN) prefers F's 'tune' and cites what could be a similar minim error at *Mac* 4.3.235, where F reads 'This time goes manly', usually emended to 'tune'. It seems, however, just as appropriate to speak of *bells* being *out of time* as 'out of tune'.

158 **stature . . . youth** form or image of youth in its full bloom. Ophelia's representation of Hamlet's youthful potential here makes him seem younger than 30 (see 5.1.135–53 and List of Roles, 1n.). F has 'Feature' for *stature*, also meaning 'form' or 'fashion'.

159 **Blasted with ecstasy** devastated by madness
  woe is me it is a misery to me, it makes me miserable

160 The corrected state of this page in Q2 has an *Exit* for Ophelia at this point, and she does leave at the equivalent moment in scene 7 of Q1, but Polonius addresses her below at 177–9. In early performance

tradition (from at least 1676) she did sometimes leave here and his lines to her were cut; the alternative (from 1723) was for her to leave and then return as if summoned by *How now, Ophelia?* at 177. Williams ('Directions', 43) suggests that she should exit after 179. If she remains onstage she is often out of earshot of the King's speech (she '*goes up the stage*' in Oxberry's 1827 acting edition), or too distressed to listen to it.

161 The King is perhaps reacting to Hamlet's expressions of distaste for life and reluctance to pass it on by 'breeding'.
  affections passions

162–3 **Nor . . . not** The double negative is not uncommon in Shakespeare (see Blake, 6.2 and 6.2.7, and Hope, 2.1.9).

164 **sits on brood** The metaphor is of a brooding bird sitting on its eggs; see *hatch* in 165.

165–6 **And . . . danger** The King indicates he has heard and understood the threat in *all but one* at 147, though his articulation of his thought is necessarily vague.

165 **doubt** fear
  hatch outcome; literally the emergence of a young bird from its shell.

---

156 what] that *F*   157 jangled] *F*; jangl'd, *Capell*   time] tune *F*   158 stature] Feature *F*   160 SD] *this edn; Enter King and Polonius. Q2uF; Exit. / Enter King and Polonius. Q2c, Q1 subst.*

Will be some danger – which for to prevent
I have in quick determination
Thus set it down. He shall with speed to England
For the demand of our neglected tribute.
Haply the seas and countries different   170
With variable objects shall expel
This something-settled matter in his heart
Whereon his brains still beating puts him thus
From fashion of himself. What think you on't?

POLONIUS

It shall do well. But yet do I believe   175
The origin and commencement of his grief
Sprung from neglected love. How now, Ophelia?
You need not tell us what Lord Hamlet said –
We heard it all. My lord, do as you please,
But if you hold it fit after the play   180
Let his Queen-mother all alone entreat him

Shakespeare also uses this metaphor in relation to the awakening of evil or conspiracy at *JC* 2.1.33 and *MM* 2.2.98.

disclose disclosure; synonymous with *hatch* (see also 5.1.276)

168 **set it down** made a decision about it

169 **neglected tribute** Some editors note a possible topical allusion here to the 'Danegeld', but this is not really necessary.

170 **Haply** perhaps

171 **variable objects** various sights, 'a change of scene'

172 **something-settled** somewhat obsessive

173 **brains . . . beating** relentless concentration; see *Tem* 1.2.176: 'For still 'tis beating in my mind.'

puts Blake (3.2.1.1g) notes that *brains* often takes a singular verb, while Hope (2.1.8a) argues that the noun clause ('the fact that his brains are still beating')

is the subject of *puts* rather than the plural noun.

174 **fashion of himself** his usual behaviour

177–9 **How . . . all** These lines could be taken to imply that Ophelia did not know her father and the King were spying, though this is difficult to reconcile with her presence onstage during the first part of the scene and the Queen's words to her at 37–41. In performance, Polonius' speech can be made to express either kindness (he spares Ophelia the pain of having to recount her experience) or cruelty (he dismisses her and her pain without further thought).

179 **do . . . please** i.e. you will act on your own judgement (Polonius puts his proposal deferentially)

181 **his Queen-mother** his mother who is the Queen

166 for] *om. F*   172 something-settled] *(something setled) F*   173–6] *F; Q2 lines* beating / himselfe. / on't? / well. / greefe, /   176 his] this *F*

To show his grief. Let her be round with him
And I'll be placed, so please you, in the ear
Of all their conference. If she find him not,
To England send him or confine him where   185
Your wisdom best shall think.
KING   It shall be so.
Madness in great ones must not unwatched go.   *Exeunt.*

[**3.2**]   *Enter* HAMLET *and three of the* Players.

HAMLET   Speak the speech, I pray you, as I pronounced
it to you – trippingly on the tongue. But if you mouth

---

182 **grief** grievance
    round forthright
183–4 **in** ... **Of** so as to overhear. Later,
    Polonius attributes the suggestion that he
    should eavesdrop on this conversation to
    the King: see 3.3.30 and n.
184 **find him not** fails to find out what is wrong
    with him
187 ***unwatched** Q2's 'vnmatcht' could perhaps
    mean 'not provided with a counterpart', i.e.
    'unopposed', but elsewhere Shakespeare's
    four uses of 'unmatched' all mean
    'matchless' (including the use at 158; which
    might have influenced Q2's reading).
3.2 The three texts: this scene runs to 237
    lines in Q1 (scene 9) and 389 in both
    Q2 and F; the same elements are present in
    all three texts but in abbreviated form in
    Q1 apart from some added examples of
    how clowns extemporize. Location and
    timing: this scene takes place in an indoor
    Court setting large enough to accommodate
    the performance of *The Murder of
    Gonzago*. There is often a dais for the
    courtiers as well as one for the players to
    use as a stage; chairs, stools or benches
    may be provided for the onstage audience
    (see 87n.). It is the evening of the
    day represented in 3.1, though some hours

may have elapsed.
0.1 *three* Only one is required to speak at this
    point but three are needed for the play at
    128–253 (excluding the '*three or four*'
    extras in the dumb-show). Although editors
    tend to comment that three are unnecessary,
    the actors would be available and Hamlet's
    speeches may work better addressed to a
    small group than to just one man; most
    recent productions seem to proceed on this
    assumption.
1   **the speech** Perhaps 'the speech I have asked
    you to insert' (see 2.2.476–8 and *my lines* at
    4), but Hamlet seems to be giving advice
    about acting in general. Onstage, the players'
    reactions range from reverential (Hamlet
    is seen as Shakespeare's spokesman) to
    tolerant (the princely amateur tries to teach
    the professionals their job).
1–2 as ... **you** T. Stern suggests (11) that this
    reflects the regular Elizabethan rehearsal
    system whereby an actor would practise his
    part in the presence of an 'instructor' such
    as the author, prompter, manager or another
    actor.
2   **trippingly** lightly. Shakespeare most
    often uses this word in relation to
    dancing: see *MND* 5.1.389–90, 'And this
    ditty after me / Sing, and dance it

---

182 grief] Greefes *F*   183 placed, ... you,] *F3;* plac'd so, please you *F*   187 unwatched] *F;*
vnmatcht *Q2*   **3.2**] *Capell*   0.1 three of the] the *Q1;* two or three of the *F*   1 pronounced] *F (*pronounc'd*);*
pronoun'd *Q2*

it as many of our players do, I had as lief the town-crier
spoke my lines. Nor do not saw the air too much with
your hand, thus, but use all gently; for, in the very   5
torrent, tempest and, as I may say, whirlwind of your
passion, you must acquire and beget a temperance that
may give it smoothness. O, it offends me to the soul to
hear a robustious periwig-pated fellow tear a passion to
tatters, to very rags, to split the ears of the groundlings,   10
who for the most part are capable of nothing but
inexplicable dumb-shows and noise. I would have such

trippingly', and *Tem* 4.1.46–7: 'Each one, tripping on his toe, / Will be here with mop and mow.'

mouth declaim; Hamlet's stated preference for a low-key, naturalistic mode of delivery here seems to contrast with his admiration of the speech about Pyrrhus in 2.2 which is usually delivered as a somewhat stylized declamation. Some performers even imitate here the gestures used earlier by the First Player (see Hapgood). Shakespeare evokes exaggerated acting styles at *MND* 1.2.22–38, where Bottom gives us an example of 'Ercles' vein', and at *1H4* 2.4.380–3, where Falstaff promises to act his part 'in King Cambyses' vein'.

3   **our players** (Danish – or English) players in general (Q1 / F's 'your' is a more colloquial usage)
     I . . . lief I would be as glad if
     town-crier one appointed to make public announcements by shouting them in the streets
5   **thus** Hamlet presumably imitates the excessive gestures he condemns.
     use all gently do everything with moderation
7   **acquire and beget** adopt and inculcate
9   **robustious** boisterous. *OED* sees the word

formed from 'robust' plus '-ious' and describes it as 'common' in the seventeenth century. Shakespeare's only other usage is in *H5*, where the Constable of France compares the English soldiers with mastiffs 'in robustious and rough coming on' (3.7.149).

periwig-pated fellow man with a periwig on his head. The assumption is that wigs at this time were associated with stage costuming, not everyday wear as they became later in the seventeenth century.

10   ***tatters** See t.n. for Q2's variant spelling.
     groundlings those who paid the lowest price for admission to the theatre and stood in the *ground* or yard around the stage (*OED*'s first use); the word has come back into use at the reconstructed London Globe.
11   **are capable** of have the capacity to appreciate
12   **inexplicable dumb-shows** meaningless spectacles. A dumb-show was usually, as at 128 SD and 128.1–11, a sort of preface in which the actors mimed some action relevant to the plot of the play to follow. Shakespeare's other references to them are derogatory (see *MA* 2.3.210–11 and *MV* 1.2.70–1),

---

3 our] your *Q1F*   town-crier] Town-Cryer had *F*   4 with] *Q1; om. F*   6 whirlwind of your] the Whirle-winde of *F*   9 hear] *Q1; see F*   10 tatters] *F (tatters), Q21 (totters)*   12 would] *Q1; could F*

a fellow whipped for o'erdoing Termagant – it out-
Herods Herod. Pray you avoid it.

PLAYER   I warrant your honour.   15

HAMLET   Be not too tame neither, but let your own
discretion be your tutor. Suit the action to the word, the
word to the action, with this special observance – that
you o'erstep not the modesty of nature. For anything
so o'erdone is from the purpose of playing whose end,   20
both at the first and now, was and is to hold as 'twere
the mirror up to Nature to show Virtue her feature,
Scorn her own image, and the very age and body of the

and they had by 1599 'almost completely
disappeared from more refined plays and
were mainly to be found in the type of
popular drama ridiculed by Hamlet' (Mehl,
114), but *Hamlet* seems to have given them
a new lease of life and they appear in
Jacobean plays by John Marston, Thomas
Middleton and John Webster.

and noise At the London Globe in 2000,
Mark Rylance paused after *dumb-shows*,
and duly elicited a noisy response from the
groundlings he had insulted.

13   **Termagant** an imaginary deity believed
by medieval Christians to be worshipped
by Muslims; the word was used generally
of a violent, ranting person. See Falstaff's
reference to Douglas as 'that hot termagant
Scot' (*1H4* 5.4.112–13). Diana Whaley
points out that, despite the natural
inference from this passage (and the
claims of *Hamlet* editors) that *Termagant*
was a dramatic personage, no such
character exists in the extant English
pre-Shakespearean drama. She suggests,
however, that there may have been such a
character in the tradition of St. Nicholas
drama, of which French versions survive
(Whaley, 23–39).

14   **Herod** King of Judea at the time of Christ's
birth, he ordered a massacre of children in
fear of a rival. Herod was regularly
represented in the medieval cycle plays as
a ranting tyrant.

15   SP Many editors specify 'First Player', but
Q2 and F have 'Player' and Q1 'players',
so we have left this open.

15   **I . . . honour** i.e. I can promise or assure
your lordship (that we will avoid it).

16   **tame** weak, understated

17, 18 **action** gesture

19   **modesty of nature** natural restraints or
limits

20   **from** remote from, contrary to
playing acting

22   **Nature** human action or behaviour
feature appearance, shape

23   **Scorn . . . image** 'the scornful person
what she looks like to others'; RP suggests the relevance of *MA* 3.1, where
Beatrice overhears Hero and Ursula
deliberately discussing her scorn for
men.

23–4 **very . . . time** Taken by Edwards as
hendiadys (= aged body of the time), but it
could mean more generally 'essential
reality of this moment in time'.

13–14 out-Herods] *(*out Herods*)*   19 o'erstep] ore-stop *F*   20 o'erdone] ouer-done *F*   22 her] her
owne *F*

time his form and pressure. Now this overdone, or
come tardy off, though it makes the unskilful laugh,   25
cannot but make the judicious grieve, the censure of
which one must in your allowance o'erweigh a whole
theatre of others. O, there be players that I have seen
play and heard others praised – and that highly – not to
speak it profanely, that neither having th'accent of   30
Christians nor the gait of Christian, pagan nor man
have so strutted and bellowed that I have thought some
of Nature's journeymen had made men, and not made
them well, they imitated humanity so abhominably.

PLAYER   I hope we have reformed that indifferently with us.   35
HAMLET   O, reform it altogether, and let those that play

---

24 **form and pressure** likeness and
impression

24–5 **this ... off** if this is exaggerated or
performed inadequately (*tardy* literally
means 'slow')

25 **unskilful** i.e. those who know nothing
about acting

26–7 **the censure ... one** the judgement of
one of whom (the judicious)

27 **in your allowance** by your admission

29 **heard others praised** perhaps 'heard that
others had praised'

30 **profanely** Hamlet acknowledges that it
might be profane to categorize these actors
as not Christian, pagan or human.
accent sound, pronunciation

31 **gait** bearing
Christian ... man These categories are
presumably intended to cover all kinds of
human beings: 'Christian, pagan nor any
other kind of man'. Oxf and Hibbard
emend F's 'or Norman' to 'nor no man';
Q1's version (see t.n.) is adopted by White
in his Q2-based edition. Marlowe uses a
comparable formula, 'any Christian,
Heathen, Turke, or Jew' in *Edward II*
(1592; 5.4.75).

33 **Nature's journeymen** i.e. not Nature
herself but some of her hired workers. A
journeyman was one who had completed
his apprenticeship at a trade but had not yet
become a master at it.

34 **abhominably** This spelling, which
seems to have been favoured by
Shakespeare (*OED* notes that it appears
18 times in F), allows for a play on *ab
homine* (from or contrary to man); see also
Holofernes' contempt for the version
without the 'h' at *LLL* 5.1.23–4. Although
this etymology is incorrect (the real root
is *ab omen*), *OED* points out that it has
'permanently affected the meaning of the
word'.

35 **indifferently** somewhat, to a moderate
extent
with us i.e. in our company

36–7 **those ... clowns** There is no clown in
this group of players; his absence is even
more conspicuous in Q1, where Hamlet
ends this speech with 'Maisters tell him of
it' (9.38). Shakespeare's company may in
reality have lacked a clown when *Hamlet*
was first performed, having recently
lost the popular Will Kempe (see 118n.)

25 makes] make *F*   26 of] of the *F*   29 praised] praise *F*   30 th'accent] the accent *F*   31 nor man]
Nor Turke *Q1;* or Norman *F*   35 us] vs, Sir *F*

your clowns speak no more than is set down for them.
For there be of them that will themselves laugh to set
on some quantity of barren spectators to laugh too,
though in the meantime some necessary question of the   40
play be then to be considered. – That's villainous and
shows a most pitiful ambition in the fool that uses it.
Go, make you ready.   [*Exeunt Players.*]

Enter POLONIUS, GUILDENSTERN *and* ROSENCRANTZ.

How now, my lord, will the King hear this piece of
work?   45
POLONIUS   And the Queen too, and that presently.
HAMLET   Bid the players make haste.   [*Exit Polonius.*]
Will you two help to hasten them?
ROSENCRANTZ   Ay, my lord.
                    Exeunt Rosencrantz and Guildenstern.

HAMLET
What ho, Horatio!

Enter HORATIO.

HORATIO   Here, sweet lord, at your service.

and not yet acquired Robert Armin (see Wiles, 57–60, and Thompson, 'Jest'). Hamlet later laments the death of Yorick, his father's jester (see 5.1.171n.).

38 **there . . . that** there are some of them who
38–9 **set on** incite
39 **barren** devoid of judgement; see *unskilful* at 25
40 **necessary question** important issue
42 It is at this point (after *uses it*) that Q1 has some examples of the sort of jokes that clowns add to their parts; Caldecott printed them in square brackets in 1832 and

Spencer includes them; Michael Pennington spoke them in John Barton's RSC production in 1980 (see Pennington, 24–5).

43 SD *not in Q2, but Hamlet clearly dismisses the players
46 **presently** immediately
47 SD *not in Q2, though Hamlet asks Polonius to go
48 **Will . . . them** Perhaps Hamlet deliberately dismisses Rosencrantz and Guildenstern because he wants to be alone with Horatio to finalize his plans.

43 SD] *Q1F subst.*   43.1] *F subst.; after 45 Q2*   44–5] *F lines* Lord, / Worke? /   47 SD] *F; not in Q21*   48 SP] *Both. F*   Ay] We will *F*   SD] *(Exeunt they two.); Exeunt. F*   49 ho] *(howe), F* (hoa*)* SD] *after 48 F*

HAMLET

Horatio, thou art e'en as just a man   50
As e'er my conversation coped withal.

HORATIO

O my dear lord –

HAMLET   Nay, do not think I flatter,
For what advancement may I hope from thee
That no revenue hast but thy good spirits
To feed and clothe thee? Why should the poor be
    flattered?   55
No, let the candied tongue lick absurd pomp
And crook the pregnant hinges of the knee
Where thrift may follow fawning. Dost thou hear?
Since my dear soul was mistress of her choice
And could of men distinguish her election   60
Sh'ath sealed thee for herself. For thou hast been

50–70 **Horatio ... thee** Hamlet praises Horatio as the ideal friend, listing a number of virtues not unlike those Henry V attributes to Lord Scroop at the moment when he reveals his former friend's treachery (*H5* 2.2.127–37).

50 **e'en** even, absolutely
just Editors regularly gloss as 'well balanced' or 'honourable', but 'judicious' is also relevant.

51 **conversation** experience of social intercourse
coped encountered

52 **O ... lord** Horatio indicates a modest denial of Hamlet's praise.

54 **revenue** (stress on second syllable) source of income

56–8 **let ... fawning** 'let the sweet-tongued flatterer direct his attention to ridiculous pomposity and bend his ever-ready knees where profit will result from his fawning behaviour'. The association of *fawning* with *candy* has been noted as a Shakespearean 'image cluster' (e.g. by Spurgeon and Armstrong) that often also includes dogs, as when Hotspur recalls the former flattery of Bolingbroke: 'Why, what a candy deal of courtesy / This fawning greyhound then did proffer me!' (*1H4* 1.3.247–8). F's 'faining' (feigning) is often rejected, though it too makes sense.

56 **candied** sugared

57 **crook** bend (as at *Oth* 1.1.45: 'a duteous and knee-crooking knave')
pregnant prompt, readily inclined (see 'supple knee' at *R2* 1.4.33)

58 **thrift** financial advantage (as at 177, and see 1.2.179n.)
Dost thou hear an intensive: 'please pay attention to this' (as at 2.2.461, 473).

60 'and could discriminate in her choice among men'

61 **Sh'ath sealed** she has selected or chosen (literally 'put a legal seal (on something or someone) as a sign of ownership')

---

52 SP2] *F; Q2 only in G4ʳ catchword*   56 tongue lick] tongue, like *F*   58 fawning] faining *F*   59 her] my *F*   61 Sh'ath] *Q5;* S'hath *Q2;* Hath *F*

As one in suffering all that suffers nothing –
A man that Fortune's buffets and rewards
Hast ta'en with equal thanks. And blest are those
Whose blood and judgement are so well co-meddled   65
That they are not a pipe for Fortune's finger
To sound what stop she please. Give me that man
That is not passion's slave and I will wear him
In my heart's core – ay, in my heart of heart –
As I do thee. Something too much of this: 70
There is a play tonight before the King –
One scene of it comes near the circumstance
Which I have told thee of my father's death.
I prithee when thou seest that act afoot,
Even with the very comment of thy soul   75
Observe my uncle. If his occulted guilt
Do not itself unkennel in one speech

62 'like a person who, having experienced everything, responds stoically to it all'
63 **buffets** blows
64 **with equal thanks** i.e. in the same equable spirit
65 **blood and judgement** passion and reason
co-meddled mixed together; a rare word, but *OED* (under 'commeddle') also gives an example from Webster's *White Devil* (1612; 3.3.39) which was presumably influenced by *Hamlet*. F's 'co-mingled' is synonymous.
66 **pipe** Hamlet returns to this idea when the players re-enter with literal pipes at 336.1
67 **she** Fortune was usually depicted as female (see 2.2.224–31, 431–5 and nn.).
69 **core** centre, but also perhaps a play on *cor*, Latin for 'heart'
70 **Something** an intensifier: 'altogether'
72 **scene** episode or sequence
circumstance details of the manner of
73 **Which . . . thee** Although Hamlet refused

to share the Ghost's revelations with his companions in 1.5, it seems that he has subsequently told Horatio the whole story. In *Fratricide Punished* (1.6) he does this at the equivalent of the end of 1.5, as soon as they are alone together (Bullough, 7.134–5).
74 **that act afoot** that action being performed
75 **the . . . soul** the most concentrated attention of your entire being. Q2's 'thy soule' is usually adopted by editors who sometimes argue explicitly that Hamlet wants Horatio's judgement to back his own; F's 'my Soule' has also been defended as implying that Hamlet wants his friend's attention to be as intense as his own.
76 **occulted** concealed
77 **itself unkennel** reveal itself. The King's guilt is seen as an animal emerging from its lair. RP suggests *unkennel* might also evoke the overflowing of a 'kennel' or gutter,

64 Hast] Hath *F*   65 co-meddled] *(comedled); co-mingled *F*   75 thy] my *F*   76 my] mine *F*

It is a damned ghost that we have seen
And my imaginations are as foul
As Vulcan's stithy. Give him heedful note,   80
For I mine eyes will rivet to his face
And after we will both our judgements join
In censure of his seeming.

HORATIO   Well, my lord
If 'a steal aught the whilst this play is playing
And scape detected I will pay the theft.   85

Enter Trumpets and Kettledrums, KING, QUEEN, POLONIUS,
OPHELIA [, ROSENCRANTZ *and* GUILDENSTERN].

although *OED* does not list this meaning for the verb. (*Unkennel* oddly echoes *uncle* in 76.)

one speech implicitly the speech Hamlet has had inserted (see 2.2.476–8 and n.), if *in* means 'during'; the implication might, however, be that the King will actually *proclaim* [*his*] *male-faction* like the *guilty creatures* Hamlet mentioned at 2.2.523–7.

78 **damned** damnèd. See 1.4.40 and n.

79 **my imaginations** i.e. my suspicions, based on the Ghost's words

foul polluted, offensive

80 **Vulcan's stithy** The workshop or forge of Vulcan, the blacksmith-god; it was reputedly situated underneath Mount Etna and hence associated with the notion of hell. Theobald emended to 'smithy' on the grounds that a stithy (which he takes to mean 'anvil') is 'not the dirtiest thing in a Smith's shop'.

heedful attentive; F has 'needfull' (necessary); either seems acceptable.

83 **In ... seeming** in deducing what we can from his appearance or behaviour

83–5 **Well ... theft** Horatio agrees to Hamlet's proposal which commits him to observation

and deduction but not to any specific action.

84 **'a** he

aught anything

85 **detected** i.e. being detected; Jenkins adopts F's 'detecting'.

pay the theft i.e. recompense the owner of the stolen goods

85.1–2 *This entry SD heralds the beginning of the sequence in *Hamlet* which requires the largest number of actors (see Appendix 5). Q2 omits Rosencrantz and Guildenstern; the former speaks at 103, the latter not until after their re-entry at 287.1, but one would expect them both to be present, given their discussion of the play with Hamlet, their role in inviting the King and Queen, and their continuing scrutiny of Hamlet. They are named in F's more elaborate SD (see t.n.), which includes '*Torches*' to remind the audience that it is now supposed to be night. Dessen & Thomson note (under 'drum') that Q2's specification of '*Kettle Drummes*' is unique for a SD, though of course Hamlet has referred to 'the kettledrum and trumpet' in the dialogue at 1.4.11.

80 stithy] *F* (Stythe) heedful] needfull *F*   83 In] To *F*   84 'a] he *F*   85 detected] detecting *F*
85.1–2 *Enter ...* OPHELIA] *Enter King, Queene, Corambis Q1; Enter King, Queene, Polonius, Ophelia F*
85.2 ROSENCRANTZ *and* GUILDENSTERN] *and other Lords. Q1; Rosincrance, Guildensterne, and other Lords attendant, with his Guard carrying Torches. Danish March. Sound a Flourish. F*

HAMLET [*to Horatio*]   They are coming to the play. I
must be idle. Get you a place.

KING   How fares our cousin Hamlet?

HAMLET   Excellent, i'faith! Of the chameleon's dish – I
eat the air, promise-crammed. You cannot feed capons   90
so.

KING   I have nothing with this answer, Hamlet. These
words are not mine.

HAMLET   No, nor mine now, my lord. [*to Polonius*] You
played once i'th' university, you say?   95

POLONIUS   That did I, my lord, and was accounted a
good actor.

HAMLET   What did you enact?

---

87   **be idle** i.e. resume my *antic disposition*
(see *idle* at 3.4.10 and in Q1 (7.88) where
Corambis uses the word to describe
Hamlet's love for Ofelia). Some
performers, notably Macready, have
behaved in an exaggerated and manic
fashion as the courtiers enter (see
Hapgood).
Get . . . place find yourself somewhere to
sit. This implies that chairs, stools or
benches have been set up, perhaps during
Hamlet's opening discussion with the
players.

88   **How fares** The King (repeating the sense
of his first words to Hamlet in their
previous encounter at 1.2.64–6) means
'How are you?', but Hamlet picks up a pun
on *fare* meaning food.

89   **Of . . . dish** i.e. I eat the same food as the
chameleon (which was thought to live on
air: Hamlet perhaps alludes to the proverb
'Love is a chameleon that feeds on air'
(Dent, L505.1), which Shakespeare had
used in *TGV* 2.1.167–8 and 2.4.25–8).

There may be a further implied pun on *air*
(90) and 'heir'.

90   **promise-crammed** (I am) stuffed with
promises. (The implied complaint seems to
relate to Hamlet's statement that he *lack[s]*
advancement at 331 – a conversation
which comes earlier in Q1.)
capons cockerels castrated and fattened for
eating

92   **I . . . with** I get nothing out of

93   **are not mine** don't answer my question,
mean nothing to me

94   **now, my lord** Q2's punctuation implies
these words are addressed to the King; F's
'Now my Lord' addresses them to
Polonius; most editors conflate, following
Q2 in putting *now* with *mine*, but following
F in the direction of *my lord*.

95   **i'th' university** On its title-page, Q1
claims that *Hamlet* had been acted 'by his
Highnesse seruants in the Cittie of London:
as also in the two Vniuersities of
Cambridge and Oxford'. (See pp. 56–7 for
a discussion of this claim.)

86–7] *Spencer; Q2F line* idle, / place. /   86 SD] *this edn*   89–95] *F; Q2 lines* yfaith, / ayre, / so. /
Hamlet, / mine. / Lord. / say, /   94 mine now] mine. Now *F*   SD] *Rowe*   96 did I] I did *F*   98 What]
Q1; And what *F*

POLONIUS   I did enact Julius Caesar. I was killed i'th'
Capitol. Brutus killed me.   100

HAMLET   It was a brute part of him to kill so capital a calf
there. Be the players ready?

ROSENCRANTZ   Ay, my lord, they stay upon your
patience.

QUEEN   Come hither, my dear Hamlet, sit by me.   105

HAMLET   No, good mother, here's metal more attractive.

POLONIUS [*to King*]   O ho, do you mark that!

HAMLET   Lady, shall I lie in your lap?

OPHELIA   No, my lord.

99–101 The puns on *Brutus/brute* and *Capitol/capital* are in all three texts. They may allude to Shakespeare's recent *JC* in which John Heminges (now Polonius) probably played Caesar and Richard Burbage (now Hamlet) played Brutus (see Appendix 5). Williams ('Romans', 47–8) notes another parallel between Hamlet and Brutus (Lucius Junius), referred to in *H5* 2.4.38 as 'Covering discretion with a coat of folly'.

100 **Capitol** Caesar was killed in the Senate House, but Shakespeare equates the two locations in *JC*, an error he may have taken from Chaucer's 'Monk's Tale': 'This Julius to the Capitolie wente / Upon a day, as he was wont to goon / And in the Capitolie anon hym hente / This false Brutus and his othere foon' (3893–6).

101 **brute part of** brutal action by (with *part* as a pun on an actor's *part* or role)
calf fool (*OED* calf I 1c)

103–4 **stay . . . patience** i.e. are waiting for you to tell them to begin

105 SP For the first time, Q2 has '*Ger.*', using it throughout 3.4 and 4.1 but reverting to '*Quee.*' in 4.5.

106 **No** Hibbard notes that Hamlet could not watch the King if he sat next to the Queen, who would be between them. In a long stage tradition, inaugurated by Edmund Kean in 1814, Hamlet began watching the play stretched out at Ophelia's feet but crawled gradually towards the King; the 'Kean crawl' survived until at least Asta Nielsen's screen performance in 1920 (see Figs. 13 and 14 and pp. 103–5).
metal more attractive (1) more magnetic substance; (2) more appealing proposition. The spellings 'metal' and 'mettle' were used indistinguishably. The exchange with Ophelia has caused criticism and embarrassment: Theobald says, 'if ever the Poet deserved Whipping for low and indecent Ribaldry, it was for this Passage; ill-tim'd in all its Circumstances, and unbefitting the Dignity of his Characters, as well as of his Audience' (*Restored*, 87). (See Taylor & Thompson.)

109–10 Ophelia indicates that she understands *lie in your lap* in a sexual sense – a meaning Hamlet denies. He aims to entrap like Ferdinand in Webster's *Duchess of Malfi* (1614) who tells his

99–102] *F; Q2 lines* Capitall, / mee. / there, / readie? /   105 dear] good *F*   106 metal] *(*mettle*) F, Q5 (*metall*);* a mettle *Q1*   107 SD] *Capell subst.* 109–10] *Ofel.* No my Lord. / *Ham.* Vpon your lap, what do you thinke I meant contrary matters? *Q1; Ophe.* No my Lord. / *Ham.* I meane, my Head vpon your Lap? / *Ophe.* I my Lord. *Ham.* Do you thinke I meant Country matters? *F*

HAMLET	Do you think I meant country matters?	110
OPHELIA	I think nothing, my lord.	
HAMLET	That's a fair thought to lie between maids' legs.	
OPHELIA	What is, my lord?	
HAMLET	Nothing.	
OPHELIA	You are merry, my lord.	115
HAMLET	Who, I?	
OPHELIA	Ay, my lord.	

HAMLET O God, your only jig-maker! What should a
man do but be merry, for look you how cheerfully my
mother looks, and my father died within's two hours! 120
OPHELIA Nay, 'tis twice two months, my lord.
HAMLET So long? Nay, then, let the devil wear black, for
I'll have a suit of sables! O heavens – die two months

sister, 'woemen like that part, which (like the Lamprey) / Hath nev'r a bone in it' and then, when she shows that she understands the sexual innuendo, rebukes her, 'Nay, / I meane the Tongue' (1.1.375–9). That a sexual sense for *lap* was current is clear from Marlowe's *Jew of Malta* (c. 1589), where Bellamira tempts Barabas' servant, 'Now, gentle *Ithimore*, lye in my lap', quickly followed by 'let's in and sleepe together' (4.2.82, 129); the invitation is repeated at 4.4.27–9, where Ithamore responds, 'let musicke rumble, / Whilst I in thy incony lap doe tumble.' In F Ophelia's 'No my Lord' is followed by Hamlet's clarification and her acceptance (see t.n.). This more decorous sense is present in the more playful context of *1H4* 3.1.207–8 and 222–3.

110 **country matters** a vulgar reference, i.e. one suitable for rustics (with a pun on 'cunt' as in Ben Jonson's reference to 'the Low Country' in *Everyman Out* (1599; 3.1.375)).

111, 114 **nothing** 'Thing' could be a euphemism for a man's penis; alternatively *nothing* (the figure nought) could refer to a

woman's vagina; again Hamlet teases or insults Ophelia.

118 **your only jig-maker** your best comedian, entertainer: Hamlet bitterly casts himself as the clown. There may be an allusion to Will Kempe, the Chamberlain's Men's famous *jig-maker*, who left the company in 1599 to undertake his marathon jig from London to Norwich (see 36–7n. and 266n.).

120 **within's** within this (i.e. these)

120–1 **two hours . . . months** Hamlet's *two hours* is rhetorical; if we assume that Ophelia is accurate, two months have passed since Hamlet lamented his father 'But two months dead' (1.2.138), so it is another two months since Hamlet encountered the Ghost (see headnote to 2.1). Klein suggests an allusion to theatrical time: the 'two hours' traffic of our stage' (*RJ* Prologue 12).

122–3 **let . . . sables** i.e. if my father has been dead so long the devil can have my mourning clothes and I'll wear furs (sable fur is also dark brown or black).

123 **sables** The word also recalls the *sable arms* of Pyrrhus at 2.2.390.

122 devil] *(deule), Q1 (diuell), F (Diuel)* for] *Q1F;* 'fore *Warburton*

ago and not forgotten yet? Then there's hope a great
man's memory may outlive his life half a year! But, 125
by'r Lady, 'a must build churches then, or else shall 'a
suffer not thinking on – with the hobby-horse whose
epitaph is 'For O! For O! The hobby-horse is forgot!'

The trumpets sounds. Dumb-show follows.

Enter [Players *as*] *a king and a queen, the queen embracing him
and he her. He takes her up and declines his head upon her*

125–6 **by'r Lady** by Our Lady (the Virgin
Mary); see 2.2.363.
126 **'a . . . 'a** he . . . he
  build   churches   See   Benedick's
  comparable cynicism in *MA*: 'If a man do
  not erect in this age his own tomb ere he
  dies, he shall live no longer in monument
  than the bell rings, and the widow weeps'
  (5.2.73–5).
127 **not thinking on** not being thought about
  hobby-horse a pantomime-type horse
  costume worn by a morris dancer; 'the
  hobby-horse is forgot' seems to have been
  a popular catchphrase (see, for example,
  the running joke in Thomas Dekker's *The
  Witch of Edmonton* (1621), 2.1 and 3.4).
  The point may be that the popular hobby-
  horse had to be left out of May games
  and other festivals because of Puritan
  disapproval.
  epitaph literally epitaph, but also refrain or
  catchphrase (see Jenkins, LN, and
  Edwards)
128 **'For . . . forgot!'** apparently a line from a

lost ballad which Shakespeare also quotes
in *LLL* (3.1.28–9)
128 SD, 128.1–11 The F SD differs in some
  details (see t.n.). It specifies '*some two
  or three Mutes*' to return with the poisoner
  as compared with Q2's '*some three or
  foure*'; both directions seem 'permissive'
  and extravagant with personnel, though
  presumably two people are needed to
  remove the body unless the poisoner and
  the Queen do it at the end of the show. Q1's
  specification that Lucianus enters '*with
  poyson in a Viall*' (see t.n.) underlines the
  re-enactment of the Ghost's story at
  1.5.59–70.
  Dumb-show follows The dumb-show has
  often been omitted in performance, partly
  in order to avoid the problem of the King's
  failure to react to it, but this leaves the
  audience ignorant of the outcome and
  especially of the role of the Queen.
128.2 **takes her up** The assumption seems
  to be that she has knelt (as in F's SD)
  and that he offers his hand to help her

125 by'r] *(ber)*   126 'a . . . 'a] he . . . he *F*   128 SD, 128.1–11 *The . . . love.*] *Enter in a Dumbe Shew, the
King and the Queene, he sits downe in an Arbor, she leaues him: Then enters Lucianus with poyson in a
Viall, and powres it in his eares, and goes away: Then the Queene commeth and findes him dead: and goes
away with the other. Q1; Hoboyes play. The dumbe shew enters. / Enter a King and Queene, very louingly;
the Queene embracing him. She kneeles, and makes shew of Protestation vnto him. He takes her vp, and
declines his head vpon her neck. Layes him downe vpon a Banke of Flowers. She seeing him a-sleepe,
leaues him. Anon comes in a Fellow, takes off his Crowne, kisses it, and powres poyson in the Kings eares,
and Exits. The Queene returnes, findes the King dead, and makes passionate Action. The Poysoner, with
some two or three Mutes comes in againe, seeming to lament with her. The dead body is carried away: The
Poysoner Wooes the Queene with Gifts, she seemes loath and vnwilling awhile, but in the end, accepts his
loue. F* 128.1 Players *as*] *this edn*

neck. He lies him down upon a bank of flowers. She seeing
him asleep leaves him. Anon come in [a Player as] another
man, takes off his crown, kisses it, pours poison in the 128.5
sleeper's ears and leaves him. The queen returns, finds the
king dead, makes passionate action. The poisoner with some
three or four [Players] *come in again, seem to condole with*
her. The dead body is carried away. The poisoner woos the
*queen with gifts. She seems harsh awhile but in the end*128.10
accepts love. [*Exeunt.*]

OPHELIA What means this, my lord?

HAMLET Marry, this munching mallico! It means 130
mischief.

OPHELIA Belike this show imports the argument of the
play.

Enter [a Player as the] Prologue.

HAMLET We shall know by this fellow. The players

---

up (see the kneeling Richard's challenge to
Lady Anne at *R3* 1.2.187: 'Take up the
sword again, or take up me').

128.3 *He ... flowers* An inventory of 1598
shows that the Admiral's Men possessed
'ij mose [mossy] banckes' as stage
properties. Q1's staging – '*he sits downe in
an Arbor*' – might imply the use of a
'discovery space' or inner stage; this would
remove the necessity for the subsequent
carrying away of the body.

128.7 *makes passionate action* i.e. makes
gestures to convey the intensity of her
grief

128.8 *condole* commiserate. The word is
synonymous with F's '*lament*', but
Shakespeare apparently ridicules it in the
mouths of Bottom in *MND* 1.2.24 and

38 and Pistol in *H5* 2.1.126. (But see
condolement at 1.2.93 above.)

128.10 *harsh* unresponsive

130 **munching mallico** An obscure phrase in
all three texts (see t.n.), apparently meaning
something like 'stealthy iniquity'. Tronch-
Pérez supports Hanmer's suggestion that
mallico may derive from Spanish
malhecho, meaning 'a wicked act'; many
editors prefer F's 'Miching', which they
relate to the noun 'micher' meaning
'truant' at *1H4* 2.4.404. Fortunately,
Hamlet follows this phrase with a further
explanation (again in all three texts).

132 **Belike** perhaps

134 **this fellow** F has 'these Fellowes',
presumably meaning the actors in general
rather than the one playing the Prologue.

128.4 *a* Player *as*] *this edn* 128.8 Players] *this edn* 128.11 Exeunt.] *F; not in Q1* 130 this] this is
Q1F; 'tis *Q3* munching] myching *Q1;* Miching *F* mallico] *(Mallico) Q1;* Malicho *F;* mallecho
Malone It] that *Q1F* 133.1] *Theobald; opp.* fellow *134 Q2; opp.* 129 *Q1; after 141 F* a Player *as the*]
this edn 134 this fellow] *Q1;* these Fellowes *F*

cannot keep council – they'll tell all. 135

OPHELIA Will 'a tell us what this show meant?

HAMLET Ay, or any show that you will show him. Be not
you ashamed to show, he'll not shame to tell you what
it means.

OPHELIA You are naught, you are naught. I'll mark the 140
play.

PROLOGUE

For us and for our tragedy,
Here stooping to your clemency,
We beg your hearing patiently. [*Exit.*]

HAMLET Is this a prologue or the posy of a ring? 145

OPHELIA 'Tis brief, my lord.

HAMLET As woman's love.

Enter [Player] King *and* [Player] Queen.

PLAYER KING

Full thirty times hath Phoebus' cart gone round

135 ***keep council** There is no reason for
Hamlet to break off his speech, so we
assume Q1/F's 'counsell' has been omitted
from Q2.

137 **any . . . show him** Hamlet implies that
what Ophelia might *show* is intimate or
sexual.

137–8 **Be not you** if you are not

140 **naught** offensive, indecent (the origin of
the modern 'naughty')
mark attend to

143 *stooping . . . clemency* bowing to [implore]
your mercy, generosity

145 **the . . . ring** the (necessarily brief) motto
inscribed inside a ring. Hamlet implies that
it is too perfunctory for a Prologue, as
Ophelia agrees. *Posy* is a syncopated form
of Q1/F's 'poesie'.

147.1 Q1 avoids the ambiguities in Q2/F (see

t.n.) of having two Kings and two Queens
onstage by calling the Players '*Duke*'
and '*Dutchesse*' after the dumbshow,
their correct titles according to Hamlet at
232–3.

148–253 As the speech about Pyrrhus (2.2.388–
456) was set apart from the surrounding
linguistic context by its elevated language,
The Murder of Gonzago is set apart by its
consistent use of rhymed couplets, which
often require distortions of word order.

148–51 *thirty . . . thirties* Strictly, the first *thirty*
times would indicate 30 days, while *thirty*
dozen moons indicates 30 years. The stress
on 30 years of marriage has not particularly
caused commentators to seize on these
lines as the insertion by Hamlet (whose
parents must have been married for 30
years), but the speech he promised to

135 council] *Q1F; not in Q2* 136 'a] they *F;* he *Q1* 137 you will] you'l *Q1F* 144 SD] *Globe* 145
posy] *(posie), Q1F (*poesie*)* 147.1 ¹Player, ²Player] *Pope subst.* King] *F;* the Duke *Q1* Queen] *Dutchesse*
Q1; his Queene *F* 148+ SP] *Steevens²; King. Q2F; Duke Q1*

Neptune's salt wash and Tellus' orbed ground
And thirty dozen moons with borrowed sheen   150
About the world have times twelve thirties been
Since love our hearts and Hymen did our hands
Unite commutual in most sacred bands.

PLAYER QUEEN

So many journeys may the sun and moon
Make us again count o'er ere love be done.   155
But woe is me, you are so sick of late,
So far from cheer and from our former state,
That I distrust you. Yet, though I distrust,
Discomfort you, my lord, it nothing must.
For women fear too much, even as they love,   160
And women's fear and love hold quantity –
Either none, in neither aught, or in extremity.
Now what my love is proof hath made you know

write at 2.2.476–8 has proved impossible to identify with any certainty (see 180–209n. and 248–53n.). (Q1 has 'forty', perhaps a more common round figure for 'a long time'.)

148 *Phoebus' cart* the chariot of the sungod, i.e. the sun

149 *Neptune's salt wash* the sea, Neptune being its god
**Tellus' orbed ground* orbèd; the rounded (orbed) earth, Tellus being its goddess (Q2 has 'Tellus orb'd the ground', with 'orb'd' as an unlikely verb.)

150 *borrowed sheen* light reflected from the sun

152 *Hymen* the god of marriage (who appears rather mysteriously at *AYL* 5.4.105)

153 *commutual* reciprocally (*OED*'s first use)

154–66 This speech in Q2 contains three lines that are not in F: 160 and 165–6; there are also several variant readings.

It has been argued that F incorporates Shakespeare's deletions and corrections (see Edwards, pp. 10–11).

158 *distrust you* fear for you

159 it must not discomfort you at all, my lord

160 This line (not in F) stands out in Q2 as an uncompleted couplet. It may be a 'false start' by Shakespeare, or it may be that its companion line has been omitted.

161 *hold quantity* are in proportion to each other

162 *Either . . . aught* Q2's *Either none* is extra-metrical, and it seems to mean the same as *in neither aught*: 'either there is no fear or love at all'.
or in extremity or there is an excess (of both)

163 *love Q2's '*Lord*' makes very strained sense ('what has already been proved has made you know') and loses the parallel with 164. '*Lord*' is a likely error, perhaps repeated from 159.

149 *orbed*] F; orb'd the *Q2*   154+ SP] *Steevens²; Quee. Q2; Dutchesse (only four speeches) Q1; Bap. F, except Bapt. 176, Qu. 221*   157 *our*] your *F* *former*] forme *F*   160] *om. F*   161 *And*] For *F hold*] holds *F*   162 *Either none*] *om. F*   163 *love*] *F, Q5;* Lord *Q2*

And, as my love is sized, my fear is so.
Where love is great, the littlest doubts are fear,   165
Where little fears grow great, great love grows there.

PLAYER KING

Faith, I must leave thee, love, and shortly too,
My operant powers their functions leave to do,
And thou shalt live in this fair world behind
Honoured, beloved, and haply one as kind   170
For husband shalt thou –

PLAYER QUEEN   *O, confound the rest!*
Such love must needs be treason in my breast.
In second husband let me be accurst:
None wed the second but who killed the first.

HAMLET   That's wormwood!   175

PLAYER QUEEN

The instances that second marriage move
Are base respects of thrift, but none of love.
A second time I kill my husband dead
When second husband kisses me in bed.

PLAYER KING

I do believe you think what now you speak.   180

---

164 **i.e.** and my fear is as great (the same size) as my love

168 ***operant powers*** vital organs or faculties
leave to do cease to perform

171 ***shalt thou*** – Presumably the line would have ended in 'find' if it had not been interrupted. The assumption that she would find a second husband, despite being old enough to have been married for 30 years, makes her case parallel to that of Hamlet's mother. This King, unlike Hamlet, seems to regard it as natural, even desirable, that a widow will remarry.
confound destroy (i.e. don't utter)

175 In Q2 both the SP and Hamlet's words are printed in the right-hand margin, perhaps a way of indicating an aside. Some performers address this line to Horatio.
wormwood literally, the plant *artemisia absinthium*, used figuratively for something bitter or mortifying. Hamlet seems to be more attentive to the reactions of the Queen than to those of the King at this point. He accuses her of *kill*[*ing*] *a king* at 3.4.27, although the Ghost has not been specific about the extent of her involvement.

176 ***instances*** reasons
move motivate

177 ***thrift*** financial advantage (as at 58, and see 1.2.179n.)

180–209 Some commentators have found this speech to stand out from the rest of *The Murder of Gonzago* and have

165–6] *om. F*   168 their] my *F*   175] *opp. 174, 176; Ham.* O wormewood, wormewood! *after 179 Q1; Ham.* Wormwood, Wormwood. *after 174 F*   180 *you think*] you sweete *Q1;* you. Think *F*

But what we do determine oft we break.
Purpose is but the slave to memory,
Of violent birth but poor validity,
Which now like fruit unripe sticks on the tree
But fall unshaken when they mellow be.   185
Most necessary 'tis that we forget
To pay ourselves what to ourselves is debt.
What to ourselves in passion we propose,
The passion ending doth the purpose lose.
The violence of either grief or joy   190
Their own enactures with themselves destroy.
Where joy most revels grief doth most lament,
Grief joys, joy grieves, on slender accident.
This world is not for aye, nor 'tis not strange
That even our loves should with our fortunes change,   195
For 'tis a question left us yet to prove
Whether Love lead Fortune or else Fortune Love.
The great man down, you mark his favourite flies,

speculated that it is the one inserted by Hamlet (see 2.2.476–8), but, while its sentiments may be generally relevant to his situation, it does not really come 'near the circumstance . . . of [his] father's death' in the way he has promised Horatio at 72–3. (See 148–51n. and 248–53n.)

182 i.e. purposes are easily forgotten

183 *Of violent birth* robust to begin with
poor validity not well founded, i.e. without staying power

184 **like fruit* Q2's 'the fruite' works for 184 if we take *purpose* as the subject which *sticks* the unripe fruit on the tree, but breaks down in 185.

186–7 'It is essential that we forget the debts we owe to ourselves.' The idea that promises (such as the one not to remarry) must necessarily be forgotten could be seen as cynical or just realistic.

190–1 i.e. violent grief and joy destroy themselves in the very act of manifesting or fulfilling themselves. See *RJ* 2.6.9: 'These violent delights have violent ends.'

191 *enactures* actions – a Shakespearean coinage. F's word is also unique; both relate to *enact* at 99.

193 **Grief . . . grieves* i.e. grief turns into joy, joy turns into grief; see *R2* 1.3.258–61 for a comparable play on the reversal of *grief* and *joy. TxC* suggests Q2's copy may have read 'Greefes ioy, ioy griefes'.
slender accident the slightest occasion

194 *aye* ever

196 *prove* resolve, answer

197 *lead* dominates, is stronger than

198 *down* disgraced, out of favour
favourite flies favoured supporter runs away, abandons him

184 *like*] F; the *Q2*   190 *either*] other *F*   191 *enactures*] ennactors *F*   193 *joys*] F; ioy *Q2*   *grieves*] F; griefes *Q2*   198 *favourite*] fauourites *F*

The poor advanced makes friends of enemies,
And hitherto doth Love on Fortune tend,   200
For who not needs shall never lack a friend,
And who in want a hollow friend doth try
Directly seasons him his enemy.
But orderly to end where I begun,
Our wills and fates do so contrary run   205
That our devices still are overthrown.
Our thoughts are ours, their ends none of our own:
So think thou wilt no second husband wed
But die thy thoughts when thy first lord is dead.

PLAYER QUEEN

Nor earth to me give food nor heaven light,   210
Sport and repose lock from me day and night.
To desperation turn my trust and hope
And anchor's cheer in prison be my scope.
Each opposite that blanks the face of joy
Meet what I would have well and it destroy.   215
Both here and hence pursue me lasting strife
If once I be a widow ever I be a wife.

HAMLET   If she should break it now!

---

201 **who not needs** the person who has no need
of one
202 **try** test, make trial of
203 **seasons him** turns him into
206 **devices** plans, intentions
still always
209 **die thy thoughts** either indicative ('your
thoughts will or may die') or imperative
('let your thoughts die')
210 **Nor . . . nor** neither . . . nor
211 **Sport** recreation, entertainment
213 **And anchor's cheer** and the fare or diet of
an anchorite, a hermit. (Theobald and others,
e.g. Jenkins and Edwards, emend 'And' to
'An', but this is not strictly necessary.)

scope portion, limit
214 **opposite** opposing quality or force
blanks either (1) blenches, turns pale, or
(2) makes blank. Shakespeare does not use
blank as a verb elsewhere.
215 'encounter and destroy everything I want
to go well'
216 **and hence** in the next world
217 **I be . . . I be** The first *I be* in Q2 may be a
'false start' or anticipatory error.
218 **i.e.** it would be particularly shocking if
she were to break her vow after these
emphatic words. As at 175, Q2 prints the
SP and Hamlet's words in the right-hand
margin.

---

210 *me give*] giue me *F*   212–13] *om. F*   213 *And anchor's*] *(*And Anchors*)*; An Anchor's *Theobald*;
And anchors' *Jennens*   217] If once a widdow, euer I be wife. *Q1F; If, once a widow, ever I be a wife.*
Ard[F]   218] *Q1 subst., F; opp. 216–17 Q2*

PLAYER KING

    'Tis deeply sworn. Sweet, leave me here awhile.

    My spirits grow dull, and fain I would beguile   220

    The tedious day with sleep.

PLAYER QUEEN   *Sleep rock thy brain,*

    And never come mischance between us twain.

                            Exit. [He sleeps.]

HAMLET   Madam, how like you this play?

QUEEN   The lady doth protest too much, methinks.

HAMLET   O, but she'll keep her word.   225

KING   Have you heard the argument? Is there no offence in't?

HAMLET   No, no, they do but jest. Poison in jest. No offence i'th' world.

KING   What do you call the play?   230

HAMLET   *The Mousetrap.* Marry, how tropically! This

---

220 *fain* willingly

222 SD Q2 has '*Exeunt*' after '*twain*', but presumably the Player King feigns sleep, as F's SD indicates; the onstage audience treat this as an interval in which they can talk.

224 The Queen's response (in a line which subsequently became quasi-proverbial) can be played so as to indicate her discomfort, her self-control, or her innocence.

    doth ... much makes too many protestations (of her determination not to marry again)

226–7 These questions are perhaps addressed to Polonius rather than to Hamlet, though the latter replies. They have been taken as evidence that the King did not attend to the dumb-show, or alternatively as evidence that he did, and is now getting suspicious.

226, 229 **offence** The word echoes from Hamlet and Horatio's conversation about the Ghost at 1.5.136–9. In 1600 a monarch might be expected to find *offence* in a play which was less than circumspect on matters of state or religion, or which offered satirical comments that might be construed personally.

228 **Poison** This is the first time poison is specifically mentioned, though of course it has featured in the dumb-show.

231 *The Mousetrap* Having previously asked the Players for *The Murder of Gonzago* (see 2.2.474), Hamlet presumably invents this title with reference to his own intention of trapping the King.

    Marry, how tropically i.e. Yes indeed, by what an appropriate trope or play on words. Jenkins defends Q2's punctuation (also found in Q1) against F's (see t.n.); Q1's 'trapically' suggests a play on 'trap'.

---

222 SD *Exit*] *Q1 (exit Lady), F; Exeunt Q2 He sleeps*] *F (Sleepes), opp. 221*   224 doth protest] protests *Q1F*   231 how tropically!] *Ard²; how tropically, Q2; how tropically: Q1; how? Tropically: F*

play is the image of a murder done in Vienna. Gonzago
is the duke's name, his wife Baptista. You shall see
anon 'tis a knavish piece of work, but what of that?
Your majesty and we that have free souls – it touches us   235
not. Let the galled jade wince, our withers are unwrung.

Enter Lucianus.

This is one Lucianus, nephew to the king.

OPHELIA   You are as good as a chorus, my lord.

HAMLET   I could interpret between you and your love if I
could see the puppets dallying.   240

232–3 **Gonzago ... name** The play's title
taken alone could be ambiguous; Gonzago
is clearly the victim of the crime in Q2 and
F; in the putative source he is one of the
murderers (see p. 62 and Bullough, 7. 172–
3). Q1 has '*Albertus*' as the victim's name,
while in *Fratricide Punished* (which lacks
any equivalent of 'Aeneas' talk to Dido' in
2.2) Hamlet names the victim as 'King
Pyrrhus' (2.8; Bullough, 7.142). The use of
duke here may relate to the putative source.

233 **Baptista** used as a male name for the father
of Katherina and Bianca in Shakespeare's
TS

235 **free** i.e. from guilt

236 **Let ... wince** let the horse that is saddle-
sore kick out (i.e. let the guilty person
object or suffer). (Edwards retains Q2/ F's
'winch'; Q1's 'wince' is the same word
according to *OED*.)

our ... unwrung i.e. we are unaffected.
The *withers* are the highest part of a horse's
back, liable to be *galled* by the saddle;
Dent cites 'Touch (rub) a galled horse on
the back and he will wince (kick)' as
proverbial (H700).

237 **nephew** The word is capitalized in Q2,
perhaps for emphasis. Neither of the
murderers is a nephew of the victim in the
source given by Bullough, nor a brother –
which would be more relevant to the
King's crime. In *Fratricide Punished*
Hamlet does indeed identify the poisoner
as 'the King's brother' (2.8; Bullough,
7.142). Perhaps Hamlet is looking forward
to (or even threatening) his own revenge on
his uncle.

238 **as good as a** Tronch-Pérez finds this 'less
direct and more submissive' than F's 'a
good'. See also 3.1.96n.

chorus an actor whose role is to mediate
the story to the audience; Shakespeare used
this device in *H5, Per* and *WT*.

239–40 i.e. I could act as a chorus between you
and your love (or lover) if I could see the
puppets performing. Hamlet sees himself
as a puppet-master who would *interpret* or
provide a commentary on the show. It
seems possible that *puppets* has a sexual
meaning, related to the use of 'poop' for
the vagina (see Hulme, 114); Q1 has
'poopies'.

---

233 duke's] *Q1F;* King's *Hudson*   234 of that] A that *Q1;* o'that *F*   236 wince] *Q1;* winch *Q2F*
unwrung] *(unwrong)*   236.1] *F; after 237 Q2*   238 as good as a] *Q1;* a good *F*

OPHELIA   You are keen, my lord, you are keen.

HAMLET   It would cost you a groaning to take off mine edge.

OPHELIA   Still better and worse.

HAMLET   So you mistake your husbands. Begin, 245 murderer: leave thy damnable faces and begin. Come, 'the croaking raven doth bellow for revenge.'

LUCIANUS

Thoughts black, hands apt, drugs fit, and time agreeing,
Considerate season else no creature seeing,

241 Ophelia puts off the innuendo as a joke.
   keen sharp, incisive
242 **groaning** variously glossed as the cry of a woman losing her virginity (Jenkins, Hibbard) or the pain of childbirth (Spencer, Edwards)
242–3 **take . . . edge** put off or deter my jokes; blunt the edge of my sexual desire
244 **better and worse** wittier and more offensive; as Theobald puts it, 'his Wit is *smarter*, tho' his Meaning is more *blunt*' (*Restored*, 90).
245 **So . . . husbands** Hamlet alludes to the Christian wedding ceremony in which bride and groom promise to take each other 'for better or for worse'; he implies that women *mistake* their husbands, i.e. take other men. Spencer adopts Q1's 'must take' for *mistake*, and so do some productions, but the play on *take/mistake* has a precedent in *R2* 3.3.10–16.
246 **damnable faces** execrable grimaces
247 **'the croaking . . . revenge'** a version of two lines from *The True Tragedy of Richard III* (*c.* 1591): 'The screeching raven sits croaking for revenge, / Whole herds of beasts come bellowing for revenge' (Bullough, 3.339, 1892–3). This play was in the repertory of the Queen's Men, to which company Shakespeare probably

belonged before 1592, and the lines are from Richard's speech before the battle of Bosworth in which he imagines his victims calling for revenge; the word 'revenge' occurs 16 times in the first 23 lines. In Shakespeare's own version of the sequence, the ghosts repeat the refrain 'despair and die' and the word 'revenge' is not used until Richard's waking soliloquy (*R3* 5.3.119–78 and 187). The murder of Gonzago is not in fact presented as a revenge killing in any of the three texts, but obviously this is appropriate to Hamlet's own situation.

248–53 Some commentators have suggested that these lines are the ones inserted by Hamlet (see 77n. and 180–209n.). Irving (see Fig. 16) and other performers of Hamlet have ('often', according to Rosenberg, 593) mouthed or spoken them along with the poisoner.

249 *Considerate* If this is right it must mean 'appropriate' or 'deliberately chosen'; Q1/F's 'Confederate' must mean 'conspiring'. Both usages are unusual and are not found elsewhere in Shakespeare. Assuming the use of a long 's', it would be easy to mistake one word for the other, especially in a printed form.
   else . . . seeing no other person present as witness

242 mine] my *F*   245 mistake] *F;* must take *Q1;* mis-take *Capell*   your] *Q1; om. F*   246 leave] poxe, leaue *Q1F*   247 'the . . . revenge'] *as quotation White*   249 *Considerate*] Confederate *Q1F*

Thou mixture rank, of midnight weeds collected,   250
With Hecate's ban thrice blasted, thrice infected,
Thy natural magic and dire property
On wholesome life usurps immediately.
   [*Pours the poison in his ears.*]

HAMLET 'A poisons him i'th' garden for his estate. His name's Gonzago. The story is extant and written in 255 very choice Italian. You shall see anon how the murderer gets the love of Gonzago's wife.

OPHELIA The King rises.

QUEEN How fares my lord?

POLONIUS Give o'er the play.   260

KING Give me some light, away.

POLONIUS Lights! Lights! Lights!

Exeunt all but Hamlet and Horatio.

250 **rank** offensive, malign; see other uses of *rank* and *ranker* at 1.2.136, 2.1.20, 3.3.36, 3.4.90, 146 and 150 and 4.4.21. **of ... collected** concocted from weeds gathered at midnight (and hence assumed to be more noxious); see also 4.7.143 and n.

251 **Hecate** goddess of witchcraft; the metre requires the name to have two syllables here, though it could also have three.
ban curse (Q1's 'bane' = poison)
thrice To repeat something three times often adds power in religious or superstitious contexts; see 'Thrice the brinded cat hath mewed' (*Mac* 4.1.1). Hecate was also known as 'triple Hecate' (see *MND* 5.1.378) because she was personified as Cynthia in heaven, Diana on earth and Proserpina in hell.
*infected Q2's 'inuected' could conceivably mean 'cursed' (as in 'invective'), but *OED* does not record 'to invect' in this sense before 1614.

252 **dire property** evil power or capacity
253 **usurps** [*On*] supplants, takes wrongfully; see 1.1.45 and n.
253 SD *from F and clearly necessary
254 **'A** he
     estate wealth, property
256 **anon** soon
258–9 Jenkins includes Hamlet's additional line from Q1/F (see t.n.), presumably on the grounds that it was an accidental omission in Q2.
260 **Give o'er** give up, abandon
261 If torches are used (see 85.1–2n.), the King may at this point snatch one of them from an attendant as he leaves, but presumably he is trying to retain his composure.
262 SP See t.n.; in performance the cry may be begun by Polonius/Corambis and taken up by others; alternatively, Polonius may demonstrate his loyalty to the King while the others watch silently.

251 ban] *F;* bane *Q1, Q5, F4*   infected] *Q1, Q3, F;* inuected *Q2*   253 usurps] *Q1;* vsurpe *F*   SD] *F; not in Q2; exit. Q1*   254 'A] He *Q1F*   for his] *Q1;* for's *F*   255 written] writ *F*   256 very] *om. F* 258] *Cor.* The king rises, lights hoe. / *Exeunt King and Lordes.* / *Ham.* What, frighted with false fires? *Q1; Ophe.* The King rises. / *Ham.* What, frighted with false fire. *F*   262 SP] *All. F*

HAMLET

> Why let the stricken deer go weep,
> The hart ungalled play,
> For some must watch while some must sleep.   265
> Thus runs the world away.
> Would not this, sir, and a forest of feathers, if the rest
> of my fortunes turn Turk with me, with provincial
> roses on my razed shoes, get me a fellowship in a cry of
> players?   270

HORATIO   Half a share.

HAMLET   A whole one, I.

---

262 SD In some productions the disconcerted
players linger for a while until Hamlet
dismisses them with a gesture or a courtier
returns to usher them off. The abrupt end to
the 'show' recalls the equally
unceremonious dismissal of the 'Worthies'
at *LLL* 5.2.715.

263–6 These lines seem to be a stanza from an
otherwise unknown ballad. The contrast
between the *stricken* (wounded) deer and
the *ungalled* (uninjured) hart continues the
metaphor of the *galled jade* introduced by
Hamlet at 236 and presumably reflects on
the contrast between the guilty King and
the innocent Prince. Dent cites 'As the
stricken deer withdraws himself to die' as
proverbial (D189), so perhaps Hamlet is
speculating optimistically on the
consequences of the King's departure.
Actors of Hamlet are usually excited and
exultant, sometimes manic and even
hysterical, at this point, recalling his
behaviour after the encounter with the
Ghost in 1.5 (see Rosenberg; Hapgood).

265 **watch** stay awake.

266 **Thus . . . away** i.e. This is the way of the
world. Wiles reads this as an explicit

reminder that Will Kempe had sold his
share in the Chamberlain's Men and thus
'danced himself out of the world' (see 36–
7n. and 118n.)

267 **this** i.e. my contribution to the play
forest of feathers Hamlet assumes that
actors favoured extravagantly plumed
hats.

268 **turn . . . me** desert me, betray me (like a
Christian renouncing his faith to become a
Muslim)

268–9 **provincial roses** rosettes in the French
style of Provins or Provence – like the
feathers of 267, an affected style (Jenkins,
LN)

269 **razed** (fashionably) slashed
fellowship share, partnership; like the one
Shakespeare had with the Chamberlain's
Men whereby he received a share of their
profits (see 266n.)
cry pack – a contemptuous expression

271 Horatio seems to evince some degree of
scepticism about the scale of Hamlet's
success, and his replies at 280 and 282 are
non-committal. In general his response to
Hamlet's elation is muted (see 5.2.56n. for
his apparent neutrality later).

---

266 Thus] *Q1;* So *F*   268 with provincial] with two Prouinciall *F*   270 players] Players sir *F* 272 A
whole one, I] *F;* Ay, a whole one *Hanmer;* A whole one; – ay *Rann (Malone)*

For thou dost know, O Damon dear,
This realm dismantled was
Of Jove himself, and now reigns here   275
A very, very pajock.

HORATIO   You might have rhymed.

HAMLET   O good Horatio, I'll take the Ghost's word
for a thousand pound. Didst perceive?

HORATIO   Very well, my lord.   280

HAMLET   Upon the talk of the poisoning.

HORATIO   I did very well note him.

HAMLET   Ah ha! Come, some music! Come, the
recorders!

    For if the King like not the comedy   285
    Why then belike he likes it not, perdie.
Come, some music!

273–6 As with the stanza at 263–6, no source has been identified.

273 **Damon** Hamlet apparently addresses Horatio as *Damon* in an allusion to the story of the ideal friendship between Damon and Pythias. (Richard Edwards's play, *Damon and Pithias*, was acted in 1564 and printed in 1571.)

274 **dismantled** deprived, divested (a metaphor from clothing)

275 **Jove himself** Hamlet is presumably comparing his father with Jove (see the comparisons with Hyperion, Jove, Mars and Mercury at 3.4.54–6).

276 **pajock** Horatio might expect Hamlet to end with 'ass'; Q2/F's 'paiock' is obscure: some commentators argue for a variant of 'peacock' (Jennens quotes Pope on the fable of the birds choosing a peacock as their king rather than an eagle; Caldecott cites a 1613 text which attributes to Circe the power to turn 'proud fooles into peacocks'); others for 'patchcock' or 'patchock', a word which is used uniquely

by Edmund Spenser with reference to the degeneration of the English in Ireland (see Jenkins, LN).

284 **recorders** wind instruments, flutes. Hamlet calls for music again at 287; the players eventually appear with recorders at 336.1. (If casting allows, an attendant should presumably leave the stage to convey Hamlet's request, but it has not been customary to add a SD.)

286 Hamlet may be alluding to a line in Thomas Kyd's *The Spanish Tragedy* (c. 1587) spoken by Hieronimo with reference to his own forthcoming play-within-the-play: 'And if the world like not this tragedy, / Hard is the hap of old Hieronimo' (4.1.197–8). Actual revenge killings occur in the course of Hieronimo's play: perhaps Hamlet changes 'tragedy' to *comedy* because he has not reached this point yet.

286 **belike** perhaps. Johnson prints '*belike* –' and comments, 'Hamlet was going on to draw the consequence, when the courtiers entered.' **perdie** by god (French *pardieu*)

274–5] *F lines* himselfe, / heere. /   276 very, very] very, very – *Warburton*   pajock] *(paiock)*, F *(Paiocke)*, F2 *(Pajocke)*; Paicock *Q6*; Pecock *Q9*; peacock *Pope*   283 Ah ha!] Oh, ha? *F*

Enter ROSENCRANTZ *and* GUILDENSTERN.

GUILDENSTERN   Good my lord, vouchsafe me a word
   with you.

HAMLET   Sir, a whole history.   290

GUILDENSTERN   The King, sir –

HAMLET   Ay, sir, what of him?

GUILDENSTERN   – is in his retirement marvellous
   distempered.

HAMLET   With drink, sir?   295

GUILDENSTERN   No, my lord, with choler.

HAMLET   Your wisdom should show itself more richer to
   signify this to the doctor, for for me to put him to his
   purgation would perhaps plunge him into more choler.

GUILDENSTERN   Good my lord, put your discourse into   300
   some frame and start not so wildly from my affair.

287.1 F's earlier placing (see t.n.) may suggest
   that the appearance of the two spying
   courtiers motivates Hamlet's further burst
   of manic behaviour (though Edwards
   suggests that he 'pointedly ignores' them).
   TxC takes Q1's agreement with the earlier
   placing of this SD as confirmation that it
   reflects stage practice.
288 **Good my lord** Guildenstern's mode of
   address is carefully deferential (see also 296,
   300, Rosencrantz at 328, and see 1.2.168n.).
   vouchsafe grant, condescend to give. It
   seems possible that Guildenstern's language
   is generally rather formal or pretentious
   here and that Hamlet mocks it in his replies,
   as he does with Osric at 5.2.68–163.
290 **history** story, narrative
293 **his retirement** his withdrawal to his
   private chambers
   marvellous marvellously; see 2.1.3n.
294 **distempered** out of temper (but it could
   also mean 'drunk', which is how Hamlet
   takes it)

296 **choler** anger
297 **more richer** much more rich or
   resourceful. Shakespeare and his
   contemporaries often use double
   comparatives (see Blake, 3.2.3.4; Hope,
   1.2.3).
298 **signify** communicate
299 **purgation** A purgation could be physical
   (medical) but Hamlet presumably also has
   in mind the spiritual sense (as in
   'purgatory': see 3.3.85n.).
301 **frame** coherent shape or order
   *start F's reading is generally adopted and
   taken to mean 'shy away' or 'move
   quickly'. Q2's 'stare' might not be
   impossible as a description of Hamlet's
   attitude or behaviour (see *R2* 5.3.23–4,
   where Henry IV asks of Aumerle: 'What
   means / Our cousin, that he stares and
   looks so wildly?'), but 'stare from' is not
   idiomatic and *e/t* is an easy misreading.
   from my affair away from my business or
   message

287.1] *after 282* F; *after 285 Johnson*   296 with] rather with *F*   298 the] his *F*   for for] *F*; for *F2*
299 more] farre more *F*   300–1] *F*; *Q2 lines* frame, / affaire. /   301 start] *F*; stare *Q2*

HAMLET   I am tame, sir, pronounce.

GUILDENSTERN   The Queen your mother in most great affliction of spirit hath sent me to you.

HAMLET   You are welcome.   305

GUILDENSTERN   Nay, good my lord, this courtesy is not of the right breed. If it shall please you to make me a wholesome answer, I will do your mother's commandment. If not, your pardon and my return shall be the end of business.   310

HAMLET   Sir, I cannot.

ROSENCRANTZ   What, my lord?

HAMLET   Make you a wholesome answer. My wit's diseased. But, sir, such answer as I can make you shall command. Or rather, as you say, my mother. Therefore   315 no more. But to the matter – my mother, you say?

ROSENCRANTZ   Then thus she says. Your behaviour hath struck her into amazement and admiration.

HAMLET   O wonderful son that can so 'stonish a mother! But is there no sequel at the heels of this mother's   320 admiration? Impart.

ROSENCRANTZ   She desires to speak with you in her closet ere you go to bed.

302 **tame** calm, subdued
   pronounce i.e. deliver your message
305 We may assume from Guildenstern's response that Hamlet's words are not in fact courteous: perhaps he says them in an exaggerated way, or indicates that the sending of Guildenstern is the end of the matter.
307 **breed** (1) kind; (2) breeding in manners
308 **wholesome** healthy, i.e. sane
309 **pardon** permission to leave
312 SP Capell explains the abrupt switch of speaker in Q2 (see t.n.) by suggesting that Hamlet's *Sir, I cannot* is spoken 'somewhat

brusquely, and the receiver [Guildenstern] makes a bow and retires: Hamlet answers to Rosencrantz without considering which of them spoke.'
315 **Or . . . mother** i.e. it is my mother who is doing the commanding (see 308–9)
318 **admiration** wonder (not necessarily approving)
319 **'stonish** astonish
323 **closet** a private chamber used for prayer, study or, in the case of Ophelia's closet at 2.1.74, needlework. A closet was not necessarily a bedroom, though it is often

310 business] my Businesse *F*   312 SP] *Guild. F*   314 answer] answers *F*   315 as you] you *F* 319 'stonish] astonish *F*   321 Impart] *om. F*

HAMLET   We shall obey, were she ten times our mother.
Have you any further trade with us?   325
ROSENCRANTZ   My lord, you once did love me.
HAMLET   And do still, by these pickers and stealers.
ROSENCRANTZ   Good my lord, what is your cause of
distemper? You do surely bar the door upon your own
liberty if you deny your griefs to your friend.   330
HAMLET   Sir, I lack advancement.
ROSENCRANTZ   How can that be, when you have the
voice of the King himself for your succession in
Denmark?
HAMLET   Ay, sir, but while the grass grows – the proverb 335
is something musty.

Enter the Players *with recorders.*

O, the recorders! Let me see one. To withdraw with
you, why do you go about to recover the wind of me, as

presented as one onstage. Jardine (150) emphasizes the privacy of closets, but Orlin modifies this view by demonstrating from letters, diaries, wills and inventories that closets served a range of purposes.

324 **We . . . our** Hamlet's first use of the royal plural may be a deliberate distancing tactic.

325 **trade** business – perhaps used contemptuously

327 **pickers and stealers** hands; so-called from the Catechism in the Book of Common Prayer where the person being catechized promises to 'keep my hands from picking and stealing'

328–9 **your . . . distemper** the cause of your illness or disorder

329 **surely . . . upon** Hibbard defends F (see t.n.) as an authorial 'second thought' which adds 'a touch of wit'.

332–4 **when . . . Denmark** i.e. when the King

himself has said you are to succeed him on the throne

335 **while . . . grows** Tilley cites 'While the grass grows the horse starves' (G423).

336 **something musty** either 'a stale thing' or 'somewhat stale'. Perhaps Hamlet means that his situation, as well as the proverb, is a familiar one.

336.1 In Q1 Hamlet simply produces a pipe himself.

337 **withdraw** be private – presumably Hamlet motions Rosencrantz and Guildenstern away from the players to address them more confidentially. Or perhaps he separates Guildenstern from Rosencrantz.

338 **recover . . . me** get to windward of me. In hunting this would be a deliberate tactic to cause the quarry to move away from the scent of the hunter and towards the trap he has prepared.

327 And] So I *F*   329 surely] freely *F*   upon] of *F*   335 sir] *om. F*   336.1] *after 334; Enter one with a Recorder. F*   337 recorders] Recorder *F*   one] *om. F*

if you would drive me into a toil?

GUILDENSTERN   O my lord, if my duty be too bold, my   340
love is too unmannerly.

HAMLET   I do not well understand that. Will you play
upon this pipe?

GUILDENSTERN   My lord, I cannot.

HAMLET   I pray you.   345

GUILDENSTERN   Believe me, I cannot.

HAMLET   I do beseech you.

GUILDENSTERN   I know no touch of it, my lord.

HAMLET   It is as easy as lying. Govern these ventages with
your fingers and thumb, give it breath with your   350
mouth, and it will discourse most eloquent music. Look
you, these are the stops.

GUILDENSTERN   But these cannot I command to any
utterance of harmony. I have not the skill.

HAMLET   Why, look you now how unworthy a thing you   355

---

339 **toil** net or trap
340–1 **if ... unmannerly** i.e. if I am too
forward in doing what I see as my duty
(asking you about your *distemper*), it is my
love for you that causes me to forget my
manners.
342 **I ... that** Hamlet presumably implies that
he has no confidence in Guildenstern's
avowed love.
342–63 **Will ... me** This was for Grigori
Kozintsev, director of the 1964 Russian
film version, 'the most important passage
in the tragedy' defining the ultimate
inability of the state and its informers to
penetrate the *mystery* of the individual
(quoted by Dawson, 187–8).
348 **know ... it** do not have the skill to play it
349 **as ... lying** 'I accept from Kittredge, but
cannot confirm, that this was proverbial'
(Jenkins).

Govern This is apparently a technical
term: see 'He hath played on this prologue
like a child on a recorder; a sound, but not
in government' (*MND* 5.1.122–3).
ventages vents or holes
350 ***fingers and thumb** Attempts to explain
Q2's reading (see t.n.) are unconvincing.
Capell prints Q2 but does not gloss.
351–2, 355 **Look you** Hamlet has used this
expression earlier in F (1.5.131) and Q1
(5.101); Edwards notes at that point that it
is 'a characteristic turn of Hamlet's
speech'.
352 **stops** the same as *ventages*: the holes
which the musician's fingers must stop or
block
354 **utterance of harmony** harmonious
(musical) sound or expression
355 **unworthy** contemptible, easy to
manipulate

---

349 It is] 'Tis *F*   350 fingers] finger *F*   thumb] *F;* the vmber *Q2;* the thumb *Q3*   351 eloquent] excellent
F

make of me: you would play upon me! You would seem
to know my stops, you would pluck out the heart of my
mystery, you would sound me from my lowest note to
my compass. And there is much music, excellent voice,
in this little organ. Yet cannot you make it speak. 360
'Sblood! Do you think I am easier to be played on than
a pipe? Call me what instrument you will, though you
fret me you cannot play upon me.

Enter POLONIUS.

God bless you, sir.

POLONIUS   My lord, the Queen would speak with you, 365
and presently.

HAMLET   Do you see yonder cloud that's almost in shape
of a camel?

---

358 **mystery** (1) secret; (2) skill at a craft or
trade (such as, here, playing an instrument)
sound me (1) play on me, cause me to
make sounds; (2) explore my depths, probe
me (see 2.1.41, 3.1.7)

358–9 **to my compass** to my limit; see 'Above
the reach or compass of thy thought' (*2H6*
1.2.46). F's reading (see t.n.) makes the
metaphor from music more explicit: see
OED compass *sb.* I 10: 'the full range of
tones which a voice or musical instrument
is capable of producing'.

360 **organ** instrument, i.e. the recorder
speak i.e. make music

361 **'Sblood** an oath (by God's blood). Some
performers break the recorder in rage at
this point.

362–3 **Call . . . me** That the metaphor 'to play
upon a person' was current is demonstrated
by parallels in Ben Jonson's *Everyman Out*
(1599; Induction, 319) and in Thomas
Dekker and Thomas Middleton's *The*

Roaring Girl (1611; 4.1.211–13).

362–3 ***you fret me** (1) you can manipulate my
'frets' (ridges to guide the fingers on lutes
or other stringed instruments – not strictly
relevant to wind instruments, as Hamlet
seems to acknowledge); (2) you can
make me angry. Q2's 'not' seems to be an
error.

364 **God . . . sir** These words are presumably
addressed to Polonius, although in all three
texts he enters after they are spoken. If they
are addressed to Guildenstern they may be
pronounced as a sarcastic dismissal, or as
part of Hamlet's generally manic
behaviour. Jenkins raises but rejects the
suggestion that they are addressed to a
player as Hamlet returns the recorder.

366 **and presently** *and* emphasizes the sense of
'immediately'.

367–73 Since this scene is supposedly set
indoors at night, it is generally played
as if Hamlet is pretending to see

---

358 to] to the top of *F*   360 speak] *om. F*   361 'Sblood] Why *F;* Zownds *Q1*   think] *Q1;* thinke, that
F   363 fret me] Ard²; fret me not *Q2;* can frett mee, yet *Q1;* can fret me, *F*   363.1] *Capell; after 364
Q2*   367 yonder] *Q1;* that *F*   368 of] *Q1;* like *F*

POLONIUS   By th' mass and 'tis like a camel indeed.

HAMLET   Methinks it is like a weasel.   370

POLONIUS   It is backed like a weasel.

HAMLET   Or like a whale?

POLONIUS   Very like a whale.

HAMLET   Then I will come to my mother, by and by.

[*aside*] They fool me to the top of my bent. – I will   375
come by and by. – Leave me, friends. – I will. Say so.
'By and by' is easily said.   [*Exeunt all but Hamlet.*]
'Tis now the very witching time of night

clouds and Polonius is humouring what he assumes to be madness. It would have made different and better sense in the open-air Globe (where indeed, in 2000, spectators looked up at the sky as Hamlet gestured). It would be possible in a modern theatre to have the actors approach (or pretend to approach) a window.

371 Its back is like that of a weasel. Either Hamlet enjoys contradicting himself and exposing Polonius' insincerity, since a weasel is very unlike a camel, or we assume that the supposed cloud is changing very rapidly, like the one evoked by Antony at *AC* 4.14.1–11. If the former, Hamlet plays the same trick on Osric in 5.2.

374 **by and by** immediately

375 **to . . . bent** to my full extent. The metaphor is from bending a bow, as at 2.2.30.

376–7 **Leave . . . said** This is all part of Hamlet's speech in Q2 and can make sense as a mixture of address to the others and private reflection. Most editors and productions however follow F in giving 'I will say so' to Polonius, and moving 'Leave me friends' to after 'easily said'. *TxC* suggests that Q2's copy was confusing

at this point; certainly H4ᵛ omits '*Ham.*' from the catchwords '*Ham.* Then' at the bottom of H4ʳ, implying that Polonius speaks everything from 374 to the end of the scene.

377 SD *Q2 has an '*Exit*' for Hamlet at the end of the scene but no exit direction for any of the others; F has an '*Exit*' for Polonius after his line 'I will say so.' It seems logical in both texts that not only Polonius but also Horatio, Rosencrantz and Guildenstern should obey Hamlet's instruction, *Leave me, friends*, and that he should be alone onstage for his final speech. Q1's SDs are the fullest here with an '*Exit*' for Rossencraft and Gilderstone before the entry of Corambis, an '*exit*' for Corambis after 'Very like a whale', and an '*exit*' for Horatio after he and Hamlet have bidden each other goodnight; Q1 is the only text to pay any attention to Horatio or give him any dialogue after the equivalent of the entry of the others at 287 SD.

378 **witching time** hour appropriate for witchcraft (see *Mac* 2.1.49–52); another opportunity for a bell to chime or a clock to strike (see 1.1.5n., 1.4.3n. and 3.4.99.1n.).

369 mass] Misse *F*   'tis] it's *F*   370, 371 a weasel] *Q1F;* an Ouzle *Pope*   371 backed] *Q1F;* black *Q3*
374–7] *Pope; Q2 lines* and by, / & by, / friends. / said, /   374 SP] *Q1F; only in H4ʳ catchword Q2* I will]
i'le *Q1;* will I *F*   375 SD] *Staunton; to Hor. Capell*   377 SD] *Steevens² subst.; Exe. / Rowe*

354

When churchyards yawn and hell itself breaks out
Contagion to this world. Now could I drink hot blood 380
And do such business as the bitter day
Would quake to look on. Soft, now to my mother.
O heart, lose not thy nature. Let not ever
The soul of Nero enter this firm bosom –
Let me be cruel, not unnatural: 385
I will speak daggers to her but use none.
My tongue and soul in this be hypocrites.
How in my words somever she be shent
To give them seals never my soul consent. *Exit.*

---

379 **yawn** open wide like mouths (to let out the dead)

379–80 **breaks out / Contagion** lets loose its pestilence or poison. Jenkins adopts F's 'breaths' for *breaks*, perhaps as a better parallel with *yawn*.

380 **drink hot blood** Witches were supposed to do this; it seems in the spirit of Lucianus' '*Thoughts black*' speech at 248–53. See also *E3*, where the Prince offers 'the blood of captive kings' as a 'restorative' to the wounded Audley (4.7.31–2). Edwards argues (52) that Hamlet is disgusted by the thought rather than relishing it.

381 **the bitter day** Perhaps 'the judgemental day', or even doomsday. F has 'bitter businesse as the day', which has been widely adopted (though not in the eighteenth century, when editors such as Warburton and Steevens objected to 'bitter business' as a 'burlesque' or 'vulgar' expression).

382 **Soft** be quiet, that's enough

383 **lose . . . nature** do not deny or betray your natural (filial) feelings

384 **Nero** the Roman emperor who had his mother Agrippina murdered. Shakespeare refers to the story that he subsequently

ripped open her womb in *KJ* 5.2.152–3. Dowden points out that Agrippina was accused of poisoning her husband and living with her brother.

firm resolved (i.e against doing violence)

385 Hamlet presumably means that it will be *cruel* to attack his mother verbally but *unnatural* to attack her physically.

386 **daggers** Most editors emend Q2's 'dagger' on the analogy of 'She speaks poniards' (*MA* 2.1.232–3); 'to speak daggers' or 'to look daggers' became proverbial (Dent, D8.1).

387 Hamlet seems to mean that he will behave hypocritically or deceitfully in merely scolding his mother when in his soul he wants to do her physical harm. Hibbard, however, paraphrases: 'let my soul pretend a savage purpose it does not feel, and let my words express it.'

388 **How . . . somever** however
shent rebuked, scolded (past participle of the archaic verb *shend*)

389 **To . . . seals** to act on them; the royal *seal* ratified the words of a decree or proclamation, requiring its enactment (see also 61n. and 3.4.59n.)

---

379 breaks] breaths *F*   381 business . . . bitter] bitter businesse as the *F*   382 Soft, now] Soft now, *F*   386 daggers] *Q1F;* dagger *Q2*   388 somever] *F;* soever *Q5*   389 SD] *Q1; om. F*

[3.3] *Enter* KING, ROSENCRANTZ *and* GUILDENSTERN.

KING

I like him not, nor stands it safe with us
To let his madness range. Therefore prepare you.
I your commission will forthwith dispatch
And he to England shall along with you.
The terms of our estate may not endure   5
Hazard so near us as doth hourly grow
Out of his brows.

GUILDENSTERN   We will ourselves provide.
Most holy and religious fear it is

3.3 The three texts: this scene runs to 33 lines in Q1 (scene 10) and 98 in both Q2 and F. Q1 omits the dialogue between the King and Rosencrantz and Guildenstern as well as the appearance of Polonius/Corambis; it begins at the equivalent of 36. Location and timing: this scene follows on immediately after 3.2. *Fratricide Punished* specifies the setting as 'A church and altar' (3.1; Bullough, 7.143) and many productions do something similar. This would be an appropriate setting for the King's attempt at prayer, though it raises questions about why Hamlet's route to the Queen's closet should pass through a church or chapel; such questions would not arise on the unlocalized Elizabethan stage.

1 **him** his condition or behaviour
 nor . . . us and it is not consistent with our (my) safety

2 **range** roam freely

3 **commission** presumably the *grand commission* Hamlet describes intercepting at 5.2.18; it is never made absolutely clear whether Rosencrantz and Guildenstern know they are conducting Hamlet not just to exile but to his death (see 5.2.57n.).
 dispatch prepare promptly

4 **along** go along; see 1.1.25.

5 **terms . . . estate** responsibilities of my

position (as king)

6 **near us** F's 'dangerous' can hardly be a misreading; with 'lunacies' in 7 it provides a stronger reading.

7 **Out . . . brows** i.e. out of his mental disorder or threatening looks, the brow being seen as revealing one's state of mind, as at *R2* 4.1.331: 'I see your brows are full of discontent' (see also 3.4.40–2 and n.) F's 'Lunacies' for *brows* is printed by Hibbard, while Edwards defends *brows*, which he glosses as 'effrontery'; Jenkins (LN) rejects both 'Lunacies' here and 'dangerous' in 6 as 'stopgaps supplied, consciously or not, by a recollection of *dangerous lunacy* in 3.1.4'. (Seary, 164, endorses Theobald's emendation to 'lunes', adopted by Malone.)

7–23 **We . . . groan** In performance, the King sometimes displays impatience (or even, appropriately, embarrassment) during these speeches which attest to an Elizabethan ideal of kingship. See also the Messenger's rhetoric at 4.5.99–108.

7 **ourselves provide** prepare or equip ourselves

8 **fear** Guildenstern must mean something like 'concern': he is not accusing the King of being afraid but rather praising his caution.

3.3] *Capell*   6 near us] *Q5;* neer's *Q2;* dangerous *F*   7 brows] Lunacies *F;* Lunes *Theobald;* brawls *Cam¹ (early edns);* braves *Parrott–Craig (Dover Wilson)*

To keep those many many bodies safe
That live and feed upon your majesty.   10

ROSENCRANTZ

The single and peculiar life is bound
With all the strength and armour of the mind
To keep itself from noyance; but much more
That spirit upon whose weal depends and rests
The lives of many. The cess of majesty   15
Dies not alone, but like a gulf doth draw
What's near it with it; or it is a massy wheel
Fixed on the summit of the highest mount
To whose huge spokes ten thousand lesser things
Are mortised and adjoined, which when it falls   20
Each small annexment, petty consequence,
Attends the boisterous ruin. Never alone
Did the king sigh but with a general groan.

9–10 The slightly grotesque image of the *many many bodies* that *live and feed* on the King seems to anticipate Hamlet's insistence on the worms that feed on Polonius in 4.3.

11 **single and peculiar** i.e. private, individual
bound obliged

13 **noyance** annoyance, harm

14 **That spirit** i.e. the King
weal welfare
depends and rests A verb frequently takes a singular form when it precedes a plural subject (see Blake, 4.2.2d, or Hope, 2.1.8a).

15 **cess of majesty** cessation or decease of royalty. Given the age of Elizabeth I and her unwillingness to name an heir, this must have been a topical issue when *Hamlet* was written.

16 **gulf** whirlpool, maelstrom
draw pull in, attract

17 **massy** massive; see 2.2.433 and n. (F omits *or*, achieving a more regular metre.)

18 *summit See 1.4.70n.

20 **mortised** fastened securely (as with a mortise and tenon joint)

21 **annexment** annex, addition. 'This word seems to be Rosencrantz's gift to the English language' (Edwards); see also 1.2.93n.
petty consequence i.e. trivial thing connected with it

22 **Attends** accompanies
boisterous tumultuous; dissyllabic, as Q2's 'boystrous' indicates
*ruin Andrews interprets Q2's 'raine' as meaning 'downpour', but *a/u* is an easy misreading. Jenkins prefers F.

22–3 **Never . . . groan** (a commonplace)

23 *with We assume an accidental omission in Q2.

---

14 weal] spirit *F*   15 cess] cease *F*   17 or it is] It is *F;* 'tis *Dyce²;* O, 'tis *Cam¹*   18 summit] *Rowe;* somnet *Q2F*   19 huge] *F;* hough *Q2*   20 mortised] *(morteist),* F *(mortiz'd)*   22 boisterous] *(boystrous)* F   22 ruin] *F;* raine Q2   23 with] *F; not in Q2*

KING

    Arm you, I pray you, to this speedy voyage

    For we will fetters put about this fear   25

    Which now goes too free-footed.

ROSENCRANTZ   We will haste us.

                Exeunt Rosencrantz and Guildenstern.

              Enter POLONIUS.

POLONIUS

    My lord, he's going to his mother's closet.

    Behind the arras I'll convey myself

    To hear the process. I'll warrant she'll tax him home

    And, as you said – and wisely was it said –   30

    'Tis meet that some more audience than a mother

    (Since nature makes them partial) should o'er-hear

    The speech of vantage. Fare you well, my liege,

    I'll call upon you ere you go to bed

    And tell you what I know.

KING   Thanks, dear my lord.   35

                        Exit Polonius.

    O, my offence is rank: it smells to heaven;

---

24 **Arm . . . to** make yourselves ready for (but perhaps in this context carrying a hint of 'take arms or weapons')
   speedy i.e. imminent or perhaps hastily planned

25 **fear** danger (cause of fear)

27 **closet** private chamber (see 3.2.323n.)

28 **arras** wall-hanging (see 2.2.160n.)
   convey place, remove; often with a suggestion of something deceitful or clandestine; see *MW* 3.3.111–12, 'if you have a friend here, convey, convey him out'.

29 **process** proceedings
   warrant guarantee, promise
   tax him home reprove him thoroughly, call him to count for his behaviour

30 **as you said** It was in fact Polonius himself who made this suggestion at 3.1.182–4; 'his transfer of responsibility for the scheme is a matter of prudence as well as deference' (Edwards).

31 **meet** appropriate

33 **of vantage** This might mean 'in addition' (to the mother), as in *Oth* 4.3.83–4, 'as many to th' vantage as would store the world they played for'; or it might mean 'from an advantageous position', as in *Mac* 1.6.7, 'coign of vantage'.

36–72 In Q1, this speech begins, 'O that this wet that falles upon my face / Would wash the crime cleere from my conscience', perhaps indicating that in

---

25 about] vpon *F*   26 SP] *Both. F*   SD] *(Exeunt Gent.) F*   35 SD] *Ard*²; *after* know. *Q2; om. F*

It hath the primal eldest curse upon't –
A brother's murder. Pray can I not:
Though inclination be as sharp as will,
My stronger guilt defeats my strong intent   40
And like a man to double business bound
I stand in pause where I shall first begin
And both neglect. What if this cursed hand
Were thicker than itself with brother's blood?
Is there not rain enough in the sweet heavens   45
To wash it white as snow? Whereto serves mercy
But to confront the visage of offence?
And what's in prayer but this twofold force
– To be forestalled ere we come to fall
Or pardoned, being down? Then I'll look up: 50

some early stagings the King appeared to weep as he spoke. Angelo in *MM* has a comparable soliloquy in which he comments on his failure to repent and pray (2.4.1–17).

36 **rank** offensive, foul-smelling; see other uses of *rank* and *ranker* at 1.2.136; 2.1.20; 3.2.250; 3.4.90, 146 and 150; 4.4.21.

37 **primal eldest curse** The first murder in Judaeo-Christian tradition is Cain's killing of his brother Abel; see Genesis, 4.11–12, and 1.2.105 and n.

38 **A brother's murder** the murder of a brother. It is perhaps notable that the King does not mention incest as another *offence* here (see 1.2.157 and n.).

39 **usually paraphrased** 'although my desire to pray is as strong as my determination to do so', which seems tautologous: could it rather mean 'although my desire to pray is as strong as my will to sin'?

41 **to ... bound** obliged to undertake two tasks at once (the problem is not that he can't do two things at once but that the two things are incompatible)

43–6 **What ... snow** Hibbard points out the

relevance of three proverbial sayings here: 'To wash one's hands of a thing', 'All the water in the sea cannot wash out this stain' and 'As white as snow' (Tilley, H122, W85, S591).

43 **cursèd** cursèd

45 See Portia's claim, 'The quality of mercy is not strain'd, / It droppeth as the gentle rain from heaven / Upon the place beneath' (*MV* 4.1.182–4).

46–7 **Whereto ... offence** 'what is the function of mercy if it does not confront guilt'

48 **what's in prayer** what is the use of prayer
   prayer two syllables

49 **forestalled** forestallèd; prevented

50 ***pardoned** i.e. to be pardoned. Q2's 'pardon' may be an error of omission: final *d* misread as *e* and then dropped. It could be interpreted as meaning 'to be given pardon', but it loses the parallel with *forestalled* in 49.
   look up: Jenkins specifically rejects F's comma after *up* on the grounds that the King's resolve to *look up* is due to his confidence in the efficacy of prayer, not in his *fault* being *past*.

50 pardoned] *F;* pardon *Q2*   up:] *(vp.), Q1 (vp.), F (vp.)*

My fault is past. But O, what form of prayer
Can serve my turn: 'Forgive me my foul murder'?
That cannot be, since I am still possessed
Of those effects for which I did the murder,
My crown, mine own ambition and my Queen.   55
May one be pardoned and retain th'offence?
In the corrupted currents of this world
Offence's gilded hand may shove by justice,
And oft 'tis seen the wicked prize itself
Buys out the law; but 'tis not so above: 60
There is no shuffling, there the action lies
In his true nature, and we ourselves compelled
Even to the teeth and forehead of our faults
To give in evidence. What then? What rests?
Try what repentance can – what can it not? –   65

---

51 **past** already committed (i.e. it is too late for sin to be *forestalled*, but there is still the possibility of *pardon*). A similar thought is expressed by Henry V on the night before Agincourt when he notes that his penitence for his father's 'fault' (also, in effect, regicide) 'comes after all' (*H5* 4.1.300): he cannot undo the murder of Richard II and he still possesses the *effects* of the crime.

54 **effects** advantages, benefits

55 **mine own ambition** i.e. the achievement of my ambition

56 **retain th'offence** i.e. keep the profits of the crime

57 **currents** i.e. procedures, ways of doing things

58 See *KL* 4.6.161–2, 'Plate sin with gold, / And the strong lance of justice hurtless breaks.'
Offence's gilded hand the gold-bearing (and guilty) hand of an offender
*****shove by** thrust aside, evade. Jenkins too follows F here; *shove by* is unique in Shakespeare, but see the Archbishop of York's complaint at *2H4* 4.2.36–7 about

the 'particulars of our grief, / The which hath been with scorn shov'd from the court', and see 61n. (Q2's 'showe by' looks like a misreading, but it could mean 'appear next to'.)

61 **shuffling** trickery (as at 4.7.135). Jenkins points out that *shuffling* is a variant of 'shovelling', supporting *shove* in 58.
the action lies the case exists (a standard legal phrase)

62 **his** its

62–4 **we … evidence** i.e. we are forced to present evidence of the worst of our sins. Possibly there is a contrast here with English law in which accused people cannot be *compelled* to incriminate themselves.

63 **teeth and forehead** The metaphor picks up the idea of 'confront[ing] the visage of offence' in 47, and perhaps that of dangers growing out of Hamlet's *brows* at 7. Bared *teeth* and frowning brow are seen as expressing defiance or anger.

64 **rests** remains, is left (to say or do)

65 **can** i.e. can achieve

---

58 shove] *F;* showe *Q2*

Yet what can it, when one cannot repent?
O wretched state, O bosom black as death,
O limed soul that struggling to be free
Art more engaged. Help, angels, make assay.
Bow, stubborn knees, and heart with strings of steel   70
Be soft as sinews of the new-born babe.
All may be well.

Enter HAMLET.

HAMLET
Now might I do it. But now 'a is a-praying.
And now I'll do it [*Draws sword.*] – and so 'a goes to
    heaven,
And so am I revenged! That would be scanned: 75
A villain kills my father, and for that

---

68 **limed** limèd; trapped, as a bird with birdlime, a sticky substance spread on the branches of trees
69 **engaged** involved, entangled
    assay effort. It is not clear whether the King is addressing the angels or himself here.
73–95 **Now . . . goes** Johnson found this speech 'too horrible to be read or uttered'; other eighteenth- and nineteenth-century editors, such as Caldecott, justified its apparent barbarity as appropriate to the historical period represented. From Garrick onwards it has frequently been cut in performance. Hamlet's stated desire not only to kill his uncle but to send his soul to hell contrasts with Othello's words to Desdemona when he tells her to pray: 'I would not kill thy unprepared spirit . . . I would not kill thy soul' (*Oth* 5.2.31–2).
73 **But** F has 'pat' = conveniently, adopted by

Jenkins without comment. *But* introduces Hamlet's doubt immediately.
'a is a-praying F's version may be easier to speak, but Hope points out (1.3.2c) that F has 'he' for Q2's ' 'a' three times in this speech (73, 74, 80) and that '*a* (assumed to relate to the dialect roots of Shakespeare, who is one of the latest citations for its usage in *OED*) is 'highly unstable textually, and liable to be changed to *he* by scribes and compositors'.
74 **And . . . it** Hamlet draws his sword at this point, as is explicit in Q1's 'come forth and work thy last'.
75 ***revenged** Q2's 'reuendge' may be a misreading of final *d* as *e*.
75 **would be scanned** needs to be scrutinized. The absence of punctuation after 'scand' in Q2 would, however, allow the syntax to continue: 'would be interpreted . . .'

---

69 Help, angels,] *Theobald (*help, angels!*); helpe Angels *Q2;* Helpe Angels, *F*   70 Bow,] *Theobald;* Bowe *Q2F*   73 But] pat, *F*   'a] he *F*   a-praying] *(*a praying*); praying *F*   74 SD] *Capell subst.* 'a] he *F*   75 revenged] *F (*reueng'd*), Q1 (*reuenged*); reuendge *Q2*

I, his sole son, do this same villain send
To heaven.
Why, this is base and silly, not revenge.
'A took my father grossly full of bread   80
With all his crimes broad blown, as flush as May,
And how his audit stands who knows, save heaven,
But in our circumstance and course of thought
'Tis heavy with him. And am I then revenged
To take him in the purging of his soul   85
When he is fit and seasoned for his passage?
No.   [*Sheathes sword.*]
Up sword, and know thou a more horrid hent
When he is drunk, asleep or in his rage,

79 **Why ... silly** F's reading (see t.n.) is generally adopted on the grounds that the Q2 reading is erroneous (see Jenkins, LN); Parrott–Craig defend Q2, pointing out that the F reading would be Shakespeare's only use of 'salary'; Mack and Boynton retain.
base and silly unworthy and weak-spirited. *Base* frequently means 'inferior' or 'illegitimate' in Shakespeare (see especially Edmund's complaint, 'Why bastard? Wherefore base?', at *KL* 1.2.6), while *silly* means 'feeble-minded' at *R2* 5.5.25.

80 **'A** he
grossly Although this relates grammatically to *took* ('he killed my father without any decency') it could also refer to the victim ('he killed my father in a state of gross sinfulness').
full of bread i.e. in a state of sensual satiety, not repentant or fasting. 'Fulnes of bread' is listed as a state of sin in Ezekiel, 16.49.

81 **broad blown** in full bloom. See 'in the blossoms of my sin' (1.5.76).
flush lusty, vigorous

82 **his** i.e. old Hamlet's
audit See *reckoning* and *account* at 1.5.78.
who ... heaven Warburton conjectured on the basis of this line that Shakespeare's 'first sketch' of the play did not contain the Ghost, who 'had told [Hamlet], very circumstantially, how his audit stood' (in 1.5).

83 **circumstance ... thought** knowledge which is necessarily limited or circumstantial

84 **'Tis ... him** i.e. his *audit* or list of sins is a weighty or large one

85 **purging** The word implies a connection between prayer in this world and the possibility of purgatory to come (see 3.2.299).

86 **seasoned** prepared

88 **hent** This could mean 'grasp' (i.e. occasion to be grasped), or it could be a variant of 'hint' = opportunity. Hamlet presumably sheathes his sword at this point.

89 **drunk, asleep** the comma implies 'drunk or asleep'; F's lack of punctuation may imply 'dead drunk' (like Q1's 'drinking drunke'?).

77 sole] foule *F*   78–9] *one line F*   79 Why] Oh *F*   base and silly] a benefit *Q1*; hyre and Sallery *F*; bait and salary *Cam¹*   80 'A] He *Q1F*   81 flush] fresh *F*   86–7] *one line F*   87 SD] *Cam¹*   89 drunk, asleep] drunke asleepe *F*

Or in th'incestuous pleasure of his bed,   90
At game a-swearing, or about some act
That has no relish of salvation in't.
Then trip him that his heels may kick at heaven
And that his soul may be as damned and black
As hell whereto it goes. My mother stays;   95
This physic but prolongs thy sickly days.   *Exit.*

KING

My words fly up, my thoughts remain below.
Words without thoughts never to heaven go.   *Exit.*

[3.4]   *Enter* QUEEN *and* POLONIUS.

90 **incestuous** See 1.2.157n.
91 **At game a-swearing** 'There can be little
    doubt about the correctness of Q2 which is
    supported by Q1 as against F's paraphrase'
    (Edwards). This time it is F that implies
    two distinct activities, gambling and
    swearing, rather than 'swearing as he
    gambles' (see 89n.).
92 **relish** hint, trace (literally, 'flavour')
93–5 **Then . . . goes** Honigmann ('First
    Quarto') notes the parallel with *Oth*
    2.1.186–7: 'Olympus-high and duck again
    as low / As hell's from heaven'.
93 **trip him** cause him to stumble and fall
    kick at heaven usually glossed 'spurn
    heaven (as he plunges headlong into hell)',
    though it also seems to carry some sense
    of 'batter (ineffectively) at the gates of
    heaven'
95 **stays** is waiting
96 Although this line is rhetorically addressed
    to the King, it cannot be heard by him.
    physic i.e. the King's prayer (or Hamlet's
    decision not to kill him at once?)
97–8 The King's final couplet reveals that his
    attempt to pray has failed, casting an ironic
    retrospective light on Hamlet's stated

reasons for sparing him.

3.4 The three texts: it has been traditional since
    Q6 to end this scene, and indeed Act 3, with
    Hamlet's exit at 3.4.215, although the
    action in Q2 and F is arguably continuous
    until the exeunt of the King and Queen at
    what is traditionally designated the end of
    4.1; in Q1 the action is continuous without
    a scene-break until the entry of Fortenbrasse
    (*sic*) at the beginning of what is traditionally
    designated 4.4; see headnote to 4.1 and
    Appendix 4 on this division. Up to Hamlet's
    exit, the scene runs to 103 lines in Q1
    (scene 11), 215 lines in Q2 and 192 lines in
    F; F omits five passages from Hamlet's
    castigating speeches (see notes on 69–74,
    76–9, 159–63 and 165–8) and his
    determination to outwit his *schoolfellows*
    (200–8). Q1 covers the same ground, but
    with some significant additions to the
    Queen's role: see 28n. and 195–7n.
    Location and timing: this scene follows
    immediately after 3.3 and takes place in the
    Queen's *closet* – a private room but
    not a bedroom, which would have
    been referred to as her 'chamber': see
    3.2.323n. Since Barrymore gave the

91 game a-swearing] *(*game a swearing*);* game swaring *Q1;* gaming, swearing *F*   **3.4]** *Capell* 0.1 SD
QUEEN] *Q1F; Gertrard Q2*

POLONIUS

'A will come straight. Look you lay home to him.
Tell him his pranks have been too broad to bear with,
And that your grace hath screened and stood between
Much heat and him. I'll silence me even here.
Pray you be round.

QUEEN   I'll warrant you, fear me not.   5
Withdraw, I hear him coming.

[*Polonius hides behind the arras.*]

scene an Oedipal reading in 1922 (see Hapgood), modern productions have often included a bed (see also p. 102). The 2000 production at the Globe did not use a bed, though Hamlet dragged a sheet on from the discovery space when he talked of 'the rank sweat of an enseamed bed' (90); he used it later to wrap and drag the body. Jones compares this scene, in which an aggressive son confronts a guilty mother and forces her to confession, with the similarly structured but comic episode in *KJ* 1.1.217–76 (*Scenic*, 99–104).

1   **'A** he
    straight immediately
    lay ... him accuse or reprove him thoroughly; see Polonius' 'I'll warrant she'll tax him home' at 3.3.29.

2   **pranks** reprehensible actions; a stronger meaning than the modern one of 'jokes'; see *1H6* 3.1.11–15, where the Duke of Gloucester accuses the Bishop of Winchester to his face of 'thy vile outrageous crimes ... thy audacious wickedness, / Thy lewd, pestiferous and dissentious pranks'.
    broad gross, excessive
    bear with tolerate

3–4 **screened ... heat** The metaphor is of a movable screen used to protect people from the direct heat of an open fire.

4   **I'll ... here** Polonius presumably gestures towards the arras he mentioned at 3.3.28 and where he is to hide at 6 SD. Both Q2/F's 'silence' and Q1's 'shrowde' are ironically apt. Edwards wonders, 'Is it conceivable that this is the one place where an authoritative change, occurring to Shakespeare when the play was in production, is preserved only in the corrupt first quarto?'

5   **round** forthright; see his earlier 'Let her be round with him' at 3.1.182. Jenkins sees F's extrametrical 'with him' as recollected from 3.1.182 and dismisses the offstage cry (see t.n.) as 'a fairly obvious stage accretion' (i.e. an actor's insertion), but Edwards argues that the latter is 'very much in character'.

5   SP Q2 uses '*Ger.*' instead of '*Quee.*' consistently throughout this scene and the next.
    *warrant you Q2's 'wait you' does yield the meaning 'watch out for you', though this is an obsolete sense according to *OED* 3a, and a misreading of an abbreviation for F's 'warrant' is more likely. (See also 1.2.241 and 3.3.29 as cited at 1n.)

6.1 It seems logical for Hamlet to enter after Polonius has hidden and the Queen has said 'I hear him coming.'

1] *F lines* straight: / him, / 'A] He *F*   4 silence me] *F*; shrowde my selfe *Q1*; 'sconce me *Hanmer* even] e'ene *F*   5 round] round with him. / *Ham. within.* Mother, mother, mother *F*   warrant] *F*; wait *Q2*; war'nt *Cam²*   6 SD] *Rowe subst.*   6.1] *F; after round 5 Q2*

Enter HAMLET.

HAMLET

Now, mother, what's the matter?

QUEEN

Hamlet, thou hast thy father much offended.

HAMLET

Mother, you have my father much offended.

QUEEN

Come, come, you answer with an idle tongue. 10

HAMLET

Go, go, you question with a wicked tongue.

QUEEN

Why, how now, Hamlet!

HAMLET   What's the matter now?

QUEEN

Have you forgot me?

HAMLET   No, by the rood, not so.

---

7   **In** Q1, Hamlet begins by asking, 'How is't with you mother?', the Queen replies, 'How is't with you?', and he answers, 'I'le tell you, but first weele make all safe', implying that he locks the door – a piece of business preserved in *Fratricide Punished* (3.5; Bullough, 7.145). Orlin demonstrates that a major feature of a *closet* in this period is that it can be locked.

8–9 **thou ... you** The pronouns reflect the usual parent-to-child and child-to-parent contrast which is more or less sustained until the Queen echoes Hamlet's *you* at 112 (see also 101–5 and n.).

8, 9 **father** The Queen means the present King, Hamlet's stepfather; Hamlet refers to the previous King, his real father.

10   **idle** possibly just 'foolish' or 'frivolous' (as at 3.2.87), but the word at this time could have a stronger sense of 'void of meaning or sense' (*OED a.* 2b).

11   **Go, go** not a standard idiom; Hamlet continues to play on the Queen's words.

13   **forgot me** forgotten that I am your mother; the Queen implies that Hamlet is being disrespectful. Later in Q1 when she describes this encounter she claims, 'then he throwes and tosses me about, / As one forgetting that I was his mother' (11.108–9). A reference by Thomas Dekker in *Lanthorne and Candlelight* (1609, H2ᵛ) to 'any mad Hamlet' who might 'smell villanie & rush in by violence' might also attest to the physical action in this scene.

the rood Christ's cross. Some nineteenth-century productions introduced a cross or other religious emblem in this scene; a *closet* was often a place for meditation and prayer.

---

11   a wicked] an idle *F*

You are the Queen, your husband's brother's wife,
And, would it were not so, you are my mother.   15

QUEEN

Nay then, I'll set those to you that can speak.

HAMLET

Come, come, and sit you down. You shall not budge.
You go not till I set you up a glass
Where you may see the inmost part of you.

QUEEN

What wilt thou do? Thou wilt not murder me –   20
Help, ho!

POLONIUS [*behind the arras*]
                    What ho! Help!

HAMLET

How now! A rat! Dead for a ducat, dead!
[*Kills Polonius.*]

POLONIUS

O, I am slain!

---

16 'If you won't respect me I'll have to confront you with others who can speak more forcefully.' Presumably she means the King.

17 **budge** move. The whole line indicates that Hamlet is forcing the Queen to sit down and prepare to listen to him. In Q1 she is explicit in her subsequent account of his behaviour (see 13n.) – but theatrical tradition has not needed the authority of this text to inject violence, often erotically charged, into this scene.

18 **glass** mirror

19 ***inmost** Q2's 'most' makes poor sense and metre and can be accounted for as a minim misreading.

22 **rat** Hibbard cites two relevant proverbs: 'The rat betrayed herself with her own

noise' (Dent, R30.1) and 'I smell a rat' (Tilley, R31). 'Rat' could also be used as an insult, cf. Coriolanus' contemptuous 'Rome and her rats are at the point of battle' (*Cor* 1.1.161). It must literally have been the case that rats hid behind curtains and in the spaces between walls in Elizabethan houses.

Dead for a ducat 'I'll bet a ducat that he is (or will be) dead.' Jenkins, however, says, 'Not a bet that he *is* dead but the price for making him dead. Cf. for two pins' (Ard²).

22 SD *Later in all three texts the Queen gives the King an account of what happens here (4.1.7–12), though as she promises to conceal that Hamlet is only *mad in craft* (186) she may exaggerate his frenzy.

---

15 And] But *F*   it] you *F*   19 inmost] *F;* most *Q2*   21 Help, ho!] *(*Helpe how.*), Q1;* Helpe, helpe, hoa. *F*   SD] *Rowe*   What ho! Help!] *(*What how helpe.*);* What hoa, helpe, helpe, helpe. *F*   22 SD] *F, after* slaine. 23*; not in Q2*1

QUEEN   O me, what hast thou done?

HAMLET

   Nay, I know not. Is it the King?

QUEEN

   O, what a rash and bloody deed is this!   25

HAMLET

   A bloody deed – almost as bad, good mother,

   As kill a king and marry with his brother.

QUEEN

   As kill a king?

HAMLET   Ay, lady, it was my word.

     [*Uncovers the body of Polonius.*]

   – Thou wretched, rash, intruding fool, farewell:

   I took thee for thy better. Take thy fortune;   30

   Thou find'st to be too busy is some danger.

   – Leave wringing of your hands. Peace, sit you down

   And let me wring your heart. For so I shall

   If it be made of penetrable stuff,

   If damned custom have not brazed it so   35

   That it be proof and bulwark against sense.

QUEEN

   What have I done that thou dar'st wag thy tongue

---

28 'It is extraordinary that neither of them takes up this all-important matter again' (Edwards). In all three texts the Queen seems shocked by the accusation; the Ghost has not specified complicity on her part in 1.5, and her relative calmness during *The Murder of Gonzago* has been taken as evidence that she is innocent of murder, which she specifically denies at this point in Q1: 'I sweare by heauen / I neuer knew of this most horride murder' (11.85–6).
  As kill as to kill

30 **thy better** i.e. the King
  Take thy fortune accept your fate
31 **busy** overactive, interfering; proverbial: 'To be too busy is dangerous' (Dent, B759.1)
34 'if it has still retained any sensitivity to emotion'
35 **damned custom** damnèd; accursed habit
  brazed it covered it as with brass (or hardened like brass?)
36 **proof and bulwark** armoured and fortified (another example of hendiadys)
  sense natural or proper feeling (i.e. guilt)
37 **wag thy tongue** i.e. scold

28 it was] 'twas *F*   SD] *this edn*   30 better] Betters *F*   35 brazed] *(*brasd*), F;* brass'd *Globe*   36 be] is *F*

In noise so rude against me?

HAMLET   Such an act
That blurs the grace and blush of modesty,
Calls virtue hypocrite, takes off the rose   40
From the fair forehead of an innocent love
And sets a blister there, makes marriage vows
As false as dicers' oaths – O, such a deed
As from the body of contraction plucks
The very soul, and sweet religion makes   45
A rhapsody of words. Heaven's face does glow
O'er this solidity and compound mass
With heated visage as against the doom,

---

38 **Such an act** In his language from here to
99 the *act* Hamlet dwells on is the Queen's
remarriage, not the murder.

39 **blurs** disfigures
  grace … modesty innocent (blushing)
  grace of a modest woman (*grace and blush*
  is another example of hendiadys)

40 **Calls virtue hypocrite** i.e. makes any
claim to virtue subject to accusations of
hypocrisy

40–2 **takes … there** As at 3.3.7, the brows or
forehead reveal the inner self; the *rose*
represents idealized love, while the *blister*
refers to the practice of branding prostitutes,
which as Edwards points out did not
literally happen in Elizabethan England,
though it had been threatened by Henry
VIII in 1531 (see also Henning, who notes
that editors after Edwards continue to assert
that it did happen). Laertes evokes the idea
again at 4.5.117–20. This passage used to
attract such fanciful explanations that
Furness felt obliged to remark, 'It is only
by keeping steadfastly in mind the many
benefits which we have received at the
hands of the early commentators that we
can listen with any patience to their dispute
about the meaning of this phrase' (see Var

for examples).

40 **off** Q2's 'of' was a common spelling for
off.

43 **dicers' oaths** the (rash) promises of
gamblers

44 **body of contraction** substance of a
(marriage) contract

45–6 **sweet … words** turns sweet religion into
a mere confusion or frenzy of words. This
is Shakespeare's only use of the word
rhapsody, which carried a more negative
meaning than it does today.

46–9 **Heaven's … act** In Q2's version, the
visage of heaven (i.e. the sky) glows red-
hot over the earth as if it were the Day of
Judgement and is *thought-sick* at the
Queen's behaviour.

47 **O'er** F's 'Yea' for *O'er* makes 'this solidity
and compound mass' (i.e. the world) the
subject of *Is thought-sick* rather than
Heaven's face as in Q2.

48 **heated** F's 'tristfull' means sorrowful;
despite his commitment to F as
Shakespeare's revision of Q2,
MacDonald comments: 'I cannot help
thinking the Q[2] reading of this passage
the more intelligible, as well as
much the more powerful.' Edwards

---

40 off] *(of), F* 42 sets] makes *F* 46 rhapsody] *(rapsedy), F (rapsidie)* does] doth *F* 47 O'er]
(Ore); Yea F; And Cam¹ 48 heated] tristfull *F* doom,] *F; doome Q2*

Is thought-sick at the act.

QUEEN   Ay me, what act

That roars so loud and thunders in the index?   50

HAMLET

Look here upon this picture, and on this,

The counterfeit presentment of two brothers:

See what a grace was seated on this brow,

assumes the Q2 compositor could not read or understand 'tristfull' and supplied *heated* from *glow*. Hibbard assumes that the F reading is an authorial revision; Jenkins retains *O'er* but prints 'tristful' on the grounds that 'so rare and eloquent a word seems beyond an improver' (LN). Against this, Shakespeare had used the word in Falstaff's comically inflated command when he is playing the king in *1H4*: 'convey my tristful Queen' (2.4.389) – if Dering's emendation of 'trustfull' to 'tristful' is correct. See the oddly similar textual difference at 2.2.489, where Q2 has 'visage wand' and F has 'visage warm'd'.

as . . . doom as if it were doomsday

49 **thought-sick** sick at the thought (or perhaps 'sick in thought')

50 Q2 gives this line to Hamlet as the first line of his speech, as if he is continuing from *the act* in 49, with the Queen's question as an interruption; most editors follow F and make it part of her question: *index* certainly seems to make more sense from her than from him.

index i.e. prologue. In Elizabethan parlance the *index* was the table of contents placed at the front of a book.

51 **this . . . this** It is clear from 52 that Hamlet is comparing a picture of his father with one of the present King; onstage, the pictures can be large formal portraits, miniatures,

coins or even photographs, depending on the overall concept of the production. Some commentators have argued that the audience needs to see the pictures to judge for themselves, but this may not be necessary, given that they have seen both the Ghost and the King in person. In *Fratricide Punished* Hamlet says, 'But look, there in that gallery hangs the counterfeit resemblance of your first husband, and there hangs the counterfeit of your present one' (3.5; Bullough, 7.145), perhaps implying that he gestures towards unseen pictures offstage. Jenkins (LN) argues plausibly with reference to the occurrence of portraits in other plays (e.g. *TNK* 4.2) that relatively small portable versions would have been used at the Globe, though the illustration in Rowe's 1709 edition showing large pictures may reflect later stage practice (and see 56n.). John Philip Kemble is credited with (re)introducing miniatures to the London stage in 1783, though his grandfather John Ward seems to have used them in the provinces (see Thompson, 'Ward'). James Henry Hackett describes a striking effect in a production in 1840 in which the Ghost seemed to step out of a full-size portrait on to the stage (Hackett, 79–80).

52 **counterfeit presentment** artificial representation; *counterfeit* did not necessarily carry a negative connotation.

49 Is] *F*; 'Tis *Pope*   49–50 Ay . . . index?] *prose F*   49 Ay] *F*; Ah *Malone*   act] *F (*act,*)*; act? *Q2* 50
That] *F (*that*)*; *Ham.* That *Q2*   loud] *F (*lowd*)*; low'd *Q2*   51 SP] *F*; *not in Q2* 53 this] his *Q3*, *F*

369

Hyperion's curls, the front of Jove himself,
An eye like Mars to threaten and command,   55
A station like the herald Mercury
New-lighted on a heaven-kissing hill,
A combination and a form indeed
Where every god did seem to set his seal
To give the world assurance of a man;   60
This was your husband. Look you now what follows:
Here is your husband like a mildewed ear
Blasting his wholesome brother. Have you eyes?
Could you on this fair mountain leave to feed

54 **Hyperion's curls** Presumably the sun-god would have golden tresses. For a preview of this idealized portrait, see 1.2.140, where Hamlet saw his father in relation to the present King as 'Hyperion to a satyr'. He now elaborates by attributing to his father all the best features and qualities of the classical gods. The list of attributes recalls Ophelia's enumeration of Hamlet's own 'eye, tongue, sword' at 3.1.150.
front of Jove forehead of Jove, the king of the gods

55 **eye like Mars** The war-god would have a dominating glare.

56 **station ... Mercury** The messenger-god would have an athletic, upright *station* or stance. This reference may indicate that Hamlet is describing (or imagining) a full-length portrait, not a head or bust as would have been more usual for a miniature. Given his use of Marlowe and Nashe's *Dido* elsewhere in *Hamlet*, Shakespeare may be recalling the appearance of 'Jove's winged messenger' to Aeneas at 5.1.25: like the Ghost later in 3.4, the purpose of the visitation is to remind the hero of his mission (and Hermes/Mercury arrives accompanied by Aeneas' son Ascanius).

57 **New-lighted** newly alighted or landed;

Mercury was regularly depicted with wings.
*****heaven-kissing** high; Q2's reading seems erroneous.

58–60 See Antony's praise of the dead Brutus: 'the elements / So mix'd in him that Nature might stand up / And say to all the world, "This was a man!" ' (*JC* 5.5.73–5).

58 **combination** i.e. of physical features

59 **set his seal** place his mark of approval or ownership (see also 3.2.61n. and 3.2.389n.)

62–3 **like ... Blasting** blighting his ear as if with mildew. The notion of an *ear* being attacked by blight also of course recalls the literal manner of the murder, though in this case the reference is presumably to an ear of corn, as in the biblical account of Pharaoh's dream (Genesis, 41.5–7), a story Shakespeare also refers to at *1H4* 2.4.467, *KL* 5.3.24 and *Cor* 2.1.113–14 (see Shaheen).

63, 65 **Have you eyes?** In Q1, Hamlet follows this with the more explicit charge 'and can you look on him / That slew my father' (11.40–1).

64–5 **mountain ... moor** The intended contrast must be between 'high' and 'low', since there would not be much difference in terms of quality of pasture.

55 and] or *F*   57 heaven-kissing] *F, Q5;* heaue, a kissing *Q2*   58 and a] and *Q4*   62 ear] *F;* deare *F2;* Deer *F3*   63 brother] breath *F*

And batten on this moor? Ha, have you eyes?   65
You cannot call it love, for at your age
The heyday in the blood is tame, it's humble
And waits upon the judgement, and what judgement
Would step from this to this? Sense, sure, you have –
Else could you not have motion. But sure, that sense   70
Is apoplexed, for madness would not err
Nor sense to ecstasy was ne'er so thralled
But it reserved some quantity of choice
To serve in such a difference. What devil was't
That thus hath cozened you at hoodman-blind?   75

65 **batten on** feed on. Hibbard argues that the *moor* provides 'an abundance of rank grass', making it preferable to the *fair mountain*, but surely Hamlet's point is that his mother's choice is an irrational one.

moor The suggestion of a pun on 'blackamoor' is supported by Hamlet's claim that the present King has 'a face like Vulcan' in Q1 at this point (11.34), Vulcan being the blacksmith of the gods whose face was darkened by the smoke of his occupation.

66 **at your age** Hamlet's assumption, in all three texts, that his mother is too old to experience sexual desire has been regularly endorsed by (male) editors, who also feel that she must be too old to excite it. Within the play, she is the same age as 'Gonzago's wife', whose remarriage is viewed with equanimity by her failing husband at 3.2.167–71.

67 **heyday ... blood** sexual excitement. The origin of the word *heyday* is obscure: *OED* says 'the second element does not seem to have been the word *day*', though 'high-day' (= noon) is how it is often understood.

68 **waits upon** is subservient to

69–74 **Sense ... difference** This passage and that at 76–9 are not in F; Edwards argues that Shakespeare was dissatisfied with

them and intended to delete them; Hibbard goes further and claims, 'They smack of self-indulgence on the part of the hero and, possibly, of the author.' Earlier editors and commentators, such as Theobald, were more open-minded; he conjectures of the first passage, 'Perhaps it was not written when he first finish'd the Play; or it was left out in the shortning the Play for the Representation' (*Restored*, 103).

69–70 **Sense ... motion** i.e. you must have some basic *sense* or apprehension or you would not be living and moving.

71 **apoplexed** struck with apoplexy, paralysed

for ... err i.e. even a mad person would not make this mistake

72 **Nor ... thralled** nor was sensibility ever so enslaved to transcendent fantasy

73 'without holding back some limited amount of the power to choose'

74 **To ... difference** to enable it to differentiate (in such a case)

75 **cozened** deceived

at hoodman-blind in a game of blind man's buff (so called because one of the players was blindfolded by wearing a hood over the head); Hamlet implies that his mother must have been blindfolded when she chose her second husband.

65 moor] *(Moore) F*   69 step] *F; stoop Collier²*   69–74 Sense ... difference] *om. F*   75 hoodman-blind] *(hodman blind), F*

Eyes without feeling, feeling without sight,
Ears without hands or eyes, smelling sans all,
Or but a sickly part of one true sense
Could not so mope. O shame, where is thy blush?
Rebellious hell,   80
If thou canst mutine in a matron's bones,
To flaming youth let virtue be as wax
And melt in her own fire; proclaim no shame
When the compulsive ardour gives the charge,
Since frost itself as actively doth burn   85
And reason pardons will.

QUEEN   O Hamlet, speak no more.
Thou turn'st my very eyes into my soul
And there I see such black and grieved spots
As will leave there their tint.

76–9 **Eyes . . . mope** Hamlet's catalogue of the senses echoes his earlier catalogue of his father's attributes (53–61). See 69–74n.

77 **sans** without

79 **so mope** behave in such an aimless way

80 **Rebellious hell** Hamlet sees sensuality as a kind of rebellion (as Laertes did at 1.3.43) and as a *hell* (as in *Son* 129).

81 **canst mutine** can mutiny, rebel
matron's bones As at 66–8, Hamlet stresses the Queen's maturity.

82–3 **To . . . fire** i.e. chastity (*virtue*) will be like wax for young people (who are naturally more sensual) and will melt in its own heat. Hamlet's language and tone here again recall the advice of Laertes and Polonius to Ophelia in 1.3.

83 **proclaim no shame** *Proclaim* and 'proclamation' regularly refer to quasi-formal public announcements in Shakespeare, as when Cinna in *JC* urges the other conspirators to 'Run hence, proclaim, cry it [the death of Caesar] about the streets' (3.1.79), or when Isabella

threatens, 'I will proclaim thee, Angelo' (*MM* 2.4.150).

84 **compulsive . . . charge** 'compelling lust gives the signal for attack'

85 **frost** i.e. age. Dent cites 'To find fire in frost' as proverbial (F283.1).
actively vigorously

86 **And . . . will** and reason forgives (or makes excuses for) passion. F's 'As Reason panders Will' makes the construction a comparative one. 'Panders' is a stronger word meaning 'prostitutes' or 'serves the gratification of'; Jenkins, Edwards and Hibbard all conflate Q2's *And* with F's 'panders'.

87 **my . . . soul** F's reading is adopted by Jenkins, perhaps because *my very eyes* (= my own eyes) seems tautologous.

88 **grieved** grievèd; grievous. F's 'grained' (ingrained) is adopted by Jenkins, even though it repeats the idea that the stain is indelible. *TxC* specifically rejects *grieved* as a minim misreading of 'greined'.

89 **As . . . tinct** as will leave their stain there. F's reading (see t.n.) repeats the

76–9 Eyes . . . mope] *om. F*   79–80 O . . . hell] *one line F*   81 mutine] mutiny *Rowe*   86 And] As *F* pardons] panders *F*   87 my very] mine *F*   soul] very soule *F*   88 grieved] grained *F*   89 leave there] not leaue *F*

HAMLET   Nay, but to live

In the rank sweat of an enseamed bed   90

Stewed in corruption, honeying and making love

Over the nasty sty –

QUEEN   O speak to me no more!

These words like daggers enter in my ears.

No more, sweet Hamlet.

HAMLET   A murderer and a villain,

A slave that is not twentieth part the kith   95

Of your precedent lord, a vice of kings,

A cutpurse of the empire and the rule,

That from a shelf the precious diadem stole

And put it in his pocket, –

QUEEN   No more!

HAMLET   – a king of shreds and patches –

---

notion in 'grained' that the stain is indelible. Jenkins points out, 'The meaning is basically the same, owing to the ambiguity of *leave*, which means either cease, give up (F) or cause to remain behind (Q2)'.

90 **rank** offensive, excessive; see 146, 150 and other uses of *rank* and *ranker* at 1.2.136, 2.1.20, 3.2.250, 3.3.36, 4.4.21. **enseamed** enseamèd. Editors gloss 'saturated with grease or animal fat' (Dover Wilson suggests that Shakespeare drew unwittingly on early memories of hog's lard used in his father's wool-dyeing trade); 'stained with semen' seems another possibility (see Rubinstein, Supplement, 345). (Olivier's Hamlet in the 1948 film replaced *enseamed* with 'lascivious'.)

91 **Stewed** smothered, steeped; brothels were referred to as 'the stews'.
honeying using love-talk, calling each other *honey*

92 **sty** pigsty. In this part of the story in Saxo Grammaticus, Amleth chops up the body of the eavesdropper and feeds it to the pigs

(Bullough, 7.65).

93 **Hamlet** has succeeded in his intention to *speak daggers* (3.2.386).

95 **not . . . kith** If *kith* is taken as a synonym of 'kin', this must mean something like 'not a twentieth part kin to him', i.e. completely unlike him. Most editors adopt F's 'tythe' for *kith*, which yields the meaning 'not a twentieth part of a tenth part', and is supported by the extreme ease of *k/t* confusion in secretary hand.

96 **vice of kings** supreme example of a vicious king. There may also be a reference to the traditional character of the Vice in the morality plays.

97 **the rule** the kingdom

98 **diadem** crown

99 **And . . . patches** Hamlet apparently continues his line, ignoring or speaking over the Queen's extra-metrical interruption.
shreds and patches i.e. ragged patchwork (as contrasted with the paragon of *your precedent lord*). Stallybrass ('Clothes', 315) points out that this line

---

90 enseamed] *(inseemed)*, F; incestuous *Q3*   93 my] mine *F*   95 kith] tythe *F*   99] *this edn (*RP*); Q2F line* pocket. / more. / patches. /

Enter GHOST.

Save me and hover o'er me with your wings,   100
You heavenly guards! What would your gracious
    figure?

QUEEN

Alas, he's mad!

HAMLET

Do you not come your tardy son to chide

---

appears in Q2 and F *after* the entry SD for
the Ghost and might apply to his apparently
diminished status (see next note) as well as
to his brother, though this hardly fits
Hamlet's *gracious figure* (101).

99.1 Q1's SD is often quoted and sometimes
adopted by editors of Q2/F reasoning that it
indicates what originally happened onstage.
Nightgowns are frequently specified in
plays of the period; Dessen & Thomson
note 40 examples under 'nightgown'.
Perhaps the appearance of Caesar in his
nightgown, accompanied by 'Thunder &
Lightning' (*JC* 2.2), and later as a ghost in a
night-time scene in Brutus' tent when
Brutus has called for his 'gown' (4.3), is a
relevant parallel, even an influence on Q1. If
we assume Q1 is correct, the contrast here
with the fully armed Ghost of Act 1 is
striking: Hibbard claims it 'modifies our
previous impression of him greatly by
bringing out his humanity'. Greenblatt
suggests that the change 'would lightly echo
those multiple hauntings in which spirits
from Purgatory displayed their progressive
purification by a gradual whitening of their
robes' (*Purgatory*, 223). A more prosaic
reason might be that, if the actor playing the
King was doubling the Ghost, a nightgown
could be put on quickly over his previous
costume and taken off again for his next
entry (in Q1 there are 21 lines between the
Ghost's exit and the King's entry at the

equivalent of the beginning of 4.1 (see Q1
11.82–103 and Appendix 5 on doubling).
Phelps (147) claims that Irving in 1874 was
the first to stage the Ghost dressed in this
way, though this was more than 50 years
after the rediscovery of Q1. Some
productions precede the Ghost's entry with
a clock striking, as in 1.1 and sometimes in
1.4; see also 3.2.378n. and Fig. 7).

100–1 **Save ... guards** Hamlet appeals to
angels for protection.

101–5 **your ... your ... your** Hamlet's
pronouns (unlike *thee/thou* at 1.4.40–52)
may explicitly acknowledge the Ghost as
his father (see 8–9n.).

101 **your gracious figure** F's reading seems
equally acceptable, and 'you'/'yor' with
final superscripts would be easy to confuse
in manuscript.

102 This response makes it clear that, unlike
Horatio, Marcellus and Barnardo in Act 1,
the Queen does not see the Ghost. A
comparable scene is *Mac* 3.4, where
Macbeth alone sees the Ghost of Banquo,
who, however, does not speak.
Occasionally in productions it is indicated
that the Queen does see the Ghost but still
denies his existence (see Dawson, 156).
Dessen (*Elizabethan*, 153) argues that the
Queen's blindness 'is designed primarily to
italicize the larger issue of *not*-seeing in
this scene and in the tragedy as a whole'.

103–5 'What can this question, asked by

99.1 *Singer; Enter the ghost in his night gowne. Q1; after* more *99 Q2F* 101 your] you *F*

That, lapsed in time and passion, lets go by
Th'important acting of your dread command?   105
O say!

GHOST   Do not forget! This visitation
Is but to whet thy almost blunted purpose.
But look, amazement on thy mother sits!
O step between her and her fighting soul.
Conceit in weakest bodies strongest works.   110
Speak to her, Hamlet.

HAMLET
How is it with you, lady?

QUEEN   Alas, how is't with you,

---

one who has only a moment before killed the man he thought was his uncle, possibly mean?' (Greenblatt, *Purgatory*, 223). Hamlet's treatment of the two murdered fathers present onstage in this scene could hardly be more different.

103 **tardy** late, i.e. procrastinating

104 **That . . . passion** Commentators agree that Hamlet is accusing himself of having wasted time, but they disagree on whether he is also saying he has allowed his original passion (for revenge) to cool. MacDonald offers six different meanings for this phrase: '1. Who, *lapsed* (fallen, guilty), lets action slip in delay and suffering; 2. Who, *lapsed* in (fallen in, overwhelmed by) delay and suffering, omits etc.; 3. *lapsed* in respect of *time*, and because of *passion* – the meaning of the preposition *in*, common to both, reacted upon by the word it governs; 4. faulty both in delaying, and in yielding to suffering, when action is required; 5. *lapsed* through having too much *time* and great suffering; 6. allowing himself to be swept along by *time* and grief.' In the immediate context it seems equally likely that he is acknowledging that

he is indulging in the wrong kind of passion – directed against his mother.

105 **important** urgent, importunate (*OED a.* 3); as at *MA* 2.1.64–5: 'If the Prince be too important, tell him there is measure in everything.'
   your dread command Q1's Hamlet is unique in using the word *revenge* at this point.

107 Perhaps the metaphor of sharpening a blunted sword implies that Hamlet has used his weapon inappropriately (by killing Polonius) and thus jeopardized his mission (see *Son* 95, 14: 'The hardest knife ill used doth lose his edge').

109 i.e. intervene in her mental or spiritual crisis

110 **Conceit** imagination. The Ghost seems to assume that the Queen is particularly vulnerable to the *amazement* (108) caused either by Hamlet's previous behaviour or by his present reaction which is incomprehensible to her.

111–12 three short lines in Q2/F: in this case the combination of the second and third into a single line seems to us better than the combination of the first and second.

105–6] *Theobald; Q2F line* say. / visitation /

That you do bend your eye on vacancy
And with th'incorporal air do hold discourse?
Forth at your eyes your spirits wildly peep,   115
And as the sleeping soldiers in th'alarm
Your bedded hair like life in excrements
Start up and stand on end. O gentle son,
Upon the heat and flame of thy distemper
Sprinkle cool patience. Whereon do you look?   120
HAMLET
On him, on him! Look you how pale he glares,
His form and cause conjoined preaching to stones
Would make them capable. [*to Ghost*] Do not look
    upon me
Lest with this piteous action you convert
My stern effects! Then what I have to do   125
Will want true colour, tears perchance for blood.

---

113 **bend** focus, direct
　vacancy empty space
114 **th'incorporal** the immaterial or
　insubstantial
　hold discourse converse
115 a vivid metaphor based on the theory that
　extreme stress or excitement could cause
　the *spirits* to come to the surface of the
　body and become visible
116 **in th'alarm** i.e. when the alert to arm
　sounds
117 **bedded hair** rooted hairs (regarded as
　plural). Hibbard glosses *bedded* as 'lying
　flat'.
　like . . . excrements as if an *excrement* or
　outgrowth of the body like hair could have
　a life of its own. This phrase was marked
　for cutting in the quartos from 1676;
　Theobald noted that Hughes omitted it in
　his 1723 text 'either because he could
　make Nothing of it, or thought it alluded to

an Image too nauseous', indicating that
excrement had taken on a narrower
meaning by then. Of Shakespeare's six
uses of the word, four are in relation to hair
(see *CE* 2.2.77, *LLL* 5.1.96, *WT* 4.4.716).
121 **how . . . glares** See 1.2.231–2. Macbeth
uses 'glare' to describe the eyes of
Banquo's Ghost (*Mac* 3.4.95).
123 **capable** i.e. of some form of response – the
following lines imply one of sympathy
or pity rather than fear or horror as in
Act 1.
123–5 **Do . . . effects** It is not clear why the
piteous looks of the Ghost should *convert*
Hamlet's *effects* (intentions) from being
stern to something else: Q1 spells out in
more detail the idea that pity would
interfere with his revenge.
126 **want true colour** The usual gloss is
'lack its proper quality or character', but
colour might also mean 'justification'

---

113 you do] thus you *Q1, F2;* you *F*   114 th'incorporal] their corporall *F;* the corporall *F2;* th'incorporeal
Q6   117 bedded] *F;* beaded *Q4* hair] *F;* hairs *Rowe*   118 Start . . . stand] *F;* Starts . . . stands *Q3*   on]
(an) F, Q6   123 SD] *Oxf*

QUEEN

To whom do you speak this?

HAMLET

Do you see nothing there?

QUEEN

Nothing at all, yet all that is I see.

HAMLET

Nor did you nothing hear?   130

QUEEN

No, nothing but ourselves.

HAMLET

Why, look you there! Look how it steals away –
My father in his habit as he lived.
Look where he goes even now out at the portal!

Exit Ghost.

QUEEN

This is the very coinage of your brain.   135
This bodiless creation ecstasy

as at *JC* 2.1.28–9: 'since the quarrel / Will bear no colour for the thing he is'. There is also the literal contrast of the colour of tears and blood here.

129 **Nothing** In *Fratricide Punished* Hamlet responds 'Indeed I believe you see nothing, for you are no longer worthy to look upon his form' (3.6; Bullough, 7.145).

132 **it** See 1.1.20 and n.

steals unnecessarily emended to 'stalks' by some nineteenth-century editors (see Var), but the Ghost's departure from this scene (and from the play) is surprisingly informal

133 **in . . . lived** either (1) in the clothes he wore when he was alive or (2) dressed as if he were alive. As with the armour in Act 1, it seems important that the actual clothing is recognizable. Some commentators find this phrase incompatible with Q1's '*night gowne*' (see 99.1n.) but presumably such a garb would have been familiar to members of the

family. Jonson has a SD in his masque *The Fortunate Isles, and Their Union* (1626), 'Enter Scogan and Skelton, in like habits as they lived' (Jonson, *Masques*, 1.193).

134 **portal** doorway. This explicit reference, found in all three texts, makes it clear that in the original staging the Ghost did not use a trapdoor at this point but left by one of the usual stage doors: see Gurr, who argues that he enters and leaves via the central space, stepping over the body of Polonius ('Globe', 162). This was how the exit was staged at the reconstructed London Globe in 2000, though Hamlet had dragged the body forward out of the way of the Ghost.

135 **very** mere

coinage invention (but here with a sense of 'forgery')

136 **bodiless creation** manufacture of fantasies or hallucinations

ecstasy madness

127 whom] who *F*   134 SD] *Exit. F*   136–7] *Pope; one line Q2F*

Is very cunning in.

HAMLET

My pulse as yours doth temperately keep time
And makes as healthful music. It is not madness
That I have uttered. Bring me to the test   140
And I the matter will reword, which madness
Would gambol from. Mother, for love of grace
Lay not that flattering unction to your soul
That not your trespass but my madness speaks.
It will but skin and film the ulcerous place   145
Whiles rank corruption mining all within
Infects unseen. Confess yourself to heaven,
Repent what's past, avoid what is to come,
And do not spread the compost on the weeds
To make them ranker. Forgive me this my virtue,   150

137 **cunning** clever, skilful
138 i.e. my pulse keeps as moderate a rate as yours. In F, Hamlet begins his next speech by repeating 'Extasie?', printed as a separate line by Hibbard. Jenkins omits it; Edwards prints it as if Hamlet is completing the Queen's line.
141 ***And ... matter** F's 'I' seems necessary for both sense and metre.
   reword repeat (as opposed to 'put into different words'): Hamlet offers to prove his sanity by being able to repeat something accurately.
142 **gambol from** shy away from, i.e. be incapable of performing. See Falstaff's slander on Poins: 'such other gambol faculties 'a has that show a weak mind' (*2H4* 2.4.250–1).
143 **unction** soothing or healing ointment. This and Laertes' reference to the poisonous *unction* he bought *of a mountebank* at 4.7.139, are Shakespeare's only uses of this word whose primary meanings, according to *OED*, relate to oil used for anointing in

religious rituals, especially 'extreme unction', the Christian sacrament for the dying.
145 **skin and film** i.e. cover thinly like a skin or film
146 **mining** burrowing, undermining. This idea of an infection working beneath the skin comes up again in the King's description of the hidden danger represented by Hamlet at 4.1.19–23. (For a fuller discussion of this and other similar metaphors in *Hamlet*, see Thompson & Thompson, 104–9.)
148 **what ... come** i.e. future sin or opportunities for sin (Hamlet elaborates on this at 157–68)
150 **ranker** more luxuriant or vigorous (here, offensively so); see 90 and 146, and other uses of *rank* at 1.2.136, 2.1.20, 3.2.250, 3.3.36 and 4.4.21.
   Forgive ... virtue 'It is perhaps a little disgusting that in the nearest thing to an apology to Gertrude for his abusive behaviour which Hamlet achieves, he stresses even further his self-righteousness'

138 My] Extasie? / My *F*   141 I] *F; not in Q21*   143 that] a *F*   146 Whiles] Whil'st *F*   mining] *F;* running *F3*   149 on] or *F;* o'er *Caldecott*   150 ranker] ranke *F*

> For in the fatness of these pursy times
> Virtue itself of Vice must pardon beg.
> Yea, curb and woo for leave to do him good.

QUEEN

> O Hamlet, thou hast cleft my heart in twain.

HAMLET

> O throw away the worser part of it   155
> And live the purer with the other half.
> Goodnight, but go not to my uncle's bed;
> Assume a virtue if you have it not.
> That monster Custom, who all sense doth eat

(Edwards). Staunton, however, argues that the line is 'an imploration to his own virtue' and is not addressed to the Queen.

151 **pursy** fat, like a swollen purse

153 **curb** bow

154 Belleforest gives the Queen's repentant thoughts at some length at this point (Bullough, 7.94–5). Many performers of the Queen are weeping by now, either from remorse or from distress at Hamlet's behaviour. Dent cites 'To cleave a heart in twain' as proverbial (H329.1).

156 ***live** This makes better sense than Q2's 'leaue', which could be repeated from 153 (though Andrews retains, glossing 'depart'); see *AC* 5.1.59 for a similar traditional emendation: 'Caesar cannot leave/live to be ungentle' (actually emended to 'lean' in Ard³).

158 Jenkins says *assume* means 'put on the garb of, adopt' and not 'simulate'; even so the Queen may find it rather surprising advice coming from the man who had earlier told her 'I know not "seems"' (1.2.76). His choice of a clothing metaphor also seems to reverse his earlier rejection of 'the trappings and the suits of woe' (1.2.86).

159–63 **That . . . on** This passage and the one at 165–8 are not in F. Again Edwards

argues that Shakespeare marked them for deletion (see 69–74n.), and Hibbard comments dismissively on 159–63: 'The general sense of this passage is conveniently summed up in two commonplace phrases: "Custom makes sin no sin" (Tilley, C934) and "Custom is overcome with custom" (Dent, C932.1). But it becomes contorted through Shakespeare's inability to resist the temptation to quibble held out by the word *habit*.' Earlier editors agree: Caldecott remarks, 'Though this passage is much in our author's manner, the folios do not seem to have omitted any thing that could better have been spared', and MacDonald says, 'This omitted passage is obscure with the special Shakespearean obscurity that comes of over-condensation. He omitted it, I think, because of its obscurity'.

159 **monster Custom** i.e. Custom who is a monster

159–60 **who . . . devil** who destroys all sensitivity to wicked or devilish practices. Theobald and many editors emend *devil* to 'evil'; Johnson and others defend *devil* because of the antithesis with *angel*. Hibbard (who prints these lines in an appendix) emends it to 'vile' on the assumption that the

151 these] this *F*   153 woo] woe *F*   him] *F; it Pope*   154] *F lines Hamlet, / twaine. /*   156 live] *F;*
leaue *Q2*   157 my] mine *F*   158 Assume] *(Assune), F*   159–63 That . . . on] *om. F*

Of habits devil, is angel yet in this,   160
That to the use of actions fair and good
He likewise gives a frock or livery
That aptly is put on. Refrain tonight
And that shall lend a kind of easiness
To the next abstinence, the next more easy.   165
For use almost can change the stamp of nature
And either shame the devil or throw him out
With wondrous potency. Once more goodnight,
And when you are desirous to be blessed
I'll blessing beg of you. For this same lord   170
I do repent, but heaven hath pleased it so

word in the manuscript. was 'vilde'; Oxf emends to 'devilish'. (See Jenkins, LN.)

161 **use** custom, habit

162 **likewise** The assumption seems to be that, if the Queen *put[s] on* the clothing or appearance of virtue, custom will make it habitual (i.e. real), just as custom has made her insensitive to sin. Hamlet also makes the link between *habit* and *livery* in his *vicious mole* speech about Danish drunkenness (1.4.23–38).

frock or livery coat or uniform

163 **aptly** readily

165–8 ²**the next . . . potency** See 159–63n.

166 **use . . . nature** 'Use [habit or custom] is another nature' was proverbial (Dent C932). Again the language recalls the *vicious mole* passage where Hamlet refers to 'the stamp of one defect / (Being Nature's livery . . .)' (1.4.31–2).

167 *****shame** It is usually assumed that there is a

word missing in Q2 and that it should provide some alternative to *throw him out*. We adopt Hudson's emendation because the proverb 'tell truth and shame the devil' (Dent, T566) is used three times by Shakespeare in *1H4* (3.1.54, 55 and 58); see t.n. for other editorial emendations. Oxf emends to 'either in the devil', explaining that this means 'take in'.

168 **With wondrous potency** with remarkable (presumably because less expected) power

169–70 **And . . . you** See *KL* 5.3.10–11: 'When thou dost ask me blessing I'll kneel down / And ask of thee forgiveness.' In both instances Shakespeare draws on the assumption that it would be normal or proper for a child to kneel to ask blessing of a parent rather than vice versa. See also *Cor* 5.3.187, where the sight of Volumnia kneeling to her son is described as 'unnatural'.

171 **heaven . . . so** i.e. such is heaven's pleasure

160 Of habits devil] Of habit's Devil *Rowe*; Of habits evil *Theobald (Thirlby)*; Oft habit's devil *Staunton*; Of habit's evil *White*; Of habits devilish *Oxf*; Of habits vile *Oxf¹ (Theobald)*   163 on.] *Q5* (on:*); on *Q2*   Refrain tonight] *F*; to refraine night *Q2*   165–8 ²the . . . potency] *om. F*   167 either shame] *Hudson*; either *Q2*; Maister *Q3*; master ev'n *Pope*; either master *Jennens*; either curb *Malone*; entertain *Cam (Monro)*; either house *Chambers² (Bailey)*; either lodge *Ard² (Clarendon)*; either . . . *Cam²*; either in *Oxf*

To punish me with this, and this with me,
That I must be their scourge and minister.
I will bestow him and will answer well
The death I gave him. So again goodnight.   175
I must be cruel only to be kind.
This bad begins and worse remains behind.
One word more, good lady!

QUEEN   What shall I do?

HAMLET

Not this, by no means, that I bid you do –
Let the bloat King tempt you again to bed,   180

---

172 Hamlet presumably means that as he has punished Polonius (by killing him), so he will be punished for the killing (either by the King or by having the murder on his conscience).

173 **their ... minister** Hamlet sees himself as the chastising agent of the gods (*their* refers back to *heaven* in 171); see Richmond's prayer, 'Make us Thy ministers of chastisement' (*R3* 5.3.114). *Scourge and minister* is another hendiadys (= scourging minister); this idea became important in a political sense in many productions of *Hamlet* in the former Soviet Union and eastern Europe, with Hamlet seen as the self-sacrificing hero who could cleanse the state of corruption and oppression (see Stříbrný, especially 115–16 on productions by Josef Svoboda before and after the 'Prague Spring' of 1968).

174 **bestow** remove, dispose of. In Q1 Hamlet says more specifically, 'Come sir, I'll provide for you a grave' (as the first half of a couplet completed with 213).
answer well make an appropriate response, i.e. explain the death or perhaps, as Jenkins suggests, atone for it. This promise is hardly fulfilled by Hamlet's behaviour in 4.2 and 4.3, or by his apology to Laertes in 5.2.

176–7 As Edwards notes, this is a reflective couplet, almost an aside, like his couplet at the end of Act 1 (1.5.186–7).

177 **This** 'the killing of Polonius, as at [172]. It is hard to see why most eds continue to prefer F's vague and feeble *Thus*' (Jenkins).
worse remains behind i.e. worse crimes or calamities will follow. Dent cites 'An ill (bad) beginning has an ill (bad) ending' as proverbial (B261).

178 **One ... lady** This line is not in F and Jenkins suggests the omission may be deliberate as 'it seems intrusive after Hamlet's couplet'. The couplet certainly sounds like an exit-line, but Hamlet has previously said *good night* three times (157, 168, 175) and then returned to his theme, very much as he repeatedly returned to Ophelia after bidding her farewell in 3.1. Eighteenth- and nineteenth-century stage tradition ended this scene at 177: see Hapgood and Appendix 4.

179 **Not ... means** Hamlet's double negative emphasizes the irony or sarcasm of his advice. In performance it is possible to play this speech as 'mad': Hamlet reverts to his *antic disposition*, partly in order to test his mother's sincerity.

180 **bloat** bloated or fat

---

177 This] Thus *F*   178 One . . . lady!] *om. F*   180 bloat] *Warburton;* blowt *Q2;* blunt *F;* fond *Pope*

Pinch wanton on your cheek, call you his mouse
And let him for a pair of reechy kisses,
Or paddling in your neck with his damned fingers,
Make you to ravel all this matter out
That I essentially am not in madness   185
But mad in craft. 'Twere good you let him know,
For who that's but a queen – fair, sober, wise –
Would from a paddock, from a bat, a gib,
Such dear concernings hide? Who would do so?
No, in despite of sense and secrecy   190
Unpeg the basket on the house's top,
Let the birds fly and like the famous ape
To try conclusions in the basket creep
And break your own neck down.

181 **Pinch wanton** give you sensual pinches or caresses (or pinch in a wanton way?)
call . . . mouse presumably an example of the *honeying* of 91; *mouse* occurs as an endearment in other texts of the period, usually between husband and wife, though Shakespeare's Rosaline uses it to address another woman, Katherine, at *LLL* 5.2.19. See also Lady Capulet's use of 'mouse-hunt' meaning 'woman-chaser' at *RJ* 4.4.11.
182 **reechy** filthy (literally 'reeky', foul-smelling)
184 **ravel . . . out** unravel, reveal
185–6 **That . . . craft** The same question arises in a very different context in *TN* when Feste asks Malvolio, 'But tell me true, are you not mad indeed? or do you but counterfeit?' (4.2.114–15).
185 that I am not really afflicted by madness
186 **in craft** by cunning or pretence
'Twere . . . know (sarcastic)
187–8 **For . . . Would** for would anyone who was just a fair, sober and wise queen
188 **paddock . . . bat . . . gib** 'The toad, bat and tom-cat, all regarded as unclean or

venomous, were supposed to be the familiars of witches, and so privy to their secrets' (Hibbard).
gib pronounced with a hard 'g' as in 'give'
189 **Such dear concernings** matters of such crucial concern to it (him)
190–4 'Oddly enough, there is no record of this fable. It more or less explains itself, however. An ape takes a birdcage onto a roof; he opens the door and lets the birds fly out. In order to imitate them, he gets into the basket, jumps out and, instead of flying, falls to the ground. It does not seem a very appropriate way of telling the queen that she will get hurt if she releases news of Hamlet's sanity' (Edwards). Daniell cites this speech as an example of the language of *Hamlet* getting out of control when driven by passion, as compared with the more rational and orderly discourse of *JC* (Daniell, 40).
193 **try conclusions** experiment
194 **down** more likely an intensifier, 'utterly' (Edwards), than 'by falling' (Jenkins, Hibbard). MacDonald speculates, 'it could hardly have been written "neck-bone" '.

184 ravel] *F;* rouell *Q2*   186 mad] made *F*

QUEEN

> Be thou assured, if words be made of breath 195
> And breath of life, I have no life to breathe
> What thou hast said to me.

HAMLET

> I must to England – you know that.

QUEEN

> Alack, I had forgot; 'tis so concluded on.

HAMLET

> There's letters sealed and my two schoolfellows – 200
> Whom I will trust as I will adders fanged –
> They bear the mandate, they must sweep my way
> And marshal me to knavery. Let it work.

195–7 In Q1 Hamlet explicitly asks the Queen to 'assist me in revenge' at this point and she promises to do so: 'I will conceale, consent, and doe my best – / What stratagem soe're thou shalt deuise' (11.95, 99–100).

198 It is not clear how or when Hamlet (or indeed the Queen) learned about this plan first mentioned by the King to Polonius at 3.1.168–9 and announced to Rosencrantz and Guildenstern at 3.3.2–4, but Shakespeare often uses the convention whereby characters can be assumed to share information known to the audience. A somewhat over-literal Trevor Nunn production (London Old Vic 2004) had Hamlet discover the plan from a paper he found in Polonius' pocket.

200–8 **There's ... meet** not in F. Edwards argues that this passage was cut by Shakespeare as part of a revision of the later part of the play; he claims that 'the determination to kill Rosencrantz and Guildenstern does not accord with 5.2.6–11' (where events are vaguely attributed to *a divinity*), but Hamlet seems to be

resolving to outwit them here, not specifically to kill them. Edwards and Hibbard agree that the omission adds to the suspense in F. In the Kozintsev film, this part of the speech is moved to the later point where Hamlet's description of his outwitting of Rosencrantz and Guildenstern (5.2.1–53) is dramatized.

202 **bear the mandate** Hibbard assumes a breach of protocol: 'the orders for what the mission is to do should be in the hands of the most important member of it, Hamlet himself, not of two underlings', but the words might be interpreted more neutrally to mean simply that they have the King's orders to go.

sweep my way prepare the way for me

203 **marshal ... knavery** conduct me towards some kind of trick or villainy (intended for me). The word *marshal* begins a train of military metaphors (*enginer ... petard ... mines*) as Hamlet sees his contest with Rosencrantz and Guildenstern in terms of siege warfare.

Let it work i.e. let their plan unfold

199] *one line F; Q2 lines* forgot. / on. / 200–8] *om. F*

For 'tis the sport to have the enginer
Hoist with his own petard, and't shall go hard   205
But I will delve one yard below their mines
And blow them at the moon. O, 'tis most sweet
When in one line two crafts directly meet.
This man shall set me packing;
I'll lug the guts into the neighbour room.   210
Mother, goodnight indeed. This councillor
Is now most still, most secret and most grave,
Who was in life a most foolish prating knave.
Come, sir, to draw toward an end with you.   214
Goodnight, mother.   *Exit [Hamlet tugging in Polonius].*

204 **enginer** maker of 'engines': bombs and other devices. We retain the Q2 spelling to draw attention to the fact that the meaning is slightly different from that of modern 'engineer' and the stress should be on the first syllable (like *pioner* at 1.5.162).

205 **Hoist ... petard** blown up by his own bomb. Jenkins adopts 'petard' as 'the more regular spelling' than Q2's 'petar', though he notes that *OED* shows Drayton rhyming it with 'far'. He does not comment on the internal rhyme with *hard* created by 'petard'.

205–6 **and't ... will** and it will be hard luck if I do not

206 **delve** dig. See 5.1.14, where the Gravedigger is addressed as *goodman delver*.
   mines tunnels used in attacking a town (the word was later used for the explosives buried in such tunnels). Shakespeare had drawn on Holinshed's description of the use of mines at the siege of Harfleur in *H5* 3.2.55–65.

208 when two pieces of cunning collide with each other (as a countermine meets a mine)

209 **set me packing** oblige me to go at once; start me plotting

210 Richard of Gloucester has a similar line addressed to Henry VI, whom he has just killed: 'I'll throw thy body in another room' (*3H6* 5.6.92).
   lug the guts This expression, together with 'draw toward an end' at 214 and F's SD at 215, implies that Hamlet drags Polonius offstage. The lines were traditionally cut as undignified in the context; Barrymore restored them in 1925 – surprisingly as his performance otherwise avoided the less attractive side of Hamlet (see Dawson, 75–6). It must always have been awkward for a lone actor to get a body off, but the unceremonious nature of the proceedings is highlighted here, as it is in Falstaff's removal of the body of Hotspur in *1H4* 5.4. Amleth's treatment of the body is worse in Saxo Grammaticus: see 92n. and pp. 69–70.

211, 215 **goodnight ... Goodnight** See 178n.

213 **most** not in F, and perhaps mistakenly repeated from 212
   prating chattering

214 **draw ... you** (1) make an end of my business with you; (2) drag you towards your grave

215 SD *Just 'Exit'* in Q2, perhaps implying that the Queen remains onstage (see Appendix 4). Jenkins argues that

205 petard] *(petar)*   213 most] *om. F*   215 SD] *F; Exit. Q2; Exit Hamlet with the dead body. Q1*

[4.1]   *Enter* KING *with* ROSENCRANTZ
                    and GUILDENSTERN.

KING

There's matter in these sighs, these profound heaves.
You must translate; 'tis fit we understand them.
Where is your son?

QUEEN

Bestow this place on us a little while.
                    [*Exeunt Rosencrantz and Guildenstern.*]

Ah, mine own lord, what have I seen tonight!   5

KING

What, Gertrude? How does Hamlet?

QUEEN

Mad as the sea and wind when both contend

F's '*tugging*' is a misprint for 'lugging', the verb Hamlet uses at 210; *in* implies 'into' the inner stage or tiring-house, i.e. offstage.

4.1 Q2's SD (see t.n.) has been taken to justify a new scene (and indeed a new act), although there has been no exit for the Queen from 3.4. The only other textual excuse for this notoriously problematic division is the King's statement at 4.1.34–5 that 'Hamlet in madness hath Polonius slain / And from his mother's closet hath he dragged him', implying a change of location from the *closet* which was the location of 3.4. The corresponding SD in F is merely '*Enter King*', which may justify the continuation of that scene at least until the *Exeunt* of the King and Queen at 4.1.45: *TxC* assumes 'a deliberate change of staging'. See Appendix 4. The three texts: this scene runs to 22 lines in Q1 where it is a continuation of scene 11, and 45 lines in Q2; the equivalent material runs to 40 lines in F where it is a continuation of

3.4 in Ard Q1/F (see 41–4n and 3.4.215 SDn.). Location and timing: in all three texts this scene follows immediately on from 3.4.

0.1–2 Rosencrantz and Guildenstern do not enter until 32 in F. In Q2 they are apparently dismissed by the Queen at 4. They are not given an exit, though they re-enter at 32.

1   **matter** substance, meaning
      heaves heavings of the breast, sobs

2   **translate** i.e. put the meaning into words

4   The Queen asks whoever has entered with the King (see 0.1–2n.) to leave, presumably wanting privacy for what she is about to reveal.

5   **mine own lord** F's 'my good Lord' seems less intimate.

6   **What, Gertrude?** perhaps a straight question ('What have you seen, Gertrude?'); perhaps an exclamation of concern ('My poor Gertrude!')

7   **Mad ... sea** proverbial (Dent, S170).

4.1] *Q6*   0.1–2] *Cam¹ subst.; Eenter King, and Queene, with Rosencraus and Guyldensterne. Q2; Enter the King and Lordes. Q1; Enter King. F*   1–3] *F lines* sighes. / heaues / them. /   1 matter] matters *F* heaues.] *Rowe;* heaues, *Q2;* heaues *F*   4] *om. F*   SD] *Q6 subst.*   5 mine own] my good *F*   7 sea] *Q1;* Seas *F*

Which is the mightier. In his lawless fit,
Behind the arras hearing something stir,
Whips out his rapier, cries 'A rat, a rat!'   10
And in this brainish apprehension kills
The unseen good old man.
KING   O heavy deed!
It had been so with us had we been there.
His liberty is full of threats to all,
To you yourself, to us, to everyone.   ˙15
Alas, how shall this bloody deed be answered?
It will be laid to us whose providence
Should have kept short, restrained and out of haunt
This mad young man. But so much was our love,
We would not understand what was most fit,   20
But like the owner of a foul disease,
To keep it from divulging, let it feed

Q2's singular *sea* consorts better with *both* than F's 'Seas' and is supported by Q1's 'Alas my lord, as raging as the sea'. The Queen seems to be obeying Hamlet's request or command at 3.4.179–86. Sometimes in performance she shrinks from the King's touch, but she has to defend him from Laertes in 4.5 so it may be inconsistent for her to express a complete change of heart.

8 **lawless** ungovernable, out of control
9 **something** In Q2 and F the Queen is vague about the source of the noise, implying that Hamlet might have thought he was killing a literal rat; in Q1, despite her stronger commitment to support and protect her son, she says, 'Corambis called', perhaps implying more explicitly that Hamlet knew what he was doing.
10 **Whips . . . rapier** The Queen omits the subject (he = Hamlet); F improves the grammar at the expense of metre.

11 **brainish apprehension** deluded (mis-) understanding
12 **heavy** serious, grievous
13, 15, 17   **us** The King emphasizes the royal plural.
13 The King does not assume that Hamlet actually thought he was killing him, and the Queen does not enlighten him (but see 4.7.4–5).
16 **answered** responded to, or perhaps accounted for
17 **laid to us** blamed on us (me)
   providence care, forethought
18 **kept short** i.e. controlled
   out of haunt away from society, secluded
20 **would not** chose not to
22 **divulging** being made known (*OED*'s first use). The King's metaphor of a secret disease recalls Hamlet's words to the Queen at 3.4.145–7.
   let Thus Q2, making *We* the subject of the verb; F's 'let's' makes *the owner* the subject.

10 Whips . . . rapier] whips me / Out his rapier, and *Q1*; He whips his Rapier out *F*   11 this] his *Q1F*
22 let] let's *F*

Even on the pith of life. Where is he gone?

QUEEN

To draw apart the body he hath killed,
O'er whom – his very madness like some ore   25
Among a mineral of metals base
Shows itself pure – 'a weeps for what is done.

KING

O Gertrude, come away.
The sun no sooner shall the mountains touch
But we will ship him hence, and this vile deed   30
We must with all our majesty and skill
Both countenance and excuse. Ho, Guildenstern!

Enter ROSENCRANTZ *and* GUILDENSTERN.

Friends both, go join you with some further aid:
Hamlet in madness hath Polonius slain
And from his mother's closet hath he dragged him.   35
Go seek him out, speak fair and bring the body

---

23 **pith** essential substance

25–7 **O'er . . . pure** The gist seems to be that even in his madness Hamlet shows evidence of his pure strain of superiority.

25 **ore** deposit or vein of [precious] metal. 'Shakespeare seems to think *ore* to be *Or*, that is, gold. Base metals have *ore* [deposits or veins] no less than precious' (Johnson).

26 **a mineral** a mine or the contents of a mine

27 **'a . . . done** As at 9, the Queen is protecting Hamlet with this inaccurate version of his response.

29–30 **The . . . hence** 'we will make him take ship as soon as dawn breaks'. These words remind us that it is still night and the King's anticipation of the dawn recalls the endings of 1.1 and 1.5.

32 **countenance and excuse** face out and offer justification. '*Majesty* will *countenance* and *skill* will *excuse*' (Edwards).

32.1 See t.n. for placing; the King's *Ho, Guildenstern!* could be a summons if it is spoken before they appear, or a greeting if after.

33 **join . . . aid** get more men to help you (see 4.2.2.1 and n.)

35 **from . . . closet** This implication that the scene is *not* now set in the Queen's closet provides a shred of justification for the traditional scene-break (see headnote and Appendix 4).

36 **speak fair** address him courteously (i.e. placate him)

25–7 whom – . . . pure –] *Ard²;* whom, . . . pure, *Q2;* whom . . . pure. *F*   25 some] *F;* fine *Furness (Walker)*   27 'a] He *F*   32] *F lines* excuse. / Guildenstern: /   32.1] Rowe; *opp. 31 Q2; opp.* excuse *F* 35 mother's closet] Mother Clossets *F*   dragged] *F;* dreg'd *Q2*

Into the chapel. I pray you haste in this.
　　　　　[*Exeunt Rosencrantz and Guildenstern.*]

Come, Gertrude, we'll call up our wisest friends
And let them know both what we mean to do
And what's untimely done. [　　　　　　　]　　40
Whose whisper o'er the world's diameter,
As level as the cannon to his blank,
Transports his poisoned shot, may miss our name
And hit the woundless air. O come away,　　　44
My soul is full of discord and dismay.　　*Exeunt.*

[**4.2**]　　　　　　　*Enter* HAMLET.

37 SD *Some equivalent of F's SD seems
　needed here.
38 **wisest friends** It is not clear who, apart
　from the dead Polonius, are the King's
　councillors, though some productions do
　supply silent courtiers for this purpose (see
　4.3.0.1).
40 **what's untimely done** what action has
　been inopportunely or improperly
　committed (by Hamlet). It is generally
　assumed that the second half of this line is
　missing in Q2; see t.n. for editors' attempts
　to provide an explicit subject for *Whose
　whisper* (41). In F the King continues *O
　come away* as at 44, omitting the
　intervening lines.
41–4 **Whose . . . air** not in F; Edwards and
　Hibbard agree these lines must have been
　marked for deletion; Edwards describes
　them as 'sententious' and relates the 'cut'
　to others in 1.1 and 1.4. MacDonald,
　however, defends the lines despite their
　obscurity, which he says results from
　'over-condensation with its tendency to
　seeming confusion – the only fault I know
　in the Poet . . . It is much as if, able to think
　two thoughts at once, he would compel his

　phrase to utter them at once'.
41 **Whose whisper** Without emendation this
　must mean 'the rumour of which deed' (i.e.
　the killing of Polonius).
　o'er . . . diameter throughout the world
42 as straight as the cannon to its target
43 **miss our name** avoid hurting our (my)
　reputation
44 **woundless** invulnerable (*OED*'s first use
　in this sense, though the word occurs
　earlier meaning 'unwounded')
4.2 The three texts: this scene runs to 28 lines
　in Q2 and 32 in F (3.5 in Ard Q1/F) with
　no major omissions or additions. In Q1
　the action is continuous from the closet
　scene (11) to the appearance of
　Fortenbrasse (*sic*); Hamlet's encounter
　with Rosencrantz and Guildenstern at
　this point is omitted, though the dialogue
　about the *apple* (or *ape*) and the *sponge*
　(10–19) has appeared earlier, near the end
　of scene 9 (3.2). Location and timing: this
　scene follows immediately after 4.1 and
　takes place in an adjacent part of the
　palace.
0.1 F delays the entry of the others (specified
　as '*Ros. and Guildensterne*') until

37 SD] *Q1 (Exeunt Lordes), F (Exit Gent.), Rowe (Exeunt Rosencrantz and Guildenstern)*　39 And] To
F　40 done. [　]] *this edn; Q2 lines* doone, /; done. For, haply, Slander *Theobald;* done: so, haply, slander
Capell; done: so viperous slander *Malone;* done. So envious slander *Ard²* 41–4 Whose . . . air.] *om. F*　**4.2**]
Pope　0.1] *F; Enter Hamlet, Rosencraus, and others. Q2*

HAMLET   Safely stowed! But soft, what noise? Who calls
on Hamlet? O, here they come!

[*Enter* ROSENCRANTZ, GUILDENSTERN *and others*.]

ROSENCRANTZ   What have you done, my lord, with the
dead body?
HAMLET   Compound it with dust, whereto 'tis kin.   5
ROSENCRANTZ   Tell us where 'tis, that we may take it
thence and bear it to the chapel.
HAMLET   Do not believe it.
ROSENCRANTZ   Believe what?
HAMLET   That I can keep your council and not mine own.   10
Besides, to be demanded of a sponge! What replication
should be made by the son of a king?
ROSENCRANTZ   Take you me for a sponge, my lord?

after *here they come* at 2. It does seem from
the first two lines that Hamlet enters alone.
1   **stowed** put away (hidden). Hamlet's action
in hiding the body is perhaps intended to
make the murder seem like the act of a
madman. Actors often behave wildly in
this scene and the next (see Hapgood).
1–2 **Who . . . Hamlet** F has '*Gentlemen within.
Hamlet*, Lord *Hamlet*' after 'Safely
stowed', described by Jenkins as 'evidently
a playhouse addition'. Hibbard thinks it is
'deliberately added to bring out the farcical
element'.
2.1 **and others** specified in Q2's opening
direction and implied by the King's 'join
you with some further aid' at 4.1.33; some
additional personnel are also required by
Q2's directions at 4.3.11 and 15.
5   **Compound . . . dust** Combined, mixed it,
with dust. Hamlet gives the impression
here that he has buried the body rather than

just moved it. Q2's 'Compound' and F's
'Compounded' were both acceptable as
past forms of the verb *c.* 1600, according to
OED. Jennens, however, suggests that
Compound must be an imperative 'if
Shakespeare did not design Hamlet to tell
an untruth here . . . he . . . bids them
compound it with dust.'
whereto 'tis kin 'Dust thou art and unto
dust shalt thou return' (Genesis, 3.19).
10   **That . . . own** 'That I can keep your secret
(namely that you are agents for the King)
and not my own.' This passage in which he
specifically refuses to answer their
questions recalls the dialogue about the
recorders at 3.2.342–63 (with which it is
combined in Q1).
11   **demanded of** interrogated by
replication reply; *OED* 2c cites a 1586
usage in a legal sense of an answer to a
charge.

1 stowed!] stowed. / *Gentlemen within. Hamlet*, Lord *Hamlet*. / *F*   But soft,] *om. F*   2.1] *Ard²; Enter Ros.
and Guildensterne. F*   5 Compound] Compounded *F*   6–7] *Ard¹; Q2F line* thence, / Chappell. /

389

HAMLET   Ay, sir – that soaks up the King's countenance,
his rewards, his authorities. But such officers do the   15
King best service in the end: he keeps them like an ape
in the corner of his jaw, first mouthed to be last
swallowed. When he needs what you have gleaned, it is
but squeezing you and, sponge, you shall be dry again!
ROSENCRANTZ   I understand you not, my lord.   20
HAMLET   I am glad of it. A knavish speech sleeps in a
foolish ear.
ROSENCRANTZ   My lord, you must tell us where the body
is, and go with us to the King.
HAMLET   The body is with the King, but the King is not   25
with the body. The King is a thing.

---

14 **countenance** benevolent countenance, i.e.
    patronage
16 ***like an ape** as an ape does. Most editors
    (apart from Dover Wilson) regard Q2's
    'like an apple' as a misreading; Elze
    comments that 'it may be surmised that
    [Q1: 'as an Ape doth nuttes'] exhibits the
    authentic words of the poet; at all events it
    presents an excellent and most noteworthy
    reading', and Jenkins remarks that the Q1
    version 'shows how well the actors
    understood'. Singer, Staunton, Hudson and
    Rolfe actually adopt the Q1 reading; some
    editors (Oxf, Hibbard, Folg) adopt
    Farmer's conjecture 'like an ape an apple'.
18–19 **When . . . again** The implication is that
    the King will take back the benefits he has
    given at his convenience.
18 **gleaned** gathered, collected. This word
    literally refers to the practice of gathering
    ears of corn left after reaping as at 2.2.16; it
    is not normally used of the liquids implied
    by the *sponge* metaphor.
21 **knavish** wicked – either because Hamlet is
    insulting Rosencrantz or because he is
    telling a cynical truth about the King

sleeps i.e. is ineffective, does no harm
25–6 **The . . . body** 'This pretty piece of
    chiasmus [the wordplay of reversing the
    parallel terms *body* and *King*] sounds
    impressive but is singularly reluctant to
    yield up a sense that can be apprehended by
    an audience in a theatre. Intended as a riddle,
    it remains a riddle' (Hibbard). Jennens,
    however, explains, 'The body, being in the
    palace, might be said to be with the king;
    though the king, not being in the same room
    with the body, was not with the body.'
    Hamlet might also mean that the King is not
    with the body in the sense that he is not (yet)
    dead. Other editors suggest an allusion to the
    theory of the king's two bodies (natural and
    political), whereby Hamlet casts doubt on
    the legitimacy of this king, implying that his
    kingship does not reside in his physical body
    (see Jenkins, LN).
26–8 **The . . . nothing** The full stop after *thing*
    (26) in Q2 implies that Hamlet is insulting
    the King by calling him an object. F has a
    long dash after *thing* which makes
    Guildenstern's question an interruption
    (usually played as shocked), or perhaps he

---

16 like an ape] *F;* like an apple *Q2;* as an Ape doth nuttes *Q1 at 9.215–16;* like an ape an apple *Parrott–
Craig (Farmer, see Steevens²)*   26 thing.] thing – *F*

GUILDENSTERN   A thing, my lord?
HAMLET   Of nothing. Bring me to him.   *Exeunt.*

[**4.3**]   *Enter* KING *and two or three.*

KING

I have sent to seek him and to find the body.
How dangerous is it that this man goes loose!
Yet must not we put the strong law on him:
He's loved of the distracted multitude,
Who like not in their judgement but their eyes,   5
And where 'tis so th'offender's scourge is weighed
But never the offence. To bear all smooth and even

expected some legal or philosophical definition of kingship which Hamlet deflates. 'A thing of nothing' recalls Psalm 144: 'Man is like a thing of nought.'

28 **Bring . . . him** F's additional line (see t.n.) is rejected by Jenkins as an actor's interpolation but defended by Hibbard as an authorial revision in the direction of the 'savage comic humour' characteristic of this scene and the next. He also suggests it is comparable to the mad Lear's abrupt exit on the line 'Come, an you get it, / You shall get it by running' (*KL* 4.6.198–9). In both Q2 and F, Hamlet seizes the initiative and avoids the indignity of a straightforward arrest (see his similar move at 4.3.51).

4.3 The three texts: this scene runs to 66 lines in Q2 and 64 lines in F (3.6 in Ard Q1/F). In Q1 the action is continuous but this section runs to 41 lines (11.126–66). Location and timing: this scene follows immediately after 4.2 and takes place in an adjacent part of the palace.

0.1 F's SD (see t.n.) turns the King's first speech into a soliloquy, a change deplored by Edwards and Klein but approved by Hibbard. Gurr & Ichikawa (145–6) suggest that 'a large body of support for the

oppressed king ought to have been essential' here, but the numbers available may have been curtailed by the need for the appearance of Fortinbras's army in 4.4. It is not clear who Q2's '*two or three*' should be: presumably the *wisest friends* of 4.1.38 and people in whom the King feels he can confide his *desperate* plans for dealing with Hamlet. The King is notably less explicit in this speech than when he is definitely alone at the end of the scene.

3 **put . . . him** punish him to the full extent of the law

4–5 This is the first we have heard of Hamlet's popularity with the people – a factor he does not mention or exploit. The King returns to the theme at 4.7.19 when he explains to Laertes that he has not acted against Hamlet because of 'the great love the general gender bear him'.

4 **distracted multitude** confused or irrational populace

5 **like . . . eyes** approve not by judgement but by appearance

6 **scourge** punishment
   weighed taken seriously

7 **bear . . . even** i.e. conduct everything so as to minimize suspicion

28 him.] him, hide Fox, and all after. *F*   **4.3**] Pope   0.1] *Enter King. F*   7 never] neerer *F*

This sudden sending him away must seem
Deliberate pause; diseases desperate grown
By desperate appliance are relieved,   10
Or not at all.

Enter ROSENCRANTZ [*and* GUILDENSTERN] *and all the rest.*

How now, what hath befallen?

ROSENCRANTZ
Where the dead body is bestowed, my lord,
We cannot get from him.

KING   But where is he?

ROSENCRANTZ
Without, my lord, guarded, to know your pleasure.

KING
Bring him before us.

ROSENCRANTZ   Ho! Bring in the lord!   15

[*Enter* HAMLET *and Attendants.*]

KING   Now, Hamlet, where's Polonius?
HAMLET   At supper.
KING   At supper! Where?
HAMLET   Not where he eats but where 'a is eaten. A

9   **Deliberate pause** usually glossed 'i.e. the result of careful deliberation', but possibly 'a deliberate suspension of judgement'. It is now the King (and soon his ally Laertes) who must wait for the right moment to act.
9–10   **diseases ... relieved** proverbial: 'A desperate disease must have a desperate cure' (Tilley, D357)
10   **appliance** application (of remedies)
11   SD *Q2 omits Guildenstern from this entry, but many editions and productions include him; F has the King summon him at 15, when he enters with Hamlet.
11   **befallen** happened; probably disyllabic, as Q2/F's spelling 'befalne' indicates
14   **Without** outside (the door)
     guarded 'Henceforward he is guarded, or at least closely watched, according to the Folio – left much to himself according to the [Second] Quarto' (MacDonald).

11   SD *and* GUILDENSTERN] *Cam¹ subst. ¹and . . . rest*] *om. F*   befallen] *(befalne) F*   15 Ho!] *(How); Hoa, Guildensterne? F*   the] my *F*   15.1] *Kittredge; They enter. Q2, opp. 15; Enter Hamlet and Guildensterne. F*   19 'a] he *Q1F*

certain convocation of politic worms are e'en at him.　20
Your worm is your only emperor for diet. We fat all
creatures else to fat us, and we fat ourselves for maggots.
Your fat king and your lean beggar is but variable
service, two dishes but to one table. That's the end.

KING　Alas, alas.　25

HAMLET　A man may fish with the worm that hath eat of
a king and eat of the fish that hath fed of that worm.

KING　What dost thou mean by this?

HAMLET　Nothing but to show you how a king may go a
progress through the guts of a beggar.　30

KING　Where is Polonius?

HAMLET　In heaven. Send thither to see. If your messenger
find him not there, seek him i'th' other place

---

20 **convocation . . . worms** generally taken to
be a punning reference to the Diet or
council of the German city of Worms made
famous in 1521 when Martin Luther
appeared to justify his Protestant views;
see Greenblatt (*Purgatory*, 241), who
argues that this passage parodies the debate
about transubstantiation, i.e. the
transformation of the body and blood of
Jesus into the bread and wine of the
Christian communion or mass.
politic shrewd, scheming (perhaps with a
reference to Polonius' own nature)

21, 23 **Your . . . your** Used colloquially (see
Blake, 3.3.4.5c or Hope 1.3.2b) in a general
rather than a personal sense, as in *your
philosophy* at 1.5.166 and *your water* at
5.1.161–2.

21 **emperor** Hamlet is playing on the
(proverbial?) saying that even an emperor
is food for worms.

21, 22 **fat** fatten

24 **variable service** various or interchangeable
dishes or courses (of a meal); *OED* service

sb. V 27b

25–7 **Alas . . . that worm** The fact that a
version of these lines appears in Q1 causes
Hibbard to assume that F's omission of
them was an error rather than a deliberate
cut.

25 **Alas, alas** In all three texts the King's
pretence of concern for Hamlet's welfare
(also at 39–40) is undermined by his
expressed determination in soliloquy
that he is sending him to his death (see
56–66).

27 **and eat** Q1's 'And a Beggar eate' seems
necessary for Hamlet's follow-up at 29–30,
though Jenkins dismisses it as 'an inferior
reading through anticipating the point'.

28 **thou** Like the Queen in 3.4 (see 3.4.8–9n.),
the King addresses Hamlet as *thou* while
Hamlet responds using *you*.

30 **progress** the term used for official journeys
by royalty

33 **i'th' other place** i.e. in hell. Hamlet's
insulting joke recalls his concern for the
King's ultimate destination at 3.3.73–95.

---

20 politic] *Q1; om. F*　22 ourselves] our selfe *F*　24 service, . . . table.] seruices, two dishes to one messe:
Q1; seruice to dishes, but to one Table *F*　25–7] *om. F*　26–7] Looke you, a man may fish with that worme
/ That hath eaten of a King, / And a Beggar eate that fish, / Which that worme hath caught. *Q1*　28 SP] *F;
King.King Q2*

yourself. But if indeed you find him not within this
month you shall nose him as you go up the stairs into   35
the lobby.

KING [*to some Attendants*]   Go, seek him there!

HAMLET   'A will stay till you come.   [*Exeunt Attendants.*]

KING

Hamlet, this deed for thine especial safety –
Which we do tender, as we dearly grieve   40
For that which thou hast done – must send thee
    hence.
Therefore prepare thyself:
The bark is ready and the wind at help,
Th'associates tend and everything is bent
For England.

HAMLET   For England?

KING   Ay, Hamlet.

HAMLET   Good.   45

KING

So is it if thou knewst our purposes.

HAMLET

I see a cherub that sees them. But come, for England.

---

35 **shall nose** must smell
36 **lobby** corridor or ante-room
37 SD, 38 SD In Q2's version the '*two or
   three*' who entered at 0.1, '*the rest*' who
   entered at 11, and whoever entered with
   Hamlet at 15 are available to obey the
   King's command here.
38 In Q1 Hamlet spells out the joke more
   explicitly: 'do not make too much haste, /
   I'le warrant you hee'le stay till you come'
   (11.145–6).
40 **tender** care for
   dearly intensely
42 F's phrase (see t.n.) at the beginning of this

short line is an 'interpolation' for Jenkins,
prompted by the phrase 'fiery expedition' in
R3 4.3.54, but 'authorial revision' for Hibbard.
43 **bark** vessel
   at help favourable
44 **tend** are waiting
   bent directed, prepared
45 **For England?** Hamlet is presumably
   expressing sardonic knowingness rather
   than surprise (see 3.4.198 and n.).
47 **I ... them** Cherubim were supposed to be
   watchful over human affairs; perhaps
   Hamlet is suggesting that the King cannot
   hide his purposes from God.

---

34 if indeed] indeed, if *F*   within] *om. F*   37 SD] *Capell*   38 'A will] hee'le *Q1;* He will *F* you] *Q1;* ye
F   SD] *Capell*   39 deed] deed of thine, *F*   42 Therefore] With fierie Quicknesse. Therefore *F*   44 is] at
F   47 them] him *F*

Farewell, dear mother.

KING   Thy loving father, Hamlet.

HAMLET

My mother. Father and mother is man and wife.

Man and wife is one flesh. So – my mother.   50

Come, for England!   *Exit.*

KING   Follow him at foot.

Tempt him with speed aboard.

Delay it not – I'll have him hence tonight.

Away, for everything is sealed and done

That else leans on th'affair. Pray you make haste.   55

                     [*Exeunt all but the King.*]

And England, if my love thou hold'st at aught

As my great power thereof may give thee sense,

Since yet thy cicatrice looks raw and red

After the Danish sword, and thy free awe

Pays homage to us, thou mayst not coldly set   60

---

48 **Farewell, dear mother** Edwin Booth claimed to have been the first Hamlet to address these words directly to the King; the traditional method was apparently to address them off-stage to the absent Queen (see Hapgood), though the King's reply makes more sense if they are addressed to him.

50 **Man ... flesh** Hamlet alludes to biblical formulations: see Genesis, 2.24, Matthew, 19.5–6, Mark, 10.8.

51 **Come, for England** As at the end of 4.2, Hamlet seems to take the initiative, although he has in fact little choice.
at foot at his heels, i.e. closely

52 **Tempt** encourage

54–5 **everything ... That else** everything ... else that

55 **leans on** depends on, appertains to

55 SD *Q1's SD is clearly necessary, as the

following lines would be surprisingly indiscreet as a public speech (see 0.1n. above).

56–66   Although *England* must mean 'the King of England', it is conceivable that the reiteration of *England* (56, 63) might encourage the actor to speak these lines as a direct address to an English audience.

56 **hold'st at aught** consider to be of any value

57 **thereof ... sense** may give you an appreciation of the importance of valuing my love

58 **cicatrice** scar, wound. The assumption is that England has recently been 'wounded' by *the Danish sword* and is therefore more likely to carry out the King's command.

59 **free awe** voluntary obedience

60 **coldly set** set aside with indifference, i.e. ignore

49–51] *prose F*   50 So –] *this edn; so Q2;* And so *Q1F*   51–2 Follow . . . aboard.] *F; one line Rowe* 55 SD] *Q1 after equivalent of 51* England!

Our sovereign process, which imports at full
By letters congruing to that effect
The present death of Hamlet. Do it, England!
For like the hectic in my blood he rages
And thou must cure me. Till I know 'tis done,   65
Howe'er my haps my joys will ne'er begin.   *Exit.*

[**4.4**]   *Enter* FORTINBRAS [*and a* Captain] *with his army
over the stage.*

FORTINBRAS
Go, Captain, from me greet the Danish King:

---

61 **sovereign process** royal command, order
    imports at full bears as its full purport or
    message
62 **congruing** conforming, agreeing. F's
    'coniuring' (= demanding) is preferred by
    some editors, perhaps because Hamlet
    refers to the King's *earnest conjuration* at
    5.2.38, but, as Jenkins points out, that
    phrase may have prompted this one. *H5*
    has the unique but related form
    'Congreeing' (1.2.182) in F, but the word
    appears in a slightly different context in its
    Q 1600 version as 'Congrueth'.
63 **present** immediate
64 **hectic** fever
66 **Howe'er my haps** however (good) my
    fortunes
    will ne'er begin Jenkins, who adopts F's
    'were ne're begun', comments, 'The
    rhyme seems to authenticate F's otherwise
    inferior reading.'
4.4 The three texts: this scene runs to 65 lines
    in Q2 and 8 lines in F (3.7 in Ard Q1/F),
    which ends it with the exit of Fortinbras,
    omitting Hamlet's conversation with the
    Captain and his last soliloquy and making
    this the most substantial single difference

between Q2 and F. Q1 is similar to F here:
scene 12 is only 5 lines long and the
Captain does not speak; the effect in both F
and Q1 is to maintain the focus on the
Court. The whole scene was frequently
omitted in performance from 1676 until the
end of the nineteenth century (see
Hapgood); more recent Hamlets have been
reluctant to give up a soliloquy, but Mark
Rylance made this sacrifice in the Folio-
based production at the London Globe in
2000. Location and timing: in all three
texts the location is out of doors,
somewhere near enough to the royal palace
for Fortinbras to send his Captain there; in
Q2 it is also on the route Hamlet is taking
to the coast to embark. In Q2 this scene
must follow very shortly after 4.3: Hamlet
is being hurried off to England. In Q1 and
F, where Hamlet does not appear, the
timing is more indeterminate. Some editors
have argued that Act 4 should begin here
(see Appendix 4).
0.2 *over the stage* i.e. marching across the stage
    (a frequent SD according to Dessen &
    Thomson: see under 'march'). Q1 introduces
    a '*Drumme*' (military drummer) here.

---

62 congruing] coniuring *F*   66 will ne'er begin] were ne're begun *F*   4.4] *Pope*   0.1–2] *Enter
Fortenbrasse, Drumme and Souldiers. Q1; Enter Fortinbras with an Armie. F   and a* Captain] *Globe
subst.*

Tell him that by his licence Fortinbras
Craves the conveyance of a promised march
Over his kingdom. You know the rendezvous.
If that his majesty would aught with us   5
We shall express our duty in his eye,
And let him know so.

CAPTAIN   I will do't, my lord.

FORTINBRAS
    Go softly on.   [*Exeunt all but Captain.*]

Enter HAMLET, ROSENCRANTZ, [GUILDENSTERN] *and others.*

HAMLET   Good sir, whose powers are these?

CAPTAIN
    They are of Norway, sir.

HAMLET
    How purposed, sir, I pray you?   10

CAPTAIN
    Against some part of Poland.

2–4 Tell ... kingdom Fortinbras is claiming the permission requested and presumably granted at 2.2.76–82 to march his army through Denmark on their (circuitous) route to Poland. Emrys Jones (*Scenic*, 80) compares his brief entry in this scene with the 'quietly emphatic' first appearance of Octavius Caesar in 4.1 of *JC*.

3   Craves F's 'Claimes' is defended by Hibbard as more appropriate to the character of Fortinbras and his use of legalistic language here, and this reading is chosen by productions which present a strong, macho Fortinbras. Certainly it is a little strange that he should 'crave' something he has already been promised, but, as a 'chillingly calm' Fortinbras in Branagh's 1996 film, Rufus Sewell spoke the line menacingly, as if 'craves' were merely a diplomatic euphemism (Branagh, 120).

conveyance granting or fulfilment (of a promise). Some editors, influenced by Q1's 'Craues a free passe and conduct', argue that it means 'escort'.

4   You ... rendezvous 'You know where we have arranged to meet' (perhaps with other forces).

5   would ... us i.e. wants any conference with us (Fortinbras uses the royal plural)

6   express ... eye 'pay our respects in his presence'

7   let ... so let him know this (*let* is a command to the Captain, parallel with *Tell* at 2).

8   softly quietly, carefully. The word seems to imply a respectful attitude towards Denmark, whereas F's 'safely' implies that the army's march will not be challenged.

powers armed forces

---

3 Craves] *Q1*; Claimes *F*   8 softly] safely *F*   SD] *Kittredge; Exit. F; exeunt all. Q1*   8.1 GUILDENSTERN
and others] *Theobald subst.; &c. Q2; not in Q1F*   8–65 Good ... worth.] *not in Q1F*

HAMLET

Who commands them, sir?

CAPTAIN

The nephew to old Norway, Fortinbras.

HAMLET

Goes it against the main of Poland, sir,

Or for some frontier?   15

CAPTAIN

Truly to speak, and with no addition,

We go to gain a little patch of ground

That hath in it no profit but the name.

To pay five ducats – five – I would not farm it,

Nor will it yield to Norway or the Pole   20

A ranker rate should it be sold in fee.

HAMLET

Why then the Polack never will defend it.

CAPTAIN

Yes, it is already garrisoned.

HAMLET

Two thousand souls and twenty thousand ducats

---

14 **it** i.e. the army
  main mainland, major part of the country
15 **for** towards
  frontier *OED* cites this as the earliest use
  of *frontier* meaning 'fortress on the
  frontier' (*sb.* 5), but the contrast with *main*
  implies it also carries the sense of 'border
  or extremity' (*sb.* 4).
16 **addition** four syllables: add-it-i-on.
  Usually glossed 'exaggeration': the
  Captain seems to mean that he is speaking
  bluntly, not augmenting his language to
  make the situation seem other than absurd.
18 **name** 'fame (of conquering it)' (Hibbard)
19 'The line places the speaker: he is a tenant

farmer in civilian life' (Mahood, *Bit Parts*, 40).
  ducats See 2.2.302–3n. (Theobald and
  others emend to 'five ducats' fine', i.e. rent
  of five ducats.)
  farm i.e. rent it as a farm
20, 22 **the Pole ... the Polack** the King of
  Poland (see 1.1.62n.)
21 **ranker** higher, more abundant; see other
  uses of *rank* and *ranker* at 1.2.136, 2.1.20,
  3.2.250, 3.3.36, 3.4.90, 146 and 150.
  in fee outright, as a freehold
23 **garrisoned** occupied by a defending army
24–5 In giving these lines to the Captain,
  Hibbard (Appendix A) follows a
  contribution signed 'As You Like It' in the

---

19 ducats – five –] *Jennens;* duckets, fiue *Q2;* ducats fine *Theobald*   23 Yes, it is] Nay 'tis *Q5;* Yes, 'tis
Pope; O, yes, it is *Capell*

398

Will not debate the question of this straw. 25
This is th'impostume of much wealth and peace
That inward breaks and shows no cause without
Why the man dies. I humbly thank you, sir.

CAPTAIN

God buy you, sir. [*Exit.*]

ROSENCRANTZ Will't please you go, my lord?

HAMLET

I'll be with you straight. Go a little before. 30
[*Rosencrantz, Guildenstern and the others move away.*]
How all occasions do inform against me

Gentleman's Magazine, 60, 403, dated May 1790.

24 **Two thousand ... twenty thousand** If Hamlet speaks these lines he must be plucking the figures out of the air; if the Captain does he may be speaking from knowledge. See also 59n.

25 **Will not debate** are not enough to contest; editors strain to make *debate* mean 'decide'. Hibbard (Appendix A) and Oxf (Additional Passages) emend *not* to 'now', which gives an easier meaning.
straw proverbial in this sense (Tilley, S918). See also 54.

26–8 **This ... dies** Hamlet expresses the commonplace that too much wealth and peace lead to war; see Tilley, P139. The metaphor of a secret disease recalls Hamlet's words to the Queen at 3.4.145–7 and the King's words about Hamlet at 4.1.21–3.

26 **impostume** abscess

29 **God buy you** See 2.1.66n.

29–30 **Will't ... before** See 30 SDn.

30 SD *There is no SD in Q2, but most editors since Rowe take everyone except Hamlet offstage here. It is perhaps surprising that Rosencrantz and Guildenstern are prepared to leave Hamlet alone, after the King's instructions to 'Follow him at foot' (4.3.51); it seems likely that they retire but observe from a distance. RP notes a similarity with *WT* 4.4.832–3 when Autolycus soliloquizes before following the others offstage.

30 **straight** immediately

31–65 MacDonald approves F's omission of this speech on the grounds that 'the author exposes his hero to a more depreciatory judgment than any from which I would justify him, and a conception of his character entirely inconsistent with the rest of the play.' Edwards (16–19) and Hibbard (362) also argue that its omission (and that of the preceding dialogue with the Captain) in Q1 and F is an authorial 'cut' that improves the play. Spencer sees it as important structurally, enabling Hamlet to make a strong impression before his absence in 4.5 to 4.7 and to reveal an increasing maturity. Pennington (112) finds it 'amazing' that 'perhaps the best of Hamlet's monologues' should be cut. Kenneth Branagh turns it into a melodramatic climax in his 1996 film (see 64–5n.), while Peter Brook's adaptation in 2000 replaced it with 'To be or not to be', indicating that this is 'Hamlet's nadir' (Lavender, 233). (See pp. 18–20.)

31–2 As at the end of 2.2, Hamlet uses his experience to comment on the larger issues he faces.

31 **occasions** occurrences, circumstances

---

29 SD] *Capell* 30 SD] *this edn; Exe. / Manet* Hamlet *Rowe*

And spur my dull revenge. What is a man
If his chief good and market of his time
Be but to sleep and feed? A beast – no more.
Sure he that made us with such large discourse,⠀⠀⠀⠀⠀35
Looking before and after, gave us not
That capability and godlike reason
To fust in us unused. Now whether it be
Bestial oblivion or some craven scruple
Of thinking too precisely on th'event⠀⠀⠀⠀⠀40
(A thought which quartered hath but one part
⠀⠀wisdom
And ever three parts coward) I do not know
Why yet I live to say this thing's to do,
Sith I have cause and will and strength and means
To do't. Examples gross as earth exhort me –⠀⠀⠀⠀⠀45
Witness this army of such mass and charge,
Led by a delicate and tender prince

inform against accuse, bring charges against

33 **market** advantage, profit (Johnson glosses *market of his time* 'that for which he sells his time')

35 **large discourse** extensive powers of thought or reasoning

36 **Looking . . . after** As he elaborates in 38–43, Hamlet distinguishes human beings from animals because they are capable of remembering the past and thinking about the future.

38 **fust** grow musty, decay

39 **Bestial oblivion** the forgetfulness or heedlessness characteristic of animals rather than people
craven cowardly

40 **Of** caused by
precisely rigorously, with attention to minute detail
event outcome (as at 49)

42–5 **I do . . . do't** Sam West, who played Hamlet in the 2001–2 RSC production

directed by Steven Pimlott, remarked (in a talk given at King's College London on 11 March 2002) on the power of these 26 monosyllables (three of which are *do*).

43 **to do** i.e. still to be done

44 **Sith** since
strength and means It is not clear why Hamlet, as he is being escorted out of the country, claims he has ample *strength and means* for his revenge.

45 **gross** palpable, obvious

46 **mass and charge** size and expense

47 **delicate and tender** These seem inappropriate adjectives to apply to Fortinbras, who is described by Horatio as being 'Of unimproved mettle, hot and full,' at 1.1.95 and whose actions in Act 5 reveal him to be politically astute; perhaps, however, the implication is that he is highly sensitive to questions of honour. Polonius has punned on *tender* at 1.3.102–8 and Shakespeare plays on 'tender heir' and 'tender chorl' in *Son* 1.

Whose spirit with divine ambition puffed
Makes mouths at the invisible event
Exposing what is mortal and unsure   50
To all that fortune, death and danger dare
Even for an eggshell. Rightly to be great
Is not to stir without great argument
But greatly to find quarrel in a straw
When honour's at the stake. How stand I then   55
That have a father killed, a mother stained,
Excitements of my reason and my blood,
And let all sleep; while to my shame I see
The imminent death of twenty thousand men
That for a fantasy and trick of fame   60
Go to their graves like beds, fight for a plot
Whereon the numbers cannot try the cause,

48 **puffed** inflated, inspired
49 **Makes mouths at** makes faces at, laughs at (as at 2.2.301)
   invisible unforeseeable
51 **dare** i.e. can threaten
52 **eggshell** proverbially worthless (Tilley, E95), like the *straw* of 25 and 54
52–5 **Rightly ... stake** On the face of it, Hamlet seems to be saying that the truly great man will not *stir* (take up arms) without an important motive, but he will if his honour is being challenged. Many editors are unhappy with this meaning and insist that *not* should be read as a double negative: 'true greatness does not consist in refraining from action when there is no compelling cause to act, but in finding a compelling cause in the merest trifle when one's honour is in question' (Hibbard). Perhaps the underlying problem is that Hamlet insists on admiring Fortinbras while at the same time acknowledging the absurdity of his actions.
53 **not to stir** Hamlet echoes the Ghost's expression 'Wouldst thou not stir' (1.5.34).
55 **honour's ... stake** Edwards says the

metaphor is from gambling – honour is at risk – but Hibbard notes that Shakespeare uses this expression in three other plays (*TN* 3.1.119, *TC* 3.3.226 and *AW* 2.3.150) and that in *TN* and *TC* it is clear that the metaphor is from bear-baiting. It became proverbial (Dent, S813.2).
56 **stained** dishonoured
57 **Excitements** motives to incite
59 **twenty thousand** 'Contrast [24]. I fear we must ascribe the confusion to Shakespeare, often lax with numbers, rather than ... to Hamlet' (Jenkins); see, for example, *H5* 1.2.57, where he copies a fairly obvious error from Holinshed. Or perhaps Hamlet is exaggerating again, as in his claims that his father has been dead for only *A little month* (1.2.147) or *two hours* (3.2.120).
60 **fantasy ... fame** illusion and imposture regarding reputation (or honour: see 52–5)
61 **Go ... beds** As in 'To be or not to be', Hamlet employs the proverbial association of sleep with death (see Dent, B192.1).
   plot piece of ground
62 which is not big enough for so many men to fight on it to decide the issue

Which is not tomb enough and continent
To hide the slain? O, from this time forth   64
My thoughts be bloody or be nothing worth.   *Exeunt.*

[**4.5**]   *Enter* HORATIO, QUEEN *and a* Gentleman.

QUEEN
I will not speak with her.
GENTLEMAN
She is importunate – indeed, distract.

---

63   **continent** container
64   **hide** i.e. provide burial space for
64–5 **O . . . worth** In Branagh's film these
words become a 'huge scream of
resolution' as the camera draws back from
the speaker revealing more and more
members of the enormous army marching
across the screen behind him (Branagh,
122). Garrick, in his 1772 acting version,
perhaps recognizing the logical difficulties
of a resolute Hamlet at this point (see 29–
30, 30 SDn. and 44n.), rewrites the last line
and adds another: 'My thoughts be bloody
all! The hour is come – / I'll fly my keepers
– sweep to my revenge.' In this drastically
abbreviated version of the play's ending,
Hamlet avoids his voyage altogether.
4.5 The texts: this scene runs to 211 lines in
Q2, 214 in F (4.1 in Ard Q1/F) and 129
lines in Q1 (scene 13), which omits both
the Gentleman and Horatio in the opening
dialogue and abbreviates the King's
reflections at 77–96 and his dialogue with
Laertes. Q1 also changes the sequence of
Ophelia's songs. Location and timing: the
scene takes place in the royal palace, in the
King's apartments from his assumption at
97 that his *Switzers* should be guarding the
doors. Some time must have passed since
the previous scene, as both Ophelia and
Laertes have heard of the death of their
father and Laertes has returned from

France. (This lapse of time is one
justification for beginning Act 4 here: see
Appendix 4.) Often there is a general
costume change: the Court has gone into
mourning for the death of Polonius.
0.1 See t.n. for Q1/F variants. This scene can
be played as an intimate domestic one,
with only the named characters present, but
many productions include more courtiers
to react to Ophelia's distress and Laertes'
forced entry, and to receive Ophelia's
flowers at 169–78. The King's command
Attend! at 96 (only in Q2) may imply that
these courtiers, if present at all, are not
onstage before that point.
1   **her** Ophelia is not named before her
appearance in Q2 or F, though she is in Q1,
where the Queen explicitly attributes her
madness to her father's death.
2, 4 SP This courtier is sometimes a woman in
modern performances. F gives the
Gentleman's speeches to Horatio and his
reply (14–16) to the Queen. Edwards,
who follows Q2's attributions, remarks that
F 'greatly coarsens the way Ophelia's
madness is introduced'; Hibbard, who
follows F, claims that it 'cuts out an
unnecessary part' (as at 4.1.0 and 4.3.0).
Horatio does not speak again in this scene
after 16 in Q2 (13 in F); many editors
and directors take him off at 74. He is
not present at all in Q1's version of this

---

65 SD] *this edn; Exit. Q2*   4.5] *Pope*   0.1] *enter King and Queene. Q1; Enter Queene and Horatio. F*
QUEEN] *(Gertrard)*   1–16] *not in Q1*   2, 4 SP] *Hor. F*   2–3] *Capell; Q2 lines* importunat, / pittied. / haue? /;
prose F

Her mood will needs be pitied.

QUEEN   What would she have?

GENTLEMAN

    She speaks much of her father, says she hears
    There's tricks i'th' world, and hems and beats her heart, 5
    Spurns enviously at straws, speaks things in doubt
    That carry but half sense. Her speech is nothing,
    Yet the unshaped use of it doth move
    The hearers to collection. They yawn at it
    And botch the words up fit to their own thoughts   10
    Which, as her winks and nods and gestures yield
      them,
    Indeed would make one think there might be thought,
    Though nothing sure, yet much unhappily.

scene (13), which avoids the problem of why he has apparently not mentioned Ophelia's madness to Hamlet when they encounter her funeral in 5.1 (see 5.1.213n.); instead, he has his own unique scene with the Queen (14) immediately after this (see headnote to 4.6).

2 **importune** persistent in her demands
    distract mad; see 16.1n.

3 **mood** state of mind
    will needs be must necessarily be
    What . . . have i.e. what does she want

5 **tricks** deceptions, plots
    hems says 'hem'. Perhaps the Gentleman implies that she makes inarticulate noises.

6 **Spurns . . . straws** i.e. reacts suspiciously to trivial things
    in doubt of doubtful or uncertain meaning

7 **nothing** i.e. nonsense

8–9 **Yet . . . collection** yet the incoherent fragments cause those who listen to find coherence in them

8 **unshaped** unshapèd

9 **yawn** gape with surprise; see Coriolanus' account of his mother's view of the common people as 'things created . . . to

yawn, be still, and wonder' (*Cor* 3.2.9–11). F's 'ayme' (= aim, guess, conjecture) is adopted by Jenkins, but Jennens and Edwards follow Q2.

10 **botch . . . thoughts** patch the words together clumsily to match their own guesses. Blake (4.2.10) classifies *botch up* as a phrasal verb and compares *TN* 4.1.55–6, 'how many fruitless pranks / This ruffian hath botch'd up.'

11 **Which** i.e. her words
    yield render, deliver (i.e. her gestures add meaning to her words)

12 **thought** Editors insist that this is a participle (= intended or supposed), though it can also be read and spoken as a noun (= thoughtful or coherent content). If the former, it is Ophelia's observers who are doing the thinking; if the latter, Ophelia herself.

13 **unhappily** perhaps just 'awkwardly', or, judging by Horatio's response, 'maliciously'. The implication seems to be that Ophelia's words may cause people with *ill-breeding minds* to question the circumstances of Polonius' death and thereby cause trouble for the King and Queen.

9 yawn] ayme *F*   12 might] would *F*

HORATIO

'Twere good she were spoken with, for she may strew
Dangerous conjectures in ill-breeding minds.   15
Let her come in.   [*Exit Gentleman.*]

Enter OPHELIA.

QUEEN [*aside*]

To my sick soul, as sin's true nature is,
Each toy seems prologue to some great amiss,

---

14 SP F gives this speech to the Queen.
Jenkins gives 14–15 to Horatio but 16 to
the Queen on the grounds that 'Only the
Queen can give this order'. If Horatio
retains 16 it is presumably spoken as a
request to which the Queen must give some
sign of assent. The role of Horatio
continues to be puzzling (see List of Roles,
10n.): the fact that he is Hamlet's close
friend and confidant does not seem to make
the King suspicious of him.

14 **strew** distribute, i.e. incite

15 **ill-breeding** fomenting evil

16 SD *Let her come in* implies that someone
leaves the stage in order to admit Ophelia;
this would seem to be the intended function
of Q2's Gentleman.

16.1 See t.n. for Q1 and F variants. The hair
being down (as in Q1) was a conventional
indication of madness or extreme distress
(see Constance's insistence on wearing her
hair loose in *KJ* 3.4). Ophelia's dishevelled
appearance recalls her description of
Hamlet at 2.1.74–81. Editors disagree
about Q1's lute: Jenkins dismisses it as 'an
actors' embellishment' while Hibbard and
Oxf find it appropriate. Given that Q1's SD
has been widely quoted and discussed even
by editors who do not adopt it, it is not

surprising that it has often influenced
theatrical tradition; some productions even
introduce the lute earlier: see 1.3.0.1n. In
the eighteenth and nineteenth centuries,
Ophelia usually wore white in this scene,
perhaps emphasizing a view of her as a
forsaken would-be bride; modern Ophelias
often enter with their clothes in disarray
and sometimes wear a coat or hat
previously worn by Polonius, putting the
stress on her as a bereaved daughter (see
Hapgood). (See pp. 26–7 for further
discussion of the representation of
Ophelia's madness and its subsequent
influence.)

17–20 Q2 prefaces each of these lines with a
quotation mark, indicating that they are
maxims or quotable commonplaces; the
rhymes also underscore this effect. The
Queen's aside indicates a new awareness of
guilt following on from 3.4.

17 **as . . . is** in accordance with the reality of
the state of sinfulness

18 **toy** trivial thing. The word may indicate
that the Queen does not yet take Ophelia's
madness seriously, or that she sees it as
merely a private matter, insignificant in a
political context.
amiss disaster

---

14 SP] *Qu. F*   14–16] *F lines* with, / coniectures / come in. /   16 SD] *Hanmer; Exit Hor. / Johnson* 16.1]
Enter Ofelia playing on a Lute, and her haire downe singing. Q1; Enter Ophelia distracted. after 20 F;
Enter Horatio, *with* Ophelia, *distracted. / Johnson*   17 SD] *Capell*   To] *F;* 'To *Q2*   18 Each] *F;* 'Each
Q2

So full of artless jealousy is guilt
It spills itself in fearing to be spilt.   20

OPHELIA

Where is the beauteous majesty of Denmark?

QUEEN

How now, Ophelia?

OPHELIA (*Sings.*)

How should I your true love know
From another one?
By his cockle hat and staff   25
And his sandal shoon.

QUEEN

Alas, sweet lady, what imports this song?

OPHELIA   Say you? Nay, pray you, mark.

---

19 **artless jealousy** unskilled (i.e. self-incriminating) apprehension

20 i.e. Guilt produces such paranoia that it betrays itself by its very own fear of betrayal.

21 **beauteous majesty** These words most obviously relate to the Queen, but, since Ophelia has just been admitted to her presence, she may be asking for the King, anticipating the gender confusion of *Sweet ladies* at 72. It is not clear how far she recognizes (or half-recognizes) the other characters throughout her two appearances in this scene; performers have explored a range of options (see Rosenberg; Hapgood).

23–40 This song is a version of a popular ballad much quoted elsewhere (see Jenkins, LN). Its theme of the woman bereft of her lover seems to indicate that her father's death is not the only cause of Ophelia's distress; in fact she alternates between lover and father. Jenkins argues that Q1's lute would be incongruous as an accompaniment to this and Ophelia's other songs but Hibbard claims that this is an argument for her using it, since 'only a mad woman would think of doing so'. The incongruity is probably lost on modern audiences precisely because of their familiarity with the lute's appearance in this scene. (See Appendix 6 for a discussion of the music traditionally used.)

25–6 **cockle ... shoon** The hat decorated with a cockle-shell (the sign of St James of Compostella), the staff and the sandals were all signs of the pilgrim, and the pilgrim was often seen as a figure or metaphor for the lover.

26 **shoon** shoes (archaic plural: see Hope, 1.3.1)

27 **what ... song** what does this song signify

28 **Say you** what did you say. Ophelia perhaps expresses irritation at being interrupted, though her madness is otherwise signalled by her lack of response to those around her. On the other hand, she may be asking the Queen to join in the song, as she does later. **mark** pay attention (also at 35)

---

19 So] *F;* 'So *Q2*   20 It] *F;* 'It *Q2*   23 SD] *(shee sings.); singing Q1, at 16.1; om., with song in italics, F*   23–6] *Q1 subst., Capell; Q2F line one, / shoone. /*   26 sandal] *(Sendall), Q1F*   28, 38, 47, 160, 182 SD] *Song. opp. lines; not in Q1; songs in italics F*

Sings.

> He is dead and gone, lady,
> He is dead and gone.   30
> At his head a grass-green turf,
> At his heels a stone.

O ho!

QUEEN

Nay, but Ophelia –

OPHELIA   Pray you mark.   35

[*Sings.*]

> White his shroud as the mountain snow –

Enter KING.

QUEEN

Alas, look here, my lord.

OPHELIA (*Sings.*)

> Larded all with sweet flowers
> Which bewept to the ground did not go
> With true-love showers.   40

KING

How do you, pretty lady?

---

33 **O ho** a conventional representation of a sigh or groan

36.1 The King enters after 32 in F and is present from the beginning of the scene in Q1. The awkwardness of his entry, the differences of personnel between Q2 and F, the different structure of the scene in Q1 and its extra scene between Horatio and the Queen suggest rewriting here.

38 **Larded** i.e. decorated (a culinary term, from the practice of inserting strips of fat or lard into meat to baste it). MacDonald comments with Victorian disapproval: 'This expression is, as Dr. Johnson says,

taken from cookery; but it is so used elsewhere by Shakspere [*sic*] that we cannot regard it here as a scintillation of Ophelia's insanity.'

39 **ground** Q1 and F have 'graue', adopted by Jenkins. Ophelia uses *ground* again at 70.
    not This unexpected and extrametrical negative occurs in all three texts and is usually explained as Ophelia's deliberate alteration of the song to suit her own experience.

41 **pretty lady** See *Pretty Ophelia* at 56; in Q1 the King calls Ofelia 'A pretty

---

29–32] *Q1 subst., Capell; Q2F line* ²gone, / stone.   33] *not in Q1F*   35–6] *F; one line Q2*   35] *F; not in Q1*   SD] *om., with 36 in italics, F*   36.1] *after 32 F; at 0.1 Q1*   38 all] *not in Q1F*   39 ground] graue *Q1F*   did not] *Q1F;* did *Pope*   41 do you] i'st with you *Q1;* do ye *F*

OPHELIA   Well, good dild you. They say the owl was a
baker's daughter. Lord, we know what we are but know
not what we may be. God be at your table.

KING

Conceit upon her father –   45

OPHELIA   Pray, let's have no words of this, but when they
ask you what it means, say you this:

> *Sings.*

Tomorrow is Saint Valentine's Day
All in the morning betime,
And I a maid at your window   50
To be your valentine.
Then up he rose and donned his clothes
And dupped the chamber door –

wretch'. Presumably he means to express sympathy, though his tone seems deprecating. The Nurse in *RJ* refers to Juliet as a 'pretty wretch' and a 'pretty fool' when describing her childhood fall (1.3.44, 31, 48). See also 181 and n.

42 **good dild you** i.e. thank you; a corruption of 'God yield [i.e. requite] you'

42–3 **owl . . . daughter** apparently a reference to a folk-tale in which a baker's daughter refused bread to the begging Jesus, who turned her into an owl. It is not clear why Ophelia should allude to this, though Edwards points out that it is a story of transformation; Jenkins (LN) suggests an allusion to the loss of virginity, and Hibbard cites Dent, who provides a 1555 reference to 'bakers daughters and such other poore whores' (B54.1). Mary Cowden Clarke helpfully has Ophelia's friend Jutha tell her a relevant story in 'Ophelia: the Rose of Elsinore'.

43–4 **Lord . . . may be** either a general maxim or a comment on the baker's daughter

44 **God . . . table** In the parodic version of Ophelia's song in *Eastward Ho* (1605), 3.2.85–90, Gertrude sings, 'God be at your labour' (see p. 58).

45 **Conceit . . . father** – fantasies about her father (i.e. her father's death); the King has entered in time to pick up the references to death in Ophelia's song and perhaps the word *daughter* in 43. Q2 and F (and most edited texts) have a full stop after *father* but it could be spoken as a question, or Ophelia may interrupt the King (as she interrupts the Queen at 35).

46 **Pray . . . this** Ophelia perhaps chides the King for interrupting her.

48–66 This song has not been found elsewhere; it depends on the belief that the first person one sees on St Valentine's day (14 February) will become one's lover. (See Appendix 6 for a discussion of the music traditionally used.)

49 **betime** early

52 **donned** put on (did on)

53 **dupped** opened (did up)

42 good dild] God yeeld *Q1*; God dil'd *F*   45 father –] *(*father.*) F*   46 Pray, let's have] Nay Loue, I pray you make *after* be. *44 Q1*; Pray you let's haue *F*   48–51] *Q1; F* lines betime, / Valentine. /   52–5] *Q1; Q2F line* doore, / more. /   52 clothes] *Q1F;* close *Q2*

Let in the maid that out a maid
Never departed more. 55
KING
Pretty Ophelia –
OPHELIA Indeed, without an oath I'll make an end on't.
[*Sings.*]
By Gis and by Saint Charity,
Alack and fie for shame, ·
Young men will do't if they come to't: 60
By Cock they are to blame.

Quoth she, 'Before you tumbled me
You promised me to wed.'
He answers:
'So would I ha' done by yonder sun 65
An thou hadst not come to my bed.'
KING
How long hath she been thus?
OPHELIA I hope all will be well. We must be patient. But
I cannot choose but weep to think they would lay him
i'th' cold ground. My brother shall know of it. And so 70
I thank you for your good counsel. Come, my coach!

---

57 **without an oath** Ophelia may be conscious of avoiding saying 'Jesus' in 58 and 'God' in 61.

58 **Gis** Jesus
Saint Charity The capital 'S' in Q2 and F (but not in Q1) implies that *Charity* is the name of a saint, but there was no such person and the expression could just mean 'holy charity', as in Chaucer's 'Knight's Tale', 1721: 'But sle me first, for seinte charitee'.

60 **do't . . . to't** i.e. have sex when opportunity offers

61 **Cock** a corruption of 'God'. Editors regularly claim an obscene double meaning here, and one might compare related expressions where *cock* means 'penis', such as 'Pistol's cock is up' (*H5* 2.1.52) and 'Pillicock sat on Pillicock hill' (*KL* 3.4.75).

62 **tumbled** had sex with (see *AC* 1.4.17: 'to tumble on the bed of Ptolemy')

66 **An** if

71 **my coach** Editors cite Marlowe's *Tamburlaine*, part 1 (*c.* 1587), 5.1.315, where the mad Zabina calls for her coach just before killing herself, but Ophelia's use of the phrase here is not necessarily inappropriate if she is intending to go out (see also 166n.).

---

57 Indeed,] Indeed la? *F* SD] *not in Q1; om., with 58–63, 65–6 in italics, F* 58 Saint Charity] *(Saint Charitie), Q1 (saint Charitie), F (S. Charity)* 62–3] *Q1F; one line Q2* 64 He answers:] *((He answers.)); not in Q1F* 65 ha'] *(a) Q1, ha F* 67 thus] this *F* 69 would] should *F*

Goodnight, ladies, goodnight. Sweet ladies, goodnight,
goodnight.   [*Exit.*]

KING

Follow her close. Give her good watch, I pray you.
                                                   [*Exit Horatio.*]

O, this is the poison of deep grief. It springs   75
All from her father's death, and now behold –
O Gertrude, Gertrude,
When sorrows come they come not single spies
But in battalions: first, her father slain;
Next, your son gone, and he most violent author   80
Of his own just remove; the people muddied,

The moment is parodied in *Eastward Ho*, 3.2.30–35, when Gertrude longs for her coach (see p. 58).

72 **Goodnight, ladies** Unless there are more courtiers present (see 0.1), the Queen is the only other *lady* onstage; if Ophelia addresses the King and/or other male courtiers here, her confusion or conflation of genders echoes that of Hamlet at 4.3.48–50. Her ominous repetition of *goodnight* also echoes Hamlet's exit at the end of 3.4 – and is itself echoed at the end of section 2 of T.S. Eliot's *The Waste Land* (1922), though he does not record the parallel in his notes.

74 The King's command echoes his words on Hamlet's exit at 4.3.51: 'Follow him at foot.' It becomes apparent, of course, that whoever follows Ophelia does not in fact 'Give her good watch'; Branagh provides an explanation of how she gets away in his 1996 film (133).

74 SD *Presumably someone obeys the King, and Horatio might well leave at this point; Jenkins and Hibbard stress that the King and Queen must be alone onstage for the King's next speech. This intimate moment of

shared apprehension comes at the beginning of the scene in Q1, before Ofelia's entry.

75 **poison ... grief** In this formulation, Ophelia dies metaphorically by poison, as old Hamlet, the Queen, the King, Laertes and Hamlet die literally by it.

75–6 **It ... death** The King does not acknowledge Hamlet's possible role in causing Ophelia's condition (see 23–40n.).

76 **and now behold** Jenkins points out that F's omission of these words regularizes the metre and Edwards sees them as a 'false start' probably marked for omission.

78–9 **When ... battalions** Dent cites 'Misfortune (evil) never (seldom) comes alone' as proverbial (M1012).

78 **spies** i.e. lone soldiers sent out in advance of the main force

79 **battalions** large armies

80 **author** instigator

81 **just remove** deserved removal

81–2 **muddied, / Thick** stirred up, confused; see Katherina's speech at the end of *TS*: 'A woman mov'd is like a fountain troubled, / Muddy, ill-seeming, thick, bereft of beauty' (5.2.143–4).

72–3] *F; Q2 lines* ²night. / ⁴night. /   73 SD] *Q1 (exit Ofelia.), F*   74] *F lines* close, / you: /   SD] *Theobald*   75–7] *Steevens*³; *prose Q2; F lines* springs / ²*Gertrude,* /   76 and now behold –] *om. F*   78 come] comes *F*   79 battalions] Battaliaes *F*

Thick and unwholesome in thoughts and whispers
For good Polonius' death, and we have done but
　greenly
In hugger-mugger to inter him; poor Ophelia
Divided from herself and her fair judgement,　　　　　85
Without the which we are pictures or mere beasts;
Last, and as much containing as all these,
Her brother is in secret come from France,
Feeds on this wonder, keeps himself in clouds
And wants not buzzers to infect his ear　　　　　　　90
With pestilent speeches of his father's death –
Wherein necessity, of matter beggared,
Will nothing stick our person to arraign

82–4 These lines are metrically awkward: we have left 83 as an alexandrine, but *For good* might be added to 82.

82 **in** Jenkins prefers F's 'in their', presumably on metrical grounds.

83 **For** because of
　　greenly foolishly, showing lack of experience; see 'like a green girl' at 1.3.100.

84 **In hugger-mugger** secretly and hastily. Shakespeare's only use of this phrase which, as Steevens points out, he may have remembered from the account of the funeral of Julius Caesar in North's Plutarch: 'Antonius thinking good his testament should be red openly, and also that his body should be honorably buried and not in hugger mugger' ('Life of Brutus', Bullough, 5.104).

86 **pictures . . . beasts** The surprising analogy between *pictures* and *beasts* depends on the fact that both lack *god-like reason* (4.4.37), which is seen as the defining characteristic of human beings; see the King's use of the picture metaphor again at 4.7.105–7.

87 **containing** comprising, importing

88 **in secret** The suggestion (absent from Q1) is that the King's spies have discovered

this, though they have presumably not anticipated Laertes' next actions, as described at 99–108.

89 **Feeds . . . wonder** Q2's reading must mean something like 'finds food (for revenge) in these amazing events'. F's 'Keepes on his wonder' seems to mean 'sustains his amazement'. Jenkins and Hibbard follow Q2 (though Jenkins suggests 'his' might be right); Spencer and Edwards (following Johnson) print 'Feeds on his wonder'; 'Keeps' is generally rejected, presumably as an anticipation of the word later in the line.
　　clouds i.e. of suspicion or uncertainty

90 **wants not buzzers** has no shortage of people stirring up trouble or spreading rumours

90–1 **infect . . . speeches** This can hardly be a conscious allusion to the King's murder of Hamlet's father, though it might suggest, for an audience or reader, a parallel with the infection of Hamlet's ear by the words of the Ghost.

92 **necessity . . . beggared** i.e. driven by necessity because of a lack of substantial evidence

93 **Will nothing stick** will in no way refuse, refrain

---

82 in] in their *F*　　84 hugger-mugger] *(hugger mugger) F*　　89 Feeds] Keepes *F*　　this] his *F*　　92 Wherein] Where in *F*　　93 person] persons *F*

In ear and ear. O my dear Gertrude, this,
Like to a murdering-piece in many places   95
Gives me superfluous death.   *A noise within*

Enter a Messenger.

Attend!
Where is my Switzers? Let them guard the door.
What is the matter?

MESSENGER   Save yourself, my lord.
The ocean overpeering of his list
Eats not the flats with more impiteous haste   100
Than young Laertes in a riotous head

person F's plural implicitly includes the Queen in the arraignment.
arraign put on trial, accuse
94 **ear and ear** one ear after another (see 90–1n.)
this i.e. all of these things
95 **murdering-piece** a small cannon capable of delivering several shots at once. Jenkins cites Fletcher and Massinger's *Double Marriage* (1620): 'like a murdering-piece, aims not at one, / But all that stand within the dangerous level' (4.2.6).
96 **Gives . . . death** i.e. kills me many times over
96 SD1 This is the first of a series of off-stage noises of alarm or distress preceeding an entry: see Ophelia's entry at 151 and the Queen's at 4.7.160. *Within* is a common stage direction (Dessen & Thomson find 800 examples) indicating the location of a sound or figure *within* the tiring-house and therefore offstage for the audience. Our practice is to retain *within* where it occurs in the early texts but to use *offstage* when we are adding a modern SD.
SD2 **Messenger** In eighteenth- and

nineteenth-century theatrical tradition, this *Messenger* was Marcellus.
96 **Attend!** not in F, which gives the Queen a line here (see t.n.): 'most modern editors illogically include both' (Jenkins). More courtiers may enter in response to the King's command (see 0.1n.).
97 **Switzers** Swiss guards, often used as mercenary soldiers by European royalty, a custom which survives today in ceremonial form at the Vatican State in Rome. Malone quotes Nashe, *Christ's Tears over Jerusalem*, 'Law, Logicke, and the *Swizers* may be hir'd to fight for any body' (2.99).
99 **overpeering . . . list** looking over (i.e. rising above) its shore or boundary. See *R2* 3.2.106–11 for a comparable use of flooding as a metaphor for rebellion.
100 **Eats . . . flats** does not consume or overrun the flat or low-lying land
impiteous often emended to 'impetuous' (from Q3), but Edwards retains it as a Shakespearean coinage meaning 'pitiless'. Tronch-Pérez notes that 'piteous' is spelt 'pittious' in both Q2 and F texts at 2.1.91.
101 **in . . . head** in a rebellious insurrection

95 murdering-piece] *(*murdring peece*)*, F *(*murdering Peece*)*   96–8] *Ard²*; *Q2 lines* death. / doore, / matter? / Lord. /; *F lines* death. / this? / *Switzers*? / matter? / Lord. /   96 Attend!] *Qu.* Alacke, what noyse is this? *F*   97 is] are *F*   Switzers] *(*Swissers*)*, F   100 impiteous] *(*impitious*)*, F *(*impittious*)*; impetuous *Q3, F2*

411

O'erbears your officers. The rabble call him lord
And, as the world were now but to begin,
Antiquity forgot, custom not known,
The ratifiers and props of every word,   105
They cry, 'Choose we: Laertes shall be king!' –
Caps, hands and tongue, applaud it to the clouds –
'Laertes shall be king! Laertes king!'

QUEEN

How cheerfully on the false trail they cry.   *A noise within*
O, this is counter, you false Danish dogs!   110

KING

The doors are broke.

Enter LAERTES *with* Followers.

LAERTES

Where is this king? Sirs, stand you all without.

103–5 There is something incongruous about the Messenger's rather grandiose invocation of *Antiquity* and *custom* on the side of this particular king, but it is not unlike the flattery voiced by Guildenstern and Rosencrantz at 3.3.7–23.

103 **as . . . begin** i.e. as if social institutions and civil government were now being invented for the first time

105 i.e. *Antiquity* and *custom* guarantee and support every *word* (*OED*'s first use of *ratifier*).

106 ***They cry** Q2's 'The cry' could mean 'the cry is', but Jenkins prefers F, and the scribe or compositor might have been misled by 105, which begins with *The*.
  Choose we 'The *distracted multitude* who were supposed to *love* Hamlet (4.3.4) have given their allegiance to Laertes, and are demanding to take over the prerogative of the electoral body which made Claudius king' (Edwards).

shall Compare *Cor* 3.1.89–90: 'Hear you this Triton of the minnows? Mark you / His absolute "shall"?'

107 **Caps** thrown into the air in salutation/celebration

109–10 The Queen's metaphor is from hunting dogs following a false or contrary (*counter*) scent. Michael Redgrave, having suggested Wanda Rotha to play the Queen in Hugh Hunt's 1950 production at the London Old Vic, in which he played Hamlet, noted that her 'trace of a German accent' made the expression *false Danish dogs* imply that she is a foreign consort – common enough in European monarchies in Shakespeare's time (Redgrave, 230).

111 **broke** broken or burst open

111.1 It is clear from 112–15 that if the *Followers* do enter they leave again very soon; many productions represent them by shouts offstage. Laertes often

106 They] *F;* The *Q2*   109 SD] *Q2c (A noise within.), Q2u ((A noise within.); Noise within. F, after*
110   111.1] *Spencer subst.; Enter Laertes with others. Q2, after 110; Enter Laertes. F, after 110, Q1 subst.*
112 this] the *F*   king? Sirs,] King, sirs? *F*

FOLLOWERS

No, let's come in.

LAERTES   I pray you give me leave.

FOLLOWERS   We will, we will.

LAERTES

I thank you, keep the door.

> [*Exeunt Followers and Messenger.*]
> •   O thou vile King,   115

Give me my father.

QUEEN   Calmly, good Laertes.

LAERTES

That drop of blood that's calm proclaims me bastard,
Cries 'Cuckold!' to my father, brands the harlot
Even here between the chaste unsmirched brow
Of my true mother.

KING   What is the cause, Laertes,   120
That thy rebellion looks so giant-like?
Let him go, Gertrude, do not fear our person.
There's such divinity doth hedge a king

---

appears in mourning, like the Danish Court (see headnote).

113 **give me leave** i.e. leave me alone with the King

115 **keep** guard

118–19 **brands . . . brow** Laertes alludes to the threat to brand prostitutes (see 3.4.40–2n.).

119 **between** in the middle of
unsmirched unsmirchèd; unstained (*OED*'s first use: see also *besmirch* at 1.3.15)

120 **my true mother** This is the play's only reference to the mother of Laertes and Ophelia; like Miranda's mother at *Tem* 1.2.56–7, she is evoked only in order to confirm her child's legitimacy.

121 **giant-like** perhaps just 'large', but perhaps an allusion to the war of the Titans which comes up again in the references to Pelion and Ossa at 5.1.242–3 and 272.

122, 126 **Let . . . Gertrude** The Queen defends the King both verbally and physically (by holding on to Laertes) in all three texts. As is emphasized by her words at 128, she has reason to be confident that he is not in fact guilty of Polonius' death.

122 **fear** be afraid for

123 **divinity . . . king** The King (outrageously) refers to the divine right which was seen as protecting monarchs; see 3.3.7–23.
hedge surround, defend

113, 114 SP FOLLOWERS] *Spencer subst.; All. Q2F* 115–16] *F lines* doore. / Father. / *Laertes.* / 115 SD *Exeunt Followers*] *Kittredge   and Messenger*] *this edn*   117] *F lines* calmes / Bastard: / that's calm] that calmes *F*   119 brow] *F;* Brows *Q6*   121 giant-like] *(*gyant like*), F*

That treason can but peep to what it would,
Acts little of his will. Tell me, Laertes, 125
Why thou art thus incensed. Let him go, Gertrude.
Speak, man.

LAERTES   Where is my father?

KING   Dead.

QUEEN
But not by him.

KING   Let him demand his fill.

LAERTES
How came he dead? I'll not be juggled with.
To hell allegiance, vows to the blackest devil, 130
Conscience and grace to the profoundest pit.
I dare damnation. To this point I stand –
That both the worlds I give to negligence.
Let come what comes, only I'll be revenged
Most throughly for my father.

KING   Who shall stay you? 135

LAERTES
My will, not all the world's.
And for my means I'll husband them so well
They shall go far with little.

---

124 **can . . . would** can only glimpse or glance
   at its objectives
125 **Acts . . . will** is able to perform little of its
   desires
129 **juggled with** manipulated, cheated
130–1   Laertes rhetorically consigns both
   his *allegiance* to the King and his *grace* of
   his standing with God to hell (see Polonius'
   conventional association of duty to God
   and duty to the King at 2.2.44–5).
131 **pit** i.e. of hell
132 **To . . . stand** I am firm in this resolve
133 **both . . . negligence** i.e. I disregard the
   consequences both in this world and

in the next.
135 **throughly** thoroughly
   stay prevent
136 **My . . . world's** Q2's reading must mean
   something like 'I'll have my will despite
   the world's will'; F's 'world' produces the
   meaning 'By my will, the world will not'
   (prevent me). Hibbard assumes Q2's
   'worlds' was suggested by the same word
   in 133.
137–8 **And . . . little** perhaps a surprising
   comment on the resources Laertes might
   need to prosecute a revenge action against
   the King

127 Where is] where's *Q1F*   136 world's] *(worlds), Pope;* world *F*

414

KING   Good Laertes,
If you desire to know the certainty
Of your dear father, is't writ in your revenge   140
That swoopstake you will draw both friend and foe,
Winner and loser?

LAERTES
None but his enemies.

KING   Will you know them, then?

LAERTES

To his good friends thus wide I'll ope my arms
And like the kind life-rendering pelican   145
Repast them with my blood.

KING   Why, now you speak
Like a good child and a true gentleman.
That I am guiltless of your father's death
And am most sensibly in grief for it
It shall as level to your judgement 'pear   150
As day does to your eye.   *A noise within*

---

140 **father, is't** Many editors conflate Q2 with F (see t.n.) by printing 'father's death, is't', but Jenkins points out that this extrametrical addition could be an anticipation of 148. Tronch-Pérez adds that the Q2 King may be more tactful.

writ in required by; see 'writ down in our duty' at 1.2.221.

141 **swoopstake ... foe** you, as in a sweepstake, draw in friend and enemy alike. The point is that the gambler 'swoops' upon or 'sweeps' up all the stakes on the table indiscriminately. Q1 has 'draw at' = draw your sword on.

144 **ope** open

145–6 **kind ... blood** The pelican was supposed to pierce its own breast with its bill and feed its young on its own blood.

146 **Repast** feed

149 **sensibly** feelingly

150 **level** straightforwardly

'pear appear (F's 'pierce' seems to Edwards a 'more Shakespearean word')

151 SD1 The *noise* is presumably of a woman or women crying out *within*, i.e. offstage. Ophelia usually enters carrying the flowers she distributes at 173–8, though some productions (and commentators) assume that the flowers exist only in her imagination. Q1's line 'I a bin gathering of floures' (13.75–6) and the entry SD in *Fratricide Punished*, 'Ophelia, with flowers' (4.7; Bullough, 7.153), may testify to early stage practice, and this would be supported by the

---

138–9 Good ... certainty] *F; one line Q2*   140 father] Fathers death *F* is't] if *F* 141 swoopstake] *Dyce;* soopstake *Q2F;* Swoop-stake-like *Q1;* sweep-stake *Pope* 141 both] *F;* at *Q1* 145 pelican] Politician *F* 149 sensibly] sensible *F* 150 'pear] *Johnson;* peare *Q2;* pierce *F* 151 SD1] *A noise within. Let her come in. F; A noise within. [Ophelia is heard singing.] Ard²*

415

Enter OPHELIA.

LAERTES   Let her come in.
How now, what noise is that?
O heat, dry up my brains, tears seven times salt
Burn out the sense and virtue of mine eye.
By heaven, thy madness shall be paid with weight   155
Till our scale turn the beam. O rose of May,
Dear maid, kind sister, sweet Ophelia,
O heavens, is't possible a young maid's wits
Should be as mortal as a poor man's life?
OPHELIA (*Sings.*)
They bore him bare-faced on the bier   160

comparable scene where Perdita distributes flowers in *WT* (4.4.73–134).

151 **Let . . . in** These words are repeated from 16. As the text of Q2 stands, we must assume that Laertes sees someone struggling to prevent Ophelia from entering (see t.n. for F's variant). Jenkins adds the command or request to the end of the King's speech, while Oxf follows Spencer in attributing it to '*Voices* (*within*)'.

152 **How . . . that** In Q1, Laertes' first line is 'Who's this, *Ofelia*?', perhaps implying that she is so changed he can scarcely recognize her.

154 **virtue** efficacy, function

155–6 **thy . . . beam** 'your madness will be revenged (by putting more weight into our side of the scale until it over-balances the other)'. Laertes asserts the Senecan view that revenge has to outdo the original crime.

156 ***Till** Q2's 'Tell' seems erroneous (as at 2.2.482).
turn the beam tilt the bar joining the two scales

159 **a poor man's life** Jenkins prefers F's 'an old mans life', which is perhaps more appropriate as an allusion to Polonius and is supported by Q1's 'an olde mans sawe' (= saying). It is possible, however, that *poor* expresses Laertes' affection or pity for his father. He has three more lines in F at this point (see Appendix 1); Edwards asks, 'Is it possible that for once the Q2 compositor noted a deletion mark overlooked by the playhouse scribe?'

160–1 apparently the first two lines of a lament, now lost (see Jenkins's extensive LNs on songs)

160 **bare-faced** The assumption is either that there is no coffin or that the coffin is open.
bier stretcher or litter on which a corpse is carried; F has an additional line (see t.n.) after *bier*, assumed to be a 'stage-addition' by Jenkins, but part of the deliberate incongruity for Edwards and Hibbard. 'Nonny, nonny' is used to signify a happy tone in the song 'Sigh no more, ladies' in *MA*: 'Converting all your sounds of woe / Into Hey nonny, nonny' (2.3.67–8).

151 SD2] *Enter Ofelia as before. Q1; after 151 F; Enter* Ophelia, *fantastically drest with Straws and Flowers. Rowe; after 152 Ard²* SP] *F; King. Ard²* Let . . . in.] *part of* 151 *SD1 F; Dan.* [*within.*] Let her come in. *Capell* 152 How] *Laer.* How *F* 155 with] by *F* 156 Till] *F;* Tell *Q2* turn] turnes *F* 159 a poor] an old *F* life?] *followed by three additional lines F (159–61)* 160 SD] (*Song., opp. 160*) bier] *Beer, / Hey non nony, nony, hey nony: F*

416

And in his grave rained many a tear.
Fare you well, my dove.

LAERTES

Hadst thou thy wits and didst persuade revenge
It could not move thus.

OPHELIA   You must sing 'a-down a-down', an you call him   165
'a-down-a'. O how the wheel becomes it. It is the false
steward that stole his master's daughter.

LAERTES

This nothing's more than matter.

OPHELIA   There's rosemary: that's for remembrance.

---

162 **Fare ... dove** If this is Ophelia's own addition to the song (see t.n.), *my dove* seems more appropriate to a lost love than to a dead father; again she is alternating between the two (and possibly mistaking Laertes for Hamlet here).

165–6 **You ... 'a-down-a'** Ophelia instructs her listeners to sing the refrain *a-down*, etc.

165 **an** if

166 **wheel** Usually interpreted as meaning 'refrain', but Ophelia may be referring to the wheel of Fortune. Mowat and Werstine suggest a spinning wheel, 'to which motion ballads were sung' (Folg²). Farley-Hills ('Crux') points out that F2 has 'How the wheeles become it' and argues that Ophelia is still thinking about a *coach* (as at 71) and that this is how the authors of *Eastward Ho* understood (and parodied) the scene (see p. 58).

166–7 **It ... daughter** Edwards comments, 'In view of Laertes' next remark, indicating that Ophelia's disconnected remarks have a special significance, it is embarrassing that no-one has been able to throw light on the false steward', but Burnett has argued for

the 'multiple contexts' of the remark in scriptural parallels and in the romance tradition, where servants steal their masters' daughters. Perhaps, however, this is just Ophelia's confusion for the steward's daughter (herself) and the false king or prince (Hamlet).

168 i.e. This seeming nonsense is more eloquent than sensible speech. See Polonius' earlier comment on Hamlet, at 2.2.202–3 and n. In this instance, Laertes has heard only two brief speeches from Ophelia and it is not clear what sense he detects behind them, so his comment may be a choric one.

169–78 Apart from Laertes, the particular recipients of the flowers are not specified in any of the three texts, but some assumptions have been made based on traditional flower symbolism: rue or herb of grace signifies repentance and may therefore be appropriate to the Queen or to the King (though not so obviously to Ophelia); daisies signify (unrequited) love and are appropriate to Ophelia herself; rosemary for

---

161 in] *on F*   rained] *raines F*   162] *not as song Capell; as song F*   163–4] *prose F*   165–7] *F; Q2 lines* downe a downe, / becomes it, / daughter. /   165–6 You ... 'a-down-a'] *this edn; no inverted commas Q21F; all as quotation Johnson; as quotation after* sing *Steevens²; only* 'Adown adown' *as quotation Cam²;* You ... *A-down a-down*, and you *Call him a-down-a Ard²*   165 an] *(And) Q1F* 166 wheel becomes it] *F;* wheeles become it *F2;* wheels become *F3*

Pray you, love, remember. And there is pansies: that's   170
for thoughts.

LAERTES

A document in madness – thoughts and remembrance
fitted!

OPHELIA   There's fennel for you, and columbines.
There's rue for you, and here's some for me. We may
call it herb of grace o'Sundays. You may wear your rue   175
with a difference. There's a daisy. I would give you
some violets, but they withered all when my father
died. They say 'a made a good end.

Sings.

                For bonny sweet Robin is all my joy.

LAERTES

Thought and afflictions, passion, hell itself   180
She turns to favour and to prettiness.

---

remembrance and pansies for thought are
offered to Laertes (see 169–71); fennel was
associated with flattery and may be given
to any courtier (or to the King); either
violets signifying fidelity or columbines
signifying infidelity may be offered to the
Queen (see John Gerard, *The Herbal*
(1597); William Langham, *The Garden of
Health* (1579); and Jenkins, LN).

172 **document** object lesson

173 **fitted** put together appropriately

175 **o'Sundays** on Sundays
   You may Jenkins prefers F's 'you must',
which is supported by Q1. *May* could be an
erroneous repetition from 174.

176 **difference** a term from heraldry, meaning a
variation in a coat of arms to distinguish
one branch of a family from another

178 **They . . . end** Sadly untrue, if we equate
the notion of *a good end* with the
opportunity for repentance and forgiveness,
as is emphasized in 1.5 and 3.3.

'a he

179 **For . . . joy** A line from a popular song
which does not survive, though it is much
alluded to elsewhere, including in *TNK*
4.1.107–8, where the Jailer's Daughter,
whose madness is clearly influenced by
Ophelia's, says, 'I can sing "The Broom" /
And "Bonny Robin" '.

180 **Thought** i.e. sad thoughts, melancholy
   afflictions F's 'Affliction' is usually
adopted by editors, presumably because
the other terms are singular.
   passion suffering

181 **favour . . . prettiness** i.e. something
charming and attractive (see the King's
pretty at 41 and 56). Laertes' comment was
perhaps taken too literally in some
nineteenth-century productions which
presented Ophelia's madness as picturesque
(see Showalter); modern Ophelias are more
likely to be painful and distressing, which
can equally make nonsense of this line.

---

170 Pray you] I pray *Q1;* Pray *F*   pansies] pansey *Q1;* Paconcies *F*   175 herb of grace] hearb a grace *Q1;*
Herbe-Grace *F*   You] *Q1;* Oh you *F*   may] must *Q1F*   178 'a] he *F*   180 Thought and afflictions]
Thoughts & afflictions *Q1, Q5;* Thought, and Affliction *F*

OPHELIA *(Sings.)*

> And will 'a not come again?
> And will 'a not come again?
> No, no, he is dead,
> Go to thy deathbed.   185
> He never will come again.
>
> His beard was as white as snow,
> Flaxen was his poll.
> He is gone, he is gone,
> And we cast away moan.   190
> God a' mercy on his soul.

And of all Christians' souls. God buy you.   *[Exit.]*

LAERTES

Do you see this, O God?

KING

Laertes, I must commune with your grief

182–91 a lament, like the fragment at 160–1, not otherwise recorded. The song is parodied in *Eastward Ho*, 3.2.85–90 (see p. 58).

188 **Flaxen . . . poll** i.e. his hair was as white as flax. Jenkins and others prefer F's 'All flaxen', which is preferable metrically and is supported by Q1, where Ofelia sings the song on her first appearance in this scene. **poll** head

190 **we . . . moan** (1) we waste or throw away our mourning; (2) we who are abandoned mourn (?)

191 **God a' mercy** God have mercy

191–2 **on . . . of** These words seem interchangeable here, perhaps because both were often abbreviated to *o'* (see Blake, 5.4.2, *Of*).

192 **God buy you** See 2.1.66n.

192 SD *Perhaps taking their cue from F's '*Exeunt*', many productions have the Queen follow her, partly out of concern for Ophelia, but also so that she does not hear about the King's conspiracy with Laertes (which is more explicit at this point in Q1). But the plural might equally indicate that she is followed by an attendant (if more courtiers are present: see 0.1n.).

193 ***see** Q2's 'Doe you this' could mean something like 'are you responsible for this?' (F's implicitly pagan plural 'gods' seems surprising in the context.)

194–5 **I . . . right** 'I have an undeniable right to talk to you in your grief'

194 **commune with** often glossed 'participate in', though Edwards suggests 'converse

---

182 SD] (*Song., opp. 182*)   182, 183 'a] he *Q1F*   184–5] *Johnson; one line Q2F*   187 was] *not in Q1F*
188 Flaxen] All flaxen *Q1F*   189–90] *Q1 subst., Johnson; one line Q2F*   189 ¹gone] *F;* dead *Q1*   191
God a' mercy] *Q1; Gramercy F*   192 Christians'] christen *Q1;* Christian *F*   souls] soules I pray God
Q1F   buy you] be with you *Q1;* buy ye *F*   SD] *Q1 (exit Ofelia.), F (Exeunt Ophelia)*   193 see] *F; not in
Q2}*   O God] you Gods *F*   194 commune] *Q2, F2;* common *F*

Or you deny me right. Go but apart,   195
Make choice of whom your wisest friends you will,
And they shall hear and judge 'twixt you and me.
If by direct or by collateral hand
They find us touched, we will our kingdom give –
Our crown, our life, and all that we call ours –   200
To you in satisfaction. But, if not,
Be you content to lend your patience to us
And we shall jointly labour with your soul
To give it due content.
LAERTES   Let this be so.
His means of death, his obscure funeral –   205
No trophy, sword nor hatchment o'er his bones,
No noble rite, nor formal ostentation –
Cry to be heard as 'twere from heaven to earth
That I must call't in question.
KING   So you shall,
And where th'offence is let the great axe fall.   210
I pray you go with me.   *Exeunt.*

with'. F's 'common' is a variant of the
same word.
195 **Go but apart** i.e. let's discuss this privately
somewhere else (a standard exit line)
196 **whom your** which of your
wisest friends When the King and Laertes
resume this conversation in 4.7, Laertes is
still unaccompanied (see also the King's
use of the same formulaic expression at
4.1.38).
198 **collateral** indirect
199 **touched** i.e. with guilt, implicated (see
Hamlet's use of the word at 3.2.235)
205 **funeral** F has 'buriall', seen as an authorial
substitution by Hibbard on the grounds that
a *funeral* as a public event cannot be

obscure. Laertes might, however, mean
that Polonius' funeral was relatively
obscure for such a prominent courtier.
206 **trophy** memorial
hatchment memorial tablet displaying the
coat of arms of the dead person
207 **ostentation** ceremony
209 **That . . . question** so that I must demand
an explanation
210 **the great axe** The axe was the traditional
implement of execution; Shakespeare
frequently refers to 'the hangman's axe'
(see especially *MM* 4.3.26–37, where
Abhorson, the 'hangman', asks Pompey if
the axe is ready) or more generally to 'the
axe of death' (e.g. *2H6* 2.4.49).

198 collateral] *(*colaturall*)*, *F*   205 funeral] buriall *F*   206 trophy, sword] *F;* trophe sword *Q2;* trophy
sword *Pope*   207 rite] *(*right*)*, *F*   209 call't] call *F*

[4.6]   *Enter* HORATIO *and* [*a* Gentleman].

HORATIO   What are they that would speak with me?
GENTLEMAN   Sea-faring men, sir. They say they have
    letters for you.
HORATIO   Let them come in.   [*Exit Gentleman.*]
    I do not know from what part of the world I should be   5
    greeted if not from Lord Hamlet.

                    Enter Sailors.

SAILOR   God bless you, sir.
HORATIO   Let Him bless thee too.
SAILOR   'A shall, sir, an please Him. There's a letter for
    you, sir – it came from th'ambassador that was bound   10

4.6 The three texts: this scene runs to 31 lines
in Q2 and F (4.2 in Ard Q1/F) with no
major variants. Q1 has a different scene of
about the same length between Horatio and
the Queen (scene 14) in which he gives her
some of the information contained in 4.6,
4.7 and the beginning of 5.2, she repeats
her expressions of support for Hamlet and
she makes it explicit that she will
deliberately deceive the King. Location
and timing: it may seem from 'Let them
come in' at 4 that this scene is set indoors,
somewhere in the royal palace or perhaps
in Horatio's own lodgings, though *come in*
could also mean 'come onstage'. Time has
obviously passed since Hamlet left for
England at the end of 4.4 (see head note to
4.5), but this scene could follow quickly
after the previous one.

0.1 There is no need for more than one
attendant here, but Hapgood cites
Granville-Barker's speculation that Q2's
'*others*' may be the King's agents keeping
watch on Horatio. In eighteenth- and

nineteenth-century theatrical tradition,
Horatio's companion at this point was
Francisco.

1   **What are they** what sort of men are they
(pronominal use of *what*: see Blake, 3.2.2.4)

4   SD *Someone presumably leaves to admit
the sailor(s). If more than one attendant has
entered at the beginning of the scene, it
seems likely that they all leave at this point,
since it would be odd for Horatio to read
Hamlet's letter aloud in the presence of
anyone who, presumably unlike the
sailor(s), would understand its significance.

5   **what ... world** i.e. what distant part
(picking up on *Sea-faring men*)

6.1 There is no need for more than one sailor,
though Horatio's and the Gentleman's use
of *they* and *them* does indicate that the
plural is correct.
    an if it

10   **th'ambassador** Editors regularly say that
Hamlet has concealed his identity from
the sailors, but he must have convinced
them   of   his   importance   to   have

4.6] *Capell*   0.1 *and a* Gentleman.] *Spencer; and others. Q2; with an Attendant. F*   2 SP] *Ser. F*   Sea-
faring men] Saylors *F*   4 SD] *Hanmer subst.*   5–6] *this edn; Q2F line* world / Hamlet. /   6.1 Sailors]
Saylor F   9 'A] Hee *F*   an] *(and); and't F*   10 came] comes *F*   th'ambassador] th'Ambassadours *F*

for England – if your name be Horatio, as I am let to
know it is.

HORATIO [*Reads.*]   *Horatio, when thou shalt have overlooked*
this, give these fellows some means to the King: they have
letters for him. Ere we were two days old at sea, a pirate of   15
very warlike appointment gave us chase. Finding ourselves
too slow of sail, we put on a compelled valour and in the
grapple I boarded them. On the instant they got clear of our
ship, so I alone became their prisoner. They have dealt with
me like thieves of mercy, but they knew what they did: I   20
am to do a turn for them. Let the King have the letters I
have sent, and repair thou to me with as much speed as thou
wouldest fly death. I have words to speak in thine ear will
make thee dumb. Yet are they much too light for the bore

negotiated for his freedom. If a sailor is
listening, he will in any case hear Hamlet's
name at the end of the letter. Perhaps
Hamlet has warned them to be cautious
until they are quite sure they are speaking to
Horatio. F's plural 'Ambassadours' could
include Rosencrantz and Guildenstern.

11–12 **let to know** informed

13 *overlooked* i.e. read

14 *means* help in approaching

15 *were . . . old* had spent two days
pirate pirate ship, i.e. one engaged in
robbery and violence

16 *appointment* equipment (especially of a
military nature)

17 *a compelled valour* i.e. a valour compelled
by necessity

17–18 *the grapple* the action of grappling,
whereby two ships in close combat lay
hold of each other (see the metaphorical
use at 1.3.62)

20 *thieves of mercy* thieves who were
nevertheless merciful

21 *a turn* Jenkins argues that F's '*good turne*'
is 'not merely superfluous but enfeebling',
but Dent cites 'One good turn asks

(requires, deserves) another' as proverbial
(T616). It is not clear quite what Hamlet
has agreed to do for the pirates in return for
his freedom. Perhaps he is supposed to be
negotiating a ransom or an amnesty of
some kind for them. Shakespeare may be
remembering the similar incident in the life
of Julius Caesar: Caesar was well treated
by the pirates and paid his ransom, but he
subsequently pursued and executed them.
(On a literal interpretation, Hamlet may
also renege on his side of the bargain, since
he does not mention the sailors in his letter
to the King in 4.7 or in his discussion of the
episode with Horatio in 5.2, but this is not
something an audience or reader has time
to worry about.)

22 *repair* come

22–3 *with . . . death* In Q1 Hamlet's message
seems less urgent, asking Horatio to meet
him '*To morrow morning*' (14.17).

24 *they* i.e. my words

24–5 *too . . . matter* too trivial for the
importance of the subject. The
metaphor is from the *bore* or calibre of
a gun: Hamlet's words are seen as

13 SP] *om. F*   SD] *F subst. (Reads the Letter.)*   17 *valour and*] *Valour. F*   21 *turn*] *good turne F*   22
speed] *hast F*   23 *thine*] *your F*   24 *bore*] *F; bord Q2*

of the matter. These good fellows will bring thee where I 25
am. Rosencrantz and Guildenstern hold their course for
England. Of them I have much to tell thee. Farewell. He
that thou knowest thine. Hamlet.
Come. I will give you way for these your letters.
And do't the speedier that you may direct me 30
To him from whom you brought them. *Exeunt.*

[**4.7**] *Enter* KING *and* LAERTES.

KING

Now must your conscience my acquittance seal
And you must put me in your heart for friend

small bullets in a large cannon. (*OED* cites
this passage under 'bore', *sb.* 2b.)

24 ***bore*** Q2's 'bord' was perhaps influenced
by *boarded* ('boorded') at 18.

25–6 ***These . . . am*** The assumption may be that
Hamlet is in hiding, but we hear no more of
this on his reappearance in 5.1. The idea
comes up in a different way in Q1, where
the Queen asks Horatio if he knows where
Hamlet is (14.14).

27 ***He*** Q2's '*So*' seems erroneous.

28–9 ***will . . . way*** give you the means of
access (as requested in 14); Q2's 'will you
way' seems defective; some editors, e.g.
Jennens, follow Q3 (see t.n.).

4.7 The three texts: this scene runs to 192 lines
in Q2 and 166 lines in F (4.3 in Ard Q1/F),
which lacks three passages: see notes on
66–80, 98–100 and 112–21. It runs to 54
lines in Q1 (scene 15), which simplifies the
plot against Hamlet, leaving out the *sword
unbated* (136); the Queen's report of
Ofelia's death and Leartes' response are
also abbreviated in Q1. Location and
timing: the scene takes place in the royal
palace; it must follow quickly on from 4.5:

at the end of that scene the King persuaded
Laertes to discuss his griefs privately and
they are now doing this. There is, however,
no mention of the *wisest friends* Laertes
was invited to consult at 4.5.196.
Occasionally on the stage (e.g. in Tyrone
Guthrie's 1963 production and in Peter
Brook's 2000 adaptation), and in the film
versions by Kozintsev and Zeffirelli, a
large part of this scene (1–160) is moved to
follow Ophelia's funeral in 5.1, presumably
to provide even more motivation for
Laertes' hostility to Hamlet.

1–5 **Now . . . life** As often in plays of this
period, the opening speech establishes that
the characters enter in the midst of
conversation. We assume here that they are
drawing towards the end of a long
discussion.

1 **conscience** The King echoes the word used
by Laertes at 4.5.131 and which resonates
through the play: see 2.2.540; 3.1.49 and
82; 5.2.57, 66 and 279.
my acquittance seal confirm my
release or discharge (i.e. accept my
innocence)

27 *He*] F; *So Q2* 28 *thine. Hamlet*] F; *thine Hamlet Q2* 29 *Come*] F; *Hor.* Come *Q2* *give*] F; *not in
Q2;* make *Q3* 4.7] *Capell*

Sith you have heard and with a knowing ear
That he which hath your noble father slain
Pursued my life.

LAERTES   It well appears. But tell me   5
Why you proceed not against these feats
So criminal and so capital in nature
As by your safety, greatness, wisdom, all things else,
You mainly were stirred up.

KING

O, for two special reasons   10
Which may to you perhaps seem much unsinewed
But yet to me they're strong. The Queen his mother
Lives almost by his looks and for myself,
My virtue or my plague, be it either which,
She is so conjunct to my life and soul   15
That as the star moves not but in his sphere

---

3   **Sith** since
    knowing i.e. understanding or receptive
5   **Pursued my life** tried to kill me; see 4.1.13
    and n.
6   **proceed not** do not take on legal
    proceedings. Jenkins adopts F's
    'proceeded', presumably either on metrical
    grounds or because of the past tense of
    were stirred up in 9.
    feats deeds, actions
7   **criminal** Jenkins adopts F's 'crimefull',
    though he quotes *Cor* 3.3.82: 'So criminal
    and in such capital kind'.
    capital punishable by death
8   **greatness** This extrametrical word is
    generally assumed to be 'a rejected first
    thought' (Jenkins).
9   **mainly . . . up** were greatly incited (to take
    action)
10–25 The King tells Laertes why he has *not*
    acted against Hamlet but conceals from
    him that he has, as he thinks, sent his

stepson to his death. It is perhaps surprising
that he does not mention Hamlet's
supposed madness as a factor.
11   **unsinewed** lacking sinews, i.e. weak
13–17 **for . . . her** The King's profession of his
    dependence on the Queen has been taken
    by some to motivate his murder of
    Hamlet's father, but he is hardly being
    honest in this speech.
14   **be . . . which** whichever of the two it may be
15   ***conjunct** intimately associated or
    coupled, as in *KL* 5.1.12–13: 'I am
    doubtful that you have been conjunct / And
    bosomed with her.' We adopt Oxf's
    speculation (*TxC*) that this might be behind
    the word printed as 'concliue' in Q2; like
    F's 'coniunctiue' (which requires the
    elision of *she is*), it carries a sense of
    astrological influence that is picked up in
    the next line.
16   **star . . . sphere** The King refers to the
    conventional (Ptolemaic) belief that

---

6 proceed] proceeded *F*   7 criminal] crimefull *F*   8 greatness] *om. F*   11 unsinewed] *(*vnsinnow'd)*, F*
*(*vnsinnowed)*   12 But] And *F*   they're] *(*tha'r)*; they are *F*   15 She is] She's *F*   conjunct] *Oxf;* concliue
Q2; coniunctiue *F*

I could not but by her. The other motive
Why to a public count I might not go
Is the great love the general gender bear him,
Who, dipping all his faults in their affection,   20
Work like the spring that turneth wood to stone,
Convert his gyves to graces, so that my arrows,
Too slightly timbered for so loud a wind,
Would have reverted to my bow again
But not where I have aimed them.   25

LAERTES

And so have I a noble father lost,
A sister driven into desperate terms
Whose worth, if praises may go back again,

---

the stars (planets) revolved around the
earth in their spheres – a concentric set of
transparent globes.

17 **I . . . her** 'I could not live without her'

18 **count** account, indictment

19 **general gender** common sort (of people)

21 **Work** operate. Q2's version requires us to
read *Work* as a main verb in parallel with
Convert (22).

     spring . . . stone This sounds like a
mythical spring, but various British
examples have been identified;
Shakespeare is referring to the way that
water in limestone areas can deposit a layer
of lime on objects placed in it. Johnson
finds the comparison surprising – 'If the
Spring had changed base metals to gold,
the thought had been more proper' – but in
this context the point may be that stone is
less vulnerable to arrows than wood.

22 **gyves** fetters. The King presumably uses
the word to mean 'faults' or 'crimes'.

23 **slightly timbered** having too light a shaft

*so loud a wind i.e. such a fierce
opposition; Shakespeare refers to the wind
being 'loud' in *Per* (3.1.48) and *Tem*
(3.3.63). Malone calls Q2's 'so loued
Arm'd' 'as extraordinary a corruption as
any that is found in [Shakespeare's] plays',
but Jennens retains it and glosses '*Too
slightly timbered for* one *so loved*, and
armed with the affections and venerations
of the people'.

24 **reverted** returned

25 **aimed** MacDonald defends F's 'arm'd',
but the Q2 reading is generally adopted. It
seems curious that the word 'arm'd' thus
disappears from this passage although it
occurs independently in both texts.

26–7 Laertes' summary of his position recalls
Hamlet's at 4.4.55–6.

27 **terms** circumstances

28 **Whose worth** F's 'Who was' is retained by
Hibbard without comment.

     go back again i.e. recall what she was
before

---

21 Work] Would *F*   22 gyves] *(Giues)*, *F (Gyues)*; crimes *Elze*; guilts *Oxf*   23 loud a wind] *F*; loued
Arm'd *Q2*   25 But] And *F*   have] had *F*   aimed] arm'd *F*   28 Whose worth] Who was *F*; Who has
Johnson

Stood challenger on mount of all the age
For her perfections. But my revenge will come.   30

KING

Break not your sleeps for that; you must not think
That we are made of stuff so flat and dull
That we can let our beard be shook with danger
And think it pastime. You shortly shall hear more.
I loved your father and we love ourself,   35
And that, I hope, will teach you to imagine –

Enter a Messenger *with letters.*

MESSENGER

These to your majesty, this to the Queen.

KING

From Hamlet! Who brought them?

---

29 **i.e.** constituted a superlative challenge to the entire age. Laertes idealizes his *desperate* sister rather as Hamlet idealizes his dead father.

     on mount set up on high

31 **Break . . . sleeps** We would say 'don't lose any sleep', i.e. don't worry.

32 **flat and dull** inert, slow to take offence

33 **That . . . shook** To shake or pluck a man by the beard was (metaphorically) to insult him: see 2.2.508.

     with by

34 **pastime** harmless sport

     You . . . more Does the audience take this as a hint that the King is about to tell Laertes about Hamlet's journey to England and its intended consequences when he is interrupted by *more* than he expected?

35 **we love ourself** The King presumably means that his own reputation and safety are involved.

36.1 In eighteenth- and nineteenth-century theatrical tradition, this Messenger was Barnardo.

37 **These** 'Letters' could be used in the plural

of just one letter, as at 4.6.3, but F's repetition of 'This' seems more consistent. Jenkins regards F's additional phrases (see t.n.) as unnecessary 'theatrical elaboration'.

     this . . . Queen This letter was not specifically mentioned in 4.6 (the apparent plural '*letters*' at 4.6.21 being ambiguous), nor do we hear any more of it. If we are to assume that Hamlet reveals the full extent of the King's treachery in it, it is surprising that he does not intercept it. In Q1, Horatio reports directly to the Queen in a unique scene (14), at which point there is no doubt that she is informed of her husband's plot. In Olivier's 1948 film the letters are delivered between Ophelia's two mad appearances (as in 4.5) and we see the King and Queen exiting separately reading them, which may encourage us to speculate on the contents of her letter.

38 **From Hamlet** In Q2 the King presumably deduces this from the inscription. (On whether the bearer knows Hamlet's identity, see 4.6.10n.)

36.1 *with letters*] *om. F*   37 MESSENGER These] How now? What Newes? / *Mes.* Letters my Lord from *Hamlet.* This *F*

MESSENGER

Sailors, my lord, they say. I saw them not.
They were given me by Claudio. He received them   40
Of him that brought them.

KING   Laertes, you shall hear them.
Leave us.   [*Exit Messenger.*]
[*Reads.*] *High and mighty. You shall know I am set naked
on your kingdom. Tomorrow shall I beg leave to see your
kingly eyes. When I shall (first asking you pardon)*   45
thereunto recount the occasion of my sudden return.
What should this mean? Are all the rest come back,
Or is it some abuse, and no such thing?

LAERTES

Know you the hand?

KING   'Tis Hamlet's character. 'Naked',
And in a postscript here he says 'alone'.   50
Can you devise me?

39–41 Sailors ... them F omits what does
seem an over-elaboration in Q2. Hibbard,
however, while following F, comments:
'The roundabout route by which the letters
reach the King testifies to Horatio's care in
ensuring that Claudius knows no more than
Hamlet wishes him to.'

40 Claudio Shakespeare's use of this name
may indicate that he did not actively think
of the King as 'Claudius' (see List of
Roles, 3n.). Some productions substitute
'Horatio', which simplifies the matter, but
Goldberg insists on the aptness of what he
calls 'a circuit from Claudio to Claudius
where all characters are lost in the letter'
(313).

43 *naked* Hamlet means 'without any
possessions', or possibly 'unarmed'.

45–6 *eyes* ... *recount* Speaking to eyes might

sound illogical, but *eyes* was a conventional
metonymy for the royal presence; see
1.2.116 and Fortinbras's 'We shall express
our duty in his eye' (4.4.6).

45 *you pardon* Jenkins prefers F's '*your
Pardon*'; *yᵘ/yʳ* is an easy error.

46 *occasion* circumstances
sudden return Jenkins adopts both F's
additions (see t.n.) but suggests the latter is
'a players' addition'.

48 abuse trick, deception
and ... thing? i.e. is the whole thing a
trick? Preferred by Hibbard to F's 'Or no
such thing?'

49 character handwriting

51 devise explain, resolve (*OED v.* 13); F's
'aduise' provides an easier meaning. (The
same spelling occurs in Q2 for 'deuise' at
62.)

41 Of ... brought them] *om. F*   41–2 Laertes ... us.] *F; one line Q2*   42 SD] *F; not in Q2*   43 SD]
Capell   45 *you*] *your F*   46 *the occasion*] *th'Occasions F   sudden*] *sodaine, and more strange
F   return.*] *returne. / Hamlet. F*   48 abuse, and] abuse? Or *F*   49–51 'Tis ... me?] *prose F*   51 devise]
aduise *F*

LAERTES

I am lost in it, my lord, but let him come.
It warms the very sickness in my heart
That I live and tell him to his teeth
'Thus didst thou.'

KING   If it be so, Laertes –   55
As how should it be so, how otherwise? –
Will you be ruled by me?

LAERTES   Ay, my lord,
So you will not o'errule me to a peace.

KING

To thine own peace. If he be now returned
As checking at his voyage, and that he means   60
No more to undertake it, I will work him
To an exploit, now ripe in my device,
Under the which he shall not choose but fall.
And for his death no wind of blame shall breathe
But even his mother shall uncharge the practice   65
And call it accident.

---

52 **lost in** baffled by

53 **warms** i.e. does good to

54 **I live** Jenkins prefers F's 'I shall live', perhaps on metrical grounds; RP suggests the F reading might be an error for 'I live and shall tell'.

55 **didst** Jenkins follows Dover Wilson in emending to 'diest', which is attractive (and supported by Q1's 'thus he dies', 15.5) but not strictly necessary.

55–6 **If ... otherwise** Presumably the King is talking about Hamlet's return and wondering whether to believe the letter or to see it as a trick. He is deciding not to grant the interview on Hamlet's terms but to exploit the situation to entrap him.

58 **So** so long as

60 ***As ... voyage** as a result of deviating from or giving up his voyage. *Check* is a term used of hawks being diverted from their prey; Dowden cites *TN* 3.1.64, 'check at every feather'. Q2's 'the King' seems an easy misreading of F's 'checking'; some editors, e.g. Jennens, adopt the Q6 reading (see t.n.). **that** i.e. if it is the case that

62 **ripe ... device** i.e. which I have fully developed as a scheme (ready to be put into effect)

65 **uncharge the practice** find the plot blameless (because undetected). *Practice* often has negative connotations: see 136 and 5.2.302.

---

52 I am] I'm *F*   54 I] I shall *F*   55 didst thou] he dies *Q1;* diddest thou *F;* diest thou *Cam¹ (1964) (Marshall)*   55–7 If ... me?] *F lines* ²so: / me? /   57–8 Ay ... peace.] *Steevens; one line Q2* Ay ... will] If so you'l *F*   60 checking] *F;* the King *Q2;* liking not *Q6*

LAERTES   My lord, I will be ruled
The rather if you could devise it so
That I might be the organ.

KING   It falls right.
You have been talked of since your travel much,
And that in Hamlet's hearing, for a quality   70
Wherein they say you shine. Your sum of parts
Did not together pluck such envy from him
As did that one, and that in my regard
Of the unworthiest siege.

LAERTES
What part is that, my lord?   75

KING
A very ribbon in the cap of youth.
Yet needful too, for youth no less becomes
The light and careless livery that it wears
Than settled age his sables and his weeds

66–80 **My . . . graveness** These lines are not in
F: 'the cut is sensitive and proper'
(Edwards); 'evidently a deliberate cut,
designed to speed up the action by
removing some of the *indirections*
Claudius has recourse to in his approach to
Laertes' (Hibbard). Pennington, however,
describes this as 'one of Shakespeare's
great temptation scenes' (123) and clearly
relished every moment of it when he
played the King. The discussion of Laertes'
parts (71) or attributes is to some extent
repeated at 5.2.91–105, when Osric
conveys the King's praise of him to
Hamlet, who responds by parodying the
style of the message; this later passage is
also omitted from F.

68 **organ** instrument
  It falls right that will fit excellently

71 **sum of parts** entire list of attributes; one

can still speak of 'a man of parts' to mean a
man with numerous good qualities.

74 **siege** rank, importance

76 **very ribbon** usually glossed 'mere
decoration', but the King is not dispraising
the attribute: he seems rather to mean 'the
absolute pinnacle of accomplishment' or
'the finishing touch' (comparable to 'On
Fortune's cap we are not the very button',
2.2.224). Q2/F's 'ribaud' is assumed to be a
turned letter error for 'riband', but it might
also suggest a link with the puzzling
'ribaudred hag of Egypt' (*AC* 3.10.10).

77 **becomes** suits (or is suited by)

78 **livery** literally 'uniform': the King likens
the fashionable art of fencing to a garment
appropriate to *light and careless* young men.

79 **sables** furs, or robes trimmed with fur (see
1.2.240, 3.2.123 and nn.)
  weeds clothes

66–80 My . . . graveness.] *om. F*   76 ribbon] *(*ribaud*)*

> Importing health and graveness. Two months since   80
> Here was a gentleman of Normandy –
> I have seen myself, and served against, the French
> And they can well on horseback, but this gallant
> Had witchcraft in't; he grew unto his seat
> And to such wondrous doing brought his horse   85
> As had he been incorpsed and demi-natured
> With the brave beast. So far he topped my thought
> That I in forgery of shapes and tricks
> Come short of what he did.

LAERTES   A Norman was't?

KING

A Norman.

LAERTES   Upon my life, Lamord!

KING   The very same.   90

80 **Importing . . . graveness** indicating a care for health and dignity. Editors have found the association of *health* (rather than 'wealth') with *age* incongruous, though one might understand *health* as 'care for one's health'; Jenkins glosses 'orderly well-being, stability'.

80 Having omitted 66–80, F begins again with 'Some two months hence', which completes the line beginning 'And call it accident' (66).

82 **I have** F's elision improves the metre.
served taken part in military action

83 **can . . . horseback** know how to ride well; for this use of *can*, Hope (2.1.2a) compares *PT* 13–14, 'Let the priest in surplice white, / That defunctive music can'. *Can* is explicitly preferred to F's 'ran' by MacDonald and adopted by Hibbard and Oxf without comment.
gallant stressed on first syllable; daring or spirited man

85 **doing** behaviour, performance

86 **As** as if
incorpsed made into one body (*OED*'s first use)

86–7 **demi-natured . . . beast** sharing, participating in the nature of the noble or fearless animal. (The King is imagining the Norman and his horse as being like the mythical Centaur, half man and half horse.)

87 ***topped my thought** exceeded my expectation; Q2's 'topt me thought' could mean something like 'excelled, as I thought', but *me/my* is a common error. Jenkins and Edwards conflate to read 'topped my thought' (as does Jennens).

88 **forgery . . . tricks** imagination of feats (of horsemanship)

89 **Come . . . did** cannot compete with what he actually performed

90 **Lamord** Editors have suggested topical references – understandably perhaps, because the matter of the Norman and his horsemanship seems

80 Two] Some two *F*   since] hence *F*   82 I have] I'ue *F*   83 can] ran *F*   84 unto] into *F*   86 had he] *F*; he had *Q5*   demi-natured] (demy natur'd), *F*   87 topped] past *F*   my] *F*; me *Q2*   90 Lamord] *Lamound F*

430

LAERTES

> I know him well. He is the brooch, indeed,
> And gem of all the nation.

KING

> He made confession of you
> And gave you such a masterly report
> For art and exercise in your defence,   95
> And for your rapier most especial,
> That he cried out 'twould be a sight indeed
> If one could match you. Th'escrimers of their nation
> He swore had neither motion, guard nor eye
> If you opposed them. Sir, this report of his   100
> Did Hamlet so envenom with his envy
> That he could nothing do but wish and beg
> Your sudden coming o'er to play with you.
> Now out of this –

LAERTES   What out of this, my lord?

rather tangential to the real skill in question, that of fencing. They have also noted the closeness of the name to *la mort* (death).

91 **brooch** ornament, 'star'

93 **made . . . you** testified to your ability; perhaps *confession* implies that the Norman was reluctant to praise the Dane.

95 **art . . . defence** skilful practice of the art of self-defence. Wright, 192, argues that *art and exercise* is another hendiadys.

96 **rapier** a fashionable weapon for duelling around 1600: see 5.2.128n.
especial four syllables; either this form or F's 'especially' could be used adverbially.

98 **If . . . you** if anyone could be found to compete with you

98–100 **Th'escrimers . . . them** Again Edwards and Hibbard argue that the F 'cut' is beneficial.

98 ***Th'escrimers** skilled fencers (French *escrimeurs*).

99 **had** would have
motion (correct or practised) movement
eye faculty of visual perception

101 **envenom** embitter (literally, poison – a characteristically Shakespearean anticipation of the literal suggestion which soon follows)

103 **coming o'er** i.e. return from France
with you F's 'with him' is more grammatical, but either makes sense.

104 **What . . . this** Laertes' interruption may imply his impatience, or perhaps that the King has paused for thought.

92 the] our *F*   96 especial] especially*ᵉ F*   98 you.] *(*you*,); you F*   98–100 Th'escrimers . . . them.] *om. F*   98 Th'escrimers] *Oxf (White);* the Scrimures *Q2*   100 Sir, this] Sir. This *F*   103 you] him *F*   104 What] Why *F*

KING

> Laertes, was your father dear to you? 105
> Or are you like the painting of a sorrow,
> A face without a heart?

LAERTES   Why ask you this?

KING

> Not that I think you did not love your father
> But that I know love is begun by time
> And that I see in passages of proof 110
> Time qualifies the spark and fire of it.
> There lives within the very flame of love
> A kind of wick or snuff that will abate it,
> And nothing is at a like goodness still,
> For goodness growing to a pleurisy 115
> Dies in his own too much. That we would do
> We should do when we would, for this 'would'
>   changes
> And hath abatements and delays as many

105–24 The King insists (even in the abbreviated F version – see 112–21n.) that revenge is a natural concomitant of love.

106 **painting . . . sorrow** The King's metaphor recalls his description of Ophelia as being like a *picture* in her madness (4.5.86) and the First Player's reference to Pyrrhus as a '*painted tyrant*' (2.2.418).

110 **passages of proof** experiences which put this to the test

111 **qualifies** modifies, i.e. reduces

112–21 Edwards regrets what he sees as a deliberate cut in F 'since the passage is of such great interest thematically, and so illuminating of Claudius' theory of life', but Hibbard thinks an audience may become 'impatient at Claudius' elaborate moralizing'.

113 **wick or snuff** The *wick* is the fibre in a lamp or candle which is ignited to provide

light; the *snuff* is the part of the wick which is slowly consumed and needs to be trimmed occasionally. The King seems to be saying that love is lessened by the very thing that feeds it (in contrast to Hamlet's observation of his mother: 'As if increase of appetite had grown / By what it fed on', 1.2.144–5).

114 **at . . . goodness** at the same level of goodness

115 **pleurisy** excess; literally an inflammation of the chest, sometimes spelt 'plurisy' and mistakenly derived from Latin *plus, pluris* (more) – hence seen as a result of an excess of humours

116–19 **That . . . accidents** Dent cites 'He that will not when he may, when he would he shall have nay' as proverbial (N54).

118 **abatements** reductions

112–21] *om. F*   113 wick] *(weeke)*   115 pleurisy] *(plurisie)*

As there are tongues, are hands, are accidents,
And then this 'should' is like a spendthrift's sigh   120
That hurts by easing. But to the quick of th'ulcer –
Hamlet comes back. What would you undertake
To show yourself in deed your father's son
More than in words?

LAERTES   To cut his throat i'th' church.

KING

No place indeed should murder sanctuarize.   125
Revenge should have no bounds. But, good Laertes,
Will you do this? Keep close within your chamber;
Hamlet returned shall know you are come home;
We'll put on those shall praise your excellence
And set a double varnish on the fame   130
The Frenchman gave you, bring you in fine together
And wager on your heads. He being remiss,

---

119 **tongues** ... **hands** i.e. other people's words and actions

120 **spendthrift's sigh** i.e. the vain regret of a man who has spent his money. Q5's 'spend-thrift sigh' is adopted by Dowden, Spencer, Jenkins, Edwards and Hibbard: in this reading the sigh itself is the *spendthrift*. *Pleurisy* (115) is characterized by difficult and painful breathing.

121 **hurts by easing** i.e. gives pain at the same time as it relieves it

quick heart, most sensitive part (see Hamlet's *ulcer* metaphor at 3.4.145–7)

123 ***in** ... **son** Malone's emendation seems justified by the contrast with *in words* in 124.

125 **should murder sanctuarize** '[The King's] remark runs in two directions at once. (1) No church should offer sanctuary and protection to a man who like Hamlet has committed murder; (2) no church should be regarded as a sanctuary where the throat-cutting you mention cannot be carried out' (Edwards). We may recall Hamlet's refusal to kill the King at prayer in 3.3.

127 **Will** ... **this** Despite the question marks in Q5 and F2 (see t.n.), Jenkins argues that this is not a question but a condition – i.e. *if* you do this, you will 'Requite him for your father' (137).

Keep close stay concealed. The King may not want to risk a chance encounter between Laertes and Hamlet (such as occurs in 5.1).

129 **put** ... **shall** organize some people who will

130 **fame** reputation

131 **in fine** in conclusion, finally

132 ***wager on** F's reading is the more idiomatic expression (see 5.2.88), and 'on' could easily be misread as 'o'r'.

132 **remiss** careless, negligent

---

120 spendthrift's] *Pope (*spend-thrift's); spend thirfts *Q2;* spend-thrifts *Q3;* spend-thrift *Q5, Ard² * 123 in ... son] *Malone;* indeede your fathers sonne *Q2;* your Fathers sonne indeed *F;* your Father's Son in deed *F4*   127 this? ... chamber;] *Q5 (*this? ... chamber,*)*; this, ... chamber, *Q2F;* this, ... Chamber? *F2*   132 on] *F;* ore *Q2*

Most generous and free from all contriving,
Will not peruse the foils, so that with ease,
Or with a little shuffling, you may choose   135
A sword unbated and in a pass of practice
Requite him for your father.
LAERTES   I will do't.
And for that purpose I'll anoint my sword.
I bought an unction of a mountebank
So mortal that, but dip a knife in it,   140
Where it draws blood no cataplasm so rare,
Collected from all simples that have virtue

133–4 **Most . . . foils** See Edmund's reflections
   on Edgar: 'a brother noble, / Whose nature
   is so far from doing harms / That he
   suspects none' (*KL* 1.2.177–9). Perhaps
   the King overlooks the evident
   'contrivance' of *The Murder of Gonzago* in
   order to make Laertes' role in the plot seem
   easier.
133 **generous** noble, free from meanness (or
   suspicion)
   contriving scheming, deception
134 **peruse** scrutinize
   foils light swords used for fencing,
   rendered comparatively harmless by the
   placing of buttons on their points
135 **shuffling** sleight of hand (mixing up of the
   foils). Some editors suggest that *shuffling*
   means 'evasive dealing' here as it does at
   3.3.61, but *OED* gives this example under
   the literal sense (*vbl. sb.* 3).
136 **unbated** not blunted, i.e. not protected by a
   button. Jenkins stresses *sword* (as opposed
   to *foil*) in this line, but Shakespeare seems
   to use 'rapier', 'foil' and 'sword' as
   synonyms in this scene and in 5.2.
   pass of practice either (1) a thrust intended
   as mere exercise (i.e. not a serious fight) or
   (2) a thrust characterized by treachery (see
   practice at 65 and at 5.2.302).
138 *****for that purpose** F's reading (adopted by

Jenkins) seems preferable metrically to
   Q2's 'for purpose'.
139–44 **an unction . . . withal** Such a
   poison seems to belong to the world of
   legend rather than reality, like the drugs
   that cause Juliet in *RJ* and Imogen in *Cym*
   to appear to be dead for a while. In Q1 it is
   the King who suggests anointing the sword
   with poison.
139 **unction** ointment; often but not exclusively
   used in religious contexts, as in 'extreme
   unction', the final rite of the Christian
   church. This and 3.4.143 are Shakespeare's
   only uses of the word.
   mountebank travelling salesman offering
   dubious cures and potions; as the name
   implies, he got up on a bench to cry his
   wares – as the principal character does in
   2.1 of Ben Jonson's *Volpone* (1606) in
   order to see Celia.
140 **mortal** deadly, fatal
   that, but dip F's 'I but dipt' may suggest
   that Laertes has previously tested the
   poison. In both readings the syntax
   changes, leaving this part of the sentence
   incomplete.
141 **cataplasm** medicinal poultice or plaster
142 **Collected from** composed of
   simples . . . virtue herbs with healing
   properties

136 pass] *(pace), F*   138 that] *F; not in Q2; the Q3*   140 that] I *F*   dip] dipt *F*

Under the moon, can save the thing from death
That is but scratched withal. I'll touch my point
With this contagion, that if I gall him slightly   145
It may be death.
KING   Let's further think of this,
Weigh what convenience both of time and means
May fit us to our shape. If this should fail
And that our drift look through our bad performance
'Twere better not essayed. Therefore this project   150
Should have a back or second that might hold
If this did blast in proof. Soft, let me see:
We'll make a solemn wager on your cunnings –
I ha't!
When in your motion you are hot and dry   155
(As make your bouts more violent to that end)
And that he calls for drink, I'll have preferred him
A chalice for the nonce, whereon but sipping,

143 **Under the moon** perhaps just 'anywhere on earth', but see 3.2.250 for Lucianus' '*mixture rank, of midnight weeds collected*'.
144 **touch my point** anoint or smear the (*unbated*) point of my sword
145 **contagion** poisonous compound
  gall graze, scratch
148 **May . . . shape** may suit us for the role we are to play
149 **drift look** intention be visible
  bad performance failed attempt
150 **essayed** put to the test, attempted
151 **back or second** back-up or second string
  hold prove effective
152 **blast in proof** go wrong (blow up) in practice
153 **your cunnings** your respective degrees of

skill. F's 'commings' may be a version of the technical fencing term *venies* (from French *venir*, to come) used in Q1 at this point (15.18).
154 **I ha't** I have it (i.e. I've thought of the solution)
156 **As** i.e. and you should
157 **preferred** offered; F's 'prepar'd', though rejected by Hibbard, is adopted by Jenkins on the grounds that Q2's 'prefard' is a misprint since the spelling is unique in Shakespeare and the F reading is supported by Q1's 'a potion that shall ready stand'.
158 **chalice** drinking cup or goblet; like *unction* (139), the word occurs often, though not exclusively, in religious contexts.
  for the nonce especially for the occasion

145–6 With . . . death.] *F; one line Q2*   148 shape. If . . . fail] *Rowe;* shape if . . . fayle, *Q2;* shape, if . . . faile; *F*   150 essayed] *(assayd), F(assaid)*   152 did] should *F*   153 cunnings] commings *F* 154–5] *Johnson; one line Q2F*   154 ha't] *(hate), F*   156 that] the *F*   157 preferred] *(prefard), Q3 (preferd); prepar'd F*

If he by chance escape your venomed stuck,
Our purpose may hold there. But stay, what noise? 160

Enter QUEEN.

QUEEN

One woe doth tread upon another's heel,
So fast they follow. Your sister's drowned, Laertes.

LAERTES

Drowned! O, where?

QUEEN

There is a willow grows askant the brook
That shows his hoary leaves in the glassy stream. 165

---

159 **stuck** thrust (with a sword). Q6's reading 'tuck', meaning a kind of sword or rapier (as at *TN* 3.4.223), was adopted by some eighteenth-century editors, e.g. Jennens.

160 **noise** Presumably sounds of lamentation made by the Queen and/or others. Hibbard has a SD '*Enter Gertrude* [*in tears*]'.

161–2 **One . . . follow** The Queen expresses the same sentiment as her husband at 4.5.78–9: 'When sorrows come they come not single spies / But in battalions.'

163 **Drowned!** Some productions and editions make this a question.

O, where? Laertes may seem impatient to rush off to find her.

164–81 **There ... death** The Queen's description of Ophelia's death provides the material for what became one of the most frequently illustrated moments in the play even before the famous 1851 painting by John Everett Millais (now in Tate Britain, London, it provides one of the gallery's bestselling posters). A similar incident is recounted in *TNK* 4.1, but in that case the Jailer's Daughter is in fact saved from drowning by the witness, her Wooer. Some

late nineteenth- and early twentieth-century productions ended this scene with a kind of tableau in which Ophelia's dripping body was carried onstage on a litter (see Hapgood). The film versions by Eleuterio Rodolfi (1917) and Laurence Olivier (1948) show the direct influence of Millais in depicting the moment; Branagh broke with cinematic tradition (and his own liking for flashbacks and other illustrations of narrated material) by *not* filming it (Jenkins, LN; see pp. 26–7; Peterson; and Figs 5 and 6).

164 **willow** The willow was traditionally associated with unrequited love; see Desdemona's 'song of willow' in *Oth* 4.3.

askant obliquely, i.e. across. This seems to be a variant of 'askance', though *OED*'s other examples date from 1633 and 1695. F's 'aslant' is a different word with a similar meaning.

165 **shows** i.e. reflects

hoary grey or white (usually associated with age or with cold as in 'hoarfrost'). F's 'hore' regularizes the metre but loses the internal rhyme.

---

159 stuck] tuck *Q6* 160 But ... noise?] How now Gertred *Q1;* how sweet Queene *F;* how now sweet Queene *F2* 162 they] they'l *F* 164 askant the] aslant a *F* 165 hoary] *(*horry*);* hore *F*

Therewith fantastic garlands did she make
Of crowflowers, nettles, daisies and long purples,
That liberal shepherds give a grosser name
But our cold maids do dead men's fingers call them.
There on the pendent boughs her crownet weeds   170
Clambering to hang, an envious sliver broke,
When down her weedy trophies and herself
Fell in the weeping brook. Her clothes spread wide
And mermaid-like awhile they bore her up,

166 Capell defends Q2 as implying that Ophelia's decision to decorate the tree was a spontaneous one and Dover Wilson adds the point that garlands made *with* willow signify 'disconsolate love'; by contrast the F reading (see t.n.) implies she 'came' *to* the tree with ready-made garlands. This could have a bearing on whether her death is accidental or premeditated. Edwards follows Q2 on the assumption that F's scribe misunderstood the line.
  fantastic elaborate
167 **crowflowers** a common name for two different kinds of wild flowers, buttercups and ragged robins
  long purples usually identified as a kind of wild orchid
168 **liberal** free-speaking
  grosser name It is generally assumed that the *grosser name* relates to the testicle-shaped tubers of these plants; Jenkins suggests 'dogstones' and 'fool's ballocks'. (The Greek 'orchis' also means 'testicle'.) Wentersdorf, however, argues that the *long purple* is wild arum or cuckoo-pint which has a 'phallic' spadix and has also attracted *gross* names.
169 *cold i.e. chaste, the opposite of *liberal*. Q2's hypermetrical 'cull-cold' persists uncorrected

in the seventeenth-century quartos and is retained by Riv (which glosses 'chaste'), but it is not listed in *OED* and Jenkins sees it as a false start in the manuscript.
170 **pendent** overhanging
  crownet weeds coronet of wild flowers
171 **Clambering** probably disyllabic, as Q2/F's 'Clambring' indicates. Before Millais, most illustrations of this scene showed Ophelia in an upright posture, often perilously poised above the water; after 1851 she was usually depicted lying down (see Figs 5 and 6).
  envious malicious
  sliver twig or splinter; like Q1's 'sprig', the word was normally used of a part of a tree or bush much smaller than that implied here.
172 **trophies** i.e. garlands
173 **Fell** In the Queen's account, Ophelia's entry into the water seems like an accident, but in 5.1 suicide is suggested.
173–4 **Her . . . up** This passage is parodied in *Eastward Ho*, 4.1.66–75, when Slitgut observes Security's wife, who eventually comes safe ashore after a shipwreck in the Thames (see p. 58).
174 **mermaid-like** Mermaids are mythical creatures, half women and half fish.

166 Therewith] There with *F*   make] come *F*   169 cold] *F;* cull-cold *Q2;* culcold *Q4*   170 crownet] *Cam¹;* cronet *Q2;* Coronet *Q3, F*   171 Clambering] (Clambring) *F*   sliver] *F;* sprig *Q1*   172 her] the *F*   174 mermaid-like] (Marmaide like), *Q1F*

Which time she chanted snatches of old lauds 175
As one incapable of her own distress,
Or like a creature native and endued
Unto that element. But long it could not be
Till that her garments, heavy with their drink,
Pulled the poor wretch from her melodious lay 180
To muddy death.

LAERTES   Alas, then she is drowned.

QUEEN

Drowned, drowned.

LAERTES

Too much of water hast thou, poor Ophelia,
And therefore I forbid my tears. But yet
It is our trick – nature her custom holds 185
Let shame say what it will. [*Weeps.*] When these are
   gone
The woman will be out. Adieu, my lord,

---

175 **Which time** during which time
   lauds hymns. Some commentators have objected to *lauds* as unlikely given (1) the songs Ophelia sings in 4.5 and (2) the suggestion of suicide. Jennens prints *lauds* as 'the kind of music she entertained herself with just before she died', and Dover Wilson asserts that 'Ophelia dies crowned with flowers and singing hymns of praise to God'. Elze prints *lauds* but prefers Q1/F's 'tunes': 'Ophelia does not sing *lauds*, which are entirely foreign to her form of mental disease, but love ditties and songs of mourning.' Edwards dismisses 'tunes' as 'an intentional simplification by the playhouse scribe' and suggests Gertrude may be 'covering up'; he adds: 'But crazy hymn-singing might well have marked Ophelia's death.'

176 **incapable** uncomprehending
177 **endued** habituated, i.e. as if native
180 **wretch** often used to indicate a mixture of pity and affection, as the Queen uses it of Hamlet at 2.2.165 above, and in the Nurse's reference to the young Juliet as a 'pretty wretch' (*RJ* 1.3.44)
   melodious lay sweet-sounding song
181 **she is drowned** Some performers take a cue from Q3/F (see t.n.) to represent Laertes as too stunned to take in the main point of the Queen's speech.
185 **our trick** the normal reflex or impulse of human beings
186 **these** these tears
187 **The ... out** i.e. this feminine weakness will be finished with. Tears were often associated with women; see Lear's 'let not women's weapons, water-drops, / Stain my man's cheeks' (*KL* 2.2.469–70).

---

175 lauds] tunes *Q1F*   177 endued] *(*indewed*), F (*indued*)   179 their] *Q1;* her *F*   180 lay] buy *F*   181 she is] *Q1;* is she *Q3, F*   drowned.] *(*drownd.*), Q1 (*drownde:*);* drown'd? *F, Q5;* drown'd! *Pope* 186 SD] *Ard²*

> I have a speech o'fire that fain would blaze
> But that this folly drowns it.   *Exit.*
> KING   Let's follow, Gertrude.
> How much I had to do to calm his rage!   190
> Now fear I this will give it start again.
> Therefore let's follow.   *Exeunt.*

[**5.1**] *Enter two Clowns* [*a* Gravedigger *and a* Second Man].

GRAVEDIGGER   Is she to be buried in Christian burial,

---

188 ***o'fire** of fire, fiery; RP suggests Q2's 'a fire' might work as 'afire' implying inverted word order ('that fain would blaze into fire').

fain would is very eager to

189 **this folly** this foolish impulse (of weeping)

drowns F's 'doubts', usually read as 'douts' meaning 'does out, puts out, extinguishes', is adopted by Dowden, Jenkins, Edwards and Hibbard.

189–92 **Let's ... follow** In some productions the Queen seems reluctant to *follow*, repelled by the King's brisk (and selfish) focus on Laertes rather than on the tragic event he has just described. In Branagh's 1996 film this was the turning point for Julie Christie's Gertrude: 'She will not follow. Never again.' (141).

5.1 The three texts: this scene runs to 288 lines in Q2, 295 lines in F (see 33n. and 100n.), and 177 lines in Q1 (scene 16). Q1 has a shorter version of the opening conversation between the '*two Clowns*' and Hamlet's conversation with the Gravedigger. Q1 also omits the insistence on Hamlet's age at 135–53 and 163–4, and its SDs at the equivalent of 70 and 247 have proved controversial. Location and timing: this scene, a favourite with illustrators, takes place in a churchyard. There must be a

small gap in time since Ophelia's death was announced at the end of 4.7, but apparently not long enough for Hamlet to have kept his engagement to meet the King '*Tomorrow*' (4.7.44). The King's reference to 'our last night's speech' in his words to Laertes at 283 may imply that this is the next day.

0.1 In all three texts the primary meaning of *clown* is 'rustic' rather than 'comedian', but here as elsewhere in Shakespeare rustic characters are used to provide comic relief (see List of Roles, 20n.). It is clear from the dialogue that the first speaker is a gravedigger (he refers to himself as a *sexton* at 153); the other is often played as a less experienced assistant, but he may be simply a passing acquaintance. His role in any case is to play the straight man or 'stooge' to allow the gravedigger to display his wit. Q6 adds '*with spades and mattocks*' to this SD: at least one such implement is needed at 29 and later, and at least two skulls must be produced from the *grave* (see 3–4 n., 70 SD and 92 SD).

1 **she** It is obvious to audience and readers (though not to Hamlet and Horatio later on) that this is Ophelia. In Saxo Grammaticus and François de Belleforest, the hero returns to find his

---

188 o'fire] *Cam²; a fire Q2; of fire F; afire Q5*   189 drowns] *Q2, F2; doubts F; douts Ard²*   **5.1**] *Q6 0.1 Enter two Clowns*] *F; enter Clowne and an other Q1*   *a* Gravedigger *and*] *Ard² subst.   a* Second Man] *this edn;* Another *Ard²*   1+ SP] *Ard²; Clowne. Q21F*

when she wilfully seeks her own salvation?

2 MAN   I tell thee she is. Therefore make her grave
straight. The crowner hath sat on her and finds it
Christian burial.   5

GRAVEDIGGER   How can that be unless she drowned
herself in her own defence?

2 MAN   Why, 'tis found so.

GRAVEDIGGER   It must be *se offendendo*. It cannot be else.
For here lies the point: if I drown myself wittingly, it   10
argues an act, and an act hath three branches – it is to
act, to do, to perform. Argal, she drowned herself
wittingly.

own obsequies being performed, Feng/
Fengon having assumed he has been killed
in England (see Bullough, 7.69 and 108,
and pp. 66–71).
Christian burial i.e. burial in consecrated
ground accompanied by Christian ritual,
traditionally denied to suicides. From the
Queen's account of the death of Ophelia in
all three texts one might deduce it was
accidental as much as wilful, but this
discussion (which parodies legal arguments)
relates to the play's wider interest in issues
of salvation and damnation.

2   **wilfully** ... **salvation** Either the
Gravedigger implies that Ophelia is
seeking heaven prematurely, or he is
confusing *salvation* for 'damnation', as
Dogberry does at *MA* 3.3.3.

3–4 **Therefore** ... **straight** The Second Man
seems to speak with some degree of
professional authority here (see 14n.
and 29n.). The *grave* was (and is) usually
represented by an open trapdoor leading to
the space under the stage.

4   **straight** immediately
crowner colloquial version of 'coroner',
an official whose job is to conduct inquests
in cases of accidental or violent death

sat on her sat in judgement on her case
4–5 **finds ... burial** i.e. adjudicates her worthy
of burial in consecrated ground
6–7 **drowned ... defence** Self-defence could
(and can) excuse murder, but is comically
inappropriate in most cases of suicide.
9   *se offendendo Q2's 'so offended' could
mean 'It must indeed be that kind of
offence' (with the Gravedigger picking up
so from the Second Man's previous line).
Most editors prefer F's reading, taking it as
the Gravedigger's error for '*se
defendendo*', Latin for 'in self-defence'.
The Q2 compositor might have had
difficulty with the Latin here, as at 12.
10   **wittingly** knowingly
11–12 **three ... perform** It is generally agreed
that Shakespeare is alluding to the famous
suicide (by drowning) of Sir James Hales
in 1554: the subsequent legal arguments
over his property involved a claim that 'the
act of self-destruction' was divided into
three parts, the imagination, the resolution
and the perfection (see Jenkins, LN).
12   *Argal therefore (a corruption of *ergo*, the
Latin form which is found in Q1). Q2 reads
'or all', but F has 'argall' here and both
texts have 'argall' at 19 and 44.

2 when she] that *F*   3+ SP] *this edn; Other. Q2F;* 2. *Q1*   Therefore] and therefore *F*   9 *se offendendo*]
F; so offended *Q2*   11–12 to act] an Act *F*   12 do] doe and *F*   Argal] *F;* or all *Q2*

2 MAN   Nay, but hear you, goodman delver.

GRAVEDIGGER   Give me leave. Here lies the water – good.   15
Here stands the man – good. If the man go to this water
and drown himself, it is, willy-nilly, he goes. Mark you
that. But if the water come to him and drown him, he
drowns not himself. Argal, he that is not guilty of his
own death shortens not his own life.   20

2 MAN   But is this law?

GRAVEDIGGER   Ay, marry is't. Crowner's 'quest law.

2 MAN   Will you ha' the truth on't? If this had not been a
gentlewoman she should have been buried out
o'Christian burial.   25

GRAVEDIGGER   Why, there thou sayst, and the more pity
that great folk should have countenance in this world to
drown or hang themselves more than their even-
Christen. Come, my spade. There is no ancient

14 **goodman delver** 'neighbour digger'. The Second Man addresses the Gravedigger by his occupation, though some have taken 'Delver' to be the man's actual (appropriate) name. In addition to being used when addressing someone by their occupation, *goodman* could be used when condescending to someone of lower social status, as when Holofernes addresses 'goodman Dull' at *LLL* 4.2.36 and 5.1.143.

15–16 **Here … good** In performance the Gravedigger can use tools and bones as props to act this out, rather as Launce acts out his farewell to his family in *TGV* 2.3 ('This shoe is my father', etc.). In Yukio Ninagawa's production at London's Barbican Centre in 1998 the Gravedigger used a bottle of mineral water at this moment.

17 **willy-nilly** whether he is willing or not (will he? nil he?)
Mark take note, remember

20 **death shortens** It is conceivable that the comma between these two words, in both Q2 and F, indicates the Gravedigger's comic timing.

22 **'quest** inquest

23 **on't** of it

24–5 **out o'** out of, outside

26 **there thou sayst** i.e. you've made a good point. The priest's reference to *great command* at 217 seems to confirm the Gravedigger's cynicism.

27 **countenance** permission, authority (i.e. they get away with it – at least as far as getting Christian burial)

28–9 **even-Christen** fellow Christians (a collective form)

29 **Come, my spade** If this is a command to the Second Man to pick up and pass the tool, the Gravedigger is now the one speaking with authority (see 3–4n. and 14n.). But he could be addressing the tool as he picks it up.
ancient venerable, well-established

14 goodman delver] *(good man deluer), F (Goodman Deluer)*   17 willy-nilly] *(will he, nill he) F*   18 that.] *(that,) that? F*   20 death shortens] *(death, shortens) F*   23 on't] *(an't), F*   25 o'] *Jennens;* a *Q2;* of *F*   28–9 their even-Christen] *F;* other people *Q1*

gentlemen but gardeners, ditchers and grave-makers.　30
They hold up Adam's profession.

2 MAN　Was he a gentleman?

GRAVEDIGGER　'A was the first that ever bore arms. I'll
put another question to thee. If thou answerest me not
to the purpose, confess thy self.　　　　　　　　　　35

2 MAN　Go to.

GRAVEDIGGER　What is he that builds stronger than
either the mason, the shipwright or the carpenter?

2 MAN　The gallows-maker, for that outlives a thousand
tenants.　　　　　　　　　　　　　　　　　　　40

GRAVEDIGGER　I like thy wit well, in good faith. The
gallows does well. But how does it well? It does well to
those that do ill. Now, thou dost ill to say the gallows is
built stronger than the church. Argal, the gallows may

30　**ditchers** men who make and repair ditches
31　**hold up** keep up (the noble reputation of)
32　**gentleman** a reference to the proverbial rhyme, 'When Adam delved and Eve span, / Who was then the gentleman?' (Tilley, A30); the rhyme implies that there were no 'gentlemen' or distinctions between people of different social classes in Eden.
33　**bore arms** had a coat of arms, the mark of a gentleman. Jenkins attributes Q2's omission of an additional passage in F (see t.n.) to a compositor's error, an eyeskip from one *arms* to another. Shakespeare apparently assisted his father in his successful attempt to obtain a coat of arms from the Heralds' College in 1596; see Honan, 228–9. Duncan-Jones (84–91) points out that his first negotiations with the Heralds took place in the mid-1590s, when his son Hamnet or Hamlet was still alive.

35　**to the purpose** i.e. correctly
　confess thyself i.e. prepare for death. Q2 has a full stop after 'thy selfe', while F has a long dash; editors tend to adopt the latter and to quote the proverb 'Confess thyself and be hanged' (Tilley, C587).
36　**Go to** shut up (a common expression indicating objection or impatience). In F, the long dash after *confess thyself* in 35 may suggest that *Go to* is an interruption.
38　**mason** i.e. stonemason
39　**gallows-maker** one who makes the frames or gallows (consisting of one or two upright posts and a crossbeam) used for hanging criminals
　that i.e. the gallows. References to 'a gallows' in the singular are common.
42　**does well** (1) makes a good answer; (2) provides a good service
44–5　**may . . . thee** i.e. may serve its purpose by punishing you

---

33　'A] He *F*　arms.] Armes. / *Other.* Why he had none. / *Clo.* What, ar't a Heathen? how dost thou vnderstand the Scripture? the Scripture sayes *Adam* dig'd; could hee digge without Armes? *F*　35 thy self] *(thy selfe.), F (thy selfe –)*　39 that] that Frame *F*

do well to thee. To't again, come.   45

2 MAN   Who builds stronger than a mason, a shipwright or
a carpenter?

GRAVEDIGGER   Ay, tell me that and unyoke.

2 MAN   Marry, now I can tell.

GRAVEDIGGER   To't!   50

2 MAN   Mass, I cannot tell.

GRAVEDIGGER   Cudgel thy brains no more about it, for
your dull ass will not mend his pace with beating. And
when you are asked this question next, say a grave-
maker. The houses he makes lasts till doomsday. Go get   55
thee in and fetch me a stoup of liquor.

[*Exit Second Man.*]

Sings.
In youth when I did love, did love,

45 **To't again** have another try
48 **unyoke** unyoke the oxen (from the
plough), i.e. put an end to your labour
49 **Marry** by (the Virgin) Mary
50 **To't** get on with it
51 **Mass** by the mass
52 **Cudgel thy brains** proverbial (Tilley,
B602)
53 **your . . . beating** a variant of the proverb
'A dull ass must have a sharp spur' (Dent,
A348.1)
55 **doomsday** See 1.1.119, 2.2.234 and nn.
56 **in and** F's '*Yaughan*' is generally taken to
be an unusual spelling of 'Johan' or
possibly 'Joan', presumably the owner of
the alehouse.
        *stoup pitcher or jug, as at 5.2.244; it is
difficult to find a relevant meaning for Q2's
'soope' (which is an easy misreading),
though Jennens defends it as 'the clownish
pronunciation of 'sup', which Riv
retains.
56 SD *There is no SD in Q2, F or Q1, but the

command (somewhat more peremptory in
Q1: 'Fetch me a stope of beere, goe') is
presumably obeyed. Mahood (*Bit Parts*,
16) notes that the liquor never arrives and
compares this rather casual handling of a
subsidiary role with the moment in *MA* 2.3
when Benedick's page never returns with
the book he has been sent to fetch.
57–60 a version of a popular song, 'The Aged
Lover Renounceth Love', written by
Thomas Lord Vaux. His first stanza reads:
'I loathe that I did love, / In youth that I
thought sweet: / As time requires for my
behove / Methinks they are not meet.' The
Gravedigger's version seems to turn this
stanza into a more straightforward
celebration of careless youth (see Jenkins,
LN, and see Appendix 6 for a discussion of
the music traditionally used). While
Hamlet finds the Gravedigger's singing
inappropriate, it quickly becomes clear that
the theme of his song is mortality. See also
67–70, 89–92.

55 houses] *Q1*; Houses that *F*   lasts] *F*; Last *Q1, Q3, F4*   56 in and] to *Yaughan F*   stoup] *Q1* (stope*),
F* (stoupe*);* soope *Q2;* sup *Riv (Kermode)*   SD] *this edn*   57, 67, 89 SD] *F; Song. opp. line Q2; not in Q1*

> Methought it was very sweet
> To contract-a the time for-a my behove,
> O, methought there-a was nothing-a meet!   60

Enter HAMLET *and* HORATIO.

HAMLET   Has this fellow no feeling of his business? 'A
sings in grave-making.

HORATIO   Custom hath made it in him a property of
easiness.

HAMLET   'Tis e'en so. The hand of little employment   65
hath the daintier sense.

GRAVEDIGGER *(Sings.)*

> But age with his stealing steps
> Hath clawed me in his clutch
> And hath shipped me into the land

59–60 **-a . . . -a** These extrametrical syllables
are either the Gravedigger's decorations of
his lyric or his grunts as he works.

59 **To . . . behove** to pass the time for my own
pleasure

60 **meet** appropriate

60.1 See t.n. for variant placings; Hamlet and
Horatio must enter in time to hear the
Gravedigger singing. In most productions
he is not aware of their presence until
Hamlet addresses him at 110–11.

61 **'A** he (also at 80, 142, 143, 155, 157, 161,
169 and 194)

63–4 **a . . . easiness** a matter of indifference (*it*
being the *business* of *grave-making*)

66 **hath . . . sense** is more sensitive
(proverbial)
*daintier Q2's 'dintier' has no relevant
meaning; *TxC* suggests it may represent an
acceptable spelling of the alternative 'ei-'
pronunciation.

67–70 The Gravedigger combines two stanzas
in Vaux's song (see 57–60n.), the relevant
lines being 'For age with stealing steps, /
Hath clawed me with his crutch; / And
lusty life away she leaps, / As there had
been none such', and 'For beauty with her
band / These crooked cares hath wrought, /
And shipped me into the land, / From
whence I first was brought.'

68 **clawed** The word is in Vaux and provides
stronger alliteration with *clutch* than F's
'caught'.

69 **shipped . . . land** transported me to the
land (of death): *age* in the Gravedigger's
version and 'beauty' in Vaux's have the
same effect. (F's 'intill' is an archaic and
originally northern form of *into* according
to Blake, 5.4.2, who notes that it is unclear
whether, since the word occurs in a song, it
is meant to indicate the character's social
or geographical background.)

59–60] *this edn;* To contract ô the time for a my behoue, / O me thought there a was nothing a meet *Q2; To
contract O the time for a my behoue, / O me thought there was nothing meete F*   60.1] *after 56 Q1 subst.;
after 51 F subst. (Enter Hamlet and Horatio a farre off.)*   61 'A] *that he F*   62 in] *at F*   66 daintier] *F;*
dintier *Q2*   68 clawed] *caught F*   69 into] *intill F*

As if I had never been such.   70
[*Throws up a skull.*]

HAMLET   That skull had a tongue in it and could sing
once. How the knave jowls it to the ground, as if 'twere
Cain's jawbone, that did the first murder. This might be
the pate of a politician which this ass now o'erreaches –
one that would circumvent God, might it not?   75

HORATIO   It might, my lord.

HAMLET   Or of a courtier which could say, 'Good
morrow, sweet lord, how dost thou, sweet lord?' This
might be my Lord Such-a-One, that praised my Lord

---

70 SD *Q1's 'he throwes up a shovel' is
adopted by Capell and defended by
Holderness and Loughrey, but it is not clear
what 'throwing up' a shovel might mean
(unless we assume, with Riv, that 'shovel'
means 'shovelful of earth'); *skull* is
supported by Hamlet's immediate response
and by his *There's another* at 93.

71–205   **That ... flaw** Holleran points out
that Hamlet's reflections on death and
mortality here in effect supply the funeral
sermon that is missing from Ophelia's
maimed rites (208). This moment in
Hamlet is clearly recalled in Charlemont's
meditations in the churchyard in 4.3 of
Cyril Tourneur's *The Atheist's Tragedy*
(1611). It may seem surprising that Hamlet
postpones his sensational revelations
('*words to speak in thine ear* [which] *will
make thee dumb*', 4.6.23–4) until the
following scene.

72   **jowls** hurls (with a pun on *jowl* meaning
'jaw')

73   **Cain's ... murder** This is the play's third
reference to the primal fratricide: see
1.2.105n. and 3.3.37n. Traditionally
(though not biblically) Cain was thought to
have killed Abel with the *jawbone* of an *ass*

(an event dramatized in the medieval cycle
plays, e.g. 'The Killing of Abel' in the
Wakefield cycle), which is relevant to
Hamlet's train of thought here. Shaheen
points out that the idea may have come
from the story of Samson killing a thousand
Philistines with an ass's jawbone in Judges,
15.15–16.

74   **pate** head
politician one who practises 'policy' in the
sense of scheming or manipulation
o'erreaches outwits, triumphs over. F's
'o're Offices' is adopted by Jenkins, who
glosses it 'lords it over (by virtue of his
office)' and comments, 'The preference of
editors and bibliographers for Q2's "ore-
reaches", an obvious substitution, is
astonishing.' Jennens, however, defends
o'erreaches, which 'seems preferable,
when applied to a politician, not as an
insolent officer, but as a *circumventing*,
scheming man'; Caldecott quotes
Johnson's opinion that both readings are
authorial.

79–80   **that ... beg it** See *Tim* 1.2.213–15:
'And now I remember, my lord, you gave
good words the other day of a bay courser I
rode on. ' 'Tis yours, because you lik'd it.'

---

70 SD] *Capell; he throwes vp a shouel. Q1, after equivalent of 69*   72 ²the] th' *F*   'twere] it were *F*   73
This] It *F*   74 now] *om. F*   o'erreaches] o're Offices *F*   75 would] could *F*   78 ²sweet] good *F*

Such-a-One's horse when 'a went to beg it, might it   80
not?

HORATIO   Ay, my lord.

HAMLET   Why, e'en so. And now my Lady Worm's –
chapless and knocked about the mazard with a
sexton's spade. Here's fine revolution an we had the   85
trick to see't. Did these bones cost no more the
breeding but to play at loggets with them? Mine ache
to think on't.

GRAVEDIGGER   (*Sings.*)

A pickaxe and a spade, a spade,
For and a shrouding-sheet,   90
O, a pit of clay for to be made
For such a guest is meet.

[*Throws up another skull.*]

HAMLET   There's another! Why, may not that be the skull
of a lawyer? Where be his quiddities now – his quillets,

80   **'a . . . it** he went to him to beg to be given
          it; Jenkins prefers F's 'meant' over *went*,
          perhaps because it is supported by Q1.
83   **my Lady Worm's** ambiguous: perhaps
          '[the skull of] my lady who is now food for
          worms' or perhaps 'my Lady Worm's
          [skull]', where 'Lady Worm' is an ironic
          title. Benedick refers to a man's conscience
          as 'Don Worm' in *MA* 5.2.79 (see 3.2.126n.
          on this parallel to Hamlet's earlier musings).
84   **chapless** Chaps or chops are the jaws or
          cheeks, the latter being relevant here. The
          term still survives in a culinary context:
          'Bath chap' is a dish made from a pig's
          head and associated with the town of Bath
          (see Grigson, 245–6).
          *****mazard** i.e. head (literally, a *mazard* or
          mazer is a drinking bowl, which the skull is
          seen to resemble); Q2's 'massene' is not

recorded by *OED*.
85   **revolution** alteration or reversal (of social
          hierarchy)
86   **trick** skill, knack
86–7   **Did . . . them?** i.e. was the value of
          bringing up these people so negligible that
          one can play games with their bones?
87   **loggets** a game rather like skittles or alley-
          bowls in which pieces of wood (loggets)
          were thrown at a post or tree
89–92 The equivalent stanza in Vaux (see 57–
          60n.) reads 'A pickaxe and a spade, / And eke
          a winding sheet, / A house of clay for to be
          made, / For such a guest most meet.'
90   **For and** 'and moreover. Not the
          gravedigger's vulgarism, but a regular
          ballad idiom (*OED* for *conj.* 5)' (Jenkins).
94   **quiddities** excessively subtle scholastic
          arguments concerning the *quidditas*

80   **'a]** he *Q1F*   **went]** meant *Q1, Q3, F*   83   **Worm's]** *(wormes), F (*Wormes)   84   **chapless]** *(Choples), F*
mazard] *F;* massene *Q2;* mazer *Q3*   85   **an]** *(and); if F*   87   **them]** 'em *F*   92   **SD]** *Capell*   93   **Why,]** *Ard²;*
why *Q21F*   **may]** mai't *Q1;* might *F*   94   **quiddities]** Quiddits *F*   94   **quillets]** *F;* quillites *Q2;* Quirkes and
quillets *Q1;* quillities *Q3*

his cases, his tenures and his tricks? Why does he suffer   95
this mad knave now to knock him about the sconce with
a dirty shovel and will not tell him of his action of
battery? Hum! This fellow might be in's time a great
buyer of land, with his statutes, his recognizances, his
fines, his double vouchers, his recoveries. To have his   100
fine pate full of fine dirt! Will vouchers vouch him no
more of his purchases and doubles than the length and
breadth of a pair of indentures? The very conveyances
of his lands will scarcely lie in this box, and must

or essence of a thing
quillets (1) small pieces of land; (2) verbal
quibbles (see entry for 'quillets' in Sokol &
Sokol).

95 **tenures** property titles
tricks The phrase 'law-tricks' was current;
John Day's play *Law Tricks* was performed
in 1604.

96 **mad** wild, i.e. irreverent. Jenkins comments,
'It is odd that editorial tradition has
preferred F's inferior *rude*.' The Q2 reading
perhaps expresses Hamlet's appreciation of
the Gravedigger's eccentricity, while the F
reading deplores his irreverence.
sconce head

97–8 **action of battery** lawsuit charging
physical assault

99–100 **his statutes . . . recoveries** Hamlet
uses legal terminology relating to
transactions in land: *statutes* were
securities for debts or mortgages,
recognizances were bonds relating to
debts, *fines* and *recoveries* were legal
fictions used in the *conveyancing* (the legal
transfer of ownership) of land, *vouchers*
and *double vouchers* were ways of securing
third parties as guarantors, and *recoveries*
were suits for obtaining possession (see
entries for 'fine and recovery' and
'conveyance' in Sokol & Sokol). Hamlet's
interest in property and inheritance in this

context seems to relate to his own position
as in effect a disinherited son (see 1.1.88n.).

100 **fines** The word, with its appropriate
connotation of finality, leads Hamlet on to
the puns *fine pate* (handsome head) and
fine dirt (powdered earth) at 101.
recoveries Jenkins includes F's additional
line (see t.n.), presumably on the grounds
that the omission was an accidental result
of eyeskip in Q2.

101 **vouchers** Jenkins prefers F's 'his
Vouchers'.

102 **doubles** Jenkins again prefers F's 'double
ones too'.

103 **a pair of indentures** Two copies of a legal
agreement would be made on a single sheet
of paper that would then be cut on a jagged
line so that each party had a copy and the
exact fit would prove authenticity. Spencer
whimsically suggests that Hamlet may be
punning with reference to the two tooth-
bearing jaws of the skull.

103–4 **conveyances . . . lands** deeds relating to
purchase of his own lands

104 **this box** presumably 'this coffin', with an
allusion to a deed-box for containing legal
documents (but Dover Wilson says the *box*
is the skull, perhaps prompted by *memento
mori* images of skulls with rolled
documents in their eye-sockets as at *MV*
2.7.63–4)

96 mad] rude *F*   100 recoveries. To] *(recoueries, to); Recoueries: Is this the fine of his Fines, and the
recouery of his Recoueries, to *F*   101 vouchers] his Vouchers *F*   102 doubles] double ones too *F*   104
scarcely] hardly *F*

th'inheritor himself have no more, ha?   105

HORATIO   Not a jot more, my lord.

HAMLET   Is not parchment made of sheepskins?

HORATIO   Ay, my lord, and of calves' skins too.

HAMLET   They are sheep and calves which seek out
assurance in that. I will speak to this fellow. Whose   110
grave's this, sirrah?

GRAVEDIGGER   Mine, sir,

    [*Sings.*]

        O, a pit of clay for to be made –

HAMLET   I think it be thine, indeed, for thou liest in't.

GRAVEDIGGER   You lie out on't, sir, and therefore 'tis not   115
yours. For my part I do not lie in't, yet it is mine.

HAMLET   Thou dost lie in't, to be in't and say it is thine.
'Tis for the dead, not for the quick. Therefore thou
liest.

GRAVEDIGGER   'Tis a quick lie, sir, 'twill away again from   120
me to you.

HAMLET   What man dost thou dig it for?

GRAVEDIGGER   For no man, sir.

---

105 **inheritor** possessor, i.e. the lawyer himself (who has not inherited his lands but bought them); see *Tem* 4.1.154: 'all which it inherit'.

107 **parchment** i.e. as used for legal documents

109–10 **They ... that** 'people who trust such documents are fools'. Dent cites 'As simple as a sheep' (S295.1) and 'As wise as a calf' (C16.1) as relevant proverbs.

110 **assurance** legal evidence of title or ownership

111 **sirrah** a variant of 'sir' which expresses an assumption of superiority on the part of the speaker. Hamlet continues to maintain

social distance by his use of *thou* to the Gravedigger's more respectful *you* at 115. The pronouns are the same in Q1 but there Hamlet's 'my friend' suggests a different tone, possibly reflecting a more genial attitude in performance.

113 ***O** Q2 has 'or' and prints this line as regular dialogue. F has '*O*' and prints this and the next line of the song (as at 92) indented and in italics; Jenkins calls this 'evidently an actor's addition'.

118 **quick** living

120 **quick** fast-moving, i.e. I can quickly put it back on to you

---

105 th'inheritor] the Inheritor *F*   108 calves' skins] *(*Calues-skinnes*) Q1;*   Calue-skinnes *F*   109 which] that *F*   111 sirrah] Sir *F*   112–13] *F; one line Q2*   112 SD] *Capell; italics as song F*   113 O] *F;* or *Q2* made –] *(*made.*); made, / for such a Guest is meete. F*   115 'tis] it is *F*   116 yet] and yet *F* 117 it is] 'tis *F*

HAMLET   What woman, then?

GRAVEDIGGER   For none, neither.   125

HAMLET   Who is to be buried in't?

GRAVEDIGGER   One that was a woman, sir, but rest her soul she's dead.

HAMLET [*to Horatio*]   How absolute the knave is! We must speak by the card or equivocation will undo us. By the   130 Lord, Horatio, this three years I have took note of it, the age is grown so picked that the toe of the peasant comes so near the heel of the courtier he galls his kibe. – How long hast thou been grave-maker?

GRAVEDIGGER   Of the days i'th' year I came to't that day   135 that our last King Hamlet overcame Fortinbras.

HAMLET   How long is that since?

GRAVEDIGGER   Cannot you tell that? Every fool can tell

---

129 **absolute** precise, strict

130 **by the card** We might say 'by the book': a *card* was a sailor's chart or compass; at 5.2.95 Osric refers to Laertes as 'the card or calendar of gentry', where *card* seems to mean 'model'.

     equivocation quibbling – an element common to both legal arguments and comic dialogue (the latter exemplified by the puns on *lie* at 114–21)

131 **this three years** Q1's 'This seauen yeares' is surprising, given its assumption of a younger Hamlet, but 'seven years' occurs in folk-tales and in the Bible as a general term for a long time.

132 **picked** usually glossed as 'refined' or 'fastidious'. Hamlet seems to be commenting on social difference and implying that it is inappropriate for a lower-class person (*the peasant*, the Gravedigger) to equivocate with a higher-class person (*the courtier*, Hamlet himself); see *MA* 3.4.62–3, where Beatrice exclaims

to Margaret, Hero's waiting woman, 'God help me, how long have you professed apprehension [i.e. made wit your profession]?', and similar comments by Lorenzo at *MV* 3.5.42–9.

133 **galls his kibe** rubs against the sore on his heel, i.e. follows him so closely that there is little distinction between them

135 **Of the days** F's 'Of all the dayes' echoes a phrase Shakespeare had used at *RJ* 1.3.25.

135–6 **that day ... Fortinbras** The Gravedigger alludes to the events described at 1.1.79–94; we now learn how long ago they occurred, and that they coincided with Hamlet's birth. The implication that Hamlet's own grave has been waiting for him since the day he was born has been staged overtly, e.g. by Yuri Lyubimov, who in 1971 introduced the Gravedigger as a kind of prologue at the very beginning of the play and kept the grave onstage throughout (see Stříbrný, 119–20).

---

129 SD] *this edn*   131 this three] This seauen *Q1;* these three *F*   took] taken *F*   133 heel] *Q1, F2;* heeles *F* ¦the] *Q1;* our *F*   134 been] been a *F*   135 Of] Of all *F*   136 overcame] o'recame *F*

that! It was that very day that young Hamlet was born
– he that is mad and sent into England.   140

HAMLET   Ay, marry. Why was he sent into England?

GRAVEDIGGER   Why, because 'a was mad. 'A shall
recover his wits there. Or if 'a do not, 'tis no great
matter there.

HAMLET   Why?

GRAVEDIGGER   'Twill not be seen in him there. There the   145
men are as mad as he.

HAMLET   How came he mad?

GRAVEDIGGER   Very strangely, they say.

HAMLET   How, strangely?

GRAVEDIGGER   Faith, e'en with losing his wits.   150

HAMLET   Upon what ground?

GRAVEDIGGER   Why, here in Denmark. I have been
sexton here, man and boy, thirty years.

HAMLET   How long will a man lie i'th' earth ere he rot?

GRAVEDIGGER   Faith, if 'a be not rotten before 'a die (as   155

---

139 **young Hamlet** As at 1.1.169, the adjective
distinguishes Hamlet from his father. It is
perhaps more surprising here, where the
Gravedigger is about to tell us that Hamlet
is in fact 30.

145 **seen** noticed

145–6 **There ... he** The joke depends on
reminding the English audience of the
play's foreign setting, as when Portia in
MV ridicules her English suitor and claims
not to understand him because 'I have a
poor pennyworth in the English' (1.2.69–
70), or when characters such as Iago (*Oth*
2.3.71) or Trinculo (*Tem* 2.2.27–8) refer to
visits to England.

148 **Very strangely** The Gravedigger implies 'in
an unusual way', but *strangely* could also
mean 'in a foreign or outlandish manner' and
may lead on to the notion of *ground* in 151.

151 **Upon what ground** Hamlet implies 'For

what reason?' but the Gravedigger
equivocates by taking him literally.

153 **sexton** a secular church official whose
duties included ringing bells and digging
graves

thirty years In Q2 and F Hamlet's age is
given clearly, by this and by the
Gravedigger's insistence at 163–71 that
Yorick (whom Hamlet remembers) has
been dead for 23 years. The Gravedigger in
Q1 omits the first statement altogether and
says Yorick's skull has lain in the earth
'this dozen yeare', perhaps indicating that
Hamlet is 18 rather than 30, an age which
would seem more appropriate to his status
as a student (see Jenkins, LN; see also List
of Roles, 1n.). The precision in Q2/F is
comparable to that in *Oth*, where Iago
declares, 'I have looked upon the world for
four times seven years' (1.3.313–14).

---

139 ²that] the *F*   140 is] was *F*   142–3 'a ... 'A ... 'a] he ... hee ... he *F*   143 'tis] *Q1* (t'is); it's
F   145 him there. There] him, there *F*   153 sexton] sixeteene *F*   155 Faith] Ifaith *Q1F* 'a ... 'a] hee ...
He *Q1F*

we have many pocky corpses that will scarce hold the
laying in) 'a will last you some eight year – or nine year
– a tanner will last you nine year.

HAMLET   Why he more than another?

GRAVEDIGGER   Why, sir, his hide is so tanned with his   160
trade that 'a will keep out water a great while. And your
water is a sore decayer of your whoreson dead body.
Here's a skull now hath lien you i'th' earth three and
twenty years.

HAMLET   Whose was it?   165

GRAVEDIGGER   A whoreson mad fellow's it was. Whose
do you think it was?

HAMLET   Nay, I know not.

GRAVEDIGGER   A pestilence on him for a mad rogue. 'A
poured a flagon of Rhenish on my head once! This   170

156 **pocky** pox-ridden, diseased. F's 'now
   adaies' after *corpses* is adopted by Jenkins
   without comment.

156–7 **hold . . . in** remain unrotten during the
   last rites and burial

158 **tanner** one who converts animal hides into
   leather by a process of 'tanning' i.e.
   steeping them in astringent solutions. It
   may be relevant that Shakespeare's father
   was a 'whittawer', a specialist in the
   preparation of soft, white leather, who
   regularly drew a pair of glover's compasses
   or a glover's stitching clamp when he made
   his mark on documents (see pp. 37–8 and
   Honan, 8).

162 **whoreson** literally 'son of a whore or
   prostitute'; used generally as an adjective
   of familiarity or contempt

163–4 **Here's . . . years** The Gravedigger is
   presumably guessing from where he found
   the skull: he cannot possibly 'recognize' it
   as Yorick's. (Branagh, however, in his
   1996 film, made such recognition possible

by casting as Yorick the comedian Ken
Dodd, known for his pronounced buck
teeth; see 174–84n.)

163 **lien** Q2's spelling 'lyen' may suggest an
   echo of the punning on *lie* at 114–21.
   you ethical dative: 'for you'

163–4 **three and twenty years** F's version
   recommends adoption of this style of
   expansion of Q2's '23'. Mullaney points
   out the parallel with Leontes in *WT* who
   says that when he looked at his son
   'methoughts I did recoil / Twenty-three
   years, and saw myself unbreech'd'
   (1.2.154–5). The 'breeching' of boys –
   dressing them in breeches or trousers – at
   the age of seven marked their transition
   from childhood into masculinity.

169–70 **'A poured . . . once** This may seem an
   odd thing for the King's jester to do to a
   gravedigger, although the latter is now
   presumably employed at the Court chapel.

170 **Rhenish** wine from the Rhine region in
   Germany

156 corpses] *(*corses*) Q1;* Coarses now adaies *F*   157 'a] He *Q1F*   161 'a] he *F;* it *Q1*   163 now] now:
this Scul *F*   hath lien you] *(*hath lyen you*);* has laine *F*   i'th'] in the *F*   163–4 three and twenty] *F;* 23.
Q2; this dozen *Q1*   166–7] *F lines* was; / was? /   169–70 'A poured] *(*a poured*), Q1 (*He powred*), F (*a
pou'rd*)*

same skull, sir, was, sir, Yorick's skull, the King's jester.

HAMLET   This?

GRAVEDIGGER   E'en that.

HAMLET   Alas, poor Yorick. I knew him, Horatio. A
fellow of infinite jest, of most excellent fancy. He hath   175
bore me on his back a thousand times, and now how
abhorred in my imagination it is. My gorge rises at it.
Here hung those lips that I have kissed I know not how
oft. Where be your jibes now – your gambols, your
songs, your flashes of merriment, that were wont to set   180
the table on a roar? Not one now to mock your own

---

171 **sir . . . sir** The additional *sir* in Q2 makes
the Gravedigger's style of speech similar to
Pompey's in *MM* 2.1.210–31.

Yorick's This is the first occurrence of the
name (perhaps a version of Jorg or Jurek)
of one of the most famous characters not to
appear in a play (but see 174–84n.).

the King's jester As Elam points out (*TN*
2.4.11n.), 'A dead man's delight in his jester
is something of a Shakespearean topos',
noting that Feste is described as 'a fool that
the Lady Olivia's father [formerly] took
much delight in' and comparing the
Countess's reference to the clown at *AW*
4.5.63–4: 'My lord that's gone made himself
much sport out of him'. As in 3.2 (see 36–
7n., 118n. and 266n.), the absence of the
clown is noted, but if there is a topical
reference here Duncan-Jones (35) argues
that it may be to Richard Tarlton, the
celebrated clown of the Queen's Men; he
died in 1588, a date that would fit better with
Q1's 'this dozen yeare' as compared with
Q2/F's *three and twenty years* at 163–4.

172 **This?** Hamlet's words in Q1 at this point 'I
prethee let me see it', imply that the
Gravedigger hands the skull to him; it
seems likely that he is holding it during his

speech at 174–84. F also clarifies this by
adding 'Let me see' at the beginning of
174.

174–84 **Hibbard** describes this as 'a superb
flashback to Hamlet's boyhood'; Kenneth
Branagh's 1996 film presented it literally
as such.

175 **fancy** invention

176–7 **bore . . . abhorred** Q2's *bore* allows a
pun on *bore/abhor*; in both Q2 and F
Hamlet is revolted by the idea of his former
physical contact with one who is now
represented by a skull.

177 **abhorred** filled with horror (a unique
usage, according to *OED*)
gorge literally 'throat' or 'stomach' but
also 'contents of the stomach'

179 **jibes** taunts or scoffs
gambols playful tricks

181–2 **mock . . . grinning** In the Q2 reading,
where *jibes* etc. are the subject, Hamlet
seems to envisage Yorick's own jokes
mocking his present condition. In F he is
saying 'Is there no one now to mock your
jeering?' F's 'Ieering' (jeering) is rejected
by Edwards and Hibbard without comment,
perhaps because Shakespeare associates
death with *grinning* elsewhere, as when

---

171 'sir] Sir, this same Scull sir *F*   was, sir] was one *Q1;* was *F*   174 Alas] prethee let me see it, alas *Q1;*
Let me see. Alas *F*   176 bore] borne *F;* caried *Q1*   now] *Q1; om. F*   177 in] *om. F*   it is] is *F*   181 Not]
No *F*

grinning, quite chapfallen. Now get you to my lady's
table and tell her, let her paint an inch thick, to this
favour she must come. Make her laugh at that. Prithee,
Horatio, tell me one thing.   185

HORATIO   What's that, my lord?

HAMLET   Dost thou think Alexander looked o'this
fashion i'th' earth?

HORATIO   E'en so.

HAMLET   And smelt so? Pah!   190

HORATIO   E'en so, my lord.

HAMLET   To what base uses we may return, Horatio!
Why may not imagination trace the noble dust of
Alexander till 'a find it stopping a bung-hole?

HORATIO   'Twere to consider too curiously to consider so.   195

HAMLET   No, faith, not a jot. But to follow him thither

Falstaff, contemplating the corpse of Sir
Walter Blunt, comments, 'I like not such
grinning honour as Sir Walter hath' (*1H4*
5.3.59–60).

182 **chapfallen** (1) lacking the cheeks or jaw
(see 84n.); (2) crestfallen, dejected

182–4 **Now . . . come** Just before the entry of
Ophelia's corpse, Hamlet repeats the
traditional misogynistic attack on
cosmetics that he voiced to her at 3.1.141–
3 (see Jenkins, LN).

183 **table** presumably 'dressing-table'. Spencer
refers to 'engravings of Death (represented
by a skeleton) coming into a young lady's
bedchamber while she sits at her toilet-
table'. F's 'chamber' is adopted by Jenkins
without comment, perhaps on the
assumption that *table* is mistakenly
repeated from 181.

184 **favour** facial appearance

187 **Alexander** Alexander the Great: a figure
very much in Shakespeare's mind around
1599–1600; his 'Life' parallels that of

Julius Caesar in Plutarch and through
Fluellen Shakespeare sets up Henry V as an
English equivalent (*H5* 4.7.11–53). The
meditation here is echoed in Middleton and
Rowley's *The Changeling* (1622), when
Diaphanta remarks, 'Earth-conquering
Alexander, that thought the world / Too
narrow for him, in the end had but his pit-
hole' (4.1.60–1).

190 **smelt so** Dowden and Jenkins note that,
according to Plutarch, Alexander's body in
his lifetime was unusually sweet-smelling,
though here the reference is to his corpse.

193–205 **Why . . . flaw** This speculation is very
like Hamlet's earlier one about the worms
eating Polonius (4.3.17–30); he seems
fascinated by the literal as well as the
spiritual 'afterlife'.

194 **bung-hole** A *bung* is the stopper for a cask
or barrel; a *bung-hole* the outlet or 'mouth'
it stops.

195 **too   curiously**   with   excessive   or
inappropriate ingenuity

---

182 grinning] leering *F*   chapfallen] *(chopfalne) F*   183 table] chamber *Q1F*   187 o'] *(a), F*   190 so?
Pah] *Q5;* so pah *Q2;* so: pah *Q3;* so? Puh *F*   193 Why] Why, *Ard²*   194 'a] he *F*   195 consider too]
consider: to *F*

with modesty enough and likelihood to lead it:
Alexander died, Alexander was buried, Alexander
returneth to dust, the dust is earth, of earth we make
loam, and why of that loam whereto he was converted   200
might they not stop a beer-barrel?
   Imperious Caesar, dead and turned to clay,
   Might stop a hole to keep the wind away.
   O, that that earth which kept the world in awe
   Should patch a wall t'expel the water's flaw.   205

Enter KING, QUEEN, LAERTES *and* [*other Lords,*
with a Priest *after*] *the corpse.*

But soft, but soft awhile, here comes the King,

197 **modesty** moderation
   it Presumably the antecedent is *imagination*
   (193).
199 **returneth to dust** As at 1.2.71 and 4.2.5,
   there is an allusion to the Church of England
   burial service: 'Earth to earth, ashes to ashes,
   dust to dust'; see also Genesis, 3.19: 'Thou
   art dust, and to dust shalt thou returne.'
200 **loam** clay moistened to make plaster
202 **Imperious** Malone cites F's 'Imperiall' as
   an example of its habit of substituting more
   familiar words. Shakespeare, however,
   seems to use both forms indifferently:
   'imperious Agamemnon' (*TC* 4.5.171),
   'imperial Caesar' (*Cym* 5.5.475), and the
   same variant between Q1 and F *Tit* occurs
   at 1.1.254.
204 **that earth** 'i.e. Caesar's body, which
   Antony calls "thou bleeding piece of earth"
   (*JC* 3.1.254)' (Hibbard).
205 **t'expel ... flaw** 'to keep out the flow of
   water', with *flaw* as a nonce variant of
   'flow' for the sake of the rhyme. F's

'winters flaw' is generally adopted (e.g. by
Jenkins), with *flaw* glossed as 'squall' or
'shower of rain'.
205.1–2 It is odd that neither Q2 nor F includes
   the Priest in this SD: see 215 SPn. Gurr
   & Ichikawa (152) argue that Osric must
   be among the '*attendants*' or '*Lords*' here
   because he 'notes Hamlet's misleading
   claim to be king, a claim he makes much of
   in the next scene' (see also pp. 136–7). The
   dialogue in all three texts indicates that if
   there is a coffin it is an open one. Many
   productions have a bell tolling at this point
   (see 222–3 and n.).
205.2 ***corpse*** In most modern productions, the
   'corpse' is the actor of Ophelia rather than
   a dummy; this becomes obvious if Laertes
   lifts the body out of the grave at 239.
   Judging by the SDs cited for *body* and
   corpse in Dessen & Thomson, actors were
   probably used in other Elizabethan and
   Jacobean productions too.
206 **soft** be silent

198 ¹Alexander] as thus of *Alexander, Alexander Q1;* as thus. *Alexander F*   199 to] into *F*   202
Imperious] *Q1;* Imperiall *F*   205 water's] winters *F*   205.1–2] *(Enter K. Q. / Laertes and / the corse.)*
opp. 206–8; Enter King and Queene, Leartes, and other lordes, / with a Priest after the coffin. Q1, after
203; Enter King, Queene, Laertes, and a Coffin, / with Lords attendant. F, after 206   206 soft awhile] soft,
aside *F*

The Queen, the courtiers. Who is this they follow?
And with such maimed rites? This doth betoken
The corpse they follow did with desperate hand
Fordo it own life. 'Twas of some estate.   210
Couch we awhile and mark.
　　[Hamlet and Horatio stand aside.]

LAERTES
　What ceremony else?
HAMLET *[aside to Horatio]*
　That is Laertes – a very noble youth, mark.
LAERTES
　What ceremony else?

208 **maimed rites** maimèd; reduced or truncated (literally, mutilated or injured) rituals. It is not clear how this would be immediately apparent to Hamlet; perhaps the procession is shockingly small for what seems to be the funeral of a person *of some estate* (210). In Q1 he seems to imply almost the opposite by asking 'What funerall's this that all the Court laments?' Lavish nineteenth-century stagings of the scene with processions of mourning virgins made nonsense of this issue.

208–10 **This . . . life** In Olivier's 1948 film Horatio spoke these words, replying to Hamlet and realizing in horror whose funeral it was.

210 **Fordo** destroy
　it its (Hope, 1.3.2c; see 1.2.215n.)
　some estate considerable class, social standing

211 **Couch . . . mark** 'Let us conceal ourselves for a while and observe what happens.' Q1 has the more common 'Stand by a while.' Presumably the Gravedigger also stands aside; some editions and productions have

him exit here, but Bristol (363) argues that his choric function would be weakened by such an exit. More prosaically, he needs to stay onstage to continue with the burial at the end of the scene.

212 **else** further (in addition to what has been performed). Like Hamlet, Laertes seems shocked by the *maimed rites*, his response here (repeated at 214) echoing his complaint about the *obscure funeral* awarded to his father (4.5.205).

213 It is surprising that Hamlet needs to explain who Laertes is to Horatio, though it is true that they have not appeared onstage together (see List of Roles, 10n.). It is even more surprising that Horatio has apparently not told Hamlet about Ophelia's madness (which he witnessed in 4.5; however, see 4.5.2, 4' SPn. on the problematic nature of his presence in that scene); presumably he has not heard of her death since he supposedly left the Court to meet Hamlet at the end of 4.6. But an audience would not have time to worry about such things.

207 this] that *F*　208 rites] *Fc*; rights *Fu*　209 desperate] *(*desprat*)*, *F (*disperate*)*　210 it] its *Q5;* it's *F3*　of] *om. F*　211 SD] *Capell subst.*　213 SD] *Oxf*

PRIEST

Her obsequies have been as far enlarged   215
As we have warranty. Her death was doubtful;
And but that great command o'ersways the order
She should in ground unsanctified been lodged
Till the last trumpet: for charitable prayers,
Flints and pebbles should be thrown on her.   220
Yet here she is allowed her virgin crants,
Her maiden strewments, and the bringing home
Of bell and burial.

LAERTES

Must there no more be done?

215 SP *Q2 has '*Doct.*', presumably short for '*Doctor*' (of Divinity), but '*Doctor*' might be misleading in a modern text, suggesting a medical practitioner; Laertes addresses him as *churlish priest* at 229.
215 **obsequies** funeral rites
   enlarged extended, prolonged
216 **we** The priest presumably speaks on behalf of the church.
   warranty authorization
   Her . . . doubtful i.e. the manner of her death gave rise to the suspicion of suicide
217 **great command** the command of powerful people; the priest sometimes looks at the King as he says this.
   o'ersways the order prevails over the normal proceeding (or possibly 'overrules the decision of the monastic order'?)
218 **should . . . been** F's reading (see t.n.) is 'a manifest attempt at "improvement"', according to Jenkins who argues that the Q2 version is idiomatic. Q1 is more explicit about *ground unsanctified*: 'She had beene buried in the open fieldes.'
219 **last trumpet** Shaheen points out that the Geneva Bible has *trumpet* in passages relating to the end of the world: 'At the last

trumpet: for the trumpet shall blowe, and the dead shal bee raised up' (1 Corinthians, 15.52; see also 1 Thessalonians, 4.16); other translations have 'trump'.
   for instead of
   prayers The plural seems more appropriate (see t.n.) in the context (and is adopted by Hibbard).
220 F's 'Shardes' (pieces of broken pottery) before *Flints* does regularize the metre, though it seems unusual for a scribe or compositor to omit the first word in a line.
221 **virgin crants** garlands appropriate to a virgin; *crants* is from German *kranz* = crown, and is cognate with 'Rosencrantz' (see List of Roles, 11n.). F's 'Virgin Rites' is assumed by Edwards to be a substitution by the playhouse scribe who did not understand the rare *crants*; Hibbard, following Caldecott, sees the author revising by using a more familiar word here.
222 **strewments** strewings, i.e. flowers scattered on the coffin or grave (a Shakespearean coinage: see 1.2.93n.)
222–3 **the . . . burial** ceremony of bringing her to her last resting place with bell-ringing and burial rites

215, 224 SP PRIEST] *Q1F; Doct. Q2*   216 warranty] warrantis *F;* warrantise *Dyce*   218 been] haue *F*   219 prayers] praier *F*   220 Flints] Shardes, Flints *F*   221 crants] Rites *F*

PRIEST   No more be done.

We should profane the service of the dead   225

To sing a requiem and such rest to her

As to peace-parted souls.

LAERTES   Lay her i'th' earth,

And from her fair and unpolluted flesh

May violets spring. I tell thee, churlish priest,

A ministering angel shall my sister be   230

When thou liest howling.

HAMLET [*aside to Horatio*]   What, the fair Ophelia?

QUEEN

Sweets to the sweet. Farewell.

I hoped thou shouldst have been my Hamlet's wife:

I thought thy bride-bed to have decked, sweet maid,

And not have strewed thy grave.

LAERTES   O, treble woe   235

Fall ten times double on that cursed head

---

226 **requiem** funeral song or chant; F's 'sage [solemn] Requiem' is adopted by Jenkins: 'Presumably the word defeated the Q2 compositor.'

227 **peace-parted souls** those who have departed in peace or died a natural death

229 **violets** previously associated with youthful love at 1.3.7 and with death or the loss of love at 4.5.177

231 **liest howling** i.e. in hell (or purgatory)

232 **Sweets ... sweet** The Queen probably places or throws flowers on the corpse or coffin as she says this.

233–4 **I hoped ... decked** The Queen again makes it clear that she had not shared the assumption of Polonius and Laertes that Ophelia would have been an inappropriate bride for Hamlet (see 3.1.37–41n.). The painful thought is like the more

explicit transformation of wedding to funeral in *RJ*, where Capulet remarks, 'Our bridal flowers serve for a buried corpse' (4.5.89).

236 **double** F's 'trebble' is generally adopted without comment as a deliberate repetition of the word in 235 (where F, confusingly, has 'terrible'); line 236 is at the top of a new page in Q2 so the compositor was not influenced by having the previous line immediately in front of him.

236–8 **that ... of** Laertes curses Hamlet, whose *wicked deed* (the murder of Polonius?) he blames for Ophelia's madness; Hamlet, who refuses to accept any blame at 278–9, never comments directly on her madness or on her *doubtful death* (see 5.2.204–21 and n.).
cursed cursèd

---

226 a] sage *F*   231 SD] *Folg²*   232 Sweets . . . sweet. Farewell] *(*sweets . . . sweet, farewell*) Q1;* Sweets, . . . sweet farewell *F*   235 have] t'haue *F*   treble woe] terrible woer *F*   236 double] trebble *F*

Whose wicked deed thy most ingenious sense
Deprived thee of. Hold off the earth awhile,
Till I have caught her once more in mine arms.
    [*Leaps in the grave.*]
Now pile your dust upon the quick and dead   240
Till of this flat a mountain you have made
T'o'ertop old Pelion or the skyish head
Of blue Olympus.

HAMLET [*Comes forward.*]   What is he whose grief
Bears such an emphasis, whose phrase of sorrow
Conjures the wandering stars and makes them stand   245
Like wonder-wounded hearers? This is I,
Hamlet the Dane.

LAERTES [*Leaps out and grapples with him.*]
                The devil take thy soul!

237 **most ingenious sense** excellent intelligence or rationality
238 **Hold . . . awhile** hold off from filling the grave with earth for a while
239 **caught . . . arms** Many productions have Laertes lift the body out of the grave at this point.
240 **quick** living
241 **flat** level ground
242–3 **Pelion . . . Olympus** mountains in Greece; Olympus was supposed to be the home of the gods; the Titans tried to reach and conquer it by piling Pelion on top of the neighbouring peak Ossa (see 272, and Ovid, *Metamorphoses*, book 1). Golding's translation (1.171–8) implies that Ossa was piled on top of Pelion, and Dent lists 'To heap Ossa upon Pelion' as proverbial (O81).
242 **skyish** close to the sky – and therefore *blue* (243) (*OED*'s first usage)
243–5 **What . . . Conjures** In Q1 it is Laertes who says 'Whats he that conjures so?'

244 **Bears . . . emphasis** is expressed in such forceful language
245 **wandering stars** planets (both Q2 and F suggest elision with their spelling 'wandring'). Irving interpreted these words literally by staging this scene at night.
    stand stand still
246 **wonder-wounded** struck with wonder
246–7 **This . . . Dane** In performance, Hamlet often throws off a cloak at this point, perhaps the *sea-gown* he refers to at 5.2.13. See the equally grim reclamation of identity towards the end of *KL*: 'My name is Edgar and thy father's son' (5.3.167). In calling himself *the Dane* Hamlet may be asserting his claim to the crown of Denmark; see 1.1.13, 1.2.44, 1.2.109 and 5.2.61.
247 SD *While F is like Q1 in having an SD instructing Laertes to leap into the grave, Q1 is alone in having a SD at

239 SD] *Q1 subst., F*   242 T'o'ertop] *(*To'retop*);* to o're top *Q1F*   243 SD] *Pope subst.*   grief] griefes *F*   245 Conjures] Coniure *F*   wandering] *(*wandring*) F*   247 SD] *this edn; Hamlet leapes / in after Leartes, Q1 opp. equivalent of 241–5; om. F*

HAMLET

Thou pray'st not well.
I prithee take thy fingers from my throat,
For, though I am not splenative rash, 250
Yet have I in me something dangerous
Which let thy wisdom fear. Hold off thy hand.

KING

Pluck them asunder.

QUEEN   Hamlet! Hamlet!

LORDS   Gentlemen!

HORATIO

Good my lord, be quiet.

HAMLET

Why, I will fight with him upon this theme 255
Until my eyelids will no longer wag.

---

this point: '*Hamlet leaves in after Leartes*'.
This piece of staging is supported by the
anonymous *Elegy on Burbage* – 'Oft have I
seen him leap into the grave' – and it could
provide a striking visual parallel with the
Ghost's behaviour in 1.1, 1.4 and 1.5 if the
trap was indeed used then, but it has been
much disputed by editors who argue that
Hamlet cannot be the aggressor here; Laertes
must come out of the grave to attack him.
(See *AYL* 1.1.51–78 for a similar situation
where editors insert SDs to make it clear that
Oliver is the aggressor rather than Orlando.)
Another consideration is visibility: at the
Globe in 2000 Hamlet did leap into the
'grave' made by the trapdoor, and the
subsequent fight was not easily visible from
the yard. For a comparative study of this
moment in all three texts, see Zitner.

249 **I prithee . . . throat** Hamlet's phrasing is
forced and cold, under the circumstances.

250 **splenative rash** hot-tempered; the spleen
was seen as the seat of various emotions
ranging from anger and melancholy to
mirth. (F's version is generally adopted.)
OED lists both 'splenative' and
'splenitive' as obsolete; the modern word is
'splenetic'.

253 Presumably the attendants obey the King
and intervene.

253 SP LORDS **Gentlemen!** This SP and
exclamation are not in F (but are added by
Oxf and Hibbard).

254 SP F gives these words to '*Gen*'[*tlemen*];
perhaps this is related to its omission of
part of 253. It seems more appropriate for
Hamlet's friend to speak them.

254 **be quiet** calm down. At this point Rowe
and other editors (e.g. Edwards) insert a
SD: '*The Attendants part them.*'

256 **wag** move. Hamlet means 'until I have no
life left at all'.

248–9] *Q1F; one line with turnover Q2* 250 For] *Q1;* Sir *F* rash] and rash *F* 251 in me something]
something in me *Q1F* 252 wisdom] *Q1;* wisenesse *F* Hold off] *Q1;* Away *F* 253 SP LORDS] *Oxf
subst.; All. Q2* Gentlemen!] *not in Q1F* 254 SP] *Gen. F*

QUEEN

O my son, what theme?

HAMLET

I loved Ophelia – forty thousand brothers
Could not with all their quantity of love
Make up my sum. What wilt thou do for her?   260

KING

O, he is mad, Laertes.

QUEEN

For love of God, forbear him.

HAMLET

'Swounds, show me what thou'lt do.
Woul't weep, woul't fight, woul't fast, woul't tear
   thyself,
Woul't drink up eisel, eat a crocodile?   265

258–60 **I . . . sum** Edwards quotes MacDonald:
'Perhaps this is the speech in all the play of
which it is most difficult to get into a
sympathetic comprehension.'

258 **forty thousand brothers** Q1's 'twenty
brothers' is approved by Poel as an actor's
emendation to remove an unnecessary
exaggeration, but *forty* could be used as a
general round figure, as 'forty winters' in
Son 2.1 and 'forty shillings' in *MW* 1.1.183
(see also *four hours together* at 2.2.157 and
Elze, 'Four hours').

262 **forbear** bear with, tolerate

263 **'Swounds** by God's wounds (a powerful
oath, censored in F)
   ***thou'lt** thou wouldst; F's 'thou'lt' (which
appears in Q2 at 272) is defended by *TxC*
as a colloquialism.

264 **Woul't** wouldst thou (colloquial)

265 **eisel** Jenkins (LN) champions Theobald
in seeing Q2's 'Esill' ('Esile' in F) as a

spelling of *eisel* meaning vinegar;
Shakespeare refers to 'Potions of eisel' as
bitter medicines in *Son* 111.10, and there
may be a reference to the 'vinegar . . .
mingled with gall' offered to Christ on the
cross (Matthew, 27.48; 'aycel' in Wyclif's
Bible). Dowden wonders whether 'eisel'
might refer to a river, perhaps the Yssel,
and Q1's 'vessels' may indicate an early
misunderstanding.

265–6 This passage may be echoed in
Eastward Ho, 4.2.349–51: 'Offer not to
speak, crocodile . . . Thou hast learnt to
whine at the play yonder'; see p. 58.

265 **eat a crocodile** Edwards suggests 'to
increase the flow of hypocritical tears' (the
meaning picked up in *Eastward Ho*), while
Hibbard says the crocodile is included 'on
account of the toughness of its skin'.
Shakespeare refers to the former association
at *2H6* 3.1.226 and at *Oth* 4.1.245.

---

263 'Swounds, show] Shew *Q1;* Come show *F*   thou'lt] *(*th'owt*), F;* thou wilt *Q1*   264 Woul't
weep] *(*Woo't weepe*) F*   woul't fight] *(*woo't fight*) F;* Wilt fight *Q1*   woul't fast] *(*woo't fast*);* wilt
fast *Q1; om. F*   woul't tear thyself] *(*woo't teare thy selfe*) F;* wilt pray *Q1*   265 Woul't] *(*Woo't*) F;*
Wilt *Q1*   eisel] *Theobald;* Esill *Q2;* vessels *Q1; Esile F*

I'll do't. Dost come here to whine,
To outface me with leaping in her grave?
Be buried quick with her, and so will I.
And if thou prate of mountains let them throw
Millions of acres on us till our ground, 270
Singeing his pate against the burning zone,
Make Ossa like a wart. Nay, an thou'lt mouth,
I'll rant as well as thou.
QUEEN This is mere madness,
And thus awhile the fit will work on him.
Anon, as patient as the female dove 275
When that her golden couplets are disclosed,
His silence will sit drooping.
HAMLET Hear you, sir,

---

266 **Dost come** defended by Jenkins as idiomatic, compared with F's 'Dost thou come', though the latter may be preferable metrically
267 **outface** overcome, defeat ('stare out' or 'stare down' in modern idiom)
268 **quick** alive (as at 118 and 240)
269 **prate** boast
270 **acres** large quantities of land (an acre is 4,840 square yards or 4,046.86 square metres)
    our ground the ground on top of us (or possibly 'Denmark')
271 **Singeing ... zone** scorching its top by touching the sun's orbit
272 **Ossa** see 242–3n.
    like a wart as small as a wart (on the skin)
    thou'lt mouth if you want to shout
273 SP F gives this speech to the King, who uses a similar metaphor at 3.1.163–6; Q1 gives a shorter version of it to him, but also has the Queen apologize to Leartes ('Alas, it is his madnes makes him thus / And not his heart') after Hamlet's exit. MacDonald

expresses uncertainty: 'It would be a fine specimen of the King's hypocrisy; and perhaps indeed its poetry, lovely in itself, but at such a time sentimental, is fitter for him than for the less guilty queen.' Edwards follows Q2 on the grounds that 'this was an error on the part of the playhouse scribe which was carried over into performance.' Some editors find the language 'motherly', and the content is consistent with the Queen's assertion of Hamlet's madness (see 4.1.7–8).
273 **mere** complete, unmitigated
274 ***thus** Q2's 'this' may be supported by 'What am I that thou shouldst contemn me this?' (*VA* 205), but 'this' may have been induced in that case by the need to rhyme with 'kiss' in *VA* 207, and *thus* is more idiomatic.
276 **golden couplets** the twin young of the dove, *golden* because covered with yellow down
    disclosed hatched (see 3.1.165)
277 **His ... drooping** i.e. he will be quiet and contemplative

---

266 Dost come] Com'st thou *Q1;* Dost thou come *F*   273 SP] *Kin. F; King. Q1*   274 thus] *F;* this
Q2   276 couplets] *(*cuplets*); Cuplet F*

What is the reason that you use me thus?
I loved you ever – but it is no matter.
Let Hercules himself do what he may,   280
The cat will mew and dog will have his day.   *Exit.*

KING

I pray thee, good Horatio, wait upon him.   *Exit Horatio.*
[*aside to Laertes*] Strengthen your patience in our
    last night's speech,
We'll put the matter to the present push.
– Good Gertrude, set some watch over your son.   285
This grave shall have a living monument.
An hour of quiet thereby shall we see;
Till then in patience our proceeding be.   *Exeunt.*

278–9 These lines may indicate that (1) Hamlet has indeed been physically attacked by Laertes rather than vice versa (see 247 SD and n.); (2) at this stage he denies any responsibility for killing Polonius or for driving Ophelia to madness and death.

280 **Let** ... **may** i.e. even Hercules (see 1.2.153n. and 1.4.83) couldn't stop me from doing what I intend to do (?). Perhaps Hamlet is deriding Laertes for ranting in 'Ercles' vein', as Bottom calls it (*MND* 1.2.37).

281 **The** ... **day** 'Every dog has his day' was proverbial (Tilley, D464); Hamlet implies that, while the fight has been stopped for the moment, it isn't necessarily over.

282–3 **thee** ... **your** The different pronouns for Horatio and Laertes in Q2 may express a different level of familiarity on the part of the King.

283 SD *The King must conceal his plan from the Queen and the others present. In Q1 Leartes responds, 'My lord, till then my soule will not bee quiet', suggesting a private exchange.

283–4 **Strengthen** ... **We'll** 'if you draw renewed patience from remembering what we plotted last night, then we'll'

284 **present push** immediate trial

286 **living monument** enduring memorial. It is not clear what the King means by this. Does he imply that one who is *living* (i.e. Hamlet) will die to provide a *monument*? In this case, Laertes' revenge will compensate for the inadequate funerals of both his father and his sister (see 4.5.205n. and 5.1.208n. above).

287 **thereby** Jennens: '*Thereby* seems to refer to the living monument, i.e. Hamlet who is to be murdered.' It might refer rather to the period of grace allowed by the *watch* specified in 285. Jenkins prefers F's 'shortly'.

281 The ... and ... his] *F;* A ... a ... a *Q1*   SD] *F; Exit Hamlet / and Horatio. Q2, opp. 281–2; Exit Hamlet and Horatio. Q1*   282 thee] you *F*   SD] *om. F*   283 SD] *Rowe*   your] you *F* 287 thereby] *Q2c, Jennens;* thirtie *Q2u;* shortly *F*

[5.2]   *Enter* HAMLET *and* HORATIO.

HAMLET

So much for this, sir. Now shall you see the other:
You do remember all the circumstance?

HORATIO

Remember it, my lord?

HAMLET

Sir, in my heart there was a kind of fighting
That would not let me sleep. Methought I lay   5
Worse than the mutines in the bilboes. Rashly –

5.2 The three texts: this scene runs to 387 lines
in Q2, 358 in F and 133 in Q1 (scene 17). F
has a shorter version of Hamlet's
conversation with Osric (see 92–120n.)
and omits that with the Lord at 174.1–186;
it has, however, an additional line after
56 and an additional passage after 66
(see Appendix 1). Q1 lacks most of the
opening conversation with Horatio (though
some of it is summarized in scene 14,
Q1's unique scene between the Queen and
Horatio); it also has a shorter version of the
conversation with the '*Bragart Gentleman*',
its equivalent of Osric, and most of the
speeches are, as usual, shorter. Location
and timing: this scene takes place in an
indoor Court apartment large enough to
accommodate the duel; it is referred to by
Hamlet as *the hall* at 154, by the Gentleman
as 'the outward pallace' in Q1. The scene
presumably follows quickly on from the
decision by the King and Laertes to put
their plans *to the present push* at 5.1.284.

1   As in other scenes (e.g. 4.7), the characters
enter in the midst of conversation. In this
case Hamlet is fulfilling the promise of his
letter ('*I have words to speak in thine ear
will make thee dumb*', 4.6.23–4): *this*
perhaps refers to what he has already told
Horatio about his experiences, *the other* to
what is to come; or *this* could be the official

letter Hamlet was bearing from the King,
the other the one he steals from his
companions. Hamlet is carrying a paper –
the *commission* he shows Horatio at 26.
Film versions from Gade and Schall (1920)
to Almereyda (2000; 116) have chosen to
show the substitution of the papers but not
the sea-fight, probably for financial reasons
(but Russell Jackson informs us (privately)
that Branagh originally intended to film the
sea-fight).

1,4   **sir** Perhaps these usages denote a slight
formality in Hamlet's tone (as of self-
justification?). Or perhaps he is just urging
Horatio to pay attention.

2   **circumstance** Shakespeare often uses this
form where we use the plural.

3   **Remember . . . lord** i.e. how could I forget
it?

5   *****Methought** it seemed to me. *OED* lists
instances of Q2's 'my thought' as a variant
in 1503 and 1621, but *methought* is the
more usual 'modernization'. The difference
would probably not be heard.

6   **mutines** mutineers
       *****bilboes** fetters; Shakespeare uses Q2's
'bilbo' (singular) twice in *MW* to mean a
sword (1.1.149, 3.5.106). Both were
named after Bilbao in Spain, whence
various iron artefacts were imported.
       Rashly – Having described his action

5.2] *Rowe*   1 shall you] let me *F*   5 Methought] *F;* my thought *Q2*   6 bilboes] *F;* bilbo *Q2*

And praised be rashness for it – let us know
Our indiscretion sometime serves us well
When our deep plots do fall – and that should learn us
There's a divinity that shapes our ends,   10
Rough-hew them how we will.

HORATIO   That is most certain.

HAMLET

Up from my cabin,
My sea-gown scarfed about me, in the dark
Groped I to find out them, had my desire,
Fingered their packet, and in fine withdrew   15
To mine own room again, making so bold,
My fears forgetting manners, to unfold

as *rash* (hasty or impulsive), Hamlet
breaks off to reflect on *rashness* before
resuming his story again at 12.
7 **let us know** i.e. we should acknowledge
8 **indiscretion** Hamlet seems to mean an
action committed without premeditation
(rather than a careless one).
   sometime Shakespeare uses this form and
   F's 'sometimes' indifferently.
9 **deep plots** It is only in Q2 (at 3.4.200–8)
   that Hamlet has given notice of
   premeditated action against Rosencrantz
   and Guildenstern.
   fall fall down, prove inadequate. F/Q2u's
   'paule' means falter or fail; Dowden
   compares Menas' reference to Pompey's
   'palled fortunes' (*AC* 2.7.82).
   learn 'F's substitution of *teach* suggests
   that *learn* in this sense, common in
   Shakespeare and still surviving in dialect,
   may already have been losing favour'
   (Jenkins).
10–11 **There's . . . will** Hamlet attributes a
   seemingly chance circumstance (his
   sleeplessness) to divine purpose, as he
   does later: 'There is special providence

in the fall of a sparrow' (197–8).
10 **ends** (1) purposes; (2) destinations
11 **Rough-hew** fashion or shape crudely or
   carelessly (the metaphor is from cutting
   timber coarsely, without smoothing or
   finishing it)
13 **sea-gown** seaman's coat
   scarfed wrapped like a scarf
14 **find out them** See the same transposition
   of the pronoun in *JC* 1.3.133–4: 'Cinna,
   where haste you so? / To find out you.'
   Perhaps 'find-out' is treated as a single
   word in both instances.
   them i.e. Rosencrantz and Guildenstern
15 **Fingered their packet** pilfered their papers
   in fine in conclusion
16 **room** cabin
16–18 **making . . . commission** Edgar in *KL*
   expresses a similar thought when opening
   the letters he has found on the body of
   Oswald, whom he has just killed: 'Leave,
   gentle wax; and manners blame us not. / To
   know our enemies' minds we rip their
   hearts, / Their papers is more lawful'
   (4.6.254–6).
17 **unfold** F's 'vnseale' is adopted by

7 praised] praise *F*   8 sometime] sometimes *F*   9 deep] deare *F*   fall] *Q2c;* paule *Q2uF;* fail *Pope*
learn] teach *F*   17 unfold] vnseale *F*

Their grand commission; where I found, Horatio,
A royal knavery, an exact command
(Larded with many several sorts of reasons   20
Importing Denmark's health, and England's too)
With – ho! – such bugs and goblins in my life,
That on the supervise, no leisure bated
– No, not to stay the grinding of the axe! –
My head should be struck off.

HORATIO   Is't possible?   25

HAMLET

Here's the commission; read it at more leisure.
But wilt thou hear now how I did proceed?

HORATIO

I beseech you.

HAMLET

Being thus benetted round with villains,
Or I could make a prologue to my brains   30
They had begun the play. I sat me down,
Devised a new commission, wrote it fair –

Jenkins without comment, perhaps because
Shakespeare uses it elsewhere of letters,
perhaps to avoid the rhyme with *bold* in 16.
Unfold could conceivably be a misreading
of MS 'vnseld'.
20 **Larded** decorated (see 4.5.38n.)
   several separate, different
21 **Importing** signifying
22 **such bugs . . . life** my continued existence
   representing such (imaginary) bugs and
   monsters
23 **supervise** looking over, reading
   no leisure bated i.e. with no time wasted
24 **stay** wait for
   grinding sharpening
26 **Here's the commission** Hamlet
   presumably hands over the document.

29 **benetted round** surrounded as by a
   net. 'Netted' is the more common
   form: *OED* records this as the first use of
   'benet'.
   villains Editors since Capell have emended
   Q2/F's 'villaines' to 'villainies' as an
   improvement to both metre and sense.
30–1 **Or . . . play** Hamlet sees himself (his
   will?) as separate from his brain. This picks
   up the idea of *rashness* (6–7) and
   emphasizes again that his action was
   impulsive rather than premeditated.
30 **Or** an older form of 'ere' = before
   make a prologue provide an outline of the
   forthcoming action (as, for example, the
   Prologue to *RJ* does)
32 **fair** in formal handwriting

19 A] Oh *F;* Ah, *Cam¹, ArdF*   20 reasons] reason *F*   22 ho!] *(hoe), F (*hoo,*)*   27 now] me *F* 29 villains]
F; villainies *Capell, ArdF*   30 Or] Ere *F*

I once did hold it as our statists do
A baseness to write fair and laboured much
How to forget that learning, but, sir, now   35
It did me yeoman's service – wilt thou know
Th'effect of what I wrote?

HORATIO   Ay, good my lord.

HAMLET
An earnest conjuration from the King,
As England was his faithful tributary,
As love between them like the palm might flourish,   40
As peace should still her wheaten garland wear
And stand a comma 'tween their amities,
And many such like 'as', sir, of great charge,
That on the view and knowing of these contents,
Without debatement further more or less,   45
He should those bearers put to sudden death,
Not shriving time allowed.

HORATIO   How was this sealed?

---

33 **statists** statesmen
34 **A baseness** something beneath me
36 **yeoman's service** the service of a faithful attendant
38–47 **An … allowed** As Hamlet describes his substituted commission, he parodies the affected language of diplomacy.
38 **conjuration** formal request
39 **tributary** a country paying tribute, usually as the result of having been defeated in some military action; Hamlet is supposed to be pursuing England's *neglected tribute* (see 3.1.168–9, 4.3.56–66).
41 **still** always (i.e. continue to – with implicit threat of war)
   wheaten garland a traditional symbol of the prosperity fostered by peace
42 **stand … amities** This seems to mean 'stand like the shortest possible pause or

impediment between their loves', a *comma* being the punctuation sign signifying the most minimal break. Theobald, following Warburton's suggestion, emended *comma* to 'commere' which he glossed as 'co-mother or guarantee', but this word does not occur in Shakespeare or in the *OED*.
43 **'as', sir** F's 'Assis' is usually printed 'as'es' or 'as-es'; both readings imply a list of clauses beginning with 'as' like those already given.
   charge burden (allowing a pun on 'asses')
45 **debatement … less** further debate (Hamlet continues to parody 'official' language)
47 **shriving time** time for confession and absolution of their sins. Hamlet's father has complained that his sudden

---

37 Th'effect] The effects *F*   40 like] as *F*   might] should *F*   43 'as', sir,] *(as sir); Assis F; As's Rowe, Ard² (*'as'es)   44 knowing] know *F*   46 those] the *F*

HAMLET

Why even in that was heaven ordinant:
I had my father's signet in my purse –
Which was the model of that Danish seal –   50
Folded the writ up in the form of th'other,
Subscribed it, gave't th'impression, placed it safely,
The changeling never known. Now the next day
Was our sea-fight, and what to this was sequent
Thou knowest already.   55

HORATIO

So Guildenstern and Rosencrantz go to't.

HAMLET

They are not near my conscience. Their defeat
Does by their own insinuation grow.

murder did not allow him time for confession (1.5.76–9), and Hamlet decided not to kill the King at 3.3.73–96 in case he was confessing his sins and therefore in a state of grace.

How ... sealed The specificity of Horatio's question might raise the further issue of the availability of paper, pen, ink and sealing-wax.

48 **ordinant** controlling, ordaining events

49 **signet** small seal in the form of a signet-ring

50 **model** likeness, copy (not necessarily a smaller version, as is implied by modern usage)

that Danish seal presumably the royal seal on the original commission

51 **writ** written document

52 ***Subscribed** F's 'Subscrib'd' seems more appropriate than Q2's 'Subscribe', as *gave't* and *placed* are both past tense.

gave't th'impression i.e. sealed it

53 **changeling** substitution. The term was used for a child substituted by fairies for

one they steal, like the changeling boy in *MND* 2.1.120.

54 **was sequent** followed

56 **go to't** i.e. go to their deaths. It is not easy to judge the tone of Horatio's comment in Q2; in F, Hamlet's reply begins with an additional line (see t.n. at 57) which may indicate that he receives it as a question or even a criticism. Edwards (14–19) argues that this was a crucial part of Shakespeare's revision; Jenkins includes it.

57 **defeat** destruction

58 **their own insinuation** their own act of winding their way in, ingratiating themselves. It is not clear whether Rosencrantz and Guildenstern know that they are supposed to be escorting Hamlet to his death; the King's instructions at 3.3.1–26 refer merely to the need to remove him from Denmark, and the fact that they continue their voyage after his capture by the pirates might imply that they think they are conveying other matters to the

48 ordinant] ordinate *F*   51 ²the] *om. F*   th'other] the other *F*   52 Subscribed] *F* (Subscrib'd); Subscribe *Q2*   54 sequent] sement *F*   55 knowest] know'st *F*   57 They] Why man, they did make loue to this imployment / They *F*   defeat] debate *F*   58 Does] Doth *F*

'Tis dangerous when the baser nature comes
Between the pass and fell incensed points   60
Of mighty opposites.

HORATIO   Why, what a king is this!

HAMLET

Does it not, think thee, stand me now upon?
He that hath killed my King and whored my mother,
Popped in between th'election and my hopes,
Thrown out his angle for my proper life   65
And with such cozenage. Is't not perfect conscience?

Enter [OSRIC,] *a courtier.*

OSRIC   Your lordship is right welcome back to Denmark.

King of England. Hamlet, however, sees them as the King's active accomplices here, as they clearly are in Saxo and Belleforest (Bullough, 7.67, 102).

60–1 **Between ... opposites** Hamlet's metaphor anticipates the coming duel.

60 **pass** sword-thrust
   fell incensed points incensèd; deadly and enraged weapons (it is of course those wielding the weapons who are *incensed*)

61 **opposites** opponents. Following on from his self-identification as *Hamlet the Dane* (5.1.246–7), Hamlet seems to see himself as the equal or rival of the King at this point.

62–6 **Does it ... Is't** The change in sentence structure is particularly marked in Q2, where the sentence begun at 66 is left incomplete.

62 'Don't you think I am now under an obligation?' Q2 leaves the precise nature of this obligation undefined: see 66n. and Appendix 1.
   think thee Hibbard notes a possible confusion between 'thinks it thee' (seems it to you) and 'thinkst thou' (what do you think).

63 **whored my mother** Hamlet now seems to see the Queen as a fellow victim of the King rather than as his dupe, as in 3.4.

64 **election** See 339 and 1.2.109 and n.

65 **angle** fishing hook and line
   my proper life my own life

66 **cozenage** deception
   Is't ... conscience? Is it (my attitude or behaviour) not morally justifiable? In F Hamlet continues, 'To quit him with this arme', and there are a further 13 lines: see Appendix 1.

66.1 OSRIC Q2 has '*Enter a Courtier*' at this point, but he is named as 'young *Ostricke*' by the Lord at 176 and addressed by the King in the same way at 236 (see List of Roles, 18n.). He enters to announce the arrival of Fortinbras at 333.1 although he has not been given an exit after his previous line at 290. The treatment of the role is similar in F; he is simply '*a Bragart Gentleman*' in Q1 (17.4.1). Like the clowns in 5.1 he provides some comic relief, though Osric is merely the butt of Hamlet's mockery; he does not hold his own like the Gravedigger.

62 think] thinkst *F;* think'st *Dyce (Walker)*   upon?] vpon *F*   66 conscience?] conscience, *F, followed by 14 additional lines of dialogue (68–81)*   66.1 OSRIC, *a courtier*] a Bragart Gentleman *Q1;* young Osricke *F*   67+ SP] *F (Osr.); Cour. Q2; Gen[t]; Q1*

HAMLET   I humbly thank you, sir. [*aside to Horatio*] Dost
   know this water-fly?
HORATIO [*aside*]   No, my good lord.   70
HAMLET [*aside*]   Thy state is the more gracious, for 'tis a
   vice to know him. He hath much land, and fertile. Let
   a beast be lord of beasts and his crib shall stand at the
   king's mess. 'Tis a chough but, as I say, spacious in the
   possession of dirt.   75
OSRIC   Sweet lord, if your lordship were at leisure I
   should impart a thing to you from his majesty.
HAMLET   I will receive it, sir, with all diligence of spirit.
   Your bonnet to his right use: 'tis for the head.
OSRIC   I thank your lordship, it is very hot.   80

68   *humbly Q2's 'humble' is recorded in an
     adverbial sense by *OED* in 1483, but does
     not occur elsewhere in Shakespeare. (If it
     is retained, Hamlet might mean 'I, who am
     humble'.)
69   water-fly i.e. superficial, trivial person.
     Thersites uses the same term to insult
     Patroclus: 'how the poor world is pestered
     with such water-flies!' (see *TC* 5.1.33–4).
     In Osric's case the word may also imply
     'gaudy'.
71   state condition, circumstances
     gracious free from sin, in a state of grace
72–4   Let . . . mess i.e. if a man is rich with
     large herds of animals (even though he is
     little better than an animal himself) he will
     be welcome at the King's table.
73   crib manger or trough for animals' food
74   mess meal-table. The term survives in
     military and naval contexts to denote a
     group of men of the same rank who eat
     together – and hence the place where they
     eat. In *LLL* 4.3.203 Shakespeare seems to
     refer to Inns of Court usage where a *mess*
     consisted of four men.

chough literally, crow or jackdaw, both
     birds which can be trained to talk – hence
     one who chatters or gossips (some editors
     also gloss 'chuff' = rustic, which does not
     seem very appropriate).
74–5   spacious . . . dirt possessing large
     tracts of land. Hamlet picks up one of
     the themes of his dialogue in 5.1 and
     derides Osric's lands by calling them mere
     dirt.
77   a thing something (as at *Oth* 3.3.305)
78   sir Hibbard includes this word, omitted
     in F.
     diligence attentiveness
79   Your . . . use put your hat to its proper use.
     Osric has presumably taken off his hat as a
     gesture of respect.
80   Since Hamlet has acknowledged but
     rejected his gesture, and he is afraid to put
     his hat on again, Osric pretends he has
     taken it off because of the heat. Many
     productions make much of this comic
     business, which echoes Hamlet's deliberate
     misunderstanding of Polonius at 2.2.169–
     214 and 3.2.367–75.

68 humbly] *F*; humble *Q2*   SD] *Capell*   70 SD] *Capell*   71 SD] *Capell*   74 chough] *(*chough*), F*
*(*Chowgh*)*; chuff *Ard²*   say] saw *F*   76 lordship] friendship *F*   78 sir] *om. F*   79 Your] put your *F*
80 it is] 'tis *F*

HAMLET   No, believe me, 'tis very cold; the wind is northerly.

OSRIC   It is indifferent cold, my lord, indeed.

HAMLET   But yet methinks it is very sultry and hot, or my complexion –   85

OSRIC   Exceedingly, my lord, it is very sultry, as 'twere – I cannot tell how. My lord, his majesty bade me signify to you that 'a has laid a great wager on your head. Sir, this is the matter –

HAMLET   I beseech you remember.   90

OSRIC   Nay, good my lord, for my ease, in good faith. Sir, here is newly come to court Laertes – believe me, an absolute gentleman, full of most excellent differences, of very soft society and great showing. Indeed, to speak sellingly of him, he is the card or calendar of gentry, for   95 you shall find in him the continent of what part a gentleman would see.

---

83   **indifferent** somewhat

84   **But yet methinks** Q2's *But yet* increases the teasing component over F's 'Mee thinkes'.

    *sultry There is no relevant meaning in *OED* for Q2's 'sully' (which could easily be a misreading), and Q2 has 'soultery' at 86.

    or If Q2 is right, Osric interrupts Hamlet in his eagerness to agree with him. F's 'for' is generally preferred.

85   **complexion** constitution

88   **'a** he

90   **I . . . remember** i.e. to put your hat on (as at *LLL* 5.1.90–2: 'I do beseech thee, remember thy courtesy: I beseech thee, apparel thy head'). Hamlet presumably points or gestures towards the hat.

92–120   **here . . . sir** Edwards and Hibbard commend F's omission of these lines, which they see as 'over-elaboration' and 'unnecessary to the plot'.

93   **absolute** complete, perfect
    differences distinguishing qualities

94   **soft society** agreeable company
    great showing impressive appearance

95   **sellingly** like a salesman. This reading of a unique word in the uncorrected state of Q2 is preferred by some editors, e.g. Steevens, Jennens and Dover Wilson. It might be supported by *TC* 4.1.76–9, where Diomed, speaking of Helen, tells Paris, 'We'll not commend, that not intend to sell.' Others prefer the corrected Q2's 'fellingly' = feelingly or forcefully. Confusion of *f* and long *s* is the obvious cause of the discrepancy.
    card or calendar literally, map or directory, hence model or exemplar (see 5.1.130)
    gentry gentility

96–7   **continent . . . see** container or possessor of whatever quality a gentleman

---

84 But yet] *om. F*   sultry] *F (*soultry*)*; sully *Q2*   hot, or] hot for *F*   87 My] but my *F*   88 'a] he *F*
91 good my lord] in good faith *F*   ²my] mine *F*   91–120 Sir . . . sir?] *om. F*   95 sellingly] *Q2u;*
fellingly *Q2c;* feelingly *Q3*   96 part] parts *Cam*¹

HAMLET Sir, his definement suffers no perdition in you,
    though I know to divide him inventorially would dazzle
    th'arithmetic of memory, and yet but yaw neither, in   100
    respect of his quick sail; but in the verity of extolment
    I take him to be a soul of great article and his infusion
    of such dearth and rareness as, to make true diction of
    him, his semblable is his mirror, and who else would
    trace him, his umbrage, nothing more.   105
OSRIC Your lordship speaks most infallibly of him.
HAMLET The concernancy, sir – why do we wrap the
    gentleman in our more rawer breath?
OSRIC Sir?

might wish to see. *Continent* also carries on the geographical metaphor in *card*, so that *part* can also mean 'region'.

98–105 Hamlet's response parodies Osric's affected style of speech, full of empty and repetitive formulas; he seems to agree with Osric's inflation of Laertes' attributes but finally reduces him to his own shadow or mirror image. The parody includes the Shakespearean coinages *definement* (98) and *extolment* (101): see 1.2.93n.

98 **his . . . you** his definition or description suffers no loss by your words

99 **divide him inventorially** list all his qualities separately (as in an inventory or financial account)
    *dazzle Q2 reads 'dazzie' in the corrected state, 'dosie' in the uncorrected one; either way *th'arithmetic of memory* is seen as being overwhelmed or bewildered. (Jenkins and Edwards print 'dozy'; Hibbard, in an appendix, follows Q3's 'dizzie'.)

100 **th'arithmetic of memory** the ability of memory to calculate

100–1 **and . . . sail** and yet only manage a roundabout voyage in comparison to his rapid sailing

100 ***yaw** a nautical expression: a ship is said to *yaw* when it deviates from a straight course. (Q2c's 'raw' is difficult to justify; Jennens retains but does not gloss; Caldecott glosses as 'unready, untrained and awkward'.)

101 **verity of extolment** truth of eulogy (i.e. to praise him truthfully)

102 **great article** significant matter or importance (continuing the language of the inventory)
    his infusion what is infused into him

103 **dearth** dearness (a synonym for *rareness*)
    to . . . diction to speak truly

104 **his semblable . . . mirror** the only person like him is his mirror image

105 **trace** follow, i.e. rival
    umbrage shadow

106 **infallibly** truthfully

107 **The concernancy** 'how is this relevant' or 'how does this concern us'. *Concernancy* is a unique usage according to *OED*.

107–8 **wrap . . . breath** i.e. clothe him in words which are too crude to do him justice

109 **Sir?** There is no question mark in Q2, but Osric is maybe puzzled by Hamlet's imitation of his own style.

99 dazzle] *(Wilson, Manuscript)*; dosie *Q2u, Ard²;* dazzie *Q2c;* dizzie *Q3*   100 yaw] *Q2u, Ard²;* raw *Q2c*

HORATIO Is't not possible to understand in another   110
tongue? You will do't, sir, really.

HAMLET What imports the nomination of this
gentleman?

OSRIC Of Laertes.

HORATIO His purse is empty already – all's golden words   115
are spent.

HAMLET Of him, sir.

OSRIC I know you are not ignorant –

HAMLET I would you did, sir. Yet, in faith, if you did, it
would not much approve me. Well, sir?   120

OSRIC You are not ignorant of what excellence Laertes is.

HAMLET I dare not confess that, lest I should compare
with him in excellence. But to know a man well were to
know himself.

OSRIC I mean, sir, for his weapon. But in the imputation   125

110–11 'Paradoxically, Horatio's interjection
is more obscure than the ridiculous
colloquy which he interrupts' (Edwards).
Horatio may be asking Osric if he can't
understand his own *tongue*, or he may be
calling on both speakers to use simpler
words. RP suggests: 'Couldn't you become
comprehensible by talking in a foreign
language?' (See Jenkins, LN.)

111 **You will do't** you will manage it (i.e. speak
more plainly)
   really Oxf (in an appendix) follows
Theobald in emending to 'rarely' (=
unusually well, splendidly), pointing out
that *really* does not occur in Shakespeare
apart from this usage and a rather different
one at *TNK* 2.1.6–7, where the Jailer
remarks, 'I would I were really that I am
delivered to be.' The use of 'real' is almost
as sparing, perhaps indicating that he
charged the word with more significance
than we do.

112 **What ... nomination** what is the
significance of naming (Hamlet continues
to use a pretentious style)

114 **Of Laertes** Again there is no question mark
in Q2, though many editors introduce one;
Osric could be asking whom Hamlet means,
or he could be confirming that Laertes is
indeed the *gentleman* in question.

119 **I would you did** 'I wish this were truly
your opinion (though you are unqualified
to hold it)' (RP)

120 **approve** advantage, commend (i.e. it
wouldn't do me any good?)

122–6 See t.n. and 92–120n.

122–4 Hamlet implies that to recognize
Laertes' excellence one would need to
match it, and that to know anyone else well
one must first know oneself.

125 *****his weapon** Q2's 'this weapon' is an
easy error. F perhaps clarifies by
omitting 122–6 and adding 'at his weapon' to 121, so this reads 'you are

---

111 do't] *Q2c* (doo't); too't *Q2u, Ard² (to't)*   121 You] Sir, you *F*   is] is at his weapon *F*   122–6] *om. F*
125 his] *Q5;* this *Q2*

472

laid on him by them in his meed he's unfellowed.

HAMLET   What's his weapon?

OSRIC   Rapier and dagger.

HAMLET   That's two of his weapons. But well.

OSRIC   The King, sir, hath wagered with him six Barbary   130
horses, against the which he has impawned, as I take it,
six French rapiers and poniards, with their assigns, as
girdle, hanger and so. Three of the carriages, in faith,
are very dear to fancy, very responsive to the hilts, most
delicate carriages and of very liberal conceit.   135

HAMLET   What call you the carriages?

HORATIO   I knew you must be edified by the margin ere

---

not ignorant of what excellence Laertes is
at his weapon'.

125–6 **in . . . meed** Osric seems to mean 'in the
estimation of those who know his merit',
though some editors take *in his meed* to
mean 'in his pay', i.e. his retainers, or
perhaps his fencing-masters.

127 **What's his weapon** Hamlet's question
seems to belie the King's insistence on his
envy of Laertes' skill with the rapier
(4.7.71–4, 93–103). Or perhaps he is just
impatient for Osric to come to the point.

128 **Rapier and dagger** These were
fashionable weapons for duelling in
England around 1600 (see *MM* 4.3.13–14:
'Master Starve-lackey the rapier and
dagger man'); Shakespeare had previously
specified the use of the *rapier* in several
plays, including (anachronistically) *Tit*
(2.1.54 and 4.2.87) and *R2* (4.1.40).

130 **Barbary** Arabian. The elided form
'Barbry' in Q2 at 142 may indicate a
colloquial pronunciation.

131 **has impawned** has wagered. F's 'impon'd'
is defended by Edwards as indicating
Osric's pronunciation, and by Hibbard as

an affected 'inkhorn' term. Osric's *as I take
it* seems to imply some uncertainty about
the word which Hamlet challenges in F
(see 145 and t.n.).

132 **poniards** daggers
assigns accessories

133 **girdle, hanger** sword-belt and its straps
and so and so on, etcetera
carriages Hamlet queries this term in all
three texts, presumably because it is
inappropriate (see 140n.). Osric explains at
139 that he means the straps that carry the
sword; possibly he is trying to avoid the
sexual innuendo of *hangers*. A similar
metaphor occurs in *TN* 3.4.222–3, when
Sir Toby advises Cesario to 'Dismount thy
tuck' (i.e. draw your sword).

134 **dear to fancy** endearing or pleasing to the
fancy, i.e. fancifully designed or decorated
responsive to matching or in keeping with

135 **liberal conceit** ingenious or lavish design

137 **edified . . . margin** instructed by a
marginal note. Horatio is saying that
he knew Hamlet would need to ask for
some explanation or annotation of
Osric's vocabulary.

---

130 King, sir] sir King *F*   hath wagered] hath layd a wager *Q1;* ha's wag'd *F*   131 has impawned]
*(*has impaund*);* impon'd *F*   133 hanger] Hangers *F*   and] or *F*   134 responsive] *Q2c F;* reponsiue
Q2u   137 margin *(margent)*   137–8] *om. F*

you had done.

OSRIC The carriages, sir, are the hangers.

HAMLET The phrase would be more germane to the 140
matter if we could carry a cannon by our sides. I would
it might be 'hangers' till then. But on. Six Barbary
horses against six French swords, their assigns and
three liberal-conceited carriages – that's the French bet
against the Danish. Why, is this all you call it? 145

OSRIC The King, sir, hath laid, sir, that in a dozen passes
between yourself and him he shall not exceed you three

---

139 ***carriages** F's plural seems to follow better than Q2's singular.

140 **germane** relevant. Hamlet is suggesting that *carriage* would be more appropriate to a larger weapon such as a *cannon* which would be transported on a gun-carriage; see *H5* 3 Prologue 26: 'Behold the ordnance on their carriages'.

142 ***might be** Q2c's 'be might' seems to result from erroneous correction which placed the missing *might* after *be* rather than before it.

But on i.e. do continue

144–5 **the French ... Danish** We are reminded that Laertes has been living in France, whence he has apparently brought the items he is wagering.

145 **Why ... it** 'If Q2 were our only text, its [reading] could be interpreted as it stands, with Hamlet ridiculing Osric's verbosity by affecting to be unable to repeat it: Why is this – all you said it was?' (Jenkins, who assumes an omission in Q2 and supplies F's 'why is this impon'd as you call it?') Oxf suggests Q2 should have read 'all what you call it', though 'all that you call it' would be an easier error, assuming compositorial omission of 'yt' (= that) as an anticipation of 'it' (see the 'it/that' variant at 148).

146–8 **The ... nine** The King is clearly

placing odds on Hamlet, but the precise terms of this wager are described by Jenkins (LN) as 'an insoluble problem' and a recent debate in the *Times Literary Supplement* (6 February 2004) failed to clarify the issue. Probably the King is betting that, in 12 bouts or *passes* (146), Laertes' total number of hits will not exceed Hamlet's total by 3. Q1 offers a simpler version: 'that yong Leartes in twelue venies / At Rapier and Dagger do not get three odues of you' (17.27–9), which seems to mean that Laertes will not achieve three hits. Oxf emends *on* (F 'one') to 'ont' (= on it), arguing that the King is laying odds not 'on' but rather 'against' the terms stated (*TxC*). Perhaps the actual details are comparatively unimportant, since we know that the King and Laertes are not going to play by the rules anyway (and none of the players will be alive to collect the stakes).

146 **laid** wagered

passes brief periods of engagement or 'rounds' as they would be called in some sports; *pass* also occurs at 4.7.136. It is called a *bout* at 266 and 4.7.156 and an *exchange* at 246. Q1 uses the more technical 'venies' or venues (15.18 and 17.28), which may also be implied by F's 'comings'; see Ard Q1/F at 4.3.128.

---

139 carriages] *F;* carriage *Q2* 141 a] *om. F;* the *Q1* 142 might be] *F;* be *Q2u;* be might *Q2c* on. Six] *(on, six);* on sixe *F* Barbary] *(Barbry). F* 144 bet] but *F* 145 all] impon'd as *F;* all 'impawned' as *Cam¹* 146 ²sir] *om. F* 147 yourself] you *F*

hits. He hath laid on twelve for nine, and it would come
to immediate trial if your lordship would vouchsafe the
answer.   150

HAMLET   How if I answer no?

OSRIC   I mean, my lord, the opposition of your person in
trial.

HAMLET   Sir, I will walk here in the hall. If it please his
majesty, it is the breathing time of day with me. Let the   155
foils be brought, the gentleman willing and the King
hold his purpose – I will win for him an I can; if not, I
will gain nothing but my shame and the odd hits.

OSRIC   Shall I deliver you so?

HAMLET   To this effect, sir, after what flourish your   160
nature will.

OSRIC   I commend my duty to your lordship.

HAMLET   Yours. 'A does well to commend it himself.

[Exit Osric.]

There are no tongues else for's turn.

HORATIO   This lapwing runs away with the shell on his   165
head.

148 **it** F's 'that' is preferred by Hibbard.
149 **immediate trial** The transformation of
the scene from one of private conversation
to a public trial of arms is like that in
AYL 1.2: see Scolnicov, who notes the
parallels between the plays in so far as
Laertes, like Charles the wrestler, seems
more likely to win, especially as we are
aware of the collusion between him and
the King, like that between Charles and
Oliver.
149–50 **vouchsafe the answer** agree to accept
the challenge (but Hamlet takes it to mean
'make a reply')
155 **breathing . . . me** my daily time for
exercise
157 **an** if

158 **the odd hits** any hits I may make (despite
losing the match)
159 **deliver you so** convey your response in
this way. F's 'redeliuer' seems more
characteristic of Osric.
160 **after what flourish** in whatever elaborate
style
161 **will** wishes, intends
162 Osric's response is a standard parting
formula.
164 **There . . . turn** i.e. no one else would serve
his purpose (by doing it for him). Hibbard
cites the proverb 'He must praise himself
since no man else will' (Dent, P545.1).
165–6 proverbial (Tilley, L69), indicating
Osric's youthful naïvety – and perhaps a
final reference to his hat

148 laid on] one *F*   nine] mine *F*   it] that *F*   155 it is] 'tis *F*   157 an] *(and);* if *F*   157–8 I will]
Ile *F*   159 deliver] redeliuer *F*   so] ee'n so *F*   163 Yours.] *Riv (Parrott–Craig);* Yours *Q2;* Yours,
yours; *F*   'A does] *Riv (Parrott–Craig);* doo's *Q2;* hee does *F*   SD] *this edn; after* Yours. *Capell*
164 turn] tongue *F*

HAMLET   'A did so, sir, with his dug before 'a sucked it.
Thus has he, and many more of the same breed that I
know the drossy age dotes on, only got the tune of
the time and, out of an habit of encounter, a kind of   170
yeasty collection, which carries them through and
through the most profane and winnowed opinions; and
do but blow them to their trial – the bubbles are out.

Enter a Lord.

LORD   My lord, his majesty commended him to you by   175

167 **'A did so** i.e. he behaved in this way. This
is not impossible, but Jenkins follows F,
remarking, 'Q2, in trouble with several
words in this passage, appears to have
surrendered on this one.' The fact that *so* is
added in the corrected version of this Q2
page may be evidence of the difficulty of
the MS here.

   his dug his mother's (or his nurse's) nipple
168 **Thus . . . breed** Spencer, Jenkins, Edwards
and Hibbard all take 'many' from Q2 and
'bevy' ('Beauvy') from F.
169 **the drossy age** the degenerate world we
live in
169–70 **only . . . time** captured merely the
fashionable style of the day
170 **out . . . encounter** from frequent social
encounters. 'F *outward*, though much
followed and superficially attractive in
reinforcing *habit* (= dress) and providing a
parallel metaphor for *tune*, would imply a
contrast with some inner worth, which a
drossy age must lack' (Jenkins).
171 *****yeasty** frothy, trivial; Q2's 'histy' is not
otherwise recorded and *h/y* is an easy
mistake in secretary hand.
   collection mixture, repertoire

171–2 **which . . . opinions** 'which allows them
to bluff their way in all companies'
172 *****profane and winnowed** i.e. both
vulgar and selective. Most editors prefer
F's 'fond and winnowed', generally
emended to 'fanned and winnowed',
with 'fanned' understood as repeating
the idea of 'sifted' already present in
winnowed. There is no such word as
Q2's 'trennowed', and *tr/w* is an
easy misreading, but Jennens prints
'tres-renowned' meaning most renowned,
following Q6's 'renowned'.
174.1–186 *Enter . . . me* 'Even Dover Wilson
admits that the excision of these lines,
which serve no useful purpose and
require an extra speaking actor, is "a
definite improvement" ' (Hibbard). But,
apart from giving notice of the approach
of the royal party, they do contain the
Queen's message to Hamlet (see 184–5n.).
They were included in the Folio-based
version at the Globe in 2000, though
Hamlet's subsequent apology to Laertes
was abbreviated.
175 **commended him** sent his commendations
or greetings

167 'A . . .'a] *(A . . . a); He . . . hee F* so, sir,] *Q2c;* sir *Q2u;* Complie *F* 168 has] had *F* many]
mine *F* breed] Beauy *F* 170 out' of an] outward *F* 171 yeasty] *F (*yesty*);* histy *Q2* 172 profane]
fond *F;* fann'd *Hanmer, Warburton, Ard[2];* profound *Tschischwitz (Bailey)* winnowed] *F;* trennowed
Q2; trennowned *Q3;* renowned *Q6* 173 trial] tryalls *F* 174.1–186 *Enter . . . me.] om. F*

young Osric, who brings back to him that you attend
him in the hall. He sends to know if your pleasure hold
to play with Laertes, or that you will take longer time.

HAMLET I am constant to my purposes. They follow the
King's pleasure. If his fitness speaks, mine is ready. 180
Now or whensoever, provided I be so able as now.

LORD The King and Queen and all are coming down.

HAMLET In happy time.

LORD The Queen desires you to use some gentle
entertainment to Laertes before you fall to play. 185

HAMLET She well instructs me. [*Exit Lord.*]

HORATIO You will lose, my lord.

HAMLET I do not think so. Since he went into France I
have been in continual practice. I shall win at the odds.
Thou wouldst not think how ill all's here about my 190
heart – but it is no matter.

HORATIO Nay, good my lord –

HAMLET It is but foolery, but it is such a kind of
gaingiving as would perhaps trouble a woman.

HORATIO If your mind dislike anything, obey it. I will 195
forestall their repair hither and say you are not fit.

178 **play** i.e. fence, duel (supposedly in sport)
  that if
179 **follow** agree with, obey
180 **his fitness speaks** his convenience suits. Hamlet identifies the King as the key figure (and his true opponent).
183 **In happy time** i.e. this is an opportune moment
184–5 **use ... entertainment** show some courtesy. Thus in Q2, though not in F, Hamlet's words at 204–21 seem prompted by the Queen.

188–9 **Since ... practice** Hamlet here contradicts his earlier claim that he has 'forgone all custom of exercises' (2.2.262–3).
189 **at the odds** i.e. given that the odds [as specified at 146–50] are advantageous to me
194 ***gaingiving** misgiving; Q2's 'gamgiuing' is assumed to be a minim error for F's 'gain-giuing', seen as related to 'gainsay', though it is a rare word which elsewhere means 'giving in return'.
196 **repair** coming

186 SD] *Theobald* 187 lose] lose this wager *F* 190 Thou] but thou *F* ill] *om. F* all's] all *F*
194 gaingiving] *F (*gain-giuing*);* gamgiuing *Q2;* game-giuing *Q3* 195 it] *om. F*

HAMLET   Not a whit. We defy augury. There is special
providence in the fall of a sparrow. If it be, 'tis not to
come. If it be not to come, it will be now. If it be not
now, yet it will come. The readiness is all, since no man   200
of aught he leaves knows what is't to leave betimes. Let
be.

*A table prepared. Trumpets, Drums and Officers with
cushions, foils and daggers. [Enter]* KING, QUEEN,
LAERTES, [OSRIC] *and all the state.*

197 **Not a whit** not at all. A *whit* was a very
small quantity; it occurred in negative
expressions like this and 'never a whit'.
augury literally, the practice of learning
secrets or predicting the future from the
flight of birds. Given that Hamlet goes on
to talk about sparrows, he is perhaps using
it in a more general sense of 'superstition'.

197–8 **special . . . sparrow** Hamlet alludes to
the Christian (Calvinist) belief in God's
direct intervention in worldly affairs (see
Matthew, 10.29).

198 **If it be** *It* is Hamlet's moment of death,
predetermined by God like 'the fall of a
sparrow'. Jenkins prefers Q1/F's 'If it be
now'. Hamlet's sentiments here echo those
of Francis Feeble, the woman's tailor,
facing possible death in battle at *2H4*
3.2.233–7: 'we owe God a death . . . and't
be my destiny, so; and't be not, so . . . he
that dies this year is quit for the next.'

200–1 **since . . . betimes** 'Since no one has any
knowledge of the life he leaves behind
him, what does it matter if one dies early
[*betimes*]?' (Edwards). The F reading
substitutes ownership for knowledge (see
Jenkins, LN).

201–2 **Let be** leave it alone; say no more.
These are the final (punning) words of
Charlotte Jones's 2001 *Hamlet*-based play
Humble Boy.

202.2 Q2's '*Cushions*' seems to indicate
that the courtiers sit to watch; chairs or
thrones may be brought on for the King
and Queen, and a table for the *stoups of
wine* at 244. F's substitution of '*Gauntlets*'
for Q2's '*daggers*' may reflect a change in
fashion; it would also facilitate the
necessary exchange of weapons at 285;
see Edelman, and Gurr & Ichikawa
(155–9) for detailed discussions of ways
of staging this fight. Both Q2 and F omit
Osric from this entry but the King
addresses him at 236 and he speaks at
243.

202.3 **all the state** the rest of the Court.
In eighteenth- and nineteenth-century
theatrical tradition, the '*state*' included
Marcellus, Barnardo and Francisco, with
Francisco playing the role of the King's
cup-bearer later in the scene. This SD
might also imply that a 'chair of state' or
throne is brought on (see 'state' in Dessen
& Thomson).

197 There is] theres a *Q1F*   198 be] be now *Q1F*   199 will] *F;* well *Q2*   201 of . . . knows] *(*of ought he
leaues, knowes*)*, ha's ought of what he leaues *F;* owes aught of what he leaues *Hanmer;* knows aught of
what he leaves, *Johnson;* of aught he leaues, knows aught *Ard²*   201–2 Let be.] *om. F* 202.1–3] *Q2 subst.
(A table prepard, Trumpets, Drums and officers with Cushions, / King, Queene, and all the state, Foiles,
daggers, / and Laertes.); Enter King, Queene, Leartes, Lordes. Q1; Enter King, Queene, Laertes and Lords,
with other Atten- / dants with Foyles, and Gauntlets, a Table and / Flagons of Wine on it. F*   202.3 OSRIC]
Theobald subst.

KING

> Come, Hamlet, come and take this hand from me.
> [*Puts Laertes' hand into Hamlet's.*]

HAMLET

> Give me your pardon, sir. I have done you wrong,
> But pardon't as you are a gentleman.   205
> This presence knows, and you must needs have heard,
> How I am punished with a sore distraction.
> What I have done
> That might your nature, honour and exception
> Roughly awake, I here proclaim was madness.   210
> Was't Hamlet wronged Laertes? Never Hamlet.
> If Hamlet from himself be ta'en away
> And when he's not himself does wrong Laertes,
> Then Hamlet does it not; Hamlet denies it.
> Who does it then? His madness. If 't be so,   215
> Hamlet is of the faction that is wronged –
> His madness is poor Hamlet's enemy.
> Let my disclaiming from a purposed evil

---

203 **this hand** The King takes Laertes' hand and places it in Hamlet's. Laertes and Hamlet shake hands, either here, or possibly not until 221 ('I am satisfied in nature'), but Laertes may let go of Hamlet's hand at 224 (*I stand aloof*).

204–21 This apology to Laertes, perhaps motivated in Q2 by the Queen's message at 184–5, has struck editors and commentators since at least Johnson in 1765 as disingenuous: Hamlet is clearly using his assumed or supposed madness as an excuse for his behaviour – and modern judicial practice still permits denial of responsibility on grounds of insanity. But the excuse is difficult to accept here, in relation to either the death of Polonius or the madness and death of Ophelia; the fact that Hamlet talks in generalities and does not spell out the crimes with which he is charged seems, to say the least, evasive.

206 **presence** audience, assembly of courtiers

207 **sore distraction** serious mental derangement

209 **exception** dissatisfaction (*OED* cites this passage as a rare example)

210 **awake** arouse

212 The mad Ophelia is described in a similar way as 'Divided from herself and her fair judgement' (4.5.85).

216 **faction** contending party

217 Jenkins includes F's additional short line.

218 **disclaiming from** denial of
purposed evil deliberate evil intention

---

203 SD] *Johnson subst., after Hanmer*   204 I have] I'ue *F*   205–8] *Rowe; Q2 lines* knowes, / punnisht / done /; *F lines* Gentleman. / knowes, / punisht / done /   207 a] *om. F*   217 enemy.] Enemy. / Sir, in this Audience, *F*

Free me so far in your most generous thoughts
That I have shot my arrow o'er the house 220
And hurt my brother.

LAERTES   I am satisfied in nature,
Whose motive in this case should stir me most
To my revenge. But in my terms of honour
I stand aloof and will no reconcilement
Till by some elder masters of known honour 225
I have a voice and precedent of peace
To keep my name ungored. But all that time
I do receive your offered love like love
And will not wrong it.

HAMLET   I embrace it freely
And will this brothers' wager frankly play. 230
Give us the foils.

LAERTES   Come, one for me.

HAMLET

I'll be your foil, Laertes. In mine ignorance
Your skill shall like a star i'th' darkest night

220 **That I have** as to imagine I have
221 **brother** F's 'Mother' is tentatively defended (though not printed) by Dowden. Given his failure to refer specifically to Ophelia in this scene, it seems unlikely that Hamlet means 'brother-in-law'.
221–9 Laertes' reply is at least as disingenuous as Hamlet's apology: Hamlet glosses over his past faults while Laertes dissimulates about his planned revenge.
221 **in nature** as far as my natural feelings are concerned. Like Hamlet, Laertes fails to name his father and sister as specific issues.
222 **Whose motive** the motivation or urging of which
223 **in . . . honour** as far as my sense of honour is concerned

224 **will** wish for, desire
225 **elder . . . honour** i.e. some experienced men who are knowledgeable about questions of honour
226 **voice . . . peace** opinion and previous example of (a similar) reconciliation
227 **To . . . ungored** to preserve my reputation from injury
   *keep F's reading seems necessary for both sense and metre.
   all F's 'till' is generally adopted, though *all* makes sense.
230 **frankly** freely, with no ill feeling
231 **Give . . . foils** F's 'Come on' after this perhaps anticipates Laertes' line.
232 **I'll . . . foil** Hamlet puns on *foil* meaning setting (as of a jewel), background or contrast.

220 my] mine *Q1F*   221 brother] *Q1;* Mother *F*   226 precedent] *(president) F*   227 keep] *F; not in Q21*   ungored] vngorg'd *F*   all] till *F*   229–30 I . . . play] *F; prose Q2*   229 I] I do *F*   230 brothers'] *(brothers) F*   231 foils.] Foyles: Come on. *F*

Stick fiery off indeed.

LAERTES   You mock me, sir.

HAMLET

No, by this hand.   235

KING

Give them the foils, young Osric. Cousin Hamlet,
You know the wager.

HAMLET   Very well, my lord.
Your grace has laid the odds o'th' weaker side.

KING

I do not fear it. I have seen you both
But since he is better we have therefore odds.   240

LAERTES

This is too heavy, let me see another.

HAMLET

This likes me well. These foils have all a length?

OSRIC

Ay, my good lord.

KING

Set me the stoups of wine upon that table.

---

234 **Stick fiery off** burn brightly in contrast.
See Lepidus on Antony: 'His faults, in him,
seem as the spots of heaven, / More fiery
by night's blackness' (*AC* 1.4.12–13), and
see 2.1.33n.

238 **has ... odds** Hamlet seems simply
to mean 'backed' or 'bet on', but some
commentators interpret this as a reference
to the advantage given to Hamlet by the
puzzling terms announced at 146–8.
o' on

239 **I ... it** i.e. I am not afraid of that

240 **better** i.e. at this sport; F's 'better'd' is
generally adopted and interpreted as
meaning either that Laertes is 'pronounced

to be better' (Jenkins) or that he has
'improved' (Edwards). Q2's reading is
acceptable, though less courteous.
we ... odds i.e. we have therefore arranged
the terms in your favour

242 **likes** pleases
have ... length are all of one (i.e. the
same) length (see Hope, 1.1.2a); Osric's
reply indicates that this is a question and
it is one which may give the King and
Laertes a moment of unease, given their
confidence that Hamlet would 'not peruse
the foils' (4.7.134).

244 **stoups** flagons, jars (as at 5.1.56)

---

234 off] *(of), F*   236–7] *F lines Osricke, / wager. /*   238 has] hath *F*   240 better] better'd *F*   242]
F lines well, / length. /   length?] length. *Prepare to play. F*

If Hamlet give the first or second hit   245
Or quit in answer of the third exchange
Let all the battlements their ordnance fire.
The King shall drink to Hamlet's better breath
And in the cup an union shall he throw
Richer than that which four successive kings   250
In Denmark's crown have worn. Give me the cups,
And let the kettle to the trumpet speak,
The trumpet to the cannoneer without,
The cannons to the heavens, the heaven to earth.

Trumpets the while

Now the King drinks to Hamlet. Come, begin.   255
And you, the judges, bear a wary eye.

245–54 **If ... earth** The King's description of how he will salute Hamlet's success recalls his acclamation of his stepson's 'gentle and unforced accord' at 1.2.121–8 and Hamlet's disapproval of the practice at 1.4.8–38.

246 **quit ... exchange** acquit himself well by winning the third bout (?). The expression is obscure: does the King mean that he will celebrate Hamlet winning the third bout, even if he has lost the first and the second?

247 **battlements** i.e. the soldiers on the fortified crenellations of the castle
ordnance cannon

248 **better breath** i.e. improved performance

249 ***union** a kind of pearl (as clarified at 264), so called because of the unique nature of each example. This F reading allows Hamlet's grim pun at 310; Edwards points out that Q2's 'Onixe' could be a mistaken correction of 'Vnice', itself a misreading of MS 'Vnio' or 'Vnione'; Q1 has 'union' at the latter point but not at the former. Parrott and Craig note that Shakespeare 'may have been thinking of the tale of Cleopatra's

throwing a pearl into a cup of wine. In *Soliman and Perseda* (ascribed to Thomas Kyd; 2 quartos were printed in 1599) this pearl is called "Cleopatra's union" [2.1.231].' Presumably the jewel either contains the poison or simply identifies Hamlet's cup (see 264n.).

252 **kettle ... trumpet** Both terms could refer to the instrument and/or to the musician who played it; *cannoneer* in 253 might indicate that the reference is to the players.

253 **cannoneer without** man in charge of the cannons outside

255 **Now ... Hamlet** Most editors put this in quotation marks, as what the King says he will do. They assume he doesn't drink until 265. It is, however, possible that he deliberately drinks from what will later be identified as *the poisoned cup* (275) before putting the pearl into it (see 264n.) or before the poison has time to dissolve.

256 **you, the judges** The only named character who takes on this role is Osric (see 262 and 284); presumably other courtiers arrange themselves as observers.

---

249 union] *F (*vnion*);* Vnice *Q2u;* Onixe *Q2c*   252 trumpet] Trumpets *F*   254 heaven] *F;* heavens *Q3*   SD] *opp.* 255–6; *om. F*

HAMLET   Come on, sir.
LAERTES   Come, my lord. [*They play.*]
HAMLET   One!
LAERTES   No!   260
HAMLET   Judgement?
OSRIC   A hit, a very palpable hit.   *Drum, trumpets and shot*
LAERTES   Well, again.
KING

    Stay, give me drink. Hamlet, this pearl is thine:
    Here's to thy health. Give him the cup.   265
HAMLET

    I'll play this bout first. Set it by awhile.   [*They play.*]
    Come, another hit! – What say you?
LAERTES   I do confess't.
KING

    Our son shall win.
QUEEN   He's fat and scant of breath.
    Here, Hamlet, take my napkin, rub thy brows –   270
    The Queen carouses to thy fortune, Hamlet.
HAMLET   Good madam.

---

258 **my lord** Q2's reading may be more deferential than F's 'sir'.

259 **One** Hamlet claims a hit (which Laertes denies).

261 **Judgement?** Hamlet appeals for adjudication, perhaps directly to Osric, who replies.

262 **palpable** tangible, i.e. definite

264 **this pearl** See 249n. If his words imply that he drinks from the cup before putting the pearl into it, the suggestion that the pearl contains the poison seems plausible. However it is handled, the audience must see and understand the poisoning of the

cup in order to follow the subsequent death of the Queen.

269 **fat** This word has been much discussed by commentators who do not want it to mean 'overweight'. Jenkins (LN) argues that, in conjunction with *scant of breath*, it must mean something like 'out of condition'; Hibbard sees the line as 'maternal solicitude' which 'becomes all the more evident if Hamlet is neither fat nor scant of breath'.

270 **napkin** handkerchief

271 **carouses** drinks a toast

272 **Good madam** Hamlet acknowledges the Queen's gesture.

---

257 sir.] *F*; sir: *a hit Q1*   258 Come, my lord.] Come on sir. *F*   SD] *F; not in Q2; opp. 260 Q1*   262 SD] *opp. 262; not in Q1F*   263 again.] *F;* again. *Florish, a peece goes off. Q2*   265 cup.] cup, / *Trumpets sound, and shot goes off. F*   266 it] *Q1; om. F*   SD] *Q1 (They play againe.) after equivalent of* Come, 267   268] I, I grant, a tuch, a tuch. *Q1;* A touch, a touch, I do confesse. *F*   270 Here . . . my] *Q1;* Heere's a *F*

KING   Gertrude, do not drink.

QUEEN

    I will, my lord. I pray you pardon me.

KING   [*aside*]

    It is the poisoned cup! It is too late.   275

HAMLET

    I dare not drink yet, madam. By and by.

QUEEN

    Come, let me wipe thy face.

LAERTES [*aside to King*]

    My lord, I'll hit him now.

KING [*aside to Laertes*]   I do not think't.

LAERTES [*aside*]

    And yet it is almost against my conscience.

HAMLET

    Come for the third, Laertes, you do but dally.   280

    I pray you pass with your best violence.

---

274 **I … lord** During the eighteenth and nineteenth centuries, the Queen's line was often altered onstage to 'I have, my lord', presumably to make it apologetic rather than defiant (see O'Brien). In Q1, the SD '*Shee drinkes*' precedes the King's prohibition. Some performers make it clear that they are drinking the poison deliberately, as Eileen Herlie did in Olivier's 1948 film (see Dawson, 182) and Diana Wynyard did in the production Olivier directed at the London Old Vic in 1963 (see Trewin, 122).

275, 278, 279 SDs *Neither Q2 nor F designates these speeches as asides, but they do seem to be speeches not intended for all to hear. See also 279 and SDn.

275 The King will let the Queen die rather than risk exposure, despite his vaunted love for her (see 4.7.13–17 and n.).

276 Hamlet's line implies that the Queen offers him the cup after drinking from it herself.

    By and by See 3.2.374n.

279 and SD In all three texts, Laertes has this moment of misgiving, perhaps redeeming himself a little in the minds of the audience / reader. It is possible that he speaks this line directly to the King rather than as an aside to the audience; Robert Holmes did so when playing an unusually sympathetic Laertes in the first modern-dress production of *Hamlet* staged by Barry Jackson and H.K. Ayliff at the Kingsway theatre in London in 1925 (see Dawson, 90).

280 **you … dally** you're only playing, i.e. you aren't competing in earnest

281 **pass** thrust, attack

    your best violence your utmost strength

---

275 SD] *Rowe*   278 SD1] *Oxf* SD2] *Oxf*   279 SD] *Rowe* it is] it goes *Q1;* 'tis *F* against] *Q1;*
'gainst *F*   280] *F lines* third. / dally. / do but dally] dally *Q1;* but dally *F*

I am sure you make a wanton of me.

LAERTES Say you so? Come on. [*They play.*]

OSRIC Nothing neither way.

LAERTES Have at you now! [*In scuffling they change* 285
rapiers.]

KING Part them – they are incensed.

HAMLET Nay, come again. [*Queen falls.*]

OSRIC Look to the Queen there, ho!

HORATIO

They bleed on both sides. How is it, my lord?

OSRIC How is't, Laertes? 290

LAERTES

Why, as a woodcock to mine own springe, Osric:
I am justly killed with mine own treachery.

HAMLET

How does the Queen?

KING She swoons to see them bleed.

---

282 **sure** F's 'affear'd' (afraid) is adopted by Jenkins, presumably on metrical grounds and as a stronger reading.

make . . . me play games with me, trifle with me. Elam points out the association of *dally, pass* and *wanton* in *TN* 3.1.14–43, where the reference to fencing is metaphorical but anticipates the actual duel in 3.4.

284 **Nothing neither way** no advantage on either side (either because there was no hit, or because two hits cancelled each other out)

285 **Have . . . now** Laertes presumably attacks and wounds Hamlet before the next bout should officially begin, though these words at least give him some warning.

285 SD *Sometimes onstage Hamlet realizes that he has been wounded with an *unbated* (302) sword and forces the exchange of weapons; or attendants may pick up the

rapiers that have been dropped and return them to the 'wrong' duellists. However it is managed, Hamlet must get the *unbated* and poisoned rapier from Laertes and wound him with it.

288 **Look . . . ho** Osric calls for other courtiers to help the Queen, who has presumably collapsed (but Jenkins interprets *ho* as a call to stop the combat).

291 **woodcock . . . springe** The woodcock was generally thought to be a stupid bird because it was easy to catch; Laertes unwittingly, but perhaps touchingly, repeats his father's proverb (see 1.3.114 and n.), combining it with another one: 'The fowler is caught in his own net' (Tilley, F626).

springe trap

293 **swoons** collapses, faints. (The King tries desperately to retrieve the situation, as he does again at 308.)

---

282 sure] affear'd *F*   283 SD] *F (Play.); not in Q1*   285 SD] *F; They catch one anothers Rapiers, and both are wounded, Leartes falls downe, the Queene falles downe and dies. Q1*   287 SD] *Capell*   289 is it] is't *F*   291] *F lines* Woodcocke / Osricke, /   own] *om. F*   293 swoons] *(sounds) F, Q5 (swounes)*

QUEEN

No, no, the drink, the drink, O my dear Hamlet,
The drink, the drink – I am poisoned.   [*Dies.*]   295

HAMLET

O villainy, ho! Let the door be locked.
Treachery! Seek it out.   [*Exit Osric.*]

LAERTES

It is here, Hamlet, thou art slain.
No medicine in the world can do thee good:
In thee there is not half an hour's life;   300
The treacherous instrument is in thy hand
Unbated and envenomed. The foul practice
Hath turned itself on me. Lo, here I lie,
Never to rise again. Thy mother's poisoned –
I can no more – the King, the King's to blame.   305

HAMLET

The point envenomed too? Then venom to thy work!
[*Hurts the King.*]

LORDS   Treason, treason!

294–5 In all three texts the Queen calls on Hamlet as she dies, warning him of the poisoned drink.

295 SD *During the eighteenth and nineteenth centuries, the Queen was often carried offstage to die (see O'Brien).

296 **Let . . . locked** Hamlet presumably intends to prevent any perpetrator of treason from escaping. Jenkins and Hibbard also take Osric off at this point (see 333.1 and n.).

298 **Hamlet** F's repetition regularizes the metre.

299 **medicine** i.e. antidote

301 ***thy hand** If Q2's 'my hand' is right, the duellists would have to switch twice to get the poisoned weapon back in Laertes' hand (or the actors could substitute *was*

for *is* in this line).

302 **Unbated** i.e. with its point unprotected (as plotted at 4.7.136)
envenomed anointed with poison
practice stratagem, trick

303 **turned itself** rebounded

305 **can** can say, can do
to blame Q2/F's 'too blame' could mean 'excessively blameworthy' (see 3.1.45n.), but Q2's 'inuenom'd to' in the next line shows that the spellings were interchangeable. The metre here encourages 'to blame', i.e. 'at fault'.

307 **Treason** The lords may be responding directly to Hamlet's attack on the King, or perhaps to what Laertes has just said (see also 309 and n.).

294–5] *F lines* ²drinke. / ⁴drinke, / poyson'd./   295 SD] *Rowe subst.*   296 ho!] *(*how*), Q1 (*ho*), Q3 (*hoe*), F (*How?*)   297 SD] *Ard*ᶠ   298 *F lines* Hamlet. / slaine, / Hamlet,] *Hamlet.* / *Hamlet,* F   300 hour's] houre of *Q1F*   301 thy] *Q1F, Q5;* my *Q2*   306 SD] *F; not in Q21*   307 SP] *Oxf subst.; All. Q2F*

KING

O, yet defend me, friends, I am but hurt.

HAMLET

Here, thou incestuous, damned Dane!
Drink of this potion. Is the union here?   310
Follow my mother.   [*King dies.*]

LAERTES   He is justly served.
It is a poison tempered by himself.
Exchange forgiveness with me, noble Hamlet,
Mine and my father's death come not upon thee,
Nor thine on me.   [*Dies.*]   315

HAMLET

Heaven make thee free of it. I follow thee.
I am dead, Horatio. Wretched Queen, adieu.
You that look pale and tremble at this chance,

309 ***Here** F's reading is supported by the similar repetition in Q1: 'Come drinke, here lies thy union, here.' Q2's 'Heare' is not, however, impossible.
incestuous, damned damnèd; F's 'incestuous, murdrous / Damned' is preferred by Jenkins, perhaps because it regularizes the metre and is more emphatic. In Q2 and F this is the first time that the *incest* accusation has been made publicly (see 1.2.157n.). The courtiers would understand F's 'murdrous' as a reference to the King's actions against Hamlet and the Queen: not even at this point does Hamlet confront the King with the murder of his father.

310 **Drink . . . potion** Hamlet forces the King to drink from the cup (though some must be left for Horatio to try to drink at 326). F's 'Drinke off' is often preferred (and *of* / *off* could simply be a spelling variant), but *Drink of* (i.e. from) seems acceptable.

312 **tempered** prepared, concocted

314 **Mine** my death
come . . . thee i.e. may they not count (at the Last Judgement) as charges against you. Perhaps Laertes means that his own villainy equals and therefore excuses Hamlet's. He dies unaware of the full extent of his accomplice the King's guilt.

315 SD *Strictly speaking, Laertes should die after Hamlet, who was wounded first, but the reversal is obviously required for dramatic reasons. (If a literal explanation is needed, one might assume that Hamlet's wound was more superficial.)

316 **free** i.e. absolved of the guilt (unlike the King)

317 **I am dead** If Hamlet is already 'dead' when he kills the King, this may be Shakespeare's solution to the moral dilemma of the blood-guilt of the successful revenger.
Wretched unhappy

318 **this chance** what has happened here (*chance* in this sense is often negative = mischance)

309 Here] *F;* Heare *Q2*   incestuous] incestuous, murdrous *F*   310 of] off *F*   the] thy *Q1F*   union] *Q1F;* Onixe *Q2*   311 SD] *Q1 subst., F*   311–12] *F; Q2 lines* mother. / himselfe, /   315 SD] *Q1 subst., F*

That are but mutes or audience to this act,
Had I but time (as this fell sergeant Death   320
Is strict in his arrest) – O, I could tell you –
But let it be. Horatio, I am dead.
Thou livest: report me and my cause aright
To the unsatisfied.

HORATIO   Never believe it.
I am more an antique Roman than a Dane: 325
Here's yet some liquor left.

HAMLET   As thou'rt a man
Give me the cup. Let go! By heaven I'll ha't!
O God, Horatio, what a wounded name,
Things standing thus unknown, shall I leave behind
    me!
If thou didst ever hold me in thy heart   330

---

319 **That . . . act** 'that are either mere *auditors* of this *catastrophe*, or at most only *mute performers* that fill the stage without any part in the action' (Johnson)
  act action; performance
320 **as** because, whereas
  fell sergeant cruel officer; Death is seen as arresting Hamlet ('Death is God's sergeant' was proverbial: Dent, D142.2), with the implication that he must appear in court, or perhaps that his destination is the *prison-house* of purgatory described by the Ghost (1.5.14).
321 **strict** precise, rigorous
323 **report . . . aright** i.e. give an accurate account of my experiences and the reasons for my actions. It is left to Horatio to explain the origins of the plot in the murder of old Hamlet.
324 **the unsatisfied** i.e. those who will demand an explanation
325 **antique Roman** Horatio claims to see suicide as heroic, like Shakespeare's Titinius and Brutus (*JC* 5.3.89 and 5.5.56–

7) and like Cleopatra, who aspires to death 'after the high Roman fashion' (*AC* 4.15.91). This attitude is unlike that of the Christians in this play and others such as *KL* (4.6.33–4, 75–7) and *Cym* (3.4.75–7).
326–33 In performance, Hamlet may grapple with Horatio and spill the rest of the poison, or Horatio may assent more quietly to his request.
328 **God** F's 'good' may be a correction, not an expurgation, since Q2 reads 'god' (it normally capitalizes *God*); Honigmann (Ard[3] *Oth*), however, emends Q 1622 *Oth* 'O Good Iago' to 'O God Iago' (4.2.150) on the opposite assumption that the capital there (together with F's alternative 'Alas Iago') indicates expurgation.
  wounded name damaged reputation
329 **shall I leave** F's 'shall liue' is metrically smoother. Hibbard emends to 'I leave', claiming that it 'has a greater urgency than either F or Q2' and that *leaue* is supported by Q1; see t.n.

---

323 livest] liu'st *F*   cause aright] causes right *F*   325 antique] *(anticke), Q1F (*antike), Q5   326–7 As . . . ha't!] *F lines* Cup. / haue't. /   327 ha't] *(hate); haue't *F*   328 God,] *(god); fie *Q1; good *F*
329 shall I leave] wouldst thou leaue *Q1;* shall liue *F*   me!] *(me?); me. *F*

Absent thee from felicity awhile
And in this harsh world draw thy breath in pain
To tell my story. *A march afar off* [*and a sound of shooting*]
        What warlike noise is this?

Enter OSRIC.

OSRIC

Young Fortinbras with conquest come from Poland
To th'ambassadors of England gives   335
This warlike volley.
HAMLET   O, I die, Horatio.
The potent poison quite o'ercrows my spirit,
I cannot live to hear the news from England,
But I do prophesy th'election lights
On Fortinbras: he has my dying voice.   340

---

331 i.e. postpone your journey from this earth
to heaven. Hamlet does not seem troubled
by the consequences of suicide for Horatio
here.

333 SD *F's '*shout*' (see t.n.) is generally taken
as an error for '*shot*': Hamlet's reference to
a *warlike noise* and Osric's to a *warlike
volley* (336) seem to require this, though the
drum referred to by Horatio at 345 could
also be construed as a *warlike noise*, since it
accompanies the march of soldiers. In any
case, the shooting represents Fortinbras's
greeting to the English ambassadors (see
334–6 and *Oth* 2.1.56 and 94) and not (as
sometimes in recent productions and films)
the beginning of an offstage battle.

333.1 Both Q2 and F have Osric enter to
announce the arrival of Fortinbras, though
neither has given him an exit since he
spoke at 290 and was addressed by Laertes
at 291 (see 296n.). Riv leaves him onstage
throughout and at this point inserts a SD,
'*Osric goes to the door and returns*', to

explain how he has acquired the news he
conveys.

335 **th'ambassadors of England** Plural in
both Q2 and F, and plural pronouns are
used in 352–6 although only one of them
speaks. Presumably they are coming to
report the news about the deaths of
Rosencrantz and Guildenstern and we are
to suppose that they have fallen in with
Fortinbras on his return from Poland.

337 **o'ercrows** triumphs over (like a victorious
cockerel: Jennens, who emends to
'o'ergrows', finds the metaphor 'a little too
ludicrous, in this place')

339 **th'election** of a new king of Denmark (see
64 and 1.2.109n.)

340 **dying voice** Words spoken on a person's
deathbed are often seen as particularly
important, and an audience living
under a hereditary monarchy would
suppose that Hamlet, having been
named as the King's heir, would have
the right to nominate his own. Having

---

333 SD *A . . . off.*] *(opp 332–3); not in Q1; March afarre off, F   and . . . shooting*] Steevens subst.; not in
Q21; and shout within. F   333.1] F; not in Q1

So tell him with th'occurrents more and less
Which have solicited. – The rest is silence.   [*Dies.*]
HORATIO
Now cracks a noble heart. Goodnight, sweet Prince,
And flights of angels sing thee to thy rest.
Why does the drum come hither?   345

Enter FORTINBRAS *with* [*his train and*] *the* Ambassadors.

FORTINBRAS
Where is this sight?

been born on the day that old Hamlet overcame old Fortinbras, young Hamlet makes restitution to young Fortinbras as he dies. (*Voice* is used here in the sense of 'vote', as in *Cor* 2.3.)

341 **th'occurrents ... less** all the events, of major and minor importance

342 **solicited** incited (i.e. me to give him my support): the sentence is unfinished.
The rest is silence *Rest* = residue, remainder, repose, but this might be heard as a pun, 'th'arrest': see *arrest* in 321. F's 'O, o, o, o' is a conventional indication of a dying groan or sigh, as at *KL* 5.3.308.

343–4 It is perhaps implied that these are the first two lines of what might have been a longer eulogy, had Horatio not been interrupted by the arrival of Fortinbras.

343 **Now ... heart** It was supposed that the heart-strings cracked at the point of death; see *R3* 4.4.365, 'Harp on it [that string] still shall I, till heart-strings break.' Shakespeare develops the idea into a nautical metaphor at the death of King John: 'The tackle of my heart is crack'd and burn'd, / And all the shrouds wherewith my life should sail / Are turned to one thread, one little hair' (*KJ* 5.7.52–4).

344 **flights** flying companies
angels As Greenblatt points out (*Purgatory*, 51–4), angels frequently appear in depictions of purgatory, assisting in the deliverance of souls; indeed, their very presence signals that the place depicted is purgatory rather than hell.

345 **drum** Fortinbras's entry is heralded by the sound of a military drum. F's SD specifies that he enters with a drummer and a standard bearer, regular features of military entrances found in over 90 plays (Dessen & Thomson, 'drum').

345.1 Fortinbras is in armour or some kind of military uniform, perhaps deliberately recalling the martial appearance of the Ghost in Act 1. Q1 adds Voltemar (*sic*) to this entry, which may indicate that the actor who played Voltemand in 1.2 and 2.2 is now playing the English Ambassador (see Appendix 5). Q1's '*train*' of soldiers (or F's '*Attendants*') are necessary for the removal of the bodies (see 385 and n.). Sometimes, most spectacularly in Branagh's 1996 film, Fortinbras and his men arrive as a sinister, invading force.

346 **this sight** Fortinbras has apparently been warned (by Osric?) what to expect. Q1 is even more explicit (see t.n.).

341 th'occurrents] the occurrents *F*   342 silence.] silence. O, o, o, o. *F*   SD] *Q1 subst., F* 343] *F* lines heart: / Prince /   cracks] cracke *F*   345.1 his train] *Q1; Drumme, Colours, and Attendants. F   and the Ambassadors*] Voltemar and the Ambassadors from England. *Q1; and English Ambassador F* 346 sight] *F;* bloudy sight *Q1*   you] ye *F*

HORATIO   What is it you would see?
  If aught of woe or wonder, cease your search.
FORTINBRAS
    This quarry cries on havoc. O proud Death,
    What feast is toward in thine eternal cell
    That thou so many princes at a shot   350
    So bloodily hast struck?
AMBASSADOR   The sight is dismal
    And our affairs from England come too late.
    The ears are senseless that should give us hearing
    To tell him his commandment is fulfilled
    That Rosencrantz and Guildenstern are dead.   355
    Where should we have our thanks?
HORATIO   Not from his mouth,
    Had it th'ability of life to thank you;
    He never gave commandment for their death.
    But, since so jump upon this bloody question
    You from the Polack wars and you from England   360
    Are here arrived, give order that these bodies
    High on a stage be placed to the view,

---

348 **This ... havoc** This pile of bodies
   proclaims that there has been a massacre.
   Quarry is a term used for the slaughtered
   animals after a hunt, as at *Cor* 1.1.197.
   Havoc is a battle-cry inciting soldiers to
   slaughter and destruction, as at *JC* 3.1.273.
349 **feast** Death is also personified as one who
   feasts on his victims in *KJ* 2.2.352–5 and
   in *RJ* 5.3.45–8.
   toward being prepared, going forward
   eternal 'Shakespeare occasionally uses
   this word as if it meant "damnable" or
   "infernal" ' (Edwards). See also 1.5.21
   and n.
351 **dismal** dreadful, disastrous (a stronger
   meaning than the modern one)
352 **affairs** business
353 **The ears** i.e. those of the King; an

appropriate way of saying that the King
is dead, given the play's obsession
with literal and metaphorical *ears* – see
1.1.30n.
356 **Where** i.e. from whom. The Ambassador
   is in effect enquiring who is now King of
   Denmark.
   his i.e. the King's
359 **jump upon** immediately after
   question quarrel, conflict
361 **give order** Fortinbras, with his conquering
   army (334), is in a position to do so.
362 **a stage** some kind of platform; Q1 has
   'a scaffold'. Steevens quotes the end
   of Arthur Brooke's *Romeus and Juliet*
   (a major source for Shakespeare's *RJ*):
   'The prince did straight ordaine, the
   corses that wer founde, / Should be set

348 This] His *F*   350 shot] shoote *F*

491

And let me speak to th' yet unknowing world
How these things came about. So shall you hear
Of carnal, bloody and unnatural acts,   365
Of accidental judgements, casual slaughters,
Of deaths put on by cunning, and for no cause,
And in this upshot purposes mistook
Fallen on th'inventors' heads. All this can I
Truly deliver.
FORTINBRAS   Let us haste to hear it   370

forth vpon a stage hye raysed from the ground' (2817–18; Bullough, 1.358).
placed placèd

363 **let me speak** We may imagine Horatio addressing the Danes and others, rather as Brutus and Antony address the Romans in *JC* 3.2.

364–9 **So ... heads** Horatio's list covers, without necessarily itemizing, most of the play's crimes and deaths; some of them could be placed in more than one category. Several critics have found the vagueness and generality of this account unsatisfactory: Horatio fails to give the onstage audience any of the specific details (about the death of old Hamlet, or the King's plots against young Hamlet, for example) that are known to the theatre audience or reader. Perhaps a feeling that this speech is somewhat equivocal (is Horatio waiting to see how Fortinbras will react?) helped to inspire some of the play's sequels in which he turns out to be secretly in league with Norway (see pp. 134–5).

365 **carnal ... acts** Horatio may agree with Hamlet in seeing the marriage of the King and Queen as incestuous, therefore *carnal* (sensual, motivated by lust); he may be thinking of the King's murder of his brother as *bloody and unnatural*.

366 **accidental judgements** judgements or punishments brought about by accident.

The death of Polonius might be viewed in this light, as well as the deaths of the Queen and Laertes.

casual slaughters killings brought about by chance

367 **put ... cunning** instigated, set up by plot or strategy. This could cover the deaths of Rosencrantz and Guildenstern as well as that of Hamlet.

for no cause This apparently repeats the idea of *casual slaughters*. F's 'forc'd cause' is generally preferred, meaning 'false or contrived cause' – a possible allusion to the King's attempt to have Hamlet executed in England.

368 **this upshot** this climax or conclusion. An *upshot* is literally the final shoot-off to decide the winner in an archery contest.

368–9 **purposes ... heads** See Hamlet's view, 'For 'tis the sport to have the enginer / Hoist with his own petard' (3.4.204–5); his *defeat* (57) of Rosencrantz and Guildenstern could fall into this category, as could Laertes' death 'as a woodcock to mine own springe' (291), and ultimately the death of the King.

370 **deliver** report, narrate

370–1 **Let ... audience** Fortinbras assumes that they will repair to some other more public location to hear Horatio's story – which gives the actors a reason to leave the stage.

363 th'yet] *F*; yet *Q2*   367 for no] forc'd *F*   369 th'inventors'] the Inuentors *F*

And call the noblest to the audience.
For me, with sorrow I embrace my fortune.
I have some rights of memory in this kingdom
Which now to claim my vantage doth invite me.

HORATIO

Of that I shall have also cause to speak   375
And from his mouth whose voice will draw no more.
But let this same be presently performed
Even while men's minds are wild, lest more mischance
On plots and errors happen.

FORTINBRAS   Let four captains
Bear Hamlet like a soldier to the stage,   380
For he was likely, had he been put on,

372–4 Fortinbras's careful balance of his *sorrow* against his eagerness to *embrace my fortune* recalls the King's similar balance between *wisest sorrow* and *remembrance of ourselves* in his opening speech at 1.2.6–7.

372 **fortune** good luck

373 **rights of memory** unforgotten or immemorial rights (?). Fortinbras is claiming (at least) the lands forfeited by his father to the elder Hamlet (see 1.1.79–94). Thanks to the actions of the King and Laertes, he is spared any obligation to revenge his father's death on the younger Hamlet.

374 **my vantage** my advantageous position

376 **whose . . . no more** Q2's reading must mean 'who has ceased to draw breath'. F's 'whose . . . on more' ('whose support will encourage further votes'; see 340 and n.) is generally accepted (e.g. by Jenkins), but it is arguable that Horatio is focused on his dead friend at this point, not on the likelihood of Fortinbras's election.

377 **this same** i.e. the public exhibition of the bodies and the permission to speak about

what has happened that Horatio requested at 361–4.

presently immediately

378 **wild** disturbed, excited

379 **On** either 'on top of' or 'arising from'

four captains Four bearers was a standard requirement for a ceremonial exit or entrance with a body, as in '*They march out with the body of the King, lying on four men's shoulders with a dead march, drawing weapons on the ground*' (Marlowe, *The Massacre at Paris*, 1593; 1.1623) or '*Enter funeral. Body borne by four Captains and Soldiers*' (Philip Massinger and Nathan Field, *The Fatal Dowry*, 1619, 2.1.47).

380–4 **Bear . . . him** In contrast to the *hugger mugger* or *obscure* burial of Polonius (4.5.84, 205) and the *maimed rites* of Ophelia (5.1.208), Hamlet is to be given a proper funeral ceremony, though it may be questionable whether a military one is appropriate.

380 **stage** See 362 and n.

381 **put on** given the opportunity (to rule as king)

---

373 rights] *Q1;* Rites *F*   374] *Q1 subst.; F lines* doth / me, / now] *Q1;* are *F*   claim] *Q1;* claime, *F*   vantage] *F;* leisure *Q1*   375 also] alwayes *F*   376] *F lines* mouth / more: /   no] on *F* 378] *F lines* wilde, / mischance /   while] whiles *F*

To have proved most royal. And for his passage
The soldiers' music and the rite of war
Speak loudly for him.
Take up the bodies. Such a sight as this   385
Becomes the field but here shows much amiss.
Go, bid the soldiers shoot.   *Exeunt.*

FINIS

382 **passage** passing (from life to death)

383 **soldiers' music** the drum that accompanies the captains marching off with the body; see Benedick's characterization of Claudio as a soldier in *MA*: 'I have known when there was no music with him but the drum and the fife' (2.3.13–14).

   ***rite of war** sound of gunshot (?). Edwards prefers Q2's 'right' to F 'rites' on the grounds that Shakespeare often uses *rite* in the singular.

384 **Speak** (imperative)

385 **bodies** See 387 SDn. Q1/F's 'bodie' presumably refers to Hamlet's body – 'the rest must lie and rot where they were' (Jennens). Hibbard follows Q2.

386 **Becomes the field** is appropriate to the battlefield

   shows much amiss is most out of place

387 'The end is a half-line after a riming [*sic*] couplet – as if there were more to come – as there must be after every tragedy' (MacDonald).

387 SD All four bodies (those of Hamlet, the King, the Queen and Laertes) would presumably have been carried off at this point; a modern production can bring down a curtain or dim the stage lights.

382] *F lines* royally: / passage, / have] *F;* a *Q1*   royal] *Q1;* royally *F*   383 rite] *Cam¹, Ard²;* right *Q2;* rites *F*   385 bodies] bodie *Q1F*   387 SD] *not in Q1; Exeunt Marching: after the which, a Peale of / Ordenance are shot off. F*

APPENDIX 1
Folio-Only Passages

This appendix contains text, textual notes and commentary for the Folio-only passages of three lines or more. These are the following four (amounting to a total of about 77 lines): F 2.2.238–67; 2.2.335–60; 4.1.159–61; and 5.2.68–81. Briefer Folio-only passages are covered in the commentary notes and/or the textual notes; see, for example, notes at 2.1.51; 2.2.208–9, 288–9, 334–5; 3.2.109–10, 128.1–11, 258–9; 3.4.5; 4.2.28; 4.3.42; 4.5.96; 4.7.37; 5.1.33, 100, 171, 172 and 174; 5.2.56 and 217.

References throughout are to the Q2 text in this edition, unless otherwise stated.

(1) F 2.2.238–2.2.267 (follows the equivalent of Q2 2.2.235 'true')

HAMLET . . . Let me question more in particular. What have you, my good friends, deserved at the hands of Fortune that she sends you to prison hither?

GUILDENSTERNE Prison, my lord?

HAMLET Denmark's a prison. 5

ROSINCRANCE Then is the world one.

HAMLET A goodly one, in which there are many confines, wards and dungeons – Denmark being one o'th' worst.

ROSINCRANCE We think not so, my lord. 10

HAMLET Why, then 'tis none to you; for there is nothing either good or bad, but thinking makes it so. To me it is a prison.

ROSINCRANCE Why, then your ambition makes it one: 'tis too narrow for your mind. 15

HAMLET O God, I could be bounded in a nutshell and count myself a king of infinite space – were it not that I have bad dreams.

---

(1) It is generally supposed (e.g. by Jenkins and Edwards) that these lines were omitted from Q2 because of the offence they might cause to Anne of Denmark, wife of James I, but Hibbard argues that they could have been added in F to 'bring out more fully the evasiveness of Rosencrantz and Guildenstern' (Oxf¹, 112). The concept of the whole state as a prison dominated a number of productions of *Hamlet* in the former Soviet Union and eastern Europe during communist rule, most notably exemplified by the 'Iron Curtain *Hamlet*' directed by Nikolai Okhlopkov in Moscow in 1954 (see Stříbrný, 100); it is prominent in the Russian film directed by Grigori Kozintsev in 1964 (see p. 118 and Fig. 18).

4, 6, SPs Guildensterne and Rosincrance are F's consistent spellings.

7 **confines** places of confinement

8 **wards** divisions or departments within a prison

11–12 **there . . . so** i.e. whether Denmark seems like a prison or not depends on your mental attitude. See Jenkins, LN, where he quotes other examples of this commonplace, such as *FQ*, 6.9.30: 'It is the mind that maketh good or ill, / That maketh wretch or happy', and refers to the proverbial 'A man is weal or woe as he thinks himself so' (Tilley, M254).

18 **bad dreams** 'As nothing develops from *bad* in the subsequent dialogue, emendation to "had" is attractive' (Spencer). Jenkins, however, notes that bad dreams were a recognized symptom of melancholia.

GUILDENSTERNE Which dreams, indeed, are ambition;
for the very substance of the ambitious is merely the   20
shadow of a dream.

HAMLET A dream itself is but a shadow.

ROSINCRANCE Truly, and I hold ambition of so airy and
light a quality that it is but a shadow's shadow.

HAMLET Then are our beggars bodies, and our monarchs   25
and outstretched heroes the beggars' shadows. Shall we
to th' Court? For, by my fay, I cannot reason.

ROSINCRANCE, GUILDENSTERNE We'll wait upon you.

HAMLET No such matter. I will not sort you with the rest
of my servants, for, to speak to you like an honest man,   30
I am most dreadfully attended.

20–1 **the very ... dream** variously glossed according to whether *very substance* is taken to mean the ambitious people themselves (Jenkins, Hibbard), or the material they live on (Edwards). Either way, Guildenstern seems to be dismissing both ambitious people and their ambitions as insubstantial. This turn of the conversation is reminiscent of the moment in *R2* when Bolingbroke suggests to Richard that 'The shadow of your sorrow hath destroy'd / The shadow of your face' (4.1.292–3), and it recalls Hamlet's insistence on the difference between the appearance and the reality of grief at 1.2.76–86.

25–6 **Then ... shadows** Hamlet seems to be saying that *beggars* alone have *bodies* (because they are not ambitious), while *monarchs* and *outstretched heroes* are merely *shadows* (because they are ambitious). It is not clear why the *monarchs* should be *the beggars' shadows*, but the social reversal implied is comparable to Hamlet's musing at 4.3.29–30 on 'how a king may go a progress through the guts of a beggar'. (Jenkins sees this speech as deliberately absurd; Hibbard quotes Coleridge: 'I do not understand this.')

26 **outstretched** extended (either in their own ambition or in the praise of others). The word may also apply to the *shadows* themselves.

26–7 **Shall ... th' Court** a slightly puzzling suggestion, since we assume from the opening of the scene that it is located at the royal *Court*. Hamlet may mean something like 'Shall we go to the royal presence?' Or perhaps *Court* means lawcourt, where this kind of quibbling would be appropriate.

27 **fay** faith

28 **wait upon** accompany, escort (but with a sense of 'serve')

29–30 **No ... servants** As in his encounter with Horatio, Marcellus and Barnardo at the end of 1.2, Hamlet claims to treat his companions as friends rather than servants.

29 **sort** classify

31 **dreadfully attended** deplorably waited on (by my servants). But Hamlet could also be referring metaphorically to his *bad dreams*; MacDonald and Adams suggest that he is referring to the King's spies, of whom Hamlet now knows that Rosincrance and Guildensterne are two.

(2) F 2.2.335–2.2.360 (follows Q2 2.2.299)

HAMLET   How comes it? Do they grow rusty?

ROSINCRANCE   Nay, their endeavour keeps in the wonted
pace. But there is, sir, an eyrie of children, little eyases
that cry out on the top of question and are most
tyrannically clapped for't. These are now the fashion,   5
and so berattle the common stages (so they call them)
that many wearing rapiers are afraid of goose-quills
and dare scarce come thither.

HAMLET   What, are they children? Who maintains 'em?

---

(2) Jenkins (LN) argues that these lines were
cut from Q2 because the so-called 'war of
the theatres' between the adult acting
companies and the Children of the Chapel,
who began performing at the Blackfriars
theatre around 1600, was no longer topical
by 1604; by the same token, it was even
less topical in 1623. Bednarz (248),
however, points out that by 1604 the
Children had become the Children of Her
Majesty's Chapel under the patronage of
Queen Anne, so this might be another
'diplomatic' cut, like the reference to
Denmark as a prison in passage 1. Hibbard
again suggests that the passage could, like
the prison one, be a deliberate addition. In
this case the purpose would be to enhance
the analogy between the fickleness of the
theatre audiences, who prefer the novelty
of the boy actors, and that of the Danish
population, who prefer the new King to
Hamlet's father.

1   **Do . . . rusty?** i.e. have their skills become
impaired or obsolete?

2–3   **their . . . pace** i.e. their efforts continue in
the same way as before (*wonted pace* =
literally, usual speed or style)

3   **eyrie** generation or brood; literally, the nest
of any bird of prey
eyases children; literally, young, untrained
hawks

4   **cry . . . question** i.e. make a louder
noise than others involved in the
controversy

5   **tyrannically** vehemently, excessively

6   ***berattle** assail with noise, clamour
against. F2's 'be ratle' is generally
preferred to F's 'be-ratled', since it is in
parallel with the other present tense verbs
in this passage and misreading of final *e*/*d*
is an easy error.
common stages public theatres (like the
Globe). The adult actors played in the
large open-air amphitheatres which were
relatively cheap for the audience; the boys
played in smaller indoor theatres which
were relatively expensive and hence
sometimes designated 'private'.
(so . . . them) Rosincrance seems to
dissociate himself from this expression
which, as Jenkins points out, is used
contemptuously in Ben Jonson's *Cynthia's
Revels* (1600) at Induction, 182, and
4.3.118.

7   **many wearing rapiers** i.e. many
fashionable young men
goose-quills pens. The assumption in 5–7
is that the poets who write for the boys'
companies have deterred the fashionable
young men from attending the *common
stages* (by attacking either the theatres or
their audiences).

---

3 eyases] *(Yases)*   6 berattle] *F2 (*be ratle*); be-ratled *F*

How are they escotted? Will they pursue the quality no   10
longer than they can sing? Will they not say afterwards
if they should grow themselves to common players – as
it is most like if their means are no better – their
writers do them wrong to make them exclaim against
their own succession?   15

ROSINCRANCE   Faith, there has been much to-do on both
sides, and the nation holds it no sin to tar them to
controversy. There was for a while no money bid for
argument unless the poet and the player went to cuffs
in the question.   20

HAMLET   Is't possible?

---

10   **escotted** provided for
    pursue the quality follow the profession
    (of acting)
10–11   **no . . . sing** only until their voices break.
    This was the point at which a boy actor
    might normally become an adult actor.
    There is much emphasis on the importance
    of a high voice for the boys playing female
    roles in the adult companies, e.g. in *TN*,
    when Orsino tells Viola/Cesario, 'thy small
    pipe / Is as the maiden's organ, shrill and
    sound' (1.4.32–3), and in the frequent
    references to 'speaking small' (e.g. *MND*
    1.2.47 and *MW* 1.1.44).
12   **to** into
13   ***most like** Like Hibbard, we follow Pope's
    emendation; Cam¹ and Oxf print 'like most
    will'.
    if . . . better if they have no better way of
    making a living. (F reads *no better*, though
    an inking space makes it look like *not
    better*, the F2 reading adopted by Cam¹.)
14–15   **exclaim . . . succession** rail at their own
    future profession. Nathan Field and John
    Underwood, who had appeared as child
    actors in *Cynthia's Revels*, and William
    Ostler, who had appeared in Jonson's

Poetaster (1601), did indeed later join the
King's Men as adults. One might also
note that Richard Burbage, the first
performer of the role of Hamlet, was in
effect the landlord of the boys' company at
the Blackfriars, creating another layer of
topical allusion for early audiences.
16   **to-do** bustle, turmoil
16–17   **on both sides** This most obviously
    means on the sides of both the *children* (3)
    and the *common players* (12), but Jenkins
    suggests a more specific opposition
    between Jonson, who wrote *Cynthia's
    Revels* for the Children of the Chapel, and
    Thomas Dekker, who wrote *Satiromastix*
    (1601) for the Lord Chamberlain's
    Company in retaliation. Bednarz (255–6
    and 275–6) dates this passage after the
    performance of Jonson's *Poetaster* in 1601.
17   **holds . . . sin** i.e. doesn't scruple
    tar provoke, incite (used elsewhere of dog-
    fights)
18–19   **no . . . argument** i.e. no fee paid by a
    theatre company for a new plot or draft of a
    play
19–20   **went . . . question** became violently
    involved in the dispute

---

13   most like] *Pope;* like most *F;* like most will, *Cam (anon)*   16 to-do] *(to do)*

499

GUILDENSTERNE   O, there has been much throwing about
    of brains.
HAMLET   Do the boys carry it away?
ROSINCRANCE   Ay, that they do, my lord – Hercules and   25
    his load too.

22–3 **throwing** ... **brains** expenditure of
    mental effort
24 **carry it away** emerge as the winners
25–6 **Hercules** ... **load** The sign of the Globe
    theatre was Hercules carrying the world on
    his shoulders (according to Steevens and
    Malone), so Shakespeare seems to be
    conceding victory to *the boys*. There was
    no serious danger that the Chamberlain's
Men could be driven from London at this
point, though the competition for the
higher-paying members of the audience
may have been real enough. Since the
Theatre was rebuilt and renamed as
the Globe in 1599, this passage has
implications for dating, though it is found
only in F (see pp. 52–4).

(3) F 4.1.159–4.1.161 (follows Q2 4.5.159)

LAERTES

  . . . Nature is fine in love, and where 'tis fine
It sends some precious instance of itself
After the thing it loves.

(3) These lines have been much criticized –
from Johnson, who called them 'obscure
and affected', to Edwards, who says the
'conceit [is] too absurd even for Laertes'.
Jenkins includes them and offers the
paraphrase: 'Human nature, when in love,
is exquisitely sensitive, and being so, it
sends a precious part of itself as a token to
follow the object of its love.' He notes that,
while the most obvious reference is to
Ophelia's love for her father, it could also
apply to her love for Hamlet. Norton
offers: 'Laertes struggles to say that
because of Ophelia's great love for her
father, her sanity departed with him.'

(4) F 5.2.68–5.2.81 (follows Q2 5.2.66)

HAMLET

> . . . To quit him with this arm? And is't not to be
> damned
> To let this canker of our nature come
> In further evil?

HORATIO

> It must be shortly known to him from England
> What is the issue of the business there.   5

HAMLET

> It will be short. The interim's mine,
> And a man's life's no more than to say one.
> But I am very sorry, good Horatio,
> That to Laertes I forgot myself,
> For by the image of my cause I see   10

---

(4) 'The absence of these lines from Q2 is difficult to explain except as an accidental omission' (Jenkins). Edwards and Hibbard both argue that they are part of an authorial revision.

1   **quit** requite, repay

damned condemned to hell. In the F reading, this picks up *perfect conscience* in Q2 5.2.66: Hamlet is arguing that it is morally justifiable to take revenge on the King and that it would be damnable to let him continue.

2   **canker** ulcer, sore (formerly the same as 'cancer')

of our nature i.e. of the human race

2–3 **come / In** enter into, commit

4–5 As at 5.2.56, Horatio's response can be performed (and read) as a relatively neutral comment, not the endorsement Hamlet seems to be seeking.

6   **It** presumably *The interim*, i.e. the time between the present moment and the enacting of Hamlet's revenge

interim's Thus F. Since Hanmer, many editors (including Jenkins and Hibbard) have emended to *interim is*, which regularizes the metre, but, as Edwards points out, there is no authority for this.

7   **a man's . . . one** a man's life is no longer than the time it takes to say *one*. Dent cites 'Man (Life) is but a figure of one' as proverbial (O50.1).

9   **I forgot myself** i.e. I behaved badly; as is clear from 12–13, Hamlet is regretting his words and actions at Ophelia's grave in 5.1.

10–11 **by . . . his** i.e. by thinking about my own obligation to revenge I recognize the same pattern in him. Despite this perception, Hamlet does not seem to see Laertes as a threat – a testimony to his nature as 'remiss / Most generous, and free from all contriving', as the King put it at 4.7.132–3. (See also Perdita at *WT* 4.4.384–5: 'By th' pattern of mine own thoughts I cut out / The purity of his.')

6–8] *Hanmer; F lines* short, / more / Horatio, /

The portraiture of his. I'll count his favours;
But sure the bravery of his grief did put me
Into a towering passion.

Enter young OSRICKE.

HORATIO   Peace, who comes here?

---

11   **count his favours** 'take note of, think
about, his favourable characteristics (*OED*
favour *sb.* 8)' (Oxf¹). Since Rowe, many
editors (including Edwards and Oxf) have
emended to 'court his favours' (which
could indeed describe the intention of
Hamlet's speech at 5.2.204–21). Jennens
notes that '*court* is not so proper a
word for *Hamlet*, when applied to his
inferior, *Laertes*', but deliberate humility is
presumably the point, and is indeed
displayed when they meet.

12   **bravery** extravagance

13.1 ***young*** OSRICKE F is alone in naming
Osricke in SDs and SPs; Q2 identifies
'*young Ostricke*' retrospectively in lines
missing from F (see 5.2.66n.) and both
Q2 and F have the King address '*young
Os(t)ricke*' later (see 236 and List of Roles
18n).

13.1] *(after 81) young* OSRICKE] *a Bragart Gentleman Q1; a Courtier Q2*

APPENDIX 2
The Nature of the Texts

THE EARLY PRINTED TEXTS

We have already provided a general account of the 'The composition of *Hamlet*' in the Introduction to this volume (pp. 76–96), briefly describing the history of the printed texts attributed to Shakespeare and the editorial principles and practice we have adopted in producing a modernized edition of the three earliest printed texts. In this appendix we offer a more detailed account of that history, explain our reasons for printing three texts when almost all previous editors have printed one, and describe how we have tackled particular editorial issues such as lineation and punctuation.

The early quartos

Only two copies of the 1603 Quarto (Q1) have survived and both came to general attention in the nineteenth century.[1] One, which lacks the final leaf, was discovered in 1823 by Sir Henry Bunbury at Barton in England,[2] subsequently became the property of the Duke of Devonshire and is now to be found in the Huntington Library in San Marino, California. The other, which lacks the title-page, was acquired in 1856 by a Dublin bookseller, who got it from a student at Trinity College, who in turn had brought it from his home in the English Midlands (probably Nottinghamshire or Leicestershire) three years

---

1 Perhaps there was a third. John Payne Collier claimed to have been offered a 'large portion of a copy' in the mid-1840s (*Athenaeum*, 4 October 1856, 1120–11), but it has never been traced.
2 In 1866 W.G. Clark and W.A. Wright referred to a note by Bunbury which gave the date of his discovery as 1821 (Cam, Preface to 8.vii).

earlier. It was bought from the Dublin bookseller by the bibliophile and scholar James Orchard Halliwell, who sold it to the British Museum in 1858. It is now in the British Library in London. In 2001 Arthur and Janet Ing Freeman filled in a little of the earlier history of this second copy, by producing evidence that the handwritten notes on some interleavings were made by an owner probably at some time between 1718 and 1733 (Freeman, 349–63). In spite of the absence of a title-page, this annotator had worked out that his or her book pre-dated any other known edition of the play.

In fact, neither of the extant copies of Q1 is complete, for the Huntington Library copy lacks the last leaf (I4), and therefore the closing lines of dialogue. But they differ in other ways too. Elizabethan printers made corrections as sheets came off the press, and, rather than waste paper, they were usually content to bind a mixture of both corrected and uncorrected states of the printed sheets to make up copies for sale. In the case of Q1, there are nine minor variants resulting from such proof-correction,[1] with all the corrected states being found only in the British Library copy.[2] All the corrections are in two formes (B outer and B inner), all are in the first two scenes, all but one are in the second scene, and none is substantive – that is, none affects the meaning of a passage. They are listed at the end of this appendix in Table 1.

The title-page of the Huntington Library copy of the First Quarto reads:

1 We have consulted both copies. Bernice Kliman has proposed a tenth variant in F inner, at F3^v.13 – 'more,' in the Huntington Library (HN) copy, corrected to 'more' in the British Library (L) copy (undated erratum slip in Bertram 1991). It is not entirely clear from the L copy that there is no trace of a comma, and identical spacing in the two copies strongly suggests the presence of a comma that has not inked in this copy, although it did in the HN copy.
2 It is, of course, a matter of deduction that a variant is an uncorrected or a corrected state (Irace, 30).

THE
Tragicall Historie of
HAMLET
Prince of Denmarke
By William Shake-speare.
As it hath beene diuerse times acted by his Highnesse ser-
uants in the Cittie of London: as also in the two V-
niuersities of Cambridge and Oxford, and else-where
[device (McKerrow 301)]
At London printed for N.L. and Iohn Trundell.
1603.

This tells us that John Trundle and Nicholas Ling were the publishers (the device is Ling's), and the headpiece at the beginning of the text indicates that the printer was Valentine Simmes. However, the copyright to *Hamlet* seems to have belonged to another stationer, James Roberts, who on 26 July of the previous year had registered 'A booke called the Revenge of Hamlett Prince Denmarke as yt was latelie Acted by the Lo: Chamberleyn his servantes' (Arber, 3.212). Roberts appears nowhere on Q1's title-page, and it would therefore seem that the 1603 edition was printed and published by persons with no rights to do so. Consequently, the First Quarto has often been described as 'pirated'. On the other hand, Roberts had a long history of working with Ling, was experiencing one of the busiest years in his career, and may well have been happy for someone else to do the work (Kastan, 27–30).

The 1603 Quarto has few admirers. Most readers find it awkward and often poorly written, and since 1909 it has suffered from being labelled by A.W. Pollard a 'bad quarto', a label devised to categorize playtexts that in his opinion had been reconstructed from memory (Pollard, 64–80). Those brought up on the better-known versions of the play are almost bound to find Q1 a disconcerting reading experience, since, in terms of both structure and language, it mixes familiar with unfamiliar material. When it was first reprinted in 1825, people initially believed they were reading Shakespeare's early draft of a play that was to become famous in a later, quite different, form. There are still scholars who would support this theory, but their view soon began to lose ground to those who saw Q1 as the work of others, either plagiarists or members of Shakespeare's own company ('his Highnesse seruants'). Opinions are still divided over the text's authorship and the nature of its printer's copy, although more scholars believe that it is a 'reported text' (i.e. a reconstruction of an original text by someone other than the author) rather than entirely Shakespeare's work.

As for the process by which a supposedly reported text would have been constructed, there is no consensus here either. Laurie E. Maguire, for example, has examined the theory that Q1 is a 'memorial reconstruction',[1] i.e. an attempt to reconstruct the play largely from memory. She is not entirely convinced but can see that a case can be made (Maguire, 325). Gary Taylor, however, is convinced, and argues from the 'mature' elements within the 'extreme variability in its verbal quality' that the text lying behind Q1 is the text lying behind the Folio text of 1623 (*TxC*, 398). His is the prevalent view, but Albert Weiner (48) and Robert E. Burkhart (23) believe that Q1 is not a memorial reconstruction but an adaptation for touring (to 'Cambridge and Oxford, and elsewhere') with a small troupe of actors.[2] Kathleen O. Irace combines these theories and concludes that touring members of Shakespeare's company reconstructed from memory a script they had originally performed in the Globe (Irace, 19–20) and adapted it to suit a less sophisticated provincial audience. It is important to record here that, whoever wrote it and however it came to be printed, for more than a century now the Q1 text has occasionally been performed and

1 The phrase was coined by W.W. Greg (Greg, *Merry Wives*, xxvii).
2 But see Appendix 5 for a consideration whether or not Q1 needs a smaller cast than Q2 or F.

has found some favour with theatre audiences both provincial and metropolitan.[1]

In 1604 Roberts began to print a second edition of *Hamlet*. Seven copies of this quarto have survived. Its title-page reads:

THE
Tragicall Historie of
HAMLET,
Prince of Denmarke.
By William Shakespeare.
Newly imprinted and enlarged to almost as much
againe as it was, according to the true and perfect
Coppie.
[device (McKerrow 301)]
AT LONDON,
Printed by I.R. for N.L. and are to be sold at his
shoppe vnder Saint Dunstons Church in
Fleetstreet.

The title and author have not changed, but Q2's text is certainly 'enlarged to almost as much againe as it was' in Q1, and there is a suggestion here that Q1's text might not have been 'true and perfect'.

Three copies, all of them currently to be found in the United States, carry the date '1604'.[2] The other four extant copies, all currently in Europe, carry the date '1605' (it seems that the printing process continued into the new year and someone altered the date while the final sheet was at press).[3] At least

---

1   See Ard Q1/F. As RP points out, however, the 'novelty factor' has to be acknowledged and there are no signs that Q1 will become the preferred stage text.
2   They are the Jennens–Howe copy in the Folger Library in Washington, DC, the Kemble–Devonshire copy in the Huntington Library in San Marino, California, and the Huth copy in the Elizabethan Club collection of the Beinecke Library at Yale University, New Haven, Connecticut.
3   These four are David Garrick's copy (lacking the final leaf) in the British Library, Edward Capell's copy in Trinity College, Cambridge, the so-called 'Gorhambury'

twenty-six variants are to be found in these seven copies (see Table 2).[1] The editor of a modernized text has little difficulty with those where an error has clearly been corrected (as at 5.1.287, where 'thirtie' is corrected to 'thereby') or miscorrected (as at 3.1.160, where the corrector mistakenly introduces the SD *'Exit.'*), or those which merely involve spelling (as at 1.3.69, where 'by' is corrected to 'buy'). But some involve difficult choices over meaning (e.g. where 'pall' is corrected to 'fall' at 5.2.9; 'sellingly' to 'fellingly' at 5.2.95; 'dosie' to 'dazzie' at 5.2.99; 'yaw' to 'raw' at 5.2.100; 'too't' to 'doo't' at 5.2.111; or 'sir' to 'so sir' at 5.2.167) and, while the uncorrected 'Vnice' at 5.2.249 may not be a meaningful alternative to the corrected 'Onixe', it may nevertheless be closer to the word in the manuscript, which could well have been 'Vnion'.

Editors' decisions can be affected by their beliefs about, among other things, the identity of the compositors who set the printed text they are dealing with. In 1955 John Russell Brown analysed the spellings of a small number of words in Q2 and concluded that Q2 had two compositors, with two different spelling habits (Brown, 17–40).[2] The compositor whom he called

copy belonging to the Earl of Verulam, in the Bodleian Library, Oxford, and, finally, a copy in Poland which was mis-catalogued in the Municipal Library in Wroclaw until it came to light in 1959 but which now belongs to the University of Wroclaw.

1 See Bertram–Kliman[2]. We have also personally consulted and collated five copies, and used the MIT Shakespeare Electronic Archive to collate the other two (Oxford and Wroclaw). John Dover Wilson (Wilson, *Manuscript*) identified eighteen variants across only seven formes, but he was unaware of the existence of the Wroclaw copy, did not personally consult all the others, and was not entirely accurate in his descriptions of what he did find. In 1964, having looked at a photocopy of the Wroclaw quarto, Charlton Hinman thought he might have found two new variants, one in inner K and the other in outer L (Greg, *Second Quarto*, 'Note', 2nd impression). But in 1982 Harold Jenkins, having inspected the copy, ruled these out (Ard[2], 53). Nevertheless, in 1987 Gary Taylor seemed to be accepting the press variants 'noted by Wilson . . . and Hinman' (*TxC*, 396).

2 This contrasts with Q1, which Alan E. Craven has demonstrated was set by just one compositor (Craven, 37–60).

X, and whom he regarded as the more error-prone, set sheets B, C, D, F, I, N, O and the first and last pages of sheet L; compositor Y set sheets E, G, H, K, most of L, and M. However, W. Craig Ferguson produced evidence in 1989 that two different founts of pica roman type were used for the printing of Q2 and that each sheet was set in one or other fount (Ferguson, 15). Brown's spelling analysis was almost entirely confirmed by the fount analysis, but, as the whole of sheet L was in one fount, Ferguson concluded that it was all set by Compositor Y (see Table 3).

An editor will normally be suspicious of corrections in the printing-house, since a proofreader might change an unusual but nevertheless authentic reading to something more conventional. But knowing the identity and error-proneness of a compositor can provide the editor with a measure of guidance when choosing between substantive variant readings. Compositor X set just over 50 per cent of the text, but his text contains 75 per cent of the corrections – and 100 per cent of those variants which present an editor with difficult choices. If X really was more error-prone than his colleague, this might encourage an editor to give more trust than usual to the press-corrector's decisions to make alterations, but that does not in itself validate the corrections he went on to make. In our edition we have favoured X's reading in two of the three problem variants identified above – 'pall' and 'sellingly' – and, while in the third we have been persuaded to go with the corrector's decision to alter X's 'dosie', we have nevertheless emended the corrector's 'dazzie' to 'dazzle'.

Q2 seems to most scholars to have the appearance of a text deriving from Shakespeare's holograph first draft, but Greg argued that, for at least the first scene, an annotated copy of Q1 served as the compositors' copy: 'After the entry of Horatio and Marcellus . . . the texts become closely parallel and, at once, a typographical correspondence is observable likewise.'[1] First,

---

1 Greg, *First Folio*, Note F, 331–2. Greg used the word 'corrected' rather than 'annotated', but he does not seem to have meant 'press-corrected'.

both texts start by not indenting the speech prefixes but then at the same moment (1.21 in Q1, 1.1.29 in Q2) they shift to indenting them:

> *Mar.* Horatio sayes tis but our fantasie,
> ... He may approoue our eyes, and speake to it.
>   *Hor.* Tut, t'will not appeare.

(Q1)

> *Mar.* Horatio saies tis but our fantasie,
> ... He may approoue our eyes and speake to it.
>   *Hora.* Tush, tush, twill not appeare.

(Q2)

Secondly, two early one-line speeches in Q2 which have a close resemblance to lines in Q1 end with a comma where they should end with a full stop, and in both cases the Q1 counterpart ends with a comma. Francisco's third speech in Q2 was printed 'you come most carefully vpon your houre,' while the First Sentinel's second speech in Q1 was printed 'O you come most carefully vpon your watch,'. Marcellus' first speech in Q2 reads 'And Leedgemen to the Dane,' while his first line (which is not, however, the whole of his speech) in Q1 reads 'And leegemen to the Dane,'. There is some force to these parallels, but it should be noted that four out of Q2's first nineteen single-line sentences end in a comma.

Thus, by 1605, there were at least two *Hamlet* texts in circulation,[1] but within six years the number of different versions had begun to expand further. Having acquired Ling's copyright on 19 November 1607, John Smethwick had Q2 reprinted in 1611 by George Eld (Lavin, 173–6) and this new edition (Q3) introduced some new variants. A few years later

---

1 Because they exhibit variants, each of the Huntington and British Library copies of Q1 provides a slightly different Q1 text. Only two out of the seven extant copies of Q2 are identical. One could therefore argue that by 1605 there were at least eight technically different texts in circulation.

Smethwick had Q3 reprinted in another, undated quarto (Q4), again introducing a small number of new variants. Jenkins assigns Q4 to 1622 (Ard², 17–18), but Eric Rasmussen has argued persuasively that, while it could have been printed as late as 1623, the likeliest date is 1621.[1] Either Q3 or Q4 was probably consulted by the compositors of the next edition of *Hamlet*, the First Folio (F), which appeared in 1623 (*TxC*, 396–7), for F has a number of readings which first appear in Q3 (and are repeated in Q4) and not all of them are obvious and necessary corrections of Q2 (*TxC*, 397). While there is no reason for believing that they have any authority, one or both of Q3 and Q4 may therefore have played a small part in the emergence of the text of *Hamlet* as we have become used to reading it and hearing it performed.[2]

The First Folio

That next edition was contained in the 1623 First Folio (F), published by a syndicate which included Smethwick. The volume's claim that the texts it prints are 'Published according to the True Originall Copies' (see Fig. 11) implicitly casts doubt on the authority of all previous editions. However, that could well have been a marketing ploy rather than an accurate description of the nature of the copy from which its compositors worked. *Hamlet* occupies pages numbered '152' to '280', but some pages have been misnumbered (we leap from 156 to 257, from 278 back to 259, and experience two pages

---

1 Rasmussen examines the progressive deterioration of a cherub's lock of hair in Smethwick's publisher's device between the printing of Michael Drayton's *Poems* of 1619 and Thomas Lodge's *Euphues Golden Legacy* of 1623, and concludes that Q4 comes approximately halfway through this process (Rasmussen, 'Date').

2 For example, at Q2 4.7.181 Laertes responds to Gertrude's description of Ophelia's death, 'Alas, then she is drownd'; F, on the other hand, has 'Alas, then, is she drown'd?', which is Q3's word order ('Alas then is she drownd') and may represent F being affected by Q3. Some modern editors (e.g. Jenkins) follow Q2, others (e.g. Spencer and Edwards) follow F, while others (e.g. Hibbard and Oxf) are closest to Q3.

numbered '280'), so that the play in fact runs to only 31 pages, not 109.

Charlton Hinman argued that five different compositors had shared the typesetting of the volume as a whole (Hinman, *Printing*, 2.511), identifying them on the basis of recurring types and distinctive spelling habits, and calling them compositors A, B, C, D and E. Since then, the case has been made for adding four more, identified as compositors F, H, I and J (Howard-Hill, 'Compositors'; Taylor, 'Shrinking'). This printing of *Hamlet* is less than satisfactory, perhaps because it seems to have been mainly set by Compositor B, the principal compositor throughout F, who is noted for inaccuracy and even for tampering with his text (Hinman, *Printing*, 2.10), and who came up with such problematic readings as 'or Norman' at F 3.2.32 and 'Politician' at F 4.1.144. Compositor E, the least skilful of Jaggard's employees (Hinman, *Printing*, 2.264), set most of Act 5 and was responsible for such unlikely readings as 'sixteene' at F 5.1.160 and 'terrible woer' at F 5.1.243. If these are misreadings, they contribute to the evidence that the compositors were working primarily from a manuscript rather than an annotated copy of Q2, Q3 or Q4.[1]

The size of the print run of the First Folio has not been precisely established, though it seems to have been printed in an edition of well under 1,000.[2] None the less, in 1963 Charlton Hinman (*Printing*, 1.243–4) published the fruits of his collation or examination of eighty copies of the 228 or so which still exist (West, 'Census', 60–73).[3] This led him to identify some

---

1 For a breakdown of the division of labour in Jaggard's shop, see Table 4.

2 Hinman estimated 1,200 (*Printing*, 1.39), but Peter Blayney has challenged this estimate, and argues that a run of about 750 copies is more likely (Introduction to Hinman, *Facsimile* 1996, xxxiii).

3 Hinman collated fifty complete and five incomplete copies in the Folger Shakespeare Library in Washington, DC, and consulted a further twenty-five. See too the first volume of Anthony James West's history of the First Folio post-publication (West, *Folio*).

400 press variants in the whole volume, which he believed resulted from corrections made by just one careless and superficial proofreader, most of whose relatively few substantive changes are 'demonstrably wrong' (Hinman, *Facsimile*, xx). However, although Hinman found thirty-seven variants in *Hamlet* (see Table 5), these face an editor of a modernized text with no real choices, since in the case of the only substantive variant (at F 2.2.82) the corrected 'thanke' makes sense and the uncorrected 'take' does not.

The major problem facing the editor of F is the whole question of the causal relationship, if any, between it and Q2. Assuming the copy for Q2 pre-dates the copy for F (an assumption which is usually made but for which there is nevertheless no hard evidence), it has been argued that F's compositors worked from a marked-up copy of the 1604–5 Quarto.[1] But the F text has so many and sometimes such extensive variants from Q2 that it seems rather unlikely that quarto pages (even when untrimmed) could have provided an annotator with sufficient space for marking up all the additional passages. F must surely derive, at least in part, from a manuscript. But what kind of manuscript? The text is quite close to Q1 at many points, and Q1 has the appearance of being some kind of representation of the play as performed. It could be that F also derives ultimately from a theatrical manuscript, but while it is certainly shorter than Q2 – many of the absent lines come from the middle of long speeches (Rasmussen, 'Revision') – it is by no means as short as Q1 and it is hard to believe that F too would not have been cut before it could serve as the script for an actual performance.

It is sometimes claimed that F has been cleansed of profanity. In 1606, at least three years after *Hamlet* was first written, an 'Acte to restraine Abuses of Playes' threatened to fine anyone in a stage play who might 'jestingly or prophanely speake or

1   This is proposed by Alice Walker (Walker, 'Reconsideration').

use the holy Name of God' (quoted in Chambers, *Shakespeare*, 4.338–9). But the Act did not apply to the printed word; neither Q3 (1611) nor Q4 (*c.* 1621) shows any evidence of such cleansing, and F *Hamlet* shows very little. On the other hand, it is certainly 'tidier' than Q2, being more consistent in its speech prefixes and more precise in its stage directions, and it makes a partial attempt in the first quarter to introduce act and scene divisions.[1] But, while the second of these characteristics seems to focus on theatrical realization, the others – along with its preference for more capitalization, heavier and more extensive punctuation, and some unsystematic 'modernization' of language – can be seen as ways of making the text more suitable for a reading public and more 'modern' literary tastes.

The quartos and folios after 1623

John Smethwick, having had a share in the publication of the 1623 Folio text, then published another quarto edition in 1637 (Q5), which, but for a handful of new emendations, is yet another reprint of the basic Q2 text, unaffected by any of the conditions that produced the different text in F. Five years later, Parliament closed the theatres, but, after the Restoration of the monarchy in 1660 and the granting of licences to two companies to put on plays again, a new quarto (Q6) claiming to represent the play 'As it is now Acted at his Highness the Duke of *York*'s Theatre' was published in 1676. Another quarto (Q7) carries the same date but may have followed Q6. These two so-called 'Players' Quartos' include emendations by Sir William Davenant, and mark those sections of the play that were cut during performances by his acting company. Reinforcing the

---

1 F marks an '*Actus Primus. Scœna Prima*', a '*Scena Secunda*' and a '*Scena Tertia*'; then, after a gap of two scenes, an '*Actus Secundus*' (see t.n.). James Hirsh argues that the division into five acts in twenty-eight of the plays in F was made by the publishers to make their edition look 'classical' (Hirsh, 227), and that the scribe Ralph Crane was probably responsible for such a division in seventeen of them, along with the introduction into *Hamlet* of '*Actus Secundus*' (229–30).

evidence of the Q1 and Q2 title-pages, we can see clearly here that *Hamlet* has always had two lives, one as an acting text and one as a text to be read.

It should be clear from this brief bibliographical history[1] that we can distinguish three 'primary' texts, Q1, Q2 and F, and springing from them two separate lines of descent – the quartos after Q1 all being reprints of Q2 and the folios all being reprints of F. In 1709, however, Nicholas Rowe effectively changed the history of the play by beginning to bring these two lines together. His edition of *The Works of Mr William Shakespear* contained a *Hamlet* which, by including readings from Q6 (such as Hamlet's soliloquy at 4.4.31) in a text based on F4, initiated the whole tradition of a *conflated* text, which was taken up and developed in such influential editions as those of Alexander Pope in 1723 and Lewis Theobald in 1733, and which has dominated the business of editing *Hamlet* right up to the present day. Conflation has almost exclusively been a matter of emending F through use of Q2 or emending Q2 through use of F, but ever since its rediscovery editors have also made occasional use of readings from Q1.

MODERN EDITORS AT WORK

The 1604–5 Quarto claims on its title-page that, unlike that of the 1603 Quarto, its text is 'true and perfect'. The 1623 First

---

1   Further editions of Davenant's text followed – Q8 in 1683, Q9 in 1695 and Q10 in 1703. In 1929 Henrietta C. Bartlett and Alfred W. Pollard identified nineteen extant copies of Q3, twenty of Q4, thirty-one of Q5, thirty-three of Q6–Q7, twenty-one of Q8, twenty-two of Q9 and fifty-one of Q10 (Bartlett & Pollard). The play's commercial success as a printed text may be further indicated by the fact that there were two separate issues (i.e. reprints with new title-pages) of each of Q8 and Q9 and five of Q10 – although a reissue with a new title-leaf might equally be a way of clearing old stock when a book was not selling well. Meanwhile, a second edition of the Folio had been published in 1632 (F2). A third edition followed in 1663 (F3, with a second, expanded issue in 1664) and then, in 1685, a fourth (F4), each containing the F *Hamlet* text, with just a few fresh emendations.

Folio addresses its readers with the news that its texts are 'perfect' (A3[r]) and asserts on its title-page that they accord to 'the True Originall Copies'. Yet Jesús Tronch-Pérez has calculated that, beyond the omission or addition of significant stretches of dialogue, there are over 1,000 variations in single words or phrases between the texts of Q2 and F (Tronch-Pérez, 16). If one includes those stretches unique to each text, by our count 2,879 of Q2's words are not found in substantively the same form and place in F, and 1,889 of F's words are not found in Q2.

Nearly 400 years later, there is still no consensus on what constitutes the true text of *Hamlet*. This can easily be illustrated by comparing editions currently on sale in bookshops. In the UK in 2005 most large bookshops stock the 1980 New Penguin Shakespeare edition by T.J.B. Spencer (reissued with a new Introduction in 2005), as well as those already mentioned by Philip Edwards (reissued in 2003), G.R. Hibbard and Harold Jenkins. If one takes the earliest (Spencer) as the base text and compares it with the other three, one finds that there is always at least one editor who disagrees with Spencer over what words to print in 20 per cent of the lines. This is partly explained by the choice of control text: while Spencer and Jenkins choose Q2, Hibbard chooses F, and Edwards moves between the two. But how can it be that even Spencer and Jenkins diverge on as many as 193 occasions? The answer is that, even where editors work from a common control text, they tend not to agree on their role, their methodology or the kind of text they are intending to produce.

The written text

In choosing Q2 as their control text, Spencer and Jenkins are following in the footsteps of John Dover Wilson, who edited *Hamlet* for the New Cambridge Shakespeare in 1934. Indeed, our predecessor in the Arden Shakespeare writes that it is Wilson who 'established' Q2 as the most authoritative text (Ard[2], 24–5).

He is clearly referring to Wilson's book, also published in 1934, *The Manuscript of Shakespeare's 'Hamlet' and the Problems of its Transmission*. This title summarizes what Wilson believes to be the editor of *Hamlet*'s project – the attempted reconstruction of the text of Shakespeare's manuscript – and Wilson and Jenkins between them lay down the foundations of the project for all subsequent editors.

As the first stage in the process of reconstruction, Wilson feels he must understand the nature and history of the manuscripts used for the printing of the earliest texts of the play, and he comes to the conclusions that Q2 was largely set directly from Shakespeare's foul papers, while F was set from a transcript of the promptbook,[1] which probably derived directly from those foul papers. As for Q1, it was set from a reported text deriving from the play in performance and, therefore, ultimately from a transcript made in the theatre by someone tidying up the text of Shakespeare's foul papers. This establishes a hierarchy of authority, with Q2 at the top because it stands at the smallest number of removes from Shakespeare's hand, and Q1 at the bottom, because it stands at the greatest number of removes. However, all three texts are 'patently imperfect', since they all regularly print readings that Wilson cannot believe Shakespeare 'intended to write' (Wilson, *Manuscript*, 5).

Wilson rejects any editorial methodology which relies merely on the editor's 'good taste and judgment' (*Manuscript*, 7). He condemns as wrong-headed those editors who try to follow one text to the exclusion of the others (e.g. Charles Jennens with Q2 in 1773 or Nicolaus Delius with F in 1854–65), yet he regards as equally wrong-headed those eclectic editors, such as William George Clark and William Aldis

---

1 The commonly accepted term, despite its being something of an anachronism (since Elizabethans called it 'the Booke', while a modern promptbook is a more detailed document).

Wright in their 1864 Globe and 1866 Cambridge editions, who pick and choose between texts 'at their own will' (12). Nevertheless, for all his commitment to the construction of a 'critical apparatus' (175) and compliance with a set of 'Editorial Principles' (177), individual literary judgements underpin Wilson's practice and methodology. When faced with two indifferent variants, one from Q2 and one from F, he chooses the one which is 'manifestly superior aesthetically' (177),[1] and his refusal to believe that Shakespeare intended certain passages does not derive from a mechanical theory of transmission but is a matter of the editor exercising the connoisseur's ability to detect 'the unmistakable impress of the master's hand' (178).

Set out in Wilson's book, we have the framework within which all modern editing of *Hamlet* operates. Our Arden predecessor, Harold Jenkins, is firmly in the Wilsonian tradition, seeking the solution to the problem posed by the unreliability of the three early texts by attempting the reconstruction of the text which lies *behind* them and the relation of that text to 'the play as Shakespeare wrote it' (Ard[2], 75).[2]

Jenkins turns to each text in turn and looks for clues to the nature of its printers' copy. Q2's stage directions are sometimes 'casual about characters' names and often indefinite about numbers' (Ard[2], 37) – as at the opening of 2.1, where Polonius enters '*with his man or two*' but the subsequent dialogue reveals there is only one man and he has a name, Reynaldo. This suggests an author who has yet to confront practical decisions about

---

1 Elsewhere, however, Wilson distances himself from Edward Capell's notion of the editor as one who wishes to improve Shakespeare and advance his 'perfectness' (Wilson, *Manuscript*, 2.179).

2 Wilson's ultimate project, however, is not so much the reconstruction of the play as Shakespeare wrote it as the construction of the play which Shakespeare set out to write. For 'where we have reason to think that the pen of Shakespeare himself slipped, there can be no harm in restoring the reading which he clearly thought he had set down on paper' (*Manuscript*, 179). The editor's job is, therefore, not simply the reconstruction of a lost historical artefact, but the creation of an ideal text, the *Hamlet* Shakespeare would have intended.

resources which will have to be made once a play is in production. Another clue is the large number of printing errors, which indicates that the manuscript was hard to read (as at 3.2.350, where Hamlet gives Guildensterne a recorder and tells him to cover the holes with his fingers '& the vmber'; F corrects this to 'and thumbe'). Some errors suggest a manuscript containing the unusually formed letters *a* and *u* which are found in the Hand D addition to *The Book of Sir Thomas More* by Anthony Munday and others, which most scholars believe was written by Shakespeare.[1] There are also some unusual spellings, all characteristic of Shakespeare,[2] the 'most striking' (Ard², 41) being the *Sc* in '*Sceneca*' (2.2.336),[3] which may reflect a predilection for *sc* at the beginning of some words normally beginning with *s* and which seems to accord with similar *sc-* spellings in *Coriolanus, 2 Henry IV* and *Troilus and*

---

1 MS Harley 7368 in the British Library. T.H. Howard-Hill feels the evidence favours Shakespeare as 'the author and hand of Addition II' (Howard-Hill, *More*, 8). John Jowett and Stanley Wells in their discussion of *Coriolanus* point out that 'An unfamiliar proper name might prove especially resistant to scribal regularization, just as it did to regularization by one of the compositors' (*TxC*, 593).

2 Jenkins believes that F sometimes followed Q2 in common errors (see the t.n. at 1.1.93 'designe', 1.2.206 'Whereas', 2.2.484 'A ro wsed', 2.2.578 'Deere', 3.3.18 'somnet', 4.3.56 'diddest', 4.3.84 't'would', 4.3.98 'indeed') as well as in unusual spellings (e.g. 1.1.15 'farwel', 1.1.39 'of', 1.1.72 'Brazon', 1.3.51 'reaks', 1.3.73 'ranck', 2.2.504 'ore-teamed', 2.2.536 'dosen', 2.2.546 'Fixion', 3.2.275 'Paiocke', 3.4.19 'boudge', 3.4.77 'Ardure', 4.5.99 'impittious', 4.5.140 'Soop-stake', 4.7.11 'vnsinnowed', 5.1.18 '&', 5.1.177 'Renish', 5.1.258 'Spleenatiue', 5.1.261 'a sunder' (Fu), 5.1.271–2 'Woo't', 5.1.272 'Crocadile' (Fu), 5.1.283 'Cuplet', 5.2.266 'How?'), some of which can be even traced back to Q1 (e.g. 1.1.62 '*Pollax*', 1.5.64 'leaperous', 1.5.67 'Allies', 1.5.156 '&', 1.5.162 'can'st', 1.5.167 'dream't', and 1.5.171 'Anticke').

3 We might note that '*Sceneca*' occurs only five words after the word 'scene'. Although '*Sceneca*' occurs on the next page (F3), both pages were set by Compositor X, and 'scene' was the last word in the last line of F2ᵛ, i.e. the key word for someone justifying the page. Unless it was added later by someone else, X still had to set the catchword: whoever did it put 'indeuidible.' when he should have put 'indeuidible,'. So we may have an example of X's mind not being entirely focused on his job, to set beside the coincidence of someone repeating a word ('scene') which has just borne a special significance. Who is to say that this not a scribe's unconscious misreading of his copy?

Cressida. In five Q2 passages (none of which appears in F) Jenkins finds Shakespeare rejecting his first thoughts, but failing to delete them clearly – with the result that the compositor mistakenly preserved them. For example, at 3.2.160–2, he believes the lines

> For women feare too much, euen as they loue,
> And womens feare and loue hold quantitie,
> Eyther none, in neither ought, or in extremitie,

contain both first and second thoughts, and that what was finally intended was a rhyming couplet reading (in modern spelling)

> For women's fear and love hold quantity,
> In neither aught, or in extremity.

Even though Jenkins calls this example 'decisive' (41), Spencer prints the lines unemended. Similarly Jenkins is sure that Shakespeare intended to remove 'greatnes' from 'As by your safetie, greatnes, wisdome, all things els' (4.7.8), but Spencer keeps it in. Jenkins calls 'Giues him threescore thousand crownes in annual fee' (2.2.73) an 'impossible line' (41), but concedes that 'Theobald defended its metre and Dover Wilson insists upon the sum' (41). He also notes that G. Blakemore Evans in his Riverside edition retains 'cull-cold' at 4.7.169, where Jenkins argues that 'cull-cold' records Shakespeare miswriting 'cull' and failing to make his intentions clear. All of this evidence persuades Jenkins that Q2's compositors were working, not from a promptbook, not from a fair copy or scribal transcript, but from Shakespeare's holograph – perhaps annotated in the playhouse in preparation for transcription as a promptbook.

Jenkins finds evidence that F, on the other hand, derives from a fair copy of Shakespeare's foul papers, transcribed by a scribe who was much more accurate than Q2's compositors, and that this fair copy underwent a second transcription which then received 'some preparation for the stage' (Ard[2], 56). He reads most of the 230-odd Q2 lines that are not in F as deliberate cuts, and most of the cuts as theatrical abridgement, and he also thinks F's text has been corrupted by actors introducing small verbal repetitions, additions and substitutions. Despite being one of the first to challenge Alice Walker's belief that F was set from an annotated copy of Q2,[1] by the time of his Arden edition Jenkins has come round to accepting that F probably depends upon a copy of Q2 which had been collated with the second transcription, and then itself transcribed again, with some alterations and embellishments. Where F differs from Q2 over particular words or phrases in the dialogue, Jenkins is struck by what he regards as the superiority of many of the F readings.[2] While F never derives directly from foul papers at any point, he believes that some of its passages that are not found in Q2 are accidental Q2 omissions, and that elsewhere F, despite the interference of actors, scribes and printers, still sometimes preserves a reading from foul papers which Q2 has obscured. (It needs to be noticed that Jenkins's preferences are not universally shared. At 5.1.78, for instance, he is delighted that F's Compositor E should have Hamlet talk of a gravedigger who 'o're Offices' a politician's skull, when Q2's Compositor Y had him talk of a gravedigger who 'ore-reaches' it (59). Yet Jenkins himself cites Charlton Hinman, who regards 'o're Offices' as a typical Compositor E mistake (*Printing*, 1.302–3; 2.257). At the same time, Jenkins finds many more cases where F alters but does *not* improve on Q2, and these he attributes either to careless typesetting or else to deliberate purification, sophistication and modernization of the text by hands other than Shakespeare's.

1 See Walker, 'Reconsideration', 328–38, and *Problems*, 121–37; Jenkins, 'Relation', 69–83; Nosworthy, *Occasional*, 144–51; Walton; Taylor, 'Folio copy', 44–61, and 'Compositors', 17–74; Hibbard, 'Errors', 55–61.
2 Identification of superiority seems to be a matter of aesthetic judgement. Jenkins provides examples of places where an 'obviously superior' F reading reveals an 'error' in Q2, but on the one occasion where he gives grounds for preferring the F variant the grounds are that it is in 'Shakespeare's finest manner' (Ard[2], 59).

As for Q1, Jenkins concludes that it derives from the same version of the play that is represented in F, and that it records most of F's variant readings and cuts, but reorders some of the scenes and introduces many cuts of its own (Ard², 21). An editor cannot dismiss the possibility that Q1 preserves readings from Shakespeare's foul papers which have been obscured in the transmission of Q2 and F (e.g. 'father' at 2.2.518).

So Jenkins reconstructs what he reckons Shakespeare wrote by printing the Q2 text along with 'anything preserved in F which I take to have been lost from Q2 . . . [except] words and phrases in F which I judge to be playhouse additions to the dialogue' (Ard², 75). Where variants appear to be indifferent the Q2 reading is usually preferred, but 'the editor must be eclectic; every variant imposes upon him the inescapable responsibility of choice' (76).

However, the editor committed to this kind of project still needs to decide how much of what has been reconstructed has a place in the completed edition. If, as Jenkins thinks, Q2 contains some of Shakespeare's first and second thoughts, side by side, the editor may preserve them all on the basis that anything by Shakespeare merits preservation. But he may decide to leave out either the first thoughts[1] or the second thoughts, on the evidence that the play reads better without them. Edwards, Wilson's successor in the New Cambridge series, observes:

> It is ironic that compositors may have unwittingly preserved a good deal of material which Shakespeare decided to dispense with. If that is in fact the case, they will have provided us with immensely valuable information about Shakespeare's methods of composition, but presented an editor with the formidable

---

1 As Jenkins does at Q2 3.2.160 (which he omits entirely) and 162 (where he deletes 'Either none,').

problem of whether he should put back into a play what Shakespeare had decided to leave out.

(Cam², 14)

The performed text

In Edwards's view, 'the nearer we get to the stage, the further we are getting from Shakespeare' (Cam², 32), but other editors are as interested in the performed text as they are in the written or intended text.[1] For some the editorial project is the reconstruction, not of the text in Shakespeare's manuscript, but of the text of the promptbook of *Hamlet* as it was performed by the acting company to which Shakespeare belonged. The fact that he was an actor and a shareholder in the company might mean that their promptbook represented the version of the play with which he was happiest. It might also be that, if we could reconstruct it, it would tell us what actually happened on stage, but we should remember that Hamlet complains that actors don't always follow their scripts.

Spencer, for one, believes that the printers of F took as their primary source either 'the prompt copy' or a transcript of it, and that F comes closer than Q2 to representing 'the play as it was performed by Shakespeare's company' (Spencer, 150). He is prepared to print many of the repetitions in Hamlet's speeches not found in Q2 which other editors have regarded as actors' interpolations. This is partly because he thinks some of them could have been penned by Shakespeare himself, since 'changes in the Folio text may represent his own minor improvements to help the actors' (151), but he also believes that 'The Folio has its own kind of authority . . . because it represents the practice

---

1   Gary Taylor and Stanley Wells explain in their General Introduction to the plays in the Oxford *Complete Works* that 'Performance is the end to which they were created, and in this edition we have devoted our efforts to recovering and presenting texts of Shakespeare's plays as they were acted in the London playhouses' (Oxf, xxxix).

of the playhouse for which Shakespeare wrote' (151). In other words, Spencer is prepared to include in his edited text words which may have been incorporated in the text without Shakespeare's approval on the grounds that they were spoken in the playhouse 'for which Shakespeare wrote'.

Similarly, Q1 'arouses suspicions that the play may have been performed soon after it was written in a text that has otherwise not come down to us, possibly an earlier version, possibly a shortened form of what we now regard as the authentic text, made conceivably for a touring company' (Spencer, 149). Q1 may therefore be a record, however imperfect, of *Hamlet* in performance during Shakespeare's lifetime, and as such may tell us something not recorded in a promptbook. For Spencer it provides the occasional 'authentic' (149) reading, some stage directions and even some passages of dialogue not to be found elsewhere.[1]

The printed text

G. Thomas Tanselle distinguishes between 'the text of a document', i.e. the printed text in its physical form, and 'the text of a work', i.e. the text as intended by the author (Tanselle, 35). Editors can choose a much narrower project than those tackled by Wilson, Jenkins or Spencer and restrict themselves simply to editing the texts of documents. In their diplomatic edition of Q1 in 1992, Graham Holderness and Bryan Loughrey entirely reject the kind of thinking illustrated by all the editors so far discussed. They dismiss as philosophically impossible any attempt 'to construct a rehabilitated text reflecting a form approximating Shakespeare's artistic vision' (Holderness & Loughrey, 8). Their project is the representation of a real, rather than imagined, text. Their text is historical, but it is also

---

1 Indeed, Spencer is prepared to break with tradition and print Q1 Hamlet's commentary on clowns after the equivalent of Q2 3.2.43 (Q1 29–40, 'And ... Well,').

extant – the text to be found in a particular library in a particular copy of a particular quarto printed in 1603 with the title *The Tragicall Historie of Hamlet Prince of Denmarke*.

They also reject the celebration of *Hamlet* as the work of an individual artist, arguing that there is no reason for privileging either the 'scriptwriter' (Holderness & Loughrey, 7) or any single script over all the other influences in the production of a play. The title of the series in which their edition appeared may be 'Shakespearean Originals', but this does not mean that the printed Q1 reflects accurately any Shakespearean autograph. Neither does it mean that they consider the word 'Shakespeare' to be more than 'a convenient if misleading shorthand term alluding to the complex material practices of the Elizabethan and Jacobean theatre industry' (8). Their copy of Q1 (the one in the British Library) is 'original' in that it is one of the documents which form the origins of what we call '*Hamlet*', a contribution to the 'rich diversity of textual variation which is shrouded by those traditional editorial practices which have sought to impose a single, "ideal" paradigm' (8). On another occasion they might have edited the Huntington Library copy of Q1, or a copy of Q2, or a copy of the *Hamlet* pages in F.

Holderness and Loughrey argue that 'there is no philosophical justification for emendation, which foregrounds the editor at the expense of the text' and they therefore try to restrict themselves to 'a minimum of editorial mediation' (9). But that minimum includes two kinds of emendation.[1] First, they modernize certain orthographic and printing conventions (long *s*, for example). Second, while at Q1 1.101 they print the word 'invelmorable', they later include in their endnotes the entry '*invelmorable*: invulnerable' (103). Had they been

---

1 By which we mean *deliberate* emendation. Unfortunately, by occasionally mistranscribing Q1, they introduced some unintended emendations. But this should not be regarded as undermining the strength of their arguments about the theory of editing Shakespeare.

explicitly emending their copy-text they would have printed 'invulnerable'. Instead, they implicitly emend by making that cryptic entry (although the absence of any explanation might lead an innocent reader to believe that 'invelmorable' is an Elizabethan word meaning 'invulnerable'). This must mean they believe that the First Quarto's compositor misread 'invulnerable' in his copy, or that it was his intention to print 'invulnerable' but he failed to do so, or else that the author of the copy intended 'invulnerable' but mistakenly wrote 'invelmorable'. Underlying their note is the assumption that none of those involved in the production of the 1603 printed text (be they author(s), actors, scribes or printers) can have intended 'invelmorable': it was therefore a mistake, and any literate Elizabethan would have corrected it to 'invulnerable'. It would seem to follow, then, that, while they are committed to a diplomatic facsimile of a copy of the First Quarto, they are also committed to reconstructing either the copy, or the intended copy, from which the compositor was working.

In his 2002 *Synoptic 'Hamlet'*, Jesús Tronch-Pérez is another editor whose project is the attempted reproduction of the printed text. However, he tackles two texts at once, printing the common text to be found in Q2 and F, and then, wherever there are variants, printing them both in parallel.[1] Rather than begin with the author's text, he prefers to begin with the reader's text. He explains that 'This is not an edition meant to offer readers a reconstruction of the *Hamlet* or *Hamlet*s its authors wrote' (Tronch-Pérez, 63). Unlike Holderness and Loughrey, he is not against emendation on principle, but he believes he serves his modern readers best by allowing the printed text every opportunity to yield up meaning: 'On facing a reading in Q2 or in F1, I have asked . . . "What does this reading mean?", rather than "Is this right or wrong?"' (63).

---

1 For an earlier attempt at a similar project, see Bernice W. Kliman's synoptic 'Enfolded *Hamlet*' (Kliman).

The multiple text

With the exception of Tronch-Pérez, each of the foregoing editors is seeking to reconstruct and print a single text of *Hamlet*. However, Holderness and Loughrey have arbitrarily selected theirs out of what they call a 'diversity of textual variation' (8), and the implication of their method is, in fact, the assertion of plurality. In the cases of Wilson, Jenkins and Spencer, nevertheless, the assumption is that Shakespeare wrote a single work called *Hamlet* (possibly emending it slightly, once it was in the process of production), that the plurality of the Q1, Q2 and F texts disguises that fact, and that an editor must dispel plurality through the recreation of singularity.

The extent of Q1's difference from the other two texts creates a potential difficulty for those committed to the twin notions that the author produced just one set of foul papers and that the public wants only one play. The problem is usually solved by calling Q1 corrupt and eliminating its text from the edition. Even so, there have been occasional voices questioning the idea that Q1 represents merely the product of a process of fragmentation and degeneration of a unitary original work. Those editors and critics who have espoused the memorial reconstruction theory[1] have never been able to agree on who all the reporters were, and indeed those sections of Q1 where the various possible candidates are present are not consistently closer to Q2 or F than those sections where they are absent. Paul Werstine ('Quartos') argues that there is no real evidence that Q1 has theatrical provenance, let alone that it was memorially reconstructed; Steven Urkowitz ('Basics') reintroduces the idea

---

1   Editors such as Jenkins, Edwards, Hibbard, Taylor and Irace (see both her edition of Q1 and *Reforming*, 118); scholars such as W.H. Widgery (see Widgery), R. Grant White (see White), W.W. Greg ('Quartos', 196–7, and *Editorial*, 66), H.D. Gray ('First Quarto', and 'Kyd', 721–35), John Dover Wilson ('Copy', 153–85, and 'Transcript', 217–47), E.K. Chambers (*Shakespeare*, 1.416), George Duthie (see Duthie), Alfred Hart (*Stolne*, 349), and J.M. Nosworthy ('Player', 74–82).

that Q1 pre-dates the foul papers behind Q2, that it is an early draft, and therefore a distinct Shakespearean work; and Eric Sams points out that Ling published both Q1 and Q2 and presumably knew the source of his manuscripts, and asks why Q2's compositors would have consulted Q1 if they didn't think it was by Shakespeare (Sams, *Shakespeare*, 126).[1] Even if it is the case that Q1 post-dates the Q2 manuscript, the contentious label 'bad' has always allowed editors to disown the 1603 Quarto if they wanted to, attributing it effectively to some anonymous actors rather than to Shakespeare.

That still leaves editors free to treat Q2 and F as expressions of an original single work. In recent years, however, some editors of major editions have begun to question this assumption. Building on E.A.J. Honigmann's 1965 proposal that Shakespeare may have introduced minor variants while copying out his own work, and may also have been prepared to rethink and rewrite (Honigmann, *Stability*), they entertain the idea that F records Shakespeare's decision to revise the text which lies behind Q2. This would mean that Q2 and F reflect distinct Shakespearean *Hamlet*s (or distinct phases in the history of a single *Hamlet*).

Edwards, for example, believes that Shakespeare could have contributed to a theatrical transcript of his foul papers, which then became the basis of a further transcript from which Jaggard printed F. He speculates that 'Shakespeare . . . made many alterations to his play, mostly reflected in cutting rather than adding material, some of which he may have made after preliminary discussions with his colleagues among the Chamberlain's men' (Cam[2], 31–2). For this reason, Edwards wishes to give F as much authority as Q2. His edition is therefore an eclectic text, which adopts readings from both Q2 and F: 'In some cases I have judged the Folio to be correct and

---

1   Richard Proudfoot answers this question: 'Because they were having trouble with the manuscript and thought initially that Q1 might help' (private correspondence).

in some cases the quarto' (32). Gary Taylor (Oxf; *TxC*) reckons that there are so many individual verbal variations between Q2 and F that Shakespeare was probably responsible for most of them. Analysis of punctuation, spelling and common errors persuades him that the compositors' copy for F was a transcript of the promptbook, that the prompt-book may well have been Shakespeare's own fair copy (appropriately annotated for the playhouse) of his foul papers, and that through that fair copy F records not just performance practice but Shakespeare's own revisions of his text. He is persuaded by Edwards's argument that F's substantive differences from Q2 are coherent and make the two texts different works of art.[1]

Hibbard adopts a similar line, arguing that, while most of the Q2 lines missing from F are cuts, these cuts are so deft they must have been the work of Shakespeare himself. Meanwhile the F lines missing from Q2 fall into two categories: the single words and brief phrases known as 'actors' additions', and three substantial passages. The former seem to Hibbard to have been 'introduced into the text at an early stage in the play's history when Shakespeare must have been taking a very active interest in it still, for they also appear in Q1' (Oxf[1], 113). As for the latter, Hibbard sees them as F additions rather than Q2 omissions, arguing that Q2 makes perfectly good sense without them, and pointing out that Davenant and his actors seem to have agreed with him, for the 1676 'Players' Quartos' were content to leave the Q2 passages virtually unaltered. He agrees with Taylor that F derives from Shakespeare's fair copy, but he

---

1   Indeed, he feels that Edwards could even have strengthened his case had he considered that F at 5.2.77–80 provides Hamlet with one motivation for reconciliation with Laertes – empathy with Laertes because they have both lost a father through murder – whereas Q2 at 5.2.184–5 provides him with a different motivation – the Lord says his mother wishes it – and that conflation renders the Lord's contribution superfluous. However, it is arguable that multiple motivation does not necessarily weaken the credibility or dramatic force of Hamlet's change of heart.

does not believe that it had served as a promptbook, preferring to imagine Shakespeare making corrections and improvements, clarifications and additions as he copied out his text.

In his edition, Hibbard notes that Q1 makes all F's cuts and also reproduces in truncated form F 2.2.335–60, one of the three passages of some length (the others being F 2.2.238–67 and 5.2.68–81), which are peculiar to F and, in his opinion, constitute F additions. More recently, Hibbard has found four examples of Q1 adapting Q2 before F further adapts it (the end of 3.4/opening of 4.1; 5.2.14; 1.2.57; and 4.4). These, he says, are places where F has cuts which, had they been available to him, the abridger responsible for Q1 would surely have adopted (Hibbard, 'Chronology', 84). Where Hibbard had earlier imagined the reporter trying to remember an abridged version of the play which derived from F (87), he now proposes that the acting version of the play represented by Q1 preceded the version represented by F.

The 1997 Norton Shakespeare, edited by Stephen Greenblatt and others, follows the Oxford *Complete Works* in printing both Q and F *King Lear*, because they seem to represent distinct authorial versions of the play. Greenblatt's team also prints a third, conflated, text, because it is 'the text on which innumerable performances of the play have been based and on which a huge body of literary criticism has been written' (Norton, xii). On similar grounds, they explain that they would have liked to have printed four texts of *Hamlet* and were only dissuaded from so doing by the perceived inappropriateness of the exercise for a largely undergraduate readership, along with 'the economics of publishing and the realities of bookbinding' (xii). The four texts, one assumes, would have included Q1 as well as Q2, F and a conflated text. What is not clearly stated is the reason for printing Q1. Is it because it reflects theatrical practice by Shakespeare's company? Or is it because, like F, Q1 derives ultimately from an authorial fair copy which includes authorial revisions of the original foul papers?

A common position?

There is, then, a lack of consensus among *Hamlet*'s editors over the nature of the editorial project. The same is true of their theories of the texts' transmission, largely because so much of the evidence is either contradictory or ambiguous. Thus, while few scholars now see in Q1 an early draft of a play by Shakespeare, the rest are still not agreed on how that text came into being. It clearly contains versions of some F passages not found in Q2 (e.g. F 2.2.335–60 on the theatre, F 5.2.75–80 on Laertes) and lacks some of the Q2 passages not found in F (e.g. Hamlet's twenty-two lines about Denmark's reputation in 1.2, and his dialogue with the Captain and subsequent soliloquy in 4.4). This suggests some kind of causal link between Q1 and F, but those who see such a link are not agreed on the precise nature of the relationship. Most believe that the original form of the text of Q1 post-dates the original form of the text of F. They find it difficult to agree, however, whether it is a memorial reconstruction or an adaptation – or a memorial reconstruction of an adaptation, or an adaptation of a memorial reconstruction – and whether what is being reconstructed or adapted is the text behind F or a performance of the text behind F.

Q2, on the other hand, has attracted near consensus in respect of certain features of its transmission. Almost all editors think the printer's copy for Q2 was Shakespeare's foul papers,[1] emended by occasional reference to a copy of Q1. It is worth noting, however, that some features of Q2 proposed as support for this position can be challenged. As we have already observed, it is not incontrovertible that Shakespeare is correcting first thoughts at 3.2.167–8. Nor is everyone entirely convinced that Hand D in *More* is Shakespeare's and that we

---

1   Richard F. Kennedy demonstrates that alternation between the speech prefixes '*Quee.*' and '*Ger.*' in Q2 arose from compositors X and Y running short of particular italic capital letters and argues that this weakens 'claims that such alternation is proof of foul papers' (Kennedy, R., 206).

know enough about Shakespeare's spelling habits to be able to discern where Q2 or F adhere to or deviate from a text in his handwriting. Furthermore, William B. Long has undermined confidence that a text containing indeterminate stage directions necessarily pre-dates theatrical performance, and Steven Urkowitz ('Basics', esp. 270–5) has even questioned the theory that a copy of Q1 was consulted by Q2's compositors.

As for F, most editors believe that the original form of the text of F post-dates the original form of the text of Q2. This in turn means that, while they accept the dates on the title-pages of all three texts, and therefore the order of printing which they imply, they believe that the order of composition of the three texts in their original forms is not Q1 > Q2 > F, but Q2 > F > Q1. Since the date on the title-page of Q1 is 1603, this means that the original forms of all three texts were in existence twenty years before F was printed. But that is the end of consensus. Editors are divided as to whether F's printer's copy was an annotated exemplar of Q2, collated with and emended against a transcript of a fair copy of Shakespeare's foul papers, or a transcript of Shakespeare's own revision of those foul papers.

Nevertheless, for all the range of disagreement among them, the editors discussed above agree on certain issues. Whatever their choice of copy-text, all incorporate readings from the rejected texts where the textual theory they have adopted supports emendation. All agree that

- Q2 derives directly, or pretty well directly, from foul papers.
- F derives directly or indirectly from some kind of transcript of foul papers.
- Q1 derives, probably at more removes than F, from the same transcript.
- Q1 was consulted in the preparation of Q2.
- Q2 directly or indirectly influenced the copy for F.

They also all agree that

- Q2 has considerable authority.
- F has at least some authority.
- Q1 may have at least some authority, even if it is only a matter of providing an insight into the play's performance history.

In addition, some think that the transcript referred to in relation to F and Q1 was prepared by Shakespeare himself, and that this gives as much authority to F as to Q2 (and, possibly, more), and increases the authority of Q1.

While editorial practice it is to some extent a function of the editor's choice of project, it is also to some extent a function of the editor's choice of transmission theory. Broadly speaking, every editor works within one of three theories, which we might call theory A, theory B and theory C. Those who adopt theory A assume a *single* lost holograph; they are obliged to choose Q2 as their copy-text. Those who adopt theory B assume *two* lost holographs; all of those discussed above choose F as their copy-text.[1]

Theory A
This theory can be expressed in simple diagrammatic form (in which derivation runs from top left to bottom right, and an asterisk indicates a Shakespeare manuscript).

---

1   Edwards adopts a compromise position, arguing that Shakespeare revised his play and incorporated the revisions in the foul papers, but Q2's compositors failed to always understand them so that some don't show up until F. He regards Q2 and F as a single copy-text, and chooses those readings he regards as the most Shakespearean. However, he rejects F whenever it leads away from Shakespeare the writer and towards the play as acted in the theatre. Taylor (Oxf; *TxC*), on the other hand, warms to the play as performed.

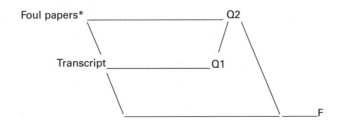

It holds that Q2 derives from Shakespeare's foul papers, while both Q1 and F derive from a transcript of those foul papers. An editor committed to producing a single edited text which reconstructs either 'the play as Shakespeare wrote it', or the play as Shakespeare intended it, will therefore take Q2 as the copy-text but, when persuaded that Q2 has misrepresented what was written in or intended by the foul papers and either Q1 or F records it more accurately, emend accordingly.

Jenkins, Wilson, Spencer and, to some extent, Edwards follow theory A. Jenkins, for example, takes Q2 as the copy-text because he believes Q2 is based on Shakespeare's foul papers. He emends when he deems it necessary, primarily with reference to F, which is based on an annotated copy of Q2 collated with and emended against a transcript of a fair copy of foul papers; Q1, which is based on a memorial reconstruction of the play in performance, can sometimes provide him with an insight into the intended text recorded in the foul papers.

Theory B

Theory B holds that Q2 derives from Shakespeare's foul papers, while both Q1 and F derive from a transcript, at least partly prepared by Shakespeare himself and incorporating his own revisions to the play. An editor committed to producing a single edited text will therefore take either Q2 or F (or even, it could be argued, Q1) as the copy-text. Nevertheless, since all three texts derive ultimately from one or both of the manuscripts in Shakespeare's hand, and the transcript is bound to carry over some material from the foul papers, any of the three texts not serving as the copy-text may be able to correct some of the copy-text's readings when the editor is persuaded that the copy-text is in error and the other Shakespearean autograph contained a 'better' version which a text other than the copy-text records more accurately. Theory B can be expressed diagramatically.

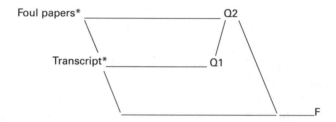

Hibbard and Taylor follow theory B, taking F as the copy-text and emending primarily with reference to Q2. Since they believe Shakespeare revised his play in a fair copy, changing its shape, content and language, they omit those sections of Q2 which do not feature in F, and try to use Q1 and Q2 to 'correct' F when it appears to go wrong in other respects. Taylor attempts to establish a dichotomy between foul papers and 'theatrical' texts, arguing that Q2 descends from one and F from the other:

> What matters, editorially, is the space between (a) the foul papers, and (b) the first theatrically motivated transcript of it. Some editors – Jenkins and Edwards, conspicuously – regard that interval as the threshold of debasement: what happens before belongs to Shakespeare, what happens afterwards belongs to someone else. We do not share their view. Instead, we regard that interval as a natural episode of authorial refinement . . . These differences in interpretation result from irreconcilably opposed ideologies of literary production.

(TxC, 400)

A possible option within theory B is not to produce a single edited text, as Hibbard and Taylor (Oxf) do, but two or even three, one based on Q2 because it derives pretty directly from the foul papers, one based on F because it derives pretty directly from the transcript in Shakespeare's hand, and possibly one based on Q1, because it too derives ultimately from the transcript.

Theory C

Theory C (if it can, indeed, be called a theory) holds that it is impossible and unnecessary to determine the origins of the three texts known as Q1, Q2 and F in the ways in which other editors have attempted, that each is of equal authority, and that an editor's job is to reproduce them verbatim and without emendation. Holderness and Loughrey fall into this category, rejecting both theories A and B as being too speculative. Perhaps the only way to express theory C diagrammatically is:

Q2

Q1

F

Holderness and Loughrey's cultural materialism regards each of the earliest printed texts as an 'authentic material object' (Holderness & Loughrey, 8), to be treated on its own terms as a Shakespearean *Hamlet*. This provides Q1 with a new authoritative status, but Spencer had begun the process when he included in his edition sections of dialogue probably supplied by the actors rather than the playwright and recorded in Q1. Whatever its origins, Q1 has now acquired enough of a theatrical history to have a claim to an edition of its own.

Our procedure as editors of Hamlet
Determining transmission

If we had only one of the three basic printed texts, we would necessarily take it as our control text, resolve the minor differences between individual copies on the basis of likelihood, and emend the resulting text only where it failed to yield a plausible meaning. Similarly, if there were only two basic texts – Q1 and just one out of Q2 or F – an editor would edit them separately, since Q1 is so very different from the others. Irace, in the Preface to her edition, begins by referring to Q1 as 'Shakespeare's first printed text of *Hamlet*' (Irace, ix), but she later appears to attribute authorship not to Shakespeare but to 'members of Shakespeare's company' (20). Either way, as a first draft by Shakespeare or as a later reconstruction *not* by Shakespeare, Q1 can clearly be edited as an independent entity.

What complicates matters is the joint existence of both Q2 and F which, while they differ from each other in many important respects, are so very much more similar to each other than either is to Q1. That degree of similarity encourages most editors to believe that, while all three texts must obviously have some common ancestry, Q2 and F have a particularly close family relationship. Such editors feel obliged to hypothesize the detailed history of transmission of at least Q2 and F from authorial first draft to printed book. And some editors, as we have already seen, produce extremely complicated hypotheses. Jenkins, for example, argues for at least eight identifiable stages of transmission from Shakespeare's first draft to F: the copy from which the compositors set Q2 was the foul papers, but they 'may obviously have still fouler papers behind them' (Ard[2], 37); Q2's compositors also referred to a copy of Q1; a fair copy of the foul papers was made, followed by a transcript of the fair copy; a copy of Q2 was then emended to conform with that transcript; and a transcript of the annotated copy of Q2 then became the copy for the compositors of F. Gary Taylor would add a further stage, when either Q3 or Q4 affected the preparation of F.

Faced with such complexity and the need for such a sophisticated degree of speculation, deduction and personal judgement, an editor may long for the simple life and look to other principles and procedures. Holderness and Loughrey settle for the reproduction of a single printed text, 'the object of which we can have direct knowledge' (Holderness & Loughrey, 8), rather than attempt to hunt down a hypothetical series of lost manuscripts. They set their faces against any kind of emendation of the text, even where it prints nonsense. Equally set against an 'author-centred' approach is Tronch-Pérez in his modernized 'synoptic' multiple edition of Q2 and F. What he offers is 'alternative interpretations of the early texts on which the author-centred editions are based' (Tronch-Pérez, 63). He is, however, prepared to emend, but only when readings have proved to be 'impossible or inexplicable' (63).

We do not feel that there is any clinching evidence to render definitive any of the competing theories outlined above. The temptation to deny that we have a theory for any one text, let alone all three, is almost overwhelming. Our disposition is agnostic, yet we know that it is philosophically impossible for an editor not to have at least a crude theory of transmission, simply because the choice of copy-text and the treatment of variants necessarily imply one. Our procedure has been to weigh the rival theories of transmission of the three texts and settle for the most probable. None is proven (or, we imagine, finally provable) and none can be dismissed out of hand. Theory A implies an edition of Q2, and one version of it implies an edition which includes as an appendix the sections in F which are not present in Q2. Theory B can imply either one edition (F) or two editions (one of Q2 and one of F) or three editions (one of Q2, one of F and one of Q1). Theory C, in turn, implies three editions. Our carefully negotiated, tentative position within a network of possibilities and probabilities is as follows.

Q1's text is sufficiently dissimilar to both Q2 and F to make it plausible that the compositor's copy could have been either an early draft by Shakespeare (or someone else) or an adaptation and/or memorial reconstruction of the text behind F – or a performance of that text – probably made by persons other than

Shakespeare. Some of Q1's entry stage directions fail to name individual characters (e.g. the 'Lordes' at 8.02 turn out to be Rossencraft and Gilderstone), a feature which Jenkins regards as characteristic of 'Shakespeare's practice in composition' (Ard[2], 37). But the stage directions *'Enter the ghost in his night gowne'* (Q1 11.57.1) and *'Enter Ofelia playing on a Lute, and her haire downe singing'* (Q1 13.14.1), while they could be regarded as designed for a reading audience, nevertheless suggest experience of actual performance and these, taken together with other evidence such as sixty possible 'actors' additions' detected by Irace, persuade us that it is slightly more probable that Q1 is a reconstruction than an early draft, and a reconstruction of a performed text than of a written text. We are therefore obliged to bear in mind that the texts behind Q2 or F may have contained readings which can correct errors in Q1.

The simplest explanation of the characteristics of the Q2 text is that the compositors' primary copy was Shakespeare's foul papers. All the editors discussed above who concern themselves with Q2 adopt this theory of its transmission and, while some of the grounds for the theory have been challenged, no more probable alternative has, to our knowledge, been advanced. They emend Q2 by reference primarily to F on the grounds that F, like Q2, derives ultimately from foul papers and may sometimes therefore record readings which can correct Q2 when it is in error.

F's text presents a much more difficult problem. In theory A, its copy was the original foul papers reinterpreted, or a transcript based on those foul papers, or an annotated copy of Q2 – or a combination of some or all of these. In theory B, whether or not any of these elements were also involved, F's copy derived from a manuscript, at one or more removes from the foul papers, recording significant (and insignificant) revisions by Shakespeare. Taylor (Oxf) and Hibbard follow theory B, choosing F as the copy-text and emending it by reference primarily to Q2, on the grounds that Shakespeare was revising only parts of the foul papers text and Q2 may record readings which can correct F when it is in error. But it could just as well be argued that theory B involves two *Hamlet*s, a first version and a second, the one represented primarily in Q2 and the other represented primarily in F, and that neither has to be the editor's preferred text. If we have to choose between these two versions of theory B, we find the second a simpler explanation of the facts and, while this is not a clinching argument, it provides a reasonable basis for preferring it.

Ours is not a strong theory of the texts' transmission but a default position arrived at by eliminating what we are persuaded are the less likely options. That position is that Q1's copy was based on an anonymous reconstruction of a performance based on the text behind F, that Q2's copy was largely based on Shakespeare's foul papers, and that F's copy was no more than one step away from a manuscript containing some significant authorial revisions to the text in the foul papers. We have arrived at a version of theory B, but it is that version which leads to three editions, since it seems to us to follow from the argument above that each of Q1, Q2 and F records a distinct *Hamlet*. We acknowledge that there is a case for a conflated edition, taking Q2 as the copy-text but incorporating the additional F material, but we have decided against this option on two practical grounds: we are restricted to the production of no more than three texts; and we have no reason to believe that we can produce a better Q2-based conflated edition than that of our predecessor, Harold Jenkins. For the reader who wants to construct a conflated edition we print as Appendix 1 the F passages absent from Q2.

Editorial principles

What we are attempting is an edition of each of three texts of *Hamlet* – those contained in the quartos of 1603 and 1604–5 and in the Folio of 1623. Our editorial approach is to produce a conservative edition of each text, while providing the reader with enough information to entertain a less conservative edition. By 'conservative edition' we mean one that keeps to the copy-text wherever it seems possible to do so without involving a degree of ingenuity which renders the refusal to emend implausible. Such a judgement involves the consideration of context, idiom, linguistic norms and our theory of the transmission of the texts,

Why are we conservative? For all that we are curious about our texts' transmission and their author's (or authors') intentions, we begin with the working assumption that each of our copy-texts reflects pretty accurately the manuscript that served as its compositor's copy. We attribute authority to the compositor's copy on the basis that, for all we know to the contrary (there being no hard evidence to go on), it is a pretty accurate record of what the author wrote and intended to write. Since all three texts claim Shakespeare as the author, since Shakespeare was resident dramatist in an acting company, and since all three texts contain publishers' references to that company as the play's provenance, the issue of whether or not 'playhouse practice' or 'actors' interpolations' have contaminated the author's text is not, for us, a major consideration.

The questions that follow from this are: how often are we going to emend, and upon what principle? Our answer is that we print the copy-text reading wherever we can reasonably defend it and emend only when, to us, it is implausible. When we emend, it is to provide the reader with a reading which makes sense in the context of a play probably written by Shakespeare in about 1600.[1] We are not assuming that behind the text we are editing lies any particular lost text, be it holograph, promptbook or performance, but we recognize that somewhere behind each text lies an authorial manuscript, and

---

1 Admittedly Q1 may technically have been authored by people other than Shakespeare, but it seems to derive ultimately from Shakespeare, and his writing therefore provides the best context for emendatory judgements.

that where our copy-text is in error there is a degree of probability (but no certainty) that one of the other texts contains a more accurate record of the author's intentions. Almost all other editors have emended much more frequently than we do, and many have used a different principle from ours. (Some of their ideas are recorded in our commentary and textual notes.)

In preparing our edition of Q1, we have found ourselves agreeing with Irace that 'in almost all cases, Q1's readings make sense' (29), and so, like her, we have resisted emending to make Q1 match Q2 or F. Nevertheless, most of our substantive emendations to Q1 are to be found, like hers, in Q2 or F. At 1.74 both her edition and ours correct 'seale' to 'sealed'; at 1.101 'invelmorable' to 'invulnerable'; at 2.5 'Yong' to 'You'; at 2.63 'teates' to 'tears'; at 2.158 'hither' to 'hitherto'; at 5.42 'fate' to 'sate'; at 5.51 'Hold' to 'Holds'; at 7.340 'Th'arganian' to 'th' Hyrcanian'; at 7.349 'calagulate' to 'coagulate'; at 9.162 'Murdred' to 'murderer'; at 16.145 'Pellon' to 'Pelion'; at 16.160 'Oosell' to 'Ossa'; at 17.64 'laught' to 'length'; at 17.132 'fight' to 'sight' (although, in fact, Q1's reading probably is 'sight'); and at 7.150 both introduce 'sooner'. In addition to these, however, Irace makes some emendations which we do not make – at 1.110 'strauagant' to 'extravagant'; at 2.2 'impudent' to 'impotent'; at 2.119 'stands' to 'Stand'; at 5.24 'that' to 'that I'; at 7.382 and 9.156 'Epiteeth' and 'Epitithe' to 'epitaph' (we emend to 'epithet'); at 9.20 'abhominable' to 'abominably'; at 9.170 'One' to 'On'; and at 16.105 'of' to 'on'. When Eric Rasmussen reviewed Irace's edition in 1999, he commented that occasionally 'Q1's seemingly defensible (albeit quirky) verbal variants are emended to conform to the standard Q2/F readings' and asked: 'should not these Q1 variants be preserved in an edition claiming to present "the first printed text of Shakespeare's *Hamlet*"?' (Rasmussen, 'Year', 312–13). Our edition preserves some of the variants Rasmussen had in mind, and, while we appear to share Irace's general principle for emendation (even if, for all we know, our reasons for turning to Q2 and F may be slightly different), our edition proves to be more conservative.

The closest to our Q2 edition is the extremely conservative multiple-text edition of Tronch-Pérez. He accepts that scribes and compositors make errors but only emends as a last resort, having used all his ingenuity to make sense of his copy-texts. As a result he makes just thirty-five substantive emendations to the dialogue in his Q2 text, whereas we make 128. Jenkins's Q2-based *Hamlet* not only incorporates all the F-only passages but goes on to emend the text on 293 occasions, with almost all of the emendations drawn from F (see Table 6 for the full list). Sometimes the decision to emend seems to be prompted because the F variant offers slightly easier sense than Q2, as when he prints 'soldier' for 'souldiers' at 1.1.15; 'be' for 'boy' at 1.3.74; 'posset' for 'possesse' at 1.5.68; 'tale' for 'talke' at 2.2.384; 'the cue' for 'that' at 2.2.496; 'music' for 'musickt' at 3.1.155; 'detecting' for 'detected' at 3.2.85; 'winter's' for 'waters' at 5.1.205; 'for' for 'or' at 5.2.84; 'comply' for 'so sir' at 5.2.167; and 'forc'd' for 'for no' at 5.2.367. Sometimes he sees in F a metrical improvement on Q2. This category includes seemingly minor emendations such as 'th'' for 'the' at 1.1.60, 1.3.44 and 2.2.447 (but 'the' for 'th'' at 2.2.392), but major emendations such as the deletion of 'Eyther none, in' at 3.2.162 and of 'greatness' at 4.7.8, or the addition of 'With fiery quickness' at 4.3.42, and 'murd'rous' at 5.2.309. At 5.2.298, despite a belief that repetition is often an indicator of actors' later additions, Jenkins introduces a repetition when he prefers F's 'Hamlet, thou' to Q2's 'thou'! Metrical matters are, of course, in the ear of the reader, and at least on occasion a matter of literary taste and judgement.

The remainder are emendations where Jenkins makes a literary judgement about what Shakespeare would have written or would have wanted to have written. He sometimes finds F to be 'noticeably inferior' to Q2 (Ard², 61), but there are many places where F is 'obviously superior' (59). For example, at 1.4.49 he prints F's 'inurn'd' for Q2's 'interred', while 'fretful' is preferred to 'fearefull' at 1.5.20, 'o'er-offices' to 'ore-reaches' at 5.1.74, and 'affear'd' to 'sure' at 5.2.282. Such judgements are sometimes reinforced by the application of a supposed 'rule', such as 'repetition of a word or small phrase suggests non-authorial actors' additions' (F's 'Well' is preferred to Q2's 'well, well' at 1.5.174, F's 'was' is preferred to Q2's 'was sir' at 5.1.171),[1] or 'the unusual reading may well be the authorial one' (F's 'crimeful' is cautiously preferred to 'criminall' at 4.7.7). A problem with these choices based on literary judgement is that editors, whom one might expect to agree sometimes do not. At 4.5.9 Jenkins emends Q2's 'yawne' to F's 'aim', but Edwards, despite being less committed to Q2 as copy-text, prints 'yawn'. Again, even though at 4.7.157 Jenkins emends Q2's 'prefard' to F's 'prepar'd', Edwards prefers 'preferred'.

Frequently, Jenkins's emendations seem to arise not because Q2 makes little sense, or offends against a metrical test, but because the existence of a variant in F provides the opportunity for expressing a literary preference. Once an editor has adopted a theory of the relationship between Q2 and F which allows the possibility that, in any instance where F has a different reading from the one in Q2, that variant may record a more authoritative reading than the one in Q2, there is an open invitation to emend Q2 by reference to F. While the choices open to Jenkins include other editors' emendations and his own independent attempts to reconstruct the lost manuscript through a knowledge of Shakespeare's other work and the mechanics of Elizabethan handwriting and printing, his belief that Q1, Q2 and F are all imperfect descendants of the single lost holograph version of the play encourages him to conceive of them as a single data

---

1 In opting for F's 'till' rather than Q2's 'all' at 5.2.227, Jenkins ignores the use of 'Till' just two lines earlier.

set. Like us, he is ultimately prepared to derive his emendations from any reasonable source, but he feels much less committed to his copy-text than we do. Q2 may be closer to his goal, the single play that Shakespeare wrote, than are the other two extant early versions, but all three nevertheless provide him with his best clues to the nature of that lost text. He argues that, even where Q2 prints nonsense, 'we might well not have seen what the true reading should be if it had not been preserved in F' (Ard², 59). Equally, it seems likely that many Q2 readings would not have been revealed to Jenkins as 'errors' had he not had access to F's 'corrections'. The result is that he feels at liberty to look beyond his copy-text and emend, not just when the copy-text presents an impossible or unlikely reading, but whenever he sees in Q1 or F a *preferable* reading.

A similar willingness to emend is to be found in the F-based editions by Hibbard (Oxf¹) and by Taylor (Oxf), both of whom draw liberally on Q2, and occasionally on Q1. Once again, there is a marked contrast with the F editions prepared by Tronch-Pérez and ourselves. Tronch-Pérez makes only twenty-nine substantive emendations to the dialogue, we make eighty-two (of which sixty-seven are to be found in Q2), but Hibbard's total is 342 (325 taken from Q2) and Taylor's 356 (337 taken from Q2). A high level of emendation is understandable where an editor's theory holds that both Q2 and F derive from a single lost holograph and there is the possibility that in any particular instance either Q2 or F could be the better record of the author's text. In such a case (for example, Jenkins's edition), the decision to emend is bound to be ultimately a matter of literary judgement. But once the editor's theory entertains two holographs, with Q2 deriving primarily from one and F deriving primarily from the other, one would expect that there would no longer be the same pressure to emend either Q2 or F, for where they diverge they could both be right.

One reason that Jenkins, Hibbard and Taylor (Oxf) all emend more frequently than we do is their commitment to certain 'rules' deriving from their wish to reconstruct a lost manuscript or performance. Jenkins, for example, writes that F 'regularly gives us *he* for the pronoun *a* which is common in Q2. It tends, though less systematically, to expand *th'* to *the*. It changes *my* and *thy* before a vowel into *mine* and *thine*' (Ard², 61).

One might expect that, given their choice of copy-text, Jenkins would prefer the Q2 form, Hibbard and Taylor (Oxf) the F form. But this is not how it always turns out. First of all, the expected pattern is not always there in the copy-texts. To take the 'my'/'mine' choice as an example, as early as 1.1.67 Q2 reads 'of mine opinion', while at the equivalent point F reads 'of my Opinion'. However, all three editors print 'my opinion'. This means that Taylor and Hibbard stick with their copy-text, while Jenkins *corrects* his on the assumption that Shakespeare habitually wrote 'my' before a vowel, and in this instance someone must have misread his handwriting. If we now turn to 1.2.151, we find that Q2 reads 'my Vncle', while F reads 'mine Vnkle'. This time the expected pattern is there. Jenkins prints 'my uncle', sticking with his copy-text as well as his belief that before a vowel Shakespeare always writes *my* rather than *mine*. Taylor again sticks with his copy-text and prints *mine*. But, despite explaining that 'where indifferent readings are concerned that of F is normally preferred to that of Q2' (Oxf¹, 131) Hibbard here overrules his copy-text, and prints Q2's 'my'. What emerges is that, given a choice between Q2 and F, and despite their allegiances to different copytexts, Jenkins and Hibbard always print 'my', even if it means emending Q2, while Taylor (Oxf) prints 'mine'. Similarly Hibbard emends 'ye' to 'you', but Taylor (Oxf) does not. However, Taylor always emends 'he' to 'a', but Hibbard does not. There are some problems here, surely. Jenkins's belief that Shakespeare preferred 'my' to 'mine' arises from the fact that Q2 has a clear preference for 'my', and Jenkins believes that Q2, unlike F, is based directly on foul papers. But, even though Jenkins always opts for 'my' when given a choice between variants, he does not print 'my' when Q2 and F agree on 'mine', so he clearly does not believe that Shakespeare *always* wrote 'my'. If Shakespeare did not always write 'my', why change 'mine' to 'my' in any particular instance? And once Taylor or Hibbard have decided F has a *new* manuscript behind it, why do we think we need Q2's readings in the argument? Only, surely, where F fails to make sense. So why change 'my' to 'mine'?

Sometimes F repeats a word within a line or two, and Q2 does not. An example is F 1.1.130–3, where F's text reads 'I haue hearde / The Cocke that is the Trumpet to the day, / Doth with his lofty and shrill-sounding Throate / Awake the God of Day.' Taylor and Hibbard silently emend F's 'day' in the second line to Q2's 'morne', presumably because 'day' is repeated two lines later, just as at 1.3.117 they reject F's 'Giues', which is followed a line later by 'Giuing'. But why would Shakespeare not be prepared to repeat a word so quickly? After all, 'giue th'assay of Armes' at 2.2.71 is followed two lines later by 'Giues him three thousand Crownes' and four lines after that by 'giue quiet passe'.

Another 'rule' relates to the view that the original text behind F may have been purged of some oaths. In the first act, for example, F at 1.2.148 and at 1.5.24 has 'O Heauen' where Q1 and Q2 have 'O God', and at 1.2.192 F has 'For Heauen's loue' where Q1 and Q2 have 'For God's loue'. If this in any way reflects a shift in public taste, that shift clearly post-dates the publication of Q2, and therefore the original form of F; what is more, Q1 shares Q2's reading, despite the fact that Q1 probably records an attempt to reconstruct the performance text of F. Both Taylor (Oxf) and Hibbard emend their copy-text at each point and print 'God'. F at 2.1.74 reads 'Heauen', Q2 at 2.1.73 has 'God', but Q1 has no equivalent phrase, and yet Taylor and Hibbard still print 'God'. They have clearly developed a rule that, irrespective of whether Q1 supports Q2's reading, where Q2 has an oath and F does not, F's reading needs replacing with

Q2's. This rule has a logic to it, and they extend the principle to all places where an oath of any kind is weaker or absent in F. But there are only twelve such places in the whole text, F still has twenty-two references to God, and on one occasion (F 4.1.195) F actually introduces 'I pray God' at a point where Q2 has no such phrase.

We have refrained from correcting the copy-text when there is no problem of meaning. We have followed the copy-text for stage directions (except where they need amplification or emendation according to Arden conventions, or when it clarifies the action, or helps the reader to visualize the play in performance). But in respect of the dialogue our rule is that, where the copy-text is implausible, we take note of the other two texts before any other potential emendatory source, and that (in light of our 'default position' theory of the texts' transmission), where we wish to choose between variants within that pool, F is a likelier authority than Q2 for emending Q1, F is a likelier authority than Q1 for emending Q2, and Q2 is a likelier authority than Q1 for emending F.

An example is provided at Q2 1.5.55–7, which in the copy-text reads:

> So but though to a radiant Angle linckt,
> Will sort it selfe in a celestiall bed
> And pray on garbage.

The equivalent in Q1 (5.41–3) reads:

> So Lust, though to a radiant angle linckt,
> Would fate it selfe from a celestiall bedde,
> And prey on garbage:

The equivalent in F (1.5.55–7) reads:

> So Lust, though to a radiant Angell link'd,
> Will sate it selfe in a Celestiall bed, & prey on
> Garbage.

We have emended Q2's 'but' (1.5.55), not because we prefer a reading in Q1 or F, but because Q2's reading makes no sense, and we are forced to look for a reading which makes sense. We have emended it to Q1/F's 'Lust', not because of a principle that, so long as it provides at least a slightly better variant, one of Q1 or F has to be our solution, but because of a principle that, where the copy-text fails to provide a plausible reading, we consider Q1 and F variants before we consider other alternatives and, in this instance, the Q1/F variant 'Lust' not only makes more sense than Q2 but actually makes very good sense. Had Q1 or F only yielded a variant which made slightly more sense, we might have tried to come up with a better alternative ourselves, and then weighed the probabilities according to our own literary/historical judgement.

Similarly, we have emended both Q1's 'fate' (5.42) and Q2's 'sort' (1.5.56) to F's 'sate', because F's reading makes excellent sense for Q2 and fairly acceptable sense (certainly better than any alternative we can think of) for Q1. As it happens, F also takes precedence in the chains of textual authority for both Q1 and Q2, and had it been competing with an equally plausible variant it would have won out. Finally, of course, confusion of ƒ and long *s* is among the easiest of misreadings and misprints.

Lineation and punctuation

We try to follow each copy-text's lineation, except where it seems to be ignoring obvious verse or obvious prose. Confronted by short verse lines where the immediately preceding or succeeding lines are blank verse,[1] we have rearranged the lineation only where the result easily makes convincing blank verse. Where dialogue between two or three speakers involves

1   'Blank verse' is the name given to unrhyming verse lines, each of which has between nine and eleven syllables and a rhythm which is iambic, i.e. generated by the regular alternation of one light, followed by one heavy, beat. A 'short line' here means one that has fewer than five heavy beats.

a run of three short lines which could make blank verse in two different ways, and neither way is much easier than the other, we have set the first two as blank verse, and left the third short.[1] If a speech, even though it has less than five feet, is clearly iambic and doesn't easily link up with another adjacent speech to create a pentameter, it stands as a line of verse. If a whole scene is almost entirely verse, it has sometimes been considered better to present as verse a speech which might otherwise be regarded as prose. In our Q1 and F texts, we have preserved their lineation where it differs from Q2 and yet makes obvious verse or prose.

We have modernized punctuation, but we have also attempted to some extent to reflect the different punctuation characteristics of the three printed texts. F is more heavily punctuated than Q1 or Q2,[2] using both more punctuation and more of the 'heavier' marks (i.e. fewer commas and more semicolons, colons, dashes, brackets, question marks, exclamation marks and full stops).[3] But there is no way of knowing the precise extent to which this reflects the manuscripts from which the printers worked rather than the different practices of the compositors employed by Valentine Simmes in 1603, James Roberts in 1604–5 and William Jaggard in 1623. Fredson Bowers found no evidence that there were printing-house rules in the Elizabethan period

---

1 Despite the fact that this is contrary to Arden practice.
2 Q1 has 3,115 punctuation marks across its 15,983 words; Q2 has 4,741 across its 28,628 words; F has 5,434 across its 27,602 words.
3 Commas make up 67 per cent of Q2's punctuation, 64 per cent of Q1's, but only 51 per cent of F's. F makes more use of each of the other punctuation marks than Q2 does, and Q1 only exceeds F in its use of the exclamation mark. Q1 has 1,987 commas, 21 semicolons, 227 colons, 5 pairs of brackets, 208 question marks, 31 exclamation marks, no dashes and 636 full stops. Q2 has 3,189 commas, 118 semicolons, 123 colons, 13 pairs of brackets, 261 question marks, 4 exclamation marks, no dashes and 1,033 full stops. F has 2,767 commas, 285 semicolons, 547 colons, 59 pairs of brackets, 445 question marks, 20 exclamation marks, 7 dashes and 1,304 full stops.

for punctuation, although some houses clearly favoured certain punctuation marks (Bowers, *Criticism*, 134n.).

Anthony Graham-White has observed that F adopts more complex punctuation than the quartos, not only because of its wish to be 'literary' but because punctuation had become more sophisticated by 1623 – particularly in relation to the intermediate marks, the colon and the semicolon (Graham-White, 34; see also Proudfoot, 'Modernizing', 26–8). The exclamation mark appears rarely in Shakespeare's plays, and compositors had more question marks in their case, so the question mark is often found where we would expect an exclamation mark: the latter is mentioned in the earliest printed English grammar, John Hart's *An Orthography* (1569), but only began regularly to replace the question mark some years after Shakespeare's death (Graham-White, 31–2).

We have taken note of each copy-text's punctuation both at a local level and at the level of the text as a whole and, where it makes acceptable sense and modern conventions allow, have tried to follow it. Modern punctuation conventions do not always give us much room for manoeuvre, however, and, for all that we attempt to retain something of the distinctive character of each text, it is unfortunately frequently impossible.

An example, not only of the punctuation characteristics of the three texts, but also of the problems posed by attempting to punctuate our editions of them, is Hamlet's first soliloquy (1.2.129–59). Q2 uses thirty-five commas, a couple of semicolons, one question mark and one full stop; F's almost identical soliloquy uses sixteen more punctuation marks: twenty-six commas, two semicolons, nine colons, a pair of brackets, four question marks, two exclamation marks and ten full stops. Thus F not only uses more punctuation but heavier punctuation – colons, full stops, question marks and exclamation marks – while Q2 tends to turn to the comma when it feels punctuation is needed. Q1's equivalent speech is very much shorter than its counterparts; it uses proportionately more punctuation than Q2, but less than F: sixteen commas, one semicolon, seven colons, no parentheses, no question marks, one exclamation mark and three full stops.[1]

Lines 5–10 of this speech run as follows in Q2:

How wary, stale, flat, and vnprofitable
Seeme to me all the vses of this world?
Fie on't, ah fie, tis an vnweeded garden
That growes to seede, things rancke and grose in
    nature,
Possesse it meerely that it should come thus

The question mark ending the second line can hardly mean that the first two lines make up a question. In our edition, therefore, we change it to an exclamation mark. It is hard to make sense of the absence of any mark after 'meerely' in the fifth line, so we introduce a full stop. We drop the comma after 'flat' in the first line, since Arden house style, in common with most British publishing practice, omits serial commas (i.e. commas before the final 'and' in lists of three or more items) unless required to avoid ambiguity, whereas such commas were more often included in seventeenth-century texts.[2] Our Q2 version runs thus at lines 133–7:

How weary, stale, flat and unprofitable
Seem to me all the uses of this world!
Fie on't, ah, fie, 'tis an unweeded garden
That grows to seed, things rank and gross in nature
Possess it merely. That it should come thus:

---

1   In Q2 the speech consists of 258 words, in F (1.2.127–57) it has 262, while Q1 (2.55–75) uses only 158. Q2 averages one punctuation mark for every 8.32 words, Q1 has one for every 5.64 words, and F has one for every 4.76 words. Another difference is in the use of marks: for example, although each of Q2 and F uses two semicolons, they do not occur at the same points in the speech.

2   We decided reluctantly not to retain this comma, which appears in both Q2 and F, although it could be argued that it was intended to signal to the actor that the line should be delivered slowly, doggedly and wearily.

F has eleven punctuation marks rather than Q2's eight, and neither of its two question marks indicates a question:

> How weary, stale, flat, and vnprofitable
> Seemes to me all the vses of this world?
> Fie on't? Oh fie, fie, 'tis an vnweeded Garden
> That growes to Seed: Things rank, and grosse in
> > Nature
> Possesse it meerely. That it should come to this:

In the first line, Arden house style again omits the serial comma before 'and'; modern conventions require us to remove the comma after 'rank' in the fourth line; but as part of a strategy to indicate that F's punctuation is both heavier than Q2's and slightly more 'expressive' (perhaps because it is a more 'literary' production), we have changed the colon at the end of the fifth line into an exclamation mark:

> How weary, stale, flat and unprofitable
> Seems to me all the uses of this world!
> Fie on't! O fie, fie, 'tis an unweeded garden
> That grows to seed: things rank and gross in nature
> Possess it merely. That it should come to this!

TEXTUAL TABLES5

TABLE 1 Variants in copies of Q1

In the following list, the uncorrected state is given first:

No.	Ard³	Forme	Line	Variant	Copy
1	1.29 SD	Bi	Biᵛ.15	(double leads below) (leads above and below)	HN L
2	2.13	Bo	B3.31	*Leartes* *Leartes,*	HN L
3	2.13	Bo	B3.31	newes news	HN L
4	2.15	Bo	B3.33	*Lea:* *Lea.*	HN L
5	2.58	Bi	B4.7	God God,	HN L
6	2.58	Bi	B4.7	moneths months	HN L
7	2.58	Bi	B4.7	maried married	HN L
8	2.98	Bo	B4ᵛ.14	father, father.	HN L
9	2.116	Bo	B4ᵛ.35	eies. eies	HN L

Key: HN = Huntington Library, San Marino; L = British Library, London

TABLE 2 Variants in copies of Q2
In the following list, the uncorrected state is given first.

No.	Ard^3	Forme	Line	Variant	Copy
1	[imprint]	Ai	A1.12	1604. 1605.	F HN Y^2 L C^2 VER Wro
2	1.1.106	Bo	$B2^v.20$	Romeage Romadge	L VER Wro F HN Y^2 C^2
3	1.2.176	Ci	C2.2	pre thee prethee	F HN Y^2 L C^2 VER Wro
4	1.2.212	Co	$C2^v.3$	watch, watch watcl	C^2 VER Wro HN Y^2 F L
5	1.3.47	Ci	$C3^v.31$	step steepe	F HN Y^2 L C^2 VER Wro
6	1.3.69	Ci	C4.15	by buy	F HN Y^2 L C^2 VER Wro
7	1.4.69	Di	D2.4	my my Lord,	HN Y^2 F L C^2 VER Wro
8	1.5.7	Do	$D2^v.4$	here[1] hear heare.	Y^2 HN F L C^2 VER Wro

1 Paul Bertram and Bernice Kliman believe they have detected this unique uncorrected state in the Yale copy (Bertram–Kliman^2).

No.	Ard³	Forme	Line	Variant	Copy
9	1.5.90	Di	D3v.9	gines gins	HN Y² F L C² VER Wro
10	2.2.522	Go	G1.10	braues braines	L Wro F HN Y² C² VER
11	3.1.160	Go	G3.38	[no SD] Exit.	L Wro F HN Y² C² VER
12	4.5.102	Lo	L1.16	Ore beares Ore-beares	L F HN Y² C² VER Wro
13	4.5.102	Lo	L1.	Officres Officers	L F HN Y² C² VER Wro
14	4.5.109	Lo	L1.23	.(A .A	L F HN Y² C² VER Wro
15	5.1.287	No	N1.18	thirtie thereby	F HN Y² Wro L C² VER
16	5.2.9	No	N1.30	pall fall	F HN Y² Wro L C² VER
17	5.2.95	No	N2ᵛ.2	sellingly fellingly	F HN Y². L Wro C² VER

(Continued)

TABLE 2 (Continued)

18	5.2.99	No	N2ᵛ.6	dosie dazzie	F HN Y² Wro L C² VER
19	5.2.100	No	N2ᵛ.7	yaw raw	F HN Y² Wro L C² VER
20	5.2.100	No	N2ᵛ.7	neither in neither,in	F HN Y² Wro L C² VER
21	5.2.111	No	N2ᵛ.17	too't doo't	F HN Y² Wro L C² VER
22	5.2.134	No	N2ᵛ.36	reponsiue responsiue	F HN Y² L Wro C² VER
23	5.2.142	No	N3.4	be be might	F HN Y² Wro L C² VER
24	5.2.167	No	N3.25	sir so sir	F HN Y² Wro L C² VER
25	5.2.249	Ni	N4.34	Vnice Onixe	F HN Y² Wro L C² VER
26	[signature]	Oi	O2	G2 O2	F HN Y² C² VER Wro

Key: F = Folger Library, Washington; HN = Huntington Library, San Marino; Y² = Beinecke Library, Yale University, New Haven; L = British Library, London; C² = Trinity College Library, Cambridge; VER = Bodleian Library, Oxford; Wro = University of Wrocław.

TABLE 3 Q2's compositors

The division of labour in Roberts's printing shop was as follows:

Compositor	Ard³	Signatures
X	1.1.1–1.5.181	B1–D4ᵛ
	2.2.158b–2.2.512	F1–F4ᵛ
	3.3.21–3.4.208	I1–I4ᵛ
	5.1.272 to end	N1–O2
Y	1.5.182–2.2.158a	E1–E4ᵛ
	2.2.513–3.3.20	G1–H4ᵛ
	3.4.209–4.5.89	K1–K4ᵛ
	4.5.90–4.7.133	L1–L4ᵛ
	4.7.134–5.1.271	M1–M4ᵛ

TABLE 4 F's compositors

The division of labour in Jaggard's printing shop was as follows.
(T.H. Howard-Hill has queried Hinman's analysis of Compositor E's
work,[1] hence the 'E?' in the following table.)

Compositor	Ard³	Signatures
B	1.1.1–1.2.162	nn4ᵛ–nn5ᵛ
	1.5.22–1.5.57	oo1b
	2.1.102–2.2.212	oo2ᵛ–oo3
	2.2.339 (fashion) – 4.3.50 (hand?)	oo4–pp4a
	4.3.71–5.1.22	pp4ᵛ
	5.2.221 (Giue) –5.2.358	qq1–qq1ᵛ
I	1.2.163–1.5.21	nn6–oo1a
	1.5.58–2.1.101	oo1ᵛ–oo2
	2.2.213–2.2.339 (the)	oo3ᵛ
B or I	4.3.50 ('Tis)–4.3.70	pp4b
E	5.1.23–5.1.272	pp5–pp5ᵛ
E?	5.1.273–5.2.221 (worne.)	pp6–pp6ᵛ

1   In two privately circulated monographs – 'Compositors B and E in the Shakespeare
First Folio and some recent studies' (1976) and 'A reassessment of compositors
B and E in the First Folio tragedies' (1977) – and in Howard-Hill, 'New light',
156–78.

TABLE 5 Variants in copies of F

In the following list, the uncorrected state is given first.[1]

No.	Compositor	Page	Signature	Line	Variant	Ard³
1	B	154	nn5ᵛ	page number	152 154	
2	B			b17	ns as	1.2.120
3	B			b33	Posseffe Possesse	1.2.135
4	B			b39	hnng hang	1.2.141
5	B			b64	friend, ■ friend,	1.2.161
6	I	155	nn6	a42	B■ By	1.2.200
7	B	260	oo2ᵛ	a31	Sinee Since	2.2.6
8	B			a64	*Hamlee* *Hamlet*	2.2.36

(Continued)

1 In Ard², Jenkins repeated his earlier claim ('The relation between the Second Quarto and the Folio text of *Hamlet*', *SB*, 7 [1955], 69–83), itself deriving from Walker (*Problems*, 124), that some copies of F read 'off' rather than 'of' at 1.1.39 (F nn4ᵛ, b3), but Hinman records no such variant. *TxC* records the King as beginning a speech with 'On' at 3.4.202 (F pp2ᵛ, a39), but the copies we have consulted suggest that it is 'Oh' with the 'h' only partly inked.

TABLE 5 (Continued)

9	B			b18	yuur / your	2.2.54
10	B			b19	othet / other	2.2.55
11	B			b48	take / thanke	2.2.82
12	I	262	oo3ᵛ	b30–1	An-/ gell? / An-/ gel?	2.2.305
13	I			b31	God the / God? the	2.2.305
14	B	265	oo5	b18	returnes. / returnes,	3.1.80
15	E	277	pp5	page number	273 / 277	
16	E			a58	iowlos / iowles	5.1.76
17	E			a60–1	Of-/fices one / Of-/fices: one	5.1.78
18¹	E			b15	hs Tricks / his Tricks	5.1.98

1 Hinman records that 'hs' was corrected to 'his' in line b15, but fails to explain which 'his' in the line ('Quillets? his Cases? his Tenures, and his Tricks? why') he is referring to. We are grateful to Georgianna Ziegler for identifying the variant 'his' by consulting the two copies which Hinman mentions as having the uncorrected forme (copies 25 and 52 of FF in the Folger Library, Washington, DC; see Hinman, *Printing*, 1.302).

No.	Compositor	Page	Signature	Line	Variant	Ard[3]
19	E	278	pp5ᵛ	a17	sirh, is sir, his	5.1.167
20	E			a20	twentyearys twenty years	5.1.171
21	E			a40	laugh■at laugh at	5.1.192
22	E			a40	pry pry-	5.1.192
23	E			a41	o-nthing one thing	5.1.193
24	E			a64	*Cooffin* *Coffin*	5.1.213.1
25	E			b1	rights rites	5.1.216
26	E			b3	For do Fore do	5.1.218
27	E			b30	Brid-bed Bride-bed	5.1.242
28	E			b30	Maide Maid	5.1.242

(Continued)

TABLE 5 (Continued)

29	E				*Laer.* *Laer.*	5.1.243
30	E			b32	*in■the* *in the*	5.1.247.1
31	E			b37	Emphasies? Emphasis?	5.1.252
32	E			b43	wisensse wisenesse	5.1.260
33[1]	E			b52	a sunder asunder	5.1.261
34	E			b53	*Qn.* *Qu.*	5.1.269
35	E			b63	forebeare forbeare	5.1.269
36[2]	E			b63	Crocadile Crocodile	5.1.272
37	B		281	b66	thee [damaged 'h'] thee ['h' replaced]	5.2.301
				qq1		
				b33		

1 Jenkins considers that F is following Q2 in its spelling 'a sunder', and then decides to correct it (Ard[2], 66).

2 Jenkins sees 'Crocadile' as another case of F following Q2, and then 'correcting' it (Ard[2], 66).

TABLE 6 Ard² Q2 emendations from F

Please note that line references are to the present edition of Ard Q2. Jenkins's emendations are printed in italics to distinguish them from words in the copy-text.

Jenkins's emendations where F makes easier sense than Q2

soldier for 'souldiers', 1.1.15; *be* for 'boy', 1.3.74; *posset* for 'possesse', 1.5.68; *no* added after 'Fayth', 2.1.28; *tale* for 'talke', 2.2.384; *the cue* for 'that', 2.2.496; *music* for 'musickt', 3.1.155; *detecting* for 'detected', 3.2.85; *winter's* for 'waters', 5.1.205; *for* for 'or', 5.2.84; *comply* for 'so sir', 5.2.167; *forc'd* for 'for no', 5.2.367.

Jenkins's emendations where F is a metrical improvement on Q2

'*th*' for 'the', 1.1.60; *th'* for 'the', 1.3.44; *like* added after 'Whiles', 1.3.48; *a* added after 'what', 1.5.47; *o'er-hasty* for 'hastie', 2.2.57; *three* for 'threescore', 2.2.73; *since* added after 'Therefore', 2.2.90; '*tis* added after 'thinke', 2.2.149; *the* for 'th'', 2.2.392; *And* added before 'Like', 2.2.419; *th'* for 'the', 2.2.447; *Let's* added after 'comming', 3.1.54; *of us all* added after 'cowards,', 3.1.82; *expectancy* for 'expectation', 3.1.151; 'Eyther none,' deleted before ''in', 3.2.162; *foolish* for 'most foolish', 3.4.213; *With fiery quickness* added before 'Therefore', 4.3.42; *their* added after ''in', 4.5.82; *proceeded* for 'proceed', 4.7.6; 'greatness' deleted after 'safetie', 4.7.8; *shall* added after 'I', 4.7.54; *and* added after 'spleenatiue', 5.1.250; *affear'd* for 'sure', 5.2.282; *Hamlet, thou* for 'thou', 5.2.298; *murd'rous* added after 'incestious', 5.2.309.

Jenkins's emendations where F is 'superior' to Q2

Question for 'Speake to', 1.1.44; *my* for 'mine', 1.1.67; *why* for 'with' and *cast* for 'cost', 1.1.72; *those* for 'these', 1.1.87; *return'd* for 'retume', 1.1.90; *cov'nant* for 'comart', 1.1.92; *at* added after 'strike', 1.1.139; *bonds* for 'bands', 1.2.24; *so* for 'so much', 1.2.67; *good* for 'coold', 1.2.77; *a* for 'or', 1.2.96; *to this* for 'thus', 1.2.137; *would* for 'should', 1.2.143; *to drink deep* for 'for to drinke', 1.2.174; *bulk* for 'bulkes', 1.3.12; *For he himself is subject to his birth* added after 1.3.18; *dulls* for 'dulleth', 1.3.76; *parley* for 'parle', 1.3.122; *inurn'd* for 'interred', 1.4.49; *frefful* for 'fearefull', 1.5.20; *pursuest* for 'pursues', 1.5.84;

(*Continued*)

TABLE (Continued)

stiffy for 'swiftly', 1.5.95; *bird* for 'and', 1.5.115; *Ah ha* for 'Ha, ha', 1.5.171; *Well* for 'well, well', 1.5.174; *i'th'* for 'with', 2.1.40; *passion* for 'passions', 2.1.102; *I* added after 'so', 2.2.5; *he is* for 'hee's', 2.2.97; *above* for 'about', 2.2.123; *winking* for 'working', 2.2.134; *a* added after 'to', 2.2.146; *suddenly contrive the means of meeting between him and* added after 'and', 2.2.208; *sir* added after 'cannot', 2.2.210; *over-happy* for 'euer happy', 2.2.223; 25 lines beginning *Let me* and ending *attended* after 'true;', 2.2.235; *even* for 'euer', 2.2.238; *woman* for 'women', 2.2.275; *the clown shall make those laugh whose lungs are tickle a th' sear* added after 'peace,', 2.2.289; 23 lines beginning *How comes* and ending *too* added after 2.2.299; *tragical-historical, tragical-comicall-historical-pastoral* added after 'Historicall Pastorall', 2.2.335; *husband's* for 'husband', 2.2.452; *a* added after 'for', 2.2.476; *dozen* for 'dosen lines', 2.2.477; *his* for 'the', 2.2.489; *scullion* for 'stallion', 2.2.522; *too* for 'two' (possibly a variant spelling), 3.1.28; *lawful espials* added after 'selfe,', 3.1.31; *dispriz'd* for 'despiz'd', 3.1.71; *the* for 'these', 3.1.98; *your honesty* for '²you', 3.1.106; *all* added after 'knaues', 3.1.128; *your* added after 'wantonnes', 3.1.144; *that* for 'what', 3.1.156; *tune* for 'time', 3.1.157; *feature* for 'stature', 3.1.158; *your* for 'our', 3.2.3; *of the* for 'of', 3.2.26; *praise* for 'praysd', 3.2.29; *Ham. I mean, my head upon your lap. / Oph. Ay, my lord* added after 3.2.109; *is* added after 'this', 3.2.130; 'women feare too much, euen as they loue, And' deleted, 3.2.160–1; *o'* for '²of', 3.2.234; *my* for 'mine', 3.2.242; *Confederate* for 'Considerat', 3.2.249; *my* added after 'of', 3.2.310; *to the top* of for 'to', 3.2.358; *breathes* for 'breaks', 3.2.379; *bitter business as the* for 'business as the bitter', 3.2.381; *pat* for 'but', 3.3.73; *hire and salary* for 'base and silly', 3.3.79; *tristful* for 'heated', 3.4.48; *panders* for 'pardons', 3.4.86; *grained* for 'greeued', 3.4.88; *not leave* for 'leaue there', 3.4.89; *tithe* for 'kyth', 3.4.95; *Compounded* for 'Compound', 4.2.5; *were ne're begun* for 'will nere begin', 4.3.66; *aim* for 'yawne', 4.5.9; *Larded* for 'Larded all', 4.5.38; *grave* for 'ground', 4.5.39; *an old* for 'a poore', 4.5.159; three lines added beginning *Nature* and ending *loves* after 4.5.159; *must* for 'may', 4.5.175; *affliction* for 'afflictions', 4.5.180; *All* added before 'Flaxen', 4.5.188; *Christian* for 'Christians', 4.5.192; *crimeful* for 'criminall', 4.7.7; *conjunctive* for 'concliue', 4.7.15 (we emend to 'conjunct'); *had* for 'haue', 4.7.25; *your* for 'you', 4.7.45; *and more strange* added after 'suddaine', 4.7.46; *prepar'd* for 'prefard', 4.7.157; *douts* for 'drownes', 4.7.189; four lines added beginning *Why, he* and ending *arms?* after 'Armes.', 5.1.33; *frame* added after 'that', 5.1.39; *to Yaughan* for 'in, and', 5.1.56; *intil* for 'into', 5.1.69; *to th'* for 'to the', 5.1.72; *o'er-offices* for 'ore-reaches', 5.1.74; *meant* for 'went', 5.1.80; *his* added after 'will', 5.1.101; *double ones too* for 'doubles', 5.1.102; *'tis* for 'it is', 5.1.117; *all* added after 'Of', 5.1.135; *o'ercame* for 'ouercame', 5.1.136; *nowadays* added after 'corses', 5.1.156; *three and twenty* for '23', 5.1.163–4; *was* for 'was sir', 5.1.171; *chamber* for 'table', 5.1.183; *Shards* added before 'Flints', 5.1.220; *sage* for 'a', 5.1.226; *treble* for 'double', 5.1.236; *wiseness* for 'wisdome', 5.1.252; *shortly* for 'thereby', 5.1.287; *unseal* for 'vnfold', 5.2.17; *Why, man, they did make love to this employment* added before 5.2.57; 12 lines added beginning *To quit* and ending *here* after 5.2.66; *bevy* for 'breede', 5.2.168; *Sir, in this audience* added after 5.2.217; *till* for 'all', 5.2.227; *better'd* for 'better', 5.2.240; *off* for 'of' (possibly a variant spelling), 5.2.310; *on* for 'no', 5.2.376.

APPENDIX 3

Editorial Conventions and Sample Passages

CONVENTIONS

Proper names

In our Q2 text, we have adopted 'conventional/traditional' spelling of names (e.g. 'Gertrude' rather than 'Gertrard', 'Osric' rather than 'Ostrick', and 'Rosencrantz' rather than 'Rosencraus'). In the other two texts, we have retained their names where they are substantively 'different' but used 'conventional/traditional' spellings of the rest.

Act and scene numbers

In Q1 we have numbered scenes consecutively 1–17 but added the act and scene numbers used in our edition of Q2 (where there is an equivalent). In F we have employed appropriate act and scene numbers, but added Q2's where they differ. In the text, square brackets are used to indicate that particular act and scene numbers or stage directions derive from sources other than Q1, Q2 or F. In the texts of Q1 and F, numbers in square brackets in the right-hand margin indicate the comparable scene in Q2.

Commentary

Q2 has full commentary notes throughout, but we have provided such notes for Q1 and F only where the text differs from Q2.

Textual notes

In the textual notes, when we cite a sequence of identical accepted or rejected readings, the copy-text reading comes first, followed by the others in chronological order. We have included in the textual notes likely or certain errors, but we have not collated obvious nonsense typos except when recording variants between corrected and uncorrected copies of the text in question. The textual notes to Q2 have been treated as if Q2, Q1 and F were collateral texts – in other words, we have collated Q1 (when close) and F, and recorded all substantive or otherwise significant emendations of Q2.

For considerable stretches of Q1 there is little match between it and Q2, and if all the differences between the two texts were to be recorded the amount of space devoted to textual notes would be disproportionately swollen. But we are clearly in danger of creating the false impression that these are the most important differences between Q1 and Q2. Nothing could be further from the truth. Take the opening of the two texts as an example: Q1 opens with an interchange between two unnamed sentinels ('Stand: who is that?', 'Tis I.'), whereas Q2 opens with five speeches from Barnardo and Francisco ('Whose there?', 'Nay answere me. Stand and vnfolde your selfe.', 'Long liue the King.', '*Barnardo*.', 'Hee.'). None of this appears in our Q2 textual notes because they have only one word ('Stand') in common.

However, the textual notes to Q2 that indicate significant differences between the three texts are not there to indicate difference as an end in itself. Their function is to supply readers of Ard Q2 *Hamlet* with the kind of information provided by the textual notes in any other Arden edition – information intended to enable readers to appreciate the nature of arguments mounted by editors of eclectic editions of the play (i.e. not the present Arden edition of *Hamlet*). Such editors make judgements based on the evidence of variants between what have been regarded as collateral texts (Q2 and F) and those passages in Q1 which are close enough to Q2 or F to be used in evidence of a theory that posits a relationship of dependency between Q1 and either of the other two texts. Appendix 2 surveys the history of such arguments and illustrates elements within them, as well as challenging the eclectic tradition.

In the Q1 textual notes, we record substantive or otherwise significant emendations of Q1, but we have not collated Q2 or F, except where the commentary refers to a reading in Q2 or F. Similarly, in the textual notes to F, we record substantive or otherwise significant emendations of F, but we have not collated Q1 or Q2, except where the commentary refers to a reading in Q1 or Q2. However, we have also included F spellings and punctuations where they might seem to derive from Q2 or, alternatively, make derivation from Q2 unlikely.

In all the textual notes, the source of a reading comes first, followed by a semicolon. If the adopted reading is taken from the control text, there is no reference to that text, and if that reading is shared with one or more of the other three texts they are cited but the control text is not. Rejected readings (including readings from the control text) are placed after the semicolon, each one followed by its source. If the reading in our printed text is not that of the control text and there is no rejected reading from the control text, this fact is recorded (e.g. '*not in Q2*'). Where a reading in a stage direction in our printed text is not from the control text, this fact is not recorded because it is indicated by square brackets in the text. The only other exception is where the reading in our printed text is from a text other than Q1, Q2 or F1, and there is no rejected reading from any of these three: in this circumstance, no mention is made of the control text. References to the control text come first, but references to other texts are taken in chronological order. Thus, in the notes to Q2, references to Q2 precede references to any other text, but references to Q1 precede references to F. The abbreviation Q12 (or Q1F, or Q21, or Q2F, or FQ1, or FQ2) refers to a common reading to be found in both Q1 and Q2 (or Q1 and F, or Q2 and Q1, or Q2 and F, or F and Q1, or F and Q2).

Where we wish to draw attention to a noteworthy spelling of a word, that spelling appears in italic brackets followed by a semicolon. In Q2, for example, if 'soul' appears in the text but the Q2 spelling is 'sole', then 'sole' will appear first in the note, within italicized brackets, thus:

soul] *(sole);*

If the Q2 spelling is also to be found in F, then 'F' will follow the brackets without any intervening comma, thus:

soul] *(sole) F;*

If, however, the F spelling is not the Q2 spelling but the modern spelling in the lemma, then a comma will intervene:

soul] *(sole), F;*

If, on the other hand, the F spelling is neither the Q2 nor the modern spelling, then the F spelling will follow 'F' inside another set of italic brackets:

soul] *(sole), F (soule);*

Where there is a textual note on a word that occurs twice or more in the same line, a superscript number indicates which use is referred to. 'Q1' or 'Q2' or 'F' refer to a reading to be found in Q1 or Q2 or F1. Where the readings of uncorrected and corrected states of a forme are collated, that is indicated (e.g. 'Fu' and 'Fc').

SAMPLE PASSAGES

Comparable sections of the texts of Q1 (13.64–86), Q2 (4.5.144–78) and F (4.1.143–81) are included at this point (see Figs 20 and 21), but we have numbered the lines of each extract (including lines that are stage directions) to begin at a notional line 1. They illustrate many of the issues raised by editing *Hamlet*. They also illustrate characteristics of the three texts and characteristic differences between them.

Q1 almost always tries to set everything as verse, although the verse is anything but regular in metre. The other two texts

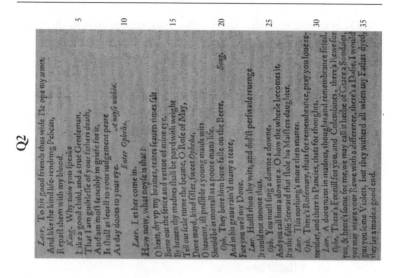

20 Sections of the playtext of Q1 13.64–86 and Q2 4.5.144–78

move between verse and prose, and the verse is usually pretty regular. Where the texts are the same (or nearly the same) in terms of words and word order, but differ in terms of lineation, or the use of verse or prose, we respect these differences as

F

La. To his good Friends, thus wide Ile ope my Armes,
And like the kinde Life-rend'ring Politician,
Repaſt them with my blood.
   King. Why now you ſpeake
Like a good Childe, and a true Gentleman,   5
That I am guiltleſſe of your Fathers death,
And am moſt ſenſible in greeſe for it,
It ſhall as leuell to your Iudgement pierce
As day do's to your eye.
              A noiſe within. Let her come in.   10
                  Enter Ophelia.
   Laer. How now? what noiſe is that?
Oh heate drie vp my Braines, teares ſeuen times ſalt,
Burne out the Sence and Vertue of mine eye,
By Heauen,thy madneſſe ſhall be payed by waight, 15
Till our Scale turnes the beame. Oh Roſe of May,
Deere Maid, kinde Siſter, ſweet *Ophelia* :
Oh Heauens, is't poſſible, a yong Maids wits,
Should be as mortall as an old mans life?
Nature is fine in Loue, and where 'tis fine,   20
It ſends ſome precious inſtance of it ſelfe
After the thing it loues,
   Ophe. They bore him bare fac'd on the Beer,
   Hey non nony,nony,hey nony :
   And on his graue raines many a teare,   25
   Fare you well my Doue.
   Laer. Had'ſt thou thy wits, and did'ſt perſwade Re-
uenge, it could not moue thus.
   Ophe. You muſt ſing downe a-downe, and you call
him a-downe-a. Oh, how the wheele becomes it? It is 30
the falſe Steward that ſtole his maſters daughter.
   Laer. This nothings more then matter.
   Ophe. There's Roſemary, that's for Remembraunce.
Pray loue remember : and there is Paconcies, that's for
Thoughts.   35
   Laer. A document in madneſſe, thoughts & remem-
brance fitted.
   Ophe. There's Fennell for you, and Columbines: ther's
Rew for you, and heere's ſome for me. Wee may call it
Herbe-Grace a Sundaies : Oh you muſt weare your Rew 40
with a difference. There's a Dayſie, I would giue you
ſome Violets, but they wither'd all when my Father dy-
ed : They ſay, he made a good end ;

21 Section of the playtext of F 4.1.143–81

being properties of the different texts. In these extracts, this difference occurs in Ofelia/Ophelia's speeches, where Q1 treats everything as verse, Q2 treats the first two speeches as verse but the remaining two as prose, and F treats the first as verse and everything else as prose. It also occurs in Laertes' speech which appears only in Q2 (at 23–4) and F (27–8): Q2 treats it as verse, F as prose.

The Q1 passage runs through roughly the same material as Q2 and F but usually more rapidly, and sometimes in a different sequence (e.g. 'rue' comes before 'rosemary' in Q1, but after it in Q2 and F). F has a three-line sequence not found in either of the other texts (20–2), and this sequence is not easy to interpret. Every editor must decide whether or not to interfere. Pope considered replacing 'fine' with 'fire', and 'instance' with 'incense', while Warburton conjectured that maybe 'fine' should be replaced with 'fal'n'. In the end they left the passage alone (see commentary).

Where there are minor differences between texts (and there are very many, as evident in this passage), they may illustrate the different spelling habits or levels of competence of the scribes or printers, they may reflect differences in the 'house styles' of the printing-houses or the periods in which the texts were printed ('a' at Q2, line 36, becomes 'he' in F, line 43), or they may result from one version having been more influenced by actors' embellishments of the text as first supplied (Ophelia's 'Hey non nony' line in her song as printed in F, line 24, or Leartes' 'O God, O God!' in Q1, line 22).

One problematic difference is that the opening speech is delivered by someone whose name is not spelled, or possibly even pronounced, in the same way in all three texts. Does an editor treat Q1's 'Leartes' (*'Lear.'* in this extract) and Q2/F's 'Laertes' as different names, or as variations on the same name (which should therefore be regularized as either one or the other)? A similar problem arises with Q1's 'Ofelia' and Q2/F's 'Ophelia' (although, in this case, pronunciation is clearly unaffected, and therefore no theatre audience will be aware of the distinction, even if an editor wishes to make one).

When the edition is more than a facsimile but intended for use by general readers, students or actors, it is one of an editor's duties to correct obvious errors in the text. So, when faced with a nonsense word like 'Paconcies' (F, line 34), we opt for 'pansies', prompted to consider it by Q1 ('pansey') and Q2 ('Pancies'), and persuaded to choose it because it makes ideal sense (pansies are 'for Thoughts', since the French for 'thoughts' is *pensées*). In another case there is slightly more difficulty. The phrase 'the kinde Life-rend'ring Politician' (F, line 2) does not make much sense, but 'politician', unlike 'Paconcies', is at least a real word and the phrase is not total nonsense. Q2's 'Pelican' provides excellent sense, however, because the pelican was reputed to feed its young with its own blood if there was no other food available. So ready sense prevails over little sense. In both cases, the error is attributable to misreading and lack of concentration by a compositor or scribe. In neither case does the solution require us to assume any particular theory of the bibliographical relationship of F to either of the other two texts. It so happens that our emendations are drawn from one or more of the quarto readings, but, had their readings been less than clinching, we would have had to look elsewhere. A third case provides much more difficulty. Is 'pierce' an error at F, line 8? And what does 'peare', the equivalent word in Q2, mean?

There is an interesting stage direction in this passage. Q1's direction at line 8 differs from the minimal '*Enter Ophelia*' at Q2, line 10, and F, line 11, in that it reads: '*Enter Ofelia as before.*' That '*as before*' is significant, because it refers us back to the stage direction for her previous entry, which reads, '*Enter Ofelia playing on a Lute, and her haire downe singing*', and provides us with an indication of how either Shakespeare or a transcriber envisaged Ofelia in this scene or else how an acting company presented her. At the comparable point F indicates something of her appearance, '*Enter Ophelia distracted*', but Q2 has the minimal '*Enter Ophelia.*' The editor has to choose whether to retain the differences between the three texts or to regularize them. If the latter, how? At the first entry, Jenkins provides Q2's direction, Edwards F's and Hibbard Q1's (but none of them gives '*as before*' at the second).

Much more problematic is the rest of this stage direction in Q2 and F. In Q1 the direction '*Enter Ofelia as before*' is followed by a speech from Leartes beginning 'Who's this, *Ofelia?*' Q2 has a two-part direction, '*A noise within*', in the right-hand margin, followed by the centred '*Enter Ophelia.*' Then follows a speech from Laertes beginning 'Let her come in. / How now, what noyse is that?' Something seems wrong here. Ophelia has entered, but her brother, who hasn't seen her since his return from Paris, gives the order to let her come in without knowing she is there, yet after her entry and before asking what the earlier noise was.

Many editors feel that F has sorted some of this out by not giving the line 'Let her come in' to Laertes, and by allowing him to ask what the noise was before saying anything about Ophelia. ('How now?' does not have to be referring to the noise, though, and might be an exclamation at the sight of Ophelia.) However, problems of interpretation still persist: Ophelia still enters before Laertes questions the noise, and 'Let her come in' is no longer obviously part of the dialogue but italicized and set to the right of '*A noise within*'.

Hardin Aasand has discussed the significance of the different solutions proposed by Rowe, Pope, Theobald, Hanmer, Warburton, Johnson and Capell to the differences in Q2's and F's presentation of Ophelia's second entry (Aasand, 'Ophelia'). Aasand argues that editorial decisions modify a text, thereby affecting readers' interpretations of that text, and that in their handling of Ophelia's entry in this extract, for example, those eighteenth-century editions reveal their own attitudes to women and to madness. Quite apart from choosing between (and interpreting, where necessary) the Q2 and F texts, Rowe, Theobald, Hanmer and Warburton decide to describe Ophelia's appearance for us as 'fantastically drest with straws and flowers'.

APPENDIX 4
The Act Division at 3.4/4.1

At 3.4.215, at the end of his conversation with his mother in her closet, Hamlet leaves the stage, having declared (in Q2): 'Ile lugge the guts [Polonius' body] into the neighbour roome.' Q2 follows its simple '*Exit*' with another SD: '*Eenter King, and Queene, with Rosencraus and Guyldensterne.*' F at this point provides a longer exit SD for Hamlet – '*Exit Hamlet tugging in Polonius*' (Harold Jenkins suggests that '*tugging*' is a misprint for '*lugging*') – and a briefer entry SD, '*Enter King.*' Q1 has '*Exit Hamlet with the dead body*' followed by '*Enter the King and Lordes.*' None of the three texts provides an exit for the Queen. In all three texts the King immediately addresses the Queen, who is in a state of distress because of her experience. It does not seem as if any time has passed, but since the 1676 Quarto this entry has been taken to signal not only the beginning of a new scene but also the beginning of a new act (4.1). The only tiny shred of justification for this comes at 4.1.34–5, where the King says (in Q2), 'Hamlet in madnes hath Polonius slaine, / And from his mothers closet hath he dreg'd him', which implies a change of location, but this is by no means a reliable indication of a new scene in Elizabethan drama, where it is common enough for location to be undefined, or to change in the course of a scene.[1]

The editorial tradition

Previous editors of *Hamlet* in the Arden Shakespeare series have expressed their doubts about the traditional division between Acts 3 and 4. Dowden, whose edition inaugurated the first Arden series in 1899, writes in his Introduction:

---

1 This appendix uses some material previously published in our chapter 'Variable texts: stage directions in Arden 3 *Hamlet*', in Aasand, *Directions*, 19–32.

The received division between III and IV is unfortunate. Mr. E. Rose proposed that III should open with Hamlet's advice to the Players (III.ii of the received arrangement), and that IV should open with the march of Fortinbras (our present IV.iv). As regards IV, this is the division of Mr. Hudson in his *Harvard Shakespeare*; and but for the inconvenience of disturbing an accepted arrangement, to which references are made in lexicons and concordances, I should in this edition follow Mr. Hudson.[1]

Harold Jenkins, whose edition concluded the second Arden series in 1982, quotes W.W. Greg in his note on the opening of 4.1: '"It is a disaster that editors have followed a late quarto in choosing this of all points at which to begin a new act" ([Greg, *First Folio*,] 333). The action is continuous, the Queen remaining on stage.' In his Longer Note (Ard², 523–4), Jenkins comments 'Instead of inventing an exit for the Queen which all three texts lack, editors would have done better to follow F in omitting Q2's superfluous entry-direction for her.' Nevertheless, he perpetuates the division, and the page layout of the Arden second series, where a new act is given a new page, gives it greater prominence; a similar convention emphasizes the break in the 1992 New Folger Library text (edited by Barbara A. Mowat and Paul Werstine), where each act has an interleaved title-page. The other editors of single-volume *Hamlet*s during the 1980s, Philip Edwards (Cam²) and G.R. Hibbard (Oxf¹), follow Jenkins's advice by omitting the entry for the Queen, but they keep the act and scene division. These editors are typical of the whole tradition; most of them deplore the break and quote Samuel Johnson approvingly: 'This division is modern and arbitrary; and is here not very happy, for the pause is made

---

1 Ard¹, xxii; see also Hudson; and Edward Rose, 'The division into acts of *Hamlet*', *Transactions of the New Shakespere Society*, series 1, vols 5–7 (1877–9), 1–10.

at a time when there is more continuity of action than in almost any other of the scenes' (Johnson, 8.247). They nevertheless retain it in the interests of ease of reference. Hibbard adds another justification: 'it serves to bring out the fact that all the traditional divisions in the play are editorial, and therefore have no authority' (Oxf¹, 288).

This reference to the wider context is apposite, though we should distinguish between different kinds of 'traditional divisions', specifically between scene divisions and act divisions. Scene divisions have real meaning (or 'authority') in the context of the pragmatics of Shakespeare's theatre and of his own dramatic writing: a scene is a unit of dramatic action that begins and ends with an empty stage. This has produced the so-called 'law of reentry' whereby an actor who has left the stage at the end of one scene cannot re-enter immediately (either in the same character or in another role) at the beginning of the next. Such immediate re-entry was not usually feasible in a theatre without either a curtain or a convention of interval breaks, and instances where it does occur, as in *The Taming of the Shrew* at 5.1/5.2, have raised questions regarding the reliability of the copy. As a practical playwright working regularly in the late 1590s for the same company with a stable number of actors, Shakespeare must have been continually aware of this convention and of the need to match his scenic structures to his casting requirements. *TxC*, however, defends the re-entry of the Queen here, arguing that 'immediate re-entry is acceptable, so long as the character enters with a new group' and further that 'The agreement of F and Q1 ... apparently results from a deliberate change of staging' (*TxC*, 407).

Act divisions are very different from scene divisions, and we would agree that in the case of *Hamlet* these have only the authority of convention. Not many scholars today would endorse the view of T.W. Baldwin in 1944 that Shakespeare, like other Elizabethans, would have assumed that all plays had five acts;[1] or that, even if this may have been a common assumption on the part of some intellectual playwrights, it would necessarily have been translated into popular theatrical practice. Gary Taylor has shown that the five-act structure began to be imposed on all plays only between 1606 and 1617, the King's Men adopting the change between 1608 and 1610, probably as a result of their use of the indoor Blackfriars theatre, where act intervals provided a convenient opportunity to trim the candles. Taylor ('Act-Intervals') argues that we should accordingly give some credence to the act breaks in Shakespeare's plays from *Coriolanus* (1608–9) onwards. There is no record of act intervals in public performances as early as 1600–1, when *Hamlet* was first performed, though changing theatrical practice may have led to their imposition on Jacobean and Caroline revivals of the play, fifty years before their appearance in print in the 1676 Quarto.

Very few editors have rejected the traditional break between 3.4 and 4.1. Henry N. Hudson, in the twenty-volume Harvard edition of 1880, as cited by Dowden, begins a new scene, 3.5, and comments in his endnotes:

> Modern editors, generally, make the fourth Act begin here. None of the old copies have any marking of the Acts and Scenes, after the second Scene of the second Act; and it seems that it is very clear that there is no sufficient interval or pause in the action to warrant the beginning of a new Act in this place. I therefore agree with Caldecott and Elze that Act IV ought to begin with the fourth scene after [i.e. at the beginning of the usual 4.4].

> (Hudson, quoted in Dowden, 330)

Thomas Caldecott, who edited *Hamlet* in 1819, and Karl Elze, who edited *Hamlet* in German in 1857 and in English in 1882,

---

1 T.W. Baldwin, *William Shakespeare's Five-Act Structure* (Urbana, Ill., 1944).

both preserve the traditional division while arguing against it. George MacDonald, who edited a Folio-based text in 1885, uses it as one of his many examples of the stupidity of the editorial tradition, remarking on the juxtaposition of the stage directions '*Exit Hamlet tugging in Polonius. / Enter King*':

> Here, according to the editors, comes 'Act IV'. For this there is no authority, and the point of division seems to me very objectionable. The scene remains the same . . . and the entrance of the king follows immediately on the exit of Hamlet. He finds his wife greatly perturbed: she has not had time to compose herself. From the beginning of Act II to where I would place the end of Act III [at the beginning of 4.4] there is continuity.

> (MacDonald, 181)

But, like the others, he keeps the division in his text.

Unfortunately, there is no unanimity about where to begin Act 4 if not in the middle of the closet scene. Caldecott, Elze, Hudson and MacDonald all recommend beginning it with '*Enter Fortinbras*' (traditionally the beginning of 4.4), though Hudson is the only one to do it. MacDonald justifies this placing with reference to the time-sequence: 'Between the third and the fourth [acts, i.e. between the traditional 4.3 and 4.4] passes the time Hamlet is away; for the latter, in which he returns, and whose scenes are *contiguous*, needs no more than one day' (MacDonald, 191). (It is important to note here that MacDonald is editing a Folio-based text, in which Hamlet does not appear in 4.4.) Joseph Quincy Adams in the 1929 edition begins Act 4 at the opening of the traditional 4.5: '*Enter Horatio, Gertrard, and a Gentleman*', commenting on the opening of his 3.5:

> In modern reprints of the play, this scene is regularly made to open Act IV. But since all the original editions – the First Quarto, the Second Quarto, and the Folio – fail to indicate act, or even scene, divisions, we are

under no obligation to perpetuate the blunder of a later edition.

He argues that the time sequence is continuous to the end of what he designates 3.8 (the exit of Hamlet at the end of the traditional 4.4), but that the next scene with the entry of Ophelia begins 'several weeks later'. A significant gap in time is a stronger argument for beginning a new act than a change in location, but here of course the texts differ: in Q2 the traditional 4.4 seems to follow soon after 4.3, since Hamlet has not yet left Denmark, while in F the very brief appearance of Fortinbras could take place either soon after the events of 4.3 or shortly before those of 4.5.

The theatrical tradition

The same starting-point for Act 4, that is with the traditional 4.5, is found in Wilson Barrett's acting edition of *Hamlet*;[1] Barrett published an essay in 1890 in which, as an actor-manager, he criticized the 'maltreatment of this glorious tragedy' by the introduction of the traditional act division which was for him the supreme example of 'false tradition' in the theatre. He deplored the way in which

> Since Betterton's time the actors have invariably finished the third act of *Hamlet* with the lines 'I must be cruel only to be kind; / Thus bad begins, but worse remains behind.' Turn to the published acting editions of the play and you will find the proof of what I say.

> (Barrett, 1–4)

By evoking Betterton he is of course referring to the 1676 Quarto, which claims to give the play 'As it is now Acted at his Highness the Duke of *York*'s Theatre'. This quarto contains the cast-list for Betterton's *Hamlet* and indicates cuts made in his

1   Wilson Barrett (ed.), *Hamlet, as Arranged for the Stage* (1884).

version; it is reasonable to assume that the act divisions were also used in Restoration performances, though as we have said, act divisions of some sort may have been introduced earlier. Barrett's return to the earliest quartos and folios, his reinstatement of their ordering of scenes and his restoration of cut lines was a direct response to his rival, Henry Irving. Irving had somewhat bypassed the 3.4/4.1 issue by cutting the first four scenes of Act 4 altogether (see Dawson, 66); Barrett argued forcefully that the resulting 'jumble' must be sorted out by ending Act 3 after Hamlet's departure for England, which would provide 'the interregnum which the dramatist intended'. Before the start of the traditional 4.4:

> Some six weeks have elapsed, there has been time to bury Polonius, time for Ophelia's grief to affect her brain, time for Laertes to travel from France, and time for Hamlet to be captured by the pirates at sea and to be released again.

> (Barrett, 1)

Granville-Barker dismissed 'The five acts of the editors' in his *Preface* to *Hamlet*, claiming that Shakespeare 'certainly did not ... think out his plays in five-act form' and that the imposition of this structure is unhelpful: 'It cannot but to some extent thwart his technique; and at one point – in the contriving of the end of a third act and a beginning for a fourth – the offence is patent and the cobbling of the clumsiest' (Granville-Barker, 33–4). In a footnote he criticizes Dowden for noticing the problem but failing to take it seriously: 'Of so little importance did this aspect of Shakespeare's stagecraft seem to him' (14–16).

Gielgud agreed with Granville-Barker in deploring Victorian and Edwardian traditions of staging Shakespeare, but in his notes on *Hamlet* he reveals some ambivalence about breaking with tradition at the end of Act 2, confessing himself unable simply to leave the stage after the soliloquy:

I suppose I was hypnotized by the famous business of Irving, when, as the curtain falls, he is seen writing madly on his tablets. One cannot help feeling that 'The play's the thing / Wherein I'll catch the conscience of the King' should be the signal for the greatest applause in the play. When I have played the part on first nights I have never been able to believe that I could succeed until this applause had come. At later performances, however, I have been, and still am, irritated by my actor's desire to make such a 'curtain' of it.

(quoted in Gilder, 159)

In the description of his performance (1936 in London), scene 10 (3.4) is set in 'the Queen's private apartment' and there was clearly another 'curtain' when the Queen 'fled from the room' leaving Hamlet alone: 'For a moment he looks after her and then, with repressed anguish, the one word, "Mother" – the cry of a child left in the dark – the hopeless cry of a creature torn from its one safe anchorage' (Gilder, 88). At the beginning of scene 11 (4.1), set in 'the King's dressing-room', 'The Queen hurries in breathless with the terror of the scene she has lived through' (88). Elsewhere in his account of this moment, Gielgud takes it for granted that the Queen has to leave the stage at the end of 3.4 (159). It is of course clear in all three texts that Hamlet leaves the stage before the Queen (if she leaves it at all) but the editors' attempts to tidy up this moment by providing an exit for her perhaps prompted directors' thoughts of another scene ending with Hamlet alone on stage.

Turning to the better-known film versions, Olivier (1948), Kozintsev (1964) and Michael Almereyda (2000) handle the end of the 'closet' scene by omitting 4.1 altogether; Tony Richardson (1969) also omits 4.1 and ends 3.4 early at 'I must be cruel only to be kind.' The BBC version directed by Rodney Bennett (1980) cuts very abruptly from 3.4 to 4.1, apparently implying a time-lapse, while Zeffirelli (1990) moves almost seamlessly from one to the other. In Branagh's 1996 film version there is a change of location from 'Gertrude's Apartments' to 'Corridor', where we encounter 'Claudius, Rosencrantz and Guildenstern plus Guards, striding along the corridor as Gertrude comes out of her apartment', though the sequence is fluid, proceeding into the King's apartments and then back into hers, indicating no lapse of time (Branagh, 103, 112–13).

Act and scene divisions are more important today as reference points for readers rather than for performers, since modern performance tends to aim for an almost cinematic fluidity as compared with the punctuation provided previously by 'curtains', both literal and figurative. In the practical experience of theatre-goers today, plays are usually divided into two parts by a single interval break; it is rare to have two intervals, and indeed the practice of having no interval at all is becoming more common with shorter tragedies such as *Julius Caesar* and *Macbeth*. In the case of such a long play as either Q2 or F *Hamlet*, drastic cutting would be required to make this possible.

Our decisions for the new Arden Hamlet

Some of the decisions we have taken with respect to editing this play have had to be governed by pragmatic considerations. Since our text of Q2 will be (we expect) much more widely used than our texts of Q1 and F, we have decided to join the queue of editors who preserve the traditional 3.4/4.1 division, muttering our disapproval at the foot of the page but conceding that a different disposition of act and scene numbers affecting not only 3.4 but the whole of Act 4 would be a serious inconvenience to readers trying to find passages quoted in the huge range of existing criticism and commentary. As we have said above, there is a minimal justification for at least a scene division in Q2, where the Queen is given an entry though not an exit. We would see this decision as being congruous with our use of the familiar names Gertrude and Rosencrantz in our edited text of Q2, even though these characters are consistently Gertrard and Rosencraus in the original.

There seems little point in trying to impose on Q1 the act and scene divisions familiar from edited versions of the other texts; we have accordingly decided simply to number the scenes, following the practice of previous editors (though unfortunately they have not agreed on the numbers). We have also devised a way of recording which sections of Q2 are relevant to the Q1 scenes. An added complication in the case of Q1 is that we have 'displaced' passages to contend with (most famously 'To be or not to be') as well as abridgement, but we have indicated the placing of 'parallel' passages at the beginning of each scene and supplemented this with commentary notes.

A similar (and more straightforward) display of conventional act and scene divisions is made in our edited text of F. Here the practical question is to decide where Act 4 begins. Once we override the traditional 3.4/4.1 division, it seems clear that 3.4 continues until the exit of the King and Queen after his couplet 'O come away, / My soul is full of discord and dismay', which is the end of the traditional 4.1. (The first half-line differs in the two texts, as F lacks three and a half of Q2's lines here.) The next two scenes, with the search for Polonius' body, follow immediately with minimal change of either time or place but, as we have said, F's version of the first appearance of Fortinbras (the traditional 4.4) is less clearly related to this sequence than Q2's version, since Hamlet does not appear in the F scene, leaving its timing in relation to the previous scene unclear. (Branagh's climactic treatment of the ending of Hamlet's soliloquy in this scene seems to support the case for an act break – certainly the intermission was very welcome – but of course his film uses Q2.)

Despite these reservations, we have begun Act 4 in our Folio text with the traditional 4.5, Ophelia's mad scene, mainly on the grounds of the 'gap in time' argument. This gives us seven scenes in Act 3 (4.1 is a continuation of 3.4; 4.2 becomes 3.5;

4.3 becomes 3.6; and 4.4 becomes 3.7), followed by three scenes in Act 4 (4.5 becomes 4.1; 4.6 becomes 4.2; and 4.7 becomes 4.3). Act 4 thus becomes noticeably shorter than the other acts, but this is not unique in Shakespeare's canon: *Love's Labour's Lost* is perhaps the most striking example with an editorial Act 5 amounting to nearly half the play. Such an imbalance provides further evidence that, at least in the Elizabethan phase of his career, Shakespeare was not writing with a five-act structure in mind. By providing conventional divisions (and, in the case of the extended 3.4, line numbers) in square brackets on the page, we have tried to minimize the inconvenience for our readers, but we do feel that an advantage of the three-text edition we are offering is that it allows us the luxury of making a change which so many of our predecessors have only contemplated before rejecting it on expedient grounds.

APPENDIX 5

Casting

We assume that the practice of doubling, whereby one actor plays more than one part, was routine on Shakespeare's stage.[1] The obvious motivation for this practice is the need to save on actors: no one believes that Shakespeare had forty-nine actors on hand to perform the Folio text of *Henry V* or, even more extravagantly, sixty-seven to perform *3 Henry VI*; indeed, editors in the third series of the Arden Shakespeare have managed to cast these plays with eighteen and seventeen actors respectively.[2] In addition to doubling for practical purposes (what Sprague (12) calls 'deficiency' doubling), some editors and scholars have argued for further 'conceptual' doubling whereby the audience is assumed to be aware of the practice and to make connections between the roles doubled. A proposed example of this would be the possible doubling in *Cymbeline* of the hero, Posthumus, with the villain, Cloten, a doubling which might suggest that the villain is the alter ego of the hero.[3] This second proposition is clearly more speculative, but it interests some directors who have found that they can use this aspect of casting as an additional means of interpreting a play.[4]

1   This appendix uses some material previously published in our chapter, '"Your sum of parts": doubling in *Hamlet*', in Lukas Erne and M.J. Kidnie (eds), *Textual Performances: The Modern Reproduction of Shakespeare's Drama* (Cambridge, 2004), 111–26.

2   See *Henry V*, ed. T.W. Craik (1995), 404–5; and *3 Henry VI*, ed. John D. Cox and Eric Rasmussen (2001), 410–20.

3   For a discussion of this example, see Stephen Booth, 'Speculations on doubling in Shakespeare's plays', in his *'King Lear', 'Macbeth', Indefinition and Tragedy* (1983), 127–55. For a discussion of 'conceptual' doubling in *Henry V*, see Thomas L. Berger, 'Casting *Henry V*', *SSt*, 20 (1988), 89–104.

4   Hugh Quarshie doubled Posthumus and Cloten in a production of *Cymbeline* at the Royal Exchange Theatre in Manchester directed by Greg Herson, James Maxwell,

We offer three texts of *Hamlet*, in which the number of speaking roles varies: Q1 has twenty-six speaking roles, Q2 and F each have thirty-one. Consequently, we provide separate casting charts for each text. We are not the first people to do this: in 1992, three scholars, David Bradley, T.J. King, and Scott McMillin ('Casting'), all went into print with doubling analyses of all three texts, and each reached a different set of conclusions. This was largely because each was using a different set of 'rules'. The rules are not always made explicit in such exercises, but variations include whether actors double both male and female roles, whether speaking actors double non-speaking roles, whether actors double parts where there are few or even no intervening lines to cover a costume change, and so forth.

Where a play survives in more than one early version, there is no necessary correlation between the length of those texts and the minimum size of the company needed to perform them. In the case of *Hamlet*, Q2 is the longest text and Q1 by far the shortest. While David Bradley and T.J. King seem influenced by the traditional assumption that 'bad' or 'short' quartos are abridged texts designed for performance by touring (and therefore smaller) companies, McMillin argues that, the longer the text, the easier doubling becomes, since there can be more time for changing costumes. He initially calculated (McMillin, *More*, 88) that Q1 needed thirteen actors whereas Q2 needed only twelve, but he later revised these figures downward (McMillin, 'Casting', 190). Acknowledging Albert Weiner's 1962 edition of Q1, which calculated that the text actually requires only twelve actors, McMillin questioned Weiner's methodology, which precluded in theory doubling within the

Braham Murray and Casper Wrede in 1984. Since Peter Brook's influential production of *A Midsummer Night's Dream* for the Royal Shakespeare Company at Stratford-upon-Avon in 1970, it has become common for the performers of Oberon and Titania to double as Theseus and Hippolyta (despite the fact that they have no time to change in 4.1), similarly suggesting a deeper parallel between the characters.

Q1 CASTING CHART

Actor	Scene 1	2	3	4	5	6	7	8	9	10	11	12	13	14	15	16	17
1	Sen–						Ros–	Ros–	–Ros–		–Ros–					Man–	–Bra
2	Bar	–Bar–				Mon–	–PDk–		PDk–			For				–Pri	–For
3	–Hor	–Hor–		Hor	–Hor				–Hor–					Hor		–Hor–	Hor
4	–Mar	Vol– Mar–		Mar	–Mar		–Vol– PPr–		PPr– PLu–								–Vol
5	–Gho–	Kin–		–Gho–	Gh–		Kin–	Kin	–Kin–	Kin	–Gho–Kin		Kin		Kin	–Kin	–Kin
6		Ham		Ham–	Ham		–Ham		Ham	–Ham–	–Ham–					–Ham–	Ham
7		Cor–	–Cor			Cor	–Cor–	Cor	–Cor–		Cor–					Gra	
8		Lea–	Lea–				Gil–	Gil–	–Gil–		–Gil–		–Lea		Lea	–Lea	–Lea
9+		Que–					Que–	Que	–Que–		Que–		Que–	Que–	–Que–	–Que	–Que
10+			Ofe			–Ofe–	–Ofe–		–Ofe–				–Ofe–				
11+		Crn–					–Crn– PDc–		PDc–								–Amb

Key:

|	= enters after beginning of scene
–	= exits before end of scene

bold	male	
italic	female	
+	boy actor	

Speaking roles in order of entry:

Sen	=	1 Sentinel	Cor	=	Corambis		
Bar	=	Barnardo	Vol	=	Voltemar		
Hor	=	Horatio	Crn	=	Cornelia		
Mar	=	Marcellus	Ofe	=	Ofelia		
Gho	=	Ghost	Mon	=	Montano		
Kin	=	King	Gil	=	Gilderstone		
Que	=	Queen	Ros	=	Rossencraft		
Ham	=	Hamlet	PDk	=	Player Duke		
Lea	=	Leartes	PDc	=	Player Duchess		

PPr	=	Player Prologue
PLu	=	Player Lucianus
For	=	Fortenbrasse
Gra	=	Gravedigger
Man	=	Second Man
Pri	=	Priest
Bra	=	Braggart Gentleman
Amb	=	Ambassador

Q2 CASTING CHART

Actor	1.1	1.2	1.3	1.4	1.5	2.1	2.2	3.1	3.2	3.3	3.4	4.1	4.2	4.3	4.4	4.5	4.6	4.7	5.1	5.2
1	Fra–						Ros–	Ros–	–Ros–	Ros–	Ros–		–Ros–	–Ros–	–Ros		–Sai		Man–	–Osr
2	Bar	–Bar–				Rey–	–PKi–		PKi–						For–	Gen–	Gen–		–Pri–	–For
3	–Hor	–Hor–		Hor	–Hor				–Hor–							Hor–	Hor		–Hor–	Hor
4	–Mar	Vol– Mar–		Mar	–Mar		–Vol– PPr–		PPr– PLu–											
5	–Gho–	Kin–		–Gho–	Gho–		Kin–	Kin	–Kin–	Kin	–Gho–	Kin	Kin	Kin		–Kin		Kin	–Kin	–Kin
6		Ham		Ham–	Ham		–Ham–	–Ham–	Ham	–Ham–	–Ham		Ham	–Ham–	–Ham				–Ham–	Ham
7		Pol–	–Pol			Pol	–Pol–	Pol	–Pol–	–Pol–	Pol				Cap–				Gra	–Lor–
8		Lae–	Lae–				Gui–	Gui–	–Gui–	Gui–		Gui–	–Gui–	–Gui–	–Gui	–Lae		Lae–	–Lae	–Lae
9+		Que–					Que–	Que–	–Que–		Que	Que				Que		–Que	–Que	–Que
10+			Oph			–Oph		Oph	–Oph–							–Oph–				
11+		Crn–					–Crn– PQu–		PQu–							–Mes–		–Mes–		–Amb

592

Key:

—	enters after beginning of scene
−	exits before end of scene

bold = male
italic = female
+ = boy actor

Speaking roles in order of entry:

Bar	=	Barnardo	Vol	=	Voltemand	For	=	Fortinbras
Fra	=	Francisco	Crn	=	Cornelius	Cap	=	Captain
Hor	=	Horatio	Oph	=	Ophelia	Gen	=	Gentleman
Mar	=	Marcellus	Rey	=	Reynaldo	Mes	=	Messenger
Gho	=	Ghost	Gui	=	Guildenstern	Sai	=	Sailor
Kin	=	King	Ros	=	Rosencrantz	Pri	=	Priest
Que	=	Queen	PPr	=	Player Prologue	Gra	=	Gravedigger
Pol	=	Polonius	PKi	=	Player King	Man	=	Second Man
Lae	=	Laertes	PQu	=	Player Queen	Osr	=	Osric
Ham	=	Hamlet	PLu	=	Player Lucianus	Lor	=	Lord
						Amb	=	Ambassador

F CASTING CHART

Actor	Scene																		
	1.1	1.2	1.3	1.4	1.5	2.1	2.2	3.1	3.2	3.3	3.4	3.5	3.6	3.7	4.1	4.2	4.3	5.1	5.2
1	Fra–						Ros–	Ros–	–Ros–	Ros–		–Ros	–Ros–			–Sai		Man–	–Osr
2	Bar	–Bar–				Rey–	–PKi–		PKi–					For				–Pri	–For
3	–Hor	–Hor–		Hor	–Hor				–Hor–						Hor–	Hor		–Hor–	Hor
4	–Mar	–Vol– Mar–		Mar	–Mar		–Vol– PPr–		PPr– PLu–										
5	–Gho–	Kin–		–Gho–	Gho–		Kin–	Kin	–Kin–	Kin	–Gho– Kin		Kin		–Kin		Kin	–Kin	–Kin
6		Ham		Ham–	Ham		–Ham	–Ham–	Ham	–Ham–	–Ham–	Ham	–Ham–					–Ham–	Ham
7		Pol–	–Pol			Pol	–Pol–	Pol	–Pol–	–Pol–	Pol			Cap		Att–		Gra	
8		Lae–	Lae–				Gui–	Gui–	–Gui–	Gui–		–Gui	–Gui–		–Lae		Lae–	–Lae	–Lae
9+		Que–					Que–	Que–	–Que–		Que				Que		–Que	–Que	–Que
10+		Oph–	Oph			–Oph		Oph	–Oph–						–Oph–				
11+		–Crn–					–Crn– PQu–		PQu–						–Mes–		–Mes–	–Gen	–Amb

Key:

| | enters after beginning of scene |
| − | exits before end of scene |

bold = male
italic = female
+ = boy actor

Speaking roles in order of entry:

Bar	=	Barnardo	Oph	=	Ophelia	For	=	Fortinbras
Fra	=	Francisco	Vol	=	Voltemand	Cap	=	Captain
Hor	=	Horatio	Crn	=	Cornelius	Mes	=	Messenger
Mar	=	Marcellus	Rey	=	Reynoldo	Att	=	Attendant
Gho	=	Ghost	Gui	=	Guildensterne	Sai	=	Sailor
Kin	=	King	Ros	=	Rosincrance	Gra	=	Gravedigger
Que	=	Queen	PPr	=	Player Prologue	Man	=	Second Man
Ham	=	Hamlet	PKi	=	Player King	Pri	=	Priest
Pol	=	Polonius	PQu	=	Player Queen	Gen	=	Gentleman
Lae	=	Laertes	PLu	=	Player Lucianus	Osr	=	Osricke
						Amb	=	Ambassador

same scene, even when an actor had ample time to exit and re-enter later in a new role. By allowing for such within-scene doubling, McMillin in 1992 found a way of casting both Q1 and Q2 with only eleven actors.

The accompanying charts list all the speaking parts and all the scenes in each of the three texts as we are printing them. Each indicates which scenes characters appear in, whether they are on stage at the beginning or at the end of the scene in question, and whether the role is male or female and therefore whether for an adult or a boy actor. Finally, each chart proposes a feasible pattern of doubling for the text in question, which, for the purposes of comparison, we make as similar as possible to the pattern we propose for the other two texts.

The charts are based on two familiar assumptions: that acting companies in Shakespeare's day wished to minimize the number of actors they employed; and that some non-speaking parts might be played by people who were not necessarily regular members of the company. The charts therefore attempt to cast all the speaking roles in each of the three texts of *Hamlet* with as few actors as possible. For the purpose of the exercise our charts obey six self-imposed 'rules'. They are as follows: (1) every line in the relevant text is performed; (2) no role is divided between different actors, but (3) one actor can play any number of roles, so long as (4) he or 'she' has time to leave the stage for at least a few minutes before returning in a new role; (5) female roles are played by boys; (6) boys can nevertheless also occasionally play adult male roles.

The first of our rules is rarely, if ever, obeyed in theatrical practice, particularly in the case of such a long text as Q2 or F *Hamlet*. The other rules are either supported by evidence or seem at least highly probable. Thus we believe that it would have been exceptional for more than one actor to play a particular role during a particular performance (rule 2). (Yet of course it can happen; for example, when the sharing of a role at the end of a play such as *The Comedy of Errors* or *The Winter's*

Tale has been imposed by doubling of characters – the two sets of twins, or Hermione and Perdita – who eventually appear in the same scene.) We have evidence that doubling was used in the Elizabethan theatre, just as in the modern theatre (rule 3). Suspension of disbelief is probably easier if time elapses between the appearances of an actor in different parts (rule 4), and any change in costume or hand-held stage properties takes time, but time is also in the hands of the actors, so there can be no hard-and-fast prescription of the amount of dialogue needed to cover such a change. Elizabethan actors were always (or almost always) male, and there is evidence that boys usually played female roles (rule 5), but there may have been exceptions. Finally, there is no reason to believe that boys (of ages extending to their late teens) could never have played adult male roles (rule 6). Inevitably they played both women and adult males in all the plays put on by the children's companies, a topic that is discussed in the Induction to John Marston's *Antonio and Mellida*, a play close in date to *Hamlet* (see p. 52). We emphasize that the underlying principle of our casting charts, namely the attempt to be as economical of the company's workforce as is mechanically and logically possible, represents a theoretical extreme, but also that the same principle and rules could produce alternative doubling patterns.

The minimum number of actors needed for speaking roles is the total number of actors on stage at that point in the play when the largest number of speaking roles is present. In many plays the last scene requires the largest cast of speaking characters, making it the starting-point for a doubling calculation. In *Hamlet*, however, it is the performance of *The Murder of Gonzago* (3.2), which needs eleven actors in all three texts. In Shakespeare's comedies the final scene is typically one in which all, or at least most, of the characters assemble for the resolution of their difficulties in reconciliation and marriage. In the tragedies, the final scene is also the opportunity to resolve the plot, but usually some characters have by this time gone missing, thus increasing opportunities for doubling. In *Hamlet*, the Players never return after the interruption of their play, the Ghost makes his last appearance in the closet scene, and Hamlet himself has a hand in the premature removal of Polonius, Ophelia, Rosencrantz and Guildenstern.

It emerges that, even though the number of speaking roles varies somewhat between them, all three texts can, at a pinch, be acted by a company made up of eight adult actors and three boys or women. This is McMillin's conclusion in his 1992 essay ('Casting') and it is ours too. Although there are other ways of achieving the same total number of actors, the distribution of roles proposed in these charts doubles Polonius/ Corambis with the Gravedigger and the Ghost with the King. The latter is a version of 'conceptual' doubling, but Hamlet himself plays with the idea, coining the term 'uncle-father' at 2.2.313. In *The Murder of Gonzago* he also confronts his uncle with his double – or, rather, his doubles, and others' doubles too. Hamlet's play is one in which every character has to be read as doubling roles in Hamlet's life: the Player King suggests his father but also his uncle; the Player Queen his mother but also (as the wife of his uncle) his aunt; and Lucianus a murdering villain and, thereby, his uncle, but also a nephew and, thereby, himself. Against the doubling of the Ghost with the King, one could of course argue that Hamlet makes much of the physical difference between his father and his uncle in 1.2 ('Hyperion to a satyr') and in 3.4 when he compares their pictures. Moreover, it may give undue prominence to the actor playing these two roles, who would be onstage for fifteen of the play's twenty scenes (though silent in two of them) and who would speak around 600 lines in Q2. Hamlet is onstage for thirteen scenes but speaks around 1,300 lines in Q2 (the King loses around thirty lines in the shorter F text, while Hamlet loses around 120 but gains around forty).

Our charts also double Marcellus with Voltemand/Voltemar. This is to accommodate (while not necessarily endorsing) a popular theory about the origins of Q1. Q2 and F are close to the wording of the first five scenes of Q1 but only occasionally close thereafter. Paul Werstine, who has explored (and to some extent challenged) the theory that Q1 is a memorial reconstruction of Q2/F, traces the theory back to 1880–1 (Werstine, 'Quartos', 317, n. 17), when Richard Grant White and W.H. Widgery independently argued that the text of Q1 derives from the attempts of the actor who played Voltemand to reconstruct the play from his memory of having performed in it. But Voltemand alone does not account for all the most similar passages, so the hunt began for an actor who would have been onstage wherever the texts coincide. Since no one character fits that bill, the theorists had to posit an actor playing more than one part. Widgery favoured someone doubling Voltemand and the Player King; W.W. Greg preferred Voltemand and Marcellus (Greg, 'Quartos'); Henry David Gray rejected Voltemand and went for Marcellus and the Player (or Players) acting the Prologue and Lucianus; John Dover Wilson reinstated Voltemand but extended the list to include a trio of the Second Gravedigger, the Priest and the English Ambassador (Wilson, 'Transcript').

Unfortunately for Dover Wilson, Voltemar and the English Ambassador are onstage at the same moment in Q1's last scene. Unfortunately for all the theorists, as Werstine points out, none of the doubling scenarios to date really covers the full facts. When these characters are present, the texts are sometimes close, but they are not uniformly so, while sometimes the texts are close when these characters are absent. In our charts we have entertained Kathleen O. Irace's theory, first mooted in 1992 ('Origins', 95–6), that the actor playing Marcellus might have doubled Voltemand, the Prologue and Lucianus (see also Irace, *Reforming*, 118–19); later, in her 1998 edition of Q1 (Irace, 7), she excluded the Prologue from this list. The charts reveal that, while such an actor would have been quite busy in the early scenes, he would thereafter have been offstage for the bulk of the play. (This could, of course, be 'corrected' if we were to adopt in part Dover Wilson's theory and also attribute to him such roles as the Second Gravedigger – our Second Man – and the Priest.) As it stands, then, the memorial reconstruction theory seems uneconomical, and does not fit with the assumption that doubling arose out of a need to save on man- and boy-power.

Four hundred years on, and, in the absence of the original constraints, doubling persists (partly, no doubt, because actors still have to be paid). In 1986, after surveying over 100 productions of *Hamlet*, Ralph Berry came to the conclusion that, even though no natural pattern of doubling is required by the play, certain permutations of doubling have become traditional. Although scholars committed to a belief in memorial reconstruction have assumed the doubling of Marcellus and Voltemand, and some even added the Prologue and Lucianus from *The Murder of Gonzago*, Berry found no clear example of this doubling actually happening on stage (R. Berry, 'Doubles'). Some companies have doubled Polonius and the Gravedigger since at least 1730 (see Sprague, 23–4, 35), but the practice of doubling the Ghost and the King is relatively modern, beginning, we believe, with Gielgud's production in 1939. The Ghost has also doubled resonantly with the Gravedigger, and even, less plausibly, with Laertes (see R. Berry, *Castings*, 15).

An acting company as large and apparently well funded as London's National Theatre was still doubling parts in 2000, when John Caird's widely acclaimed production of *Hamlet*, starring Simon Russell Beale, not only doubled the Ghost with the Player King, but doubled Polonius with the Gravedigger, Reynaldo with Francisco, Osric with a player, and Barnardo with the Priest. A year later, Steven Pimlott's RSC production, starring Sam West, again doubled Polonius with the Gravedigger, but more unusually employed what Michael Dobson ('2001') called 'cunning thematic casting' by doubling two landowners (the Ghost with Osric), and two proxies for Hamlet (Lucianus with Fortinbras). In 2004, Trevor Nunn's production at the London Old Vic, starring Ben Whishaw, doubled the Ghost with the King, while in the same year in Michael Boyd's RSC production, starring Toby Stephens, Greg Hicks played the Ghost, the Player King and the Gravedigger. A different kind of 'conceptual' doubling occurred in Andrzej Wajda's production at the Stary Theatre in Krakow in 1989. Teresa Budzisz-Krzyzanowska, who played Hamlet, commented on how the doubling reflected the reality of martial law in Poland, when many actors boycotted the mass media: 'The First Player later becomes a gravedigger, just as Krzysztof Kolberger became a waiter and others taxi drivers.'[1]

On Shakespeare's stage, the boy playing Ophelia could possibly have doubled Osric, a suggestion made recently by Andrew Gurr and Mariko Ichikawa (Gurr & Ichikawa, 152), which would have been unthinkable for long stretches of the play's history. In recent years gender has again diminished as a determinant in casting: in Peter Zadek's 1999 production at the Vienna Festival, Ophelia doubled Fortinbras; and in the same year, in Red Shift's production of Q1, Ofelia doubled the Second Gravedigger (our Second Man). Cinema, with its greater emphasis on naturalistic casting and its commitment to close-up photography, might seem to offer little scope for actors to double parts, but film technology makes it very easy for one actor to play twins, as in A. Edward Sutherland's *The Boys from Syracuse* (1940) or James Cellan Jones's BBC television *Comedy of Errors* (1983) – or indeed for twins to play one character, as in Celestino Coronado's 1976 *Hamlet*. Perhaps it even offers the ultimate actor's dream (indeed Bottom's dream in *A Midsummer Night's Dream*, 1.2) in Peter Greenaway's *Prospero's Books* (1991), which begins with one actor, John Gielgud, speaking all the parts.

---

1 Quoted in Howard, 196

It could be argued that a special kind of spectral or virtual 'doubling' occurs when the same actor plays different parts in different plays, or different parts in the same play on different nights, and the audience is likely to recognize this fact. Having star actors alternate in the roles of Othello and Iago was a feature of several nineteenth-century productions of *Othello* (and even of productions as late as the 1950s) that is unlikely to be revived today, when black casting of black roles has become a new constraint. In *Hamlet*, Polonius recalls playing Julius Caesar in a play at university (3.2.94–102): many readers have interpreted this as a joking allusion by Shakespeare to his own play of that name, performed in 1599. In his 1982 Arden edition, Harold Jenkins glossed Polonius' statement, 'Brutus killed me', with the note: 'It is likely enough that the roles of Caesar and Brutus . . . were taken by the same actors as now played Polonius and Hamlet; so that "Hamlet" would already have killed "Polonius" in a previous play, and, ironically, is to do the same "brute part" in this' (Ard², 294n.). The Hollywood star system, and its equivalent in the theatre dating back to Garrick and beyond, has always assumed that audiences, in this sense, see a 'double' when they 'recognize' a particular actor, and directors cast according to type, or deliberately against type.

How, then, does an appreciation of doubling inform our larger project in editing these texts? For editors of *Hamlet*, whether of eclectic, single-text or multiple-text editions, doubling has been an essential element in the discussion of the relationship between the three texts, since the theory that Q1 was a memorial reconstruction usually assumes that the reconstructors were actors. However, beyond any such textual implications, these doubling charts stimulate thinking about the original conditions of performance, and those of subsequent ages including our own. They can also reflect not just the play's mechanical structure but also its thematic organization, and its implicit treatment of such things as age, gender and even sexuality.

Our own analysis and speculations on the casting of the three *Hamlet* texts have led us to ponder some characteristics of the plays' anatomies. For all their differences in length and in language, Q1 and the other two texts of *Hamlet* are extraordinarily similar in their casting patterns. They provide virtually the same doubling possibilities and they need exactly the same number of actors to cover all the parts. In this perspective, the three texts of *Hamlet* share essentially the same structure, deploying as they do a similar distribution of parts across a similar pattern of scenes. The long tradition of doubling certain parts reinforces *Hamlet*'s self-conscious concern with the theatre and with theatricality. It also seems to call attention to Hamlet's 'crisis of identity' and his own mental habit of seeing the portraiture of one person, or one role, in another.

Finally, while working on these charts, we have been struck by the parts that *cannot* be doubled: one thing which all three texts of *Hamlet* have in common is the fact that the actors who play Hamlet, the Queen and Horatio are very unlikely to double any other parts. The actor who plays Hamlet could conceivably double Francisco in the opening scene, Reynaldo/Montano in 2.1, the Captain in F's equivalent of 4.4 or the Sailor in 4.6. So, for that matter, could the boy who plays the Queen. The actor least able to double is the one who plays Horatio (who could only double Reynaldo/Montano or the Captain in F's equivalent of 4.4). This 'marking' of these three roles may call for an explanation. That the actor who plays Hamlet should be a special case is unsurprising. The centrality and dominance of the role within the play, and for us the modern cultural significance of the role of Hamlet and those who play it, seem to have prepared us for it. The Queen's marking could be read as the marking not of her individuality but of her relationship with Hamlet, and therefore reinforces conventional interpretations of the centrality of that relationship to the play's meanings. But the fact that the actor who plays Horatio should be someone who can never be anyone else is striking. Does his marking, like the Queen's, call attention to his relationship with Hamlet (and in Q1, because of the unique Scene 14, with the Queen in relation to Hamlet)? Does it reinforce our sense that he is to a remarkable degree unengaged with the action of the play? Or does it reinforce Hamlet's own view of Horatio as an ever-fixed mark, who must be encouraged to go on being himself to the end of the play?

APPENDIX 6

Music

Hamlet has seventeen musical stage directions and at least six songs,[1] of which Ophelia sings the first five[2] and the Gravedigger the sixth:

1 'How should I your true love know' (4.5.23–6, 29–32, 36, 38–40)

2 'Tomorrow is Saint Valentine's Day' (4.5.48–55, 58–66)

3 'They bore him bare-faced on the bier' (4.5.160–1)

4 'For bonny sweet Robin is all my joy' (4.5.179)

5 'And will 'a not come again?' (4.5.182–91)

6 'In youth when I did love' (5.1.57–60, 67–70, 89–92, 113)

Unfortunately, there is no real evidence of the original melodies to which these songs were sung on the Elizabethan stage, but Frederick W. Sternfeld and Peter J. Seng agree that, while songs 2 and 5 are associated with tunes sung at Drury Lane in the late eighteenth century, songs 1 and 3 may have used the popular Elizabethan melody 'Walsingham', which is found in the *Fitzwilliam Virginal Book* in versions by John Bull and William Byrd, and song 4 probably used another popular Elizabethan tune, which is found in six printed sources between 1597 and 1621. Since *A Gorgeous Gallery of Gallant Inventions* of 1578 refers to 'the Tune of I lothe that I did loue', it is reasonable to

---

1 Frederick W. Sternfeld's *Music in Shakespearean Tragedy* (Oxford, 1963), his *Songs from Shakespeare's Tragedies* (Oxford, 1964) and Peter J. Seng, *The Vocal Songs in the Plays of Shakespeare: A Critical History* (Cambridge, Mass., 1967) all discuss the music for the play's six songs.

2 For a gender-based discussion of Ophelia's songs, see Leslie C. Dunn, 'Ophelia's songs in *Hamlet*: music, madness, and the feminine', in Leslie C. Dunn and Nancy A. Jones (eds), *Embodied Voices* (Cambridge, 1994), 50–64.

conclude that song 6 may have used either the tune for these words found in BM Add. MS 4900 or another which was found in 1814 in a (now lost) copy of Richard Tottel's famous 1557 anthology of *Songs and Sonnets* (known as *Tottel's Miscellany*).

Since its original performances, Shakespeare's *Hamlet* has generated much music, partly because directors and composers have given these songs new settings or set other passages to music. Samuel Pepys commissioned a recitative setting of 'To be or not to be', and there were nine metrical and musical adaptations of Hamlet's letter to Ophelia between 1786 and 1861.[1] Stage and film productions have given rise to specially composed incidental or mood music, and the play as a whole or in part has inspired operas (most famously, by Ambroise Thomas in 1868), musicals (such as Ben M. Jerome and Edward Madden's *Mr Hamlet of Broadway* in 1908, and Cliff Jones's *Rockabye Hamlet* in 1974), and concert pieces (including those by Frédéric Chopin in 1833, Hector Berlioz in 1844 and 1848, Franz Liszt in 1858, Peter Tchaikovsky in 1888 and Duke Ellington in 1957).[2] Some composers have kept returning to *Hamlet* for inspiration: Dmitri Shostakovich (whose Fifth Symphony was often dubbed the 'Hamlet Symphony' in the former Soviet Union) wrote incidental music for a stage production by Nikolai Akimov at the Vakhtangov Theatre in Moscow in 1932, and then for another production by Grigori Kozintsev at the Leningrad Pushkin Theatre in 1954; the latter led on to the score for Kozintsev's 1964 film, and subsequent ballets in 1969, 1971 and 1975. Similarly, William Walton

---

1   Alfred Roffe, 'Shakespeare's music', *N&Q*, 2nd series, 12, 5 October 1891, 265–6.
2   Frédéric Chopin's Nocturne Op. 15 was originally inscribed 'After a performance of Hamlet'; Hector Berlioz composed a *Marche funèbre pour la dernière scène d'Hamlet* in 1844, as well as his 1842 song 'La Mort d'Ophélie', which was arranged for orchestra in 1848; Franz Liszt composed a symphonic poem entitled *Hamlet*, and Peter Tchaikovsky composed an overture with the same title; Duke Ellington's suite *Such Sweet Thunder* includes a movement entitled 'Madness in great ones'.

followed up his 1947 score for Olivier's film with a *Funeral March* of 1963 and *Hamlet and Ophelia: A Poem for Orchestra* of 1967. By 1988, at least 1,406 *Hamlet*-related pieces of music had been written, including 'Tuba or not tuba', 'Something's rockin' in Denmark', and a dramatic overture, inspired by Ernesto Rossi's performance as the prince in 1874 and composed by William Shakespeare (1849–1931).[1]

1   Bryan N.S. Gooch, David Thatcher and Odean Long (eds), *A Shakespeare Music Catalogue* (Oxford, 1991), vol. 1.

ABBREVIATIONS AND REFERENCES

Place of publication in references is London unless otherwise stated. Quotations and references relating to *Hamlet* are keyed to this edition. All other works of Shakespeare are cited from *The Arden Shakespeare: Complete Works*, ed. Richard Proudfoot, Ann Thompson and David Scott Kastan (rev. edn, 2004). *OED* references are to *OED¹*. Biblical quotations are from the Bishops' Bible (1573), STC 2108, unless otherwise noted.

ABBREVIATIONS

ABBREVIATIONS USED IN NOTES

*	precedes commentary notes involving readings altered from the text on which this edition is based
conj.	conjectured (by)
LN	longer notes
n.	(in cross-references) commentary note
n.d.	no date
om.	omitted
opp.	opposite
SD	stage direction
SP	speech prefix
subst.	substantially
this edn	a reading adopted for the first time in this edition
t.n.	textual note
( )	surrounding a reading in the textual notes indicates original spelling; surrounding an editor's or scholar's name indicates a conjectural reading

WORKS BY AND PARTLY BY SHAKESPEARE

AC	*Antony and Cleopatra*
AW	*All's Well That Ends Well*
AYL	*As You Like It*
CE	*The Comedy of Errors*

608

Cor	*Coriolanus*
Cym	*Cymbeline*
E3	*King Edward III*
Ham	*Hamlet*
1H4	*King Henry IV, Part 1*
2H4	*King Henry IV, Part 2*
H5	*King Henry V*
1H6	*King Henry VI, Part 1*
2H6	*King Henry VI, Part 2*
3H6	*King Henry VI, Part 3*
H8	*King Henry VIII*
JC	*Julius Caesar*
KJ	*King John*
KL	*King Lear*
LC	*A Lover's Complaint*
LLL	*Love's Labour's Lost*
Luc	*The Rape of Lucrece*
MA	*Much Ado About Nothing*
Mac	*Macbeth*
MM	*Measure for Measure*
MND	*A Midsummer Night's Dream*
MV	*The Merchant of Venice*
MW	*The Merry Wives of Windsor*
Oth	*Othello*
Per	*Pericles*
PP	*The Passionate Pilgrim*
PT	*The Phoenix and Turtle*
R2	*King Richard II*
R3	*King Richard III*
RJ	*Romeo and Juliet*
Son	*Sonnets*
STM	*Sir Thomas More*
TC	*Troilus and Cressida*
Tem	*The Tempest*
TGV	*The Two Gentlemen of Verona*
Tim	*Timon of Athens*
Tit	*Titus Andronicus*
TN	*Twelfth Night*
TNK	*The Two Noble Kinsmen*
TS	*The Taming of the Shrew*
VA	*Venus and Adonis*
WT	*The Winter's Tale*

REFERENCES

EDITIONS OF SHAKESPEARE COLLATED

Adams	*Hamlet*, ed. Joseph Quincy Adams (1929)
Alexander	*The Complete Works*, ed. Peter Alexander, 4 vols (London and Glasgow, 1951)
Andrews	*Hamlet*, ed. John F. Andrews, Everyman Shakespeare (1993)
Ard¹	*Hamlet*, ed. Edward Dowden, Arden Shakespeare (1899)
Ard²	*Hamlet*, ed. Harold Jenkins, Arden Shakespeare (1982)
Bailey	Samuel Bailey, *On the Received Text of Shakespeare's Dramatic Writings and its Improvement*, 2 vols (1862–6)
Bantam	*Hamlet*, ed. David Bevington, Bantam Shakespeare (New York, 1988)
Bertram–Kliman	*The Three-Text Hamlet: Parallel Texts of the First and Second Quartos and First Folio*, ed. Paul Bertram and Bernice W. Kliman (New York, 1991)
Bertram–Kliman²	*The Three-Text Hamlet: Parallel Texts of the First and Second Quartos and First Folio*, ed. Paul Bertram and Bernice W. Kliman, 2nd edn (New York, 2003)
Boswell	*The Plays and Poems of William Shakespeare, with . . . a life of the Poet . . . by the late Edmond Malone*, ed. James Boswell [The Third Variorum, or the Malone–Boswell], vol. 7 (1821)
Caldecott	*Hamlet, and As You Like It, a Specimen of a New Edition of Shakespeare*, ed. Thomas Caldecott (published anonymously, 1819; rev. 1832)
Cam	*Hamlet*, ed. W.G. Clark, J. Glover and W.A. Wright, Cambridge Shakespeare (1863–6), vol. 8 (1866); rev. edn, W.A. Wright (1891–3), vol. 7 (1892)
Cam¹	*Hamlet*, ed. John Dover Wilson, New Shakespeare (Cambridge, 1934; 2nd edn, 1936; rev. 1954, 1964)
Cam²	*Hamlet*, ed. Philip Edwards, New Shakespeare (Cambridge, 1985)
Capell	*Mr William Shakespeare, his Comedies, Histories, and Tragedies*, ed. Edward Capell, vol. 10 (1768)
Chambers	*Hamlet*, ed. E.K. Chambers, Warwick Shakespeare (1894)
Chambers²	*Hamlet*, ed. E.K. Chambers, Red Letter Shakespeare (1907)

Clarendon	*Hamlet*, ed. W.G. Clark and W.A. Wright, Clarendon Press Shakespeare (1872)
Clark, Glover & Wright	See Cam
Collier	*The Works of William Shakespeare*, ed. John Payne Collier, 8 vols (1842–4)
Collier²	*The Plays of Shakespeare*, ed. John Payne Collier, 8 vols (1853)
Delius	*Shakspere's Werke*, ed. Nicolaus Delius, 7 vols (Elberfeld, 1854–65)
Dover Wilson	See Cam¹
Dowden	See Ard¹
Dyce	*The Works of William Shakespeare*, ed. Alexander Dyce, 6 vols (1857)
Dyce²	*The Works of William Shakespeare*, ed. Alexander Dyce, 2nd edn, 9 vols (1864–7)
Edwards	See Cam²
Elze	*Shakespeare's Tragedy of Hamlet*, ed. Karl Elze (Halle, 1882)
F, F1	*Mr William Shakespeares Comedies, Histories, and Tragedies*, The First Folio (1623)
Fc	Corrected state of F
Fu	Uncorrected state of F
F2	*Mr William Shakespeares Comedies, Histories, and Tragedies*, The Second Folio (1632)
F3	*Mr William Shakespeares Comedies, Histories, and Tragedies*, The Third Folio (1663, 1664)
F4	*Mr William Shakespear's Comedies, Histories, and Tragedies*, The Fourth Folio (1685)
Farnham	*William Shakespeare; the Complete Works*, Pelican Text Revised, *Hamlet*, ed. Willard Farnham (1969)
Folg	*Hamlet*, ed. L.B. Wright and V.A. LaMar, Folger Library General Reader's Shakespeare Series (New York, 1958)
Folg²	*Hamlet*, ed. Barbara A. Mowat and Paul Werstine, New Folger Library (New York, 1992)
Furness	See Var
Globe	*The Works of William Shakespeare*, ed. William George Clark and William Aldis Wright, Globe Edition (1864)
Halliwell-P	*The Works of William Shakespeare*, ed. James O. Halliwell[-Phillipps] (1853–65), vol. 14 (1865)
Hanmer	*The Works of Shakespeare*, ed. Sir Thomas Hanmer, 6 vols (Oxford, 1743–4)

Hapgood	*Hamlet*, ed. Robert Hapgood, Shakespeare in Production (Cambridge, 1999)
Herford	*The Works of Shakespeare*, ed. C.H. Herford, Eversley Edition, vol. 8 (1899)
Hibbard	See Oxf[1]
Holderness & Loughrey	*The Tragicall Historie of Hamlet Prince of Denmarke*, ed. Graham Holderness and Bryan Loughrey, Shakespearean Originals (Hemel Hempstead, 1992)
Hoy	*Hamlet*, ed. Cyrus Hoy, Norton Critical Edition (1963)
Hubbard	*The First Quarto Edition of Shakespeare's 'Hamlet'*, ed. Frank G. Hubbard (Madison, Wis., 1920)
Hudson	*The Complete Works of William Shakespeare*, ed. Henry N. Hudson, 11 vols (1851–6)
Irace	*The First Quarto of Hamlet*, ed. Kathleen O. Irace, New Cambridge Shakespeare: The Early Quartos (Cambridge, 1998)
Jenkins	See Ard[2]
Jennens	*Hamlet . . . collated with the old and modern editions*, ed. Charles Jennens (1773)
Johnson	*The Plays of William Shakespeare ... with the corrections and illustrations of Various Commentators; to which are added notes by Samuel Johnson*, 8 vols (1765)
Keightley	*The Works of William Shakespeare*, ed. Thomas Keightley, 6 vols (1864)
Kittredge	*Hamlet*, ed. George Lyman Kittredge (Boston, Mass., 1939)
Klein	*Hamlet: Englisch / Deutsch*, ed. Holger M. Klein, 2 vols (Stuttgart, 1984)
Kliman	'The Enfolded *Hamlet* edited by Bernice W. Kliman', *Shakespeare Newsletter*, extra issue, 1–44 (1996) <http://www.global-language.com/enfolded.html>
MacDonald	*The Tragedie of Hamlet, Prince of Denmarke: A Study with the Text of the Folio of 1623*, ed. George MacDonald (London, 1885)
Malone	*The Plays and Poems of William Shakespeare*, ed. Edmond Malone, 10 vols (1790)
Mowat & Werstine	See Folg[2]
Munro	*The London Shakespeare: A New Annotated and Critical Edition of the Complete Works*, ed. John Munro, vol. 5 (1958)

Norton	*The Norton Shakespeare based on the Oxford Edition*, ed. Stephen Greenblatt, Walter Cohen, Jean E. Howard and Katharine Eisaman Maus (New York, 1997)
Oxf, Oxford	William Shakespeare, *The Complete Works*, ed. Stanley Wells and Gary Taylor, with John Jowett and William Montgomery (Oxford, 1986)
Oxf[1]	*Hamlet*, ed. G.R. Hibbard (Oxford, 1987)
Oxf OS	William Shakespeare, *The Complete Works: Original-Spelling Edition*, ed. Stanley Wells and Gary Taylor (Oxford, 1986)
Parrott–Craig	*The Tragedy of Hamlet: A Critical Edition of the Second Quarto*, ed. Thomas Marc Parrott and Hardin Craig (1938)
Pope	*The Works of Shakespear*, ed. Alexander Pope, 6 vols (1723–5)
Pope[2]	*The Works of Shakespear*, ed. Alexander Pope, 8 vols (1728)
Q1	*The Tragicall Historie of Hamlet Prince of Denmarke. By William Shake-speare*, The First Quarto (1603)
Q1c	Corrected state of Q1
Q1u	Uncorrected state of Q1
Q2	*The Tragicall Historie of Hamlet, Prince of Denmarke. By William Shakespeare. Newly imprinted and enlarged . . . according to the true and perfect Coppie*, The Second Quarto (1604–5)
Q2c	Corrected state of Q2
Q2u	Uncorrected state of Q2
Q3	*The Tragedy of Hamlet Prince of Denmarke. By William Shakespeare. Newly imprinted and enlarged . . . according to the true and perfect Coppy* (1611)
Q4	*The Tragedy of Hamlet Prince of Denmarke. Newly Imprinted and inlarged, according to the true and perfect Copy lastly Printed. By William Shakespeare* (*c.* 1621)
Q5	[Substantially as Q4.] (1637)
Q6	*The Tragedy of Hamlet Prince of Denmark. As it is now Acted at . . . the Duke of York's Theatre. By William Shakespeare* (1676)
Q7	[Substantially as Q6.] (1676)
Q8	*The Tragedy of Hamlet Prince of Denmarke. As it is now Acted at . . . the Duke of York's Theatre. By William Shakespeare* (1683)

Q9	*The Tragedy of Hamlet Prince of Denmark. As it is now Acted at the Theatre Royal. By William Shakespeare* (1695)
Q10	*The Tragedy of Hamlet Prince of Denmarke. As it is now Acted at the Theatre Royal. By William Shakespeare* (1703)
Rann	*The Dramatic Works of Shakespeare*, with notes by Joseph Rann, vol. 6 (1786[–94])
Reed	*The Plays of William Shakespeare. With . . . Notes by Samuel Johnson and George Steevens*, 5th edn, revised and augmented by Isaac Reed [The First Variorum, so called], vol. 18 (1803)
Ribner	*Hamlet*, ed. George Lyman Kittredge, rev. M.R. Ribner (1967)
Ridley	*Hamlet*, New Temple Shakespeare, ed. M.R. Ridley (1934)
Riv	*The Riverside Shakespeare*, ed. G. Blakemore Evans and others (Boston, Mass., 1974)
Riv²	*The Riverside Shakespeare*, ed. G. Blakemore Evans and others, 2nd edition (Boston, Mass., 1997)
Rolfe	*Hamlet*, ed. William J. Rolfe (New York, 1890)
Rowe	*The Works of Mr William Shakespear*, ed. Nicholas Rowe, 6 vols (1709)
Serpieri	*William Shakespeare: Il primo Amleto*, ed. Alessandro Serpieri (Venice, 1997)
Singer	*The Dramatic Works of William Shakespeare*, ed. Samuel Wells Singer, 10 vols (1856) [a revision of Singer's edition of 1826]
Sisson	*William Shakespare, The Complete Works*, ed. Charles Jasper Sisson (1954)
Spencer	*Hamlet*, New Penguin Shakespeare, ed. T.J.B. Spencer (Harmondsworth, 1980; reissued with a new introduction, 2005)
Staunton	*The Plays of Shakespeare*, ed. Howard Staunton (1858–60), vol. 3 (1860)
Steevens	*The Plays of William Shakespeare*, ed. Samuel Johnson and George Steevens, 10 vols (1773)
Steevens²	*The Plays of William Shakespeare*, ed. Samuel Johnson and George Steevens, 2nd edn, 10 vols (1778)
Steevens³	*The Plays of William Shakespeare*, ed. Samuel Johnson and George Steevens, 4th edn, 15 vols (1793)

Theobald	*The Works of Shakespeare*, ed. Lewis Theobald, 7 vols (1733)
Theobald[2]	*The Works of Shakespeare*, ed. Lewis Theobald, 8 vols (1740)
Theobald, *Restored*	Lewis Theobald, *Shakespeare Restored* (1726)
Tronch-Pérez	*A Synoptic 'Hamlet'*, ed. Jesús Tronch-Pérez (Valencia, 2002)
Tschischwitz	*Shakspere's Hamlet, Prince of Denmark*, ed. Dr Benno Tschischwitz (Halle, 1869) (English text, with commentary in German)
Var	*Hamlet*, ed. Horace Howard Furness, New Variorum Shakspeare, 2 vols (Philadelphia, 1877)
Verity	*Hamlet*, ed. A.W. Verity (1904)
Walker	W.S. Walker, *A Critical Examination of the Text of Shakespeare*, ed. W.N. Lettsom, 3 vols (1860)
Warburton	*The Works of Shakespear*, ed. Alexander Pope and William Warburton, 8 vols (1747)
Weiner	*Hamlet: The First Quarto 1603*, ed. Albert B. Weiner (1962)
White	*The Works of William Shakespeare*, ed. Richard Grant White, 12 vols (1857–65)

OTHER WORKS CITED

Aasand, *Directions*	Hardin L. Aasand (ed.), *Stage Directions in 'Hamlet'* (Madison, Wis., 2003)
Aasand, 'Ophelia'	Hardin L. Aasand, '"The young, the beautiful, the harmless, and the pious": contending with Ophelia in the eighteenth century', in Joanna Gondris (ed.), *Reading Readings: Essays on Shakespeare Editing in the Eighteenth Century* (1998), 223–43
Ackroyd	Peter Ackroyd, *Shakespeare: The Biography* (2012)
Adelman	Janet Adelman, *Suffocating Mothers: Fantasies of Maternal Origin in Shakespeare's Plays, 'Hamlet' to 'The Tempest'* (1992)
Aebischer	Pascale Aebischer, *Shakespeare's Violated Bodies: Stage and Screen Performances* (Cambridge, 2004)
Aers	David Aers, 'A whisper in the ear of Early Modernists; or, reflections on literary critics writing the "History of the Subject"', in David Aers (ed.), *Culture and History 1350–1600: Essays on English Communities, Identities and Writing* (Detroit, 1992), 177–201

Almereyda   *William Shakespeare's 'Hamlet'*, adapted by Michael
                     Almereyda (2000)
Arber   *A Transcript of the Registers of the Company of
                     Stationers of London, 1554–1640* AD, ed. Edward
                     Arber, 5 vols (1875–94)
Armstrong   Edward A. Armstrong, *Shakespeare's Imagination*
                     (1946)
Atwood   Margaret Atwood, *Good Bones* (1992)
Bachelard   Gaston Bachelard, *L'Eau et les rêves* (Paris, 1942)
Bains, 'Corrupt'   Y.S. Bains, 'The incidence of corrupt passages in the
                     First Quarto of Shakespeare's *Hamlet*', *N&Q*, 40
                     (1993), 186–92
Barrett   Wilson Barrett, 'The sanity and age of Hamlet',
                     Lippincott's Magazine (April 1890)
Barrie   Robert Barrie, '*Telmahs*: carnival laughter in *Hamlet*',
                     in Burnett & Manning, 83–100
Bartlett & Pollard   Henrietta C. Bartlett and Alfred W. Pollard, *A Census
                     of Shakespeare's Plays in Quarto 1594–1704* (New
                     York, 1939)
Bate, 'Case'   Jonathan Bate, 'The Case for the Folio', www.
                     rscshakespeare.co.uk
Bate, *Soul*   Jonathan Bate, *Soul of the Age: The Life, Mind and
                     World of William Shakespeare* (2008)
Bate & Rasmussen   Jonathan Bate and Eric Rasmussen (eds), *The RSC
                     Shakespeare Complete Works* (London, 2013)
Beaumont &   *The Dramatic Works in the Beaumont and Fletcher
   Fletcher   Canon*, gen. ed. Fredson Bowers, 10 vols (Cambridge,
                     1966–96)
Bednarz   James P. Bednarz, *Shakespeare and the Poets' War*
                     (New York, 2001)
Belsey   Catherine Belsey, 'Sibling rivalry, *Hamlet* and the
                     first murder', in *Shakespeare and the Loss of Eden*
                     (Basingstoke, 1999), 129–74
Bentley   Eric Bentley, 'A directors' theatre', in *What is
                     Theatre?* (Boston, Mass., 1956)
Berkoff   Steven Berkoff, *I am Hamlet* (1989)
Bernhardy   William Bernhardy, 'Shakespeare's *Hamlet*: Ein
                     literar-historisch kritischer Versuch', *Hamburger
                     literarisch-kritische Blätter*, 49 (1857), 103; cited in
                     Cohn, cxx
Berry, 'Ear'   Philippa Berry, 'Hamlet's ear', *SS 50* (1997), 57–64
Berry, *Endings*   Philippa Berry, *Shakespeare's Feminine Endings*
                     (1999)

Berry, *Castings*	Ralph Berry, *Shakespeare in Performance: Castings and Metamorphoses* (New York, 1993)
Berry, 'Doubles'	Ralph Berry, 'Hamlet's doubles', *SQ*, 37 (1986), 204–12
Bevington	*Troilus and Cressida*, ed. David Bevington, Arden Shakespeare (1998)
Blake	Norman F. Blake, *A Grammar of Shakespeare's Language* (Basingstoke, 2002)
Blayney	Peter Blayney, 'Publication of playbooks', in John D. Cox and David Scott Kastan (eds), *A New History of Early English Drama* (New York, 1997), 393–4
Bliss	Lee Bliss, 'Scribes, compositors, and annotators: the nature of the copy for the First Folio text of *Coriolanus*', *SB*, 50 (1997), 224–61
Bloom	Harold Bloom, *Shakespeare: The Invention of the Human* (New York, 1998)
Boaden	James Boaden (ed.), *The Private Correspondence of David Garrick with the Most Celebrated Persons of his Time*, 2 vols (1831–2)
Boehrer	Bruce Thomas Boehrer, *Monarchy and Incest in Renaissance England: Literature, Culture, Kinship, and Kingship* (Philadelphia, 1992)
Booth	Stephen Booth, 'Close reading without readings', in McDonald, 42–55
Bourus	Terri Bourus, *Young Shakespeare's Young Hamlet: Print, Piracy and Performance* (London, 2014).
Bowers, *Criticism*	Fredson Bowers, *Textual and Literary Criticism* (Cambridge, 1959)
Bowers, *Tragedy*	Fredson Bowers, *Elizabethan Revenge Tragedy 1587–1642* (Princeton, NJ, 1940)
Bradley, A.C.	A.C. Bradley, *Shakespearean Tragedy* (1904)
Bradley, D.	David Bradley, *From Text to Performance in the Theatre: Preparing the Play for the Stage* (Cambridge, 1992)
Branagh	Kenneth Branagh, *Hamlet: Screenplay and Introduction* (1996)
Brigden	Susan Brigden, *New Worlds, Lost Worlds: The Rule of the Tudors 1485–1603* (2000)
Briggs	Julia Briggs, 'Virginia Woolf reads Shakespeare; or, her silence on Master William', *SS* 58 (2005), 118–29
Bristol	Michael D. Bristol, '"Funeral bak'd meats": carnival and the carnivalesque in *Hamlet*', in Susanne L.

617

Wofford (ed.), *'Hamlet': Case Studies in Contemporary Criticism* (New York, 1994), 348–67

Brown   John Russell Brown, 'The compositors of *Hamlet* Q2 and *The Merchant of Venice*', *SB*, 7 (1955), 17–40

Bruster   Douglas Bruster, *To Be Or Not To Be* (London, 2007)

Bullough   Geoffrey Bullough (ed.), *Narrative and Dramatic Sources of Shakespeare*, 8 vols (London and New York, 1957–75)

Burkhart   Robert E. Burkhart, *Shakespeare's Bad Quartos: Deliberate Abridgements Designed for Performance by a Reduced Cast* (The Hague and Paris, 1973)

Burnett, 'Ophelia'   Mark Thornton Burnett, 'Ophelia's "false steward" contextualised', *RES*, 46 (1995), 48–56

Burnett, *Cinema*   Mark Thornton Burnett, *Shakespeare and World Cinema* (Cambridge, 2013)

Burnett, *Filming*   Mark Thornton Burnett, *Filming Shakespeare in the Global Marketplace* (Basingstoke, 2007)

Burnett, *Translating*   Mark Thornton Burnett, *Translating 'Hamlet': Travels in World Cinema* (forthcoming)

Burnett & Manning   Mark Thornton Burnett and John Manning (eds), *New Essays on 'Hamlet'* (New York, 1994)

Burton   Hal Burton, *Great Acting* (New York, 1967)

Callaghan   Dympna Callaghan, 'Buzz Goodbody: directing for change', in Jean I. Marsden (ed.), *The Appropriation of Shakespeare* (Brighton, 1991), 163–81

Campbell   Kathleen Campbell, 'Zeffirelli's *Hamlet*: Q1 in performance', *Shakespeare on Film Newsletter*, 16 (1991), 7–8

Carlson   Marvin Carlson, 'Daniel Mesguich and intertextual Shakespeare', in D. Kennedy, 213–31

Cartelli   Thomas Cartelli, 'Channelling the Ghosts: The Wooster Group's Remediation of the 1964 Electronovision *Hamlet*', *SS 61* (2008), 147–60

Cartmell   Deborah Cartmell, '*Hamlet* 2000: Michael Almereyda's city comedy', in Dieter Mehl, Angela Stock and Anne-Julie Zwierlein (eds), *Plotting Early Modern London: New Essays on Jacobean City Comedy* (Aldershot, 2004), 209–16

Cathcart, '*Dominion*'   Charles Cathcart, '*Lust's Dominion; or, The Lascivious Queen*: authorship, date', *RES*, 52 (2001), 360–75

Cathcart, '*Hamlet*'   Charles Cathcart, '*Hamlet*: date and afterlife', *RES*, 52 (2001), 341–59

Cavell	Stanley Cavell, '*North by Northwest*', in *Themes out of School: Effects and Causes* (San Francisco, 1984), 152–72
Chambers, *Shakespeare*	E.K. Chambers, *William Shakespeare: A Study of Facts and Problems*, 2 vols (Oxford, 1930)
Chambers, *Stage*	E.K. Chambers, *The Elizabethan Stage*, 4 vols (Oxford, 1923)
Chapman	*The Plays of George Chapman: The Tragedies*, gen. ed. Allan Holaday (Cambridge, 1987)
Chaucer	Geoffrey Chaucer, quotations from Thomas Speght's 1598 edn; line numbers from *The Works of Geoffrey Chaucer*, ed. F.N. Robinson, 2nd edn (1957)
Chedgzoy, 'Prince'	Kate Chedgzoy, 'The (pregnant) prince and the show-girl', in Burnett & Manning, 249–69
Chedgzoy, *Queer*	Kate Chedgzoy, *Shakespeare's Queer Children: Sexual Politics and Contemporary Culture* (Manchester, 1995)
Clare	Janet Clare, *Shakespeare's Stage Traffic: Imitation, Borrowing and Competition in Renaissance Theatre* (Cambridge, 2014)
Clary, 'Mousetrap'	Frank N. Clary, Jr, 'Hamlet's mousetrap and the play-within-the-anecdote of Plutarch', in Joanna Gondris (ed.), *Reading Readings: Essays on Shakespeare Editing in the Eighteenth Century* (Madison, NJ, 1997), 164–87
Clayton	Thomas Clayton (ed.), *The 'Hamlet' First Published (Q1, 1603): Origins, Form, Intertextualities* (Newark, Del., 1992)
Coddon	Karin S. Coddon, '"Such strange desyns": madness, subjectivity and treason in *Hamlet* and Elizabethan culture', *RD*, 20 (1989), 51–75
Cohn	Albert Cohn, *Shakespeare in Germany in the Sixteenth and Seventeenth Centuries* (1865)
Conklin	Paul S. Conklin, *History of 'Hamlet' Criticism 1601–1821* (New York, 1947)
Cook	Patrick Cook, *Cinematic 'Hamlet'* (Athens, OH, 2011)
Cowden Clarke	Mary Cowden Clarke, 'Ophelia: the Rose of Elsinore', *The Girlhood of Shakespeare's Heroines* (1852)
Craven	Alan E. Craven, 'Simmes's Compositor A and five Shakespearean quartos', *SB*, 26 (1973), 37–60
Cripps	A.R. Cripps
Critchley & Webster	Simon Critchley and Jamieson Webster, *The Shakespeare Doctrine* (London and New York, 2013).

Croall	Jonathan Croall, *'Hamlet' Observed: The National Theatre at Work* (2001)
Cummings	Brian Cummings, *Mortal Thoughts: Religion, Secularity and Identity in Shakespeare and Early Modern Culture* (Oxford, 2014)
Curran	John E. Curran, *'Hamlet', Protestantism, and the Mourning of Contingency* (Farnham, 2006)
Dane	Joseph A. Dane, 'Perfect order and perfected order: the evidence from press-variants of early seventeenth-century quartos', *Papers of the Bibliographical Society of America*, 90, no 3 (1996), 272–320
Daniell	*Julius Caesar*, ed. David Daniell, Arden Shakespeare (1998)
Davison	Richard Allan Davison, 'The readiness was all: Ian Charleson and Richard Eyre's *Hamlet*', in Lois Potter and Arthur F. Kinney (eds), *Shakespeare: Text and Theater* (Newark, Del., 1999), 170–82
Dawson	Anthony B. Dawson, *Shakespeare in Performance: 'Hamlet'* (Manchester, 1995)
Dekker	*The Dramatic Works of Thomas Dekker*, gen. ed. Fredson Bowers, 4 vols (Cambridge, 1953–61)
Dent	R.W. Dent, *Shakespeare's Proverbial Language* (Berkeley, Calif., 1981)
Dering	*The History of King Henry the Fourth, as Revised by Sir Edward Dering, Bart.*, ed. George Walton Williams and Gwynne Blakemore Evans (Charlottesville, Va., 1974)
Dessen, *Elizabethan*	Alan C. Dessen, *Elizabethan Stage Conventions and Modern Interpreters* (Cambridge, 1984)
Dessen, 'Options'	Alan C. Dessen, 'Weighing the options in *Hamlet* Q1', in Clayton, 65–78
Dessen & Thomson	Alan C. Dessen and Leslie Thomson, *A Dictionary of Stage Directions in English Drama 1580–1642* (Cambridge, 1999)
Deubel	Werner Deubel, *Der deutsche Weg zur Tragödie* (Dresden, 1935)
Dido	Christopher Marlowe and Thomas Nashe, *Dido, Queen of Carthage* (1594)
Dobson, '2000'	Michael Dobson, 'Shakespeare performances in England, 2000', *SS 54* (2001), 246–82
Dobson, '2001'	Michael Dobson, 'Shakespeare performances in England, 2001', *SS 55* (2002), 285–321

Dobson, '2006'	Michael Dobson, 'Shakespeare Performances in England, 2006', *SS 60* (2007), 284–319
Donaldson	Peter S. Donaldson, 'Olivier, Hamlet and Freud', in *Shakespearean Films/Shakespearean Directors* (Boston, Mass., 1990), 31–67
DSK	David Scott Kastan, private communication
Duncan-Jones, *Ungentle*	Katherine Duncan-Jones, *Ungentle Shakespeare: Scenes from his Life* (2001)
Duncan-Jones, *Upstart*	Katherine Duncan-Jones, *Shakespeare: Upstart Crow to Sweet Swan, 1592–1623* (2011)
Duthie	G.I. Duthie, *The 'Bad' Quarto of Hamlet: A Critical Study* (Cambridge, 1941)
Dutton	Richard Dutton, '*Hamlet, An Apology for Actors*, and the sign of the Globe', *SS 41* (1989), 35–43
Eagleton	Terry Eagleton, *William Shakespeare* (Oxford, 1986)
Eastward Ho	George Chapman, John Marston and Ben Jonson, *Eastward Ho* (1605)
Edelman	Charles Edelman, *Brawl Ridiculous: Swordfighting in Shakespeare's Plays* (Manchester, 1992)
Eden & Opland	Avrim R. Eden and Jeff Opland, 'Bartolommeo Eustachio's *De Auditus Organis* and the unique murder plot in Shakespeare's *Hamlet*', *New England Journal of Medicine*, 307 (22 July 1982), 259–61
Edward III	*Edward III*, ed. Giorgio Melchiori (Cambridge, 1998)
Egan	Gabriel Egan, 'The editorial problem of press variants: Q2 *Hamlet* as a test case', *The Papers of the Bibliographical Society of America*, 106, no 3 (2012), 311–55
Elam	Keir Elam (ed.), *Twelfth Night*, Arden Shakespeare (2007)
Eliot	T.S. Eliot, *Selected Prose of T.S. Eliot*, ed. Frank Kermode (1975)
Ellrodt	R. Ellrodt, 'Self-consciousness in Montaigne and Shakespeare', *SS 28* (1975), 37–50
Elze, 'Four hours'	Karl Elze, 'You know sometimes he walks four hours together, here in the lobby', *SJ*, 11 (1876), 288–94
Engle	Ron Engle, 'Audience, style and language in the Shakespeare of Peter Zadek', in D. Kennedy, 93–105
Erne	Lukas Erne, *Shakespeare as Literary Dramatist* (Cambridge, 2003)
Evans	G. Blakemore Evans, 'An echo of the *Ur-Hamlet*?', *N&Q*, 246 (2001), 266

Eyre   Richard Eyre, *Utopia and Other Places* (1993; rev. edn, 1994)

Farley-Hills, *Critical*   David Farley-Hills (ed.), *Critical Responses to 'Hamlet' 1600–1900*, 4 vols (New York, 1995–)

Farley-Hills, 'Crux'   David Farley-Hills, 'Another *Hamlet* crux', *N&Q*, 243 (1998), 334–6

Farmer   Richard Farmer

Ferguson   W. Craig Ferguson, *Pica Roman Type in Elizabethan England* (1989)

Fiedler   Lisa Fiedler, *Dating Hamlet* (2002)

Fink   Bruce Fink, 'Reading *Hamlet* with Lacan', in Willy Apollon and Richard Feldstein (eds), *Lacan, Politics, Aesthetics* (New York, 1996), 181–98

Fleay   Frederick Gard Fleay, *Shakespeare Manual* (1878)

Fletcher, John   See Beaumont & Fletcher

Foakes, 'Ghost'   R.A. Foakes, '"Armed at point exactly": the Ghost in *Hamlet*', *SS 58* (2005), 34–47

Foakes, *Hamlet*   R.A. Foakes, *Hamlet versus Lear* (Cambridge, 1993)

Foster, 'Forged'   William Foster, 'Forged Shakespeariana', *N&Q*, 134 (1900), 41–2

Foster, 'Replies'   William Foster, 'Replies', *N&Q*, 195 (1950), 414–15

FQ   Edmund Spenser, *The Faerie Queene*, ed. Thomas P. Roche, Jr (Harmondsworth, England, 1978)

Freeman   Arthur and Janet Ing Freeman, 'Did Halliwell steal and mutilate the First Quarto of Hamlet?', *Library*, 7th series, 24 (December 2001), 349–63

Froula   Christine Froula, 'Virginia Woolf as Shakespeare's sister: chapters in a woman writer's autobiography', in Novy, *Re-Visions*, 123–42

Garber   Marjorie Garber, *Shakespeare's Ghost Writers: Literature as Uncanny Causality* (1987)

Garner   Shirley Nelson Garner, '"Let her paint an inch thick": painted ladies in Renaissance drama and society', *RD*, 20 (1989), 123–39

Gibson   James M. Gibson, *The Philadelphia Shakespeare Story* (New York, 1990)

Gilder   Rosamond Gilder, *John Gielgud's Hamlet: A Record of Performance, with 'The Hamlet Tradition' by John Gielgud* (1937)

Goethe   Johann Wolfgang von Goethe, *Wilhelm Meister's Apprenticeship*, trans. Eric A. Blackall (Princeton, NJ, 1989)

Goldberg	Jonathan Goldberg, 'Hamlet's hand', *SQ*, 39 (1988), 307–27
Golding	See Ovid 1965
Gottschalk	Paul Gottschalk, *The Meanings of 'Hamlet': Modes of Literary Representation since Bradley* (Albuquerque, N. Mex., 1972)
Grady, *Impure*	Hugh Grady, *Shakespeare and Impure Aesthetics* (Cambridge, 2009)
Graham-White	Anthony Graham-White, *Punctuation and its Dramatic Value in Shakespearean Drama* (Newark, Del., 1995)
Granville-Barker	Harley Granville-Barker, *Prefaces to Shakespeare: Third Series: 'Hamlet'* (1936)
Gray, 'First Quarto'	Henry David Gray, 'The First Quarto "Hamlet"', *MLR*, 10 (1915), 171–80
Gray, 'Kyd'	Henry David Gray, 'Thomas Kyd and the First Quarto of *Hamlet*', *PMLA*, 42 (1927), 721–35
Gray, 'Reconstruction'	Henry David Gray, 'Reconstruction of a lost play', *PQ*, vol. 7, no. 3 (1928), 254–74
Grazia, de, *'Hamlet'*	Margreta de Grazia, *'Hamlet' Without Hamlet* (Cambridge, 2007)
Grazia, de, 'Soliloquies'	Margreta de Grazia, 'Soliloquies and wages in the age of emergent consciousness', *Textual Practice*, 9 (1995), 67–92
Grazia, de, 'Teleology'	Margreta de Grazia, 'Teleology, delay and the "old mole"', *SQ*, 50 (1991), 251–67
Grazia, de, 'Time'	Margreta de Grazia, '*Hamlet* before its time', *Modern Language Quarterly*, 62 (2001), 355–75
Greenblatt, 'Hamnet'	Stephen Greenblatt, 'The death of Hamnet and the making of *Hamlet*', *New York Review of Books*, vol. 51, no. 16 (21 October 2004), 42–7
Greenblatt, *Purgatory*	Stephen Greenblatt, *Hamlet in Purgatory* (Princeton, NJ, 2001)
Greenblatt, 'Remnants'	Stephen Greenblatt, 'Remnants of the sacred in Early Modern England', in Margreta de Grazia, Maureen Quilligan and Peter Stallybrass (eds), *Subject and Object in Renaissance Culture* (Cambridge, 1996), 337–45
Greenblatt, *Will*	Stephen Greenblatt, *Will in the World: How Shakespeare Became Shakespeare* (2004)
Greer	Germaine Greer, *Shakespeare's Wife* (New York, 2007)
Greetham	David C. Greetham, *Textual Scholarship* (New York, 1992)

Greg, *Editorial*	W.W. Greg, *The Editorial Problem in Shakespeare* (Oxford, 1942)
Greg, *First Folio*	W.W. Greg, *Shakespeare's First Folio: Its Bibliographical and Textual History* (Oxford, 1955)
Greg, *First Quarto*	W.W. Greg, *Hamlet: The Quarto of 1603*, Shakespeare Quarto Facsimiles no. 7 (Oxford, n.d. [1951]; 2nd impression, 1964)
Greg, *Merry Wives*	*The Merry Wives of Windsor, 1602*, ed. W.W. Greg (Oxford, 1910)
Greg, 'Quartos'	W.W. Greg, 'The *Hamlet* Quartos, 1603, 1604', *MLR*, 5 (1910), 196–7
Greg, *Second Quarto*	W.W. Greg, *Hamlet: The Quarto of 1604–5*, Shakespeare Quarto Facsimiles no. 4 (Oxford, 1940; 2nd impression, 1964)
Grigson	Jane Grigson, *Charcuterie and French Pork Cookery* (1967)
Guilfoyle	Cherrell Guilfoyle, *Shakespeare's Play within Play* (Kalamazoo, Mich., 1990)
Gurr, 'Auto da fe'	Andrew Gurr, '*Hamlet* and the auto da fe', *Around the Globe*, 13 (Spring 2000), 14–15
Gurr, 'Globe'	Andrew Gurr, 'Staging at the Globe', in J.R. Mulryne and Margaret Shewring (eds), *Shakespeare's Globe Rebuilt* (Cambridge, 1997), 159–68
Gurr, *Playgoing*	Andrew Gurr, *Playgoing in Shakespeare's London* (Cambridge, 1987)
Gurr & Ichikawa	Andrew Gurr and Mariko Ichikawa, *Staging in Shakespeare's Theatres* (Oxford, 2000)
Hackett	James Henry Hackett, *Notes, Criticisms and Correspondences upon Shakespeare's Plays and Actors* (New York, 1863)
Hansen	William F. Hansen, *Saxo Grammaticus and the Life of Hamlet* (Lincoln, Nebr., 1983)
Hart, *Homilies*	Alfred Hart, *Shakespeare and the Homilies and Other Pieces of Research into the Elizabethan Drama* (Melbourne, 1934)
Hart, 'Number'	Alfred Hart, 'The number of lines in Shakespeare's plays', *RES*, 8 (1932), 19–28
Hart, *Stolne*	Alfred Hart, *Stolne and Surreptitious Copies: A Comparative Study of Shakespeare's Bad Quartos* (Melbourne, 1942)
Hawkes, *Meaning*	Terence Hawkes, *Meaning by Shakespeare* (1992)
Hawkes, 'Telmah'	Terence Hawkes, 'Telmah', *That Shakespeherian Rag* (1986), 92–119

Heilbrun	Carolyn Heilbrun, *Hamlet's Mother and Other Women* (New York, 1990)
Henning	Standish Henning, 'Branding harlots on the brow', *SQ*, 51 (2000), 86–9
Henslowe	*Henslowe's Diary*, ed. R.A. Foakes, 2nd edn (Cambridge, 2002)
Heppenstall & Innes	Rayner Heppenstall and Michael Innes, *Three Tales of Hamlet* (1950)
Hibbard, 'Chronology'	G.R. Hibbard, 'The chronology of the three substantive texts of Shakespeare's *Hamlet*', in Clayton, 79–89
Hibbard, 'Errors'	G.R. Hibbard, 'Common errors and unusual spellings in *Hamlet* Q2 and F', *RES*, n.s. 37 (1986), 55–61
Hillman	David Hillman, *Shakespeare's Entrails: Belief, Scepticism and the Interior of the Body* (2007)
Hinman, *Facsimile*	*The First Folio of Shakespeare*, Norton Facsimile, ed. Charlton Hinman (New York, 1968; 2nd edn, 1996)
Hinman, *Printing*	Charlton Hinman, *The Printing and Proof-Reading of the First Folio of Shakespeare*, 2 vols (Oxford, 1963)
Hirsh, 'Act'	James Hirsh, 'Act divisions in the Shakespeare First Folio', *PBSA*, 96 (June 2002), 219–56
Hirsh, '*Hamlet*'	James Hirsh, '*Hamlet* and empiricism', *SS* 66 (2013), 330–43
Hirsh, 'To be'	James Hirsh, 'The "To be, or not to be" speech: evidence, conventional wisdom, and the editing of *Hamlet*', *Medieval and Renaissance Drama in England* 23 (2010), 34–62
Hodgdon	Barbara Hodgdon, 'The critic, the poor player, Prince Hamlet, and the lady in the dark', in McDonald, 259–93
Holderness, *Prince*	Graham Holderness, *The Prince of Denmark* (Hertfordshire, 2001)
Holderness, 'Skull'	Graham Holderness, '"I covet your skull": death and desire in *Hamlet*', *SS* 60 (2007), 223–36
Holland	Peter Holland, 'Film editing', in Grace Ioppolo (ed.), *Shakespeare Performed: Essays in Honour of R.A. Foakes* (Newark, Del., 2000), 273–98
Holleran	James V. Holleran, 'Maimed funeral rites in *Hamlet*', *English Literary History*, 19 (1989), 65–93
Holmes	Jonathan Holmes, 'Noble memories: playing Hamlet', in *Merely Players? Actors' Accounts of Performing Shakespeare* (2004), 95–140

Honan	Park Honan, *Shakespeare: A Life* (Oxford, 1998)
Honigmann, Ard³ *Oth*	*Othello*, ed. E.A.J. Honigmann, Arden Shakespeare (1996)
Honigmann, 'Date'	E.A.J. Honigmann, 'The date of *Hamlet*', *SS* 9 (1956), 24–34
Honigmann, 'First Quarto'	E.A.J. Honigmann, 'The First Quarto of *Hamlet* and the date of *Othello*', *RES*, 44 (1993), 211–19.
Honigmann, *Stability*	E.A.J. Honigmann, *The Stability of Shakespeare's Text* (1965)
Hope	Jonathan Hope, *Shakespeare's Grammar* (2003)
Horwich	Richard Horwich, '*Hamlet* and *Eastward Ho*', *Studies in English Literature*, 11 (1971), 223–33
Howard	Tony Howard, *Women as Hamlet: Performance and Interpretation in Theatre, Film & Fiction* (Cambridge, 2007)
Howard-Hill, 'Compositors'	T.H. Howard-Hill, 'The compositors of Shakespeare's Folio Comedies', *SB*, 26 (1973), 62–106.
Howard-Hill, *More*	T.H. Howard-Hill (ed.), *Shakespeare and 'Sir Thomas More': Essays on the Play and its Shakespearean Interest* (Cambridge, 1989)
Howard-Hill, '*New light*'	T.H. Howard-Hill, 'New light on Compositor E of the Shakespeare First Folio', *Library*, 6th series, 2 (1980), 156–78
Howlett	Kathy M. Howlett, *Framing Shakespeare on Film* (Athens, Ohio, 2000)
HS	*Hamlet Studies*
Hulme	Hilda M. Hulme, *Explorations in Shakespeare's Language: Some Problems of Lexical Meaning in the Dramatic Text* (1962)
Hunter	Joseph Hunter, *New Illustrations of the Life, Studies, and Writings of Shakespeare, Supplementary to All the Editions*, 2 vols (1845)
Ingleby	C.M. Ingleby, Lucy Toulmin Smith and F.J. Furnivall, *The Shakespere Allusion Book*, 2 vols (1909)
Irace, 'Origins'	Kathleen O. Irace, 'Origins and agents of Q1 *Hamlet*', in Clayton, 90–122
Irace, *Reforming*	Kathleen O. Irace, *Reforming the 'Bad' Quartos: Performance and Provenance of Six Shakespearean First Editions* (Newark, Del., 1994)
Jackson	MacDonald P. Jackson, 'The manuscript copy for the Quarto (1598) of Shakespeare's *1 Henry IV*', *N&Q*, 231 (1986), 353–4

Jardine	Lisa Jardine, 'What happens in *Hamlet*?', in *Reading Shakespeare Historically* (1996), 148–57
Jenkins, 'Relation'	Harold Jenkins, 'The relation between the Second Quarto and the Folio text of *Hamlet*', *SB*, 7 (1955), 69–83
John	Juliet John, 'Dickens and Hamlet', in Gail Marshall and Adrian Poole (eds), *Victorian Shakespeare*, vol. 2: *Literature and Culture* (Basingstoke, 2003), 46–60
Jolly	Margrethe Jolly, *The First Two Quartos of 'Hamlet': a New View of the Origins and Relationships of the Texts* (Jefferson, North Carolina, 2014)
Jones, Ernest	Ernest Jones, *Hamlet and Oedipus* (New York, 1949); extract in John Jump (ed.), *Shakespeare: 'Hamlet': A Casebook* (1968)
Jones, *Scenic*	Emrys Jones, *Scenic Form in Shakespeare* (Oxford, 1971)
Jones, 'Sequences'	Emrys Jones, 'The sense of occasion: some Shakespearean night sequences', in Kenneth Muir, Jay L. Halio and D.J. Palmer (eds), *Shakespeare, Man of the Theater* (Newark, Del., 1983), 98–104
Jonson, *Everyman In*	Ben Jonson, *Every Man In His Humour*, in Jonson, *Works*
Jonson, *Everyman Out*	Ben Jonson, *Every Man Out of His Humour*, ed. Helen Ostovich, Revels Plays (Manchester, 2001)
Jonson, *Masques*	*Ben Jonson: The Complete Masques*, ed. Stephen Orgel (New Haven, Conn., and London, 1969)
Jonson, *Works*	Ben Jonson, *Works*, ed. C.H. Herford and Percy and Evelyn Simpson, 11 vols (Oxford, 1925–52)
Jorgens	Jack J. Jorgens, *Shakespeare on Film* (Bloomington, Ind., 1977)
Kastan, *Book*	David Scott Kastan, *Shakespeare and the Book* (Cambridge, 2001)
Kastan, *Religion*	David Scott Kastan, *A Will To Believe: Shakespeare and Religion* (Oxford, 2014)
Kehler	Dorothea Kehler, 'The First Quarto of *Hamlet*: reforming widow Gertred', *SQ*, 46 (1995), 398–413
Kelly	Charles Adams Kelly, *The Evidence Matrix for the 1st Quarto of Shakespeare's Hamlet* (Triple Anvil Press, Ann Arbor, MI, 2007)
Kemble	Frances Ann Kemble, *Records of a Girlhood* (New York, 1879)
Kennedy, D.	Dennis Kennedy (ed.), *Foreign Shakespeare: Contemporary Performance* (Cambridge, 1993)

Kennedy, R.	Richard F. Kennedy, 'Speech prefixes in some Shakespearean quartos', *The Papers of the Bibliographical Society of America*, 92 (June 1998), 177–209
Kermode	Frank Kermode
Kermode, *Language*	Frank Kermode, *Shakespeare's Language* (2000)
Kiasashvili	Nico Kiasashvili, 'The martyred knights of Georgian Shakespeariana', *SS 48* (1995), 185–90
King	T.J. King, *Casting Shakespeare's Plays: London Actors and Their Roles, 1590–1642* (Cambridge, 1992)
Kinney	Arthur F. Kinney (ed.), *'Hamlet': New Critical Essays* (2002)
Klein	Lisa Klein, *Ophelia* (2006)
Knowles	Ronald Knowles, '*Hamlet* and counter-humanism', *Renaissance Quarterly*, 52 (1999), 1046–69
Knutson	Roslyn Lander Knutson, *The Repertory of Shakespeare's Company, 1594–1613* (Fayetteville, Ark., 1991)
Kottman	Paul A. Kottman, *Tragic Conditions in Shakespeare* (Baltimore, 2009)
Kozintsev	Grigori Kozintsev, *Shakespeare: Time and Conscience*, trans. Joyce Vining (New York, 1966)
Kurland	Stuart M. Kurland, '*Hamlet* and the Scottish succession', *Studies in English Literature*, 34 (1994), 279–300
Kyd	Thomas Kyd, *Works*, ed. F.S. Boas (Oxford, 1901)
Lacan	Jacques Lacan, 'Desire and the interpretation of desire in *Hamlet*' (1959), trans. Jacques-Alain Miller, repr. in Shoshana Felman (ed.), *Literature and Psychoanalysis* (Baltimore, Md., 1982), 11–52
Lavender	Andy Lavender, *Hamlet in Pieces: Shakespeare Reworked by Peter Brook, Robert Lepage, Robert Wilson* (New York, 2001)
Lavin	J.A. Lavin, 'The printer of *Hamlet* Q3', *SB*, 25 (1972), 173–6
Lee	John Lee, *Shakespeare's 'Hamlet' and the Controversies of Self* (Oxford, 2000)
Lesser	Zachary Lesser, *'Hamlet' After Q1: An Uncanny History of the Shakespearean Text* (Philadelphia, 2015)
Lesser & Stallybrass	Zachary Lesser and Peter Stallybrass, 'The first literary *Hamlet* and the commonplacing of professional plays', *SQ* 59, 4 (2008), 371–420

Levin	Richard Levin, 'Hamlet, Laertes, and the dramatic function of foils', in Kinney, 215–30
Lewis	C.M. Lewis, *The Genesis of 'Hamlet'* (New York, 1907)
Livy	Livy, *History of Rome*, books 1 and 2, trans. B.O. Foster (Cambridge, Mass., 1919)
Loewenstein	Joseph Loewenstein, 'Plays agonistic and competitive: the textual approach to Elsinore', *RD*, 19 (1988), 63–96
London	John London, 'Non-German drama in the Third Reich', in John London (ed.), *Theatre Under the Nazis* (Manchester, 2000), 222–61
Long	William B. Long, 'Stage directions: a misinterpreted factor in determining textual provenance', *TEXT*, 2 (1985), 121–37
Loomba	Ania Loomba, 'Shakespearian transformations', in John J. Joughin (ed.), *Shakespeare and National Culture* (Manchester, 1997), 109–41
Lowe	Robert W. Lowe (ed.), *An Apology for the Life of Mr Colley Cibber* (1740), vol. 1 (1889)
Macfaul	Tom Macfaul, *Problem Fathers in Shakespeare and Renaissance Drama* (Cambridge, 2012)
McCabe	Richard A. McCabe, *Incest, Drama and Nature's Law* (Cambridge, 1993)
McDonald	Russ McDonald (ed.), *Shakespeare Reread: The Texts in New Contexts* (Ithaca, NY, 1994)
Mack & Boynton	Maynard Mack and Robert W. Boynton (eds), *The Tragedy of Hamlet* (Montclair, NJ, 1981)
McKerrow	Ronald Brunlees McKerrow, *Printers' and Publishers' Devices in England and Scotland, 1485–1640* (1913)
McMillin, 'Casting'	Scott McMillin, 'Casting the *Hamlet* quartos: the limit of eleven', in Clayton, 179–94
McMillin, *More*	Scott McMillin, *The Elizabethan Theatre and 'The Book of Sir Thomas More'* (Ithaca, NY, 1987)
Maguire	Laurie E. Maguire, *Shakespearean Suspect Texts: The 'Bad' Quartos and their Contexts* (Cambridge, 1996)
Maher	Mary Z. Maher, *Modern Hamlets and their Soliloquies* (Iowa City, 1992; expanded 2nd edn, 2003)
Mahood, *Bit Parts*	M.M. Mahood, *Playing Bit Parts in Shakespeare* (1998); earlier version published as *Bit Parts in Shakespeare's Plays* (Cambridge, 1992)
Mahood, *Wordplay*	M.M. Mahood, *Shakespeare's Wordplay* (1957)
Mallin	Eric S. Mallin, *Godless Shakespeare* (London, 2007)

Mare & Quarrell	M.L. Mare and W.H. Quarrell (eds), *Lichtenberg's Visits to England* (Oxford, 1938)
Marino, 'Ghost'	James J. Marino, 'Shakespeare's Father's Ghost', *English Literary Renaissance* 44.1 (2014), 56–77
Marino, *Owning*	James J. Marino, *Owning William Shakespeare: the King's Men and Their Intellectual Property* (Philadelphia, 2011)
Marlowe	*The Complete Works of Christopher Marlowe*, ed. Fredson Bowers, 2nd edition, 2 vols (Cambridge, 1981)
Marshall	Frank A. Marshall, *A Study of Hamlet* (1875)
Marston, *Plays*	*The Selected Plays of John Marston*, ed. MacDonald P. Jackson and Michael Neill (Cambridge, 1986)
Marston, *Revenge* (1965)	John Marston, *Antonio's Revenge*, ed. G.K. Hunter (1965)
Marston, *Revenge* (1978)	John Marston, *Antonio's Revenge*, ed. W. Reavley Gair (Manchester, 1978)
Massinger	*The Poems and Plays of Philip Massinger*, ed. Philip Edwards and Colin Gibson, 5 vols (Oxford, 1976)
Matthiesson	F.O. Matthiesson, *The American Renaissance: Art and Expression in the Age of Emerson and Whitman* (New York, 1941)
Mehl	Dieter Mehl, *The Elizabethan Dumb Show* (Cambridge, Mass., 1965)
Melchiori	Giorgio Melchiori, '*Hamlet*: the acting version and the wiser sort', in Clayton, 195–210
Menzer	Paul Menzer, *The 'Hamlets': Cues, Qs, and Remembered Texts* (Newark, Delaware, 2008)
Middleton & Rowley	Thomas Middleton and William Rowley, *The Changeling*, in *Thomas Middleton: Five Plays*, ed. Bryan Loughrey and Neil Taylor (Harmondsworth, England, 1988)
Miller	Jonathan Miller, *Subsequent Performances* (New York, 1986)
Mills	John A. Mills, *Hamlet on Stage: The Great Tradition* (Westport, Conn., 1985)
Miola, *Reading*	Robert S. Miola, *Shakespeare's Reading* (Oxford, 2000)
Miola, *Tragedy*	Robert S. Miola, *Shakespeare and Classical Tragedy* (Oxford, 2002)
MLR	*Modern Language Review*
Monro	C.J. Monro
Montaigne	Michel de Montaigne, *The Essayes*, trans. John Florio, 3 vols (1910)

Montrose	Louis Adrian Montrose, '"Shaping fantasies": figurations of gender and power in Elizabethan culture', *Representations*, 1 (1983), 61–94
Moretti	Franco Moretti, *Distant Reading* (London and New York, 2013)
Mowat	Barbara Mowat, 'The form of *Hamlet*'s fortunes', *RD*, 19 (1988), 97–126
Mullaney	Steven Mullaney, 'Mourning and misogyny: *Hamlet, The Revenger's Tragedy*, and the final progress of Elizabeth I, 1600–1607', *SQ*, 45 (1994), 139–62
Murphy	Andrew Murphy, *Shakespeare in Print: A History and Chronology of Shakespeare Publishing* (Cambridge, 2003)
N&Q	*Notes and Queries*
Nashe	Thomas Nashe, *Works*, ed. Ronald B. McKerrow, repr. with corrections by F.P. Wilson, 5 vols (Oxford, 1966)
Neill	Michael Neill, *Issues of Death: Mortality and Identity in English Renaisance Tragedy* (Oxford, 1997)
Newell	Alex Newell, 'The etiology of Horatio's inconsistencies', in Maurice Charney (ed.), *'Bad' Shakespeare: Revaluations in the Shakespeare Canon* (Rutherford, NJ, 1988), 143–56
Nosworthy, *Occasional*	J.M. Nosworthy, *Shakespeare's Occasional Plays* (New York, 1965)
Nosworthy, 'Player'	J.M. Nosworthy, '*Hamlet* and the player who could not keep counsel', *SS 3* (1950), 74–82
Novy, *Differences*	Marianne Novy (ed.), *Cross-Cultural Performances: Differences in Women's Re-Visions of Shakespeare* (Urbana, Ill., 1993)
Novy, *Engaging*	Marianne Novy, *Engaging with Shakespeare: Responses of George Eliot and Other Women Novelists* (Athens, Ga., 1994)
Novy, *Re-Visions*	Marianne Novy (ed.), *Women's Re-Visions of Shakespeare: On the Responses of Dickinson, Woolf, Rich, H.D., George Eliot, and Others* (Urbana, Ill., 1990)
O'Brien	Ellen J. O'Brien, 'Revision by excision: rewriting Gertrude', *SS 45* (1992), 27–35
OED	*Oxford English Dictionary*
Olivier	Laurence Olivier, *On Acting* (New York, 1987)
Olson et al.	Donald W. Olson, Marilynn S. Olson and Russell L. Doescher, 'The stars of *Hamlet*', *Sky and Telescope* (November 1998), 68–73

Orlin   Lena Cowen Orlin, 'Gertrude's closet', *SJ*, 134 (1998), 44–67

Ovid 1965   *Ovid's Metamorphoses: The Arthur Golding Translation (1567)*, ed. John Frederick Nims (New York, 1965)

Ovid 1977   Ovid, *Metamorphoses*, 2 vols, Loeb Classical Library, 3rd edn, trans. Frank Justus Miller (1977)

Ovid, *Fasti*   Ovid, *Fasti*, trans. and ed. A.J. Boyle and R.D. Woodard (2000)

Oxberry   William Oxberry (ed.), *Hamlet*, Oxberry's New English Drama (1827)

Oya   Reiko Oya, 'A dream of passion: representation and reception of Shakespearean tragedy in the age of Garrick and Kean', unpublished PhD thesis, University of London, 2003

Parker, 'Dilation'   Patricia Parker, '*Othello* and *Hamlet*: dilation, spying, and the "secret places" of woman', in McDonald, 105–46

Parker, *Fat Ladies* Patricia Parker, *Literary Fat Ladies; Rhetoric, Gender, Property* (New York, 1987)

Paul   Henry N. Paul, *The Dram of Esile and The Ennobled Queen* (Philadelphia, 1933)

PBSA   *Publications of the Bibliographical Society of America*

Pennington   Michael Pennington, *'Hamlet': A User's Guide* (1996)

Petersen   Lene Petersen, *Shakespeare's Errant Texts: Textual Form and Linguistic Style in Shakespearean 'Bad' Quartos and Co-authored Plays* (Cambridge, 2013)

Peterson   Kaara Peterson, 'Framing Ophelia: representation and the pictorial tradition', *Mosaic*, 31 (1998), 1–24

Peterson & Williams   Kaara L. Peterson and Deanne Williams (eds), *The Afterlife of Ophelia* (London, 2012)

Pfister   Manfred Pfister, 'Hamlets made in Germany, East and West', in Michael Hattaway, Boika Sokolova and Derek Roper (eds), *Shakespeare in the New Europe* (Sheffield, 1994), 76–91

Phelps   Henry P. Phelps, *Hamlet from the Actors' Standpoint* (New York, 1890)

PMLA   *Publications of the Modern Language Association of America*

Poel   William Poel, 'The First Quarto of *Hamlet*, an Elizabethan actor's emendations', *N&Q*, 12 (1922), 301–3

| Pollard | A.W. Pollard, *Shakespeare's Folios and Quartos: A Study in the Bibliography of Shakespeare's Plays 1594–1685* (1909) |

Pollard — A.W. Pollard, *Shakespeare's Folios and Quartos: A Study in the Bibliography of Shakespeare's Plays 1594–1685* (1909)

Poole — Adrian Poole, *Shakespeare and the Victorians* (2004)

Potter — Lois Potter, 'Fire in the theater: a cross-cultural code', in Tetsuo Kishi, Roger Pringle and Stanley Wells (eds), *Shakespeare and Cultural Traditions* (Newark, Del., 1994), 266–73

Potter, *Life* — Lois Potter, *The Life of William Shakespeare: A Critical Biography* (Oxford, 2012)

PQ — *Philological Quarterly*

Proudfoot, 'Conscience' — Richard Proudfoot, '*Hamlet* and the conscience of the Queen', in John W. Mahon and Thomas A. Pendleton (eds), *Fanned and Winnowed Opinions: Shakespearean Essays Presented to Harold Jenkins* (1987), 160–83

Proudfoot, 'Modernizing' — R. Proudfoot, 'Modernizing the printed play-text in Jacobean London: some early reprints of *Mucedorus*', in Linda Anderson and Janis Lull (eds), *'A Certain Text': Close Readings and Textual Studies on Shakespeare and Others in Honor of Thomas Clayton* (Newark, Del., 2002), 26–8

Race — Sydney Race, 'J.P. Collier's fabrications', *N&Q*, 195 (1950), 345–6

Rasmussen, 'Date' — Eric Rasmussen, 'The date of Q4 *Hamlet*', *PBSA*, 95 (March 2001), 21–9

Rasmussen, 'Revision' — Eric Rasmussen, 'The revision of scripts', in John D. Cox and David Scott Kastan (eds), *A New History of Early English Drama* (New York, 1997), 441–60

Rasmussen, 'Year' — Eric Rasmussen, 'The year's contribution to Shakespeare Studies', *SS 52* (1999), 311–14

RD — *Renaissance Drama*

Redgrave — Michael Redgrave, *In My Mind's Eye* (1983)

REED: Cambridge — *Records of Early English Drama: Cambridge*, ed. Alan H. Nelson, 2 vols (Toronto, 1989)

RES — *Review of English Studies*

Roffe — Alfred Roffe, 'Shakespeare's music', *N&Q*, 2nd series, 12 (October 1891), 265–6

Rose — Jacqueline Rose, 'Sexuality in the reading of Shakespeare: *Hamlet* and *Measure for Measure*', in John Drakakis (ed.), *Alternative Shakespeares* (1985), 95–118

Rosenbaum	Ron Rosenbaum, 'The Year in Culture ... 2006', *Slate* [The Washington Post] (8 January 2007)
Rosenberg	Marvin Rosenberg, *The Masks of Hamlet* (Newark, Del., 1992)
Rosenblatt	Jason P. Rosenblatt, 'Aspects of the incest problem in *Hamlet*', *SQ*, 29 (1978), 349–64
RP	Richard Proudfoot, private communication
Rubinstein	Frankie Rubinstein, *A Dictionary of Shakespeare's Sexual Puns and their Significance*, 2nd edn (Basingstoke, 1989)
Russell	E.R. Russell, *Irving as Hamlet* (1875)
Rutter	Carol Rutter, 'Snatched bodies: Ophelia in the grave', in *Enter the Body: Women and Representation on Shakespeare's Stage* (2001), 27–56
Rutter, '2010'	Carol Chillington Rutter, 'Shakespeare Performances in England, 2010', *SS 64* (2011), 340–77
Sams, *Shakespeare*	Eric Sams, *The Real Shakespeare: Retrieving the Early Years, 1564–1594* (1995)
Sams, 'Taboo'	Eric Sams, 'Taboo or not taboo: the text, dating and authorship of *Hamlet*, 1589–1623', *HS*, 10 (1988), 12–46
Sanders	Julie Sanders, *Novel Shakespeares: Twentieth-Century Women Novelists and Appropriation* (New York and London, 2001)
SB	*Studies in Bibliography*
Schiesari	Juliana Schiesari, *The Gendering of Melancholia* (Ithaca, NY, 1992)
Schleiner	Louise Schleiner, 'Latinized Greek drama in Shakespeare's writing of *Hamlet*', *SQ*, 41 (1990), 29–48
Scofield	Martin Scofield, *The Ghosts of 'Hamlet': The Play and Modern Writers* (Cambridge, 1980)
Scolnicov	Hanna Scolnicov, '"Here is the place appointed for the wrestling"', in François Laroque (ed.), *The Show Within: Dramatic and Other Insets*, 2 vols (Montpellier, 1992), vol. 1, 141–52
Scott	Clement Scott, *'The Bells' to 'King Arthur'* (1896)
Seary	Peter Seary, *Lewis Theobald and the Editing of Shakespeare* (Oxford, 1990)
Shaheen	Naseeb Shaheen, *Biblical References in Shakespeare's Plays* (Newark, Del., 1999)
Shand	C.B. Shand, 'Gertred, captive queen of the First Quarto', in Jay L. Halio and Hugh Richmond (eds),

	Shakespearean Illuminations: Essays in Honor of Marvin Rosenberg (Newark, Delaware, 1998), 33–49
Shapiro, *1599*	James Shapiro, *1599: A Year in the Life of William Shakespeare* (London, 2005)
Shapiro, 'Biography'	James Shapiro, 'Toward a new biography of Shakespeare', *SS 58* (2005), 9–14
Shattuck	Charles H. Shattuck, *The Hamlet of Edwin Booth* (Urbana, Ill., 1969)
Showalter	Elaine Showalter, 'Representing Ophelia: women, madness, and the responsibilities of feminist criticism', in Patricia Parker and Geoffrey Hartman (eds), *Shakespeare and the Question of Theory* (New York, 1985), 77–94
Shurbanov & Sokolova	Alexander Shurbanov and Boika Sokolova, *Painting Shakespeare Red: An East-European Appropriation* (Newark, Del., 2001)
SJ	*Shakespeare Jahrbuch*
Smith	Emma Smith, 'Ghost writing: *Hamlet* and the *Ur-Hamlet*', in Andrew Murphy (ed.), *The Renaissance Text: Theory, Editing, Textuality* (Manchester, 2000), 177–90
Smith, P.	Peter Smith, 'A world of kin unkind', *Times Higher Education Supplement* (16 December 2010), 45
Snyder	Susan Snyder, *The Comic Matrix of Shakespeare's Tragedies* (Princeton, NJ, 1979)
Sokol & Sokol	B.J. Sokol and Mary Sokol, *Shakespeare's Legal Language: A Dictionary* (2000)
Spenser	See *FQ*
Sprague	Arthur Colby Sprague, *The Doubling of Parts in Shakespeare's Plays* (1966)
Spurgeon	Caroline F.E. Spurgeon, *Shakespeare's Imagery and What It Tells Us* (Cambridge, 1935)
SQ	*Shakespeare Quarterly*
SS	*Shakespeare Survey*
SSt	*Shakespeare Studies*
Stachan & Penrose	M. Stachan and B. Penrose (eds), *The East India Journals of Captain William Keeling and Master Thomas Bonner, 1615–1617* (Minneapolis, Minn., 1971)
Stallybrass, 'Clothes'	Peter Stallybrass, 'Worn worlds: clothes and identity on the Renaissance stage', in Margreta de Grazia, Maureen Quilligan and Peter Stallybrass (eds), *Subject*

	and Object in Renaissance Culture (Cambridge, 1996), 289–320
Stallybrass, 'Mole'	Peter Stallybrass, '"Well grubbed, old mole": Marx, *Hamlet*, and the (un)fixing of representation', *Cultural Studies*, 12 (1998), 3–15
Stern, T., *Rehearsal*	Tiffany Stern, *Rehearsal from Shakespeare to Sheridan* (Oxford, 2000)
Stern, T., 'puppets'	Tiffany Stern, '"If I could see the puppets dallying": *Der Bestrafte Brudermord* and Hamlet's encounter with the puppets', *Shakespeare Bulletin* 31.3 (2013), 337–52
Stern, T., 'Sermons'	Tiffany Stern, 'Sermons, plays and note-takers: *Hamlet* Q1 as a "noted" text', *SS* 66 (CUP, 2013), 1–23
Stern, V.	Virginia F. Stern, *Gabriel Harvey: His Life, Marginalia and Library* (Oxford, 1980)
Stewart, 'Closet'	Alan Stewart, 'The Early Modern closet discovered', *Representations*, 50 (1995), 76–100
Stewart, *Letters*	Alan Stewart, *Shakespeare's Letters* (Oxford, 2008)
Stoppard	Tom Stoppard, *Rosencrantz and Guildenstern Are Dead* (1967)
Stříbrný	Zdenek Stříbrný, *Shakespeare and Eastern Europe* (Oxford, 2000)
Tanselle	G. Thomas Tanselle, *A Rationale of Textual Criticism* (Philadelphia, 1989)
Tassi	Marguerite A. Tassi, *Women and Revenge in Shakespeare: Gender, Genre, and Ethics* (Selinsgrove, Pennsylvania, 2011)
Taylor, 'Act-intervals'	Gary Taylor, 'The structure of performance: act-intervals in the London theatres, 1576–1642', in Gary Taylor and John Jowett, *Shakespeare Reshaped 1606–23* (Oxford, 1993), 3–50
Taylor, 'Africa'	Gary Taylor, '*Hamlet* in Africa 1607', in Ivo Kamps and Jyotsna G. Singh (eds), *Travel Knowledge: European 'Discoveries' in the Early Modern Period* (Basingstoke, 2001), 223–48
Taylor, 'Bard'	Gary Taylor, 'The incredible shrinking bard', in Christy Desmet and Robert Sawyer (eds), *Shakespeare and Appropriation* (1999), 197–205
Taylor, 'Compositors'	Gary Taylor, 'Folio compositors and Folio copy: *King Lear* in its context', *PBSA*, 79 (1985), 17–74
Taylor, 'Folio copy'	Gary Taylor, 'The Folio copy for *Hamlet, King Lear*, and *Othello*', *SQ*, 34 (1983), 44–61

Taylor, 'Red Dragon'   Gary Taylor, 'The Red Dragon in Sierra Leone', in
                       Ivo Kamps and Jyotsna G. Singh (eds), *Travel
                       Knowledge: European 'Discoveries' in the Early
                       Modern Period* (Basingstoke, 2001), 211–22
Taylor, 'Shrinking'   Gary Taylor, 'The shrinking Compositor A of the
                       Shakespeare First Folio', *SB*, 34 (1981), 96–117
Taylor, ' 'Swounds'   Gary Taylor, ' 'Swounds revisited: theatrical, editorial
                       and literary expurgation', in Gary Taylor and John
                       Jowett, *Shakespeare Reshaped 1606–23* (Oxford,
                       1993), 51–106
Taylor & Thompson   Neil Taylor and Ann Thompson, 'Obscenity in *Hamlet*
                       3.2: "country matters"', *Textus* (English Studies in
                       Italy), 9 (1996), 485–500
Taylor & Warren   Gary Taylor and Michael Warren (eds), *The Division
                       of the Kingdoms: Shakespeare's Two Versions of
                       'King Lear'* (Oxford, 1983)
Tennenhouse   Leonard Tennenhouse, 'Violence done to women on
                       the Renaissance stage', in Nancy Armstrong and
                       Leonard Tennenhouse (eds), *The Violence of
                       Representation* (1989), 77–97
Thirlby   Styan Thirlby
Thompson, 'Canon'   Ann Thompson, '*Hamlet* and the canon', in Kinney,
                       193–205
Thompson, 'Jest'   Ann Thompson, 'Infinite jest: the comedy of *Hamlet,
                       Prince of Denmark*', *SS 56* (2003), 93–104
Thompson,   Ann Thompson, '*The New Wing at Elsinore, The
  'New Wing'   Redemption of the Hamlet*s and other sequels, prequels
                       and off-shoots of *Hamlet*', in Boika Sokolova and
                       Evgenia Pancheva (eds), *Renaissance Refractions:
                       Essays in Honour of Alexander Shurbanov* (Sofia,
                       Bulgaria, 2001), 217–29
Thompson, 'Teena'   Ann Thompson, 'Teena Rochfort Smith, Frederick
                       Furnivall, and the New Shakspere Society's four-text
                       edition of *Hamlet*', *SQ*, 49 (1998), 125–39
Thompson, 'Ward'   Ann Thompson, '"I'll have grounds more relative
                       than this": the puzzle of John Ward's *Hamlet*
                       promptbooks', *Yearbook of English Studies*, 29
                       (1999), 138–50
Thompson &   Ann Thompson and Neil Taylor, '"Your sum of parts":
  Taylor, 'Doubling'   doubling in *Hamlet*', in Lukas Erne and Margaret
                       Jane Kidnie (eds), *Textual Performances: The Modern
                       Reproduction of Shakespeare's Drama* (Cambridge,
                       2004), 111–26

Thompson & Taylor, 'Paternity'	Ann Thompson and Neil Taylor, '"Father and mother is one flesh": *Hamlet* and the problems of paternity', in Lieve Spaas (ed.), *Paternity and Fatherhood: Myths and Realities* (Basingstoke, 1998), 246–58
Thompson & Taylor, 'Text'	Ann Thompson and Neil Taylor, '"O that this too too XXXXX text would melt": *Hamlet* and the indecisions of modern editors and publishers', *TEXT*, 10 (1997), 221–36
Thompson & Thompson	Ann Thompson and John O. Thompson, *Shakespeare, Meaning and Metaphor* (Brighton and Iowa City, 1987)
Tilley	Morris Palmer Tilley, *A Dictionary of the Proverbs in England in the Sixteenth and Seventeenth Centuries* (Ann Arbor, Mich., 1950)
Tobin, 'Elements'	J.J.M. Tobin, 'More elements from Nashe', *HS*, 5 (1983), 52–8
Tobin, 'Harvey'	J.J.M. Tobin, 'Gabriel Harvey: "Excellent matter of emulation"', *HS*, 7 (1985), 94–100
Tobin, '*Lenten*'	J.J.M. Tobin, '*Hamlet* and Nashe's *Lenten Stuffe*', *Archiv*, 219 (1982), 388–95
Tobin, 'Nashe'	J.J.M. Tobin, 'Nashe and *Hamlet*, yet again', *HS*, 2 (1980), 35–46
Tobin, '*Salary*'	J.J.M. Tobin, 'Hamlet and *salary*', *N&Q*, 30 (1983), 125–6
Tobin, '*Teares*'	J.J.M. Tobin, '*Hamlet* and *Christs Teares over Jerusalem*', *Aligarh Journal of English Studies*, vol. 6, no. 2 (1981), 158–67
Todd	Richard Todd, *Iris Murdoch: The Shakespearean Interest* (1979)
Trafford	Jeremy Trafford, *Ophelia* (Thirsk, North Yorkshire, 2001)
Traub	Valerie Traub, 'Rainbows of darkness: deconstructing Shakespeare in the works of Gloria Naylor and Zora Neale Hurston', in Novy, *Differences*, 150–64
Trewin	J.C. Trewin, *Five and Eighty Hamlets* (New York, 1987)
TxC	Stanley Wells and Gary Taylor, with John Jowett and William Montgomery, *William Shakespeare: A Textual Companion* (Oxford, 1987)
Urkowitz, 'Basics'	Steven Urkowitz, 'Back to basics: thinking about the *Hamlet* First Quarto', in Clayton, 257–91
Urkowitz, 'Good news'	Steven Urkowitz, 'Good news about "bad" quartos', in Maurice Charney (ed.), *'Bad' Shakespeare* (Cranbury, NJ, 1988), 189–206

Urkowitz, *Lear*   Steven Urkowitz, *Shakespeare's Revision of 'King Lear'* (Princeton, NJ, 1980)

Urkowitz,   Steven Urkowitz, '"Well-sayd olde mole": burying
  'Old mole'   three *Hamlets* in modern editions', in Georgianna Ziegler (ed.), *Shakespeare Study Today* (New York, 1986), 37–70

Van Fossen   *Eastward Ho by George Chapman, Ben Jonson and John Marston*, ed. R.W. Van Fossen (Manchester, 1979)

Vickers   Brian Vickers, review of Arden editions of *Hamlet* and *Hamlet: The Texts of 1603 and 1623*, edited by Ann Thompson and Neil Taylor, in *Editionen in der Kritik*: Editionswissenschaftliches Rezensionsorgan, II (Berlin, 2007), 15–42

Vining   Edward P. Vining, *The Mystery of Hamlet: An Attempt to Solve an Old Problem* (Philadelphia, Pa., 1881)

Walaszek   Joanna Walaszek, 'Andrzej Wajda, Hamlet four times', in Marta Gibinska and Jerzy Limon (eds), *Hamlet East–West* (Gdansk, 1998), 108–17

Walker, *Problems*   Alice Walker, *Textual Problems of the First Folio: Richard III, King Lear, Troilus and Cressida, 2 Henry IV, Hamlet, Othello* (Cambridge, 1953)

Walker,   Alice Walker, 'The textual problem of *Hamlet*: a
  'Reconsideration'   reconsideration', *RES*, 2 (1951), 328–38

Walton   J.K. Walton, *The Quarto Copy for the First Folio of Shakespeare* (Dublin, 1971)

Warley   Christopher Warley, 'Specters of Horatio', *ELH* 75 (Winter 2008), 1023–1050

Watermeier   Daniel J. Watermeier, *Between Actor and Critic: Selected Letters of Edwin Booth* (Princeton, NJ, 1971)

Watson   Robert N. Watson, *The Rest is Silence: Death as Annihilation in the English Renaissance* (Berkeley, Calif., 1994)

Webster   *The Works of John Webster*, ed. F.L. Lucas, 4 vols (1927)

Weimann, 'Divided'   Robert Weimann, 'A divided heritage: conflicting appropriations of Shakespeare in (East) Germany', in John J. Joughin (ed.), *Shakespeare and National Culture* (Manchester, 1997), 173–205

Weimann, *Pen*   Robert Weimann, *Author's Pen and Actor's Voice: Playing and Writing in Shakespeare's Theatre* (Cambridge, 2000)

Weis	René Weis, *Shakespeare Revealed: A Biography* (2007)
Weitz	Morris Weitz, *'Hamlet' and the Philosophy of Literary Criticism* (Chicago, 1964)
Wells, *Anthology*	Stanley Wells, *Shakespeare in the Theatre: An Anthology of Criticism* (Oxford, 1997)
Wells, *Re-editing*	Stanley Wells, *Re-editing Shakespeare for the Modern Reader* (Oxford, 1984)
Wells & Taylor	Stanley Wells and Gary Taylor, 'The Oxford Shakespeare re-viewed', *Analytical and Enumerative Bibliography*, 4 (1990), 6–20
Wells & Taylor, *Companion*	Stanley Wells and Gary Taylor, with John Jowett and William Montgomery (eds), *William Shakespeare: A Textual Companion* (Oxford, 1987)
Welsh	Alexander Welsh, *Hamlet in his Modern Guises* (Princeton, NJ, 2001)
Wentersdorf	Karl P. Wentersdorf, '*Hamlet*: Ophelia's long purples', *SQ*, 29 (1978), 413–17
Werner	Sarah Werner, 'Two *Hamlets*: Wooster Group and Synetic Theater', *SQ* 59 (2008), 323–9
Werstine, 'Mystery'	Paul Werstine, 'The textual mystery of *Hamlet*', *SQ*, 39 (1988), 1–26
Werstine, 'Quartos'	Paul Werstine, 'A century of "bad" Shakespeare quartos', *SQ*, 50 (1999), 310–33
Werstine, *Scripts*	Paul Werstine, *Early Modern Playhouse Scripts and the Editing of Shakespeare* (Cambridge, 2013)
West, 'Census'	Anthony James West, 'Provisional new census of the Shakespeare First Folio', *Library*, 6th series, 17 (1995), 1, 60–73
West, *Folio*	Anthony James West, *The Shakespeare First Folio: The History of the Book* (Oxford, 2001)
Whaley	Diana Whaley, 'Voices from the past: a note on Termagant and Herod', in John Batchelor, Tom Cain and Claire Lamont (eds), *Shakespearean Continuities* (New York, 1997), 23–39
Whitaker	V.K. Whitaker, *Shakespeare's Use of Learning* (San Marino, Calif., 1953)
White, 'Two *Hamlets*'	Richard Grant White, 'The two *Hamlets*', *Atlantic Monthly*, 48 (1881), 467–79
Whiter	*Walter Whiter: A Specimen of a Commentary on Shakespeare (1794)*, ed. Alan Over and Mary Bell (1967)
Widgery	W.H. Widgery, *The First Quarto Edition of 'Hamlet', 1603*, one of *Two Essays to which the Harness Prize*

was *Awarded* [the other by C.H. Herford] (1880), 87–204

Wilcock — Mike Wilcock, *'Hamlet': The Shakespearean Director* (Dublin, 2002)

Wiles — David Wiles, *Shakespeare's Clown: Actor and Text in the Elizabethan Playhouse* (Cambridge, 1987)

Williams, 'Directions' — George Walton Williams, 'Exit by indirection, finding directions out', in Aasand, *Directions*, 42–6

Williams, 'Romans' — George Walton Williams, 'Antique Romans and modern Danes in *Julius Caesar* and *Hamlet*', in Vincent Newey and Ann Thompson (eds), *Literature and Nationalism* (Liverpool, 1991), 41–55

Wilson — Richard Wilson, *Shakespeare in French Theory: King of Shadows* (London, 2007)

Wilson, 'Copy' — John Dover Wilson, 'The copy for *Hamlet*, 1603', *Library*, 3rd series, 9 (1918), 153–85

Wilson, *Manuscript* — John Dover Wilson, *The Manuscript of Shakespeare's Hamlet and the Problems of its Transmission*, 2 vols (Cambridge, 1963)

Wilson, 'Transcript' — John Dover Wilson, 'The *Hamlet* transcript, 1593', *Library*, 3rd series, 9 (1918), 153–85 and 217–47

Worthen, *Performance* — W.B. Worthen, *Shakespeare and the Force of Modern Performance* (Cambridge, 2003)

Worthen, 'Wooster' — W. B. Worthen, '*Hamlet* at Ground Zero: The Wooster Group and the Archive of Performance', *SQ* 59 (2008), 303–22

Woudhuysen — *Love's Labour's Lost*, ed. H.R. Woudhuysen, Arden Shakespeare (Walton-on-Thames, 1998)

Wright — George T. Wright, 'Hendiadys and *Hamlet*', *PMLA*, 96 (1981), 168–93

Zitner — Sheldon P. Zitner, 'Four feet in the grave', *TEXT*, 2 (1985), 139–48

INDEX

This index covers the Introduction, the commentary notes and the Appendices; it excludes references in the textual notes and it excludes references to the OED. The abbreviation 'n.' is used only for footnotes in the Introduction and Appendices; it is not used for commentary notes. Italic numbers refer to illustrations.

Aasand, Hardin 576, 577n.
Ackroyd, Peter 143
act and scene divisions 177, 231, 240–1, 363, 385, 402, 421, 423, 577–87
actors 2–8, 97–111, 161–8, 247, 288–90, 292, 293, 294–7, 298, 302–3, 325–8, 582–5 (*see also* child actors and under names of characters)
Adams, Joseph Quincy 497, 581
Adelman, Janet 29–30
Aebischer, Pascale 117n.
Aers, David 20
Aeschylus
  Agamemnon 65, 72
  Oresteia 64–5
Akimov, Nikolai 606
Al-Bassam, Sulayman, 121
Alday, John 75
Alexander the Great 453
allusions (early) 45–54, 58–9, 146, 200, 211, 241, 282–3. 291, 314–15, 331, 365, 408–9, 417, 419, 437, 445, 453, 460
Almereyda, Michael 114, 116, 123, 166, 195, 286, 463, 584
Andrews, John F. 245, 357, 379
Anne of Denmark (wife of James I) 53, 233, 285, 496, 498
Aramburo, Diego 165
Arcand, Denys 19
Armin, Robert 58, 174, 328–9
Armstrong, Edward A. 330
Arumagam, Vaneshran 163
Atkinson, Kate
  Human Croquet 131
Atwood, Margaret 129
  Cat's Eye 133
  'Gertrude Talks Back' 133, 133n.
Austen, Jane 129
authorial revision 10, 19–20, 59, 82, 84–7, 91, 140, 147–54, 158, 233, 239,

283, 285, 289, 339, 351, 371, 381, 399, 402, 409, 429, 431, 432, 456, 470, 476, 496, 498, 501, 502, 524, 529–31, 533, 534–7, 540–1
Ayliff, H.K. 111, 112, 113, 200, 484

'bad' quartos 86, 147–54, 506, 528–9, 589
Bachelard, Gaston 26
Bains, Y.S. 86n.
Baldwin, T.W. 579–80
ballet 124, 606
Banks, Anthony 166
Barker, Howard 124
Barrie, Robert 58
Barrett, Wilson 583
Barrymore, John 3, 108, 110, 111, 363–4, 384
Bartlett, Henrietta C. 516n.
Bartolezzi, Francesco 28
Barton, John 329
Bate, Jonathan 143, 147, 148–9
Baty, Gaston 7
Baynton, Henry 3
Beale, Simon Russell 2, 27, 111, 114, 307, 600
Beaumont, Francis and John Fletcher
  Scornful Lady, The 59, 315
  Woman Hater, The 58, 241
Bednarz, James P. 53, 498, 499
Beerbohm-Tree, Herbert 103, 110
Belleforest, François de 46, 68–72, 171, 172, 208, 244, 379, 439–40, 468
Belsey, Catherine 33–4
Bennett, Rodney 113, 584
Benson, Frank 110, 115
Benthall, Michael 18n., 111
Bentley, Eric 7
Berger, Thomas L. 588n.
Bergman, Ingmar 117
Berkoff, Steven 19n.
Berlioz, Hector 606
Bernhardt, Sarah 111

643